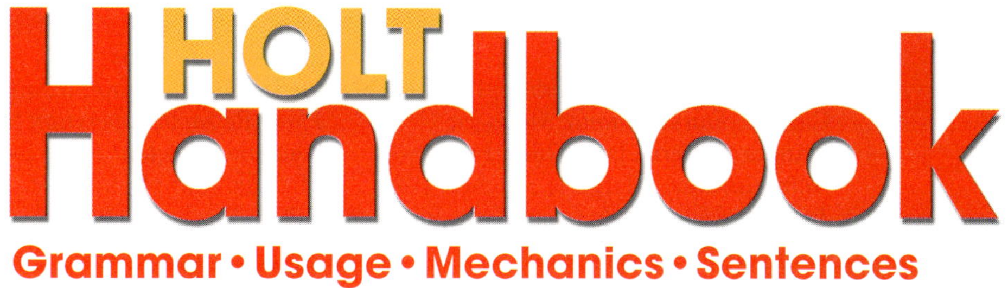

Holt Handbook

Grammar • Usage • Mechanics • Sentences

Third Course

ANNOTATED TEACHER'S EDITION

Instructional Framework by

John E. Warriner

HOLT, RINEHART AND WINSTON

A Harcourt Education Company

Austin • Orlando • Chicago • New York • Toronto • London • San Diego

AUTHOR JOHN E. WARRINER

JOHN E. WARRINER taught for thirty-two years in junior and senior high schools and in college. He was a high school English teacher when he developed the original organizational structure for his classic *English Grammar and Composition* series. The approach pioneered by Mr. Warriner was distinctive, and the editorial staff of Holt, Rinehart and Winston have worked diligently to retain the unique qualities of his pedagogy in the *Holt Handbook.* John Warriner also co-authored the *English Workshop* series and edited *Short Stories: Characters in Conflict.*

STAFF CREDITS

EDITORIAL

Executive Editor
Robert R. Hoyt

Program Editor
Marcia L. Kelley

Project Editors
Eileen Joyce, Kathryn Rogers

Writing and Editing
David Bradford, Thomas Browne, Gail Coupland, Gabrielle Field, Scott Hall, Suzi Hunn, Karen Kolar, Sondra Maze, Theresa Reding, Jennifer Schwan

Copyediting
Michael Neibergall, *Copyediting Manager;* Mary Malone, *Copyediting Supervisor;* Elizabeth Dickson, *Senior Copyeditor;* Christine Altgelt, Joel Bourgeois, Emily Force, Julie A. Hill, Julia Thomas Hu, Jennifer Kirkland, Millicent Ondras, Dennis Scharnberg, *Copyeditors*

Project Administration
Marie Price, *Managing Editor;* Lori De La Garza, *Editorial Finance Manager;* Jennifer Renteria, Janet Riley, *Project Administration;* Margaret Sanchez, *Word Processing Supervisor;* Casey Kelly, Joie Pickett, *Word Processing*

Editorial Permissions
Janet Harrington, *Permissions Editor*

ART, DESIGN, AND PHOTO

Book Design
Diane Motz, *Senior Design Director;* Sally Bess, *Designer*

Graphic Services
Kristen Darby, *Manager*

Image Acquisitions
Joe London, *Director;* Jeannie Taylor, *Photo Research Supervisor;* Sarah Hudgens, *Assistant Photo Researcher;* Michelle Rumpf, *Art Buyer Supervisor;* Gillian Brody, *Art Buyer*

Cover Design
Bruce Bond, *Design Director*

PRODUCTION

Belinda Barbosa Lopez, *Senior Production Coordinator*
Carol Trammel, *Production Supervisor*
Beth Prevelige, *Senior Production Manager*

MANUFACTURING/INVENTORY

Shirley Cantrell, *Manufacturing Supervisor*
Mark McDonald, *Inventory Planner*

For acknowledgments, see page 550, which is an extension of the copyright page.

Printed in the United States of America

ISBN 0-03-066137-4

1 2 3 4 5 6 7 8 9 048 05 04 03 02

CONTENTS IN BRIEF

CONTENTS

CHAPTER 3

The Phrase

CHAPTER 4

The Clause

CHAPTER 6

Using Verbs Correctly

CHAPTER 7

Using Pronouns Correctly

CHAPTER 8

Using Modifiers Correctly

CHAPTER 9

A Glossary of Usage

CHAPTER 10

Capital Letters

CHAPTER 11

Punctuation

The Granger Collection, New York.

Punctuation

Punctuation

CHAPTER 16

Spelling

CHAPTER 17

Correcting Common Errors

PART 3 Resources

John Warriner: In His Own Words

The name of John Warriner has long been associated with a rather formal style of teaching traditional school grammar. Interestingly, however, John Warriner did not consider himself primarily a grammarian but rather an English teacher. Also, he did not consider his books primarily grammar textbooks but rather reference handbooks for students and teachers of composition.

In his prefaces to *Handbook of English: Book One* and *Handbook of English: Book Two* (published in 1948 and 1951, respectively), Warriner articulated his vision of what his textbooks were intended to do and how they might best be used. What he had to say might surprise you.

First, Warriner's goal in preparing these books was to create "a completely flexible teaching tool adaptable to . . . any individual classroom." He did *not* design his books to be teaching texts in which the class moves sequentially from chapter to chapter, every student doing all the exercises along the way. In fact, he asserted just the opposite: "[A] book of this kind is not intended for methodical coverage from cover to cover. The book contains more material than any one class can handle in a single year. Teachers will teach those chapters that a particular class needs and will assign exercises in proportion to the need."

John Warriner: In His Own Words

In the 1940s and '50s, John Warriner (1907–1987) published his first grammar and composition textbooks. Mr. Warriner's goal as a teacher and as a writer was to help students learn to use English effectively in order to be successful in school and in life. Throughout the years that followed, Mr. Warriner revised his original books and wrote others, creating the series on which this textbook is based. Included in Mr. Warriner's books were a number of short essays to his students. In these essays, Mr. Warriner explored the role of language in human life, the importance of studying English, and the value of mastering the conventions of standard English.

We could tell you what John Warriner thought about the study of English, but we'd rather let you read what he himself had to say.

Language Is Human

"Have you ever thought about how important language is? Can you imagine what living would be like without it?

"Of all creatures on earth, human beings alone have a fully developed language, which enables them to communicate their thoughts to others in words, and which they can record in writing for others to read. Other creatures, dogs, for example, have ways of communicating their feelings, but they are very simple ways and very simple feelings. Without words, they must resort to mere noises, like barking, and to physical actions, like tail wagging. The point is that one very important difference between human beings and other creatures is the way human beings can communicate with

Warriner's first grammar and composition textbooks, published in the 1940s and '50s.

one another by means of this remarkable thing called language. When you stop to think about it, you realize that language is involved to some extent in almost everything you do.”

(from *English Grammar and Composition: First Course,* 1986)

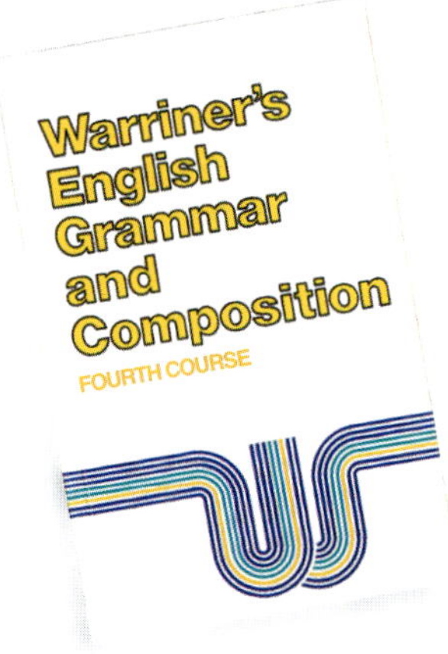

***Warriner's English Grammar and Composition: Fourth Course,* 1977**

Why Study English?

“The reason English is a required subject in almost all schools is that nothing in your education is more important than learning how to express yourself well. You may know a vast amount about a subject, but if you are unable to communicate what you know, you are severely handicapped. No matter how valuable your ideas may be, they will not be very useful if you cannot express them clearly and convincingly. Language is the means by which people communicate. By learning how your language functions and by practicing language skills, you can acquire the competence necessary to express adequately what you know and what you think.”

(from *English Grammar and Composition: Fourth Course,* 1977)

Why Study Grammar?

“Grammar is a description of the way a language works. It explains many things. For example, grammar tells us the order in which sentence parts must be arranged. It explains the work done by the various kinds of words—the work done by a noun is different from the work done by a verb. It explains how words change their form according to the way they are used. Grammar is useful because it enables us to make statements about how to use our language. These statements we usually call rules.

“The grammar rule that the normal order of an English sentence is subject-verb-object may not seem very important to us, because English is our native tongue and we naturally use this order without thinking. But the rule would be very helpful to people who are learning English as a second language. However, the rule that subjects and verbs ‘agree’ (when the subject is plural, the verb is plural), and the rule that some pronouns (*I, he, she, we, they*) are used as subjects while others (*me, him, her, us,*

***Warriner's English Grammar and Composition: Third Course,* 1982**

Warriner was also attuned to the needs of individual students within a class, acknowledging that "students arrive with greatly varying degrees of mastery of language essentials. One student may be weak in sentence sense, another in pronoun usage. But each student requires for his [or her] special weakness a full text explanation, a wealth of examples, and practice material," which Warriner endeavored to provide.

To organize his material, Warriner separated language instruction into sections, choosing to present grammar before usage. His rationale for doing so was that a working understanding of grammar terms and concepts would provide students and teachers a common vocabulary for discussing usage concepts. However, Warriner was not comfortable with the implications of such a separation: "This is not to imply that grammar can be separated from usage in practice. *The only valid reason for teaching grammar at all is to apply it to specific usage problems* [emphasis added]."

Finally, in spite of his reputation as a grammar curmudgeon, John Warriner had some rather modern ideas about language. He believed that English was an evolving language and that appropriate usage varied according to the situation. In fact, Warriner was adamant that a language arts textbook "must make clear to students that correctness in English is not fixed, but variable, that there are levels of usage, and that any living language suffers change."

them) are used as objects—these are helpful rules even for native speakers of English.

"Such rules could not be understood—in fact, they could not be formed—without the vocabulary of grammar. Grammar, then, helps us to state how English is used and how we should use it. ”

(from *English Grammar and Composition: Third Course*, 1982)

Why Is Punctuation Important?

"The sole purpose of punctuation is to make clear the meaning of what you write. When you speak, the actual sound of your voice, the rhythmic rise and fall of your inflections, your pauses and hesitations, your stops to take breath—all supply a kind of 'punctuation' that serves to group your words and to indicate to your listener precisely what you mean. Indeed, even the body takes part in this unwritten punctuation. A raised eyebrow may express interrogation more eloquently than any question mark, and a knuckle rapped on the table shows stronger feeling than an exclamation point.

"In written English, however, where there are none of these hints to meaning, simple courtesy requires the writer to make up for the lack by careful punctuation.”

(from *English Grammar and Composition: Fourth Course*, 1973)

English Grammar and Composition: Fourth Course, 1973

Why Learn Standard English?

"Consider the following pair of sentences:

1. George don't know the answer.

2. George doesn't know the answer.

"Is one sentence clearer or more meaningful than the other? It's hard to see how. The speaker of sentence 1 and the speaker of sentence 2 both convey the same message about George and his lack of knowledge. If language only conveyed information about the people and events that a speaker is discussing, we would have to say that one sentence is just as good as the other. However, language often carries messages the speaker does not intend. The words he uses to tell us about events often tell us something about the speaker himself. The extra, unintended message conveyed by 'George don't know the answer' is that the speaker does not know or does not use one verb form that is universally preferred by educated users of English.

"Perhaps it is not fair to judge people by how they say things rather than by what they say, but to some extent everyone does it. It's hard to know what is in a person's head, but the language he uses is always open to inspection, and people draw conclusions from it. The people who give marks and recommendations, who hire employees or judge college applications, these and others who may be important in your life are speakers of educated English. You may not be able to impress them merely by speaking their language, but you are likely to impress them unfavorably if you don't. The language you use tells a lot about you. It is worth the trouble to make sure that it tells the story you want people to hear.”

(from *English Grammar and Composition: Fourth Course*, 1973)

TO OUR STUDENTS

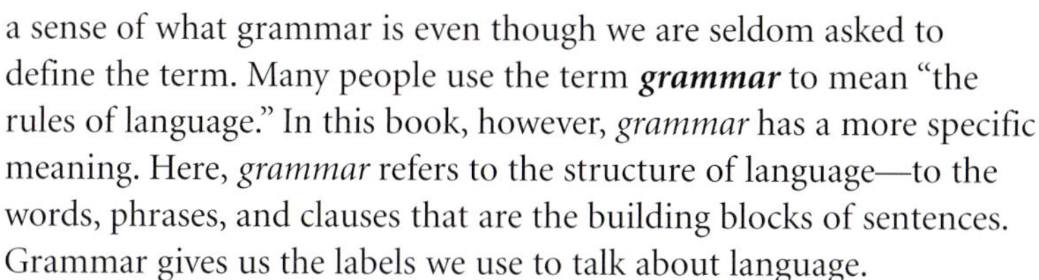

What is grammar?

That seems like a simple question, doesn't it? Most of us have a sense of what grammar is even though we are seldom asked to define the term. Many people use the term ***grammar*** to mean "the rules of language." In this book, however, *grammar* has a more specific meaning. Here, *grammar* refers to the structure of language—to the words, phrases, and clauses that are the building blocks of sentences. Grammar gives us the labels we use to talk about language.

What about the rules that govern how language is used in various social situations? In this book, these rules are called usage. Unlike grammar, **usage** determines what is considered standard ("isn't") or nonstandard ("ain't") and what is considered formal ("why") or informal ("how come"). Usage is a social convention, a behavior or rule customary among members of a group. As a result, what is considered acceptable usage can vary from group to group and from situation to situation.

To speak standard English requires a knowledge of grammar and of standard usage. To write standard English requires something more—a knowledge of mechanics. ***Mechanics*** refers to the rules for written, rather than spoken, language. Spelling, capitalization, and punctuation are concepts we don't even think about when we are speaking, but they are vital to effective written communication.

Why should I study grammar, usage, and mechanics?

Many people would say that you should study grammar to learn to root out errors in your speech and writing. Certainly, the *Holt Handbook* can help you learn to avoid making errors and to correct the errors you do make. More importantly, though, studying grammar, usage, and mechanics gives you the skills you need to take

sentences and passages apart and to put them together, to learn which parts go together and which don't. Instead of writing sentences and passages that you hope sound good, you can craft your sentences to create just the meaning and style you want.

Knowing grammar, usage, and mechanics gives you the tools to understand and discuss your own language, to communicate clearly the things you want to communicate, and to develop your own communication style. Further, mastery of language skills can help you succeed in your other classes, in future classes, on standardized tests, and in the larger world—including, eventually, the workplace.

How do I use the *Holt Handbook*?

The skills taught in the *Holt Handbook* are important to your success in reading, writing, speaking, and listening.

Not only can you use this book as a complete grammar, usage, and mechanics textbook, but you can also use it as a reference guide when you work on any piece of writing. Whatever you are writing, you can use the *Holt Handbook* to answer your questions about grammar, usage, capitalization, punctuation, and spelling.

How is the *Holt Handbook* organized?

The *Holt Handbook* is divided into three main parts:

PART 1 The **Grammar, Usage, and Mechanics** chapters provide instruction on and practice using the building blocks of language—words, phrases, clauses, capitalization, punctuation, and spelling. Use these chapters to discover how to take sentences apart and analyze them. The last chapter, **Correcting Common Errors,** provides additional practice on key language skills as well as standardized test practice in grammar, usage, and mechanics.

PART 2 The **Sentences** chapters include Writing Complete Sentences, Writing Effective Sentences, and Sentence Diagramming. **Writing Complete Sentences** and **Writing Effective Sentences** provide instruction on and practice with writing correct, clear, and interesting sentences. **Sentence Diagramming** teaches you to analyze and diagram sentences so you can see how the parts of a sentence relate to each other.

PART 3 The **Resources** section includes **Manuscript Form,** a guide to presenting your ideas in the best form possible; **The History of English,** a concise history of the English language; **Test Smarts,** a handy guide to taking standardized tests in grammar, usage, and mechanics; and **Grammar at a Glance,** a glossary of grammatical terms.

How are the chapters organized?

Each chapter begins with a Diagnostic Preview, a short test that covers the whole chapter and alerts you to skills that need improvement, and ends with a Chapter Review, another short test that tells you how well you have mastered that chapter. In between, you'll see rules, which are basic statements of grammar, usage, and mechanics principles. The rules are illustrated with examples and followed by exercises and reviews that help you practice what you have learned.

What are some other features of this textbook?

- **Oral Practice**—spoken practice and reinforcement of rules and concepts
- **Writing Applications**—activities that let you apply grammar, usage, and mechanics concepts in your writing
- **Tips & Tricks**—easy-to-use hints about grammar, usage, and mechanics
- **Meeting the Challenge**—questions or short activities that ask you to approach a concept from a new angle
- **Style Tips**—information about formal and informal uses of language
- **Help**—pointers to help you understand either key rules and concepts or exercise directions

Holt Handbook on the Internet

As you move through the *Holt Handbook,* you will find the best online resources at **go.hrw.com.**

Teaching Strands

Connecting Grammar and Writing
This teaching-strand chart shows you some ways to connect grammar instruction and writing instruction.

The *Holt Handbook* is designed to be a flexible teaching tool that accommodates many teaching philosophies and styles. For example, some teachers will prefer to use the handbook as a reference source, having students refer to it only as the need for explicit grammar instruction arises. Others will use the handbook as a teaching text, having their classes work through the instruction, examples, and exercises in a more methodical fashion. Your personal teaching style and the needs of your students will determine the best way for you to teach this material.

GO TO: go.hrw.com

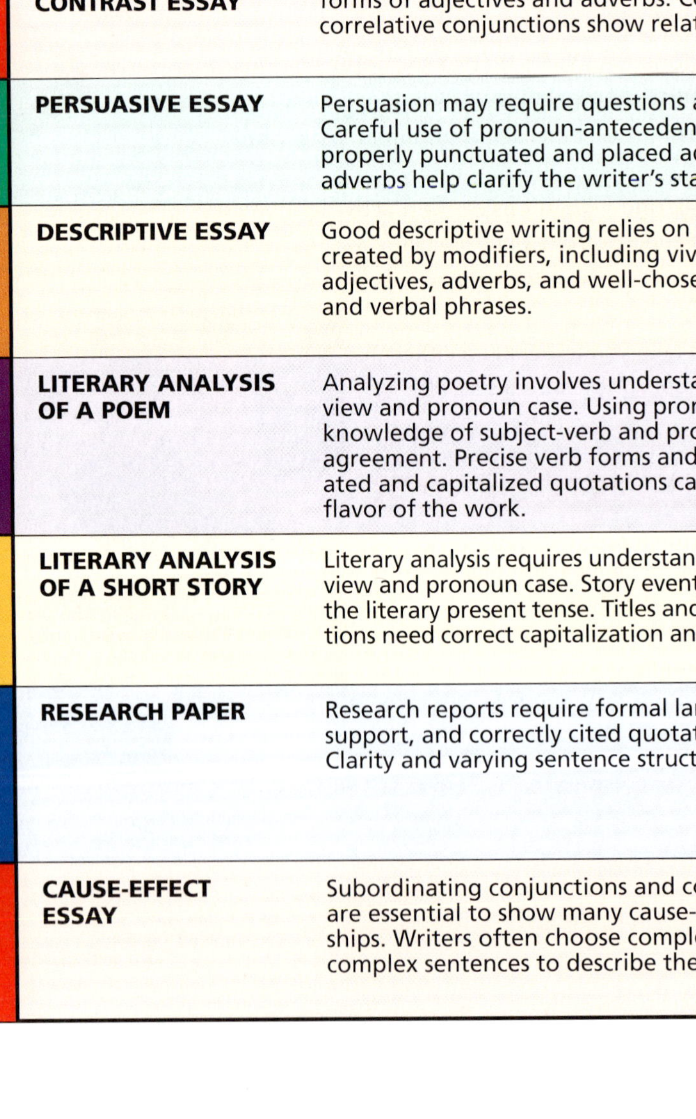

Writing Assignments	Rationale
AUTOBIOGRAPHICAL NARRATIVE	Autobiographical narratives call for clear depiction of people (subjects) and their actions (verbs). To keep such writing lively, writers often use active-voice verbs. Autobiographical narratives may involve dialogue; therefore, correctly using contractions, apostrophes, quotation marks, and commas is essential.
SHORT STORY	Action and conflict may develop through correctly punctuated dialogue containing informal contractions and dialects. Similes and metaphors may use prepositions and predicate nominatives.
NONFICTION ANALYSIS	Carefully chosen words can capture a work's essence. Citations of titles, details, and direct quotations must be properly capitalized and punctuated. Using adjective clauses eliminates short, choppy sentences.
COMPARISON-CONTRAST ESSAY	Comparing and contrasting calls for comparative forms of adjectives and adverbs. Coordinating and correlative conjunctions show relationships of ideas.
PERSUASIVE ESSAY	Persuasion may require questions and exclamations. Careful use of pronoun-antecedent agreement and properly punctuated and placed adjectives and adverbs help clarify the writer's stance.
DESCRIPTIVE ESSAY	Good descriptive writing relies on the precise images created by modifiers, including vivid single-word adjectives, adverbs, and well-chosen prepositional and verbal phrases.
LITERARY ANALYSIS OF A POEM	Analyzing poetry involves understanding point of view and pronoun case. Using pronouns requires knowledge of subject-verb and pronoun-antecedent agreement. Precise verb forms and correctly punctuated and capitalized quotations can capture the flavor of the work.
LITERARY ANALYSIS OF A SHORT STORY	Literary analysis requires understanding of point of view and pronoun case. Story events may be related in the literary present tense. Titles and supporting quotations need correct capitalization and punctuation.
RESEARCH PAPER	Research reports require formal language, detailed support, and correctly cited quotations and credits. Clarity and varying sentence structure are important.
CAUSE-EFFECT ESSAY	Subordinating conjunctions and conjunctive adverbs are essential to show many cause-effect relationships. Writers often choose complex and compound-complex sentences to describe these relationships.

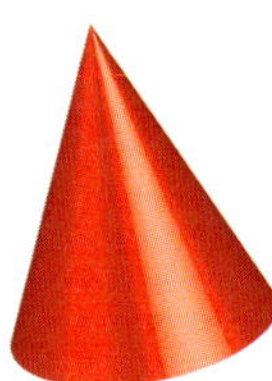

Links to Grammar	Links to Usage	Links to Mechanics
subjects, predicates (Ch. 2)	subject-verb agreement (Ch. 5)	apostrophes with contractions (Ch. 14)
action verbs, linking verbs (Ch. 1)	active voice (Ch. 6)	punctuating dialogue (Ch. 13)
pronouns (Ch. 1)	pronoun-antecedent agreement (Ch. 5)	apostrophes with possessives (Ch. 14)
pronouns, prepositions (Ch. 1)	pronoun-antecedent agreement (Ch. 5); *like, as* (Ch. 9)	punctuating dialogue (Ch. 13); contractions (Ch. 14)
predicate nominatives (Ch. 2)	pronoun case (Ch. 7)	
adjective clauses, relative pronouns (Ch. 4)	placement of adjective clauses (Ch. 8)	punctuating essential and nonessential clauses (Ch. 11);
kinds of sentences (Ch. 2); sentence structure (Ch. 4)		capitalizing and punctuating titles and quotations (Ch. 10 & Ch. 13)
adjectives, adverbs (Ch. 1)	modifiers (Ch. 8)	spelling with suffixes (Ch. 16)
conjunctions (Ch. 1); compound sentences (Ch. 4)	subject-verb agreement with compound subjects (Ch. 5)	punctuating compound sentences (Ch. 11 & Ch. 12)
sentences classified by purpose (Ch. 2)	pronoun-antecedent agreement (Ch. 5)	end marks (Ch. 11)
adjectives, adverbs (Ch. 1)	placement of modifiers (Ch. 8)	punctuating items in a series (Ch. 11)
adjectives, adverbs (Ch. 1)	comparison of modifiers (Ch. 8)	punctuation of items in a series (Ch. 11)
phrases (Ch. 3)	placement of phrase modifiers (Ch. 8)	punctuation of introductory and nonessential phrases (Ch. 11)
pronouns (Ch. 1)	agreement (Ch. 5); case forms of personal pronouns (Ch. 7)	quotation marks (Ch. 13); capitalizing titles (Ch. 10)
verbs (Ch. 1)	active, passive voice (Ch. 6)	spelling with suffixes (Ch. 16)
pronouns (Ch. 1)	pronoun case, person (Ch. 7)	capitalization of *I* (Ch. 10)
verbs (Ch. 1)	literary present tense (Ch. 6); subject-verb agreement when using literary titles (Ch. 5)	capitalization of titles (Ch. 10); punctuation of quotations and titles (Ch. 13)
independent and subordinate clauses (Ch. 4)	pronoun case, person (Ch. 7)	punctuating with commas, semicolons, colons (Ch. 11 & Ch. 12)
sentences classified by structure (Ch. 4)	formal English (Ch. 9)	quotation marks (Ch. 13); italics, hyphens, dashes, parentheses, ellipsis points, brackets (Ch. 15)
subordinate clauses (Ch. 4)	placement of clause modifiers (Ch. 8)	punctuation of introductory and nonessential phrases (Ch. 11)
subordinating conjunctions (Ch. 4)		punctuating sentences with semicolons and commas (Ch. 11 & Ch. 12)

By Amy Benjamin

Dispelling the Myths about Grammar Instruction

I know an excellent English teacher whose students, many years after graduation, remember her for her grammar lessons. Unfortunately, instead of being proud of this, she is chagrined. . . . "*Grammar*!? Of all things in my class to remember! Why *grammar*? Why can't they remember me for all the wonderful literature I taught them? for what I taught them about composition? expression? creativity? Why just *grammar*? I don't even teach *grammar* anymore. I teach the *writing* process."

Perhaps these students remembered their grammar lessons because of the usefulness of those lessons or because of the satisfaction that they derived from learning challenging material. Perhaps they remembered because those lessons in syntax, placement, word classification, and the subtleties of style helped them to be better writers, more efficient readers, clearer thinkers.

It is not uncommon for English teachers as well as their trainers and supervisors to hold that the teaching of grammar is quaint and unnecessary at best, prejudicial and exclusionary at worst.

How lamentable it is that teaching writing through a process approach has become an orthodoxy in which the grammatical strand of English language arts is pitted against the literary strand, as if the two are not intertwined. Who set up this false dichotomy? The notion that grammar instruction is antithetical to the writing process is specious. My purpose in this essay is to debunk some of the myths about grammar instruction and to refurbish its tarnished reputation.

It is not uncommon for English teachers as well as their trainers and supervisors to hold that the teaching of grammar is quaint and unnecessary at best, prejudicial and exclusionary at worst. The problem begins with muddy terminology. Some people conflate the terms *grammar, usage,* and *mechanics,* as well as the terms *correct/incorrect* and *standard/ non-standard.* Before I turn my fire extinguisher on the grammar myths, let me clarify my terms: By *grammar,* I refer to the rules which govern how words function in a sentence to make meaning. That *man bites dog* means something different from *dog bites man* is a function of grammar. By *usage,* I refer to the social conventions that determine what is considered standard. By *standard,* I do not mean *correct.* I mean that style of the English language which most educated people accept in formal circumstances. By *mechanics,* I refer to physical manifestations of language such as spelling, punctuation, capitalization and other conventions. In the case of *mechanics,* the terms *correct* and *incorrect* are more appropriate than they are when we are talking about matters of usage, but even spelling is not without gray areas.

Reasonable people can disagree over matters of content and methodology in teaching. However, I think everyone would agree that to understand a complicated system we need to know the names of its parts, their forms and functions, how the parts relate to the whole, and where these parts belong if the system is to operate at maximum efficiency. That said, here's what some people say about grammar instruction, and why I disagree with them.

Myth #1:

The explicit teaching of grammar does not improve writing ability, so time spent on grammar is time not spent on more worthy pursuits in the English classroom.

Think about it. Suppose my car is making a funny noise. Suppose I have no better understanding of what is going on under the hood than that. I take it to my mechanic, trusting his knowledge, integrity, and skill. He'll figure out what's wrong with my car and fix the problem. I'll pay the bill, and if all is not well, I'll get either another mechanic or another car. That is how many car owners (myself included) operate. We don't have the time or the inclination to learn the taxonomy, nomenclature, and anatomy of our cars.

When we don't speak explicitly to students about grammar, syntax, diction, and coherence, we have to resort to the "funny noise" method: We have to say "This part just doesn't sound right here," or "You're not saying this clearly." We may be able to help writers fix the sentence, but we haven't given them the generality that will allow them to apply what they've learned to similar circumstances.

On the other hand, I can know the names of all the tools in my toolbox, what each is for, and how they relate to one another; but if I don't use them to facilitate an actual job in progress, then my knowledge does not fulfill its intended purpose. For many of us, the grammar lessons that we learned in school were about "picking out." We'd "pick out" all kinds of structures: the parts of speech, subjects and predicates, simple subjects, helping verbs. Later, we'd hunt down adverbial clauses, subject complements, infinitives. We'd underline and double underline. We'd diagram. The trouble with our instruction was not that it was misguided, but that it was unfinished. Having learned to spot prepositional phrases, we may not have learned why doing so could improve our discourse.

How can we *use* our ability to identify grammatical structures such as prepositional phrases in our own reading and writing? We may have learned that the object of a preposition must be in the objective case, and that the object of a preposition is never the subject of the sentence. This knowledge helps us solve some usage problems, but that is not its main value. Knowing how to discern the subject and verb can help us read dense prose. When reading dense prose, the reader needs strategies. One such strategy is to reduce the sentence to its subject and verb. That done, the reader sees prepositional phrases for what they are: details. Beyond that, knowing about prepositions helps writers add sentence variety, as they learn not to begin sentence after sentence with the subject. Beginning a sentence with a prepositional phrase can set the stage for the action, but we have to be judicious: Sometimes, that prepositional phrase can be distracting or redundant. As modifiers, prepositional phrases can be movable, and their placement affects meaning, rhythm, and emphasis. Prepositional phrases, "time and place words," add detail and dimension. The novice writer who has difficulty fleshing out a topic can do well to consciously add more prepositional phrases. It is knowing what prepositional phrases can and can't do for you that makes being able to identify them worthwhile. Selecting standard pronoun case, creating purposeful variety in sentence structure, adding detail and dimension, and eliminating redundancy are some good reasons for being able to recognize prepositional phrases.

It is knowing what prepositional phrases can and can't do for you that makes being able to identify them worthwhile.

Recognition of a grammatical structure is only the beginning. If we think of grammar instruction as building an awareness of language choices available to the careful writer, then we view such instruction in two phases: recognition and application. Too often, the application phase does not happen. When it does not, the recognition phase seems to lack practicality. Thus does grammar instruction fall out of favor.

Myth #2:

Grammar instruction applies only to the editing phase of the writing process.

When people operate under this myth, they are confusing grammar with usage and mechanics. Usage and mechanics may be seen as "touch-ups," part of the finishing-off of a written piece. As such, they are not essential to the real intellectual work of the process, although no one should minimize their importance. Usage and mechanics can determine the first and last impressions that the reader gets of the writer's work. The point is that we should not limit our understanding of grammar to the surface features of usage and mechanics.

Along with diction and rhetoric, grammar (unlike usage and mechanics) is *organic* to the crafting of sentences and text. Writers with an awareness of grammar can make informed choices about how word order affects meaning. Picture a carpenter. He doesn't just blindly reach into his toolbox, pull out a screwdriver, try to make it do the work of a wrench, and figure he'll just sand down the rough spots later. We can make our students better writers if we teach them to use grammatical knowledge consciously as they match their syntax to their intentions.

We understand the power of graphic organizers in both reading and writing for many learners. We teach students to map their ideas as a prewriting strategy. We teach them to make Venn diagrams to show similarities and differences, and flowcharts to express sequence. Sentence structures are patterns. We can think in terms of certain grammatical templates, containers, that work well for certain types of ideas. Parallel structure and compound sentences or simple sentences with compound constituents are good containers for *like* elements bearing equal importance. Complex sentences are good containers to use when we need to show the backgrounding and foregrounding of elements that do not bear equal importance. Sentence structure selections occur in the drafting and revision stages of the writing process, as the writer searches for the clearest, most efficient way to express thoughts.

Many writers have an intuitive sense of what kinds of containers work best with what kinds of ideas. When we bring this underlying awareness of grammar to the conscious level, we help students manage inchoate ideas in the same way that a graphic organizer, such as a Venn diagram, might. Indeed, there is much to be said for using one of the many versions of graphic organizers *along with* sentence structure templates. The writer can then look at a branch diagram or a cluster, decide how the ideas are related, and then consider an array of syntactical containers to suit them.

What I've described is a way of understanding the role of grammar in the writing process that is deeper than what is commonly thought, i.e., that grammatical thinking enters the picture only as the cleanup man. In fact, we already make intuitive grammatical choices as we compose our thoughts. Those intuitive choices may or may not be the best ones for the purpose. By building awareness of sentence and textual structure, we can increase our chances that our message is clear, efficient, and graceful.

Myth #3:

Grammar is boring.

There are many ways to make our classrooms boring. We can "cover material" in a perfunctory way, "going over" the exercises done for homework or as seatwork. We can convey to students that their language is "wrong" and ours is "right." We can be language prudes, fainting and blanching at every double negative or misplaced modifier that dares to show its face in our presence. We can insist that the answer key is always the authority and that grammar is a "no discussion" subject. We can isolate the study of grammar, treat it as something we "have to get through" before moving on to literature. We can fail to make any connection between grammar and journalism, grammar and advertising, grammar and novels, grammar and drama, grammar and music, grammar and poetry. These are ways to make grammar boring.

I've heard teachers claim that grammar instruction interferes with creativity.

I've heard teachers claim that grammar instruction interferes with creativity. "Grammar is boring," they say. "And writing should be fun and interesting." This is a misguided notion, because creativity thrives within structure. The sonneteer works within a strictly prescribed structure, choosing that structure because it is the best container for particular ideas. The sonnet form is not constraining but liberating: The format frees the writer from decisions about rhythm and rhyme scheme. Because of the structure, half the work is done. I can't think of any creative pursuit—music, fine arts, dance, photography, drama, writing—that does not demand mastery of technique. I can't think of any creative pursuit in which there is no terminology, no anatomy, no structure, no tradition, no rules. Why would learning any kind of writing, much less creative writing, be detached from the fundamentals? Knowledge of structure is not a hindrance, but a guide that enables, rather than impedes, creativity.

Sometimes, grammar instruction is thought of as "drill and kill." This pejorative implies that the instruction will consist of lower level thinking skills, mindless repetition, and lack of application to authentic language. We picture fill-in-the-blank workbook-type questions in which there is one right answer. The book that you have in your hands is an extremely useful, in fact indispensable, tool for the teaching of language. However, any grammar text is most effective when used *along with*, not in place of, literature and student writing. It might seem that students would naturally make the crossover from what they learn in grammar exercises to their own language use, but such is not necessarily the case. As teachers, we have to make that crossover happen very deliberately, pointing out structures that students have learned and how those structures are used to make meaning in authentic contexts. Thus does grammar instruction transcend the practice exercises that illustrate targeted concepts.

Everybody loves language; children and teenagers love it especially, because they are in the process of defining their own culture by laying claim to words and expressions all their own. When we invite students to analyze their own neologisms, grammatical idiosyncrasies, and dialectical styles, we enliven grammar lessons immeasurably. As English teachers, we embrace all forms of the English language even while we recognize that mastery of standard English is essential for success in certain precincts of society.

Another way to make grammar instruction interesting is to let students discover how language changes right before our eyes. Movies and novels set in various pockets of the English-speaking world are museums of linguistic anthropology. Compare the idioms of *To Kill A Mockingbird* to those of *The Color Purple.* Analyze the language of a movie set in New Orleans and compare it to the language of a movie set in Los Angeles.

There are many ways to make our classrooms interesting. Our love of the subject is contagious. Grammar is exciting and rewarding to learn not because we get the answers right, but because we've applied logic and found patterns, and because there may be more than one answer, depending on the circumstances, audience, and purpose. Contrary to myth, a good grammar lesson can invite a lively discussion about ambiguities in meaning and the best way to express thought in a particular context. It can even ignite a discussion about social power structures, prejudices, and immigration. This is not boring stuff.

Myth #4:

Grammar applies only to English classes.

For lack of a better term, we refer to subjects other than English as "content areas." Aside from the obvious expectation that we use standard English in school, how can students apply grammar to their content area classes?

Every teacher wants students to be better readers. A law student told me recently that she was glad that she knew something about grammar, because she needed it to read complex materials in her courses. She found that by mentally pulling out the subject and verb, she could follow the lines of technical text.

Needless to say, grammatical knowledge of the English language is essential for learning another language. Just as grammar has fallen out of favor in many English classes, it has suffered a similar blow in the pedagogy of learning other languages as well, where grammar instruction has been supplanted by "conversation." The predictable consequence has been much confusion and frustration for both teachers, who feel that their hands are tied, and students, many of whom are bewildered by the gymnastics of the French verb when they don't even know how English verbs behave.

What about science, math, social studies, the arts? All teachers love words. The biology teacher is fussy about the difference between *osmosis* and *diffusion.* Getting students to make fine distinctions is an important part of teaching students to think like scientists. Teachers want to give away the words of their subject areas the way grandmothers want to give away food. We want to invite our students into the professional conversation of our subject areas.

Teachers want to give away the words of their subject areas the way grandmothers want to give away food.

As English teachers, we love words about words, language about language. To us, there is a vast difference between an action verb and a linking verb, a predicate nominative and a direct object, a transitive verb and an intransitive verb. In teaching students to talk the talk, we turn them into licensed operators, not just amateurs. A licensed operator can make the machinery run more efficiently, can anticipate potential problems, and can fix what is wrong. An amateur *hopes* that the sentence "sounds good."

Grammar should be the permeable membrane that allows knowledge learned in English class to transform into skill in the content area classes. Active voice may be preferable in English classes where the subject is often *people doing things* (S-V-O). In composing a lab report, however, passive voice may be the better choice. *The difference in pressure was recorded* might sound more scientific than *I recorded the difference in pressure.* In the language of lab reports, the fact that the technician did the action is irrelevant. A radiologist writes her report in the passive voice: *No abnormalities were found,* rather than *I found no abnormalities.* In English class, we show students the difference in tone between active and passive voice.

It is important to learn to think in action verbs in all subject areas. A student who is writing about the Reformation needs to focus on who did what: *Martin Luther translated the Bible into the German vernacular. His translation enabled more people to read the Bible.* The action verbs tell the story. They give students a starting point when writing and a focus when reading. All subject areas use this concept; it is we English teachers who actually teach it in our grammar lessons.

The social studies teacher and the science teacher may not know it, but the benefits of grammar instruction are carried through the student's entire day.

Myth #5:

Grammar instruction is ethnocentric and prejudicial.

As English teachers, we need to avoid giving the impression that we are the designated Keepers of the Language. We can teach the etiquette of standard English without denying a student the right to his or her own dialect.

An educated person has that social thermostat that linguists call code-switching. The metaphor of table manners is apt: What we are expected to do at an outdoor barbecue differs from what we're expected to do at Thanksgiving dinner. Those of us who can't tell the difference, who can't code-switch, are socially awkward. This is not to say that standard English is better than any particular dialect. Standard English is not more expressive, more poetic, or even more accurate. It is simply the expected currency of mainstream society in formal situations. We don't have to use it all of the time, but if we *can't* use it when it is expected, then we are at a cultural disadvantage that our education should remedy.

We are constantly making impressions that indicate our understanding of our social context. Those who are successful in their chosen fields, indeed, those for whom a chosen field is an option in the first place, know how to control the impression that others have of them. People judge our status and education levels not only through language, but also through dress, manners, and gesture.

Once we acknowledge that standard English is just another form of English that is appropriate for certain situations but not for all, then we are free to enjoy the dialects of English that we find in authentic literature, regional speech, song lyrics, and casual conversation. We can look at new coinages, popular metaphors, slang, and jargon with the interest of a linguist rather than the arrogance of a pedant.

We can teach the etiquette of Standard English without denying a student the right to his or her own dialect.

That language is a changing social contract is evidenced by grammar books of yore. Even in one generation, the *who/whom* distinction has attenuated, as has the use of the past perfect tense of verbs. Certain usages, such as the nominative case after a linking verb, sound stuffy. We have yet to solve the problem that exists because we lack a generic singular pronoun: *He,* once preferred, is thought to be sexist; *one* sounds stilted and British; *they* is a grammatical mismatch. That leaves *he or she*, which can seem awfully conspicuous. It's interesting to have students compare the style guides of various publications on sensitive points such as this.

Myth #6:

As native speakers, we don't have to learn grammar.

It is true that we already know grammar intuitively. Native speakers learn, quite naturally, how to put words together to make meaning. What we don't learn naturally is the metalanguage, that is, the language of language. Absent that, we can't explain what we mean about what we are trying to say, and others are at a loss to help us.

Terminology is powerful.

Recently, I worked with a group of elementary school teachers who were looking for teaching strategies that would improve their students' writing skills. When I suggested that they develop a scope and sequence in grammar skills, they were skeptical. "They already know how to use adjectives, nouns, and verbs," one teacher said. "Why do they have to know the *names* of these things?" "That just isn't the way we teach anymore," said another with a wave of her hand. "We don't want to interfere with the children's creativity. Teaching them grammar would interrupt their flow." A fourth-grade teacher added, "But that isn't on the state test, and we really don't have time for anything that doesn't get the scores up." Here's what I would answer:

Terminology is powerful. We can't improve our sentences until we understand the crucial role played by verbs. We certainly can't understand that role until we know how to identify verbs in context and that verbs come in various flavors: finite verbs, infinitives, participles, gerunds.

Further, creativity and "flow" are enhanced, not impeded, by knowledge of language structure and what certain kinds of phrases and sentences can and can't do. When the reader has to stumble over and re-read awkward, redundant, convoluted, or misplaced structures within sentences, does it matter how creative the writer was? Doesn't the logic of grammar *improve* the flow of prose?

To answer the last objection, the statewide tests may or may not have explicit questions regarding grammar. Some do; some don't, and the nature of those tests can and will change. What will not change is that a writer who knows where commas belong makes the job easier on the reader, as does the writer who understands subordination, agreement, and overall sentence management. If we acknowledge that the whole purpose of writing is to communicate, and that communication is accomplished by writing clearly, then we can see the application of grammar to writing. Of course, if grammar instruction never makes the leap from identification of a structure to its effective application, then these teachers are right to reject it as largely irrelevant.

What Knowing Grammar Can Do for Writers

Finally, here is a list of what you can do when you know a few things about grammar:

- If you know how to use parallel structure, you can make your message smoother, clearer, easier on the reader, more logical, and more memorable.
- If you know when to use active voice and when to use passive voice, you can control the directness or indirectness of your message. You control the power and impact of your words. You can also avoid the trouble that comes from being too direct or accusatory.
- If you know how to use verb tense consistently, you can guide your reader through the tangle of time in your narrative.
- If you know how to vary the grammatical constructs in your sentence structure, you can make your flow of sentences more musical, more nuanced, less choppy.
- If you know the difference between a phrase, a clause, and a sentence, you can guide your reader by using well-placed punctuation.

Like poetry, grammar is about the beauty of expressing exactly what we mean by placing the words just right.

Understanding how grammar works puts the writer on the right path. When writers begin a definition by saying "Osmosis is *when* . . ." they are failing to apply the concept that a subject complement, not an adverbial clause, must follow a linking verb. The "*is when* . . ." definition is going to fall on its face because the key term has not been handled properly in the sentence. Definitions call for classification. First, we must place the term in its proper realm: "Osmosis is a . . . process? means? phenomenon?" The writer must stop and think about what *kind* of thing osmosis is. Such categorical thinking is absolutely essential to the scientist, but it does not happen with the ungrammatical ". . . *is when*" structure. This example demonstrates the relationship between grammar and the logical progression of ideas.

Knowing grammar is useful, but even if it weren't, learning it would still be worthwhile because it is interesting. Like chess, grammar is about how power and proximity govern relationships and possibilities. Like engineering, grammar is about structure, balance, efficiency and strength. Like mathematics, grammar is about patterns and forms. Like geology, grammar is at once eternal and dynamic. Like poetry, grammar is about the beauty of expressing exactly what we mean by placing the words just right. ■

Amy Benjamin is an English teacher at Hendrick Hudson High School in Montrose, New York. In addition, she is a consultant to teachers, administrators, staff developers, and people in the business world. Amy specializes in showing people how to use clear, concise language. She has written several books about teaching literacy skills in all subject areas, as well as two plays (Romeo and Juliet Will Not Be Performed Tonight *and* Romeo and Juliet: Still Not Dead) *and a young adult novel* (Russell Kim: My Real Name). *Amy lives in Fishkill, New York, with her husband Howard and son Mitch.*

By Brock Haussamen

Grammar: Why Teach It?

Why should students learn—and teachers teach—grammar? Simply memorizing the parts of speech doesn't, by itself, make students better writers. Worrying about errors can quickly dampen student enthusiasm for a writing project. Over the past three decades, grammar's reputation has suffered. Is grammar useful? Why teach it?

I believe the central reason for teaching and learning grammar is that it gives all of us a language for talking about language, and certainly the ability to talk about language is a fundamental educational goal. It is difficult to discuss sentences without knowing basic grammar in the same way that it is difficult to talk about a sport or a science or politics without knowing the names of its elements and how they are organized. Knowing basic grammar is what enables students to discuss the sentences in a book they are reading or in a paper they are writing, and to discuss their native language or a second language.

Think of grammar as having two faces. One is its public face, which can be quite formal. The other face is private and more friendly.

The Two Faces of Grammar

To teach grammar effectively, we need to show students how to put it to use. The language of grammar—the names for the parts of speech and other sentence components that appear in the grammar section of this textbook—has two distinct kinds of uses. Think of grammar as having two faces. One is its public face, which can be quite formal. The other face is private and more friendly.

Public Grammar

The public face of grammar consists of all the rules we teach students to follow in their writing and all the errors we tell them to avoid making. In this textbook it is the material in the sections on usage and mechanics. I call usage and mechanics "public grammar" because they identify the conventions of the standard American dialect in which our society carries on its formal writing and speaking. There are many good reasons to teach these conventions. Such a standard dialect helps people from different places and different backgrounds to communicate clearly. The conventions of public grammar help sustain the uniformity of our writing system, on which our society depends utterly. Finally, they reflect the language of economic power. In general, people who can write and speak according to the standard conventions have a better chance at participating in the influential core of our society. People who do not master those conventions will likely face obstacles at every turn.

It is important for us to remember and to remind our students that public grammar is different from, not inherently better than, the language students normally use. The do's and don'ts of public grammar create an illusion that they are rigorously logical, like the rules of mathematics, and that they are permanent. Neither of these claims is true. The do's and don'ts are sometimes illogical, and they change. Just a few decades ago, grammar textbooks like this one would have insisted on the distinction between *will* and *shall*; today that distinction is all but gone. A few decades into the future, a book such as this will probably simplify and may even omit the distinction between *who* and *whom*, which is already fading in informal English.

The "right" clothes, like the "right" grammar, depend on what is appropriate or expected in a given situation.

Try explaining to your students that their grammar is like the clothes they wear. The "right" clothes, like the "right" grammar, depend on what is appropriate or expected in a given situation. Around their friends, students talk and dress in particular ways. At formal occasions or in the workplace, they will be required to dress, to talk, and to write in other ways. This approach will less likely demean those students who do not routinely hear and use standard English. It also gives grammatical correctness a practical value and encourages your students to see language differences as an example of social diversity and opportunity.

Private Grammar

The other face of grammar is much more personal. By "private grammar," I mean the language structure that all of us already carry around in our heads and put to use when we communicate or think. In contrast to the study of public grammar, which has evolved over centuries, the description of our inherent language ability has grown from the work of linguists over the last several decades. Such grammar is private in the sense that it operates inside our heads, so quickly we are not even conscious of it. You won't find questions about private grammar on standardized tests; it is what students possess in order to read the tests in the first place.

If using public grammar can be compared to wearing socially acceptable formal clothes, private grammar can be compared to doing what comes naturally, to physical skills such as walking or running or throwing. Ask students to take a statement and turn it into a question in their native language. They can do it easily. They can fit new slang words into sentences fluidly. They know quickly when the language they hear or read sounds confusing or clear, choppy or smooth. They do all this with their private grammar.

Private grammar can be compared to doing what comes naturally, to physical skills such as walking or running or throwing.

If they can do all this already, how will studying grammar help them do more? The answer is that any skill that already comes somewhat naturally, like throwing a ball or making music, will improve if we learn about it and practice it. Students will be using the language of grammar to some degree when they revise and combine sentences in the section on "Writing Effective Sentences" in this textbook. They will do so to a greater degree whenever you show them how to improve the style of their writing by finding active verbs or expanding sentences with participles or prepositional phrases.

Putting Grammar to Use

As you can see from these descriptions of public and private faces, the language of basic grammar has many uses. Nonetheless, it is a difficult language for students to grow comfortable with; its vocabulary looks large and forbidding; many of the terms combine with each other in ways that seem strange to students ("adjective clause"); and because it is a language about language, it strains the verbal skills of many of its students, both children and adults. So, like any language it must be practiced often and put to use in a variety of contexts. Here are some general suggestions.

Use Private Grammar to Teach Public Grammar

As language users, we all have an intuitive sense that sentences are made up of sections. Give students a sentence and ask them to divide it into chunks and to group the words that go together. This approach can remain basic or can become more refined as students divide and cluster clauses and phrases.

This sort of activity easily leads to sentence diagramming. If you are not familiar with diagramming, see Chapter 20. I teach students not the whole of it but just the basic components; even elementary diagrams help many students see the subject-predicate core of a sentence more clearly. If you choose to teach diagramming more thoroughly, students will be able to analyze difficult sentences that they encounter in reading and will build their comprehension. Many students enjoy constructing the diagrams; the activity taps students' visual and spatial skills in addition to their verbal ones.

Another way to draw on students' private grammatical ability is to provide them with practical shortcuts for getting at the essential points of grammar. Grammarians over the years have assembled a number of these simple methods, and your students will love you for telling them about these methods. One good book on the subject is Rei Noguchi's *Grammar and the Teaching of Writing: Limits and Possibilities* (NCTE). Students find the shortcuts practical, and they also appreciate the positive reinforcement of their grammatical instincts.

Use Grammar for Reading

Although grammar is most closely associated with writing, students can put grammar to use when they read.

Knowing grammatical terminology gives students the tools they need to discuss a difficult sentence in a story or a poem. Ask students to pick out the main verb and then the simple subject; finding these can help them figure out the rest of the sentence. Poets bend sentences around a good deal, but most poetry consists of recognizable sentences and sentence parts. Often you can help students move beyond their perplexity about a poem by reminding them to look for the sentences and their basic parts.

In discussing with students what they enjoy or don't enjoy about a writer's style, look for the grammatical characteristics of the writer's sentences. What parts of speech stand out in the sentences? Some writers specialize in strong, active verbs, with few forms of the verb *be*. In other writers' texts, *is* and *are* abound, but the nouns stand out. In still others', the adjectives and adverbs catch the reader's attention.

Another approach is to ask students how long a writer's sentences are, on average. What characteristic sentence lengths do students notice among types of writers, or the writers of different periods? This approach can lead to a discussion of the different structures that make up a writer's sentences. Some writers like to add modifiers, phrases, and clauses; other writers keep sentences short to highlight the main nouns and verbs. Some start a sentence with long introductory word groups; others go right to the subject.

Bring grammar into the reading of advertisements, political language, and the World Wide Web. Advertisements provide good examples of sentence fragments, imperative verbs, and words that look like nouns but act like adjectives ("a Labor Day sofa sale"). Political speeches and slogans make interesting use of *we* and other personal pronouns. E-mail seems to encourage sentences that are variously clipped, casual, funny, skillful, and careless. Ask students to bring in examples for discussion.

Use Grammar for Revision

When students write, help them use grammar not just in the final editing stage, when they hunt out their violations of public grammar, but in the revising stage as well, when they can experiment with private grammar to develop their style as writers.

This textbook shows students how to combine sentences by inserting words or using conjunctions. Students can use some of the same methods to build a single sentence. They can build their sentences by adding participles (especially *–ing* participles that function half as an active verb, half as an adjective) and also by adding appositives. "A spider, **a repulsive, hairy creature, no bigger than a tarantula,** crawled into the room. . . . **Hands trembling, sweat dripping from his face,** he flung the magazine left and right, **trying to kill the spiders,** but there were too many." That example of an eighth-grader's work is from Harry Noden's *Image Grammar: Using Grammatical Structures to Teach Writing,* an excellent source for these and other techniques. Students can also add phrases, especially prepositional phrases, and clauses to a sentence, expanding the information about their main point, giving more details in order to paint a picture, building, and penetrating further into their topic. (The sentence that you just read is one example; you can find more—and better ones—in the work of most accomplished writers.) Students may think at first that they are merely making sentences longer, but they will quickly find that they are also saying more.

Conclusion

The suggestions in this essay are only a sample of the good ideas for using the language of grammar to help students become better readers and writers. The books I have mentioned will lead you to other ideas. And your colleagues in language arts can provide you with many other suggestions for using grammar in the classroom. If you think of grammar as a language for talking about language and you keep in mind the differences

between public and private grammar, you can make grammar a valuable part of your students' language education.

For Further Reading

Assembly for the Teaching of English Grammar. www.ateg.org.

Berk, Lynn M. *English Syntax: From Word to Discourse.* New York: Oxford UP, 1999.

Haussamen, Brock. *Revising the Rules: Traditional Grammar and Modern Linguistics.* 2nd ed. Dubuque: Kendall/Hunt, 2000.

Kolln, Martha. *Rhetorical Grammar: Grammatical Choices, Rhetorical Effect.* 3rd ed. Boston: Allyn and Bacon, 1998.

Kolln, Martha, and Robert Funk (contributor). *Understanding English Grammar.* 5th ed. Needham: Allyn and Bacon, 1998.

Noden, Harry R. *Image Grammar: Using Grammatical Structures to Teach Writing.* Portsmouth: Heinemann/Boynton Cook, 1999.

Noguchi, Rei. *Grammar and the Teaching of Writing: Limits and Possibilities.* Urbana: NCTE, 1991.

Weaver, Constance. *Teaching Grammar in Context.* Portsmouth: Boynton/Cook, 1996.

William, Joseph M. Style: *The Lessons in Clarity and Grace.* 6th ed. New York: Longman, 2000. ■

Brock Haussamen has taught at Raritan Valley Community College in New Jersey since 1968. He is the author of Revising the Rules: Traditional Grammar and Modern Linguistics *(Kendall/Hunt) and also of a book on the history of the local New Jersey railroads. He began serving as president of the Assembly for the Teaching of English Grammar in 2000. His hobby and passion recently is playing ragtime piano.*

By Rei R. Noguchi

Getting Down to Basics:

Using What Students Already Know

Like sentences, subjects and verbs are among the most basic elements of grammar and writing instruction.

Too often we struggle in teaching basic grammar to our students. Yet what really are the basics and how should we teach them? The most basic—the rock-bottom minimum—are sentence, verb, and subject. Surprisingly, we can teach these three basic elements by taking advantage of the unconscious linguistic knowledge that students already possess, their private grammar, so to speak. By tapping this unconscious knowledge, we can help students identify more easily the three basic elements, and, more important, help them better understand subsequent instruction in grammar, usage, and mechanics.

Why are the sentence, verb, and subject the very basics of grammar instruction? Take the notion of sentence. The sentence constitutes the most important unit in written texts, particularly in writing for school. A shaky grasp of what counts as a written sentence inevitably and unintentionally leads to distracting sentence fragments, fused sentences, and comma splices. Clearly, to master formal written English, students need to differentiate between a genuine sentence and an inappropriate nonsentence. Like sentences, subjects and verbs are among the most basic elements of grammar and writing instruction. Besides helping to define a sentence, subjects and verbs constitute elements on which a great deal of grammar and writing instruction builds. Without a reliable way of identifying subject and verb, students can almost certainly expect rough going.

How can we teach the concepts of subject, verb, and sentence so that students can identify them easily? I would suggest that, rather than relying solely on semantic definitions, we take fuller advantage of what we often ignore or downplay in our teaching of grammar, namely, the tremendous unconscious knowledge that all fluent or near-fluent speakers of English bring to the classroom every day. Put more bluntly, our students know a great deal more about grammar than many of us think. This grammar is not school grammar but their "private grammar," the system of rules unconsciously learned and unconsciously used by all fluent speakers of English in everyday conversation. We cannot teach this personal underlying grammar for the simple reason that our students already know it. All we can do is bring this knowledge to the surface and exploit it to the fullest.

Identifying the Sentence

Exploiting the unconscious linguistic knowledge of students is the key to teaching the very basics of grammar. For students unaccustomed or resistant to working with abstract definitions, identifying sentences and fragments may prove difficult. To identify fragments, students must, at minimum, understand that a fragment is an "incomplete sentence"; to apply this definition, however, students must understand what a sentence is. To understand what a sentence is, students must understand such terms as subject, predicate, and independent clause. Each of these terms may require further definitions yet.

Exploiting the unconscious linguistic knowledge of students is the key to teaching the very basics of grammar.

To avoid the chain of seemingly endless definitions to identify sentences and fragments, teachers can take advantage of their students' unconscious knowledge of what constitutes a complete sentence. Teachers can, for example, use the following frame to help students tap what they already know.

Sentence Frame:
They liked the idea that

____________________.

Many word groups will fit in the frame, but whatever they are, they will all be genuine declarative sentences. Students can try out fragments you provide, such as *Thinking of joining the team* or *Because he joined the team,* as well as any suspicious word groups they themselves may write. If students discover a fragment, they can add or delete words to make it fit into the frame and thereby change the fragment into a genuine sentence. There is no need to define a sentence formally at this stage. If students can perform the simple test given here, they already unconsciously know what a sentence is, and with that knowledge they can easily identify fragments, which are just parts of sentences. With a bit of guidance and exploration, students will discover that fused sentences and comma splices won't fit in the empty slot either.

Identifying Verbs

If we tap the private grammar of our students, we can also help them identify specific and important parts of the sentence. Below are two frames that will help students identify words that can serve as main verbs.

Main-Verb Frame 1:
They might _____ (it) now.

Main-Verb Frame 2:
They aren't _____-ing (it) now.

Any word that fits in the empty slots above will be the base form (infinitive) of the main verb, the form listed in the dictionary (e.g., *eat, collect, finish, sleep*). There is no need here to define *main verb.* If the word fits in the empty slot, it's a word that English speakers and writers can and do use as a main verb in sentences.

Because verbs don't always occur in the base form in actual sentences, students need other strategies to identify verbs, especially in the sentences they compose. Here again, we can take advantage of the unconscious linguistic knowledge of students, this time their uncanny ability to produce negative sentences and yes-no questions, to assist students in identifying helping verbs.

If we examine the following sentences, we see that a helping verb is a word that immediately precedes the negative element (*–n't* or *not*) in negated sentences or the word that gets fronted in yes-no questions.

EXAMPLES

1. Jim should go to the football game. *[Transform this into a negative sentence or a question.]*

   Jim **should**n't go to the football game.

   Should Jim go to the football game?

2. Jim went to the football game.

   Jim **did**n't go to the football game.

   Did Jim go to the football game?

If we have students transform declarative sentences into either negative sentences or yes-no questions, we can help them identify helping verbs. Again, there is no need to define *helping verb* formally. Though students may have never heard of the term *helping verb* (or *auxiliary verb*) before, they already unconsciously know what it is if they can produce a corresponding negative sentence or a corresponding yes-no question from a declarative sentence. Making such transformations requires complex linguistic knowledge. Yet, remarkably, we don't have to teach students how to do this. If students are fluent or near-fluent in spoken English, they already know it, as amply demonstrated in their daily speech. What we need to do, however, is to take advantage of this knowledge in teaching the basics of grammar.

Main Verb *Be*

The main verb *be* (as in *They were friends*) is especially tricky because, unlike other main verbs, it moves to the front in yes-no questions (*Were they friends?*). It also takes the negative element in negative sentences (*They weren't friends*). The main verb *be* can thus masquerade as the helping verb *be* (compare *They were friends* to *They were running*). To make matters worse, the main verb *be* appears frequently in student writing. Indeed, when we complain that our students write with too many *be* verbs, we really mean the main verb *be*, not the helping verb *be*. This gives all the more reason for students to be able to identify the main verb *be*. Teaching students to use the main-verb frames and the helping-verb transformations can reduce confusion over the function of *be* in a sentence. Further, having students memorize the main-verb forms of *be* can reduce the confusion even more.

Identifying Subjects

Once students have identified the verb of a sentence, they can easily identify the subject. To identify the latter, they can insert the verb in the question frame below and then answer the question.

Simple-Subject Frame:
Who or what __________?

In most cases, the answer to the question will be the subject of the sentence.

Applying Knowledge of Subjects and Verbs

Being able to identify subjects and verbs brings considerable payoffs. It will help students understand *clause*, which, in turn, will help them understand *independent* (or *main*) *clause* and *subordinate* (or *dependent*) *clause.* Understanding these terms will help them better understand the notion of *sentence*, which, in turn, will help them better understand and correct any unintentional fragment or run-on sentence. (Think also of all the punctuation rules that directly or indirectly refer to these structures.) Being able to identify subjects and verbs will certainly help students identify errors in subject-verb agreement, errors in verb-tense consistency, and even the overuse of main verb *be*. This skill can also help students identify verbs in the passive voice and can help students choose the correct case of personal pronouns. In short, knowing how to identify subjects and verbs leads to an understanding of a host of other concepts.

Conclusion

For many language arts teachers, teaching grammar is both a labor of love and a love of labor. Many of us like the notion of grammar as a system, the wholes and parts fitting into place. Yet too often we struggle with difficult concepts and often with indifferent students. We can make the labor of teaching grammar less—and, hopefully, the love of grammar more for both teacher and student—if we take advantage of the prodigious private linguistic knowledge that all fluent speakers of English, native and non-native, bring to the language arts classroom every day.

Further References

DeBeaugrande, Robert. "Forward to the Basics: Getting Down to Grammar." *College Composition and Communication* 35 (1984): 358–67.

Noguchi, Rei R. *Grammar and the Teaching of Writing: Limits and Possibilities.* Urbana, IL: National Council of Teachers of English. 1991. ■

Rei R. Noguchi, Professor of English and Linguistics at California State University, Northridge, has taught courses in linguistics to practicing and prospective language arts teachers for over seventeen years. He is the author of Grammar and the Teaching of Writing: Limits and Possibilities *(NCTE). When not teaching or writing, he enjoys reading, bicycling, and following various kinds of sports, particularly baseball.*

By Billy T. Boyar, Ph.D.

Raising Expectations:

The Importance of Teaching Grammar to ESL Students

In the sixth grade, my class was taught sentence diagramming. Trying to superimpose our simple schoolbook diagrams on the infinity of language felt mysterious. Studying grammar in such a systematic way was like mapping the stars: We named unidentified words and charted their relationships. Words and phrases depended on other words like moons held to planets by gravity, and verbs sparkled like stars. I was not surprised, years later, to learn that the word *grammar* is etymologically related to *glamour* and *gramarye*,

Studying grammar in such a systematic way was like mapping the stars: We named unidentified words and charted their relationships.

suggesting magic. To me, the study of grammar has always been interesting and provocative in its own right. There are, however, important practical reasons for studying grammar and even more important practical reasons for ESL students to study it.

In the past, some people have disparaged the formal, systematic teaching of grammar to the ESL student. When people emphasize the importance of the natural way of learning language, beginning with hearing and mimicking, I agree with them. When they stress the necessity of creating a relaxed noncritical environment in which the ESL student feels free to practice speaking his or her new language, I agree with them. I agree that the study of literature and written composition is crucial. I even agree that grammar, if taught to young children or to ESL beginners of any age, should be fun and games, or should not be taught at all. However, when people advocate such approaches to the exclusion of a formal program of grammar for ESL students who are at least on an intermediate level and at least in the sixth grade, their argument is extreme, and I disagree with them.

Why is the study of grammar, usage, and mechanics important for appropriately mature and advanced ESL students?

Avoiding False Analogies

A study of English grammar, usage, and mechanics helps ESL students to avoid developing English language habits based on false analogies with the rules for their primary language. A comparative study of different languages shows that the basic patterns of grammar, conventions such as punctuation and capitalization, and the special uses of words can be vastly different. For example, a Spanish sentence doesn't necessarily need a subject (the subject can be implied by the verb); Spanish uses the present tense where English would sometimes use the past tense; question marks and exclamation points are placed both at the beginning and at the end of sentences; and a double negative is considered standard usage. English is even further from the grammatical expectations of Chinese and other non-Western ESL students.

In the past, some people have disparaged the formal, systematic teaching of grammar to the ESL student.

In my composition class, a Mexican American student submitted an essay that contained this sentence: "The Christmas party resulted well." The cognates *to result* (English) and *resultar* (Spanish) have confusingly similar meanings, yet their usage is distinctly different. Here, *resultar* could be translated *to turn out.* My student meant that the party turned out well, but she was basing her English usage on a false analogy with Spanish usage.

Not only does the ESL student tend to base English grammar rules on such false analogies, but also he or she often hears nonstandard usage repeated by friends and family. Being continually reinforced, the false analogy becomes an ingrained habit. Without the formal, systematic study of English grammar, usage, and mechanics, the ESL student may always have difficulty with standard English.

Promoting Academic Success

Teaching grammar to ESL students will help them succeed academically, especially if they plan to attend college. I have taught ESL and English at both high school and college. In composition classes, which also often contain ESL students, I frequently need to explain a point of grammar in order to help students understand why I am asking them to revise their papers. I want them to understand the principle so that they can avoid committing the same error over and over in future essays. For example, I ask them not to separate the subject and verb with only one comma (as in *Sara, who lives nearby is on my soccer team.*). This comment inevitably requires a further explanation: "Here you have inserted a nonessential clause between the subject and verb."

"But Mister," asks one ESL student, "what do you mean . . . *nonessential?*"

"A nonessential clause is a clause that can be removed. . . ."

"But what's a clause?"

"A clause contains a subject and a verb—it can be independent or subordinate. There are three kinds of subordinate . . ."

"What do you mean *subordinate?*"

"I mean that they have a subject and verb but that they cannot stand . . ."

"So what's a subject?"

"A subject is the noun or pronoun doing the . . ."

"Noun?"

The problem is that trying to teach a little bit of grammar is like trying to paint a little bit of a wall: It doesn't work.

I encounter situations like this all the time—and of course, ESL students aren't the only ones who don't know formal English grammar. The problem is that trying to teach a little bit of grammar is like trying to paint a little bit of a wall: It doesn't work. In a college composition class, instructors typically explain points of grammar, usage, and mechanics as they are related to essays submitted by students. However, it would not be appropriate to stop the composition class in order to devote the rest of the course to the basics of grammar. The result is that the ESL student who knows no formal English grammar is poorly served because he or she cannot take full advantage of the instructor's explanations.

Like many a native English speaker's, the ESL student's grammar and usage may never be perfect. Rather than perfection, the goal is a workable compromise. If students can communicate effectively in English, does it matter that they speak with an accent? The lives of ESL students will not be destroyed, for example, if they do not master the subjunctive mood. As teachers, we must demand excellence, but at the same time, we should carefully consider what exactly we want students to master.

Supporting Career Success

Studying grammar will help ESL students succeed professionally. Recently, a city employee asked me to tutor him in English. He had started out as a garbage collector, but after a few years his bosses recognized his ability and promoted him, then promoted him again. He suddenly found himself having to write memos and job descriptions. Now, in order to keep the job, he was required to improve his English grammar, usage, and mechanics.

The reality is that proficiency in standard English is a badge required for acceptance in many careers and professions in the United States. Teachers, lawyers, doctors, and so forth may not be given the respect and trust they deserve if their use of language departs too far from the standard. Beyond this country, English has become the foremost international language. The dialect of the neighborhood, rightly cherished, will not succeed very well in commerce on the World Wide Web. The formal, systematic study of grammar, usage, and mechanics helps the ESL student separate neighborhood dialect from public language, in order to develop that public language in a clear and conscious way. Being truly bilingual, of

> **The reality is that proficiency in standard English is a badge required for acceptance in many careers and professions in the United States.**

course, is more than merely owning a badge. Coupling a career or professional training with authentic bilingualism will broaden opportunities in ways that are numerous and unforeseen: as a police officer, nurse, doctor, lawyer, salesperson, diplomat, translator, flight attendant, psychotherapist, teacher, construction supervisor, municipal work supervisor, governor, or president. In any of these careers and professions and countless others, a refined bilingualism can open doors to wider possibilities.

Increasing Language Ownership

ESL students will benefit from the formal study of English because a better understanding of language patterns, a confidence in punctuation, and a command of the special uses of words will help them internalize English as a language of their own. Language ownership is an important topic. Language is a huge part of personal identity. It is a major reference point in our understanding of who we are. However, it should be emphasized that we can own more than one language; we can have two or more languages and dialects as expressions of our identity. It is helpful, healing, and sane for ESL students whose home is the United States to adopt English and care for it as their own. The problem is that immigrants have not always been welcomed with open arms, which is ironic in a land of immigrants. Our ESL students may therefore feel somewhat alien and sense that the English language is the language of others. One category of ESL students speaks English most of the time. They speak English in school; they speak it in their after-school jobs; and they even speak it most of the time at home: with brothers and sisters nearly all of the time, with parents some of the time, but with grandparents not at all. Even though these students speak English most of the time, they paradoxically still consider English their second language. In addition, since they use their "primary" (home) language less and less, it does not grow.

The knowledge of grammar, usage, and mechanics is one tool in many, but we should not underestimate its importance.

These ESL students can be left in a world of little language indeed. A systematic study of grammar, usage, and mechanics in a friendly environment will tend to cut through the cycle of alienation. In the same way that we may feel better about our own cars when we learn how they work and can repair them ourselves, ESL students can learn how English works and can feel the pride of ownership.

Conclusion

Finally, ESL students are in the advantageous position of having a head start on bilingualism. If they continue to grow in their first language and if we give them the tools that they need for their second language, they will become truly bilingual. They need many tools in their language tool kits: the training to hear English phonemes, so that they can be good listeners; the skill of pronunciation, so that they can speak clearly; the knowledge of literature, so that they can contemplate the values of English-language cultures and the cultures of the rest of the world; and the art of writing compositions, so that they can express their own truths. The knowledge of grammar, usage, and mechanics is one tool in many, but we should not underestimate its importance. For ESL students, grammatical knowledge is a *sine qua non* of becoming bilingual on a professional level. On this level of bilingualism, the advantages are many, but it seems we and our students sometimes set our sights too low. Perhaps we have been guilty of not expecting our ESL students to accomplish as much as other students. They can aspire to the same—or better—careers and professions and can partake richly of the larger culture. Beyond these avenues, however, from the point of view of those of us who love language, ESL students will be able to look at language from a higher vantage point. From this aerial view, perhaps some will even rediscover the old meaning of grammar: magic. ■

Billy Boyar has taught composition, literature, and ESL in high schools and community colleges for twenty years. Billy lives in Austin, Texas, where he teaches at Austin Community College. He has worked with juvenile offenders, volunteered with Hospice, and mediated as an ombudsman in nursing homes. In his free time, he enjoys studying Spanish and reading philosophy and finds his garden rewarding and a great way to unwind. He believes that a formal, systematic study of grammar is an important part of an ESL program.

Holt Handbook

Your **Road Map** to Grammar, Usage, and Mechanics Mastery

Now more than ever before, there is a demand for students at all grade levels to develop competence in the language arts and facility with the English language. Students need to be able to access information with ease, to appreciate the literary arts, and perhaps most importantly, to apply their language skills at levels demanded in the twenty-first century.

GIVING ALL STUDENTS ACCESS TO LANGUAGE SKILLS

Students in each classroom—including those at grade level, special education students, students with learning difficulties, advanced learners, and English-language learners—are at varying levels of preparation and have different strengths and needs. Giving these students all the tools they need to succeed is no easy task. That's where the ***Holt Handbook*** comes in.

The motivating force behind this program's organization and instructional delivery is the desire to offer teachers and students a method of focusing on written and oral language conventions and to provide a compelling and effective way to teach and learn grammar, usage, and mechanics skills. Based on John Warriner's time-tested model for instruction, the ***Holt Handbook*** can be an integral part of any balanced language arts program, or it can stand alone as a powerful tool for giving students access to the language skills they need most.

Covering All Your Students Need to Know About **Grammar, Usage,** and **Mechanics**

THREE MAIN PARTS COVER THE BASICS

PART I: GRAMMAR, USAGE, AND MECHANICS chapters help students use and practice using the building blocks of language—words, phrases, clauses, capitalization, punctuation, and spelling. The last chapter, **Correcting Common Errors,** gives students more practice building key language skills and taking tests in standardized formats.

PART II: The **SENTENCES** section covers the building blocks of constructing sentences, such as writing complete sentences, writing effective sentences, diagramming sentences, and improving sentence style.

PART III: The **RESOURCES** chapters include **The History of English,** a concise history of the English language; **Test Smarts,** a guide to taking standardized tests in grammar, usage, and mechanics; and **Grammar at a Glance,** a glossary of grammatical terms. In addition, grades 9–12 include **Manuscript Form,** a section that covers basic guidelines for preparing and presenting manuscripts and offers a sample research paper as a model.

Pupil's Edition

Instructional Delivery That Keeps Students on Track

Each chapter in the ***Holt Handbook*** is carefully sequenced so that students are introduced to and taught new rules and skills at the right time. Each chapter includes an entry-level diagnostic preview; direct instruction of the rules followed immediately by examples and exercises; ongoing assessment; and application of new knowledge through writing. This direct and practical instructional approach allows you to keep track of your students' pace and progress.

CHAPTER

2

Parts of Speech Overview

Noun, Pronoun, Adjective

Diagnostic Preview

A. Identifying Nouns, Pronouns, and A

Tell whether each italicized word or word group in sentences is used as a *noun*, a *pronoun*, or an *adjecti*

EXAMPLE 1. *Each* student is required to take a forei *language.*

1. *Each—adjective; language—noun*

1. *That* drummer is the *best* performer.
2. That *German shepherd* puppy is a sweet-nature rascal.
3. *Everybody* says that *high school* will be more work but more fun, too.
4. *This* is the greatest year the junior varsity volleyball *team* has ever had.
5. *Who* can tell me whose bicycle *this* is?
6. Jenna prepared a special breakfast for her parents and *herself* this *morning.*
7. This is their fault because *they* ignored all the *danger* signals.
8. *We* received word that they aren't in *danger.*
9. *Each* of these clubs decorated a float for the Cinco de Mayo *parade.*
10. The runner *Carl Lewis* won several Olympic *medals.*

DIAGNOSTIC PREVIEW offers a short test that covers the whole chapter and lets you pretest for the most essential knowledge and skills.

The Independent Clause

6b. An ***independent*** (or ***main***) ***clause*** expresses a complete thought and can stand by itself as a complete sentence.

EXAMPLES

S V
The sun set an hour ago. [This entire sentence is an independent clause.]

S V
Jean Merrill wrote *The Pushcart War,* and

S V
Ronni Solbert illustrated the book. [This sentence contains two independent clauses.]

S V
After I finish studying, **I will go to the** sentence contains one subordinate clau independent clause.]

RULE, EXAMPLE, EXERCISE sequence introduces a new rule and follows it immediately with examples and exercises.

Exercise 1 Identifying Subjects and Verbs in Independent Clauses

Identify the subject and verb in each italicized independent clause in the following sentences.

EXAMPLE 1. Before she left for college, *my sister read the comics in the newspaper every day.*

1. *sister—subject; read—verb*

1. *She told me* that Jump Start was her favorite.
2. Since she liked it so much, *I made a point of reading it, too.*
3. *The comic strip was created by this young man, Robb Armstrong,* who lives and works in Philadelphia.
4. *Jump Start features a police officer named Joe and his wife, Marcy,* who is a nurse.

Jump Start reprinted by permission of United Feature Syndicate, Inc.

Review B **Proofreading for Words Often Confused**

Identify and correct each error in words often confused in the following sentences.

EXAMPLE 1. Anne Shirley, here portrayed by actress Megan Follows, found a pieceful life and a loving family on Prince Edward Island.

1. *pieceful—peaceful*

1. Does the scenery shone in the picture on this page appeal to you?
2. My family enjoyed the green hillsides and rugged seashore during our two-weak vacation there last summer.
3. Prince Edward Island is quite a beautiful spot, and its Canada's smallest province.
4. Everyone who lives there calls the island PEI, and now I do, to.
5. During our visit, the weather was quite pleasant, so I lead my parents all over PEI on foot.
6. We walked to several places of interest in Charlottetown, the capitol.
7. I got to chose our first stop, and I selected the farmhouse that's the setting for the novel *Anne of Green Gables.*
8. That novel's main character, Anne Shirley, is someone who's ideas I admire.
9. Walking around "The Garden Province," we passed many farms; the principle crop is potatoes.
10. Take my advise and visit Prince Edward Island if you get the chance.

REVIEW EXERCISES offer both reinforcement of newly learned concepts and cumulative assessment.

Chapter Review

A. Using Irregular Verbs

Write the correct past or past participle form of the italicized irregular verb provided before each sentence.

1. *break* The thunder ___ the silence.
2. *ring* Who ___ the fire alarm so quickly?
3. *shrink* This shirt must have ___ in the dryer.
4. *throw* You've ___ the ball out of bounds!
5. *lead* Julio ___ the parade last year, so now it's my turn.
6. *rise* The sun ___ over the pyramids of Giza in Egypt.
7. *swim* We have ___ only three laps.
8. *choose* Vera was ___ as captain of the volleyball team.
9. *go* I have ___ to visit the Grand Canyon twice.
10. *sit* The tiny tree frog ___ motionless.
11. *write* Joan has ___ a story about aliens fr Andromeda galaxy.
12. *do* During class, Jorge ___ the first five homework assignment.
13. *steal* Three runners ___ bases during the
14. *break* This summer's heat wave has ___ al
15. *drink* Have you ___ all of the tomato juic
16. *sink* The log had slowly ___ into the qui
17. *lie* The old postcards have ___ in the b
18. *drive* Have you ever ___ across the state o
19. *begin* Our local PBS station ___ its fund-
20. *set* Have you ___ the paper plates and picnic table?
21. *throw* Who ___ the ball to first base?
22. *know* I have ___ some of my classmates f
23. *take* Kadeem ___ the role of Frederick D
24. *tear* My mother ___ the paper to make
25. *come* We ___ close to winning the tourna

CHAPTER REVIEWS provide additional practice and opportunities for ongoing assessment.

Writing Application

Using Verbs in a Story

Verb Forms and Tenses A local writers' club is sponsoring a contest for the best "cliffhanger" opening of an adventure story. Write an exciting paragraph to enter in the contest. Your paragraph should leave readers wondering "What happens next?" In your paragraph, use at least five verbs from the lists of Common Irregular Verbs in this chapter.

Prewriting First, you will need to imagine a suspenseful situation to describe. Jot down several ideas for your story opening. Then, choose the one you like best. With that situation in mind, scan the lists of irregular verbs. Note at least ten verbs you can use. Include some lively action verbs like *burst, swing,* and *throw.*

Writing As you write your rough draft, think of your readers. Choose words that create a suspenseful, believable scene. Remember that you have only one paragraph to catch your readers' interest.

Revising Ask a friend to read your paragraph. Does your friend find it interesting? Can he or she picture the scene clearly? If not, you may want to add, delete, or revise some details.

Publishing Check your spelling, usage, punctuation, and grammar. Check to make sure the forms of verbs are correct and the tenses are consistent. You may want to exchange your cliffhanger with a partner, and complete each other's stories. With your teacher's permission, you can then read the completed stories aloud to the class.

WRITING APPLICATIONS guide students in applying grammar, usage, and mechanics skills with end-of-chapter writing activities.

Pupil's Edition

Instruction Based on **Warriner's** Model

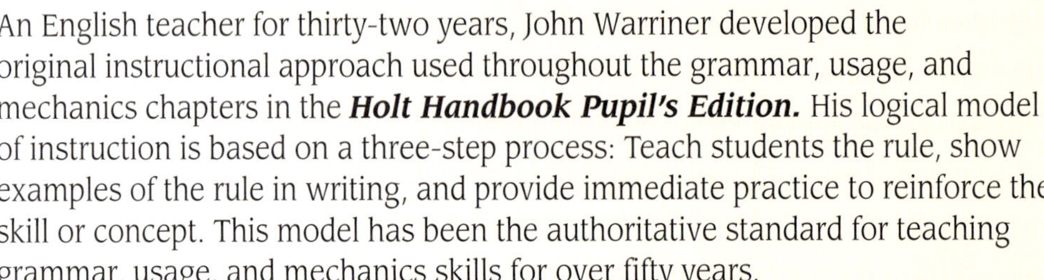

An English teacher for thirty-two years, John Warriner developed the original instructional approach used throughout the grammar, usage, and mechanics chapters in the ***Holt Handbook Pupil's Edition.*** His logical model of instruction is based on a three-step process: Teach students the rule, show examples of the rule in writing, and provide immediate practice to reinforce the skill or concept. This model has been the authoritative standard for teaching grammar, usage, and mechanics skills for over fifty years.

RULE is always clearly stated and presented in red.

EXAMPLES illustrate the language skill or concept being taught in various student-friendly sentences.

HELP

Most regular verbs that end in e drop the e before adding *–ing*. Some regular verbs double the final consonant before adding *–ing* or *–ed.*

EXAMPLES
shake—shak**ing**
hug—hu**gged**

USAGE

Reference Note

For more about **spelling rules,** see Chapter 16. For information on **standard and nonstandard English,** see page 245.

Regular Verbs

9b. A ***regular verb*** forms its past and past participle by adding *–d* or *–ed* to the base form.

Base Form	Present Participle	Past	Past Participle
clean	[is] cleaning	cleaned	[have] cleaned
hope	[is] hoping	hoped	[have] hoped
inspect	[is] inspecting	inspected	[have] inspected
slip	[is] slipping	slipped	[have] slipped

One common error in forming the past or the past participle of a regular verb is to leave off the *–d* or *–ed* ending.

NONSTANDARD Our street use to be quieter.
STANDARD Our street **used** to be quieter.

Another common error is to add unnecessary letters.

NONSTANDARD The swimmer almost drownded in the riptide.
STANDARD The swimmer almost **drowned** in the riptide.

NONSTANDARD The kitten attackted that paper bag.
STANDARD The kitten **attacked** that paper bag.

Oral Practice 1 **Using Regular Verbs**

Read each of the following sentences aloud, stressing the italicized verbs.

1. We are *supposed* to meet at the track after school.
2. The twins *happened* to buy the same shirt.
3. They have already *called* me about the party.
4. Do you know who *used* to live in this house?
5. I had *hoped* they could go to the concert with us.

"*The strongest motive in the preparation of the* **Handbook of English** *was the desire to create a book that would fit any course of study. The goal was a completely flexible teaching tool adaptable to any course of study or to any individual classroom.*"

—John Warriner
from Introduction to *Warriner's Handbook of English, Book One* © 1948

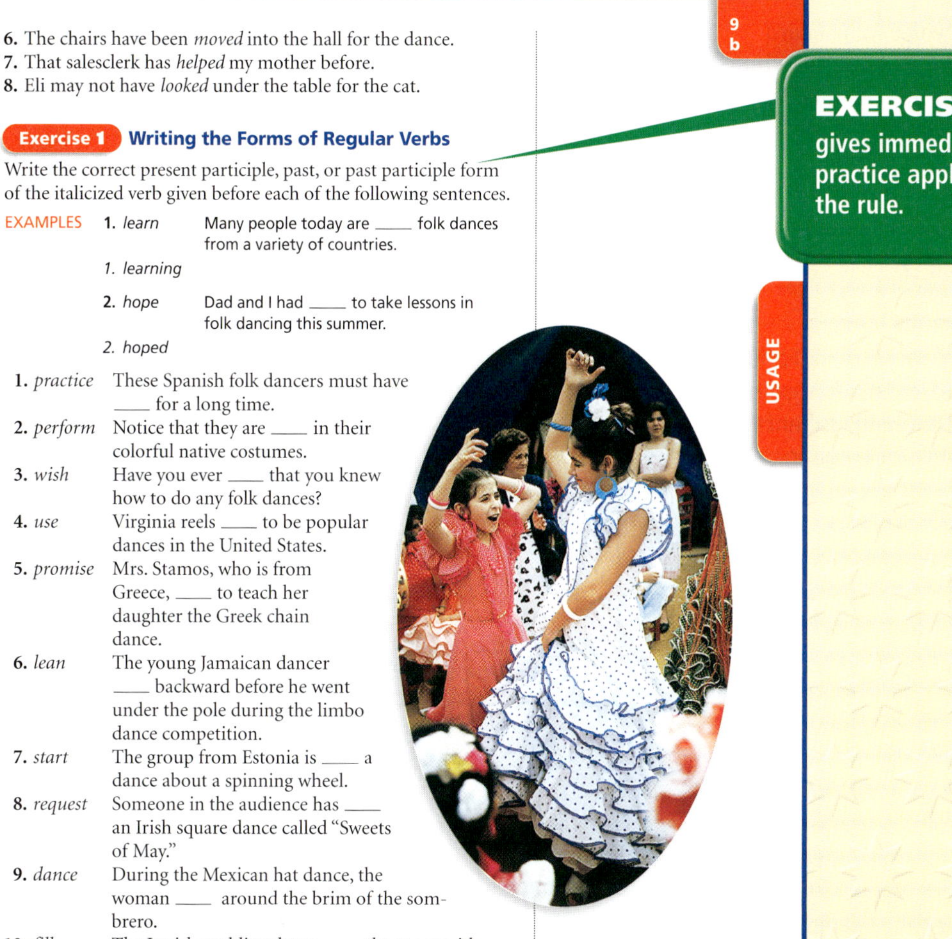

9 b

6. The chairs have been *moved* into the hall for the dance.
7. That salesclerk has *helped* my mother before.
8. Eli may not have *looked* under the table for the cat.

Exercise 1 Writing the Forms of Regular Verbs

Write the correct present participle, past, or past participle form of the italicized verb given before each of the following sentences.

EXAMPLES 1. *learn* Many people today are ____ folk dances from a variety of countries.
1. *learning*
2. *hope* Dad and I had ____ to take lessons in folk dancing this summer.
2. *hoped*

1. *practice* These Spanish folk dancers must have ____ for a long time.
2. *perform* Notice that they are ____ in their colorful native costumes.
3. *wish* Have you ever ____ that you knew how to do any folk dances?
4. *use* Virginia reels ____ to be popular dances in the United States.
5. *promise* Mrs. Stamos, who is from Greece, ____ to teach her daughter the Greek chain dance.
6. *lean* The young Jamaican dancer ____ backward before he went under the pole during the limbo dance competition.
7. *start* The group from Estonia is ____ a dance about a spinning wheel.
8. *request* Someone in the audience has ____ an Irish square dance called "Sweets of May."
9. *dance* During the Mexican hat dance, the woman ____ around the brim of the sombrero.
10. *fill* The Jewish wedding dance ____ the room with both music and movement.

USAGE

EXERCISE gives immediate practice applying the rule.

Pupil's Edition

Features That Help Students Along the Way

Oral Practice 5 **Using Forms of *Rise* and *Raise* Correctly**

Read the following sentences aloud, stressing the italicized verbs.

1. Mount Everest *rises* over 29,000 feet.
2. He *raises* the flag at sunrise.
3. The TV reporter *raised* her voice to be heard.
4. She *rose* from her seat and looked out the window.
5. The constellation Orion had not yet *risen* in the southern sky.
6. They had *raised* the piñata high in the tree.
7. I hope the bread is *rising*.
8. He will be *raising* the bucket from the well.

ORAL PRACTICE reinforces rules and concepts with spoken practice exercises.

TIPS & TRICKS

Sometimes a fragment is really a part of a nearby sentence. You can correct the fragment by attaching it to the sentence that comes before or after it.

SENTENCE WITH FRAGMENT
Mark is practicing his hook shot. Because he wants to try out for the basketball team.

SENTENCE
Mark is practicing his

TIPS & TRICKS offer easy-to-use hints that help students master language skills.

STYLE TIP

To avoid the awkward use of *his or her*, try to rephrase the sentence.

AWKWARD
Each of the actors had memorized **his or her** lines.

REVISED
All of the actors had memorized **their** lines.

STYLE TIPS guide students in making sound decisions about style and usage.

HELP

Some of the subjects and verbs in Review B are compound.

MEETING THE CHALLENGE

Write a poem, correctly using each of the six troublesome verbs, *sit, set, rise, raise, lie,* and *lay*. Be sure to check your poem for correct usage of the troublesome verbs.

MEETING THE CHALLENGE provides questions and short activities that ask students to approach a concept from a new angle.

HELP gives pointers that help students understand key rules or exercise directions.

Extend Grammar, Usage, and Mechanics Learning via the **Internet**!

GO.HRW.COM

Internet references throughout the ***Pupil's Edition*** direct students to **go.hrw.com,** a Web site that links students to resources related to concepts, rules, and assignments in the ***Holt Handbook.***

HOW IT WORKS

When students see the **go.hrw.com** logo in the textbook, they can go to the **go.hrw.com** site to find resources that support the grammatical concept or rule they are studying.

INTERACTIVE EXERCISES IN GRAMMAR, USAGE, AND MECHANICS

Among the resources available to students on the ***Holt Handbook*** site are interactive exercises in grammar, usage, and mechanics. Students can practice skills with interactive exercises and then complete a chapter test that is scored immediately, giving students instant feedback on their progress.

Annotated Teacher's Edition

Unique Strategies That Make **Planning Lessons** Easy

The ***Holt Handbook Annotated Teacher's Edition*** helps you organize your lessons into manageable segments—preteaching, direct teaching, and reteaching, for example—so that students build skills in a systematic way. Suggestions for differentiating instruction are integrated with lessons to help you support students with special learning needs, including advanced learners, students with learning difficulties, and English-language learners. Features that direct you to program resources for each chapter and lesson are also there to help you along the way.

> **PRETEACHING**
>
> **Lesson Starter**
>
> **Prior Knowledge.** Ask students to supply words that describe the similarities and differences between an orange and a baseball. Students might begin by saying that both objects are round. You might want to draw a Venn diagram on the chalkboard and ask students to suggest words that describe both items and words that

PRETEACHING offers strategies that help you identify prerequisite skills and build on the prior knowledge of your students.

> **DIRECT TEACHING**
>
> **Modeling and Demonstration**
>
> **Identifying Nouns.** Model how to identify nouns by using the example *self-esteem.* First, ask whether the word names a person, place, thing, or idea. [*idea*] *Self-esteem* names an idea; therefore, *self-esteem* is a noun. Now, have a volunteer use another example from this chapter to demonstrate how to identify a noun.

DIRECT TEACHING helps you present content with strategies that include modeling and demonstrating new concepts.

Reteaching

Pronouns

Activity. Ask students to write five descriptive sentences about a celebrity without ever mentioning the celebrity's name. Have two or three volunteers read their sentences, and let classmates try to guess the celebrity. Then, lead students to see that a common word in many of the sentences is *he* or *she.* Point out that pronouns like *he* and *she* are used in place of a noun, common or proper.

RETEACHING provides techniques to help you present material from a fresh perspective.

Extension

Critical Thinking

Metacognition. Point out to students that there are probably too many pronouns to memorize all of them by type. Ask students what their strategies are for remembering the different types of pronouns. Have students describe and rate the effectiveness of their strategies. Students having trouble with pronouns should develop new strategies. Have students meet in groups to share and compare their ideas.

EXTENSION activities and strategies ask students to make new connections between what they are learning and what they already know.

Differentiating Instruction

Advanced Learners

Have students read and discuss John Gardner's "Dragon, Dragon" or another folk tale that uses common nouns rather than proper names for its characters. Ask students to consider why the author uses common nouns rather than proper ones for the characters in the story. [*Students may say that there are so many characters in the story that it is easier for the reader to remember them with descriptive common nouns than with proper ones. Common nouns may also make the characters seem more universal.*]

DIFFERENTIATING INSTRUCTION helps you reinforce language skills with the wide variety of learners in your classroom, including advanced learners, on-level learners, learners having difficulty, special education students, and English-language learners.

CHAPTER RESOURCES

Internet

- Web resources: go.hrw.com

go.hrw.com

Practice & Review

- *Language & Sentence Skills Practice,* pp. 2–16; 17–20
- *Language & Sentence Skills Practice Answer Key,* pp. 1–7, 7–9

Application & Enrichment

- *Language & Sentence Skills Practice,* pp. 1, 21–22, 23
- *Language & Sentence Skills Practice Answer Key,* pp. 1, 9–10

CHAPTER RESOURCES BOXES list all materials that support each chapter lesson.

Teaching Suggestions and Resources

Teaching Suggestions That Help Students Make Connections

Because language arts skills are so interconnected, the ***Annotated Teacher's Edition*** provides a variety of extension and application strategies that help students make connections between the grammar, usage, and mechanics skills you're teaching them and the writing, science, and social studies skills they need to succeed in other classes. In addition, the ***Annotated Teacher's Edition*** gives you suggestions for facilitating an invaluable element of your students' learning experience—their families and communities.

MINI-LESSON Mechanics *Conti*

Punctuating Adjectives in a Series. Often two or more adjectives are used before a noun to make its meaning more specific. Remind students of the rules regarding comma usage with series of adjectives.

MINI-LESSON helps students link various grammar, usage, and mechanics skills to one another through a variety of practical lessons.

Learning for Life

Writing a Personal Profile. For various reasons, adults are sometimes asked to write personal profiles, which require careful attention to verb tense. Ask your students to write profiles of themselves, including only material they are comfort-

LEARNING FOR LIFE offers real-world suggestions that help students relate grammar, usage, and mechanics skills to their own lives and to workplace skills they'll need in the future.

CONTENT-AREA CONNECTIONS

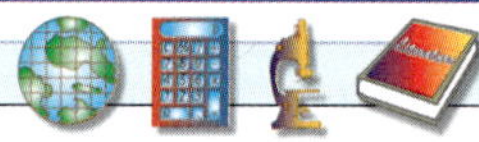

Social Studies

Places and Names. To give students practice in naming proper nouns, have students complete a team race on a social studies topic that they are studying. Divide the class into groups of four. Give each group a social studies category, and have the groups write as many proper nouns as they can in five minutes. All group members are responsible for generating answers. (Possible categories include states and their capitals, continents, oceans, rivers, countries, presidents, and

CONTENT-AREA CONNECTIONS suggest a variety of extension activities that reinforce the relevance of language arts skills to other disciplines, such as science and social studies.

FAMILY/COMMUNITY ACTIVITY

Introductions. Most students have had or will have opportunities to introduce people to each other. In doing so, students will use complements. Provide the following examples:

1. Hi! I'm Ms. King. I teach language arts at Carson Middle School.
2. Maria, this is Tom Jones. Tom is new to our school. Tom, this is Maria Gomez. Maria is my best friend.

FAMILY/COMMUNITY ACTIVITY provides a real-world forum for students' language arts skills.

Additional **Practice** and **Strategies** to Help Students Succeed

LANGUAGE & SENTENCE SKILLS PRACTICE

These worksheets provide practice, reinforcement, and extension for topics covered in the ***Holt Handbook***. Traditional worksheets offer additional practice for every rule taught in the ***Pupil's Edition.*** **Language in Context** worksheets let students apply and extend their study of grammar, usage, and mechanics to other areas in the language arts and to content in other disciplines. These worksheets include **Choices** worksheets, **Proofreading Application** worksheets, **Literary Model** worksheets, and **Writing Application** worksheets.

DEVELOPMENTAL LANGUAGE & SENTENCE SKILLS: GUIDED PRACTICE

These worksheets provide developmental learners with instruction, practice, and reinforcement to supplement lessons in the ***Holt Handbook*** and in ***Language & Sentence Skills Practice.*** Targeted to those students who have not yet mastered specific concepts taught in the ***Holt Handbook***, special features of this workbook include **Tips** that help students grasp abstract concepts with mnemonic devices, identification tests, and recognition strategies; **Points of Instruction** that explain how the rule applies to the examples provided; and **Guided Practice** that helps students with the first items of each exercise by asking guiding questions.

HOLT HANDBOOK CHAPTER TESTS

This booklet contains chapter tests in standardized test format for the grammar, usage, mechanics, and sentences chapters in the ***Holt Handbook***. Presented in multiple-choice format, each test offers a sound means of assessing your students' grasp of key English-language conventions and, at the same time, offers students opportunities to practice their test-taking skills. The answer key provides useful references to specific rules that tie the answers to relevant instruction in the ***Holt Handbook.*** It also helps you pinpoint those skills and concepts students have mastered and those that need further attention.

Instructional Resources: Chapter by Chapter

This chart outlines the chapters of the *Holt Handbook* and the resources available to help you teach these chapters. The chart lists materials appropriate for use with on-level students, advanced students, learners having difficulty, special education students, and English-language learners. Many of the resources listed are available at go.hrw.com.

Holt Handbook Chapter	Differentiating Instruction	
	Advanced Learners	On-Level Learners
1 Parts of Speech Overview	• Teacher's Edition, p. 9 • Language and Sentence Skills Practice, pp. 29–30, 31	• Teacher's Edition, pp. 2–39 • Language and Sentence Skills Practice, pp. 1–31
2 The Parts of a Sentence	• Teacher's Edition, p. 64 • Language and Sentence Skills Practice, pp. 57–58, 59	• Teacher's Edition, pp. 40–67 • Language and Sentence Skills Practice, pp. 32–59
3 The Phrase	• Language and Sentence Skills Practice, pp. 84–85, 86	• Teacher's Edition, pp. 68–95 • Language and Sentence Skills Practice, pp. 60–86

Differentiating Instruction		Assessment
Learners Having Difficulty	**English-Language Learners & Special Education Students**	
• Teacher's Edition, pp. 22, 24, 28 • Developmental Language & Sentence Skills Guided Practice, pp. 1–24	• Teacher's Edition, (English-Language Learners) pp. 7, 8, 10, 12, 22; (Special Education Students) pp. 4, 22	• Holt Handbook Chapter Tests, pp. 1–2, 52
• Teacher's Edition, pp. 42, 50, 54, 56, 58, 60, 62, 64 • Developmental Language & Sentence Skills Guided Practice, pp. 25–38	• Teacher's Edition, (English-Language Learners) pp. 44, 45, 46, 47, 48, 52, 56, 59; (Special Education Students) pp. 44, 46, 52	• Holt Handbook Chapter Tests, pp. 3–4, 52
• Teacher's Edition, pp. 80, 83, 91 • Developmental Language & Sentence Skills Guided Practice, pp. 39–50	• Teacher's Edition, (English-Language Learners) pp. 71, 74, 77, 81, 85; (Special Education Students) p. 75	• Holt Handbook Chapter Tests, pp. 5–6, 52

(continued on next page)

Holt Handbook Chapter	Differentiating Instruction	
	Advanced Learners	**On–Level Learners**
4 The Clause	• Language and Sentence Skills Practice, pp. 108–109, 110	• Teacher's Edition, pp. 96–117 • Language and Sentence Skills Practice, pp. 87–110
5 Agreement	• Teacher's Edition, p. 123 • Language and Sentence Skills Practice, pp. 133, 134–135, 136	• Teacher's Edition, pp. 118–143 • Language and Sentence Skills Practice, pp. 111–136
6 Using Verbs Correctly	• Teacher's Edition, pp. 155, 171 • Language and Sentence Skills Practice, pp. 159, 160–161, 162	• Teacher's Edition, pp. 144–175 • Language and Sentence Skills Practice, pp. 137–162
7 Using Pronouns Correctly	• Teacher's Edition, p. 188 • Language and Sentence Skills Practice, pp. 185, 186–187, 188	• Teacher's Edition, pp. 176–197 • Language and Sentence Skills Practice, pp. 163–188

Differentiating Instruction		Assessment
Learners Having Difficulty	**English-Language Learners & Special Education Students**	
• Teacher's Edition, pp. 100, 102, 107, 108 • Developmental Language & Sentence Skills Guided Practice, pp. 51–60	• Teacher's Edition, (English-Language Learners) pp. 100, 105, 107	• Holt Handbook Chapter Tests, pp. 7–8, 52
• Teacher's Edition, pp. 125, 127, 128, 136, 138 • Developmental Language & Sentence Skills Guided Practice, pp. 61–68	• Teacher's Edition, (English-Language Learners) pp. 120, 123, 137; (Special Education Students) pp. 123, 127, 130	• Holt Handbook Chapter Tests, pp. 9–10, 52
• Teacher's Edition, pp. 150, 153, 167, 170 • Developmental Language & Sentence Skills Guided Practice, pp. 69–82	• Teacher's Edition, (English-Language Learners) pp. 146, 149, 156, 163, 164, 169; (Special Education Students) p. 161	• Holt Handbook Chapter Tests, pp. 11–12, 52
• Teacher's Edition, pp. 182, 188 • Developmental Language & Sentence Skills Guided Practice, pp. 83–92	• Teacher's Edition, (English-Language Learners) pp. 178, 179, 182, 188; (Special Education Students) p. 179	• Holt Handbook Chapter Tests, pp. 13–14, 52

(continued on next page)

Holt Handbook Chapter	Differentiating Instruction	
	Advanced Learners	On-Level Learners
8 Using Modifiers Correctly	• Language and Sentence Skills Practice, pp. 214, 215–216, 217	• Teacher's Edition, pp. 198–221 • Language and Sentence Skills Practice, pp. 189–217
9 A Glossary of Usage	• Teacher's Edition, p. 236 • Language and Sentence Skills Practice, pp. 229, 230–231, 232	• Teacher's Edition, pp. 222–243 • Language and Sentence Skills Practice, pp. 218–232
10 Capital Letters	• Teacher's Edition, p. 250 • Language and Sentence Skills Practice, pp. 250, 251–252, 253	• Teacher's Edition, pp. 244–263 • Language and Sentence Skills Practice, pp. 233–253
11 Punctuation: End Marks, Abbreviations, and Commas	• Teacher's Edition, pp. 269, 276 • Language and Sentence Skills Practice, pp. 272, 273–274, 275	• Teacher's Edition, pp. 264–293 • Language and Sentence Skills Practice, pp. 254–275

Differentiating Instruction		Assessment
Learners Having Difficulty	**English-Language Learners & Special Education Students**	
• Teacher's Edition, pp. 202, 203, 209, 210, 216 • Developmental Language & Sentence Skills Guided Practice, pp. 93–98	• Teacher's Edition, (English-Language Learners) pp. 203, 208, 209	• Holt Handbook Chapter Tests, pp. 15–16, 52
• Teacher's Edition, pp. 226, 229, 234 • Developmental Language & Sentence Skills Guided Practice, pp. 99–104	• Teacher's Edition, (English-Language Learners) pp. 225, 228, 238; (Special Education Students) p. 225	• Holt Handbook Chapter Tests, pp. 17–18, 52
• Teacher's Edition, pp. 253, 259 • Developmental Language & Sentence Skills Guided Practice, pp. 105–118	• Teacher's Edition, (English-Language Learners) pp. 247, 248, 249, 256, 257; (Special Education Students) p. 255	• Holt Handbook Chapter Tests, pp. 19–20, 52
• Teacher's Edition, pp. 273, 274, 275, 279, 280, 282, 287 • Developmental Language & Sentence Skills Guided Practice, pp. 119–128	• Teacher's Edition, (English-Language Learners) pp. 266, 273, 275, 279; (Special Education Students) pp. 273, 284	• Holt Handbook Chapter Tests, pp. 21–22, 52

(continued on next page)

Holt Handbook Chapter	Differentiating Instruction	
	Advanced Learners	**On-Level Learners**
12 Punctuation: Semicolons and Colons	• Teacher's Edition, p. 297 • Language and Sentence Skills Practice, pp. 286, 287–288, 289	• Teacher's Edition, pp. 294–309 • Language and Sentence Skills Practice, pp. 276–289
13 Punctuation: Italics and Quotation Marks	• Teacher's Edition, p. 321 • Language and Sentence Skills Practice, pp. 303, 304–305, 306	• Teacher's Edition, pp. 310–325 • Language and Sentence Skills Practice, pp. 290–306
14 Punctuation: Apostrophes	• Teacher's Edition, p. 337 • Language and Sentence Skills Practice, pp. 319, 320–321, 322	• Teacher's Edition, pp. 326–341 • Language and Sentence Skills Practice, pp. 307–322
15 Punctuation: Hyphens, Dashes, Parentheses, Brackets, Ellipsis Points	• Teacher's Edition, p. 353 • Language and Sentence Skills Practice, pp. 335, 336–337, 338	• Teacher's Edition, pp. 342–357 • Language and Sentence Skills Practice, pp. 323–338
16 Spelling	• Teacher's Edition, p. 390 • Language and Sentence Skills Practice, pp. 366, 367–368, 369	• Teacher's Edition, pp. 358–393 • Language and Sentence Skills Practice, pp. 339–369

Differentiating Instruction		Assessment
Learners Having Difficulty	**English-Language Learners & Special Education Students**	
• Teacher's Edition, pp. 298, 300, 302, 305 • Developmental Language & Sentence Skills Guided Practice, pp. 129–132	• Teacher's Edition, (English-Language Learners) pp. 297, 305	• Holt Handbook Chapter Tests, pp. 23–24, 52
• Teacher's Edition, pp. 318, 321 • Developmental Language & Sentence Skills Guided Practice, pp. 133–138	• Teacher's Edition, (English-Language Learners) pp. 312, 316; (Special Education Students) p. 319	• Holt Handbook Chapter Tests, pp. 25–26, 52
• Teacher's Edition, pp. 329, 337, 338 • Developmental Language & Sentence Skills Guided Practice, pp. 139–140	• Teacher's Edition, (English-Language Learners) pp. 330, 336	• Holt Handbook Chapter Tests, pp. 27–28, 52
• Teacher's Edition, p. 351 • Developmental Language & Sentence Skills Guided Practice, pp. 141–144	• Teacher's Edition, (English-Language Learners) pp. 344, 348	• Holt Handbook Chapter Tests, pp. 29–30, 52
• Teacher's Edition, pp. 361, 364, 366, 375, 377, 381 • Developmental Language & Sentence Skills Guided Practice, pp. 145–156	• Teacher's Edition, (English-Language Learners) pp. 360, 361; (Special Education Students) pp. 360, 365	• Holt Handbook Chapter Tests, pp. 31–32, 52

(continued on next page)

Holt Handbook Chapter	Differentiating Instruction	
	Advanced Learners	On–Level Learners
17 Correcting Common Errors	• Language and Sentence Skills Practice, pp. 407, 408–409, 410	• Teacher's Edition, pp. 394–429 • Language and Sentence Skills Practice, pp. 370–410
18 Writing Complete Sentences	• Teacher's Edition, p. 439	• Teacher's Edition, pp. 432–447 • Language and Sentence Skills Practice, pp. 411–424
19 Writing Effective Sentences	• Teacher's Edition, p. 467	• Teacher's Edition, pp. 448–473 • Language and Sentence Skills Practice, pp. 425–450
20 Sentence Diagramming	• Teacher's Edition, pp. 474–487	• Teacher's Edition, pp. 474–487
Resources Manuscript Form		• Language and Sentence Skills Practice, pp. 451–452

Differentiating Instruction		Assessment
Learners Having Difficulty	**English-Language Learners & Special Education Students**	
• Teacher's Edition, pp. 401, 403, 418 • Developmental Language & Sentence Skills Guided Practice, pp. 157–158	• Teacher's Edition, (English-Language Learners) p. 402	• Holt Handbook Chapter Tests, pp. 33–34, 53
• Teacher's Edition, p. 438 • Developmental Language & Sentence Skills Guided Practice, pp. 159–162	• Teacher's Edition, (English-Language Learners) pp. 436, 438	• Holt Handbook Chapter Tests, pp. 35–38, 52
• Teacher's Edition, pp. 453, 462, 463 • Developmental Language & Sentence Skills Guided Practice, pp. 163–176	• Teacher's Edition, (English-Language Learners) pp. 452, 453, 459	• Holt Handbook Chapter Tests, pp. 39–43, 52
• Teacher's Edition, pp. 474–487	• Teacher's Edition, (English-Language Learners) pp. 474–487; (Special Education Students) pp. 474–487	
• Developmental Language & Sentence Skills Guided Practice, pp. 177–178		

PART 1

Grammar, Usage, and Mechanics

Grammar

Usage

Mechanics

Grammar, Usage, and Mechanics 1

CHAPTER

INTRODUCING THE CHAPTER

- This chapter classifies English words by defining the eight parts of speech according to function. Because usage rules, punctuation rules, and revision suggestions often mention parts of speech, you may want to refer students to this chapter throughout the year.
- The chapter closes with a **Chapter Review,** which includes a **Writing Application** feature that asks students to write a paragraph using specific adjectives.
- For help in integrating this chapter with writing assignments, use the **Teaching Strands** chart on pp. T24–T25.

CHAPTER

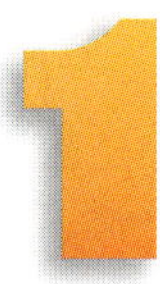

Parts of Speech Overview

The Work That Words Do

Diagnostic Preview

HELP

Some items in the Diagnostic Preview have more than one italicized word. These words work together as a single part of speech.

Numbers in brackets refer to rules tested by the items in the Diagnostic Preview.

1. adj. [1c]	**2.** verb [1d]
3. prep. [1f]	**4.** adj. [1c]
5. adj. [1c]	**6.** adv. [1e]
7. verb [1d]	**8.** noun[1a]
9. conj.[1g]	**10.** prep.[1f]
11. noun[1a]	**12.** pro. [1b]
13. int. [1h]	**14.** adj. [1c]
15. pro. [1b]	**16.** conj.[1g]
17. adv. [1e]	**18.** noun[1a]
19. adj. [1c]	**20.** noun[1a]

Identifying Parts of Speech

Write the part of speech (*noun, pronoun, adjective, verb, adverb, preposition, conjunction,* or *interjection*) of the italicized words in the paragraph below.

EXAMPLE Pioneers **[1]** *learned* how to recognize danger.

1. verb

The [1] *first* pioneers on the Great Plains [2] *encountered* many kinds [3] *of* dangerous animals. Grizzly bears and [4] *huge* herds of bison were menaces to [5] *early* settlers. One of the [6] *most* ferocious beasts of the plains [7] *was* a [8] *grizzly* protecting her cubs. However, [9] *neither* the bison *nor* the grizzly was the most feared animal [10] *on* the frontier. Not even the deadly [11] *rattlesnake*—nor [12] *any* of the other prairie creatures—was dreaded as much as the skunk. You may think, [13] "*Oh,* that is [14] *ridiculous.*" However, it is true. Skunks were feared not because [15] *they* smelled bad [16] *but,* instead, because they [17] *so* often carried [18] *rabies.* Since there was no vaccine for rabies in [19] *those* days, the bite of a rabid skunk spelled certain [20] *doom* for the unlucky victim.

CHAPTER RESOURCES

Internet

- Web resources: go.hrw.com

Practice & Review

- *Language & Sentence Skills Practice,* pp. 2–28
- *Language & Sentence Skills Practice Answer Key,* pp. 1–15

Application & Enrichment

- *Language & Sentence Skills Practice,* pp. 1, 29–31
- *Language & Sentence Skills Practice Answer Key,* pp. 1, 15–16

The Noun

1a. A *noun* is a word or word group that is used to name a person, a place, a thing, or an idea.

Persons	Sharon, Major Brown, hairstylist, joggers
Places	Iowa, districts, Mars, Antarctica, library
Things	okra, Great Pyramid, toothpicks, merry-go-round
Ideas	peace, truth, artistry, excellence, beauty

Common and Proper Nouns

A ***proper noun*** names a particular person, place, thing, or idea and is capitalized. A ***common noun*** names any one of a group of persons, places, things, or ideas and is generally not capitalized.

Reference Note

For more information on **capitalizing proper nouns,** see page 248.

Common Nouns	Proper Nouns
scientist	Marie Curie, Charles Drew
woman	Coretta Scott King, Rita Moreno
city	Cairo, St. Louis, Paris
building	World Trade Center, Eiffel Tower
continent	North America, South America, Africa
day	Monday, Thursday, Labor Day

Oral Practice Classifying Nouns

Read the following nouns aloud, and identify each one as a *common noun* or a *proper noun.* If the noun is proper, name a corresponding common noun.

Corresponding common nouns may vary.

EXAMPLE 1. Zora Neale Hurston
1. proper noun—writer

1. man 1. c.
2. month 2. c.
3. Vietnam 3. p.
4. singer 4. c.
5. Athena 5. p.
6. city 6. c.
7. gumbo 7. c.
8. self-esteem 8. c.
9. Virginia 9. p.
10. ocean 10. c.
11. Mount Hood 11. p.
12. Australia 12. p.
13. Detroit 13. p.
14. street 14. c.
15. Amelia Earhart 15. p.
16. mercy 16. c.
17. cousin 17. c.
18. automobile 18. c.
19. blues 19. c.
20. Christopher Columbus 20. p.

3. country
5. goddess
9. state
11. mountain
12. continent
13. city
15. pilot
20. explorer

GRAMMAR

ASSESSING

Entry-Level Assessment

Diagnostic Preview. The **Diagnostic Preview** requires students to identify the parts of speech of twenty words used in a paragraph. This **Diagnostic Preview** can be used to indicate the amount of reteaching needed. If only a few students are unable to demonstrate mastery, you could have them read the definitions and work on the exercises together. You will probably want to check their answers periodically to determine progress.

The Noun

Rule 1a *(pp. 3–6)*

OBJECTIVES

- To identify and classify common and proper nouns and give examples of both
- To identify nouns and compound nouns used in sentences

Differentiating Instruction

- *Developmental Language & Sentence Skills Guided Practice,* pp. 1–24
- *Developmental Language & Sentence Skills Guided Practice Teacher's Notes and Answer Key,* pp. 1–6

Assessment

- *Holt Handbook Chapter Tests with Answer Key,* pp. 1–2, 52

PRETEACHING

Lesson Starter

Prior Knowledge. To make students aware of how they figure out the parts of speech, ask them to begin a chart to show what questions to use to determine the part of speech of a word. Students can add to the chart as they study successive parts of speech in this chapter.

EXAMPLE

Noun: Is it the name of a person, place, thing, or idea? Does the word make sense with *the* or *a* in front of it?

DIFFERENTIATING INSTRUCTION

Special Education Students

Students might better understand the concept of nouns if they associate the various kinds of nouns with familiar words. Have the students fill in the following chart with names of persons, places, things, and ideas that have personal meaning. Students might need help filling in the *Idea* column.

PERSON	PLACE	THING	IDEA

BORN LOSER reprinted by permission of Newspaper Enterprise Association, Inc.

Concrete and Abstract Nouns

A ***concrete noun*** names a person, place, or thing that can be perceived by one or more of the senses (sight, hearing, taste, touch, and smell). An ***abstract noun*** names an idea, a feeling, a quality, or a characteristic.

Concrete Nouns	cloud, poison ivy, thunder, silk, yogurt, Sarah
Abstract Nouns	freedom, well-being, beauty, kindness, Buddhism

Exercise 1 Identifying and Classifying Nouns

Write all the nouns that you find in each sentence. Then, circle the proper nouns.

EXAMPLE
1. English grows daily with the addition of new words.
1. *English, addition, words*

1. Some words come from other languages, such as Spanish and French.
2. Books, music, and movies often feature new words that are then added to everyday English.
3. Many useful and amusing words came into our language during World War II.
4. Now these words are familiar throughout the United States.
5. One of these words is *gremlin.*
6. Fliers were often troubled by mysterious mechanical problems.
7. Not knowing what caused these problems, they joked that gremlins—small, mischievous creatures—were in the aircraft.
8. According to Grandpa Leroy, these gremlins could be helpful as well as harmful.
9. Many fliers claimed that they had miraculously escaped danger only because the gremlins had come to their rescue.
10. Artists drew the imps as little men with beards and funny hats who played all over the planes.

Compound Nouns

A ***compound noun*** consists of two or more words used together as a single noun. The parts of a compound noun may be written as one word, as separate words, or as a hyphenated word.

RESOURCES

The Noun

Practice

- *Language & Sentence Skills Practice,* pp. 2–4

Differentiating Instruction

- *Developmental Language & Sentence Skills,* pp. 1–2

One Word	firefighter, Iceland, newspaper
Separate Words	prime minister, Red River Dam, fire drill
Hyphenated Word	sister-in-law, Port-au-Prince, pull-up

NOTE If you are not sure how to write a compound noun, look in a dictionary. Some dictionaries may give more than one correct form for a word. For example, you may find the word *vice-president* written both with and without the hyphen. As a rule, use the form the dictionary lists first.

Exercise 2 Identifying Compound Nouns

Each of the sentences below contains at least one compound noun. Write the compound noun(s) in each sentence.

EXAMPLE 1. My cousin John is a political scientist.
1. political scientist

1. I use a word processor or a typewriter in class.
2. We went swimming in the Gulf of Mexico.
3. My sister and my brother-in-law live in Council Bluffs, Iowa.
4. My Old English sheepdog is still a puppy.
5. Some almanacs give exact times for sunrises and sunsets.
6. We used to play hide-and-seek in the old barn.
7. Sitting Bull was the war chief who masterminded the Sioux victory at the Battle of the Little Bighorn.
8. Meet me at the bowling alley near the post office.
9. The fountain pen is not as popular as the ballpoint.
10. Luís Valdez is a playwright, actor, and director.

Collective Nouns

A ***collective noun*** is a word that names a group.

People	audience, chorus, committee, crew
Animals	brood, flock, gaggle, herd
Things	assortment, batch, bundle, cluster

Reference Note

For more on **collective nouns,** see page 129.

GRAMMAR

DIRECT TEACHING

Correcting Misconceptions

Compound Nouns. Students may believe that all compound nouns should be written as one word. Point out that the typical pattern is for the hyphen to be used in a compound when it is new, but for it to be dropped after the word becomes familiar. For example, *school-boy* became *schoolboy.*

You may wish to ask students to hunt for new compound words to put on the bulletin board. Suggest that they use several different dictionaries to see if the words are treated differently.

MINI-LESSON Mechanics

Capitalizing Proper Nouns. Explain that proper nouns, including ones that consist of more than one word, are capitalized.

Write on the chalkboard items 1–3 and have students correct the capitalization. For additional help or practice, refer students to **Chapter 10: Capital Letters.**

1. ohio state fair
2. mayor gernhardt
3. *webster's new world dictionary*

GRAMMAR

The Pronoun

Rule 1b *(pp. 6–9)*

OBJECTIVE

- To identify pronouns and their antecedents in sentences

RETEACHING

Pronouns

Ask students to write five descriptive, favorable sentences about a classmate without ever mentioning the person's name. Have two or three volunteers read their sentences, and let classmates try to guess the person's name. Then, lead students to see that a common word in many of the sentences is *he* or *she*. Point out that pronouns like *he* and *she* are used in place of a noun, common or proper.

Exercise 3 **Identifying Nouns**

Identify the twenty-five nouns in the sentences below.

EXAMPLE 1. To enter the wildlife park, we walked through the mouth of a huge fake alligator.

1. park, mouth, alligator

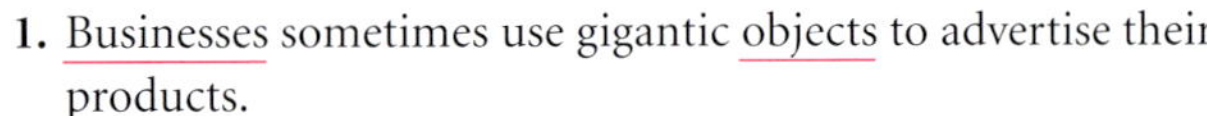

1. Businesses sometimes use gigantic objects to advertise their products.
2. A stand that sells fruit might look like an enormous orange, complete with doors and windows.
3. A restaurant in Austin, Texas, has a delivery van shaped like a dinosaur.
4. Huge dogs, windmills, and figures of Paul Bunyan are formed with cement or fiberglass to help sell chain saws, trucks, and souvenirs.
5. An old hotel in New Jersey was even built to look like an elephant!

The Pronoun

1b. A *pronoun* is a word that is used in place of one or more nouns or pronouns.

EXAMPLES Stan bought a suit and an overcoat. **He** will wear **them** tomorrow. [The pronoun *He* stands for the noun *Stan*. The pronoun *them* stands for the nouns *suit* and *overcoat*.]

Several of the horses have gone into the stable because **they** are hungry. [The pronoun *Several* refers to the noun *horses*. The pronoun *they* stands for the pronoun *Several*.]

Reference Note

For more information about **antecedents,** see page 135.

The word that a pronoun stands for or refers to is called the ***antecedent*** of the pronoun. In the following examples, the arrows point from the pronouns to their antecedents.

EXAMPLES The tour guide showed the **students** where **they** could see Mayan pottery.

Why did **Oscar** give **his** camera to the film school?

Darius scored a **field goal. It** was his first of the season.

Notice that a pronoun may appear in the same sentence as its antecedent or in a nearby sentence.

RESOURCES

The Pronoun

Practice

- *Language & Sentence Skills Practice,* pp. 5–9

Differentiating Instruction

- *Developmental Language & Sentence Skills,* pp. 3–10

Personal Pronouns

A ***personal pronoun*** refers to the one speaking (first person), the one spoken to (second person), or the one spoken about (third person).

First Person	I, me, my, mine, we, us, our, ours
Second Person	you, your, yours
Third Person	he, him, his, she, her, hers, it, its, they, them, their, theirs

EXAMPLES **I** hope that **they** can find **your** apartment by following **our** directions.

She said that **we** could call **them** at home.

He asked **us** to help **him** clear away the fallen branches from **his** backyard.

Their dog obeyed **them** immediately and went to **its** bed.

NOTE In this book, the words *my, your, his, her, its,* and *their* are called pronouns. Some authorities prefer to call these words adjectives. Follow your teacher's instructions on labeling these words.

Exercise 4 Identifying Antecedents

Give the antecedent for each italicized pronoun in the following paragraph.

EXAMPLE In about A.D. 1150, a historian wrote down a strange tale English villagers had told **[1]** *him.*

1. him—historian

Since numerous people told the same story, the historian believed [1] *it*. Supposedly, a young boy and girl with bright green skin had been found wandering in the fields. [2] *They* spoke a foreign language and wore clothing made of an unknown material. At first, the two children would eat only green beans, but after [3] *they* learned to eat bread, [4] *their* skin gradually lost [5] *its* greenness. After learning English, the girl said [6] *she* and [7] *her* brother had come from a land called Saint Martin. The story sounds like science fiction, doesn't [8] *it*? Perhaps the villagers invented [9] *it* to amuse [10] *their* friends and fool historians.

Reference Note

For information on **choosing pronouns that agree with their antecedents,** see page 135. For information on **clear pronoun reference,** see page 193.

STYLE TIP

To keep your readers from getting confused, place pronouns near their antecedents—generally within the same sentence or in the next sentence.

CONFUSING

Please hand me the scissors. I also need some strapping tape. They are in the top drawer on the left. [Does *They* refer to the scissors or to both the scissors and the strapping tape?]

CLEAR

Please hand me the **scissors. They** are in the top drawer on the left. I also need some strapping tape. [Only the scissors are in the top drawer on the left.]

DIFFERENTIATING INSTRUCTION

GRAMMAR

English-Language Learners

Cantonese. Cantonese does not make a distinction between masculine and feminine pronouns, so Cantonese speakers may have problems with the pronouns *he* and *she.* Even when speakers of Cantonese recognize these pronouns and understand them, the difficulty of pronouncing the /sh/ sound may cause confusion in speech. You can help Cantonese speakers understand the meanings of these pronouns by asking them to match pictures of male and female figures with sentences such as these:

She said that we could call them.
He asked us to help clear away fallen branches from his yard.

You may also want to emphasize the pronunciation of /sh/.

Exercise 4 Identifying Antecedents

ANSWERS

1. story
2. boy, girl
3. children
4. children
5. skin
6. girl
7. girl
8. story
9. story
10. villagers

CONTENT-AREA CONNECTIONS

Art

Computer Graphics. As students complete their parts of speech charts by including pronouns, ask those who are interested in art or computer graphics to create a chart for the classroom. If several students are interested in this project, ask them to divide the tasks: creating icons for each part of speech; selecting a color to identify each part of speech; working out placement on the chart; editing the text for spelling, parallelism, and other usage and mechanics points.

GRAMMAR

Differentiating Instruction

English-Language Learners

Spanish. Because Spanish has more verbs that require reflexive pronouns than English does, Spanish-speaking students may overuse reflexive pronouns and may think that certain English verbs take reflexive pronouns because their Spanish counterparts do. For example, the Spanish equivalent of *repent* is *arrepentirse,* which translates literally as "to repent oneself" (the ending *se* makes the verb reflexive).

Spanish. The English pronouns *your, his, her, its,* and *their* can all be translated in formal Spanish as *su* (or *sus* if more than one thing is possessed). *Your* can be expressed as *tu* (singular) or *tus* (plural) familiarly, among family and close friends. *Yourself, himself, herself, itself,* and *themselves* can all be translated as *se.* Watch for any difficulties Spanish-speaking students may have distinguishing among pronouns in their written work.

TIPS & TRICKS

To find out if a pronoun is reflexive or intensive, leave it out of the sentence. If the meaning of the sentence stays the same without the pronoun, the pronoun is intensive.

EXAMPLES

Ron looked at himself in the mirror. [*Ron looked at in the mirror* doesn't mean the same thing. The pronoun is reflexive.]

Jenny painted the room herself. [*Jenny painted the room* means the same thing. The pronoun is intensive.]

Reflexive and Intensive Pronouns

A ***reflexive pronoun*** refers to the subject of a sentence and functions as a complement or as an object of a preposition. An ***intensive pronoun*** emphasizes its antecedent and has no grammatical function.

First Person	myself, ourselves
Second Person	yourself, yourselves
Third Person	himself, herself, itself, themselves

EXAMPLES Elena treated **herself** to a snack. [reflexive]

Albert **himself** organized the fund-raiser. [intensive]

Demonstrative Pronouns

A ***demonstrative pronoun*** is used to point out a specific person, place, thing, or idea.

this that these those

EXAMPLES **That** is Soon-Hee's favorite restaurant in San Francisco.

The tacos I made taste better than **those.**

Interrogative Pronouns

An ***interrogative pronoun*** introduces a question.

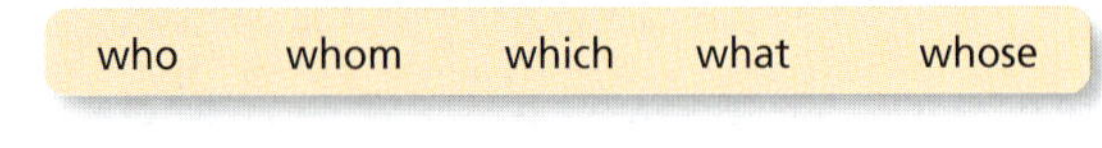
who whom which what whose

EXAMPLES **Which** of the songs is your favorite?

What is your parakeet's name?

Relative Pronouns

A ***relative pronoun*** introduces a subordinate clause.

that which who whom whose

EXAMPLES The ship **that** you saw is sailing to Greece.

Isabel is my friend **who** is training for the Boston marathon.

Reference Note

For more information on **relative pronouns,** see page 101. For information on **subordinate clauses,** see page 99.

Indefinite Pronouns

An ***indefinite pronoun*** refers to one or more persons, places, ideas, or things that may or may not be specifically named.

all	each	most	one
another	either	much	other
any	everyone	neither	several
anybody	everything	nobody	some
anyone	few	none	somebody
anything	many	no one	something
both	more	nothing	such

EXAMPLES Angelo has **everything** he will need to go rock climbing.

Is **anyone** at home?

Most of the birds had already flown south for the winter.

HELP—

Many of the pronouns you have studied so far may also be used as adjectives.

EXAMPLES

this street
whose puppy
many acorns

Reference Note

For more about using **pronouns,** see Chapter 7.

Exercise 5 Identifying Pronouns

Identify all the pronouns in the sentences below.

EXAMPLE [1] My friend Hideko invited me to a Japanese tea ceremony at her house.

1. My, me, her

[1] The tea ceremony at Hideko's house was more like some I have seen in movies than the traditional one shown in this picture. [2] "What happens during the tea ceremony, Hideko?" I asked as we entered the house. [3] According to Hideko, the purpose of the tea ceremony, a custom that dates back hundreds of years, is to create a peaceful mood. [4] In the ceremony, everyone sits quietly and watches the tea being made. [5] Before entering the room for the ceremony, I reminded myself to take off my shoes. [6] During the ceremony, each of us kneeled on a straw mat. [7] Hideko's mother was our tea hostess, the person who conducts the ceremony and prepares all of the tea. [8] She prepared the tea and served it in bowls that had been in the family for generations. [9] Then she served us sweet cakes called *kashi* (KAH-shee). [10] Afterward, Hideko herself gave me a box of tea leaves to take home with me.

GRAMMAR

Differentiating Instruction

Advanced Learners

Students might not realize that English is more closely related to German than to Latin-based languages like French or Spanish. During the Middle Ages, as the sounds of English changed, English nouns lost most of their Germanic case endings. Only possessive nouns and certain pronouns, such as *he, his,* and *him,* still indicate case.

Ask students who are studying Latin or German to give the class a presentation showing case endings of nouns in an inflected language. Students should start with a simple English sentence showing a noun used as a subject, direct object, and so forth, and provide the translation into the inflected language to show how the endings change.

Exercise 5

DISTRIBUTED REVIEW

Have students review nouns by finding the following items in the third sentence:

1. two plural nouns [*hundreds, years*]

2. a proper noun [*Hideko*]

GRAMMAR

The Adjective

Rule 1c *(pp. 10–14)*

OBJECTIVES

- To distinguish between adjectives and nouns
- To add appropriate adjectives to sentences

DIFFERENTIATING INSTRUCTION

English-Language Learners

General Strategies. In English, adjectives usually precede the nouns they modify, as in *big house.* However, in many languages, such as Khmer, Portuguese, Spanish, Tigre, and Vietnamese, adjectives usually follow the noun, as in *casa grande* ("house big"). Speakers of these languages may try to identify adjectives in English by their position, so they might think *big* is the noun and *house* is the adjective.

DIRECT TEACHING

Modeling and Demonstration

The Adjective. Model how to distinguish between adjectives and nouns by using the example *Greg buys old bicycles.* First, ask what part of speech the word *bicycles* is. [*noun*] Next, ask if there is a word that tells what kind, which one, or how many *bicycles* Greg repairs. [*yes;* old] Ask what part of speech *old* is. [*adjective*] Point out that a *noun* names a person, place, or thing, while an *adjective* describes a *noun* to make its meaning more definite. Now, have a volunteer use another example from this chapter to demonstrate how to distinguish between nouns and adjectives.

TIPS & TRICKS

The phrase *these five interesting books* can help you remember the questions an adjective can answer: Which books? These books. How many books? Five books. What kind of books? Interesting books.

The Adjective

1c. An *adjective* is a word that is used to modify a noun or a pronoun.

To ***modify*** a word means to describe the word or to make its meaning more definite. An adjective modifies a noun or a pronoun by telling *what kind, which one,* or *how many.*

What Kind?	**gray** skies **far-fetched** tale	**Irish** lace **lowest** price
Which One?	**either** way **next** day	**those** girls **last** chance
How Many?	**five** fingers **one** river	**fewer** hours **some** problems

Demonstrative Adjectives

This, that, these, and *those* can be used both as adjectives and as pronouns. When they modify nouns or pronouns, they are called ***demonstrative adjectives.*** When they take the place of nouns or pronouns, they are called ***demonstrative pronouns.***

Reference Note

For more information about **demonstrative pronouns,** see page 8.

Demonstrative Adjectives	Did Jennifer draw **this** picture or **that** one? Let's take **these** sandwiches and **those** apples on our picnic.
Demonstrative Pronouns	**This** is mine and **that** is his. **These** are much more expensive than **those** are.

Pronoun or Adjective?

Some words may be used as either pronouns or adjectives. When used as pronouns, these words take the place of nouns or other pronouns. When used as adjectives, they modify nouns or pronouns.

RESOURCES

The Adjective

Practice

- *Language & Sentence Skills Practice,* pp. 10–13

Differentiating Instruction

- *Developmental Language & Sentence Skills,* pp. 11–12

Pronoun	Adjective
I like **that.**	I like **that** shirt.
Either will do.	**Either** car will do.
Which is yours?	**Which** one is yours?
Whose is it?	**Whose** hat is it?

NOTE In this book, demonstrative, interrogative, and indefinite terms, such as those in boldface in the preceding chart, are called pronouns when they function as pronouns and are called adjectives when they function as adjectives.

The words *my, your, his, her, its, our,* and *their* are called possessive pronouns throughout this book. Some authorities, however, prefer to call these words adjectives. Follow your teacher's instructions on labeling these words.

HELP Possessive forms of nouns are also sometimes referred to as adjectives. Follow your teacher's instructions regarding these forms.

Noun or Adjective?

Many words that can stand alone as nouns can also be used as adjectives modifying nouns or pronouns.

Common Nouns	Adjectives
cheese	**cheese** sandwich
snow	**snow** sculpture
winter	**winter** sale
weather	**weather** report
steel	**steel** girder

Adjectives formed from proper nouns are called ***proper adjectives.***

Proper Nouns	Proper Adjectives
Choctaw	**Choctaw** tradition
Texas	**Texas** coast
Picasso	**Picasso** painting
Dublin	**Dublin** streets
Roosevelt	**Roosevelt** administration

APPLICATION

GRAMMAR

Overused Adjectives

Activity. Explain to students that overused adjectives, such as *nice* and *great,* can sometimes weaken a description. Have students work in groups of four to fill in the blank in the following sentence with at least five vague or overused adjectives:

Love is ________. [*nice, awesome, terrible, neat, wonderful*]

Then, have each group member suggest one adjective that is more specific [*blissful, troublesome, turbulent, fickle, romantic*].

Have each student make a list of specific adjectives on a specified topic—color, size, beauty, shape, and so on. Then, have the group discuss the lists and add to them. Post completed lists on the bulletin board.

GRAMMAR

TEACHING TIP

Exercise 6 Direct students' attention to the **Note** above the exercise. Remind students that a compound noun consists of two or more words used together as a single noun.

DIFFERENTIATING INSTRUCTION

English-Language Learners

Cantonese. Cantonese does not have the articles *a, an,* or *the.* Help students understand the difference between the definite and indefinite articles by putting the sentences in the text into a context.

> Example: Twelve boys and fourteen girls competed in the 400-meter race. **A** girl won.
>
> A boy and a girl raced each other from one end of the playground to the other. **The** girl won.

Although articles seem like a basic and easy element of English, they are often among the last features of the language acquired by English-language learners. Don't be discouraged if English-language learners continue to make mistakes with articles after several explanations and chances to practice. Because articles are unstressed in English, learners often won't hear them in normal conversation. Prompt students for articles in speech through a gesture or sign, and have students proofread written work, perhaps with the help of a native speaker, for article errors.

Reference Note

For information about **capitalizing proper adjectives,** see page 248. See page 4 for more on **compound nouns.**

NOTE Sometimes a proper adjective and a noun are used together so frequently that they become a compound noun: *Brazil nut, French bread, Christmas tree, Swiss cheese.*

Exercise 6 Identifying Nouns and Adjectives

Indicate whether each italicized word or word group in the paragraph below is used as a *noun* or an *adjective.*

EXAMPLE Do you want to see my new **[1]** *baseball* card?

1. *baseball—adjective*

I love anything that has to do with [**1**] *baseball.* I save the [**2**] *money* I make mowing the golf course, and then I go to the [**3**] *card* [**4**] *store.* The [**5**] *store* owner sold me a terrific [**6**] *Don Mattingly* [**7**] *card* today. It came in its own [**8**] *plastic* case. I'll display my new card with my other favorites in a special [**9**] *glass* [**10**] *case* on the wall in my room.

1. noun	6. adj.
2. noun	7. noun
3. adj.	8. adj.
4. noun	9. adj.
5. adj.	10. noun

Articles

The most frequently used adjectives are *a, an,* and *the.* These words are usually called ***articles.***

A and *an* are called ***indefinite articles*** because they refer to any member of a general group. *A* is used before words beginning with a consonant sound. *An* is used before words beginning with a vowel sound.

EXAMPLES **A** girl won.

They are having **a** one-day sale. [Even though *o* is a vowel, the term *one-day* begins with a consonant sound.]

An elephant escaped.

This is **an** honor. [Even though *h* is a consonant, the word *honor* begins with a vowel sound. The *h* is not pronounced.]

The is called the ***definite article*** because it refers to someone or something in particular.

EXAMPLES **The** girl won.

The one-day sale is on Saturday.

Where is **the** elephant?

The honor goes to her.

MINI-LESSON Mechanics

Punctuating Adjectives Before Nouns. Explain to students that a comma is generally used to separate two or more adjectives that come before a noun, as in *I rode a gentle, old horse.*

Sometimes when the final adjective in a series is closely linked to the noun, a comma is not needed before the final adjective: *Maya is a respected broadcast journalist.*

Adjectives in Sentences

An adjective usually comes before the noun or pronoun it modifies.

EXAMPLES Ms. Farrell tells **all** students that **good** workers will be given **special** privileges.

A **sweating, exhausted** runner crossed the line.

In some cases, adjectives follow the word they modify.

EXAMPLE A dog, **old** and **overweight,** snored in the sun.

Other words may separate an adjective from the noun or pronoun it modifies.

EXAMPLES Beverly was **worried.** She felt **nervous** about the play.

Cheered by the crowd, the band played an encore.

NOTE An adjective that is in the predicate and that modifies the subject of a clause or sentence is called a ***predicate adjective***.

Reference Note

For more information about **predicate adjectives,** see page 201.

Exercise 7 Revising Sentences by Using Appropriate Adjectives

Add adjectives to make two entirely different sentences from each of the sentences below.

EXAMPLE 1. The waiter showed the woman to a table in the corner.

1. The kindly waiter showed the shy woman to a pleasant table in the sunny corner.

The haughty waiter showed the elegant woman to a private table in the shadowy corner.

1. The blossoms on the trees filled the air with a scent.
2. As the clouds gathered in the sky, the captain spoke to the crew.
3. At the end of the hall were stairs that led to a room.
4. The car has a stereo and an air conditioner.
5. The singers and comedians gave a performance for the audience.
6. The birds flew to the birdhouse near the barn.
7. Theresa's interest in science began when she attended the class.
8. The house in the valley was constructed by builders.
9. The curtains on the windows added to the look of the room.
10. As the waves washed onto the shore, the children ran away.

COMPUTER TIP

Using a software program's thesaurus can help you choose appropriate adjectives. To make sure that an adjective has exactly the connotation you intend, look up the word in a dictionary.

To test whether the final adjective and the noun are closely linked, have students insert the word *and* between the adjectives. If *and* makes sense, they should use a comma.

Ask students to find a piece of their own writing and to check for the proper punctuation of two or more adjectives preceding a noun. For further instruction and practice, refer students to **Chapter 11: Punctuation.**

GRAMMAR

Exercise 7 Revising Sentences by Using Appropriate Adjectives

POSSIBLE ANSWERS

1. The [*delicate; purple*] blossoms on the [*young; enormous*] trees filled the [*misty; humid*] air with a [*sweet; heavy*] scent.
2. As the [*dark; billowy*] clouds gathered in the [*threatening; evening*] sky, the [*confident; enthusiastic*] captain spoke to the [*frightened; inexperienced*] crew.
3. At the end of the [*long; cluttered*] hall were [*steep; narrow*] stairs that led to a [*hidden; storage*] room.
4. The [*sports; flashy*] car has a [*state-of-the-art; cheap*] stereo and a [*high-performance; leaky*] air conditioner.
5. The [*talented; solemn*] singers and [*silly; angry*] comedians gave a [*creative; poor*] performance for the [*appreciative; confused*] audience.
6. The [*tired; mother*] birds flew to the [*tiny; gray*] birdhouse near the [*dilapidated; scarlet*] barn.
7. Theresa's interest in [*biological; physical*] science began when she attended the [*zoology; meteorology*] class.
8. The [*stone; ranch*] house in the [*lush; hidden*] valley was constructed by [*master; amateur*] builders.
9. The [*tattered; lace*] curtains on the [*grimy; sparkling*] windows added to the [*forsaken; gracious*] look of the [*dingy; inviting*] room.
10. As the [*crashing; foamy*] waves washed onto the [*forlorn; sandy*] shore, the [*frightened; giggling*] children ran away.

GRAMMAR

Review A Identifying Nouns, Pronouns, and Adjectives

Indicate whether each of the italicized words in the following paragraph is used as a noun, a pronoun, or an adjective.

EXAMPLE [1] Most high school *students* read at least *one* play by William Shakespeare.

1. *students—noun; one—adjective*

1. adj. / noun
2. noun / adj.
3. adj. / pro.
4. pro. / adj.
5. noun / pro.
6. noun / pro.
7. adj. / adj.
8. noun / pro.
9. adj. / pro.
10. pro. / noun

[1] *This* article tells about Shakespeare's *life.* [2] *Shakespeare,* perhaps the most *famous* playwright of all time, was born in Stratford-on-Avon in 1564. [3] He was baptized in the *small* church at Stratford shortly after *his* birth. [4] In 1616, *he* was buried in the *same* church. [5] If you visit his grave, you can find an *inscription* placing a curse on *anyone* who moves his bones. [6] Out of *respect* for his wish or because of fear of his curse, *nobody* has disturbed the grave. [7] As a result, his remains have never been moved to Westminster Abbey, where many *other* famous *English* writers are buried. [8] Visitors to *Stratford* can also see the house in *which* Shakespeare was born. [9] At *one* time tourists could visit the large house that Shakespeare bought for *himself* and his family. [10] *This* was where they lived when he retired from the London *theater.*

The Verb

1d. A *verb* is a word that is used to express action or a state of being.

In this book verbs are classified in three ways—(1) as main or helping verbs, (2) as action or linking verbs, or (3) as transitive or intransitive verbs.

Main Verbs and Helping Verbs

A ***verb phrase*** consists of at least one ***main verb*** and one or more helping verbs. A ***helping verb*** (also called an ***auxiliary verb***) helps the main verb express action or a state of being.

Besides all forms of the verb *be,* the following verbs can be used as helping verbs.

can	do	has	might	should
could	does	have	must	will
did	had	may	shall	would

The Verb

Rule 1d *(pp. 14–21)*

OBJECTIVES

- To identify main verbs, helping verbs, and verb phrases
- To write action verbs
- To identify linking verbs and words they link
- To add linking verbs to sentences
- To write sentences with action verbs and linking verbs
- To use transitive and intransitive verbs

RESOURCES

The Verb

Practice

- *Language & Sentence Skills Practice,* pp. 14–18

Differentiating Instruction

- *Developmental Language & Sentence Skills,* pp. 13–18

Notice how helping verbs work together with main verbs to form complete verb phrases.

EXAMPLES **is** leaving **had** seemed **might have** remained

Sometimes the parts of a verb phrase are interrupted by other parts of speech.

EXAMPLES She **had** always **been thinking** of her future.
Has my sister **played** her new CD for you?

NOTE The word *not* is an adverb. It is never part of a verb phrase, even when it is joined to a verb as the contraction *–n't*.

EXAMPLES She **should** not **have borrowed** that necklace.
She **should**n't **have borrowed** that necklace.

Reference Note

For information about **contractions,** see page 335.

Exercise 8 Identifying Main Verbs and Helping Verbs

Identify all the main verbs and helping verbs in each of the following sentences.

EXAMPLE 1. How well did your brother recover from his back injury?
1. recover—main; did—helping

1. Fortunately, he didn't need surgery.
2. His physical therapist has designed an exercise program for him.
3. Before exercise, he must spend at least five minutes warming up.
4. He will be using a back-extension machine.
5. Does he walk indoors on a treadmill or outdoors on a track?
6. At home, he will be exercising on a treadmill.
7. The doctor is always reminding my brother about proper techniques for lifting.
8. When lifting heavy objects, my brother must wear a back brace.
9. Should he try acupuncture or massage therapy?
10. Without physical therapy, he might not have healed as quickly.

Exercise 9 Identifying Verbs and Verb Phrases

Identify all the verbs and verb phrases in the sentences on the next page. Include all helping verbs, even if the parts of a verb phrase are separated by other words.

EXAMPLE 1. We will probably go to the movie if we can finish our assignment.
1. will go, can finish

EXTENSION

Relating to Literature

If your literature book contains Emily Dickinson's poem "A Bird Came Down the Walk," read the poem to students. Have them listen for verbs and tell how Dickinson's choice of verbs contributes to the poem.

[*The use of action verbs gives the reader a sense of the bird's quick and definite movements. The poet writes concisely, taking full advantage of each verb to create an effective image.*]

GRAMMAR

GRAMMAR

DIRECT TEACHING

Action Verbs

Activity. Divide the class into groups of four to play a game with action verbs. Give each group five index cards with one of the following sentences on each card:

1. Mom drove through the traffic.
2. Al walked across the stage.
3. Pedro sang for the audience.
4. The team came onto the field.
5. Maya threw the ball too hard.

The object of the five-minute game is for the groups to replace the verbs on the cards with as many specific verbs as possible. After five minutes, have the groups share their sentences with the rest of the class.

Exercise 10 Writing Action Verbs

POSSIBLE ANSWERS

1. catch
2. throw
3. eat
4. walk
5. read
6. study
7. stay
8. dance
9. ski
10. sing
11. listen
12. strum
13. display
14. jog
15. bounce
16. suppose
17. ponder
18. analyze
19. realize
20. yearn

1. Mr. Jensen always sweeps the floor first.
2. Then he washes the chalkboards.
3. He works slowly but steadily.
4. The weather forecaster had not predicted rain.
5. All morning the barometer was dropping rapidly.
6. The storm was slowly moving in.
7. Your dog will become fat if you feed it too much.
8. Dogs will usually eat everything you give them.
9. Generally, cats will stop when they have had enough.
10. After our team has had more practice, we will win.

Action Verbs and Linking Verbs

An ***action verb*** expresses either physical or mental action.

Physical Action	write describe	sit receive	arise go
Mental Action	remember consider	think understand	believe know

EXAMPLES The audience **cheered** the lead actors.
The children **hoped** for sunshine.

Exercise 10 Writing Action Verbs

Write twenty action verbs, not including those previously listed. Include and underline at least five verbs that express mental action.

EXAMPLES 1. *soar* 2. *imagine*

A ***linking verb*** connects the subject to a word or word group that identifies or describes the subject. The most commonly used linking verbs are forms of the verb *be.*

be	shall be	should be
being	will be	would be
am	has been	can be
is	have been	could be

(continued)

MINI-LESSON Grammar

Subject Complements. Explain to students that a subject complement is a noun, pronoun, or adjective that completes the meaning of a linking verb and identifies or describes the subject. If the complement is a noun or pronoun, it is called a *predicate nominative;* if it is an adjective, it is called a *predicate adjective.* Write sentences 1–3 on the chalkboard. Ask students to label each subject complement *predicate nominative*

(continued)

are	had been	should have been
was	shall have been	would have been
were	will have been	could have been

Here are some other frequently used linking verbs.

appear	grow	seem	stay
become	look	smell	taste
feel	remain	sound	turn

The noun, pronoun, or adjective that is connected to the subject by a linking verb completes the meaning of the verb and refers to the verb's subject.

EXAMPLES The answer **is** "three." [The verb *is* links *answer* and *"three."*]

The answer **is** correct. [The verb *is* links *answer* and *correct.*]

The winners **are** they. [The verb links *winners* and *they.*]

The winners **are** happy. [The verb links *winners* and *happy.*]

Many linking verbs can be used as action verbs as well.

EXAMPLES The wet dog **smelled** horrible. [The linking verb *smelled* links *dog* and *horrible.*]

The dog **smelled** the baked bread. [action verb]

The motor **sounded** harsh. [The linking verb *sounded* links *motor* and *harsh.*]

The engineer **sounded** the horn. [action verb]

The chef **tasted** the casserole. [action verb]

The casserole **tasted** strange. [The linking verb *tasted* links *casserole* and *strange.*]

Even *be* is not always a linking verb. Sometimes *be* expresses a state of being and is followed only by an adverb.

EXAMPLE I **was** there. [*There* tells *where.* It does not identify or describe the subject *I.*]

To be a linking verb, the verb must be followed by a ***subject complement***—a noun or a pronoun that names the subject or an adjective that describes the subject.

Reference Note

For a discussion of **adverbs,** see page 21.

Reference Note

For more on **subject complements,** see page 57.

EXTENSION

GRAMMAR

Relating to Writing

Students often use linking verbs in their writing when action verbs would be more concise. For example, a student might write "I am a fast runner and a high jumper" instead of "I run fast and jump high."

Ask each student to write a one-paragraph character sketch about an admired person. Tell students that when they revise their paragraphs, they should each replace all but two linking verbs. Make sure that students understand that there is nothing wrong with using forms of *be* if necessary but that action verbs often provide more specific images.

or *predicate adjective.*

1. Mario is a good soccer *player.* [*predicate nominative*]
2. The hyacinths along the path smelled *sweet.* [*predicate adjective*]
3. The one who called this morning was *she.* [*predicate nominative*]

For more information on subject complements, refer students to **Chapter 2: The Parts of a Sentence.**

GRAMMAR

PRACTICE

Guided and Independent

Exercises You may wish to have the class work through **Exercise 11** as guided practice and **Exercise 12** as independent practice.

HOMEWORK

Exercise 11 Identifying Linking Verbs and the Words They Link

Identify the linking verb in each of the sentences below. Then, give the words that are linked by the verb.

EXAMPLE 1. Dixie can be a very obedient dog.
1. can be—Dixie, dog

1. He felt foolish when his car ran out of gas.
2. Suddenly, it turned very dark, and the wind began to blow fiercely.
3. We had waited so long for dinner that anything would have tasted wonderful.
4. The plot of that fantasy novel seems awfully childish to me now.
5. Kevin and I stayed best friends throughout middle school.
6. I am happy that you won the chess match.
7. If the coach had let me play, this game would have been my first one with the Tigers.
8. My father thinks that you should become a lawyer.
9. After practicing hard, Stef's band sounded great in the concert.
10. For a moment, Dr. Kostas thought the planet's rings appeared smaller.

Exercise 12 Writing Appropriate Linking Verbs

Choose a linking verb for each blank. Try to use a different verb for each sentence. Verbs will vary.

EXAMPLE 1. The baby ____ sleepy after he was fed.
1. The baby grew sleepy after he was fed.

1. That building ____ the new public library. 1. is
2. The car ____ funny. 2. sounds
3. The moose ____ huge. 3. was
4. I ____ very nervous about the driving test. 4. felt
5. Her garden ____ dried and brown in the drought. 5. became
6. Let's hope the evening ____ cool. 6. will be
7. We can eat the raspberries when they ____ red. 7. turn
8. Burt ____ grouchy early in the morning. 8. would be
9. The soup ____ too salty. 9. tasted
10. The puppy ____ healthy and playful. 10. appears

Learning for Life

Giving Accurate Directions. People are often called upon to give directions to others for getting to a specific place. Ask students to choose a public place, such as a library or a shop, and write directions aimed at a specific audience. Students might choose to direct a child from a grade school to a public library, or a newcomer from a residence to the power company or the Department of Motor Vehicles. Ask them to use nouns, pronouns, adjectives, and verbs that are specific and that describe the landmarks a person will

Exercise 13 **Writing Sentences with Action Verbs and Linking Verbs**

Choose five nouns from the numbered items below. For each noun, write two sentences, using the noun as the subject of each sentence. Use an action verb in one sentence and a linking verb in the other. Indicate which sentence contains the action verb and which contains the linking verb.

EXAMPLE **1.** fireworks

1. *The fireworks filled the night sky with bursts of color.—action verb*

The fireworks grew more colorful toward the end of the program.—linking verb

1. pilot	**4.** skater	**7.** foghorn	**9.** movie
2. locomotive	**5.** football	**8.** Mrs. Wu	**10.** Lincoln
3. taco	**6.** coins		

Transitive and Intransitive Verbs

A ***transitive verb*** is a verb that expresses an action directed toward a person, place, or thing. The action expressed by a transitive verb passes from the doer—the subject—to the receiver of the action. Words that receive the action of a transitive verb are called ***objects.***

EXAMPLES When **will** Neil **ring** the bell? [The action of the verb *will ring* is directed toward the object *bell.*]

Juanita **mailed** the package. [The action of the verb *mailed* is directed toward the object *package.*]

Tell the truth. [The action of the verb *Tell* is directed toward the object *truth.*]

An ***intransitive verb*** expresses action (or tells something about the subject) without the action passing to a receiver, or object.

EXAMPLES Last Saturday we **stayed** inside. [The verb *stayed* does not pass the action to an object.]

After their long walk, the children **ate** quickly. [The verb *ate* does not pass the action to an object.]

When she told her story, my, how we **laughed**! [The verb *laughed* does not pass the action to an object.]

Reference Note

For more about **objects and their uses in sentences,** see page 59.

GRAMMAR

Exercise 13 **Writing Sentences with Action Verbs and Linking Verbs**

ANSWERS

Sentences will vary, but students should correctly label the action verbs and linking verbs that they use in their sentences.

DIRECT TEACHING

Modeling and Demonstration

The Verb. Model how to identify transitive and intransitive verbs by using the example *When she told her story, my, how we laughed.* First, ask which words in the sentence are verbs. [*told, laughed*] Next, ask if *told* expresses an action directed toward a person, place, or thing. [*yes;* story] Then, ask if *laughed* expresses an action toward a person, place, or thing. [*no*]. Explain that a transitive verb's action passes from the doer (the subject) to the receiver (the object), but that an intransitive verb's action tells something about the subject without passing the action to a receiver. Point out that in this sentence *told* is transitive, while *laughed* is intransitive. Now, have a volunteer use another example from this chapter to demonstrate how to identify transitive and intransitive verbs.

encounter in following the directions.

After students have completed their directions, allow them to work in groups of four to test how accurate their directions are. Have each student read his or her directions aloud to the group, and let group members add, delete, or amplify aspects of the directions to make them clearer and easier to follow.

GRAMMAR

PRACTICE

Guided and Independent

Exercises You may wish to have the class work through **Exercise 14** as guided practice and **Exercise 15** as independent practice.

HOMEWORK

EXTENSION

Relating to Literature

Popular novels and magazines often use strong, specific verbs like those listed for **Exercise 15.** Direct students to stories such as Toni Cade Bambara's "Blues Ain't No Mockin Bird" to demonstrate the creative use of such verbs in speaker tags. Ask students to bring to class examples of effective verb usage that they find in their reading. Tell them to be ready to share the examples with the class.

Exercise 15 **Revising Dialogue Using Verbs**

ANSWERS

Answers will vary, but students should be careful to follow the context clues of the sentences in order to choose appropriate verbs.

HELP

Because they do not have objects (words that tell who or what receives the action of the verb), linking verbs are considered intransitive.

Reference Note

For more about **intransitive verbs,** see page 14.

A verb may be transitive in one sentence and intransitive in another.

EXAMPLES Marcie **studied** her notes. [transitive]
Marcie **studied** very late. [intransitive]

The poet **wrote** a sonnet. [transitive]
The poet **wrote** carefully. [intransitive]

Exercise 14 Using Transitive and Intransitive Verbs

Choose a verb from the following list for each blank in the paragraph below. Then, identify each verb as *transitive* or *intransitive.*

drifted	landed	watched	experienced
floated	rode	met	admired
climbed	arrived	left	did
awaited	suggest	tried	drove

EXAMPLE Can you **[1]** _____ an activity for this weekend?
1. suggest—transitive

Aunt Pam and I [1] _____ something really different last summer. We [2] _____ on inner tubes down a river in the wilderness. A guide [3] _____ our group with a truckful of giant tubes and picnic lunches and [4] _____ us about twenty miles upstream. Then everyone [5] _____ into a tube in the water. The guide [6] _____ in the truck for a picnic spot downstream, halfway back to the base. All morning, we [7] _____ lazily along in the sunshine and [8] _____ the wildlife along the shore. When we [9] _____ at the picnic spot, a delicious lunch [10] _____ us.

Verbs will vary.
1. did—tr.
2. rode—int.
3. met—tr.
4. drove—tr.
5. climbed—int.
6. left—int.
7. floated—int.
8. admired—tr.
9. landed—int.
10. awaited—tr.

Exercise 15 Revising Dialogue Using Verbs

Using a variety of verbs can make dialogue more interesting. Rewrite the dialogue on the next page. In six of the ten items, replace *said* with one of the verbs from the following list. In the other four items, choose your own verbs.

wailed	bellowed	gloated	reported
responded	teased	soothed	confessed
exclaimed	replied	whined	accused
snapped	cried	muttered	called
howled	roared	pleaded	snapped

EXAMPLE
1. "Mom, I'm home!" said Tony, sprinting in the door.
   1. *"Mom, I'm home!" bellowed Tony, sprinting in the door.*
2. "I've got great news!" he said.
   2. *"I've got great news!" he shouted.*

Verbs will vary.

1. "Guess what? I won the spelling bee," he ~~said~~. — 1. shouted
2. "Honey, that's wonderful," ~~said~~ his mother. — 2. cried
3. "I spelled 'expeditious' when no one else could, not even Stephanie Greenblatt," ~~said~~ Tony. — 3. reported
4. "I'm so proud of you," ~~said~~ his mother. — 4. responded
5. "Who cares?" ~~said~~ his sister Amy. — 5. whined
6. "You're just jealous," ~~said~~ Tony. — 6. accused
7. "I am not!" Amy ~~said~~, running out of the kitchen. — 7. snapped
8. "Don't let her bother you," ~~said~~ his mother. "You should enjoy your success." — 8. whispered
9. "I am enjoying it," ~~said~~ Tony, "but I wish I could share my happiness with Amy." — 9. replied
10. "She'll come around," his mother ~~said~~. "Meanwhile, sit down and tell me all about it." — 10. soothed

GRAMMAR

The Adverb

1e. An *adverb* modifies a verb, an adjective, or another adverb.

An adverb tells *where, when, how,* or *to what extent* (*how long* or *how much*). Just as an adjective makes the meaning of a noun or a pronoun more definite, an adverb makes the meaning of a verb, an adjective, or another adverb more definite.

Adverbs Modifying Verbs

In the following examples, each boldface adverb modifies a verb.

Where?	When?
We lived **there**.	May we go **tomorrow**?
Please step **up**.	Water the plant **weekly**.
I have the ticket **here**.	We'll see you **later**.
Put that **down**.	He arrived **early**.

HELP

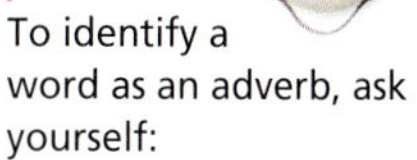

To identify a word as an adverb, ask yourself:

Does this word modify a verb, an adjective, or an adverb?

Does it tell *when, where, how,* or *to what extent*?

The Adverb

Rule 1e *(pp. 21–27)*

OBJECTIVES

- To complete sentences by adding appropriate adverbs
- To identify adverbs that modify adjectives and to name the adjectives modified
- To revise phrases and sentences by adding adverbs that modify adjectives
- To identify adverbs that modify other adverbs and to identify the words modified
- To revise sentences by using appropriate adverbs

RESOURCES

The Adverb

Practice

- *Language & Sentence Skills Practice,* pp. 19–21

Differentiating Instruction

- *Developmental Language & Sentence Skills,* pp. 19–20

GRAMMAR

Differentiating Instruction

Learners Having Difficulty

Some students will benefit from hearing and answering the adverb questions *How?*, *When?*, *Where?*, or *To what extent?* Start by saying "Jane walked . . ."

Ask students *how* she walked. Have them supply adverbs until they run out of ideas. [*slowly, tiredly, sluggishly*] Then, ask *when* she walked. Students should again supply adverbs. [*today, yesterday, Tuesday, then*] Continue with *where* and *to what extent.*

Special Education Students

Adverbs can be especially difficult for some students because an adverb can modify so many parts of speech and can easily be confused with a preposition. You may want to pair students who are having difficulty with advanced students who can answer questions, read the text aloud, and clarify concepts.

English-Language Learners

Spanish. Point out to your Spanish-speaking students that the English *–ly* suffix is equivalent to the Spanish *–mente* suffix. Both convert adjectives to adverbs. (In French the suffix is *–ment.*)

How?	To What Extent?
She **quickly** agreed.	Fill the tank **completely.**
The rain fell **softly.**	He **hardly** moved.
Drive **carefully.**	Did she hesitate **slightly**?
He sang **beautifully.**	They **partly** completed the form.

As you can see in the preceding examples, adverbs may come before or after the verbs they modify. Sometimes adverbs interrupt the parts of a verb phrase.

Adverbs may also introduce questions.

EXAMPLE **Where** in the world did you ever find that pink-and-purple necktie? [The adverb *Where* introduces the question and modifies the verb phrase *did find.* The adverb *ever* interrupts the verb phrase and also modifies it.]

NOTE Although many adverbs end in *–ly,* the *–ly* ending does not necessarily mean that a word is an adverb. Many adjectives also end in *–ly*: the *daily* newspaper, an *early* train, an *only* child, a *lonely* person. Also, some words, such as *now, then, far, already, somewhat, not,* and *right,* are often used as adverbs, yet they do not end in *–ly.*

Exercise 16 Completing Sentences by Supplying Appropriate Adverbs

Complete each of the following sentences by supplying an appropriate adverb. The word or phrase in parentheses tells you what information the adverb should give about the action. Adverbs will vary.

EXAMPLE 1. He moved his hand (*how*).

1. gracefully

1. The soldiers must travel (*how*). 1. quietly
2. You will probably sleep well (*when*). 2. tonight
3. They whispered (*how*) to Mr. Baldwin. 3. cautiously
4. Tonya took a deep breath and dove (*where*). 4. in
5. Did you study (*to what extent*)? 5. much
6. Handle the ducklings (*how*). 6. carefully
7. My uncle Hans is (*when*) in a bad mood. 7. never
8. Your taxi should be (*where*) soon. 8. here
9. I could (*to what extent*) taste the tangy pizza. 9. almost
10. (*When*), you should paste the pictures on the poster. 10. First

Adverbs Modifying Adjectives

EXAMPLES Beth did an **exceptionally** fine job. [The adverb *exceptionally* modifies the adjective *fine,* telling *to what extent.*]

Slightly cooler temperatures are forecast. [The adverb *slightly* modifies the adjective *cooler,* telling *to what extent.*]

Mr. Lomazzi is an **especially** talented chef. [The adverb *especially* modifies the adjective *talented,* telling *to what extent.*]

Exercise 17 Identifying Adverbs That Modify Adjectives

Identify the adverbs that modify adjectives in the sentences below. For each adverb, give the adjective it modifies.

EXAMPLE 1. The compass I bought was incredibly cheap.

1. incredibly—cheap

1. If you are ever really lost in the woods at night, knowing how to find the North Star may be extremely important.
2. Here is one method that is quite useful.
3. First, find the Big Dipper, which is surprisingly easy to spot.
4. It consists of seven rather bright stars in the northern sky that are arranged in the shape of a large dipper.
5. Do not confuse it with the Little Dipper, which is somewhat smaller.
6. After you have found the Big Dipper, you must be very careful to sight along the two stars that form the front of the dipper bowl.
7. They are two points on an almost straight line to the North Star.
8. This method for getting your bearings is completely reliable—except when the clouds are so dense that you cannot see the stars.
9. It would be especially wise to check the weather forecast before going on a hike.
10. Remember to take a compass, water, and a fully stocked first-aid kit.

STYLE TIP

The most frequently used adverbs are *too, so, really,* and *very*. In fact, these words are often overworked. To make your speaking and writing more interesting, replace these general adverbs with more specific ones, such as *completely, especially,* and *quite*.

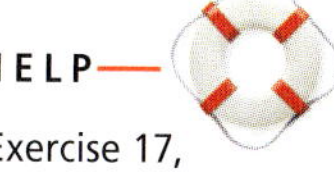

HELP

In Exercise 17, a sentence may contain more than one adverb modifying an adjective.

GRAMMAR

DIRECT TEACHING

Modeling and Demonstration

The Adverb. Model how to identify adverbs modifying adjectives by using the example *Beth did an exceptionally fine job.* First, ask what part of speech the word *job* is. [*noun*] Next, ask if there is a word that tells what kind of *job* Beth did. [*yes;* fine] Then, ask if there is a word describing where, when, how, or to what extent the *job* was *fine.* [*yes;* exceptionally] Explain that *fine* is an adjective because it modifies the noun *job.* Point out that *exceptionally* is an adverb because it modifies the adjective *fine,* telling to what extent *Beth did a fine job.* Now, have a volunteer use another example from this chapter to demonstrate how to identify adverbs modifying adjectives.

Correcting Misconceptions

Activity. Students may think that the proper place for an adverb is at the beginning of a sentence or next to a verb. Students might be unaware of how much the position of an adverb can affect the meaning of a sentence. Read the following sentences to the class. Have volunteers comment on how the position of *only* affects the meaning of each sentence.

1. The teacher *only* looked at me as I prepared to give my speech.
2. The teacher looked *only* at me as I prepared to give my speech.
3. The teacher looked at me *only* as I prepared to give my speech.

[*The first sentence indicates that all the teacher did was look at me. The second indicates that the teacher focused her attention on me. The third tells when the teacher looked at me.*]

GRAMMAR

DIFFERENTIATING INSTRUCTION

Learners Having Difficulty

Activity. To help students review adverbs before they tackle **Exercise 18**, pair them to play a game that focuses on adverbs and vocabulary development. Because the game is challenging, you may wish to pair learners having difficulty with advanced ones, but be willing to monitor activity to see that all students are making progress.

The object of the game is for each pair to come up with an adverb and a word for it to modify (verb, adjective, or other adverb) beginning with each letter of the alphabet. Some examples are *always active; bashfully brings; carefully cuts; delightfully delicious; exceedingly edgy;* and *fairly frequently.*

Give students ten minutes to work on their lists. Encourage them to use a dictionary. When time is up, have pairs exchange lists to check for accuracy.

Exercise 18 Revising with Adverb Modifiers

Make each of the phrases and sentences below more descriptive by adding one adverb that modifies each of the italicized adjectives. Use a different adverb in each item. Adverbs will vary.

EXAMPLE 1. a *confusing* sentence
1. an especially confusing sentence

1. a *sharp* turn 1. quite
2. *playful* kittens 2. extremely
3. an *easy* question 3. unusually
4. a *swept* floor 4. cleanly
5. Her little brother has a *bright* smile. 5. cheerily
6. Terri felt *satisfied* that she had done her best. 6. completely
7. The old mansion was *silent.* 7. eerily
8. Robert became *sick* and had to leave early. 8. terribly
9. Had Clara been *safe?* 9. especially
10. Most of the questions on the test were *difficult.* 10. dreadfully

Adverbs Modifying Other Adverbs

EXAMPLES Calvin was **almost** never there. [The adverb *almost* modifies the adverb *never,* telling *to what extent.*]

We'll meet **shortly** afterward. [The adverb *shortly* modifies the adverb *afterward,* telling *to what extent.*]

She slept **too** late. [The adverb *too* modifies the adverb *late,* telling *to what extent.*]

Reference Note

For information about **compound sentences,** see page 109. For information on **adverb clauses,** see page 104.

NOTE One kind of adverb—the ***conjunctive adverb***—is an adverb used as a connecting word between independent clauses in a compound sentence.

EXAMPLE We tried to be at the stadium by 6:30 P.M.; **however,** we arrived at the wrong time.

Another kind of adverb—the ***relative adverb***—is often used to introduce adjective clauses.

EXAMPLES Uncle Lionel told us about the time **when** he drove across the country.

In 1815, Napoleon was sent into exile on the island of St. Helena, **where** he died in 1821.

MINI-LESSON Grammar

Unnecessary Adverbs in Writing. Unnecessary adverbs can clutter students' writing. Copy the following paragraph on the chalkboard, underlining the adverbs as shown. Have students determine which adverbs seem necessary, and why.

I would <u>really</u> enjoy taking a vacation to a sunny beach. My idea of paradise is lying <u>quietly</u> and <u>peacefully</u> in the sun

Noun or Adverb?

Some words that can be used as nouns can also be used as adverbs.

EXAMPLES **Tomorrow** never seems to arrive. [*noun*]

We will leave **tomorrow.** [*Tomorrow* is used as an adverb telling *when*.]

Think of this place as your **home.** [*noun*]

He was eager to come **home.** [*Home* is used as an adverb telling *where*.]

When identifying parts of speech, remember: A word used to modify a verb, an adjective, or another adverb is called an adverb.

"I miss the good old days when all we had to worry about was nouns and verbs."

Exercise 19 Identifying Adverbs That Modify Other Adverbs

Identify all the adverbs that modify other adverbs in the sentences below. After each adverb, give the adverb it modifies.

EXAMPLE 1. Brian is so terribly shy that he blushes when people speak to him.

1. so, terribly

1. The cat leapt to the windowsill quite agilely.
2. The books were stacked rather haphazardly.
3. Corrie knew she'd have to get up incredibly early to watch the eclipse tomorrow.
4. The tornado almost completely destroyed the barn.
5. The famous diamond was more heavily guarded than any other exhibit at the museum.
6. My brother is nearly always finished with his paper route before I am finished with mine.
7. She registered too late to be eligible for the classes she wanted.
8. In the final four minutes of the game, Isiah Thomas shot extremely accurately.
9. Usually it seems that each month goes more rapidly than the month before.
10. They walked onto the stage most calmly, as if they felt completely relaxed.

and watching the clouds drift lazily overhead. Of course, going snorkeling and watching brightly colored fish swim rapidly through the ocean would surely be fun, too. I certainly hope I get to go, because I know it'll be totally great.

[*Students will probably agree that* peacefully, lazily, overhead, brightly, *and* too *enhance the paragraph.*]

GRAMMAR

PRACTICE

Guided and Independent

Exercises You may wish to have the class work through **Exercise 20** as guided practice and **Exercise 21** as independent practice.

HOMEWORK

EXTENSION

Relating to Writing

Before students do **Exercises 20** and **21**, have them write free-verse poems about their favorite holidays. Tell them to use at least seven adverbs.

Poems will vary greatly, but you may want to use the following student poem as an example:

Fourth of July

Rockets scream *angrily*
through the sky.

Fireworks explode *brightly.*

Flags wave *proudly.*

Crowds cheer *wildly.*

Trumpets blare *loudly.*

Drums beat *rhythmically.*

Then the parade begins.

Exercise 20 Identifying Adverbs and the Words They Modify

Identify the adverb or adverbs in each of the following sentences. Then, give the word or expression that each adverb modifies. If a sentence does not contain an adverb, write *none.*

EXAMPLE 1. Have you ever thought about writing a movie script?
1. ever—have thought

1. Successful movie scripts, or screenplays, are written according to a very rigid formula.
2. The main character and the action of the story must grab an audience's interest quickly.
3. Almost exactly twenty-five minutes into the movie comes a "plot point."
4. A plot point is a surprising event that swings the story around in another direction.
5. Most of the action and conflict occurs in the next hour of the movie.
6. Then comes another plot point, about eighty-five minutes into the movie.
7. Finally, the audience learns what happens to the characters.
8. The last time I went to a movie I really liked, I checked my watch.
9. It was quite interesting to find that the movie's timing matched this formula.
10. Try this test yourself sometime.

3. *Exactly* is modified by *Almost* and modifies *twenty-five.*

5. *none*

Exercise 21 Revising Sentences by Using Appropriate Adverbs

Revise each of the sentences below by adding at least one appropriate adverb. Try not to use the adverbs *too, so, really,* and *very.*

Adverbs will vary.

EXAMPLE 1. Dana, bring me the fire extinguisher!
1. Dana, bring me the fire extinguisher now!

1. Angelo promised me that he would try to meet the train.
2. My coat was torn during the long hike, so Barbara lent me her plastic poncho.
3. Engineering degrees are popular with students because job opportunities in engineering are good.
4. The Wallaces are settled into a new house, which they built by themselves.

1. definitely
2. badly
3. particularly
4. comfortably

5. When the baseball season begins, I will be ^ attending games every day. 5. happily
6. Ronald ^ dribbled to his left and threw the ball into a crowd of defenders. 6. hastily
7. Visits to national monuments and parks remind us that our country has an ^ exciting history. 7. especially
8. We returned the book to Marcella, but she ^ had planned her report without it. 8. already
9. Georgia O'Keeffe displayed her paintings and ^ received the admiration of a large audience. 9. later
10. The recipe calls for two eggs, but I ^ did not have time to buy any at the store. 10. certainly

Review B Identifying Nouns, Pronouns, Adjectives, Verbs, and Adverbs

Indicate whether the italicized words in the paragraph below are used as *nouns, pronouns, adjectives, verbs,* or *adverbs.*

EXAMPLE **[1]** *You* may know that Brazil is the *largest* country in South America.

1. *You—pronoun; largest—adjective*

[1] My *best* friend's mother just *came* back from visiting her family in Brazil. [2] *She* showed us *some* pictures she took in Brasília, the capital, and told us about it. [3] It was amazing to learn that *this* area had been *jungle* until construction began in the 1950s. [4] At first, few people lived in Brasília because it was so *isolated.* [5] However, over the *years* hundreds of thousands of people *have* moved *there.* [6] Several other Brazilian cities *also* lie within one hundred *miles* of Brasília. [7] *A* number of *good* highways *connect* Brasília with other major cities. [8] Residents enjoy the wide streets and open spaces *that* are *shown* in this picture. [9] *One* of Brasília's *most* striking features is its bold architecture. [10] Aren't the government buildings at the *Plaza* of the Three Powers *fantastic?*

GRAMMAR

Review B Identifying Nouns, Pronouns, Adjectives, Verbs, and Adverbs

ANSWERS

1. adj./v.
2. pro./adj.
3. adj./n.
4. adj.
5. n./v./adv.
6. adv./n.
7. adj./v.
8. pro./v.
9. pro./adv.
10. n./adj.

GRAMMAR

The Preposition

Rule 1f *(pp. 28–31)*

OBJECTIVES

- To identify prepositions and their objects in sentences
- To complete sentences by adding appropriate prepositions

DIFFERENTIATING INSTRUCTION

Learners Having Difficulty

Activity. Some prepositions show direction. To reinforce what students have learned about prepositions, have students play a game called Treasure Hunt.

Divide the class into two groups. Have one group hide something (a poster or a book, for example) somewhere in the classroom and create clues that will eventually lead the other team to the hidden item. Each clue should include a preposition. The clues should cause the hunters to wander in many different directions before reaching the hidden item. [*Sample direction*: *Go* to *the back* of *the room. Look* inside *the third desk* from *the rear.*]

MEETING THE CHALLENGE

Prepositional phrases are generally used as modifiers. You can use prepositional phrases to add specific details to your sentences and so make the sentences more interesting. To see the difference that well-chosen prepositional phrases make, write a paragraph or poem describing a friend of yours—but without using any prepositional phrases. Then, write a second version of your paragraph or poem, this time using five or more prepositional phrases. Underline each prepositional phrase in the second version.

ANSWER

Poems and paragraphs will vary, but the first version should have no prepositional phrases while the second version should have at least five underlined prepositional phrases.

The Preposition

1f. A *preposition* is a word that shows the relationship of a noun or a pronoun to another word.

By changing the prepositions in the following examples, you can change the relationship of *Saint Bernard* to *bed* and *Everything* to *beach.*

The Saint Bernard slept **near** my bed.	Everything **about** the beach was wonderful.
The Saint Bernard slept **under** my bed.	Everything **except** the beach was wonderful.
The Saint Bernard slept **on** my bed.	Everything **from** the beach was wonderful.
The Saint Bernard slept **beside** by bed.	Everything **on** the beach was wonderful.

The noun or pronoun that a preposition relates another word to is called the *object of the preposition.* In the examples above, *bed* and *beach* are the objects of the prepositions.

Commonly Used Prepositions

aboard	below	from	since
about	beneath	in	through
above	beside	inside	throughout
across	besides	into	till
after	between	like	to
against	beyond	near	toward
along	but (meaning *except*)	of	under
amid		off	underneath
among	by	on	until
around	concerning	onto	up
as	down	out	upon
at	during	outside	with
before	except	over	within
behind	for	past	without

RESOURCES

The Preposition

Practice

- *Language & Sentence Skills Practice,* p. 22

Differentiating Instruction

- *Developmental Language & Sentence Skills,* pp. 21–22

NOTE Many words in the preceding list can also be used as adverbs. To be sure that a word is used as a preposition, ask whether the word relates a noun or a pronoun to another word. Compare the following sentences:

Welcome **aboard.** [adverb]
Welcome **aboard** our boat. [preposition]

The runner fell **behind.** [adverb]
The paper fell **behind** the cabinet. [preposition]

STYLE TIP

In casual speech and informal writing, people often end sentences with prepositions. However, in formal speech and writing, it is best to avoid doing so.

GRAMMAR

Prepositions that consist of two or more words are called ***compound prepositions.***

Compound Prepositions	
according to	in place of
as of	in spite of
aside from	instead of
because of	next to
by means of	on account of
in addition to	out of
in front of	prior to

NOTE As a rule, the object of the preposition follows the preposition.

EXAMPLE Add a teaspoon of freshly ground **cinnamon.**
[*Cinnamon* is the object of the preposition *of.*]

Sometimes, however, the object of the preposition comes before the preposition.

EXAMPLE He is a singer **whom** I've never heard of before.
[*Whom* is the object of the preposition *of.*]

Objects of prepositions may be compound.

EXAMPLES Kyoko called to **Nancy** and **me.**
[Both *Nancy* and *me* are objects of the preposition *to.*]

The marbles were scattered under the **table** and **chairs.**
[Both *table* and *chairs* are objects of the preposition *under.*]

The Preposition 29

The preposition, its object, and any modifiers of the object together form a ***prepositional phrase.*** Notice in the following examples that modifiers of the object of the preposition can come before or after the object.

Reference Note

For more information about **prepositional phrases,** see page 70.

EXAMPLES Joe went **to the nearest store.** [The noun *store* is the object of the preposition *to.* The adjectives *the* and *nearest* modify the noun *store.*]

Is she one **of those trailing behind**? [The pronoun *those* is the object of the preposition *of. Those* is modified by the participial phrase *trailing behind.*]

The kitten hopped **into the big paper bag that Anita brought.** [The noun *bag* is the object of the preposition *into. Bag* is modified by the adjectives *the, big,* and *paper* and by the subordinate clause *that Anita brought.*]

Reference Note

For more information about **infinitives,** see page 85.

NOTE Be careful not to confuse a prepositional phrase that begins with *to* (*to town, to her club*) with an infinitive that begins with *to* (*to run, to be seen*). Remember: A prepositional phrase always has a noun or a pronoun as an object.

Exercise 22 Identifying Prepositions and Their Objects

HELP Sentences in Exercise 22 may have a compound object of a preposition.

Identify each preposition and its object in the following sentences.

EXAMPLE 1. I've been studying Spanish in school for three years.

1. *in—school; for—years*

1. Last week, my Spanish class went on a field trip to Monterrey, 140 miles southwest of Laredo, where we live.
2. Señora Ayala, our teacher, wanted us to practice speaking and reading Spanish outside the classroom.
3. Everyone was supposed to speak only Spanish during the trip.
4. We first went to the *Museo de la Historia Mexicana* and saw colorful displays of art and crafts and many other cultural exhibits.
5. J. D., Leo, Yolanda, and I looked around the museum and read the information about each exhibit.
6. Besides the museum, we visited the *Barrio Antiguo,* a beautiful district that dates from the seventeenth century.
7. Later, we decided to go to a restaurant near the *Gran Plaza,* the big square.
8. As Señora Ayala walked among our tables, she listened to us order our tacos, enchiladas, and frijoles in Spanish.

30 Parts of Speech Overview

9. We walked around the *Gran Plaza* and then went into the cathedral, which was completed in the eighteenth century.
10. As we got ready to leave, we chatted in Spanish about all of the interesting things we had seen.

Exercise 23 **Using Appropriate Prepositions**

Use appropriate prepositions to fill the blanks in the following sentences. Prepositions may vary.

EXAMPLE 1. Tasty, fresh lobster is a treat, ____ many diners.
1. *Tasty, fresh lobster is a treat, according to many diners.*

1. Lobsters are large, green or gray, bottom-dwelling shellfish that live ____ the sea. **1.** in
2. The people who fish ____ these creatures are hardy and very determined folk. **2.** for
3. Using small, specially built boats and a number ____ cratelike traps made ____ wood, they go to work. **3.** of / from
4. Lobster fishing ____ the United States has been practiced only ____ the last century; before that time people thought lobster was not good to eat. **4.** throughout / within
5. For centuries, farmers used the plentiful lobsters as fertilizer ____ their gardens. **5.** for
6. To catch lobsters, the fishers first lower traps ____ chunks ____ bait ____ the sea. **6.** with / of / into
7. Then the fishers mark the location ____ colorful floats that identify the owners. **7.** with
8. If the fishers are lucky, the lobster enters the trap ____ the part called the *kitchen,* tries to escape ____ another opening called the *shark's mouth,* and then is trapped ____ the section called the *parlor.* **8.** by means of / through / inside
9. Fishers call a lobster ____ only one claw a *cull;* one ____ any claws is called a *pistol* or a *buffalo.* **9.** with / without
10. By law, undersized lobsters must be returned ____ the sea. **10.** to

The Conjunction

1g. A *conjunction* is a word that joins words or word groups.

A ***coordinating conjunction*** joins words or word groups that are used in the same way.

The Conjunction

Rule 1g *(pp. 31–33)*

OBJECTIVE

- To identify and classify conjunctions

RESOURCES

The Conjunction

Practice

- *Language & Sentence Skills Practice,* p. 23

Differentiating Instruction

- *Developmental Language & Sentence Skills,* pp. 23–24

You can remember the coordinating conjunctions as FANBOYS:

For
And
Nor
But
Or
Yet
So

Coordinating Conjunctions			
and	but	or	nor
for	yet	so	

EXAMPLES streets **and** sidewalks [two nouns]

on land **or** at sea [two prepositional phrases]

Judy wrote down the number, **but** she lost it. [two independent clauses]

Correlative conjunctions are pairs of conjunctions that join words or word groups that are used in the same way.

Correlative Conjunctions	
both . . . and	not only . . . but also
either . . . or	neither . . . nor
whether . . . or	

Reference Note

A third kind of conjunction—the **subordinating conjunction**—is discussed on page 105.

EXAMPLES **Both** Jim Thorpe **and** Roberto Clemente were outstanding athletes. [two proper nouns]

We want to go **not only** to Ontario **but also** to Quebec. [two prepositional phrases]

Either we will buy it now, **or** we will wait for the next sale. [two independent clauses]

Neither Mark Twain **nor** James Joyce won the Nobel Prize in literature. [two proper nouns]

We should decide **whether** to stay **or** to go. [two infinitives]

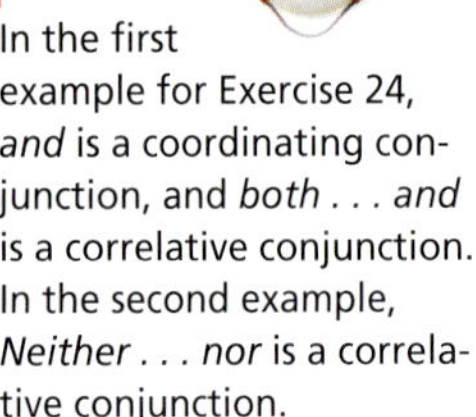

In the first example for Exercise 24, *and* is a coordinating conjunction, and *both . . . and* is a correlative conjunction. In the second example, *Neither . . . nor* is a correlative conjunction.

Exercise 24 Identifying and Classifying Conjunctions

Identify all the coordinating and correlative conjunctions in the sentences below. Be prepared to tell which ones are *coordinating conjunctions* and which ones are *correlative conjunctions.*

EXAMPLES

1. For my family and me, moving is both an exciting and a dangerous experience.

1. and, both . . . and

2. Neither my father nor I have a sense of our limitations.

2. Neither . . . nor

1. When we bought our new house, my mother wanted to hire movers, but my father and I said we could do the moving more efficiently by ourselves.
2. We said that doing the job ourselves would be not only much faster and easier but also far less expensive than having movers do it for us.
3. Neither my mom nor my brother was enthusiastic, but at last Dad and I convinced them.
4. Luckily, Uncle Waldo and my cousin Fred volunteered to help, for they thought it was a great idea.
5. Both Uncle Waldo and Fred lift weights, and they love to show off their muscles.
6. The rental truck we had reserved wasn't large enough, so we had to make several trips.
7. At the new house, we could get the sofa through neither the back door nor the front door, and Uncle Waldo strained his back trying to loosen the sofa from the door frame.
8. On the second load, either Fred or my father lost his grip, and the refrigerator fell on Dad's foot.
9. By the end of the day, all of us were tired and sore, but we had moved everything ourselves.
10. Whether we saved money or not after paying both Uncle Waldo's and Dad's medical bills and having the doorway widened is something we still joke about in our family.

The Interjection

1h. An *interjection* is a word that expresses emotion. An interjection has no grammatical relation to the rest of the sentence.

ah	hurrah	uh-oh	wow
aha	oh	well	yahoo
boy-oh-boy	oops	whew	yikes
hey	ouch	whoa	yippee

Since an interjection is not grammatically related to other words in the sentence, it is set off from the rest of the sentence by an exclamation point or by a comma or commas.

GRAMMAR

The Interjection

Rule 1h *(pp. 33–34)*

OBJECTIVE

- To use interjections in sentences and to select correct punctuation for interjections

RESOURCES

The Interjection

Practice

- *Language & Sentence Skills Practice,* p. 24

Differentiating Instruction

- *Developmental Language & Sentence Skills,* pp. 23–24

GRAMMAR

1i

STYLE TIP

Interjections are common in casual conversation. In writing, however, they are usually used only in informal notes and letters, in advertisements, and in dialogue. When you use an interjection, make sure the punctuation after it reflects the intensity of emotion you intend. Use an exclamation point to indicate strong emotion and a comma to indicate mild emotion.

EXAMPLES **Hey!** Be careful of that wire!

There's a skunk somewhere**, ugh!**

Well, I guess that's that.

I like that outfit, but**, wow,** it's really expensive.

Oops! The stoop is slippery.

Our team won the playoff! **Yippee!**

Exercise 25 Using Interjections

In the following dialogue, Jason is telling his friend Michelle about a concert he attended. Use appropriate interjections to fill in the numbered blanks. Be sure you punctuate each interjection that you use.

EXAMPLES [1] "_____ You mean you actually got to go?" Michelle gasped.

1. *"Wow! You mean you actually got to go?" Michelle gasped.*

[2] "_____ I wish I could have gone!"

2. *"Boy-oh-boy! I wish I could have gone!"*

1. Well,
2. Ugh!
3. Come on!
4. Wow!
5. Man,

[1] "_____ how was the concert?" asked Michelle. "Tell me all about what happened."

Jason shook his head. "The opening act was terrible. [2] _____ It seemed as if they played forever!"

"How was the rest of the show, though? [3] _____ Give me some details, Jason!"

"The drummer was fantastic. [4] _____ He acted like a wild man. He was all over the drums! But the best part was Stevie's twenty-minute guitar solo. [5] _____ he really let loose. The crowd went crazy!"

Determining Parts of Speech

Rule 1i *(pp. 34–36)*

OBJECTIVES

- To identify the parts of speech of words in sentences
- To apply knowledge of parts of speech to individual sentences

Determining Parts of Speech

1i. The way a word is used in a sentence determines what part of speech the word is.

The same word may be used as different parts of speech. To figure out what part of speech *well* is in each of the sentences on the next page, read the entire sentence. What you are doing is studying the word's ***context***—the way the word is used in the sentence.

RESOURCES

Determining Parts of Speech

Practice

- *Language & Sentence Skills Practice,* p. 25

EXAMPLES At the bottom of the old **well** were more than five thousand pennies. [noun]

Whenever the reunion was mentioned, tears of joy would **well** in her eyes. [verb]

Well, you may be right. [interjection]

Do you really speak four languages **well**? [adverb]

Fortunately, the baby is quite **well** now. [adjective]

Exercise 26 Identifying Words as Different Parts of Speech

Read each of the sentences below. Then, identify the part of speech of the italicized word. Be ready to justify your answer by telling how the word is used in the sentence.

EXAMPLE **1.** Aunt Shirley got a *raise.*

1. noun

1. Did Gander Pond *ice* over last year? **1.** verb
2. An *ice* storm struck. **2.** adjective
3. *Many* of these items are on sale. **3.** pronoun
4. The light flashed *on* and we entered the garage. **4.** adverb
5. We rode *on* the subway. **5.** preposition
6. The radio is *on.* **6.** adjective
7. They went to the *park.* **7.** noun
8. We can *park* the car here. **8.** verb
9. We waited, *oh,* about five minutes. **9.** interjection
10. We are all here *but* Natalya. **10.** preposition
11. I slipped, *but* I didn't fall, thank goodness. **11.** conjunction
12. *Off* the road they could see a light. **12.** preposition
13. The shop was *off* the main street. **13.** preposition
14. The deal was *off.* **14.** adjective
15. "Can you climb *up* that tree?" asked Yolanda. **15.** preposition
16. The sun was already *up* when they left for work. **16.** adjective
17. Ernesto lives a few miles *up* the coast. **17.** preposition
18. We had a long wait before the show started, but, *wow,* it was worth it! **18.** interjection
19. *Most* cats dislike taking baths. **19.** adjective
20. Did they go all the way *through* the town? **20.** preposition

PRACTICE

Guided and Independent

Exercises You may wish to have the class work through **Exercise 26** as guided practice and **Exercise 27** as independent practice.

HOMEWORK

GRAMMAR

CONTENT-AREA CONNECTIONS

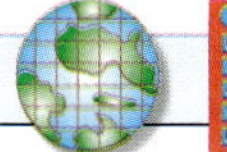

History

Essay Questions. To help students elaborate when they answer essay questions, show them how to use the parts of speech to build sentences. First, give the class the name of a historical figure or of an event they have recently studied in history class.

Then, have students build the sentence by adding words that answer these questions:

1. Who did it? [*noun or pronoun*]

2. What did that person do? [*verb*]

Continued on p. 36

GRAMMAR

HELP

Each missing word in Exercise 27 is a different part of speech.

Exercise 27 Determining Parts of Speech

A soldier in the American Revolution brings his general this spy message he found in a hollow tree. Unfortunately, termites have eaten holes in the paper. For each hole, supply one word that makes sense, and give its part of speech. Answers may vary.

EXAMPLE Please ____ this message to General Baxter immediately.
deliver—verb

Alas (interjection)
and (conjunction)
capture (verb)
beside (preposition)
encampment (noun)
early (adjective)
you (pronoun)
immediately (adverb)

! The Redcoats are chasing me, I expect them
to me soon. They are camped the river and
they are well rested. They will attack your at
dawn's light tomorrow. General, must
prepare your troops to leave .
Yours in haste, John Cadrain

Review C Writing Sentences Using the Same Words as Different Parts of Speech

ANSWERS
Sentences will vary, but students should correctly label the part of speech used in each of their pairs of sentences.

Review C Writing Sentences Using the Same Words as Different Parts of Speech

HELP

Some words may be used as more than two parts of speech. You need to give only two uses for each word in Review C.

Write forty sentences, using each of the words in the list below as two different parts of speech. Underline the word, and give its part of speech in parentheses after each sentence.

EXAMPLE 1. up
1. *We looked up. (adverb)*
We ran up the stairs. (preposition)

1. light	**6.** ride	**11.** help	**16.** that
2. run	**7.** in	**12.** drive	**17.** right
3. over	**8.** love	**13.** plant	**18.** signal
4. line	**9.** below	**14.** well	**19.** home
5. cook	**10.** picture	**15.** for	**20.** one

CONTENT-AREA CONNECTIONS

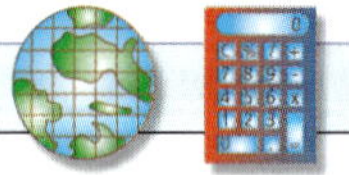

Continued from p. 35

3. When did the person do it? [*adverb or prepositional phrase*]

4. What kind of person was this? [*adjective or prepositional phrase*]

5. What else did this person do? [*conjunction*]

[Possible sentence: *In the 1930s, the determined Franklin Delano Roosevelt quickly took firm control over the government and set up many programs to help people hurt by the Great Depression.*]

Numbers in brackets refer to rules tested by the items in the Chapter Review.

1. v. [1d]
2. pro. [1b]
3. pro. [1b]
4. pro. [1b]
5. adj. [1c]
6. pro. [1b]
7. int. [1h]
8. pro. [1b]
9. adj. [1c]
10. n. [1a]
11. n. [1a]
12. n. [1a]
13. v. [1d]
14. v. [1d]
15. adv. [1e]
16. pro. [1b]
17. prep. [1f]
18. conj. [1g]
19. n. [1a]
20. pro. [1b]

Chapter Review

A. Identifying Parts of Speech

In each of the following sentences, identify the italicized word or word group as a *noun, pronoun, adjective, verb, adverb, conjunction, preposition,* or *interjection.*

1. Kofi Annan, who *became* secretary-general of the United Nations in 1997, is from Ghana.
2. *All* of the episodes of that show have been interesting.
3. I made *myself* a pimento cheese sandwich to take along.
4. This copy of the magazine is *hers.*
5. I wondered *whose* sculptures were on exhibit at the Dallas Museum of Art.
6. *That* is the third time Luisa has called me today.
7. "*Wow,* that was the fastest fly ball I've ever seen!" exclaimed Ernesto.
8. Rajiv *himself* was planning to show them around Kashmir.
9. Which of the liquids in the *smaller* beakers is clear?
10. Are those the bonsai trees *Mr. Yamamoto* told you about?
11. One of the oldest poems in the collection deals with the concept of *honor.*
12. The *cast* of the film includes many genuine descendants of Napoleon.
13. Erika and Mike *wrote* the screenplay together.
14. *Should* the alarm clock *have been set* to go off at 6:00 A.M.?
15. Those Italian clothes are well-made and *extremely* stylish.
16. *We* had been warned not to be late, yet by the time we arrived the show had already begun.
17. Warn Selena and him *about* the fire ants in the backyard before it's too late!
18. Marcel was coming down with a cold, *but* he felt obliged to keep his appointments.
19. Nancy enjoys reading about current affairs because it helps to broaden her general *knowledge.*
20. The gorilla admired *itself* in the mirror.

ASSESSING

Monitoring Progress

Chapter Review. To assess student progress, you may want to compare the types of items missed on the **Diagnostic Preview** to those missed on the **Chapter Review.** You may want to work out specific goals with individual students who are still having difficulty mastering essential information.

GRAMMAR

RESOURCES

Parts of Speech Overview

Review

- *Language & Sentence Skills Practice,* pp. 26–28

Assessment

- *Holt Handbook Chapter Tests with Answer Key,* pp. 1–2, 52

B. Identifying Parts of Speech

In each of the following sentences, identify the italicized word or word group as a *noun, pronoun, adjective, verb, adverb, conjunction, preposition,* or *interjection.*

21. verb [1d]
22. conj. [1g]
23. adv. [1e]
24. noun [1a]
25. prep. [1f]
26. pro. [1b]
27. adv. [1e]
28. adj. [1c]
29. pro. [1b]
30. int. [1h]

21. Football's most important contest *is* the annual Super Bowl game.
22. Thousands attend the game at the stadium, *and* millions watch it on television.
23. Professional football began with no system for *fairly* choosing a championship team.
24. Later, the *National Football League* was formed.
25. The two NFL teams *with* the best records play a championship game.
26. In the late 1950s, the American Football League was formed, and *it* also held a championship game every year.
27. *Eventually,* the AFL and NFL championship teams played each other at the end of the season.
28. Ever since the *first* Super Bowl was played in Los Angeles in 1967, the competition has continued to improve.
29. Do *you* know any amazing records set by NFL players?
30. *Amazing!* Fran Tarkenton threw over three hundred touchdown passes in his professional football career.

C. Identifying Parts of Speech

Identify the part of speech of each italicized word or word group in the following paragraph.

31. pro. [1b]
32. noun [1a]
33. adj. [1c]
34. adj. [1c]
35. verb [1d]
36. adj. [1c]
37. prep. [1f]
38. noun [1a]
39. prep. [1f]
40. verb [1d]
41. conj. [1g]
42. pro. [1b]
43. noun [1a]
44. verb [1d]
45. adj. [1c]
46. adv. [1e]
47. verb [1d]
48. noun [1a]
49. int. [1h]
50. adv. [1e]

For **[31]** *me,* no **[32]** *spot* is **[33]** *better* than the beach. On **[34]** *hot,* sunny days, when the sand **[35]** *burns* my feet, I am always **[36]** *careful* **[37]** *about* putting on **[38]** *sunscreen.* I like to run **[39]** *through* the foaming surf and later relax under a beach umbrella. Most of the time, I **[40]** *enjoy* **[41]** *both* being with friends *and* being by **[42]** *myself.* With only **[43]** *strangers* around me, I **[44]** *feel* free to think my **[45]** *own* thoughts. I wander **[46]** *slowly* along the waterline, looking at all the interesting things that the sea **[47]** *has* washed up. Once I accidentally stepped on a **[48]** *jellyfish* and couldn't help but yell **[49]** "*ouch!*" when it stung my foot. Since then, I've learned to be **[50]** *more* careful about where I step.

Writing Application

Writing a Descriptive Paragraph

Using Specific Adjectives Your class visited a wildlife park, but one of your friends was sick and could not go. Write a paragraph telling your friend about the field trip. Use specific adjectives to help your friend picture what he or she missed.

Prewriting Make a list of the animals and the scenes that will interest your friend. Beside each item on your list, write one or two specific adjectives.

Writing You may want to look at pictures of wildlife in magazines or books to help you think of exact descriptions as you write your first draft. Use a thesaurus to find adjectives that will help your reader visualize the animals you are describing.

Revising Have a friend or classmate read your paragraph to see if you have created clear images. Revise your paragraph by adding specific adjectives if any descriptions are unclear or too general.

Publishing Check your paragraph for errors in spelling and punctuation. Be sure that you have capitalized any proper adjectives. You and your classmates may want to create a wildlife-park bulletin board or multimedia presentation.

Reference Note

For more about **proper adjectives,** see page 248.

GRAMMAR

APPLICATION

Writing Application

Prewriting Tip. Students might find it difficult to get away from stereotypes in describing animals. Some adjectives seem almost automatic: ferocious lion, long-necked giraffe, enormous elephant, silly monkey.

To have students think critically in applying learned material to new situations, tell them to think of other aspects of these animals that they could include to develop the descriptions more fully. For example, a lion might also be *sinewy, massive,* or *regal.* The animals could include a *gangling* giraffe, a *swaying* elephant, and a *screeching* monkey. Emphasize the importance of finding adjectives that convey a sensory impression of the animal described.

Writing Tip. The writing assignment asks students to create a word-picture about a field trip to a wildlife habitat. To spark their imaginations, students might benefit from using resource books with colorful pictures.

Scoring Rubric. While you will want to pay particular attention to students' use of adjectives, you will also want to evaluate overall writing performance. You may want to give a split score to indicate development and clarity of the composition as well as grammar skills.

CHAPTER

2

INTRODUCING THE CHAPTER

- The chapter begins by covering sentences and sentence fragments. It then covers major parts of sentences (subjects, predicates, and complements) and discusses how the parts fit together to form sentences. The chapter continues with the classification of sentences by purpose and the use of end punctuation.
- The chapter closes with a **Chapter Review** including a **Writing Application** feature that asks students to use action verbs to write a summary of an incident.
- For help integrating this chapter with writing assignments, use the **Teaching Strands** chart on pp. T24–T25.

CHAPTER

2 The Parts of a Sentence

Subject, Predicate, Complement

Diagnostic Preview

A. Identifying the Parts of a Sentence

In the following paragraphs, identify each of the numbered italicized words, using these abbreviations:

s.	subject	**p.a.**	predicate adjective
v.	verb	**d.o.**	direct object
p.n.	predicate nominative	**i.o.**	indirect object

EXAMPLE Are you a mystery **[1]** *fan?*

1. p.n.

Sir Arthur Conan Doyle certainly gave [1] *readers* a wonderful [2] *gift* when he [3] *created* the character of Sherlock Holmes. [4] *Holmes* is a [5] *master* of the science of deduction. He [6] *observes* seemingly insignificant [7] *clues,* applies logical reasoning, and reaches simple yet astounding conclusions. The Hound of the Baskervilles is an excellent [8] *example* of how Holmes solves a baffling [9] *mystery.* The [10] *residents* of a rural area are afraid of a supernatural dog that [11] *kills* people at night. Helpless against this beast, they seek the [12] *services* of Sherlock Holmes. Using logic, he solves the mystery and relieves the people's [13] *fear.* This story is [14] *one* of Conan Doyle's best because it is both [15] *eerie* and mystifying.

Numerals in brackets refer to rules tested by the items in the Diagnostic Preview.

1. i.o. [2k, h]
2. d.o. [2j, h]
3. v. [2d, b]
4. s. [2c, b]
5. p.n. [2i(1), h]
6. v. [2d, b]
7. d.o. [2j, h]
8. p.n. [2i(1), h]
9. d.o. [2j, h]
10. s. [2c, b]
11. v. [2d, b]
12. d.o. [2j, h]
13. d.o. [2j, h]
14. p.n. [2i(1), h]
15. p.a. [2i(2), h]

CHAPTER RESOURCES

Internet

- Web resources: go.hrw.com

Practice & Review

- *Language & Sentence Skills Practice,* pp. 33–56
- *Language & Sentence Skills Practice Answer Key,* pp. 17–27

Application & Enrichment

- *Language & Sentence Skills Practice,* pp. 32, 57–59
- *Language & Sentence Skills Practice Answer Key,* pp. 17, 27–28

B. Identifying and Punctuating the Kinds of Sentences

Copy the last word of each of the following sentences. Then, punctuate each with the correct end mark. Classify each sentence as *imperative, declarative, interrogative,* or *exclamatory.*

EXAMPLE **1.** Sherlock Holmes has many dedicated fans

1. fans.—declarative

16. How clever Sherlock Holmes is!
17. Sir Arthur Conan Doyle wrote four novels and fifty-six short stories about Holmes.
18. Have you read any of these stories?
19. I particularly like the stories in which Holmes confronts the evil Professor Moriarty.
20. Read just one of these stories, and see why millions of mystery fans love Sherlock Holmes.

16. exc. [2l(4)]
17. dec. [2l(1)]
18. int. [2l(3)]
19. dec. [2l(1)]
20. imp. [2l(2)]

The Sentence

In casual conversation, people often leave out parts of sentences. In writing, however, it is better to use complete sentences most of the time. They help to make meaning clear to the reader.

2a. A *sentence* is a word or word group that contains a subject and a verb and that expresses a complete thought.

A ***sentence fragment*** is a word or word group that is capitalized and punctuated as a sentence but that does not contain both a subject and a verb or does not express a complete thought.

FRAGMENT Was waiting by the door. [no subject]
SENTENCE The clerk was waiting by the door.

FRAGMENT The room with the high ceiling. [no verb]
SENTENCE The room with the high ceiling glowed in the sunset.

FRAGMENT After you have finished the test. [not a complete thought]
SENTENCE Exit quietly after you have finished the test.

Some sentences contain an understood subject (*you*).

EXAMPLES [You] Stop!
[You] Pass the asparagus, please.

Reference Note

For information on **how to correct sentence fragments,** see Chapter 18. For information on **punctuating sentences,** see page 265.

COMPUTER TIP

Many style-checking software programs can help you identify sentence fragments. If you have access to such a program, use it to help you evaluate your writing.

Reference Note

For more about **understood subjects,** see page 51.

ASSESSING

Entry-Level Assessment

Diagnostic Preview. The **Diagnostic Preview** focuses on identifying the parts of sentences, classifying sentences by purpose, and using correct end punctuation. You may wish to compile data on your class's most common mistakes. If only a few students are unable to demonstrate mastery, you could have them review the instruction and examples and together work the exercises of the most troublesome sections. Check their answers periodically to determine progress.

The Sentence

Rule 2a *(pp. 41–42)*

OBJECTIVE

- To distinguish between fragments and sentences, revise the fragments to form complete sentences, and use correct capitalization and punctuation

Differentiating Instruction

- *Developmental Language & Sentence Skills Guided Practice,* pp. 25–38
- *Developmental Language & Sentence Skills Guided Practice Teacher's Notes and Answer Key,* pp. 7–9

Assessment

- *Holt Handbook Chapter Tests with Answer Key,* pp. 3–4, 52

GRAMMAR

PRETEACHING

Lesson Starter

Motivating. Introduce the topic of sentences and sentence fragments by comparing a sentence to a complete baseball game and a fragment to an inning. Ask students what they would know by the end of the game that they would not know after the first inning. [*Students may say that they will know the final score, the winner, the final outcome of the game. After one inning, they have only partial information about the game.*] Explain that similarly a fragment gives only partial information about a subject, while a sentence gives complete information. Ask volunteers first for a list of nouns pertaining to a baseball game and then for verbs relating to the action of the game. Write students' suggestions on the chalkboard in two separate lists. Have students combine the subjects and verbs to practice forming sentences about a baseball game.

DIFFERENTIATING INSTRUCTION

Learners Having Difficulty

To assist students with **Exercise 1,** help them formulate questions to determine whether a group of words is a sentence.

EXAMPLES

1. Is there a verb? (Is there a word that tells the action or indicates state of being?)
2. Is there a subject? (Is there a word that tells who or what is doing the action?)
3. Does the group of words express a complete idea?

Exercise 1 Identifying Sentences and Revising Fragments

Decide whether each of the following word groups is a sentence or a sentence fragment. If the word group is a sentence, correct its capitalization and punctuation. If the word group is a sentence fragment, revise it to make a complete sentence. Be sure to use correct capitalization and punctuation. Revisions will vary.

EXAMPLES
1. here are your glasses
1. *Here are your glasses.*
2. before going out
2. *Before going out, I always turn off the lights.*

1. on Monday or later this week 1. , the hunters will return.
2. patiently waiting for the mail carrier. 2. Our neighbors are
3. will you be there tomorrow?
4. four people in a small car. 4. We saw
5. just yesterday I discovered 5. the missing shoes.
6. two strikes and no one on base. 6. The team has
7. it runs smoothly.
8. leaning far over the railing 8. , the guide helped grab the lines.
9. give me a hand.
10. while waiting in line at the theater 10. , we were drenched with rain.
11. on the way to the science fair. 11. Karen struggled with her boxes
12. stand up. [*or* !]
13. learning English. 13. Otto listens carefully because he is
14. when is the marathon?
15. it is time.
16. to the left of the spiral staircase. 16. The door is
17. romping along the shore this morning. 17. The dogs enjoyed
18. it is theirs.
19. you surprised me, Ellen!
20. how you are. 20. Jennifer was asking

Subject and Predicate

Sentences consist of two basic parts: *subjects* and *predicates.*

2b. The *subject* tells whom or what the sentence is about, and the *predicate* says something about the subject.

RESOURCES

The Sentence

Practice

- *Language & Sentence Skills Practice,* pp. 33–34

RESOURCES

Subject and Predicate

Practice

- *Language & Sentence Skills Practice,* pp. 35–38

Differentiating Instruction

- *Developmental Language & Sentence Skills,* pp. 25–28

In the following examples, the subjects are separated from the predicates by blue vertical lines. Notice that the subject and the predicate may be only one word each, or they may be more than one word.

Coyotes | were howling in the distance.

The telephone in the lobby | rang.

The woman wearing the red blouse | is my aunt.

In these three examples, the words that appear to the left of the vertical line make up the *complete subject.* The words to the right of the vertical line make up the *complete predicate.*

The subject may appear anywhere in the sentence—at the beginning, in the middle, or at the end.

EXAMPLES In the dim light, **the eager scientist** examined the cave.

Does **Brian's car** have a CD player?

On the table stood **a silver vase.**

HELP— The order and relationship of the parts of sentences is known as ***syntax.***

Exercise 2 Identifying the Complete Subject

Identify the complete subject of each of the following sentences.

EXAMPLE 1. The art of quilting has been popular in the United States for a long time.

1. *The art of quilting*

1. Ever since colonial times, Americans have made quilts.
2. Traditional designs, with names like Honeycomb, Tumbling Blocks, and Double Diamond, have been handed down from generation to generation.
3. The designs on this page are quilt blocks from a modern quilt.
4. They certainly don't look like Great-grandmother's quilts!
5. However, quilting techniques have stayed basically the same for well over a hundred years.
6. Small scraps of bright cloth are still painstakingly stitched together to create each block.
7. As in many antique quilts, each quilt block shown here was designed and sewn by a different person.
8. Some of the designs are simple.
9. In others, colorful details bring circus scenes to life.
10. A dark background is sometimes chosen to set off the brilliant colors of a quilt.

Subject and Predicate

Rules 2b–d *(pp. 42–47)*

OBJECTIVES

- To identify complete subjects in sentences
- To form complete sentences by adding complete predicates to fragments
- To form complete sentences by adding complete subjects to fragments
- To identify complete predicates and verbs in sentences
- To make sentence fragments into sentences by adding subjects or verbs or both

GRAMMAR

DIRECT TEACHING

Modeling and Demonstration

Subject and Predicate. Model how to identify the complete subject and complete predicate in a sentence by using the example: *Does Brian's car have a CD player?* First, ask what the simple subject is in the sentence. [*car*] Explain that the complete subject also includes all the words, phrases, or clauses modifying the simple subject. Then, ask what the complete subject is. [*Brian's car*] Next, ask what the simple verb is here. [*Does . . . have*] Explain that the complete verb also includes all the words that modify or complete the simple verb's meaning. Ask what the complete verb is in this sentence. [*Does . . . have a CD player*] Now, have a volunteer use another example from this chapter to demonstrate how to identify the complete subject and the complete verb in a sentence.

GRAMMAR

Exercise 3 **Writing Complete Predicates**

POSSIBLE ANSWERS

1. Justice is one of democracy's ideals.
2. Some commercials use several methods of persuasion.
3. Is the store on the corner closed permanently?
4. The woman next door sells pecans.
5. One way to study is to use memory aids.
6. These guitars are expensive.
7. Is the bicycle on the porch yours?
8. The family reunion will be held late this year.
9. A band marched onto the field.
10. The best route is not always the shortest.

DIFFERENTIATING INSTRUCTION

Special Education Students

Give students pictures of people running, playing, swimming, and so on. Have students working in pairs take turns asking one another to state what action is being performed and who is doing the action.

English-Language Learners

Japanese and Korean. In Japanese, the subject is always followed by the functional word *wa* or *ga*. In Korean, the subject is always followed by *i* (ee) or *ga*. Speakers of these languages should consider which word(s) in English sentences would be followed by one of these functional words in their language.

Exercise 3 **Writing Complete Predicates**

Rewrite each of the following items, adding a complete predicate to make a complete sentence. Be sure to use correct capitalization and punctuation.

EXAMPLE 1. that famous painting

1. *That famous painting sold for three million dollars.*

1. justice
2. some commercials
3. the store on the corner
4. the woman next door
5. one way to study
6. these guitars
7. the bicycle on the porch
8. the family reunion
9. a band
10. the best route

The Subject

2c. The main word or word group that tells whom or what the sentence is about is called the *simple subject.*

The ***complete subject*** consists of the simple subject and any words, phrases, or clauses that modify the simple subject.

Reference Note

A compound noun, such as *Gloria Estefan,* is considered one noun. For more about **compound nouns,** see page 4.

EXAMPLES A triumphant Gloria Estefan stepped up to the microphone.

complete subject A triumphant Gloria Estefan

simple subject Gloria Estefan

Out of the beaker rose a foul smelling foam.

complete subject a foul-smelling foam

simple subject foam

Did you make the grits, Travis?

complete subject you

simple subject you

NOTE In this book, the term *subject* generally refers to the simple subject unless otherwise indicated.

Exercise 4 **Writing Complete Sentences**

Make each of the following fragments a sentence by adding a complete subject. Underline each simple subject. Answers will vary.

EXAMPLE 1. Did _____ watch the Super Bowl?

1. *Did your little brother watch the Super Bowl?*

MINI-LESSON Grammar

Placement of Adverbial Modifiers. Students may expect the complete subject always to begin a sentence. Point out to students sentence 1, **Exercise 2.** Explain that the sentence begins with adverbial modifiers—words that modify the verb and are therefore not part of the complete subject.

Present the following sentence:

After many long years of experimentation, the mad scientist invented a youth-restoring potion.

Explain that the first phrase is an adver-

1. _____ was baying at the moon. 1. A black wolf
2. _____ can make the pizza. 2. The club officers
3. _____ is needed for this recipe. 3. Buttermilk
4. Was _____ the person who won the match? 4. your son
5. _____ rose and soared out over the sea. 5. The wandering albatross
6. _____ stood on the stage singing. 6. The military choir
7. _____ were late for their classes. 7. Sara and James
8. Over in the next town is _____. 8. the county courthouse
9. Buzzing around the room was _____. 9. a large mosquito
10. In the middle of the yard grew _____. 10. some beautiful red roses

The Predicate

2d. The *simple predicate,* or *verb,* is the main word or word group that tells something about the subject.

The ***complete predicate*** consists of a verb and all the words that describe the verb and complete its meaning.

EXAMPLES The ambulance raced out of the hospital driveway and down the street.

complete predicate raced out of the hospital driveway and down the street

simple predicate raced

Diego may have borrowed my book.

complete predicate may have borrowed my book

simple predicate may have borrowed

Are you following Mr. Fayed's advice?

complete predicate Are following Mr. Fayed's advice

simple predicate Are following

Notice that the simple predicate may be a single verb or a ***verb phrase*** (a verb with one or more helping verbs).

Commonly Used Helping Verbs				
am	did	has	might	was
are	do	have	must	were
can	does	is	shall	will
could	had	may	should	would

TIPS & TRICKS

When you are identifying the simple predicate in a sentence, be sure to include all parts of a verb phrase.

EXAMPLE

Should Marshal Ney **have used** the infantry at Waterloo? [The simple predicate is the verb phrase *Should have used.* The complete predicate is *Should have used the infantry at Waterloo.*]

Exercise 4

DISTRIBUTED REVIEW

To help students review the parts of speech, have them find the verbs in sentences 1, 5, and 7.

1. was baying

5. rose; soared

7. were

GRAMMAR

DIFFERENTIATING INSTRUCTION

English-Language Learners

General Strategies. In many languages, nouns, verbs, and adjectives may be inflected to show number, person, tense, gender, and/or case. The meaning of an English sentence is much less dependent on the order of the words; therefore, the ordering of the sentence elements is much less restricted in some languages other than English. It may help English-language learners to notice that, in most cases, the simple subject comes before the simple predicate in declarative English sentences.

bial modifier; it tells *when* the action of the verb happened. Therefore, it is part of the complete predicate.

Refer students who want more information about adverbial modifiers to Prepositional Phrases, p. 70, **Chapter 3.**

GRAMMAR

DIFFERENTIATING INSTRUCTION

Advanced Learners

Advanced students may want to work with higher-level sentence structures. You may want to remind them that good writers are able to vary sentence beginnings, placing different parts of the sentence first for variety's sake.

Direct students to **Exercise 5,** and ask them to write each sentence in as many ways as possible, beginning the sentence in a different way each time. Each version should give the same information, but forms of words may be changed.

Here is an example using the first sentence:

a. Surfing, a warm-weather sport, makes use of the force of incoming waves.

b. Making use of the force of incoming waves, surfing is a warm-weather sport.

Special Education Students

Group students in pairs to work on **Exercise 6.** Work with pairs to brainstorm ideas for item 1. Ask students to tackle item 2 individually and then to compare sentences with their partners to see whether they used the same constructions or took different approaches. Students may prefer tape-recording answers to writing them.

NOTE In this book, the word *verb* refers to the simple predicate unless otherwise indicated.

Exercise 5 Identifying the Complete Predicate and Verb

For each of the following sentences, write the complete predicate. Then, underline the verb or verb phrase in each complete predicate.

EXAMPLE **1.** Surfing and snow skiing are different in many ways.

1. are different in many ways

1. The warm-weather sport of surfing uses the force of incoming waves.
2. The wintertime activity of snow skiing relies on gravity.
3. Surfers can pursue their sport with only a surfboard, a flotation vest, a swimsuit, and a safety line.
4. A skier's equipment includes ski boots, skis with bindings, safety cables, ski poles, warm clothing, and goggles.
5. Under their own power, surfers paddle out to their starting places, far from shore.
6. Must a skier buy a ticket for a ski-lift ride to the top of the mountain?
7. Oddly enough, some important similarities exist between surfing and skiing.
8. Both depend on the cooperation of nature for pleasant weather and good waves or good snow.
9. Do both surfing and snow skiing require coordination and balance more than strength?
10. In fact, each of these sports would probably make an excellent cross-training activity during the other's off-season.

Exercise 6 Writing Complete Sentences

Make each of the following sentence fragments a complete sentence by adding a subject, a predicate, or both. Be sure to add correct capitalization and punctuation. Sentences will vary.

EXAMPLE **1.** the barking dog

1. We were kept awake by the barking dog.

1. the trouble with my class schedule 1. is that I have no lunch period.
2. the legs of the table 2. were scarred by dogs and children.
3. appeared deserted. 3. The dark school building
4. my billionaire aunt from Detroit 4. bought us all tickets for a cruise.
5. thousands of screaming fans 5. welcomed the team at the airport.

6. ^my grandparents in Oaxaca. 6. We visited
7. ^thought quickly. 7. Called on to answer the question, Aaron
8. after the intermission^ 8. they returned to their seats.
9. ^until sunset. 9. The offer is good only
10. ^the science fair. 10. Jaime's project was a great success at

Review A **Distinguishing Between Sentence Fragments and Sentences; Identifying Subjects and Predicates**

Identify each word group as a sentence (*S*) or a sentence fragment (*F*). Then, for each sentence, write the simple subject, underlining it once, and the simple predicate (verb), underlining it twice.

EXAMPLE 1. The talented musicians played well together.
1. S—musicians—played

1. Jazz music filled the room. 1. S
2. Supporting the other instruments, the piano carried the melody. 2. S
3. The saxophonist, with lazy, lingering notes. 3. F
4. Beside him, the bass player added depth to the band. 4. S
5. A female vocalist with a deep, rich voice. 5. F
6. Charmed the audience with her delivery. 6. F
7. The band's star performer was the drummer. 7. S
8. For most of the evening, she stayed in the background. 8. S
9. Until the last half-hour. 9. F
10. Then she dazzled everyone with her brilliant, high-speed technique. 10. S

Finding the Subject

To find the subject of a sentence, find the verb first. Then, ask "Who?" or "What?" before the verb.

EXAMPLES Here you can swim year-round. [The verb is *can swim.* Who can swim? *You* can swim. *You* is the subject.]

There is Aunt Ivory's new truck. [What is there? *Truck* is. *Truck* is the subject.]

Into the pond jumped the frog. [What jumped? *Frog* jumped. *Frog* is the subject.]

Please close the window. [Who is to close the window? *You* are—that is, the person spoken to. *You* is the understood subject.]

MEETING THE CHALLENGE

Write a passage of ten or more sentences about something that interests you. In five sentences, underline the complete subject and circle the simple subject. In the other sentences, underline the complete predicate and circle the simple predicate.

Answer
Passages will vary but should consist of at least ten sentences, five of which should have the complete subject underlined and the simple subject circled and the rest of which should have the complete predicate underlined and the simple predicate circled.

Reference Note
For information on the **understood subject,** see page 51.

Differentiating Instruction

English-Language Learners

Vietnamese. Vietnamese has no equivalent of the verb *be,* so Vietnamese speakers will tend to make sentences such as "There Aunt Ivory's new truck." It may be difficult for them to identify as fragments sentences missing the verb *be.* They can work with sample sentences containing and missing the verb *be* such as the following:

There are many jazz musicians in New Orleans.

New Orleans in Louisiana, in the southern part of the United States.

The Blues another kind of music found in the south.

Both jazz and the blues are blends of African and European musical forms.

GRAMMAR

Finding the Subject

Rule 2e *(pp. 47–51)*

OBJECTIVES

- To identify subjects and verbs in sentences
- To write sentences that are requests or commands

RESOURCES

Finding the Subject

Practice
- *Language & Sentence Skills Practice,* pp. 39–40

Differentiating Instruction
- *Developmental Language & Sentence Skills,* pp. 25–26

GRAMMAR

DIRECT TEACHING

Modeling and Demonstrating

The Subject. Model how to identify the subject of a sentence by using the example *Here you can swim year-round.* First, ask students to identify the verb of the sentence. [*can swim*] Next, ask who can swim. [*You*] Explain that *You* is the subject of the sentence. Now, have a volunteer use another example from this chapter to demonstrate how to identify the subject of a sentence.

DIFFERENTIATING INSTRUCTION

English-Language Learners

General Strategies. Help students find the subjects of sentences by first identifying the verbs for them. Suggest they find the subject of each sentence by asking "Who or what does the action?"

Exercise 7 Identifying Subjects and Verbs

Identify the verb and its subject in each of the following sentences. Be sure to include all parts of a verb phrase.

EXAMPLE 1. Long before the equal rights movement of the 1960s, U.S. women were excelling in their professions.

1. were excelling—verb; women—subject

1. Anne Bissell ran a carpet sweeper business in the late 1800s.
2. For a time, she served as corporation president.
3. Under her direction, the company sold millions of sweepers.
4. In the late nineteenth century, a journalist named Nellie Bly reported on social injustice.
5. On assignments, she would often wear disguises.
6. Ida Wells-Barnett became editor and part owner of the *Memphis Free Speech* in 1892.
7. By the early 1930s, she had been crusading for forty years against racial injustice and for suffrage.
8. At the end of her fourth term as general of the Salvation Army, Evangeline Booth retired in 1939.
9. Booth's efforts helped to make the Salvation Army financially stable.
10. She also improved many Salvation Army services.

Prepositional Phrases

2e. The subject of a verb is never in a prepositional phrase.

EXAMPLES **Most** of the women voted. [Who voted? *Most* voted. *Women* is the object in the prepositional phrase *of the women.*]

One of the parakeets in the pet shop looks like ours. [What looks? *One* looks. *Parakeets* and *pet shop* are each part of a prepositional phrase.]

Are **two** of the books missing? [What are missing? *Two* are missing. *Books* is the object in the prepositional phrase *of the books.*]

Reference Note

For more information about **prepositional phrases,** see page 70.

A ***prepositional phrase*** includes a preposition, the object of the preposition, and any modifiers of that object.

EXAMPLES

next to Jorge	by the open door	on the floor
of a good book	at intermission	after class
in the photograph	for all of them	instead of this

Prepositional phrases can be especially misleading when the subject follows the verb.

EXAMPLE Around the corner from our house is a **store.** [What is? *Store* is. Neither *corner* nor *house* can be the subject because each is part of a prepositional phrase.]

Exercise 8 Identifying Verbs and Subjects

Identify the verb and the subject in each of the following sentences.

EXAMPLE 1. Most of the students in our class have enjoyed discussing our town's folklore.

1. have enjoyed—verb; Most—subject

1. Many regions of the United States have local legends.
2. One pine-forested area in New Jersey is supposedly inhabited by the Jersey Devil.
3. This fearsome monster reportedly chases campers and wayward travelers through the woods.
4. In contrast, Oregon is haunted by numerous legends of the less aggressive Bigfoot.
5. This humanlike creature supposedly hides in heavily forested areas.
6. Its shaggy coat of hair looks like a bear's fur.
7. According to legend, Bigfoot is gentle and shy by nature, avoiding contact with strangers.
8. Stories from the Lake Champlain area tell about a monster resembling a sea serpent in the depths of the lake.
9. Many sightings of this beast have been reported to authorities.
10. No one, however, has ever taken a convincing photograph of the monster.

Sentences That Ask Questions

Questions often begin with a verb, a helping verb, or a word such as *what, when, where, how,* or *why.* The subject of a question usually follows the verb or helping verb.

EXAMPLES How is the **movie** different from the book?

Where is the **CD** I gave you?

Does **she** have a ride home?

In questions that begin with a helping verb, like the third example above, the subject comes between the helping verb and the main verb.

TIPS & TRICKS

In many sentences, you can find the subject and the verb more easily if you cross out any prepositional phrases.

EXAMPLE
Several ~~of the puzzle pieces~~ are ~~under the sofa~~.

SUBJECT
Several

VERB
are

GRAMMAR

FAMILY/COMMUNITY ACTIVITY *Continued on pp. 50–51*

Recognizing Unspoken Imperatives. You may want to make students aware that they often face silent commands that correspond to the spoken imperative sentence. Tell students that they will prepare a lesson to teach the commands that younger children can find in traffic signs. Students may present a lesson to a class of grade-school children or to younger relatives.

Have groups of four or five discuss the assignment and create a lesson plan based on the outline on p. 50.

Differentiating Instruction

Learners Having Difficulty

Before students begin **Exercise 9,** point out pitfalls in finding the subjects of sentences by listing the following items with examples on the chalkboard:

1. prepositional phrases [*A few of the deer jumped the fence.*]
2. questions [*Are you ready to go to the mall?*]
3. sentences beginning with *there* [*There were many sports fans in the crowded auditorium.*]
4. understood subjects [*Please answer the phone.*]

Encourage students to check for these constructions before deciding on the subject.

Reteaching

Simple Predicates

Students may be better able to understand verb phrases and simple predicates if they start by building sentences around them. Arrange students in groups of three. Have one member of each group write *action verbs* on index cards labeled *AV.* Have another member write *helping verbs* on other index cards, labeled *HV.* The third member should write *linking verbs* on cards labeled *LV.* Have each group then practice combining one *AV* or *LV* card with one or two *HV* cards to compose four sentences that contain verb phrases made from the verbs on the index cards. Students may need to review helping verbs and linking verbs on pages 14 and 16. Ask each group to read its sentences aloud.

You can find the subject by turning the question into a statement and then finding the verb and asking "Who?" or "What?" before it.

EXAMPLES Was the train late? becomes The train was late. [What was late? The *train* was.]

Has she answered the letter? becomes She has answered the letter. [Who has answered? *She* has.]

Sentences Beginning with *There* or *Here*

The word *there* or *here* is almost never the subject of a sentence. Both *there* and *here* may be used as adverbs telling *where.* To find the subject in a sentence beginning with *there* or *here,* ask "Who?" or "What?" before the verb and the adverb.

EXAMPLES There are my cousins. [Who are there? *Cousins* are.]

Here is your backpack. [What is here? *Backpack* is.]

NOTE Sometimes *there* starts a sentence but does not tell where. In this use, *there* is not an adverb but an expletive. An ***expletive*** is a word that fills out a sentence's structure but does not add to its meaning.

EXAMPLES There is (V) a drawbridge (S) over the river. [*There* adds no information to the sentence, which could be rewritten as *A drawbridge is over the river.*]

There are (V) insects (S) in our garden. [The sentence could be rewritten as *Insects are in our garden.*]

To find the subject in such a sentence, omit *there* and ask "Who?" or "What?" before the verb.

EXAMPLE There was a clerk at the counter. [Who was? A *clerk* was.]

Exercise 9 Identifying Subjects and Verbs

Identify the subjects and the verbs in the following sentences.

EXAMPLE 1. Will you help me study for my history test?
1. you—subject; will help—verb

1. There are many questions on American history in my book.
2. Naturally, there are answers, too.
3. Under whose flag did Columbus sail?
4. Here is Plymouth Rock, Anita.
5. How much do you know about the Lost Colony?

Family/Community Activity

Continued from p. 49

Sample Lesson Plan
Purpose: [*To make children aware of the implications of signs*]
Materials: [*Pictures of outlines of signs, paper, crayons*]
Activities: [*Present child with signs and allow child to explain his or her response.*]
Sample answer: [***STOP.*** *Stop your car, your bicycle, or yourself when you reach this sign. Don't move until there is no danger from traffic.*]

6. What does *squatter's rights* mean?
7. In what area did most of the early Dutch colonists settle?
8. Was there disagreement among settlers in Massachusetts?
9. What kinds of schools did the colonists' children attend?
10. How did people travel in colonial America?

The Understood Subject

In a request or a command, the subject of a sentence is usually not stated. In such sentences, *you* is the ***understood subject.***

REQUEST Please answer the phone. [Who is to answer? *You* are—that is, the person spoken to.]

COMMAND Listen carefully to his question. [Who is to listen? *You*—the person spoken to—are.]

Sometimes a request or a command includes a name.

EXAMPLES Amber, please send us your new address.
Line up, class.

Amber and *class* are not subjects in the sentences above. These words are called ***nouns of direct address.*** They identify the person spoken to or addressed. *You* is the understood subject of each sentence.

EXAMPLES Amber, [you] please send us your new address.
[You] line up, class.

Exercise 10 Writing Requests or Commands

Using the following five situations, write sentences that are requests or commands. In two of your sentences, use a noun of direct address.

EXAMPLES

	Setting	Person Speaking	Person Addressed
1.	castle	queen	wizard
2.	kitchen	parent	teenager

1. *Wizard, make this straw into gold.*
2. *Please don't drink out of the carton.*

	Setting	*Person Speaking*	*Person Addressed*
1.	desert oasis	Aladdin	genie
2.	courtroom	judge	defense attorney
3.	child's room	child	baby sitter
4.	spaceship	alien invader	crew member
5.	forest	Big Bad Wolf	Little Red Riding Hood

GRAMMAR

DIRECT TEACHING

Correcting Misconceptions

Understood Subjects. Students may believe that each sentence must have a stated subject. Explain that in sentences that are requests or commands, the subject may be understood. Then, before students begin **The Understood Subject** lesson, write the following imperative sentence on the chalkboard:

Take the dog outside, please.

Then, ask for a volunteer to name the subject of the sentence [*you, understood*].

Review understood subjects with the class. Then, ask students to list as many situations as they can in which an understood subject would be used (such as recipes, directions for VCR programming, directions on tests or exercises, or "how-to" books). Ask students to bring examples of these items to class. Allow contributors to create a bulletin board display or a booklet of examples.

Exercise 10 Writing Requests or Commands

POSSIBLE ANSWERS

1. Bring me water!
2. Mr. Nye, approach the bench.
3. Please help me clean up.
4. Go into orbit around the planet.
5. Let me escort you through the woods.

Evaluation: [*Have the child draw a picture showing his or her response to each sign. To show sequence of actions, children might create comic strips.*]

If students actually teach the lesson, they should create an oral or written evaluation of their teaching experience to show what they taught and what they learned.

Compound Subjects and Compound Verbs

Rules 2f, g *(pp. 52–55)*

OBJECTIVES

- To identify compound subjects and their verbs in sentences
- To identify compound verbs and their subjects in sentences
- To identify complete subjects and predicates

DIFFERENTIATING INSTRUCTION

English-Language Learners

Spanish. Inform students that in English, a comma is commonly used before *and* or *or* when there are three or more parts of a compound subject. In Spanish a comma is not used.

Special Education Students

Have students create their own sentences with compound subjects and compound verbs. Give them patterns to imitate, and then have them work with a helper who can write the sentences down as students say them aloud. The following are some possible patterns:

1. Joe and Elena wiped the tables.
2. The drummer, guitarist, and lead singer joined the band.
3. Two bears slept and ate in their dens.
4. The driver signaled but did not turn.

Encourage students to keep copies of these patterns in their notebooks for future reference.

Reference Note

For more information about **conjunctions,** see page 31. For more about using **commas between words in a series,** see page 272.

Compound Subjects

2f. **A *compound subject* consists of two or more subjects that are joined by a conjunction and that have the same verb.**

The conjunctions most commonly used to connect the words of a compound subject are *and* and *or.*

EXAMPLE **Antony** and **Mae** baked the bread. [Who baked the bread? Antony baked it. Mae baked it. *Antony* and *Mae* form the compound subject.]

When more than two words are included in the compound subject, the conjunction is generally used only between the last two words. Also, the words are separated by commas.

EXAMPLE Antony**,** Mae**,** **and** Pamela baked the bread. [compound subject: *Antony, Mae, Pamela*]

Correlative conjunctions, such as *neither . . . nor* and *not only . . . but also*, may be used with compound subjects.

EXAMPLE **Either** Antony **or** Mae baked the bread. [compound subject: *Antony, Mae*]

Exercise 11 Identifying Compound Subjects and Their Verbs

Identify the compound subjects and their verbs in the following sentences.

EXAMPLE 1. Roast turkey and cranberry sauce are often served at Thanksgiving.

1. turkey, sauce—compound subject; are served—verb

1. Gerbils and goldfish make good, low-maintenance pets.
2. April, May, and June provide the best opportunity for studying wildflowers in Texas and Oklahoma.
3. Kettles of soup and trays of sandwiches sat on the counter.
4. Both you and I should go downtown or to the movies.
5. Either *Macbeth* or *Othello* features witches in its plot.
6. In that drawer lay her scissors, ruler, and markers.
7. Star-nosed moles and eastern moles live in the United States.
8. There are many good jokes and riddles in that book.
9. Where will you and your family go on vacation this year?
10. There were eggs and milk in the refrigerator.

RESOURCES

Compound Subjects and Compound Verbs

Practice

- *Language & Sentence Skills Practice,* pp. 41–43

Differentiating Instruction

- *Developmental Language & Sentence Skills,* pp. 25–28

Compound Verbs

2g. **A *compound verb* consists of two or more verbs that are joined by a conjunction and that have the same subject.**

EXAMPLES Jim Thorpe **entered** and **won** several events in the 1912 Olympics.

The committee **met, voted** on the issue, and **adjourned.**

My sister **will buy** or **lease** a car.

Both the subject and the verb may be compound.

EXAMPLES The **students** and **teachers wrote** the play and **produced** it.

Either **Jan** or **Beverly will write** the story and **send** it to the newspaper.

NOTE There are other cases in which a sentence may contain more than one subject and verb.

EXAMPLES The **defeat** of the Germans at Verdun in 1916 **was** a victory for France, but the **battle cost** each side nearly half a million casualties. [This kind of sentence is called a *compound sentence.*]

Because **crocodiles are** descended from dinosaurs, **they are** the nearest living relatives of birds. [This kind of sentence is called a *complex sentence.*]

Before the **movie started, Siva offered** to buy popcorn; **Melissa said** that **she would save** his seat. [This kind of sentence is called a *compound-complex sentence.*]

Exercise 12 Identifying Subjects and Compound Verbs

Identify the compound verbs and the subjects in the following sentences. Be sure to include helping verbs. If a sentence contains an understood subject, write *(You)*.

EXAMPLE **1.** Should I buy this pair of jeans now or wait for a sale?

1. compound verb—should buy, wait; subject—I

1. Tony rewound the cassette and then pressed the playback button.
2. Toshiro sings, acts, and dances in the show.
3. At the fair, Dan ran faster than the other boys and won the prize of twenty-five dollars.

STYLE  TIP

The helping verb may or may not be repeated before the second part of a compound verb if the helping verb is the same for both parts of the verb.

EXAMPLES

My sister **will buy** or **will lease** a car.

My sister **will buy** or **lease** a car.

Reference Note

For more about **compound, complex, and compound-complex sentences,** see page 109.

EXTENSION

Relating to Literature

Explain to students that compound structures, such as compound subjects and verbs, should be parallel. Refer students to **Chapter 19.** Have students look through the poetry section of their literature books to find poetry with compound subjects or verbs. ("I Never Saw a Moor" by Emily Dickinson and "Kidnap Poem" by Nikki Giovanni have examples of compound verbs.) Ask students to share with the class samples of compound verbs and subjects they have found in poems. Have students explain how the compound structures are parallel. Ask students to explain what is being emphasized through the use of compound subjects or verbs. [*This style usually emphasizes the equal importance of the compound components.*]

As students proceed through the chapter, have them return to the poems and look for other compounds, such as compound direct objects, predicate nominatives, and prepositional phrases. Have them read to the class examples they have found and discuss the effectiveness of the usage. Students might want to rewrite the section of poetry, eliminating the compound elements, and discuss the change in the effect of the language.

GRAMMAR

DIFFERENTIATING INSTRUCTION

Learners Having Difficulty

Activity. On the chalkboard or overhead projector, create a two-column graphic organizer using the following labels:

Subject	Predicate

Ask students to fill in both columns for **Exercise 13.** You may want to adapt this format to three columns for **Exercise 16** on p. 58.

PRACTICE

Guided and Independent

Exercise You may wish to have the class work through **Exercise 13** as guided practice and **Review B** as independent practice.

HOMEWORK

4. Will you walk home or wait for the four o'clock bus?
5. This kitchen appliance will slice, dice, and chop.
6. Velma will not only bring the salad but also bake bread for the party.
7. Please pick your socks up and put them either in the hamper or downstairs by the washing machine. 7. (You)
8. The marching band practiced hard and won the state competition.
9. Visit, rest, and relax. 9. (You)
10. The newborn calf rose to its feet with a wobble and stood.

Exercise 13 Identifying Subjects and Predicates

Write each of the following sentences, underlining the complete subject once and the complete predicate twice. Be sure to include all parts of compound subjects and compound verbs.

EXAMPLE 1. Gary Soto and Amy Tan are my favorite authors.

1. Gary Soto and Amy Tan are my favorite authors.

1. Soto's poetry and short stories often are about his life.
2. Will he read from his works and sign books here tonight?
3. Carlos, Ted, and I will find front-row seats.
4. Where is your copy of *Too Many Tamales*?
5. Here is Gary Soto's latest collection of poetry.
6. His realistic way of presenting life appeals to me.
7. This particular poem brings back childhood memories.
8. Something similar happened to me in the first grade.
9. There are Sandra Cisneros and Rudolfo Anaya, other successful Hispanic American authors.
10. Their stories reflect a rich cultural heritage.

HELP — Not all steps apply to every sentence in Review B.

Review B Finding Subjects and Verbs

Copy each of the sentences in the following paragraph. Then, complete steps A through D to find the subject and the verb in each sentence.

A. Cross out all prepositional phrases to help you isolate the verb and the subject.
B. Cross out *Here* or *There* at the beginning of a sentence to eliminate these words as possible subjects.
C. Underline all verbs twice, including all helping verbs and all parts of any compound verbs.

D. Underline all subjects once, including all parts of any compound subjects. If a sentence contains an understood subject, write and underline *you.*

EXAMPLE [1] Quicksand can be dangerous to a hiker.

1. Quicksand can be dangerous ~~to a hiker~~.

[1] ~~In quicksand~~, you must remain calm. [2] Violent movement, ~~such as kicking your legs~~, will only worsen the situation. [3] ~~There~~ are several steps ~~to escaping from quicksand~~. [4] First, discard your backpack or any other burden. [5] Next, gently fall ~~onto your back~~ and spread your arms. [6] ~~In this position~~, you will be able to float. [7] Only then should you slowly bring your feet ~~to the surface~~. [8] Perhaps a companion or someone else nearby can reach you ~~with a pole or a rope~~. [9] Are you alone? [10] Then you should look ~~for the shortest distance to solid ground~~ and paddle slowly ~~toward safety~~.

4. (you)
5. (you)

Complements

2h. A *complement* is a word or word group that completes the meaning of a verb.

Some groups of words need more than a subject and a verb to express a complete thought. Notice how the following sentences need the boldface words to complete their meaning. These boldface words are called *complements.*

EXAMPLES It is a good **car** even though it is **old.**

Who gave **Mr. Garcia** the **present**?

A complement may be compound.

EXAMPLES Aunt Edna looks **happy** and **relaxed** today.

My cats enjoy **eating** and **napping.**

A complement may be a noun, a pronoun, or an adjective.

EXAMPLES Marcella (S) might become (V) a **chemist** (C).

The raccoon (S) watched (V) **us** (C) gardening in the backyard.

The clerks (S) at that store are (V) **helpful** (C).

Complements

Rule 2h *(pp. 55–57)*

OBJECTIVES

- To identify subjects, verbs, and complements in sentences
- To form complete sentences by adding complements to groups of words

GRAMMAR

DIRECT TEACHING

Modeling and Demonstration

Recognizing Complements. Model how to recognize complements by using the example *Dad made himself a work bench.* First, ask which words are the subject and verb. [Dad—*subject;* made—*verb*] Next, ask whether the subject and verb express a complete thought by themselves. [*no*] Then, ask for whom Dad made the bench. [*himself*] Then, ask what Dad made. [*bench*] Tell students that both the noun *bench* and pronoun *himself* complete the meaning of the verb *made;* therefore, both are complements. Now, have a volunteer use an example from this chapter to demonstrate how to recognize complements.

RESOURCES

Complements

Practice

- *Language & Sentence Skills Practice,* p. 44

Differentiating Instruction

Learners Having Difficulty

Give students oral practice adding complements to the sentence base. Make flashcards for students out of 3" x 5" cards. On one side of the cards, put a subject, an action verb, and a blank, or put a subject, a linking verb, and a blank. On the back put possible complements. Here are some sample cards:

1. Dogs chew [bones].
2. Mom gave [me] a hug.
3. A bear is [furry].
4. Robbie is a [Boy Scout].

Have students work in pairs to complete the sentences.

English-Language Learners

Spanish. Because English has one verb for *to be* while Spanish has both *estar* and *ser,* Spanish-speaking students may have difficulty understanding sentences using forms of *be* such as those in sentences 6 and 8 in **Exercise 14.** Before students can find subject complements in the exercises, you may need to focus on vocabulary with them.

Reference Note

For information on **adverbs,** see page 21.

An adverb is not a complement.

EXAMPLES Where did we go wrong? [*Wrong* is used as an adverb, not a complement.]

That answer is not **wrong.** [*Wrong,* an adjective, is a complement in this sentence.]

Reference Note

For information on **prepositional phrases,** see page 70.

Sentence complements are never in prepositional phrases.

EXAMPLES She watched the **cardinals.** [*Cardinals* is the complement.]

She watched **all** of the cardinals. [*Cardinals* is part of the prepositional phrase *of the cardinals.*]

Reference Note

For information on **independent and subordinate clauses,** see Chapter 4.

NOTE Both independent and subordinate clauses contain subjects and verbs and may contain complements.

EXAMPLES This **kitten** (S) **is** (V) the **one** (C) **that** (S) **climbed** (V) the **curtains** (C).

Before **Eli** (S) **rides** (V) his **bicycle** (C), **he** (S) **checks** (V) his **tires** (C).

Exercise 14 Identifying Subjects, Verbs, and Complements

Identify the subject, verb, and complement in each of the following sentences.

EXAMPLE 1. Many modern slang expressions sound okay to my great-grandfather.

1. *expressions—subject; sound—verb; okay—complement*

1. Like every generation, my great-grandfather's generation had its own [slang.]
2. He still uses [it] all the time, particularly in stories about his youth.
3. Great-grandpa played the [trombone] in a jazz band in the 1930s.
4. He and other musicians developed many slang [expressions.]
5. Their language became [*jive talk*.]
6. Many of Great-grandpa's expressions are [sayings] of the entertainer Cab Calloway.
7. Great-grandpa uses [phrases] such as Calloway's *beat to my socks* (tired) and *out of this world* (perfect).
8. Great-grandpa's speech is [full] of words like *hepcat* (a lover of jazz music) and *hip* (wise) and *groovy* (wonderful).
9. Such language became [popular] all over the United States.
10. My great-grandfather, at least, still uses [it.]

Exercise 15 Writing Sentence Complements

Write ten sentences by adding a complement to each of the following word groups. Be sure to punctuate each sentence correctly.

Sentences will vary.

EXAMPLE 1. The puppy is

1. *The puppy is playful.*

1. Jesse usually seems 1. confident.
2. Tomorrow the class will hear 2. a speech from the principal.
3. That broiled fish looks 3. hot and delicious.
4. Last week our class visited 4. the art museum.
5. Do you have 5. change for a dollar?
6. Coretta finished the 6. assignment.
7. The winners felt 7. exhausted.
8. Saturday the museum will sell 8. replicas of the statue.
9. Fruits and vegetables filled the 9. plates and trays.
10. How do you like 10. your new apartment?

The Subject Complement

2i. A *subject complement* is a word or word group in the predicate that identifies or describes the subject.

EXAMPLES Mark Twain's real name was **Samuel Clemens.** [*Samuel Clemens* identifies *name*.]

The surface felt **sticky.** [*Sticky* describes *surface*.]

Subject complements may be compound.

EXAMPLES The prizewinners are **Jennifer, Marcus,** and **Raul.**

That winter seemed especially **mild** and **sunny.**

Subject complements sometimes precede the subject of a sentence or a clause.

EXAMPLES I know what a **treat** this is for her. [*Treat* is a predicate nominative identifying *this*.]

How **kind** he is! [*Kind* is a predicate adjective describing *he*.]

NOTE Subject complements always complete the meaning of linking verbs. A word that completes the meaning of an action verb is not a subject complement.

HELP

To find the subject complement in an interrogative sentence, rearrange the sentence to make a statement.

EXAMPLE
Is Darnell the treasurer?
Darnell is the **treasurer.**

To find the subject complement in an imperative sentence, insert the understood subject *you*.

EXAMPLE
Be good.
(You) Be **good.**

Reference Note

For more about **action and linking verbs,** see page 15.

The Subject Complement

Rule 2i *(pp. 57–59)*

OBJECTIVES

- **To identify subject complements as predicate nominatives or predicate adjectives**
- **To complete sentences by adding subject complements to groups of words and to identify these complements as predicate nominatives or predicate adjectives**

GRAMMAR

DIRECT TEACHING

Modeling and Demonstration

The Subject Complement. Model how to identify predicate nominatives and predicate adjectives by using the examples: *He is a doctor* and *The soup is hot.* Ask which word is the subject in the first sentence. [*He*] Then, ask what the complete verb or predicate is. [*is a doctor*] Ask whether there is a word in the predicate that identifies the subject *He*. [*yes;* doctor] Explain that *doctor* is a predicate nominative because it is a word in the predicate that identifies the subject. Next, ask if there is a word in the predicate of the second sentence that modifies the subject *soup*. [*yes;* hot] Point out that *hot* is a predicate adjective because it is in the predicate and modifies *soup*. Now, have a volunteer use another example from this chapter to demonstrate how to identify predicate nominatives and predicate adjectives.

RESOURCES

The Subject Complement

Practice

- *Language & Sentence Skills Practice,* pp. 45–47

Differentiating Instruction

- *Developmental Language & Sentence Skills,* pp. 29–32

GRAMMAR

Differentiating Instruction

Learners Having Difficulty

Tell students that a linking verb is like an equal sign (=) because it links the subject to its complement, whereas an action verb shows the relationship between the subject and a direct object through some action.

Ask students to create four sentences of their own using only linking verbs. Two should have predicate nominatives, and two should have predicate adjectives. Students might want to put the sentences on index cards, add illustrations, and keep the cards as study tools.

STYLE TIP

The use of the nominative-case pronoun, as in the last example of the predicate nominative, is uncommon in everyday speech. You will often hear *It is him,* rather than *It is he*. Remember that in formal English you should use the nominative-case pronoun.

Reference Note

For more about the **nominative case**, see page 178.

(1) A *predicate nominative* is a word or word group that is in the predicate and that identifies the subject or refers to it.

EXAMPLES Has she become a **dentist**?

Friendship is **what I value most.**

The new teacher is **he**—the man in the blazer.

(2) A *predicate adjective* is an adjective that is in the predicate and that modifies the subject.

EXAMPLES The soup is **hot.** [hot soup]

That soil seems **dry** and **crumbly.** [dry and crumbly soil]

How **expensive** are those shoes? [expensive shoes]

Exercise 16 Identifying Subject Complements

Each of the following sentences has at least one subject complement. For each sentence, give the complement or complements and tell whether each is a *predicate nominative* or a *predicate adjective.*

EXAMPLE 1. Gloria is my favorite character on the show.

1. character—predicate nominative

1. p.a. — 1. Does the lemonade taste too sour?
2. p.a. — 2. The chirping of the birds became more and more shrill as the cat approached.
3. p.a. — 3. The window washers on the fifteenth floor appeared tiny.
4. p.a. — 4. Why does he always look so serious?
5. p.n. — 5. Our candidate for the city council was the winner in the primaries.
6. p.a. — 6. You should feel proud of yourself.
7. p.n. — 7. Will the hall monitors for Wednesday be Charlene and LaReina?
8. p.a. — 8. Soft and cool was the grass under the catalpa tree.
9. p.n. — 9. Be a friend to animals.
10. p.a. — 10. The crowd grew quiet when Governor Markham spoke.

Exercise 17 Writing Subject Complements

Make complete sentences of the following word groups by adding nouns, pronouns, or adjectives as subject complements. Use five compound complements. Identify each subject complement as a *predicate nominative* or a *predicate adjective.*

EXAMPLE 1. The sky turned

1. The sky turned cloudy and dark. —predicate adjectives

1. The artist frequently was
2. Those are
3. Sara Brown became
4. It could be
5. The house looked
6. Are you
7. The weather remained
8. The test seemed
9. Manuel had always felt
10. That recording sounds

Objects

Objects are complements that do not refer to the subject. Objects follow transitive verbs—verbs that express an action directed toward a person, place, or thing.

EXAMPLE Lee Trevino sank the **putt.** [The object *putt* does not explain or describe the subject *Lee Trevino. Sank* is a transitive verb, not an intransitive verb.]

NOTE Transitive verbs may express mental action (for example, *believe, trust, imagine*) as well as physical action (for example, *give, hit, draw*).

EXAMPLE Now I remember your name. [Remember *what*? Name.]

Reference Note

For more about **transitive and intransitive verbs,** see page 14.

2j. A *direct object* is a noun, pronoun, or word group that tells who or what receives the action of a verb or shows the result of the action.

A direct object answers the question "Whom?" or "What?" after a transitive verb.

EXAMPLES

S V DO
Germs cause **illness.** [Germs cause *what*? Germs cause illness. *Illness* shows the result of the action of the verb.]

S V DO
Peter said ***Gesundheit.*** [Peter said *what*? Peter said *Gesundheit. Gesundheit* receives the action of the verb.]

S V DO
Lucy visited **me.** [Lucy visited *whom*? Lucy visited me. *Me* receives the action of the verb.]

DO S V
What a scary **movie** we saw! [We saw *what*? We saw a movie. *Movie* receives the action of the verb.]

S V DO
They were taking **whatever was left.** [They were taking *what*? They were taking whatever was left. *Whatever was left* receives the action of the verb.]

Exercise 17 Writing Subject Complements

POSSIBLE ANSWERS

1. The artist frequently was cold and hungry. p.a.
2. Those are my shoes and John's boots. p.n.
3. Sara Brown became my partner. p.n.
4. It could be a whole new idea. p.n.
5. The house looked lonely and cold. p.a.
6. Are you the substitute teacher? p.n.
7. The weather remained sunny and clear. p.a.
8. The test seemed endless. p.a.
9. Manuel had always felt honored and respected. p.a.
10. That recording sounds ancient. p.a.

GRAMMAR

Objects

Rules 2j, k *(pp. 59–63)*

OBJECTIVE

- To identify direct objects and indirect objects in sentences

DIFFERENTIATING INSTRUCTION

English-Language Learners

Spanish. In Spanish, the direct object pronoun generally precedes the verb. Ask a student to write a short sentence in Spanish on the board. Tell the student that the sentence should contain a direct object. Ask the student to label the parts and rewrite the sentence in English. Label the parts of the English sentence, emphasizing the difference in the position of the direct object.

RESOURCES

Objects

Practice

- *Language & Sentence Skills Practice,* pp.48–51

Differentiating Instruction

- *Developmental Language & Sentence Skills,* pp. 33–36

GRAMMAR

Differentiating Instruction

Learners Having Difficulty

To introduce indirect objects, give pairs of students slips of paper with sample sentences such as "He gave her a book." Have pairs act out or pantomime the sentence. Ask a volunteer to create a sentence based on the scene. Write the sentence on the board, and label the parts. Follow the same procedure as other students act out or pantomime other sentences that have direct and indirect objects. Students could create labeled stick-figure drawings on index cards to use as study guides.

Direct objects are generally not found in prepositional phrases.

EXAMPLES Josh was riding on his bicycle. [*Bicycle* is part of the prepositional phrase *on his bicycle*. The sentence has no direct object.]

Josh was riding his **bicycle.** [*Bicycle* is the direct object.]

Exercise 18 Identifying Direct Objects

Identify the direct object in each of the following sentences.

EXAMPLE **1.** I enjoy this magazine very much.
1. magazine

1. This article gives interesting facts about libraries.
2. The city of Alexandria, in Egypt, had the most famous library of ancient times.
3. This library contained the largest collection of plays and works of philosophy in the ancient world.
4. The Roman emperor Augustus founded two public libraries.
5. Fire destroyed all of these libraries.
6. Readers could not borrow books from either the library in Alexandria or the Roman libraries.
7. During the Middle Ages, the monastery libraries introduced a circulating library.
8. By the sixth century, Benedictine monks were borrowing books from their libraries for daily reading.
9. In the United States, we now have thousands of libraries.
10. Readers borrow millions of books from them every year.

HELP — Indirect objects generally precede direct objects.

2k. An *indirect object* is a noun, pronoun, or word group that often appears in sentences containing direct objects. An indirect object tells *to whom* or *to what* (or *for whom* or *for what*) the action of a transitive verb is done.

EXAMPLES

S V IO DO
Natalie knitted her **friend** a sweater. [Natalie knitted a sweater for whom? For her *friend*.]

S V IO DO
My little sister sang **me** a song. [My little sister sang a song to whom? To *me*.]

S V IO DO
Uncle Gene sends **whoever requests it** a pamphlet on earthworms. [Uncle Gene sends a pamphlet to whom? To *whoever requests it*.]

Reference Note
For information on **transitive verbs,** see page 14.

Content-Area Connections

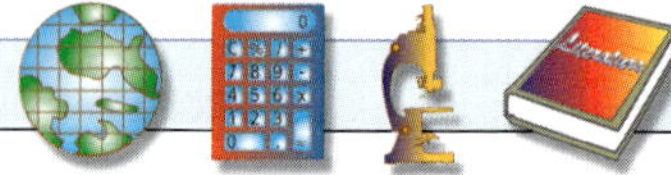

Social Studies

Note Taking. Students can improve their note-taking skills by using these basic sentence structures: subject/verb/direct object, subject/ verb/ predicate nominative, and subject/verb/predicate adjective.

From a social studies teacher, get a time line of the unit students are studying. Have students use the basic sentence structures to write sentences about events during the time period.

If the word *to* or *for* is used, the noun or pronoun following it is part of a prepositional phrase and not an indirect object.

OBJECTS OF PREPOSITIONS — My teacher showed the bird's nest to the **class.**
I left some dessert for **you.**

INDIRECT OBJECTS — The teacher showed the **class** the bird's nest.
I left **you** some dessert.

Both direct and indirect objects may be compound.

EXAMPLES Lydia sold **cookies** and **lemonade.** [compound direct object]
Lydia sold **Geraldo, Freddy,** and **me** lemonade. [compound indirect object]

NOTE Do not mistake an adverb in the predicate for a complement.

ADVERB — Go **inside,** Skippy. [*Inside* is an adverb telling *where.*]

COMPLEMENT — Tamisha sanded the **inside** of the wooden chest. [*Inside* is a noun used as a direct object.]

Reference Note
For information on **prepositional phrases and objects of prepositions,** see page 70.

Reference Note
For information on **adverbs,** see page 21.

Oral Practice — Identifying Direct Objects and Indirect Objects

Read the following sentences aloud, and identify the direct and indirect objects. Make sure that you give all parts of compound direct and indirect objects.

EXAMPLE 1. Sometimes I read my little brother stories from Greek mythology.
1. indirect object—brother; direct object—stories

1. In one myth, the famous artist and inventor Daedalus built the king of Crete a mysterious building known as the Labyrinth.
2. The complicated passageways of this building give us the word *labyrinth* ("a maze or confusing structure").
3. After the completion of the Labyrinth, the king imprisoned Daedalus and his son, whose name was Icarus.
4. To escape, Daedalus made Icarus and himself wings out of feathers and beeswax.
5. He gave Icarus careful instructions not to fly too near the sun.
6. However, Icarus soon forgot his father's advice.
7. He flew too high, and when the sun melted the wax in the wings, he plunged to his death in the ocean.

HELP
Not every sentence in the Oral Practice contains an indirect object.

GRAMMAR

EXTENSION

Relating to Writing

Based on the information in the sentences for **Oral Practice** or from the story of Daedalus and Icarus found in a literature book, have the class write an epitaph for Icarus of at least eight lines, using direct objects and indirect objects in at least four lines. Explain that an epitaph is an inscription used to mark a burial place.

Sample sentences about Nelson Mandela in South Africa:

1. Nelson Mandela had been a prisoner for many years. (S-V-PN)
2. He was considered dangerous to the current government. (S-V-PA)
3. After his release, he helped his people greatly. (S-V-DO)

GRAMMAR

DIFFERENTIATING INSTRUCTION

Learners Having Difficulty

You may want to use diagramming to illustrate the structure of a sentence. Diagramming may help students to visualize an abstract concept. For examples of diagramming, see p. 474. Encourage students to break down sentences in **Review D** (p. 62) into simple sentences and to diagram the basic parts of the simple sentences.

SAMPLE DIAGRAMS

1. Before this winter, I couldn't draw a human face well.

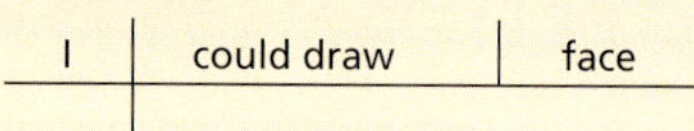

2. However, our neighbor, Mr. Teng, is a portrait painter.

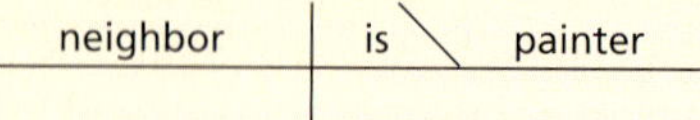

3. He has been giving me some instructive tips.

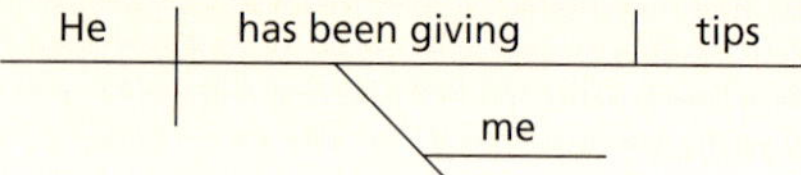

PRACTICE

Guided and Independent

Review D You may wish to have the class work through the first ten items in **Review D** as guided practice and assign the remaining items as independent practice.

HOMEWORK

8. Though saddened by the death of his son, Daedalus flew on and reached Sicily in safety.
9. Mythology tells us other stories of his fabulous inventions.
10. Even today, the name Daedalus suggests genius and inventiveness.

HELP Not every sentence in Review C contains a complement; some sentences contain more than one.

Review C Identifying Complements

Identify the complements in the following sentences. Then, tell whether each complement is a *predicate nominative,* a *predicate adjective,* a *direct object,* or an *indirect object.* If a sentence does not contain a complement, write *no complement.*

EXAMPLE [1] My brother Bill gave Mom a birthday surprise.

1. *Mom—indirect object; surprise—direct object*

[1] My brother made Mom a birthday cake. [2] However, the project soon became a fiasco. [3] First, Bill cracked three eggs into a bowl. [4] Unfortunately, bits of the shells went in, too. [5] Then he added the flour and other dry ingredients. [6] The electric mixer whirled the batter right onto the ceiling. [7] The batter was so sticky that it stayed there and didn't fall off. [8] Bill did not clean the ceiling immediately, and the sticky substance hardened overnight. [9] Mom was not angry, but she did give Bill a suggestion for a gift. [10] "A clean kitchen would be a great birthday present."

1. i.o./d.o.	**2.** p.n.	**3.** d.o.	**4.** n.c.
5. d.o./d.o.	**6.** d.o.	**7.** p.a.	**8.** d.o.
9. p.a./i.o./d.o.	**10.** p.n.		

HELP Remember that subordinate clauses contain subjects and verbs and may also contain complements.

Review D Identifying the Parts of a Sentence

Identify the italicized words in the following passage. Use these abbreviations.

s.	subject	***p.a.***	predicate adjective
v.	verb	***d.o.***	direct object
p.n.	predicate nominative	***i.o.***	indirect object

EXAMPLE When you draw faces, do they look **[1]** *realistic*?

1. *p.a.*

Before this winter, I couldn't draw a human [1] *face* well. However, our [2] *neighbor,* Mr. Teng, is a portrait [3] *painter,* and he has been giving [4] *me* some instructive [5] *tips.* He says that the most important

1. d.o.	**2.** s.
3. p.n.	**4.** i.o.
5. d.o.	

[6] *thing* is the correct [7] *placement* of the eyes. Apparently, most [8] *people* draw the [9] *eyes* too high. In fact, [10] *they* should be placed halfway down the head. Many people also [11] *make* the ears too small. The [12] *top* of each ear [13] *should align* with the eyebrow, and the [14] *bottom* should align with the tip of the nose. Getting the width of the face right is also [15] *important.* Mr. Teng says, "Use one eye's [16] *width* as a unit of measure and make the head five eye-widths wide." There are many other [17] *guidelines,* but these tips from Mr. Teng are the most [18] *basic.* By following them, I can now draw a human [19] *face* that [20] *looks* realistic.

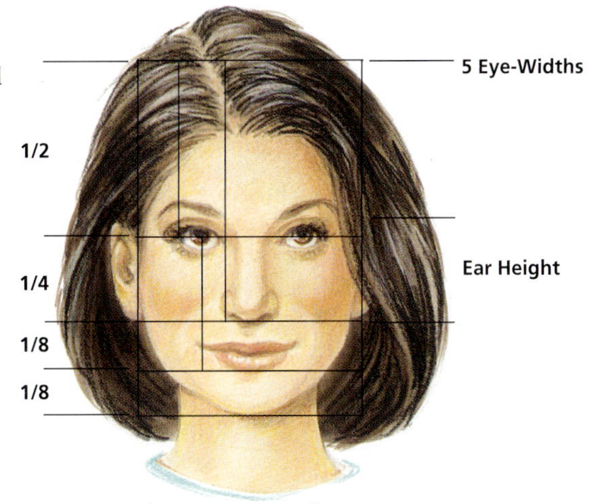

6. s. 7. p.n. 8. s 9. d.o. 10. s. 11. v. 12. s.
13. v. 14. s. 15. p.a. 16. d.o. 17. s. 18. p.a. 19. d.o. 20. v.

Classifying Sentences by Purpose

2l. **A sentence may be classified, depending on its purpose, as *declarative, imperative, interrogative,* or *exclamatory.***

(1) A *declarative sentence* makes a statement and ends with a period.

EXAMPLES Jody Williams won the Nobel Peace Prize in 1997**.**

That one-celled organism is an amoeba**.**

(2) An *imperative sentence* gives a command or makes a request. Most imperative sentences end with a period. A strong command ends with an exclamation point.

EXAMPLES Please keep to the right**.** [request]

Take care of your little brother, Rick**.** [command]

Stop**!** [strong command]

Notice in these examples that a command or a request has the understood subject *you.*

Reference Note

For more information about **understood subjects,** see page 51.

GRAMMAR

Classifying Sentences by Purpose

Rule 2l *(pp. 63–64)*

OBJECTIVE

- To choose the correct end punctuation for sentences and to classify them according to type

DIRECT TEACHING

Modeling and Demonstration

Classifying Sentences by Purpose. Model how to classify sentences by using the examples: *That one-celled organism is an amoeba; Don't do that; Are they here; I can't believe it.* First, ask whether the first sentence is a statement, a command, a question, or an exclamation. [*statement*] Explain that a declarative sentence makes a statement and should end with a period. Next, repeat the question for the second sentence. [*command*] Point out that an imperative sentence gives a command or makes a request and ends with a period. Strong commands end with an exclamation point. Then, repeat the first question for the third sentence. [*question*] An interrogative sentence asks a question and ends with a question mark. Finally, repeat the question for the fourth sentence. [*exclamation*] Explain that an exclamatory sentence makes an exclamation and ends with an exclamation point. Now, have a volunteer use another example from this chapter to demonstrate how to classify sentences.

RESOURCES

Classifying Sentences by Purpose

Practice

- *Language & Sentence Skills Practice,* p. 52

Differentiating Instruction

- *Developmental Language & Sentence Skills,* pp. 37–38

GRAMMAR

Differentiating Instruction

Learners Having Difficulty

Use the following information to help students associate sentence classification terms with more familiar words.

- **Declarative:** form of *declare*, meaning "to make a statement"
- **Interrogative:** form of *interrogate*, meaning "to ask questions"; associated with interrogating criminals or spies
- **Imperative:** think of an emperor giving commands
- **Exclamatory:** form of *exclaim*, meaning "to cry out"

Students can illustrate these terms with cartoons to use as study aids.

Advanced Learners

Students might enjoy knowing about other designations for punctuation marks. An *interrobang (‽)* is a combination of a question mark (interrogative) and an exclamation point (called a "bang" in printers' slang). It indicates a sentence that is both a question and an exclamation. (Students might enjoy creating such sentences.) A *screamer* is another slang term for an exclamation point. Challenge students to create their own humorous slang terms for punctuation.

STYLE TIP

Sometimes writers use both a question mark and an exclamation point to express the combined emotions of surprise and disbelief or wonder.

EXAMPLE
Is it really you?!

Such usage is appropriate only in informal situations and in dialogue, to convey the speaker's emotions.

(3) An *interrogative sentence* asks a question and ends with a question mark.

EXAMPLES Can they finish in time?

How did she find Yoshi and Sarah?

(4) An *exclamatory sentence* shows excitement or expresses strong feeling and ends with an exclamation point.

EXAMPLES What a good friend you are!

The battery is dead!

I can't believe this is happening!

NOTE In conversation, any sentence may be spoken so that it becomes exclamatory or interrogative. When you are writing dialogue, use periods, exclamation points, and question marks to show how you intend a sentence to be read.

EXAMPLES They won. [declarative]
They won! [exclamatory]
They won? [interrogative]

Exercise 19 Identifying the Four Kinds of Sentences

Punctuate each of the following sentences with an appropriate end mark. Classify each sentence as *imperative, declarative, interrogative,* or *exclamatory.*

EXAMPLE 1. There are many delicious foods from India
1. *period—declarative*

1. Do you like spicy food? 1. int.
2. Some Indian food is hot, and some isn't. 2. dec.
3. *Sambar* is a soup made with lentils and vegetables. 3. dec.
4. Save me some of those curried shrimp. 4. imp.
5. What is that wonderful bread called? 5. int.
6. *Palek alu* is a spicy dish of potatoes. 6. dec.
7. Watch out for the hot chilies. [*or* !] 7. imp.
8. Isn't this yogurt drink called *lassi* good? 8. int.
9. Be sure to add the curry and other spices to the onions. 9. imp.
10. How tasty this rice-and-banana pudding is! 10. exc.

Chapter Review

Numerals in brackets refer to rules tested by the items in the Chapter Review.

A. Identifying Types of Sentences and Sentence Fragments

Identify each of the following word groups as a *declarative sentence*, an *interrogative sentence*, an *imperative sentence*, an *exclamatory sentence*, or a *sentence fragment*. Supply the appropriate end mark after the last word of each item that is *not* a sentence fragment.

1. int. [2l(3)]
2. exc. [2l(4)]
3. frag. [2a]
4. dec. [2l(1)]
5. imp. [2l(2)]
6. dec. [2l(1)]
7. imp. [2l(2)]
8. dec. [2l(1)]
9. frag. [2a]
10. exc. [2l(4)]

1. Why don't we go to the wildlife park tomorrow?
2. What a good time we'll have!
3. The big cats especially at feeding time
4. Actually, I enjoy the entire park.
5. Meet me at the front gate at ten o' clock.
6. We'll first go see the elephants.
7. Don't forget the camera.
8. My favorite animal is Bonzo the baboon.
9. His amazing stunts and antics
10. How graceful the gazelles are!

B. Identifying the Complete Subject and the Simple Subject

Identify the complete subject in each of the following sentences. Then, underline the simple subject.

11. [2c, b, e]
12. [2c, b]
13. [2c, b]
14. [2c, b]
15. [2c, b]
16. [2c, b]
17. [2c, b]

11. (One of the first advocates of medical hygiene and the use of antiseptics) was Ignaz Semmelweis.
12. (This German-Hungarian physician) was born in 1818.
13. In 1844, (he) earned a degree from Vienna University.
14. (His first position) was as an assistant at the obstetric clinic in Vienna.
15. (Semmelweis) was appalled by the high mortality rate among his patients.
16. (He) taught medical staff members always to wash their hands in a chlorine solution and by doing so soon reduced the mortality rate.
17. (Semmelweis, who was a true pioneer,) lobbied the medical establishment to make antiseptic operating conditions a top priority.

ASSESSING

Monitoring Progress

Chapter Review. The **Chapter Review** requires students to identify sentences by purpose as well as to identify the function of specific words in sentences. The results of this review can be compared to those of the **Diagnostic Preview** (p. 40) to assess student progress.

RESOURCES

The Parts of a Sentence

Review

- *Language & Sentence Skills Practice*, pp. 53–56

Assessment

- *Holt Handbook Chapter Tests with Answer Key*, pp. 3–4, 52

18. [2c, b, e]
19. [2c, b]
20. [2c, b, e]

18. (The medical establishment in many countries) remained hostile to Semmelweis for many years.

19. In 1865, the year of Semmelweis's death, (a famous British surgeon named Joseph Lister) performed his first antiseptic operation.

20. (The method introduced by Semmelweis) made medicine safer and more humane.

HELP — In Part C of the Chapter Review, the simple predicate may be compound.

C. Identifying Complete Predicates and Simple Predicates (Verbs)

Identify the complete predicate in each of the following sentences. Then, underline the simple predicate (or verb).

21. [2d, b]
22. [2d, b]
23. [2d, b]
24. [2d, b]
25. [2g, d, b]
26. [2g, d, b]
27. [2d, b]
28. [2d, b]
29. [2d, b]
30. [2d, b]

21. (Have) you (met my brother Lewis)?

22. (Then listen to this.)

23. My brother (often dawdles.)

24. He (chooses odd times for some activities.)

25. (One day last week,) Lewis (gathered all of the pencils in the house and sharpened them.)

26. (Today) he (woke early and completely rearranged his room).

27. (Then) my poor little brother (was almost late for the school bus.)

28. I (reminded him, however, of his first-period test.)

29. (Somehow,) Lewis (finishes all his chores and assignments.)

30. I (might buy him a book about time management, though.)

D. Identifying Sentence Parts

Identify each italicized word in the following paragraphs as a *subject,* a *verb,* a *predicate nominative,* a *predicate adjective,* a *direct object,* or an *indirect object.*

31. s. [2c, b]
32. p.n. [2i(1), h]
33. v. [2d, b]
34. s. [2c, b]
35. p.a. [2i(2), h]
36. v. [2d, b]
37. s. [2c, b]
38. i.o. [2k, h]

A **[31]** *carwash* can be a good **[32]** *fund-raiser.* The freshman class **[33]** *planned* a carwash for last Saturday. On Saturday morning, the **[34]** *sky* did not look **[35]** *good.* In fact, the weather forecast **[36]** *predicted* thunderstorms. Did **[37]** *any* of this send **[38]** *us* a message? Yes, but we had our **[39]** *carwash* anyway. Our first **[40]** *customer,* at 9:00 A.M., was a **[41]** *woman* in a pickup truck. Glancing at the sky, she paid **[42]** *us* a compliment. "You're really **[43]** *brave,*" she said. The rain **[44]** *began* as she was speaking, and our disappointment must have been **[45]** *obvious.* "Don't worry," she added. "There is **[46]** *nothing* like a rainwater rinse." We **[47]** *charged* her only one **[48]** *dollar* because she had cheered us up so much. The morning was intermittently **[49]** *rainy.* Later, however, the clouds parted and the weather was **[50]** *perfect.*

39. d.o. [2j, h]
40. s. [2c, b]
41. p.n. [2i(1), h]
42. i.o. [2k, h]
43. p.a. [2i(2), h]
44. v. [2d, b]
45. p.a. [2i(2), h]
46. s. [2c, b]
47. v. [2d, b]
48. d.o. [2j, h]
49. p.a. [2i(2), h]
50. p.a. [2i(2), h]

Writing Application

Using Verbs in a Summary

Fresh, Lively Verbs Your little sister likes you to tell her exciting stories. You have told her so many stories that you have run out of new ones. To get ideas for new stories, you think about events you have read about or seen. Write a summary of an exciting incident from a book, a movie, or a television show. Use action verbs that are fresh and lively. Underline these verbs.

Prewriting Think about books that you have read recently or movies and television shows that you have seen. Choose an exciting incident from one of these works. Freewrite what you remember about that incident.

Writing As you write your first draft, think about how you are presenting the information. When telling a story, you usually should use chronological order (the order in which events occurred). This method would be easiest for your young listener to follow, too. Try to use fresh, lively action verbs.

Revising Imagine that you are a young child hearing the story for the first time. Look over your summary and ask yourself if you could follow this account of the story.

Publishing Read over your summary again, looking for any errors in grammar, usage, and mechanics. You may want to share your story with a younger sibling or with children at a local preschool or kindergarten.

GRAMMAR

APPLICATION

Writing Application

Prewriting Tip. Illustrate the difference between a strictly objective description and a description using sensory details. Have students picture a doctor's office; then, ask them how the picture would change from the perspective of a health care professional or a young patient. [*The scene would change according to the feelings of the person describing it. A health care professional might describe a clean, sterile, efficient clinic, while a child might describe needles and the cries of patients. In other words, sensory details are reflections of the writer's judgment.*]

Scoring Rubric. While you will want to pay particular attention to students' use of parts of the sentence, you will want to evaluate the students' overall writing performance. You may want to give a split score to indicate development and clarity of the composition as well as grammar skills.

CHAPTER 3

INTRODUCING THE CHAPTER

- This chapter looks at three types of phrases: prepositional phrases, verbal phrases, and appositive phrases.
- The chapter concludes with a **Chapter Review** including a **Writing Application** feature that asks students to write instructions using both adverb and adjective phrases.
- For help in integrating this chapter with writing assignments, use the **Teaching Strands** chart on pp. T24–T25.

CHAPTER

The Phrase

Prepositional, Verbal, and Appositive Phrases

HELP—Some sentences in Part A have more than one prepositional phrase.

Numerals in brackets refer to rules tested by the items in the Diagnostic Preview.

1. adj. [3b, d, a]
2. adj. [3b, d, a]
3. adj./adv. [3b, d, e, a, c]
4. adv. [3b, e, a]
5. adj. [3b, d, a]
6. adj./adj. [3b, d, a]

Diagnostic Preview

A. Identifying and Classifying Prepositional Phrases

Identify each prepositional phrase in the following sentences. After each phrase, write the word(s) it modifies and the type of phrase it is (*adj.* for adjective phrase, *adv.* for adverb phrase).

EXAMPLE 1. The museums of different cities are fascinating to tourists.

1. *of different cities—museums—adj.*
to tourists—fascinating—adv.

1. New York City offers tourists a number of museums.
2. Perhaps the best-known museum is the American Museum of Natural History.
3. This huge museum has exhibits on human history and culture and also shows animals, even dinosaurs, in natural-looking displays, called dioramas.
4. The museum houses the Hayden Planetarium, which teaches visitors about the heavens.
5. Exhibits about earth and space interest young and old alike.
6. The entire complex of exhibits is popular because it offers something for everyone.

CHAPTER RESOURCES

Internet

- Web resources: go.hrw.com

Practice & Review

- *Language & Sentence Skills Practice,* pp. 61–83
- *Language & Sentence Skills Practice Answer Key,* pp. 29–40

Application & Enrichment

- *Language & Sentence Skills Practice,* pp. 60, 84–86
- *Language & Sentence Skills Practice Answer Key,* pp. 29, 40–41

7. The city's other museums, which are also fascinating, attract visitors who are interested in specific topics.
8. New York is home to the Museum of Broadcasting, which is filled with old films and radio broadcasts.
9. One of the city's newest museums, Ellis Island Immigration Museum, opened during 1990 and displays many artifacts that had been owned by immigrants who entered the United States through Ellis Island.
10. People who enjoy art can visit museums like the Metropolitan Museum of Art and the Museum of Modern Art.

7. adv. [3b, e, a]
8. adj./adj./adv. [3b, d, c, e, a]
9. adj./adv./adv./adv. [3b, d, e, a]
10. adj./adj./adj. [3b, d, a, c]

B. Identifying Verbals and Appositives

In the following sentences, identify each italicized word or word group as a *participle*, a *gerund*, an *infinitive*, or an *appositive*.

EXAMPLES
1. For some reason, *cleaning* a room, that *dreaded project,* always seems *to create* new projects.
1. *cleaning—gerund; dreaded—participle; project—appositive; to create—infinitive*

11. John began with every intention of *cleaning* his entire room, the official disaster *area* of his home.
12. He first tackled the pile of CDs *lying* near his *unused* sound system.
13. *Sorting* through them, he found them mostly *outdated.*
14. John decided that his *broken* stereo system, a *gift* from his parents, was the reason.
15. By *repairing* the stereo, he could give himself a reason *to update* his music collection.
16. *Trained* in electronics, John soon saw the problem and began *to work* on it.
17. Some hours later, John had a *working* stereo system but an *uncleaned* room.
18. He had just started *playing* a CD when his sister announced, "Mom's coming *to see* how your room looks!"
19. A tough *taskmaster,* Mom wanted him *to have* it spotless.
20. She applauded his success in *fixing* his stereo but insisted that he clean the room before *doing* anything else.

11. ger./app. [3h, l]
12. part./part. [3f(1, 2)]
13. part./part. [3f(1, 2)]
14. part./app. [3f(2), l]
15. ger./inf. [3h, j]
16. part./inf. [3f(2), j]
17. part./part.[3f(1, 2)]
18. ger./inf. [3h, j]
19. app./inf. [3l, j]
20. ger./ger. [3h]

GRAMMAR

ASSESSING

Entry-Level Assessment

Diagnostic Preview. You may want to compile data on your class's most common mistakes on the **Diagnostic Preview** and use this information as a guide for instruction. After students have completed the chapter, you might compare scores on the **Diagnostic Preview** with those on the **Chapter Review** to assess progress.

Differentiating Instruction

- *Developmental Language & Sentence Skills Guided Practice,* pp. 39–50
- *Developmental Language & Sentence Skills Guided Practice Teacher's Notes and Answer Key,* pp. 10–12

Assessment

- *Holt Handbook Chapter Tests with Answer Key,* pp. 5–6, 52

GRAMMAR

What Is a Phrase?

Rule 3a *(p. 70)*

OBJECTIVE

- To identify phrases

PRETEACHING

Lesson Starter

Motivating. Ask students to suggest humorous answers to the question "Where would be a dangerous place to have a party?" Start students off by writing *on an anthill, under water, in a freezer.* Write students suggestions on the chalkboard, and then point out that the groups of words are all prepositional phrases that tell where the action happens. If added to the sentence *Do not have a party . . . ,* each of the phrases would modify *Do have.*

Prepositional Phrases

Rules 3b–e *(pp. 70–76)*

OBJECTIVES

- To identify adjective phrases and the word or words they modify
- To identify adverb phrases and the word or words they modify

What Is a Phrase?

3a. A *phrase* is a group of related words that is used as a single part of speech and that does not contain both a verb and its subject.

EXAMPLES could have been [no subject]

instead of Debra and him [no subject or verb]

A group of words that has *both* a verb and its subject is not a phrase.

EXAMPLES **We found** your pen. [*We* is the subject of *found.*]

if **she will go** [*She* is the subject of *will go.*]

Reference Note

For more about **clauses,** see Chapter 4.

NOTE If a group of words contains both a verb and its subject, it is called a ***clause.***

Oral Practice **Identifying Phrases**

Read each of the following groups of words aloud, and identify it as a *phrase* or *not a phrase.*

EXAMPLES **1.** with a hammer **2.** because we agree

1. phrase *2. not a phrase*

1. was hoping 1. p.
2. if she really knows 2. n. p.
3. with Abdullah and me 3. p.
4. will be writing 4. p.
5. inside the house 5. p.
6. since Mallory wrote 6. n. p.
7. after they leave 7. n. p.
8. has been cleaned 8. p.
9. on Miriam's desk 9. p.
10. as the plane lands 10. n. p.

Prepositional Phrases

3b. A *prepositional phrase* includes a preposition, the object of the preposition, and any modifiers of that object.

Reference Note

For a list of **commonly used prepositions,** see page 28.

EXAMPLES **to** the pool **at** the Jacksons' house **instead of** them

Notice that one or more modifiers may appear in a prepositional phrase. The first example contains *the*; the second contains *the Jacksons'.*

3c. The noun or pronoun in a prepositional phrase is called the *object of the preposition.*

EXAMPLE Clarice went to the **ballet.** [The noun *ballet* is the object of the preposition *to.*]

70 Chapter 3 The Phrase

RESOURCES

What Is a Phrase? and Prepositional Phrases

Practice

- *Language & Sentence Skills Practice,* pp. 61–65

Differentiating Instruction

- *Developmental Language & Sentence Skills,* pp. 39–42

NOTE Do not be misled by a modifier coming after the noun or pronoun in a prepositional phrase. The noun or pronoun is still the object.

EXAMPLE Heidi and Mrs. Braun worked **at the polls** today. [*Polls* is the object of the preposition *at.* The adverb *today* tells when and modifies the verb *worked.*]

Objects of prepositions may be compound.

EXAMPLES On the plaza, a guitarist sang for **Victor** and **me.** [The preposition *for* has a compound object: *Victor* and *me.*]

In A.D. 79, the city of Pompeii was buried beneath **lava, rocks,** and **ashes.** [The preposition *beneath* has a compound object: *lava, rocks,* and *ashes.*]

A prepositional phrase can modify the object of another prepositional phrase.

EXAMPLE Next to the door **of the old barn** stood two horses. [The prepositional phrase *of the old barn* modifies *door,* which is the object of the compound preposition *Next to.*]

A prepositional phrase can contain another prepositional phrase.

EXAMPLE Meet us **at the Museum of Science and Industry.** [The prepositional phrase *at the Museum of Science and Industry* contains the prepositional phrase *of Science and Industry.*]

NOTE Sometimes a prepositional phrase is combined with a noun to form a compound noun.

EXAMPLES

Strait of Hormuz	hole in one
Stratford-on-Avon	University of Pittsburgh

The Adjective Phrase

3d. A prepositional phrase that modifies a noun or pronoun is called an *adjective phrase.*

EXAMPLE The members **of the club** want sweatshirts **with the club emblem.** [The prepositional phrase *of the club* is used as an adjective to modify the noun *members. With the club emblem* is used as an adjective to modify the noun *sweatshirts.*]

TIPS & TRICKS

Be careful not to confuse the preposition *to* with the *to* that is the sign of the verb's infinitive form: *to swim, to know, to see.*

Reference Note

For more about **infinitives,** see page 85.

Reference Note

For more about **compound nouns,** see page 4.

DIFFERENTIATING INSTRUCTION

GRAMMAR

English-Language Learners

General Strategies. Some English-language learners might have difficulty sorting out the meanings of the various prepositions. To help eliminate this confusion, have students act out the following prepositional phrases.

across the room
on the chair
in her purse
from me
to you
at the pencil sharpener
between the two desks
in front of the chalkboard
behind the door

If you notice that students are confusing one preposition with another in their writing, explain the correct uses of both the preposition they used and the preposition they should have used, providing examples and a simple definition of each one. Then, have students draw simple illustrations to show the distinction between the words that they are confusing.

GRAMMAR

DIRECT TEACHING

Modeling and Demonstration

Prepositional Phrases. Model how to identify adjective phrases and the words they modify by using the example *The members of the club want sweatshirts with the club emblem.* First, ask whether the sentence contains any prepositional phrases. [*yes;* of the club, with the club emblem] Next, ask what word or words *of the club* modifies. [*members*] Ask what part of speech *members* is. [*noun*] Explain that *of the club* is an adjective phrase because it modifies the noun *members.* Then, ask what *with the club emblem* modifies. [*sweatshirts*] Next, ask what part of speech *sweatshirts* is. [*noun*] Ask what kind of prepositional phrase *with the club emblem* is. [*adjective phrase*] Now, have a volunteer use another example from this chapter to demonstrate how to identify adjective phrases.

Unlike a one-word adjective, which usually precedes the word it modifies, an adjective phrase almost always follows the noun or pronoun it modifies.

ADJECTIVE Amy closed the **cellar** door.
ADJECTIVE PHRASE Amy closed the door **to the cellar.**

More than one adjective phrase may modify the same word.

EXAMPLE Here's a letter **for you from Aunt Martha.** [The prepositional phrases *for you* and *from Aunt Martha* both modify the noun *letter.*]

An adjective phrase may also modify the object of another prepositional phrase.

EXAMPLE The horse **in the trailer with the rusted latch** broke loose. [The phrase *in the trailer* modifies the noun *horse. Trailer* is the object of the preposition *in.* The phrase *with the rusted latch* modifies *trailer.*]

Often you can convert the objects of adjective phrases into adjectives. Doing so makes your writing less wordy.

Adjective Phrases	Nouns Used as Adjectives
The light **in the kitchen** is on.	The **kitchen** light is on.
The airports **in Chicago and New York** are crowded.	The **Chicago** and **New York** airports are crowded.

However, not all adjective phrases can be changed into one-word modifiers that make sense. Sometimes, changing an adjective phrase makes a sentence awkward and ungrammatical.

CLEAR Please hand me the book on the table.
AWKWARD Please hand me the table book.

HELP—Some sentences in Exercise 1 contain more than one adjective phrase.

Exercise 1 **Identifying Adjective Phrases**

Identify the adjective phrases in the following paragraph, and give the word that each modifies.

EXAMPLE **[1]** A few years ago our family visited South Dakota and saw a famous monument to great American leaders.

1. *to great American leaders—monument*

[1] My mom took the pictures on the next page when we were visiting this scenic spot at Mount Rushmore National Memorial. [2] As

you can see, the mountainside behind us is a lasting tribute to George Washington, Thomas Jefferson, Theodore Roosevelt, and Abraham Lincoln. [**3**] The figures on the granite cliff were carved under the direction of Gutzon Borglum, an American sculptor. [**4**] Looking at the sculpture, I can certainly believe that this is one of the world's largest. [**5**] The faces are sixty feet high and show a great deal of detail and expression. [**6**] Each president symbolizes a part of United States history. [**7**] Washington represents the founding of the country, and Jefferson signifies the Declaration of Independence. [**8**] Lincoln symbolizes an end to slavery, and Roosevelt stands for expansion and resource conservation. [**9**] Tourists on the viewing terrace must gaze up nearly five hundred feet to see this art. [**10**] As both symbols for the nation and works of art, these massive faces are an inspiration to all who visit Mount Rushmore.

The Adverb Phrase

3e. A prepositional phrase that modifies a verb, an adjective, or an adverb is called an *adverb phrase.*

An adverb phrase tells *how, when, where, why,* or *to what extent.*

EXAMPLES

Britney answered **with a smile.** [The adverb phrase *with a smile* tells *how* Britney answered.]

They sailed **across the lake** yesterday. [The adverb phrase *across the lake* tells *where* they sailed.]

By Wednesday Christopher will be finished. [The adverb phrase *By Wednesday* tells *when* Christopher will be finished.]

The calculations erred **by more than two inches.** [*By more than two inches* is an adverb phrase telling *to what extent* the calculations erred.]

In the examples above, the adverb phrases all modify verbs.

GRAMMAR

Exercise 1

DISTRIBUTED REVIEW
Have students find the following items:

1. a compound proper noun used in a prepositional phrase and referring to a place [*sentence 1: Mount Rushmore National Memorial*]
2. a two-word proper adjective [*sentence 6: United States*]
3. a compound proper noun used as a direct object [*sentence 7: Declaration of Independence; sentence 10: Mount Rushmore*]

EXTENSION

Relating to Writing

Divide the class into small groups. Have each group collaborate to write a brief description of Mount Rushmore. Give each student in the group the chance to add one or two prepositional phrases. Then, have each group edit its description collaboratively. Volunteers may read completed descriptions to the class.

Differentiating Instruction

English-Language Learners

Cantonese. In Cantonese, adverbials tend to come at the beginning of the sentence. Cantonese speakers will often say:

With a smile, Britney answered.
Across the lake they sailed yesterday.

While this syntax is sometimes acceptable in English, it is not the most common pattern. Discuss the difference in emphasis that occurs when the adverbial comes at the beginning versus the end of the sentence. Ask students to write sentences containing adverbials about their own lives, and discuss when they might put the adverbial at the beginning for emphasis.

Example: All week long I go to school and study at night. So on Saturday, I like to play soccer to relax.

STYLE TIP 

Be sure to place phrases carefully so that they express the meaning you intend.

EXAMPLES

The conductor complimented Lia's performance after the concert. [Did Lia perform after the concert was over?]

After the concert, the conductor complimented Lia's performance. [The compliment was made after the concert.]

HELP

Some sentences in Exercise 2 contain more than one phrase.

An adverb phrase may modify an adjective or an adverb.

EXAMPLES Melissa is good **at tennis** but better **at volleyball.** [The adverb phrase *at tennis* modifies the adjective *good.* The adverb phrase *at volleyball* modifies the adjective *better.*]

Is the water warm enough **for swimming**? [The adverb phrase *for swimming* modifies the adverb *enough.*]

Adjective phrases almost always follow the words they modify, but an adverb phrase may appear at various places in a sentence.

EXAMPLES **Before noon** the race started.

The race started **before noon.**

Like adjective phrases, more than one adverb phrase may modify the same word.

EXAMPLE **During summers,** my older sister works **at the museum.** [The adverb phrases *During summers* and *at the museum* both modify the verb *works.* The first phrase tells *when* my sister works; the second phrase tells *where* she works.]

Exercise 2 Identifying Adverb Phrases

Identify the adverb phrases in the following sentences, and give the word or words each phrase modifies.

EXAMPLE
1. The concept of time has inspired many figures of speech over the years.
1. *over the years—has inspired*

1. We use time expressions in everyday speech.
2. In conversation, you may have heard the expression "time out of mind," which means "long ago."
3. When you fall in love, you may feel that "time stands still."
4. Is twenty minutes too long for a "time-out"?
5. If something happens "in no time," it happens very fast.
6. Have you ever noticed that "time flies" when you are chatting with your friends?
7. However, if you are sitting in a waiting room, "time drags."
8. Are you keeping someone's secret "until the end of time"?
9. Do people stop you on the street to ask if you "have the time"?
10. In the meantime, "time marches on" under the steady gaze of "Father Time."

CONTENT-AREA CONNECTIONS

Art

Adverb Phrases. After students complete **Exercise 2,** ask them to select one of the adverb phrases from the exercise and create an artwork that illustrates the meaning of the sentence. Encourage students to be as creative as possible, and remind them that representing the relationship indicated by the adverb phrase is more important than the quality of their drawings. You can point out that even stick figures can communicate the meaning of an adverb phrase.

Review A **Writing Sentences Using Adjective and Adverb Phrases**

You are a reporter for your school newspaper. The Young Business Leaders Club has given you an announcement for its upcoming banquet. Write an article about this event, using the information from the announcement below. Use five adjective phrases and five adverb phrases to help you include the necessary information in your article.

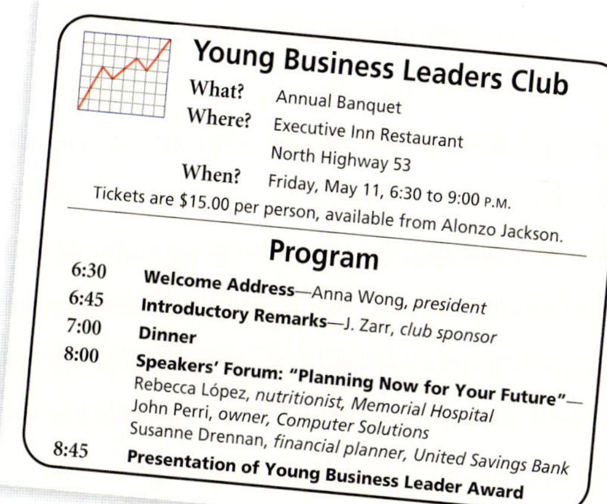
Young Business Leaders Club

What? Annual Banquet
Where? Executive Inn Restaurant
North Highway 53
When? Friday, May 11, 6:30 to 9:00 P.M.
Tickets are $15.00 per person, available from Alonzo Jackson.

Program

6:30 **Welcome Address**—*Anna Wong, president*
6:45 **Introductory Remarks**—*J. Zarr, club sponsor*
7:00 **Dinner**
8:00 **Speakers' Forum: "Planning Now for Your Future"**—
Rebecca López, *nutritionist, Memorial Hospital*
John Perri, *owner, Computer Solutions*
Susanne Drennan, *financial planner, United Savings Bank*
8:45 **Presentation of Young Business Leader Award**

Review B **Identifying Adjective and Adverb Phrases**

Identify each italicized prepositional phrase in the following paragraph as an adjective phrase or as an adverb phrase. Then, identify the word or words each phrase modifies.

EXAMPLE I enjoy reading all sorts **[1]** *of myths and legends.*

1. *adjective phrase—sorts*

Have you heard the Greek myth [1] *about Narcissus and Echo*? It is a story rich [2] *in irony.* Narcissus was a handsome young man [3] *with many admirers.* However, he rejected everyone who loved him, including the nymph Echo. As punishment [4] *for his arrogant behavior,* the gods sentenced Narcissus to stare forever [5] *at his own reflection* [6] *in a pond.* [7] *For days,* Narcissus gazed adoringly [8] *at himself.* Echo the nymph stayed [9] *with him* until she wasted away. Finally Narcissus, too, wasted away, and when he died he turned [10] *into the narcissus flower.*

MEETING THE CHALLENGE

You can use adjective phrases and adverb phrases to add necessary detail in your writing. Write directions from one place in your school to another. In your directions, use at least five adjective phrases and five adverb phrases. Check your directions, and make sure that your directions are detailed enough that even someone completely new to your school could follow them.

ANSWERS

Directions will vary but should contain at least five adverb phrases and five adjective phrases.

1. adj.
2. adv. 3. adj.
4. adj.
5. adv. 6. adj.
7. adv. 8. adv.
9. adv.
10. adv.

DIFFERENTIATING INSTRUCTION

GRAMMAR

Special Education Students

Have students visualize the banquet referred to in **Review A.** Have a helper ask students what they see and record on tape or list on paper the phrases they use.

The helper may need to prompt students with questions such as "Where are the tables?" or "How many people are attending?"

Once the list is complete, have students use the phrases to create their articles. Students who have difficulty writing may record their stories on audiotape or dictate them to a helper, who can record the information in writing or on a computer.

Review A **Writing Sentences Using Adjective and Adverb Phrases**

POSSIBLE ANSWERS

Adjective phrases are underlined once; adverb phrases are underlined twice.

The Young Business Leaders Club announced yesterday the date and program for its annual banquet. The event will be held at the Executive Inn Restaurant, North Highway 53, on Friday, May 11, at 6:30 P.M.

A speakers' forum on the subject of "Planning Now for Your Future" will follow the dinner. Participants are Rebecca López, a nutritionist at Memorial Hospital; John Perri, owner of Computer Solutions; and Susanne Drennan, a financial planner for United Savings Bank. Presentation of the Young Business Leader Award will follow the forum.

Tickets may be purchased from Alonzo Jackson for $15.00 each.

GRAMMAR

RETEACHING

Prepositional Phrases

If students have difficulty understanding the concept that a sentence develops by adding chunks of information, use specific colors to denote parts of the sentence and the prepositional phrases. For example, make the simple subject red, the verb or verb phrase yellow, the complements blue, and prepositional phrases green.

Show sentence 1 from **Review C** written on a transparency, and let students identify the parts of the sentence and prepositional phrases and tell which color to use to highlight them. [*Edwin Hubble:* red; *discovered:* yellow; *the existence:* blue; *About seventy years ago:* green; *of galaxies:* green; *outside the Milky Way:* green.]

You may wish to have students use this color coding to continue **Review C** on their own or in pairs. You may also want to have students use a similar color-coding technique as they work with other types of phrases in the chapter.

HELP — In the example for Review C, *about the universe* modifies *Theories,* and *over the years* modifies *have changed.*

1. adv./adj./adj.
2. adv./adj.
3. adj./adj.
4. adv./adj.
5. adv./adv.
6. adv./adv./adj./adj.
7. adv./adj.
8. adv./adv./adj.
9. adv./adv.
10. adv./adj./adj. [*or* would be amazed]

Review C Identifying and Classifying Prepositional Phrases

List all the prepositional phrases in each of the following sentences. Write *adj.* if the phrase is used as an adjective; write *adv.* if the phrase is used as an adverb. Be prepared to identify the word each phrase modifies.

EXAMPLE **1.** Theories about the universe have changed over the years.

1. about the universe—adj.; over the years—adv.

1. In 1929, Edwin Hubble discovered the existence of galaxies outside the Milky Way.
2. Now we know that perhaps a million galaxies exist inside the bowl of the Big Dipper alone.
3. Astronomers believe that our galaxy is only one among billions throughout the universe.
4. Knowledge has expanded since 500 years ago, when most people believed that the earth was the center of the entire universe.
5. By the 1500s, the Polish astronomer Copernicus suggested that the earth and other planets revolved around the sun.
6. In 1633, the Italian scientist Galileo was tried and convicted for the crime of teaching that the sun is the center of the universe.
7. The Catholic Church condemned Galileo because in his teachings earth and humans were not the center of all things.
8. In Galileo's time, people knew of only five planets besides our own—Mercury, Venus, Mars, Jupiter, and Saturn.
9. Since then we have identified the planets Uranus, Neptune, and Pluto, and we have sent probes into our solar system.
10. Galileo, Copernicus, and other early astronomers would be amazed at the extent of our knowledge of space today.

Verbals and Verbal Phrases

Verbals are formed from verbs. Like verbs, they may have modifiers and complements. However, verbals are used as nouns, adjectives, or adverbs, not as verbs. The three kinds of verbals are *participles, gerunds,* and *infinitives.*

The Participle

3f. A *participle* is a verb form that can be used as an adjective.

EXAMPLES We saw the raccoon **escaping** through the back door. [The participle *escaping,* formed from the verb *escape,* modifies the noun *raccoon.*]

Waxed floors can be dangerously slippery. [The participle *Waxed,* formed from the verb *wax,* modifies the noun *floors.*]

Two kinds of participles are *present participles* and *past participles.*

(1) Present participles end in *–ing.*

EXAMPLES We ran inside to get out of the **pouring** rain. [The present participle *pouring* modifies the noun *rain.*]

Watching the clock, the coach became worried. [The present participle *watching* modifies the noun *coach.*]

Although participles are forms of verbs, they cannot stand alone as verbs. Participles need to be joined to a helping verb to form a verb phrase. When a participle is used in a verb phrase, it is part of the verb and is not an adjective.

VERB PHRASES The rain **was pouring.**

The coach **had been watching** the clock.

(2) Past participles usually end in *–d* or *–ed.* Other past participles are formed irregularly.

EXAMPLES A **peeled** and **sliced** cucumber can be added to a garden salad. [The past participles *peeled* and *sliced* modify the noun *cucumber.*]

The speaker, **known** for her strong support of recycling, was loudly applauded. [The irregular past participle *known* modifies the noun *speaker.*]

Reference Note

For a discussion of **irregular verbs,** see page 147.

GRAMMAR

The Participle and the Participial Phrase

Rules 3f, g *(pp. 77–81)*

OBJECTIVES

- **To identify participles and the words they modify**
- **To complete sentences by supplying appropriate participles**
- **To identify participial phrases and the words they modify**

DIFFERENTIATING INSTRUCTION

English-Language Learners

Vietnamese. Vietnamese lacks the suffixes that often change the form of a word in English from a verb to an adjective, or a noun to a verb. Vietnamese speakers may tend to use the base form of a word in all positions, such as:

Wax floors can be dangerously slippery.
The cucumber was **peel** and **slice.**

Suffixes such as *–ed* may be hard to hear in natural speech. A good way to call students' attention to the suffixes and their use is to write words on cards or slips of paper and have students arrange them into sentences, adding the suffixes where appropriate.

The Participle and the Participial Phrase

Practice

- *Language & Sentence Skills Practice,* pp. 66–68

Differentiating Instruction

- *Developmental Language & Sentence Skills,* pp. 43–44

GRAMMAR

Direct Teaching

Correcting Misconceptions

Participial Phrases. Students may think that words ending in *–ing, –ed,* or *–en* are always part of the main verb. To help students confused by participial phrases, have them begin by finding one-word participles in sentences 1, 3, 7, and 10 in **Exercise 3.** [1. *prancing;* 3. *swaggering, boasting;* 7. *banging (students may also spot* walking, *which is part of a participial phrase);* 10. *stirring (students may also spot* marching, *which is part of a participial phrase)*].

Have students approach the exercise by first finding and color-coding the subject and verb for the sentences designated above, as students did for the reteaching activity on p. 76. Then, have students find each participle and the noun or pronoun it modifies.

To help students recognize that participles act as adjectives, have them substitute adjectives for participles (for example, *gray* for *prancing* in sentence 1).

Exercise 3

DISTRIBUTED REVIEW

To review verbs, have students list the verbs or verb phrases in sentences 1, 4, 7, 9, and 10 of **Exercise 4.**

1. were applauded
4. was postponed
7. thought, was
9. turned, fled
10. crossed

Like a present participle, a past participle can also be part of a verb phrase. When a past participle is used in a verb phrase, it is part of the verb and is not an adjective.

VERB PHRASES I **have peeled** and **sliced** the cucumber.

The speaker **was known** for her strong support of recycling.

Reference Note

For more about the **passive voice,** see page 163.

NOTE Notice in the second example above that a past participle used with a form of the verb *be* creates a *passive-voice* verb. A verb in the passive voice expresses an action done to its subject.

EXAMPLE The goal **was made** by Josh. [The action of the verb *was made* is done to the subject *goal.*]

Exercise 3 Identifying Participles and the Words They Modify

HELP — Some sentences in Exercise 3 contain more than one participle used as an adjective.

Identify the participles used as adjectives in each of the following sentences. After each participle, write the noun or pronoun it modifies.

EXAMPLES
1. We searched the island for buried treasure.
   1. buried—treasure
2. The speeding train raced past the platform.
   2. speeding—train

1. The prancing horses were loudly applauded by the audience.
2. Colorful flags, waving in the breeze, brightened the gloomy day.
3. Swaggering and boasting, the new varsity quarterback made us extremely angry.
4. The game scheduled for tonight was postponed because of rain.
5. Leaving the field, the happy player rushed to her parents sitting in the bleachers.
6. Branches tapping on the roof and leaves rustling in the wind made an eerie sound.
7. We thought the banging shutter upstairs was someone walking in the attic.
8. Painfully sunburned, I vowed always to use sunscreen and never to be so careless again.
9. Terrified by our dog, the burglar turned and fled across the yard.
10. The platoon of soldiers, marching in step, crossed the field to the stirring music of the military band.

MINI-LESSON Mechanics

Punctuating Participial Phrases. Explain to students that commas are used to set off nonessential participial phrases. Then, write the following sentences on the chalkboard, and discuss them with the class.

1. Written by hand, the essay was messy. [*Introductory participial phrases always require a comma.*]
2. Tenth-graders entering the essay contest should go to the auditorium. [*The phrase*

Exercise 4 Using Appropriate Participles

For each blank in the following sentences, provide a participle that fits the meaning of the sentence.

EXAMPLE 1. The ____ tide washed over the beach.

1. *rising*

Answers will vary.

1. Mr. Ortiz explained the effects of pollution and drought on plants ____ in a rain forest. **1.** growing
2. ____ from the point of view of a firefighter, the story is full of accurate details. **2.** Told
3. The tiger, ____ from the hunters, swam across the river to safety. **3.** running
4. ____ at the traffic light, the driver put on his sunglasses. **4.** Waiting
5. The tourists ____ in the hotel were given a free meal. **5.** staying
6. ____ as an excellent place to camp, the park lived up to its reputation. **6.** Known
7. ____ by a bee, Steven hurried to the infirmary. **7.** Stung
8. The poem describes a spider ____ on a thread. **8.** dangling
9. We stumbled off the racecourse, ____. **9.** gasping
10. ____, I quickly phoned the hospital. **10.** Aching

Reference Note

For information on **punctuating participial phrases,** see page 281. The participle as a **dangling modifier** is discussed on page 213. For information on **using participles to combine sentences,** see page 453.

The Participial Phrase

3g. A *participial phrase* is used as an adjective and consists of a participle and any complements or modifiers the participle has.

EXAMPLES **Seeing the cat,** the dog barked loudly.

The cat hissed at the dog **barking in the yard next door.**

The dog **noisily barking at the cat** had to be brought in.

In each of the following sentences, an arrow points from the participial phrase to the noun or pronoun that the phrase modifies.

EXAMPLES **Switching its tail,** the mountain lion paced back and forth. [participle with object *tail*]

She heard me **sighing loudly.** [participle with the adverb *loudly*]

Living within his budget, Adam never needs to borrow money. [participle with adverb phrase *within his budget*]

Quickly grabbing the keys, I dashed for the front door. [participle with preceding adverb *Quickly* and object *keys*]

HELP

A participial phrase should be placed very close to the word it modifies. Otherwise, the phrase may appear to modify another word, and the sentence may not make sense.

MISPLACED

He saw a moose riding his motorcycle through the woods. [The placement of the modifier *riding his motorcycle* calls up a silly picture. He, not the moose, is riding the motorcycle.]

IMPROVED

Riding his motorcycle through the woods, he saw a moose.

entering the essay contest *is necessary to the meaning of the sentence.*]

3. The Carters' house, built in the early 1950s, has beautiful hardwood floors. [*The phrase* built in the early 1950s *contains information that is not needed to understand the meaning of the sentence.*]

For more information on punctuating participial phrases, refer students to **Chapter 11: Punctuation.**

GRAMMAR

Differentiating Instruction

Learners Having Difficulty

Sometimes students have trouble seeing that a participial phrase functions as an adjective in a sentence. Write the following pairs of sentences on the chalkboard, and have students compare how participles are used in them. Be sure to explain that the participle in each pair modifies the same word.

1. The confused contestant failed to answer in time.

   Confused by the tricky question, the contestant failed to answer in time.

2. The damaged boat rocked wildly.

   Damaged by the storm, the boat rocked wildly.

Extension

Relating to Writing

To extend students' experience using verbals, ask them to write descriptive paragraphs about a journey from one place to another. The paragraphs may describe a real event, such as taking the wrong bus home from school or traveling on a family vacation, or an imaginary account of a fictional character's adventure. Instruct students to use participles and participial phrases to add detail and give variety to their sentences.

Exercise 5 Identifying Participial Phrases

Identify the participial phrases in the following sentences, and give the word each phrase modifies.

EXAMPLE 1. The sight of skyscrapers towering against the sky always impresses me.

1. towering against the sky—skyscrapers

1. How are skyscrapers created, and what keeps them standing tall?
2. As the drawing shows, columns of steel or of concrete reinforced with steel are sunk into bedrock beneath the building.
3. If a layer of rock isn't present, these columns are sunk into a thick concrete pad spread across the bottom of a deep basement.
4. From this foundation rises a steel skeleton, supporting the walls and floors.
5. This cutaway drawing shows how this skeleton, covered with a "skin" of glass and metal, becomes a safe working and living space for people.
6. This method of building, first developed in the United States, is used now in many other places in the world.
7. Chicago, nearly destroyed by fire in 1871, was later rebuilt with innovative designs.
8. The first skyscraper constructed on a metal frame was built there during this period.
9. Architects, using the latest materials, were glad to design in new ways.
10. Chicago, known as the site of the original 10-story skyscraper, now is home to the 110-story Sears Tower.

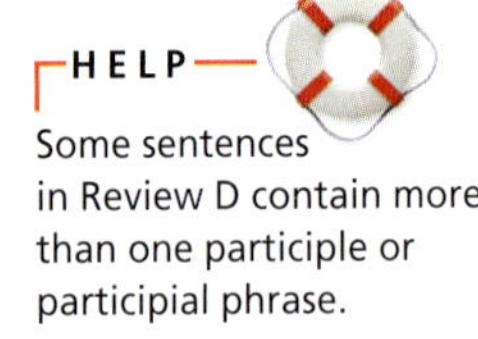

HELP—Some sentences in Review D contain more than one participle or participial phrase.

Review D Identifying Participles and Participial Phrases

Identify the participial phrases and participles that are used as adjectives in the following sentences. Then, give the words they modify.

EXAMPLE 1. Cats, known for their pride and independence, are supposedly hard to train.

1. known for their pride and independence—Cats

1. One day I was giving Chops, my spoiled cat, treats.
2. Standing on her hind legs, she reached up with her paw.
3. Chops, grabbing for my fingers, tried to bring the tasty morsel closer.

Mini-Lesson Usage

Misplaced Modifiers. Remind students that participles, like adjectives, must be placed near the words they modify. A participle placed by the wrong word is called a **misplaced modifier.**

Have students try to correct the following misplaced modifier: *Rising above the horizon, the scientists viewed the full moon.* [*The scientists viewed the full moon rising above the horizon.*] A volunteer might draw cartoon-style illustrations of both the sentence with the misplaced modifier and the corrected version.

4. Pulling my hand back a little, I tugged gently on her curved paw, and she stepped forward.
5. Praising my clever cat, I immediately gave her two treats.
6. The next time I held a treat up high, Chops, puzzled but eager, repeated the grab-and-step movement.
7. Soon Chops was taking steps toward treats held out of her reach.
8. I now have an educated cat who can walk on two legs.
9. Grabbing the treats and gobbling them down, she has learned that certain moves always get her a snack.
10. Sometimes after Chops has had her treat, she just sits and looks at me, no doubt thinking that humans are truly a strange bunch!

The Gerund

3h. A *gerund* is a verb form ending in *–ing* that is used as a noun.

Like other nouns, gerunds are used as subjects, predicate nominatives, direct objects, indirect objects, and objects of prepositions.

EXAMPLES The **dancing** was fun. [subject]

My favorite part of the show was his **juggling.** [predicate nominative]

Shauna tried **climbing** faster. [direct object]

Give **winning** the game your best. [indirect object]

We worked better after **resting.** [object of a preposition]

Like other nouns, gerunds may be modified by adjectives and adjective phrases.

EXAMPLES We listened to **the beautiful** singing **of the famous soprano.** [The article *the,* the adjective *beautiful,* and the adjective phrase *of the famous soprano* modify the gerund *singing. Singing* is used as the object of the preposition *to.*]

The Mallorys enjoy talking **about their vacation.** [The adjective phrase *about their vacation* modifies the gerund *talking,* which is the direct object of the verb *enjoy.*]

The harsh clacking **of the tappets** alerted us to a serious problem in the car's engine. [The article *The,* the adjective *harsh,* and the adjective phrase *of the tappets* modify the gerund *clacking.*]

GRAMMAR

The Gerund and the Gerund Phrase

Rules 3h, i *(pp. 81–84)*

OBJECTIVES

- **To identify and classify gerunds**
- **To identify and classify gerund phrases**

DIFFERENTIATING INSTRUCTION

English-Language Learners

General Strategies. Before introducing the gerund, you may want to review the basic functions of nouns. Remind students of the following points:

- A subject is the main part of a sentence or a clause and must have a predicate; it is the doer of the action.
- A predicate nominative is usually placed after a linking verb and explains or identifies the subject.
- A direct object answers the question *what* or *whom* after the verb.

RESOURCES

The Gerund and the Gerund Phrase

Practice

- *Language & Sentence Skills Practice,* pp. 69–72

Differentiating Instruction

- *Developmental Language & Sentence Skills,* pp. 45–46

GRAMMAR

Direct Teaching

Modeling and Demonstration

The Gerund and the Gerund Phrase. Model how to identify and classify gerunds by using the example *Swimming is my second-favorite sport, after cycling.* First, ask which word is the main verb. [*is*] Next, ask which words in the example are verbals. [*swimming, cycling*] Then, ask what the subject of the sentence is. [*swimming*] Explain that *swimming* is a gerund because it is a verbal acting as a noun. Ask if *cycling* is also a gerund in this sentence. [*yes*] Point out that, like a noun, *cycling* acts as the object of the preposition *after.* Now, have a volunteer use another example from this chapter to demonstrate how to identify and classify gerunds.

Application

Gerunds

Divide the class into four teams, and assign each team one of these four categories: subject, predicate nominative, direct object, and object of a preposition.

Write the following gerunds on the chalkboard:

asking	leaping	swinging
diving	marching	tumbling
flying	skipping	twirling

Ask each team to write sentences using these gerunds according to the team's designation (the subject team will use the gerunds only as subjects, and so on). Allow a time limit of fifteen minutes, and then have teams share their sentences with the rest of the class.

Like verbs, gerunds may also be modified by adverbs and adverb phrases.

EXAMPLES Reading **widely** is one way to acquire judgment, maturity, and a good education. [The gerund *Reading* is the subject of the verb *is.* The adverb *widely* modifies the gerund *Reading.*]

Floating **lazily in the pool** is my favorite summer pastime. [The gerund *Floating* is used as the subject of the sentence. It is modified by the adverb *lazily* (telling *how*) and also by the adverb phrase *in the pool* (telling *where*).]

Brandywine likes galloping **briskly on a cold morning.** [The gerund *galloping* is the direct object of the verb *likes.* The adverb *briskly* (telling *how*) and the adverb phrase *on a cold morning* (telling *when*) both modify *galloping.*]

Gerunds, like present participles, end in *–ing.* To be a gerund, a verbal must be used as a noun. In the following sentence, three words end in *–ing,* but only one of them is a gerund.

EXAMPLE **Circling** the runway, the pilot was **preparing** for **landing.** [*Circling* is a present participle modifying *pilot. Preparing* is part of the verb phrase *was preparing.* Only *landing,* used as the object of the preposition *for,* is a gerund.]

Exercise 6 Identifying and Classifying Gerunds

Identify each gerund in the following sentences. Then, write how each is used: as a *subject,* a *predicate nominative,* a *direct object,* or an *object of a preposition.*

EXAMPLE 1. Instead of driving, let's walk.

1. driving—object of a preposition

1. subj. 1. Her laughing attracted my attention.
2. o.p. 2. By studying, you can improve your grades.
3. d.o. 3. Why did the birds stop chirping?
4. subj. 4. Writing in my journal has helped me understand myself better.
5. d.o. 5. Smiling, Dad said that we would all go to a movie when we had finished the cleaning.
6. p.n. 6. What Joseph liked best was hiking to the peak.
7. o.p. 7. Before leaving the beach, we sat and watched the fading light.
8. d.o. 8. Yesterday, Mrs. Jacobs was discussing having a garage sale.
9. p.n. 9. One of Alvin's bad habits is boasting.
10. o.p. 10. Without knocking, the crying child threw open the door.

The Gerund Phrase

3i. A *gerund phrase* consists of a gerund and any modifiers or complements the gerund has. The entire phrase is used as a noun.

EXAMPLES **The gentle pattering of the rain** was a welcome sound. [The gerund phrase is the subject of the sentence. The gerund *pattering* is modified by the article *The,* the adjective *gentle,* and the prepositional phrase *of the rain.* Notice that the modifiers preceding the gerund are included in the gerund phrase.]

I feared **skiing down the mountain alone.** [The gerund phrase is used as the object of the verb *feared.* The gerund *skiing* is modified by the prepositional phrase *down the mountain* and by the adverb *alone.*]

My dog's favorite game is **bringing me the newspaper.** [The gerund phrase is used as a predicate nominative. The gerund *bringing* has a direct object, *newspaper,* and an indirect object, *me.*]

Evelyn Ashford won a gold medal for **running the 100-meter dash.** [The gerund phrase is the object of the preposition *for.* The gerund *running* has a direct object, *dash.*]

STYLE TIP

A noun or a pronoun that comes before a gerund should be in the possessive form.

EXAMPLES

My playing the radio loudly is a bad habit.

Ed's constant TV watching interferes with **our** studying.

Exercise 7 Identifying and Classifying Gerund Phrases

Find the gerund phrases in the following sentences. Then, tell how each phrase is used: as a *subject,* a *predicate nominative,* a *direct object,* or an *object of a preposition.*

EXAMPLE 1. My favorite hunting trophies are the ones I get by photographing wild animals.

1. *photographing wild animals—object of a preposition*

HELP

Sentences in Exercise 7 may contain more than one gerund phrase.

1. Exciting and challenging, wildlife photography is surprisingly similar to pursuing prey on a hunt. 1. o.p.
2. In both activities, knowing the animals' habits and habitats is vital to success. 2. subj.
3. Scouting out locations is important to both the hunter and the nature photographer. 3. subj.
4. This preparation gives you time for figuring out the best natural light for photography. 4. o.p.

GRAMMAR

DIFFERENTIATING INSTRUCTION

Learners Having Difficulty

Provide pieces of construction paper, glue sticks, and strips of brown, red, blue, green, and yellow paper. Tell students they will be using the art materials to color-code sentence parts and prepositional phrases. Tell students to begin by finding the verb in the first sentence of **Exercise 7** and writing it on a strip of brown paper. Then, assign red to subjects, blue to direct objects, yellow to predicate nominatives, and green to prepositional phrases. Ask students to re-create these portions of the sentences by writing the words on appropriate strips, arranging the strips on the construction paper, and gluing them into place. Students may want to write the missing parts of the sentences in the appropriate places using a standard lead pencil.

GRAMMAR

Differentiating Instruction

Advanced Learners

You may give advanced students revision practice by asking them to rewrite a sentence in two ways, once with a present participle and once with a gerund.

Here are two sentences you might use:

1. Dad is preparing tonight's dinner.

[*Possible revisions: We could hear Dad preparing tonight's dinner. (Part.) Preparing tonight's dinner was Dad's idea. (Ger.)*]

2. His first priority is to prepare for final exams.

[*Possible revisions: Preparing for final exams, he saw grades as his first priority. (Part.) Preparing for final exams is his first priority. (Ger.)*]

Challenge students to show their flexibility with language by finding and rewriting other sentences.

5. Other important skills are being quiet and keeping your aim very steady. **5.** p.n./p.n.
6. In photography, you must also consider choosing the correct film. **6.** d.o.
7. Photographers often like taking pictures of animals feeding near ponds and rivers. **7.** d.o.
8. Setting up a tripod and camera in underbrush nearby is a way to be ready when the animals come. **8.** subj.
9. Advance preparation often makes the difference between getting good pictures and getting great ones. **9.** o.p./o.p.
10. Your patience and skill are rewarded when you "capture" a wild creature without scaring it. **10.** o.p.

Review E **Identifying and Classifying Gerunds and Gerund Phrases**

Identify the gerunds or gerund phrases in the following sentences. Then, tell how each is used: as a *subject,* a *predicate nominative,* a *direct object,* or an *object of a preposition.*

EXAMPLE **1.** Drawing a good caricature is hard to do.

1. Drawing a good caricature—subject

1. A caricature is a picture, usually of a person, that draws attention to key features by emphasizing them. **1.** o.p.
2. Usually, caricature artists enjoy poking fun at famous people. **2.** d.o.
3. Looking at caricatures is an entertaining way to capture the "feel" of a historical period. **3.** subj.
4. No one looking at this sketch of Teddy Roosevelt can help smiling. **4.** d.o.
5. The artist began by simplifying the shape of his subject's head. **5.** o.p.
6. Then he started outlining the temples and round cheeks with bold strokes of his pen. **6.** d.o.
7. As you probably realize, magnifying reality is very important to good caricature. **7.** subj.
8. By enlarging Roosevelt's engaging grin and bristly mustache, the artist emphasizes these features and suggests Roosevelt's energetic, outgoing personality. **8.** o.p.
9. The artist also uses his subject's narrowed eyes and oval glasses for comic effect by drawing them closer together than they really were. **9.** o.p.
10. Exaggerating Roosevelt's features has resulted in an amusing but unmistakable likeness. **10.** subj.

The Infinitive

3j. An *infinitive* is a verb form that can be used as a noun, an adjective, or an adverb. Most infinitives begin with *to*.

Infinitives can be used as nouns.

EXAMPLES **To fly** is glorious. [*To fly* is the subject of the sentence.]

Brandon wanted **to work** on the play. [*To work* is the object of the verb *wanted*.]

Infinitives can be used as adjectives.

EXAMPLES The place **to visit** is Williamsburg. [*To visit* modifies the noun *place*.]

That record was the one **to beat.** [*To beat* modifies the pronoun *one*.]

Infinitives also can be used as adverbs.

EXAMPLES Sabina jumped **to look.** [*To look* modifies the verb *jumped*.]

Ready **to go,** we soon loaded the car. [*To go* modifies the adjective *Ready*.]

NOTE *To* plus a noun or a pronoun (*to school, to him, to the beach*) is a prepositional phrase, not an infinitive.

Exercise 8 Identifying and Classifying Infinitives

Identify the infinitives in the following sentences. Then, tell how each infinitive is used: as a *noun*, an *adjective*, or an *adverb*.

EXAMPLE 1. I would like to help you.
1. to help—noun

1. Tamisha's ambition is to teach. 1. n.
2. To persist can sometimes be a sign of stubbornness. 2. n.
3. Chen has learned to tap dance. 3. n.
4. I am happy to oblige. 4. adv.
5. An easy way to win at tennis does not exist. 5. adj.
6. We need to weed the garden soon. 6. n.
7. The hockey team went to Coach Norton's house to study last night. 7. adv.
8. We met at the lake to swim. 8. adv.
9. That is not the correct amount of paper to order for this project. 9. adj.
10. According to the map, the road to take is the one to the left. 10. adj.

STYLE TIP

A ***split infinitive*** occurs when a word is placed between the sign of the infinitive, *to*, and the base form of a verb. Although split infinitives are common in informal speaking and writing, you should avoid using them in formal situations.

SPLIT
The bear seemed to suddenly appear from the shadows.

REVISED
The bear seemed **to appear** suddenly from the shadows.

Reference Note

For more about **prepositional phrases,** see page 70.

COMPUTER TIP

Some software programs can identify and highlight split infinitives in a document. Using such a feature will help you eliminate split infinitives from your formal writing.

The Infinitive and the Infinitive Phrase

Rules 3j, k *(pp. 85–89)*

OBJECTIVES

- To identify and classify infinitives
- To identify and classify infinitive phrases

GRAMMAR

Differentiating Instruction

English-Language Learners

Spanish and French. Point out to students that in Spanish the infinitive ends in *–ar, –er,* or *–ir* (for example, *hablar, vender, partir*); in French, it ends in *–er, –ir, –oir,* or *–re* (for example, *aimer, finir, recevoir, rompre*).

Extension

Relating to Literature

If your literature textbook contains the poem "At Woodward's Gardens" by Robert Frost, have students read it. Ask them to identify the six infinitives that include *to.* Ask students what the effect of the infinitive form is. [*The infinitive form helps sustain the rhythm of the poem, giving it movement and vitality.*]

RESOURCES

The Infinitive and the Infinitive Phrase

Practice

- *Language & Sentence Skills Practice,* pp. 73–77

Differentiating Instruction

- *Developmental Language & Sentence Skills,* pp. 47–48

GRAMMAR

Extension

Critical Thinking

Analysis. To help students become familiar with some English-language patterns, have them use the following sentences to fill in a three-column chart like the one below.

I enjoy swimming.
I need to work.

VERB	DIRECT OBJECT	VERBAL
enjoy	swimming	gerund
need	to work	infinitive

Have students add to the chart by writing their own sentences using *enjoy* and *need*. Ask students to try forming a generalization about the types of verbals that will follow these verbs. [*After some practice, students should realize that* enjoy *is followed by a gerund and* need *by an infinitive.*]

Then, tell students that in general, verbs that involve a future action will be followed by an infinitive, while verbs that involve the completion of an action will take a gerund. Some examples of verbs that usually go with infinitives are *want, plan, expect,* and *ask.* Verbs such as *avoid, finish, deny,* and *admit* most often have gerunds following them.

Students might want to make two new charts, one for verbs and infinitives and one for verbs and gerunds, and complete them using combinations of the verbs above and appropriate verbals.

TIPS & TRICKS

To find out if an infinitive phrase is being used as a noun, replace the phrase with *what.*

EXAMPLES

To fix an air conditioner is my next project. [What is my next project? *To fix an air conditioner is my next project.* The infinitive is a noun.]

In New York, we went to see Gramercy Park. [We went what? This question makes no sense. The infinitive is not a noun. It is used as an adverb modifying the verb *went.*]

The Infinitive with *to* Omitted

Sometimes the sign of the infinitive, *to,* is omitted in a sentence.

EXAMPLES
She's done all her chores except [to] **feed** the cat.
I'll help you [to] **pack.**
The dogs like **to roam** in the field and [to] **chase** rabbits.
Fuel injection helps cars [to] **run** better and [to] **last** longer.

The Infinitive Phrase

3k. An ***infinitive phrase*** consists of an infinitive and any modifiers or complements the infinitive has. The entire phrase can be used as a noun, an adjective, or an adverb.

EXAMPLES

To make tamales quickly was hard. [The infinitive phrase is used as a noun, as the subject of the sentence. The infinitive has a direct object, *tamales,* and is modified by the adverb *quickly* and by the predicate adjective *hard.*]

Chris is the player **to watch in the next game.** [The infinitive phrase is used as an adjective modifying the predicate nominative *player.* The infinitive is modified by the adverb phrase *in the next game.*]

We are eager **to finish this project.** [The infinitive phrase is used as an adverb modifying the predicate adjective *eager.* The infinitive has a direct object, *project.*]

NOTE An infinitive may have a subject. An ***infinitive clause*** consists of an infinitive with a subject and any modifiers and complements of the infinitive. The entire infinitive clause functions as a noun.

EXAMPLES

I wanted **him to help me with my algebra.** [The entire infinitive clause is the direct object of the verb *wanted. Him* is the subject of the infinitive *to help.* The infinitive *to help* has a direct object, *me,* and is modified by the adverb phrase *with my algebra.*]

Would Uncle Jim like **us to clear the brush in the backyard**? [The entire infinitive clause is the direct object of the verb *Would like. Us* is the subject of the infinitive *to clear.* The infinitive *to clear* has a direct object, *brush,* which is modified by the adjective phrase *in the backyard.*]

Notice that a pronoun that functions as the subject of an infinitive clause is in the objective case.

Learning for Life

Having a Conversation. To show students that verbals are a part of their everyday lives, ask them to have a conversation and analyze it. Divide the class into groups of four or five students with like interests so that each group can have a conversation on a topic that interests all the group members. Each group should choose a topic, such as sports, movies, school activities, or hobbies, on which they can have an informal conversation. Ask students to talk together for five to ten minutes and to

Exercise 9 Identifying and Classifying Infinitives and Infinitive Phrases

Identify the infinitives and infinitive phrases in the following sentences. After each, tell whether it is used as a *noun*, an *adjective*, or an *adverb*.

EXAMPLE 1. Scott is the person to elect.
1. to elect—adjective

1. To dance gracefully requires coordination. 1. n.
2. Raymond wanted to join the team. 2. n.
3. Sandy needs to study. 3. n.
4. I'm going to the pond to fish. 4. adv.
5. A good way to stay healthy is to exercise often. 5. adj./n.
6. After our long vacation, we needed to get back in training. 6. n.
7. The best way to get there is to take the bus. 7. adj./n.
8. Don't you dare open that present before your birthday. 8. n.
9. Juanita and Matt tried to find the perfect gift. 9. n.
10. He lives to swim and water-ski. 10. adv.

HELP—The sign of the infinitive, *to,* is sometimes omitted. Also, a sentence in Exercise 9 may contain more than one infinitive or infinitive phrase.

Exercise 10 Identifying and Classifying Infinitive Phrases

Identify the infinitive phrases in the following sentences. Then, tell how each phrase is used: as a *noun*, an *adjective*, or an *adverb*.

EXAMPLE 1. To create a miracle fabric was the aim of the chemist Joe Shivers.
1. To create a miracle fabric—noun

1. He succeeded with spandex, and athletes of all shapes and sizes have learned to appreciate the qualities of his "power cloth." 1. n.
2. This material has the ability to stretch and snap back into shape. 2. adj.
3. Its sleek fit lessens friction to give the wearer faster movement through air or water. 3. adv.
4. Its slick surface makes an athlete such as a wrestler hard to hold. 4. adv.
5. To say that spandex has athletes covered is not stretching the truth. 5. n.
6. Spandex is just one of many synthetic fibers to meet today's fashion needs. 6. adj.
7. Nylon was the first synthetic; it originally was made to take the place of silk in women's garments. 7. adv.
8. To replace silk was also the purpose of rayon, another early, low-priced synthetic. 8. n.

HELP—In Exercise 10 the sign of the infinitive, *to,* is sometimes omitted.

Exercise 9

DISTRIBUTED REVIEW

Ask students to find the following sentence parts in the designated sentences.

1. complete subject [*To dance gracefully*]
2. direct object [*to join the team*]
5. predicate nominative [*to exercise often*]

GRAMMAR

tape-record their conversations.

Next, have them play their conversations back slowly, stopping frequently to note the sentences used and to write down all sentences with verbals. Once all the sentences with verbals are listed, ask students to study the verbals in context and identify them as participles, gerunds, or infinitives.

9. Polyester, developed later, often is combined with natural fibers to reduce wrinkling. 9. adv.

10. To distinguish synthetic fibers (most made from plastic) from natural fibers is not easy. 10. n.

Review F Identifying Infinitives and Infinitive Phrases

HELP

In Review F, the sign of the infinitive, *to,* is sometimes omitted.

Identify the infinitives and infinitive phrases in the following paragraph.

EXAMPLE **[1]** Laurel and Hardy are a comic team to remember.

1. to remember

[**1**] Together, Stan Laurel and Oliver Hardy have made millions of moviegoers laugh. [**2**] In their day, to be funny in the movies required the use of body language. [**3**] Both of them were geniuses in their ability to keep audiences laughing. [**4**] For his famous head scratch, Stan grew his hair long so that he could scratch and pull it to make a comic mess. [**5**] Stan also developed a hilarious cry that he used to show his character's childish nature. [**6**] He would shut his eyes tightly, pinch up his face, and begin to wail. [**7**] Ollie, too, had an uncanny ability to create his own distinctive mannerisms. [**8**] For example, he was known for the long-suffering look he used to express frustration. [**9**] He would also waggle his tie at a person he and Stan had managed to offend and then start giggling nervously. [**10**] Ollie's intent was to make the person less angry, but his gesture usually had the opposite effect.

Review G Identifying and Classifying Verbals and Verbal Phrases

Identify each verbal or verbal phrase in the following paragraph as a *participle, participial phrase, gerund, gerund phrase, infinitive, infinitive phrase,* or as a part of an *infinitive clause.*

EXAMPLE **[1]** Building the railroad across the United States in the late 1800s required thousands of workers.

1. Building the railroad across the United States in the late 1800s—gerund phrase

[**1**] The government commissioned two companies to build railway tracks between Omaha, Nebraska, and Sacramento, California. [**2**] Building eastward from Sacramento, the Central Pacific Railroad relied on Chinese workers. [**3**] One fourth of the Chinese immigrants

Review G Identifying and Classifying Verbals and Verbal Phrases

ANSWERS

1. inf. cl.
2. part. phr.

88 The Phrase

in the United States in 1868 helped with laying the track. [4] The terrain was difficult to cover, but the laborers rose to the challenge. [5] Known for their dependability, the Chinese were strong workers. [6] Complaining was a problem with some workers, but seldom with Chinese laborers. [7] It was often necessary to blow up parts of mountains, and the Chinese workers became experts at this task. [8] Chinese and Irish workers set a record on April 28, 1869, by spiking ten miles and fifty-six feet of track in twelve hours. [9] The railroad company divided the Chinese immigrants into working groups, or gangs, each with twelve to twenty men. [10] Keeping many of their traditional ways, Chinese workers ate food that was shipped to them from San Francisco's Chinatown.

Appositives and Appositive Phrases

3l. An *appositive* is a noun or a pronoun placed beside another noun or pronoun to identify or describe it.

EXAMPLES The sculptor **Isamu Noguchi** has designed sculpture gardens. [The appositive *Isamu Noguchi* identifies the noun *sculptor*.]

Eric, a talented **musician,** plans to study in Europe. [The appositive *musician* describes the noun *Eric*.]

Those, the **ones** on the right, are on sale. [The appositive *ones* identifies the pronoun *Those*.]

3m. An *appositive phrase* consists of an appositive and any modifiers it has.

EXAMPLES Lucy Sánchez, **my longtime friend from my old neighborhood,** has a new Scottish terrier.

Dr. Jackson has a degree in entomology, **the scientific study of insects.**

NOTE Sometimes, an appositive phrase precedes the noun or pronoun to which it refers.

EXAMPLE **The terror of our block,** little Anthony was on the rampage.

Review G **Identifying and Classifying Verbals and Verbal Phrases**

ANSWERS continued

3. ger. phr.
4. inf.
5. part. phr.
6. ger.
7. inf. phr.
8. ger. phr.
9. part.
10. part. phr.

GRAMMAR

Appositives and Appositive Phrases

Rules 3l, m *(pp. 89–92)*

OBJECTIVE

- To identify appositives and appositive phrases in sentences

DIRECT TEACHING

Modeling and Demonstration

Identifying Appositives. Model how to identify appositives by using the example *The sculptor Isamu Noguchi has designed sculpture gardens.* First, identify the nouns and pronouns. [*sculptor, Isamu Noguchi, garden*] Next, ask if any of the nouns are next to each other. [*sculptor* and *Isamu Noguchi*] Then, ask if *sculptor* and *Isamu Noguchi* refer to the same person. [*yes*] Explain to students that *Isamu Noguchi* is an appositive identifying *sculptor.* Now, have a volunteer use another example in this chapter to demonstrate how to identify an appositive.

RESOURCES

Appositives and Appositive Phrases

Practice

- *Language & Sentence Skills Practice,* pp. 78–80

Differentiating Instruction

- *Developmental Language & Sentence Skills,* pp. 49–50

Reference Note

For more about **essential and nonessential phrases,** see page 276.

Appositives and appositive phrases that are not essential to the meaning of the sentence are set off by commas. If the appositive is essential to the meaning, it is generally not set off by commas.

EXAMPLES My teacher, **Mr. Byrd,** trains parrots. [The writer has only one teacher. The appositive is not necessary to identify the teacher. Because the information is nonessential, it is set off by commas.]

My teacher **Mr. Byrd** trains parrots. [The writer has more than one teacher. The appositive is necessary to tell which teacher is meant. Because this information is essential to the meaning of the sentence, it is not set off by commas.]

NOTE Commas are generally used with appositives that refer to proper nouns.

EXAMPLE Linda, **the editor,** assigned the story.

However, a word or phrase that is commonly accepted as part of a person's name or title is not set off by a comma.

EXAMPLE The Roman Army defeated Attila **the Hun** in A.D. 451.

Exercise 11 Identifying Appositives and Appositive Phrases

HELP — A sentence in Exercise 11 may contain more than one appositive or appositive phrase.

Identify the appositives and appositive phrases in the following sentences. Then, give the noun or pronoun that each appositive or appositive phrase identifies or describes.

EXAMPLE 1. I usually write haiku, poems in a traditional Japanese form.

1. poems in a traditional Japanese form—haiku

1. Our community has a new organization, a writers' club called Writers, Inc.
2. Marquita Wiley, a college instructor, started the group at the request of former students.
3. A published author, she conducts the meetings as workshops.
4. The writers meet to read their works in progress, fiction or poetry, and to discuss suggestions for improvement.
5. The members, people from all walks of life, have varied interests.
6. A mechanic by trade, J. D. Ellis writes funny poems about his hobby, bird-watching.
7. My friend Lusita just had a short story about her people, the Zuni, published in a national magazine.

90 The Phrase

8. Next week, we'll meet at our regular time, 3:30 P.M.
9. Our guest speaker is Pat Mora, a Mexican American poet whose work emphasizes harmony between cultures.
10. Have you read her poem "Bribe"?

Review H Identifying Verbal Phrases and Appositive Phrases

Find the verbal phrases and appositive phrases in the following sentences. Identify each phrase as a *participial phrase,* a *gerund phrase,* an *infinitive phrase,* or an *appositive phrase.*

EXAMPLE 1. Automobiles have been partly responsible for drastically changing life in the twentieth century.

1. drastically changing life in the twentieth century—gerund phrase

HELP— A sentence in Review H may contain more than one verbal or appositive phrase.

1. Developing the automobile was actually the creative work of many people, but Henry Ford deservedly receives much credit. **1.** g.p.
2. Ford's company, using an assembly line and interchangeable parts, first produced the Model T in 1909. **2.** p.p.
3. Many people in the early 1900s wanted to buy cars because of their low prices and novelty. **3.** i.p.
4. By giving people an alternative to mass transit, automobiles did much to change the social and business scene of the United States. **4.** g.p./i.p.
5. No longer dependent on streetcars and trains, the first motorists used automobiles for going on recreational and family trips. **5.** g.p.
6. Clearly overjoyed with their vehicles, many Americans regarded automobiles as necessities by the 1920s. **6.** p.p.
7. One writer, a famous historian, noted that the automobile industry led to such new businesses as gas stations, repair garages, tire companies, and motels. **7.** a.p.

8. To get a clear idea of changes in automobile designs over the years, look at the picture to the right. **8.** i.p.
9. The photo shows Henry Ford, looking contented and proud, in his first car. **9.** p.p.
10. What are some of the main differences between Ford's car, one of the most advanced vehicles of its day, and modern cars? **10.** a.p.

GRAMMAR

PRACTICE

Guided and Independent

Review H You may wish to use the first five items of **Review H** as guided practice. Then, have students complete the review as independent practice.

HOMEWORK

DIFFERENTIATING INSTRUCTION

Learners Having Difficulty

To help students who may be having difficulty with appositives, first review the use of commas with appositives, using examples from **Review H.** Then, have students write the following sentences on strips of white paper, and have them write the appositives on strips of yellow paper.

SENTENCES

1. Jose wrote a paper about George Washington.
2. Lasagna was served for dinner.
3. California has over 800 miles of coastline.
4. Toni Morrison has written a new book.

APPOSITIVES

the largest state on the Pacific coast
an Italian food
a general and president
a famous author

Have students cut apart each sentence and insert an appositive where it makes sense, using commas where required.

Review I

Writing Appropriate Phrases

POSSIBLE ANSWERS

1. of the oranges—prep.
2. to the music—prep.
3. my former football coach—appos.
4. to see the Mayan ruins—inf.
5. Forgotten in the rush—part.
6. in the mud—prep.
7. Exercising every day—ger.
8. from the reservation—prep.
9. To win the championship—inf.
10. shown in the catalog—part.
11. hanging at the window—part.
12. in the basket—prep.
13. from the oven—prep.
14. An inline six-cylinder—appos.
15. struggling to keep up—part.
16. a well-known radio personality —appos.
17. waiting to see Dr. Patel—part.
18. To pass the exam—inf.
19. in Ms. Walter's class—prep.
20. Observing a strict diet—ger.

HELP—Although several possible answers are given in the example in Review I, you need to write only one sentence for each item.

Review I Writing Appropriate Phrases

Rewrite each of the following sentences, supplying an appropriate prepositional, verbal, or appositive phrase to fill in the blank. Use each type of phrase at least twice. Identify each phrase you use as *prepositional, participial, infinitive, gerund,* or *appositive.*

EXAMPLE
1. We have room for only a single passenger _____.
1. *We have room for only a single passenger weighing less than one hundred fifty pounds. — participial*

or

We have room for only a single passenger in the boat. — prepositional

or

We have room for only a single passenger, a small one! — appositive

or

We have room for only a single passenger to come aboard. — infinitive

1. Only one _____ was left on the plate.
2. Joyfully, she danced _____.
3. Richard, _____, is moving back to the town!
4. During the whole trip to Mexico, her goal was _____.
5. _____, the new computer still sat in boxes on the floor.
6. At the bottom of the river, a huge old catfish lay _____.
7. _____ made them strong enough for the race.
8. Navajo dancers _____ stepped lightly into the open circle.
9. _____ became their goal for the rest of the year.
10. All the clothes _____ had been made in the United States.
11. The lace curtains _____ were not for sale.
12. Are these puppies _____ all yours?
13. What a marvelous aroma is rising _____!
14. _____, the engine finally started.
15. With a glance at the other runners _____, Gretchen pulled ahead.
16. Bill Briggs, _____, greeted the enthusiastic fans.
17. Everyone _____ should move down one seat.
18. _____ was the thought of each student in the class.
19. The children _____ made mud pies.
20. _____ gave them the endurance they needed.

Chapter Review

A. Identifying Phrases

In each of the following sentences, identify each italicized phrase as *prepositional, participial, gerund, infinitive,* or *appositive.*

1. Now I would like *to tell you about my sister Alexandra.*
2. She likes *arriving at school early.*
3. By *doing so,* she can spend extra time preparing for her day.
4. She will resort to anything to get *to school* early, including waking me up, too.
5. For example, when *the beeping of my alarm* woke me yesterday, the sky was as dark as night.
6. I soon realized that Alexandra, *a volunteer crossing guard at school,* had adjusted the alarm.
7. It was, I could see, an occasion for *applying my special technique.*
8. *Called my slow-motion technique,* it always achieves the result I want.
9. I moved *around the house* as if I were underwater; Alexandra watched until she could stand it no longer.
10. Then, I moved faster; I certainly did not want *to be late for school.*

B. Identifying and Classifying Prepositional Phrases

Identify the prepositional phrases in the following sentences. Identify the word or words modified by each phrase. Then, state whether the prepositional phrase is an *adjective phrase* or an *adverb phrase.*

11. A daily newspaper has something for almost everyone.
12. In addition to news, the paper offers entertainment, classified ads, and much more.
13. Our entire family reads the newspaper in the morning.
14. Dad always begins with the sports pages; Mom prefers the general news.
15. My sister's favorite part of the newspaper is the lifestyle section.
16. She enjoys features like "How-to Hints."
17. I find the editorial and opinion pages interesting, especially when a debate between two sides develops.
18. Sometimes I see the logic behind an argument.

HELP

In the Chapter Review, if a phrase contains a shorter phrase, identify only the longer phrase.

Numerals in brackets refer to rules tested by items in the Chapter Review.

1. inf. [3k, j]
2. ger. [3i, h]
3. ger. [3i, h]
4. prep. [3b]
5. ger. [3i, h]
6. app. [3m, l]
7. ger. [3i, h]
8. part. [3g, f]
9. prep. [3b]
10. inf. [3k, j]

11. adj. [3b, d]
12. adv. [3b, e]
13. adv. [3b, e]
14. adv. [3b, e]
15. adj. [3b, d]
16. adj. [3b, d]
17. adj. [3b, d]
18. adj. [3b, d]

GRAMMAR

ASSESSING

Monitoring Progress

Chapter Review. The **Chapter Review** requires students to identify the different kinds of phrases within sentences. The results of this review can be compared to those of the **Diagnostic Preview** (pp. 68–69) to assess student progress.

TEACHING TIP

Chapter Review. Remind students that a compound noun consists of two or more words used together as a single noun. Prepositional phrases need not be identified within compound nouns such as *American Museum of Natural History, lady-in-waiting,* and *Stratford-on-Avon.*

RESOURCES

The Phrase

Review

- *Language & Sentence Skills Practice,* pp. 81–83

Assessment

- *Holt Handbook Chapter Tests with Answer Key,* pp. 5–6, 52

19. adv. [3b, e]
20. adj. [3b, d]

19. Other times I wonder why grown people argue about a trivial issue.
20. I also like to read news about local events.

C. Identifying Verbals

Identify each italicized verbal in the following sentences as a *participle,* a *gerund,* or an *infinitive.*

21. inf. [3j]
22. part. [3f(2)]
23. ger. [3h]
24. inf. [3j]
25. ger. [3h]
26. ger. [3h]
27. part. [3f(2)]
28. ger. [3h]
29. part. [3f(1)]
30. inf. [3j]

21. Many amateur athletes want *to earn* medals for their abilities.
22. *Enjoyed* by people throughout history, amateur athletic competitions can be very beneficial.
23. *Winning* an event is only part of the reason athletes compete.
24. When talented amateurs compete *to test* their skills, they learn a great deal about their sport.
25. In addition, the love of a sport, the best reason for *entering* into competition, usually grows as an athlete's performance improves.
26. Furthermore, *sharing* hard work with teammates leads a person to appreciate cooperative efforts.
27. Competitions *organized* on many levels give amateur athletes a motive for increased practice.
28. *Participating* in state, national, and international competitions is important to many amateur athletes.
29. *Wanting* to be recognized for their talent, the athletes compete against their peers in such events.
30. These competitions also provide athletes with opportunities *to put* their abilities to the test.

D. Identifying Verbal Phrases

In each of the following sentences, identify the italicized verbal phrase as a *participial phrase,* an *infinitive phrase,* or a *gerund phrase.*

31. ger. [3i, h]
32. inf. [3k, j]
33. part. [3g, f(1)]
34. inf. [3k, j]
35. part. [3g, f(1)]

31. Maxine gets her exercise by *dancing for at least three hours a week.*
32. Eddie likes *to make pizza for his friends.*
33. The mother baboon watched her infant *eating a berry.*
34. Yolanda went *to get her book.*
35. Is the man *pushing the grocery cart* an employee or a customer?

36. *Winning the contest* was a thrill for our cheerleaders.
37. I made a tote bag *to hold my gym clothes.*
38. Richard's summer job is *delivering groceries to the hospital.*
39. Enzo Ferrari became famous by *building fast and stylish cars.*
40. *Preparing for that play* took quite a long time.
41. Samantha overheard Tina and Sue *talking about their vacation plans.*
42. Prepare *to run your fastest.*
43. *Excited by the thought of the trip,* we finished packing early.
44. Koalas get most of their nutrition by *eating eucalyptus leaves.*
45. *Tired of the noise outside,* we closed the window.

36. ger. [3i, h]
37. inf. [3k, j]
38. ger. [3i, h]
39. ger. [3i, h]
40. ger. [3i, h]
41. part. [3g, f(1)]
42. inf. [3k, j]
43. part. [3g, f(2)]
44. ger. [3i, h]
45. part. [3g, f(2)]

Writing Application

Using Prepositional Phrases in a Game

Adjective and Adverb Phrases You are planning a treasure hunt for a group of neighborhood children. The treasure hunt will include six stops for clues. For each clue, write a sentence containing at least one prepositional phrase. Use a combination of adjective and adverb phrases.

Prewriting First, think about your neighborhood and pick a good place to hide a treasure. Then, think of six places to hide clues.

Writing Write a sentence giving a clue about each location. The final sentence should lead the children directly to the hidden treasure.

Revising Ask someone who is familiar with the area of the treasure hunt to look over your clues. Revise any clues that are not clear. Be sure that each clue contains at least one prepositional phrase and that you have used both adjective and adverb phrases in your clues.

Publishing Check to be sure that your prepositional phrases are properly placed. An adverb phrase may occur at various places in a sentence. Proofread your sentences for correct capitalization and punctuation. You may want to organize a treasure hunt for younger children in your family or for children that you baby-sit.

APPLICATION

Writing Application

Prewriting Tip. Brainstorm with students, and have them write as many hiding places as they can. Then, tell them to choose six of the most appealing spots. Remind them of their youthful audience. Suggest that students write their rough drafts without being concerned about whether all the prepositional phrases are included. Tell them that they can add the required phrases in the revision stage.

Scoring Rubric. While you will want to pay particular attention to students' use of adjective and adverb phrases, you will also want to evaluate overall writing performance. You may want to give a split score to indicate development and clarity of the composition as well as grammar skills.

Chapter Review 95

CHAPTER

INTRODUCING THE CHAPTER

- This chapter will help students add complexity and variety to their sentence structures. The first part of this chapter explains clauses and the differences between subordinate and independent clauses. Subordinate clauses are further explained by type—the adjective clause, the adverb clause, and the noun clause. Finally, classifying sentences according to structure (simple, compound, complex, and compound-complex) is discussed.
- The chapter concludes with a **Chapter Review** including a **Writing Application** feature that asks students to write a letter using varied sentence structure.
- For help in integrating the chapter with writing assignments, use the **Teaching Strands** chart on pp. T24–T25.

CHAPTER

The Clause

Independent and Subordinate Clauses

Diagnostic Preview

A. Identifying and Classifying Subordinate Clauses

Identify the subordinate clause in each of the following sentences. Then, classify each subordinate clause as an adjective clause (*adj.*), an adverb clause (*adv.*), or a noun clause (*n.*). If the clause is used as an adjective or adverb, write the word or phrase it modifies. If the clause is used as a noun, indicate whether it is used as a subject (*subj.*), a direct object (*d.o.*), an indirect object (*i.o.*), a predicate nominative (*p.n.*), or an object of a preposition (*o.p.*).

EXAMPLES
1. After our last class, Elena, Frieda, and I agreed that we would go bicycling in the park.
   1. *that we would go bicycling in the park—n.—d.o.*
2. As we set out for the park, we had no idea of the difficulties ahead.
   2. *As we set out for the park—adv.—had*

Numerals in brackets refer to rules tested by items in the Diagnostic Preview.

1. adv. [4c, e]
2. adj. [4c, d]
3. adv. [4c, e]
4. n.—subj. [4c, f]
5. n.—o.p. [4c, f]
6. n.—d.o. [4c, f]
7. adv. [4c, e]

1. Since none of us own bicycles, we decided to rent them there.
2. The man who rented us the bikes was helpful.
3. After we had bicycled six miles, Frieda's bike got a flat tire.
4. What we found was a nail in the tire.
5. We decided to take the bike to whatever bike shop was the nearest.
6. The woman at the bike shop told us that she could fix the tire.
7. After we had paid for the repair and gotten a receipt, we rode back to the park and bicycled for an hour.

CHAPTER RESOURCES

Internet

- Web resources: go.hrw.com

go.hrw.com

Practice & Review

- *Language & Sentence Skills Practice,* pp. 88–107
- *Language & Sentence Skills Practice Answer Key,* pp. 42–52

Application & Enrichment

- *Language & Sentence Skills Practice,* pp. 87, 108–110
- *Language & Sentence Skills Practice Answer Key,* pp. 42, 51–52

8. Our only worry was that the man at the rental shop might not pay us back for the repair.
9. When we returned our bikes, we showed the man the receipt.
10. He refunded the money we had spent to fix the tire.

8. n.—p.n. [4c, f]
9. adv. [4c, e]
10. adj. [4c, d]

B. Classifying Sentences According to Structure

Classify each of the following sentences as *simple, compound, complex,* or *compound-complex.* Be sure that you can identify all subordinate and independent clauses.

EXAMPLES
1. Amanda now plays the violin because of a winter concert that she heard when she was in the third grade.
   1. *complex*
2. The concert featured a talented, young violinist from Russia and a famous local pianist.
   2. *simple*

11. Amanda loved the sound of the orchestra at her school's winter concert, and she decided then to study the violin.
12. Amanda's first violin was not the standard size, for she was still quite small.
13. When she started the sixth grade, however, Amanda was playing a full-sized violin.
14. She did not always enjoy the many hours of practice, but they were necessary because playing the instrument is complicated.
15. Amanda knew that playing the proper notes could be especially difficult on a violin.
16. On a keyboard instrument, you simply press a key and hear the note for that key.
17. On a violin, however, the placement of a finger on a string can affect the pitch of a note.
18. If the pitch of each note is not exact, even a common tune can be difficult to recognize.
19. Once a student has mastered finger placement to some extent, he or she still has a great deal to think about; posture, hand position, and bowing technique all require great concentration.
20. When students can actually create music with this stubborn instrument, they have reason to be proud.

11. cd. [4g(2)]
12. cd. [4g(2)]
13. cx. [4g(3)]
14. cd.-cx. [4g(4)]
15. cx. [4g(3)]
16. s. [4g(1)]
17. s. [4g(1)]
18. cx. [4g(3)]
19. cd.-cx. [4g(4)]
20. cx. [4g(3)]

GRAMMAR

Assessing

Entry-Level Assessment

Diagnostic Preview. You may wish to use the **Diagnostic Preview** to gauge students' familiarity with clauses. However, even students who have mastered the identification of various clauses and sentence structures might not consciously transfer this knowledge to their writing. Therefore, you may wish to take the diagnosis one step further by evaluating actual writing samples to identify the students who vary their sentence structure.

Differentiating Instruction

- *Developmental Language & Sentence Skills Guided Practice,* pp. 51–60
- *Developmental Language & Sentence Skills Guided Practice Teacher's Notes and Answer Key,* pp. 13–15

Assessment

- *Holt Handbook Chapter Tests with Answer Key,* pp. 7–8, 52

GRAMMAR

Preteaching

Lesson Starter

Motivating. To make students aware that the sentence structures presented in this chapter appear frequently in printed material, you may want to give each student a copy of a newspaper or magazine story to use while working on this chapter. As students study each type of clause and each sentence classification, ask them to look for examples in the story. Ask them to underline and label each example they find.

You might expand the discovery approach by asking students to bring to class examples of each structure from their own outside reading. You may want to bring personal or library copies of newspapers and magazines to use as a classroom resource.

What Is a Clause?

Rules 4a–c *(pp. 98–100)*

OBJECTIVE

- To identify independent and subordinate clauses

Direct Teaching

Modeling and Demonstration

What Is a Clause? Model how to identify independent and subordinate clauses by using the example *When you arrive at the airport in Dallas, call us.* Explain that an independent clause expresses a complete thought and can stand alone as a sentence. Ask which part of the sentence can stand by itself as a sentence. [*call us*] Then, ask which words make up the first clause. [*When you arrive at the airport in Dallas*] Ask whether this clause can stand alone as a complete sentence. [*no*] Next, ask what kind of clause this is. [*subordinate*] Explain

(continued)

What Is a Clause?

4a. **A *clause* is a word group that contains a verb and its subject and that is used as a sentence or as part of a sentence.**

Although every clause contains a subject and a verb, not every clause expresses a complete thought. Clauses that do are called ***independent clauses.*** Clauses that do not express a complete thought are called ***subordinate clauses.***

INDEPENDENT CLAUSE	The people left the building
SUBORDINATE CLAUSE	when the fire alarm sounded
SENTENCE	When the fire alarm sounded, the people left the building.

HELP — A subordinate clause that is capitalized and punctuated as a sentence is a ***sentence fragment.***

Reference Note — For information about **correcting sentence fragments,** see page 434.

The Independent Clause

4b. **An *independent* (or *main*) *clause* expresses a complete thought and can stand by itself as a sentence.**

In the following examples, each boldface clause has its own subject and verb and expresses a complete thought.

EXAMPLES **Ms. Santana works in a law office in downtown Concord.**

Ms. Santana works in a law office that has a view of downtown Concord.

Ms. Santana works in a law office in downtown Concord, and **she has a successful practice.**

In the last example, the independent clauses are joined by a comma and the coordinating conjunction *and.* The clauses also could be written with a semicolon between them:

Ms. Santana works in a law office in downtown Concord**;** she has a successful practice.

or with a semicolon, a conjunctive adverb, and a comma:

Ms. Santana works in a law office in downtown Concord**;** **indeed,** she has a successful practice.

or as separate sentences:

Ms. Santana works in a law office in downtown Concord**.** She has a successful practice.

Reference Note — For a list of **coordinating conjunctions,** see page 32. For more about using **semicolons** and **conjunctive adverbs** to join independent clauses, see page 298.

RESOURCES

What Is a Clause?

Practice

- *Language & Sentence Skills Practice,* pp. 88–91

The Subordinate Clause

4c. A *subordinate* (or *dependent*) *clause* does not express a complete thought and cannot stand by itself as a sentence.

Words such as *when, whom, because, which, that, if,* and *until* signal that the clauses following them are likely to be subordinate. *Subordinate* means "lesser in rank or importance." To make a complete sentence, a subordinate clause must be joined to an independent clause. Like phrases, subordinate clauses can be used as adjectives, adverbs, or nouns.

SUBORDINATE CLAUSES
when you arrive at the airport in Dallas
which grow only locally
that he had granted us an interview

SENTENCES
When you arrive at the airport in Dallas, call us.
These wildflowers, **which grow only locally,** are of interest to scientists.
Did you know **that he had granted us an interview**?

As the preceding examples show, subordinate clauses may appear at the beginning, in the middle, or at the end of a sentence. The placement of a subordinate clause depends on how the clause is used in the sentence.

NOTE Many subordinate clauses contain complements (such as predicate nominatives, predicate adjectives, direct objects, or indirect objects), modifiers, or both.

EXAMPLES **what** it is . . . [*What* is a predicate nominative: It is *what*?]

because you look **tired** . . . [*Tired* is a predicate adjective modifying *you*.]

that you chose . . . [*That* is the direct object of *chose*.]

before he gave **us** the **quiz** . . . [*Us* is the indirect object of *gave; quiz* is the direct object of *gave*.]

that I bought **yesterday** . . . [*Yesterday* is an adverb modifying *bought*.]

when the coach was calling **to her** . . . [*To her* is an adverb phrase modifying *was calling*.]

Reference Note

For more about **sentence complements,** see page 55. For more information on **modifiers,** see Chapter 8.

that a subordinate clause does not express a complete thought and cannot stand by itself as a sentence. Then, ask what the independent clause is. [*call us*] Now, have a volunteer use an example from this chapter to identify independent and subordinate clauses.

GRAMMAR

DIRECT TEACHING

Correcting Misconceptions

The Subordinate Clause. Students might find it confusing that although a subordinate clause has a subject and a verb, it cannot stand alone as a sentence. Therefore, you may wish to write subordinate clauses on the chalkboard to help students see that more information is needed to form complete thoughts.

Sample clauses:

Because the road was slick

What we need for the picnic

That you are reading

Have students suggest ways to make the clauses complete sentences. Point out that they may add independent clauses to form complete thoughts.

GRAMMAR

Differentiating Instruction

English-Language Learners

Spanish. Emphasize to students that in English the subject usually precedes the verb. Because word order in Spanish is often different from that used in English, some Spanish-speaking students might have a tendency to invert subjects and verbs in subordinate clauses. You may wish to have students locate the subject and verb in each subordinate clause in **Exercise 1** to emphasize this structural difference.

Vietnamese. In Vietnamese, an introductory clause may be followed by a "balancing" word in the main clause, as in the following.

When you arrive at the airport in Dallas, **therefore** call us.

Often the word *also* is used to create this balance, so students may tend to write sentences like the following.

Because you look tired, you should **also** go to bed.

Show students how subordinate clauses can usually be moved from the front of the sentence to the back and vice versa, and that no other connecting word is needed. Draw their attention to subordinate clauses in their readings and their own compositions.

Learners Having Difficulty

You may wish to read aloud the examples in this lesson and the italicized clauses in **Exercise 1.** Students may be better able to hear the difference between complete and incomplete thoughts than to recognize the difference visually.

HELP

Although short, simple sentences can be effective, a variety of sentence structures is usually more effective. To make choppy sentences into smoother writing, combine shorter sentences by changing some into subordinate clauses. Also, avoid unnecessary repetition of subjects, verbs, and pronouns.

CHOPPY
I enjoy feta cheese. It comes from Greece. It is traditionally made from sheep's or goat's milk.

SMOOTH
I enjoy feta cheese, which comes from Greece and is traditionally made from sheep's or goat's milk.

In the example above, two of the short sentences are combined into a single subordinate clause.

Exercise 1 Identifying Independent and Subordinate Clauses

For each of the following sentences, identify the clause in italics as independent or subordinate.

EXAMPLE 1. *When you think of baseball,* you may think of lightning-fast pitches, bat-splitting home runs, or secret hand signals from coaches and catchers.

1. *subordinate*

1. *Baseball is a game* that generally depends on good eyesight as well as athletic skill.
2. For this reason, until recently, playing the great American game has been something *that people with visual impairments found virtually impossible.*
3. Only sighted players could participate *until an engineer named Charley Fairbanks invented beep baseball.*
4. *In this version of baseball, the ball beeps and the bases buzz* so that players like the one pictured here can tell when to swing and where to run.
5. Each team has a sighted pitcher and a sighted catcher, *who never get a turn at bat,* and six fielders who wear blindfolds so that they don't have a visual advantage.
6. The pitcher shouts "Ready!" *before the ball is pitched* and "Pitch!" when the ball is released.

7. When the bat strikes the ball, the umpire activates the buzzer in first base, *to which the batter must then run.*
8. When a team is on defense, the pitcher and catcher cannot field the batted ball themselves; *they can only shout directions to the fielders.*
9. *Beep baseball is fun to play,* and its challenges create a bond between sighted players and players with visual impairments.
10. Sighted players *who put on blindfolds and join in* come away from a game with a new respect for the abilities of their visually impaired teammates.

The Adjective Clause

4d. An *adjective clause* is a subordinate clause that modifies a noun or a pronoun.

An adjective clause usually follows the word or words it modifies and tells *what kind* or *which one.* An ***essential*** (or ***restrictive***) clause is necessary to the basic meaning of the sentence; it is not set off by commas. A ***nonessential*** (or ***nonrestrictive***) clause gives only additional information and is not necessary to the meaning of a sentence; it is set off by commas.

EXAMPLES This is the new music video **that I like best.** [The clause *that I like best* is necessary to tell which video is being mentioned. Because this information is essential to the meaning of the sentence, it is not set off by commas.]

Griffins, **which are mythological beasts,** are included on many coats of arms. [The clause *which are mythological beasts* is not necessary to identify *Griffins.* Because this information is nonessential to the meaning of the sentence, it is set off by commas.]

Reference Note

For help in deciding whether a clause is **essential or nonessential,** see page 276.

Relative Pronouns

Adjective clauses are often introduced by relative pronouns.

Common Relative Pronouns	who, whom, whose, which, that

These words are called ***relative pronouns*** because they *relate* an adjective clause to the word that the clause modifies. Besides introducing an adjective clause and relating it to another word in the sentence, the relative pronoun has a grammatical function within the adjective clause.

EXAMPLES Luís, **who enjoys running,** has decided to enter the marathon. [The relative pronoun *who* relates the adjective clause to *Luís. Who* also functions as the subject of the adjective clause.]

The students questioned the data **on which the theory was based.** [The relative pronoun *which* relates the adjective clause to *data* and functions as the object of the preposition *on.*]

We met the singer **whose new CD was released this week.** [The relative pronoun *whose* relates the adjective clause to *singer. Whose* functions as a possessive pronoun in the adjective clause.]

Reference Note

For more information on **using *who* and *whom*** correctly, see page 187. For more about **using *that* and *which*** correctly, see page 235.

The Adjective Clause

Rule 4d *(pp. 101–104)*

OBJECTIVES

- **To identify adjective clauses, relative pronouns, and relative adverbs**
- **To revise sentences by adding adjective clauses**

GRAMMAR

DIRECT TEACHING

Modeling and Demonstration

The Adjective Clause. Model how to identify adjective clauses by using the example *Luis, who enjoys running, has decided to enter the marathon.* First, ask what the independent clause is. [*Luis has decided to enter the marathon*] Next, ask what the subordinate clause is. [*who enjoys running*] Then, ask which word this subordinate clause modifies. [*Luis*] Ask what kind of subordinate clause this is. [*adjective clause*] Explain that a subordinate clause modifying a noun is an adjective clause, and point out that the relative pronoun *who* relates this adjective clause to the proper noun *Luis.* Now, have a volunteer use another example from this chapter to demonstrate how to identify adjective clauses.

RESOURCES

The Adjective Clause

Practice

- *Language & Sentence Skills Practice,* pp. 92–94

Differentiating Instruction

- *Developmental Language & Sentence Skills,* pp. 51–52

GRAMMAR

Extension

Relating to Writing

You may want to illustrate how using adjective clauses can help students add sentence variety and reduce the number of short, simple sentences in their writing. Have students combine the following sentences, using the relative pronouns in parentheses.

1. Pedro is the candidate. Pedro got the most votes. (who) [*Pedro is the candidate who got the most votes.*]
2. I interviewed a man. His daughter is an astronaut. (whose) [*I interviewed a man whose daughter is an astronaut.*]
3. Do you enjoy the music? The orchestra is playing it. (that) [*Do you enjoy the music that the orchestra is playing?*]

Encourage students to find two sentences in a piece of their writing and combine them using adjective clauses.

Differentiating Instruction

Learners Having Difficulty

Write the following adjective/noun pairs on the chalkboard, and draw arrows from the adjectives to the nouns they modify.

1. the tasty soup
2. the curious child

Then, rephrase the pairs using adjective clauses, as in the following examples. Draw arrows from the clauses to the nouns they modify.

1. the soup (that was tasty)
2. the child (who was curious)

Conclude by telling students that, in most cases, an adjective clause immediately follows the word it modifies.

Janice, **whom I have known for years,** is my lab partner this semester. [The relative pronoun *whom* relates the adjective clause to *Janice. Whom* functions as the direct object of the verb phrase *have known* in the adjective clause.]

In many cases, the relative pronoun in the clause may be omitted. The pronoun is understood and still has a function in the clause.

EXAMPLES Here is the salad **you ordered.** [The relative pronoun *that* is understood. The pronoun relates the adjective clause to *salad* and functions as the direct object of the verb *ordered* in the adjective clause.]

He is the one **I met yesterday.** [The relative pronoun *whom* or *that* is understood. The pronoun relates the adjective clause to *one* and functions as the direct object of the verb *met* in the adjective clause.]

Occasionally an adjective clause is introduced by the word *where* or *when*. When used in such a way, these words are called ***relative adverbs.***

EXAMPLES They showed us the stadium **where the game would be held.**

Saturday is the day **when I mow the lawn.**

Exercise 2 Identifying Adjective Clauses

Each of the following sentences contains an adjective clause. Write the adjective clause, and underline the relative pronoun or relative adverb that introduces it. If the relative pronoun has been omitted, write it in parentheses and then underline it.

EXAMPLE 1. Do you know anyone who is familiar with briffits, swalloops, and waftaroms?

1. *who is familiar with briffits, swalloops, and waftaroms*

1. Cartoonists use a variety of unusual names for the symbols that commonly appear in comic strips.
2. For example, a *briffit* is the little puff of dust hanging in the spot where a swiftly departing character was previously standing.
3. For times when cartoonists want to make something appear hot or smelly, they use wavy, rising lines called *waftaroms.*
4. *Agitrons* are the wiggly lines around an object that is supposed to be shaking.

Mini-Lesson Usage

Placement of Adjective Clauses. An adjective clause placed incorrectly can create a confusing sentence.

First, write this sentence on the chalkboard:

There is a picture of a dragon in the literature book that breathes fire.

Ask students to identify the adjective clause. [*that breathes fire*] Then, ask students to identify which noun or pronoun the clause modifies—[*dragon*]—and underline the word *dragon.* Point out that the adjective clause, as placed, appears to modify *book.*

5. The limbs of a character who is moving are usually preceded or trailed by a set of curved lines called *blurgits* or *swalloops*.
6. *Plewds,* which look like flying droplets of sweat, are drawn around the head of a worried character.
7. In fact, there are very few motions or emotions for which cartoonists have not invented a clever, expressive symbol.
8. Almost everyone who likes to doodle and draw has used some of these symbols, probably without knowing the names for them.
9. Look at the example cartoon, where you will find the names of other common symbols from the world of cartooning.
10. Now you know a "language" almost nobody outside the cartooning profession knows! **10.** (that)

Exercise 3 Revising Sentences by Supplying Adjective Clauses

Revise the following sentences by substituting an adjective clause for each italicized adjective. Add specific details to make your sentences interesting. Underline the adjective clauses in your sentences.

EXAMPLE **1.** The *angry* citizens gathered in front of City Hall.

1. The citizens, who were furious over the recent tax increase, gathered in front of City Hall.

1. As I entered the building, a *colorful* painting caught my eye.
2. The *patient* photographer sat on a small ledge all day.
3. The two attorneys argued all week over the *important* contract.
4. The team of mountain climbers decided to try to reach the top of the *tallest* peak.
5. At the assembly, Ms. León made two *surprising* announcements.
6. Saburo and his friends cautiously entered the *dark* cave.
7. Edna Jackson easily won her *first* political campaign.

GRAMMAR

Exercise 3 Revising Sentences by Supplying Adjective Clauses

POSSIBLE ANSWERS

1. As I entered the building, a painting that used every color in the spectrum caught my eye.
2. The photographer, whose patience was legendary, sat on a small ledge all day.
3. The two attorneys argued all week over the contract, which was important to both of them.
4. The team of mountain climbers decided to try to reach the top of the peak, which was the tallest on the continent.
5. At the assembly, Ms. León made two announcements that surprised everybody in the room.
6. Saburo and his friend cautiously entered the cave, which was completely dark.
7. Edna Jackson easily won her political campaign, which was the first ever launched by a woman in that district.

Exercise 3

DISTRIBUTED REVIEW

Have students find the following constructions in sentences 2, 4, and 9.

2. prepositional phrase [*on a small ledge*]

4. two infinitive phrases [*to try, to reach the top*]

9. participle modified by prepositional phrases [*Dodging to his left, to his right*]

Remind the students that an adjective clause should be placed just after the word that it modifies; in this case, the sentence should read "In the literature book there is a picture of a dragon that breathes fire."

For more information on placement of modifiers, refer students to **Chapter 8: Using Modifiers Correctly.**

Exercise 3 **Revising Sentences by Supplying Adjective Clauses**

POSSIBLE ANSWERS continued

8. The trainer spoke harshly to the dog, who had been disobedient for the entire session.
9. Dodging to his left and then to his right, Manuel scored the goal that won the game.
10. The veterinarian told Pamela that he was taking good care of her horse, which was lame.

The Adverb Clause

Rule 4e *(pp. 104–106)*

OBJECTIVE

- To identify and classify adverb clauses

EXTENSION

Relating to Writing

You might explain to students that they can often switch the placement of adverb clauses to change the structure of the sentence. To make this point clear, write the following sentences on the chalkboard or an overhead transparency.

1. I feverishly practiced my lines until it was my turn to speak.
2. When my name was called, I looked for a place to hide.
3. Unless a miracle happens, I have no way out!

Have students rewrite each sentence, switching the position of the adverb clause and the main clause. Point out the use of a comma after an introductory adverb clause. Encourage students to check their writing for opportunities to vary the position of adverb clauses.

8. The trainer spoke harshly to the *disobedient* dog.
9. Dodging to his left and then to his right, Manuel scored the *winning* goal.
10. The veterinarian told Pamela that he was taking good care of her *lame* horse.

The Adverb Clause

4e. An *adverb clause* is a subordinate clause that modifies a verb, an adjective, or an adverb.

An adverb clause generally tells *how, when, where, why, how much, to what extent,* or *under what condition* the action of a verb takes place.

EXAMPLES **After I had proofread my paper,** I input the corrections. [The adverb clause *After I had proofread my paper* tells *when* I input the corrections.]

Because crêpes are delicious, Joy makes them on special occasions. [*Because crêpes are delicious* tells *why* Joy makes them on special occasions.]

You and your brother may come with us **if you want to.** [*If you want to* tells *under what condition* you and your brother may come with us.]

Reference Note

For more about using **commas** to set off introductory elements, see page 280.

NOTE As you can see in the first two examples above, introductory adverb clauses are usually set off by commas.

Like adverbs, adverb clauses may also modify adjectives or adverbs.

EXAMPLES Have computers made office work easier **than it was before**? [The adverb clause *than it was before* modifies the adjective *easier,* telling *to what extent* work is easier.]

My cousin Adele reads faster **than I do.** [The adverb clause *than I do* modifies the adverb *faster,* telling *how much* faster my cousin Adele reads.]

Reference Note

For more about **complete comparisons,** see page 211.

NOTE When using adverb clauses to make comparisons, be sure your comparisons are complete.

INCOMPLETE I like dancing better than you. [Do I like dancing better than I like you? Do I like dancing better than you like dancing?]

COMPLETE I like dancing better **than you do.**

RESOURCES

The Adverb Clause

Practice

- *Language & Sentence Skills Practice,* pp. 95–98

Differentiating Instruction

- *Developmental Language & Sentence Skills,* pp. 53–54

Subordinating Conjunctions

Adverb clauses are introduced by ***subordinating conjunctions***—words that show the relationship between the adverb clause and the word or words that the clause modifies.

Common Subordinating Conjunctions			
after	because	since	when
although	before	so that	whenever
as	even though	than	where
as if	if	though	wherever
as long as	in order that	unless	whether
as soon as	once	until	while

Some subordinating conjunctions, such as *after, before, since,* and *until,* may also be used as prepositions.

EXAMPLES Be sure to hand in your report **before the end** of class today. [prepositional phrase]

Be sure to hand in your report **before class ends today.** [adverb clause]

Exercise 4 Identifying and Classifying Adverb Clauses

Identify each adverb clause in the following sentences. Then, write what the clause tells: *when, where, how, why, to what extent,* or *under what condition.* A sentence may have more than one adverb clause.

EXAMPLE 1. When you see the humble man on the next page, can you believe that he is considered one of the twentieth century's greatest leaders?

1. When you see the humble man on the next page—when

1. If you look through newspapers from the first half of the twentieth century, you will see many pictures of Mohandas K. Gandhi.
2. This man led India to independence from Britain, and he took his spinning wheel wherever he went.
3. He did so because he viewed spinning as a symbol of the peaceful, traditional Indian lifestyle.
4. He also hoped to encourage the Indian people to make their own clothes so that they would not have to depend on British industry.
5. As a form of protest, he led marches or fasted until the government met his requests.

STYLE  TIP

Because an adverb clause does not have a fixed location in a sentence, you must choose where to put the clause. Write different versions of a sentence containing an adverb clause. Then, read aloud each version to see how the placement of the clause affects flow, rhythm, and overall meaning.

EXAMPLES

After we leave for school, Mom works on her novel.

Mom works on her novel after we leave for school.

COMPUTER TIP 

If you use a computer to write compositions, you can easily experiment with the placement of adverb clauses in sentences.

GRAMMAR

DIFFERENTIATING INSTRUCTION

English-Language Learners

General Strategies. Hearing and writing numerous adverb clauses will help students who are accustomed to a different syntax. Students can practice writing adverb clauses by writing a sentence containing an adverb clause for each subordinating conjunction on the list of common subordinating conjunctions. You may want to have students share sentences in small groups.

Cantonese. In Cantonese, adverb clauses are followed by a coordinating conjunction in the main clause:

After I proofread my paper, **and** I made the corrections.

Because crepes are delicious, **so** Joy makes them on special occasions.

Draw students' attention to sentences containing adverb clauses in their readings. Show them that in English, no coordinating conjunction is needed. Ask them to find the unnecessary connecting words in their own compositions and cross them out.

Exercise 4 Identifying and Classifying Adverb Clauses

POSSIBLE ANSWERS

1. under what condition
2. where
3. why
4. why
5. to what extent

CONTENT-AREA CONNECTIONS

Science

Lab Reports. To reinforce that what students learn in one course applies to other subjects, you might work with the students' science teachers to help students write lab reports. You can emphasize that adverb clauses are especially useful to establish the order of events and to show cause and effect.

GRAMMAR

Exercise 4 Identifying and Classifying Adverb Clauses

POSSIBLE ANSWERS continued

6. to what extent
7. under what condition
8. why; when
9. when
10. why

6. Gandhi's nonviolent methods were more powerful than anyone could have predicted.
7. As India's Congress and people increasingly supported Gandhi's nonviolent program, the British government was forced to listen.
8. Gandhi was well qualified to represent India as a diplomat since he had studied law in London before he became involved in India's freedom movement.
9. After independence was assured, Gandhi turned his attention to helping India's many poor people.
10. Because he was loved throughout India and the world, Gandhi was called *Mahatma,* meaning "Great Soul."

The Noun Clause

Rule 4f *(pp. 106–108)*

OBJECTIVE

- To identify and classify noun clauses

EXTENSION

Critical Thinking

Analysis. Have students work in small groups to create noun clauses, using the introductory words listed on p. 106. Ask students to create sentences using the noun clauses. Then, have them analyze which introductory words work with clauses used as subjects, as predicate nominatives, as subjects, as predicate nominatives, as direct objects, as indirect objects, and as objects of prepositions. Students could organize their findings in a five-column chart as follows:

SUBJ	DO	IO	PN	OP
that	that		that	

The Noun Clause

4f. A *noun clause* is a subordinate clause that is used as a noun.

A noun clause may be used as a subject, as a complement (such as a predicate nominative, direct object, or indirect object), or as the object of a preposition.

SUBJECT	**What Mary Anne did to rescue the injured bird** was brave.
PREDICATE NOMINATIVE	The winner of the race will be **whoever runs fastest in the final stretch.**
DIRECT OBJECT	She finally discovered **what the answer to her question was.**
INDIRECT OBJECT	Give **whatever parts need cleaning** a rinse in detergent.
OBJECT OF PREPOSITION	He checks the ID cards of **whoever visits.**

Reference Note

For more information on **subjects, predicate nominatives, direct objects,** and **indirect objects,** see Chapter 2. For more about **objects of prepositions,** see page 70.

Noun clauses are usually introduced by the following words.

that	when	whether	whom
what	whenever	who	whomever
whatever	where	whoever	why

106 Chapter 4 The Clause

RESOURCES

The Noun Clause

Practice

- *Language & Sentence Skills Practice,* pp. 99–101

Differentiating Instruction

- *Developmental Language & Sentence Skills,* pp. 55–56

Sometimes these words have a grammatical function in the noun clause. Other times they just introduce the clause and have no other function in it.

EXAMPLES They did not know **who it could be.** [The introductory word *who* is the predicate nominative of the noun clause—*it could be who.* The entire clause is the direct object of the verb *did know.*]

Show us **what you bought.** [The introductory word *what* is the direct object in the noun clause—*you bought what.* The entire clause is the direct object of the verb *show.*]

What you learn is your decision. [The introductory word *what* is the direct object in the noun clause—*you learn what.* The entire clause is the subject of the verb *is.*]

She wished **that she were older.** [The introductory word *that* simply introduces the noun clause and has no function within the noun clause. The entire clause is the direct object of the verb *wished.*]

Sometimes the word that introduces a noun clause is omitted. In such cases, the introductory word is understood.

EXAMPLE Didn't you know **the party was canceled?** [The introductory word *that* is understood.]

Exercise 5 Identifying and Classifying Noun Clauses

Most of the following sentences contain noun clauses. If a sentence contains a noun clause, identify that clause. Then, tell how the clause is used: as a *subject,* a *predicate nominative,* a *direct object,* an *indirect object,* or an *object of a preposition.* If a sentence does not contain a noun clause, write *no noun clause.*

EXAMPLE 1. We moved to Massachusetts and did not know what we would find there.

1. what we would find there—direct object

1. What surprised me first was the yellowish green fire engine. 1. subj.
2. I had thought fire engines were always red. 2. d.o.
3. Our neighbors explained that this color keeps the fire engines from being confused with other large red trucks. 3. d.o.
4. My sister Michelle made another discovery at the bowling alley. 4. no noun clause
5. The small grapefruit-sized bowling balls with no holes were not what she was used to! 5. p.n.
6. We learned that this sport is called candlepin bowling. 6. d.o.

GRAMMAR

Differentiating Instruction

English-Language Learners

Spanish. Some Spanish-speaking students might have difficulty with the omission of the introductory word *that* in noun clauses. You may wish to write the following sentences on the chalkboard and have students read them aloud, omitting *that* in parentheses.

1. I wish (that) I could fly.
2. I understand (that) you will be moving soon.
3. The principal said (that) she would visit our class.

Learners Having Difficulty

To teach noun clauses from another perspective, you could write the following clauses on the chalkboard, asking pairs of students to use each noun clause in a sentence and identify how each clause is used.

1. that the train was late
   [*The conductor announced that the train was late.* direct object]
2. what we plan to do
   [*What we plan to do will surprise Mother.* subject]
3. whatever you need
   [*Ask the counselor for whatever you need.* object of preposition]
4. whomever I choose
   [*I will give whomever I choose the gift certificate.* indirect object]

GRAMMAR

DIFFERENTIATING INSTRUCTION

Learners Having Difficulty

Some students will understand sentence structure more clearly by marking the clauses. You could ask students to copy the sentences in **Review A** and use a different colored highlighter to mark each type of subordinate clause, leaving the independent clause unmarked.

You may want to demonstrate the first sentence on an overhead transparency.

If you stop to think about it (*adverb clause*)
why painters had a problem (*noun clause*)

7. subj.
8. o.p.
9. i.o.
10. no noun clause

7. Whoever can knock down the pins with one of those bowling balls must be an expert.
8. Later, I was surprised by how delicious the baked beans were.
9. Someone should give whoever invented Boston baked beans an award for this marvelous creation.
10. Now, after we have lived in New England for a year, both Michelle and I are happy in our new home.

Review A Identifying Subordinate Clauses

For most of the sentences in the following paragraph, identify the subordinate clause or clauses. Then, tell whether each clause is an *adjective clause*, an *adverb clause*, or a *noun clause*. If a sentence has no subordinate clauses, write *none*.

EXAMPLE **[1]** In paintings created before 1880, horses are usually shown in poses that now look quaint and unnatural.
1. *that now look quaint and unnatural—adjective clause*

1. adv./n.
2. adv./n.
3. adv./adj.
4. none
5. n.
6. adj.
7. adj
8. adv.
9. n.
10. n.

[1] If you stop to think about it, you can see why painters had a problem. **[2]** Stop-action photography had not yet been invented, and when painters looked at rapidly moving horses, they could not possibly see where the legs and hooves were at any one instant. **[3]** Whenever painters wanted to portray a galloping horse, they made up a position they thought suggested speed. **[4]** The horses in some paintings had both front legs extended far to the front and both hind legs stretched far behind. **[5]** Today, we know that this is an impossible position for a horse. **[6]** Stop-action photography was first used in the 1870s by a Californian named Eadweard Muybridge, who took this series of photographs of a galloping horse. **[7]** Along a racetrack, he set up many cameras whose shutters were controlled by threads stretched across the track. **[8]** As the horse ran by, it broke the threads and tripped the cameras' shutters one after the other. **[9]** Painters of the time thought this new technology was truly amazing! **[10]** They were the first artists in history to know what a horse really looked like at each point in its stride.

Sentences Classified According to Structure

Sentences may be classified according to purpose as declarative, imperative, interrogative, or exclamatory. Sentences may also be classified according to structure. The term ***structure*** refers to the number and types of clauses in a sentence.

Reference Note

For more on **classifying sentences by purpose,** see page 63.

4g. Depending on its structure, a sentence can be classified as simple, compound, complex, or compound-complex.

In the following examples, independent clauses are underlined once. Subordinate clauses are underlined twice.

(1) A *simple sentence* contains one independent clause and no subordinate clauses. It may have a compound subject, a compound verb, and any number of phrases.

EXAMPLES The boys [S] wanted [V] to take a vacation last summer.

Ray [S] and Joe [S] worked [V] and saved [V] enough for a trip to Ohio.

(2) A *compound sentence* contains two or more independent clauses and no subordinate clauses.

The independent clauses in a compound sentence may be joined by a comma and a coordinating conjunction; by a semicolon; or by a semicolon, a conjunctive adverb, and a comma.

EXAMPLES Originally, they [S] wanted [V] to ride bikes all the way**, but** they [S] decided [V] to take the train instead.

Ray [S] looked [V] forward to seeing his cousins**;** Joe [S] was [V] eager to play with his uncle's band.

Uncle James [S] played [V] in a country-music band**; however,** Joe [S] preferred [V] rock music.

STYLE TIP

Paragraphs in which all the sentences have the same structure can be monotonous to read. To keep your readers interested in your ideas, evaluate your writing to see whether you've used a variety of sentence structures. Then, use revising techniques—adding, cutting, replacing, and reordering—to enliven your writing by varying the structure of your sentences.

Sentences Classified According to Structure

Rule 4g *(pp. 109–114)*

OBJECTIVE

- **To classify sentences as simple, compound, complex, or compound-complex**

GRAMMAR

DIFFERENTIATING INSTRUCTION

English-Language Learners

General Strategies. You may wish to remind students that in English a clause contains both a subject and a verb. (In some languages, such as Spanish, clauses do not always require expressed subjects.) Have students pay particular attention to the subject and verb for each clause in the example sentences on p. 109.

DIRECT TEACHING

Modeling and Demonstration

Sentences Classified According to Structure. Model how to classify sentences according to structure by using the example *The band played at a dance, and Ray was pulled into a line dance that was starting.* First, ask how many independent clauses are in this sentence. [*two;* the band played at a dance, Ray was pulled into a line dance] Next, ask if there is a subordinate clause in this sentence. [*yes;* that was starting] Then, ask what kind of sentence this is according to its structure. [*compound-complex*] Point out that a compound-complex sentence contains two or more independent clauses and at least one subordinate clause. Now, have a volunteer use another example from this chapter to demonstrate how to classify sentences according to structure.

RESOURCES

Sentences Classified According to Structure

Practice

- *Language & Sentence Skills Practice,* pp. 102–103

Differentiating Instruction

- *Developmental Language & Sentence Skills,* pp. 57–60

GRAMMAR

EXTENSION

Relating to Writing

To illustrate how different types of sentences are constructed, write the following sentences on the chalkboard or on a transparency and have students use the words in parentheses to combine the sentences. Then, ask students to identify the structures of new sentences.

1. Eric read an article about book groups. He started a science fiction club. (after) [*After Eric read an article about book groups, he started a science fiction club.—complex*]
2. The members chose a book. The book appealed to everyone. A local bookstore ordered multiple copies. (that; and) [*The members chose a book that appealed to everyone, and a local bookstore ordered multiple copies.—compound-complex*]

Point out that the revised sentences are less choppy than the originals. Then, you may want to ask students to use these same patterns to create original sentences.

Exercise 6

DISTRIBUTED REVIEW

Have students identify the verbs in the independent clauses in sentences 1, 3, and 4.

1. have **3.** comes **4.** are

PRACTICE

Guided and Independent

Exercise 6 You may wish to use the first five items of **Exercise 6** as guided practice. Then, have students complete the second five items as independent practice.

HOMEWORK

NOTE Don't confuse a simple sentence that contains a compound predicate with a compound sentence. Compound sentences always have two or more complete clauses.

COMPOUND PREDICATE — **Joe** (S) **considered** (V) country music corny and **said** (V) so.

COMPOUND SENTENCE — **Joe** (S) **considered** (V) country music corny, and **he** (S) **said** (V) so.

COMPUTER TIP

A word processor can help you check for varied sentence structure in your writing. Make a copy of your document to work on. By inserting a return or a page break after every period, you can view the sentences in a vertical list and compare the structures of all the sentences in a particular paragraph. Make any revisions on the properly formatted copy of your document.

(3) A *complex sentence* contains one independent clause and at least one subordinate clause.

EXAMPLES

Because Joe (S) wanted (V) to keep his guitar with him, they (S) decided (V) against taking a plane.

If they (S) took (V) a train, they (S) could see (V) all the sights, too.

(4) A *compound-complex sentence* contains two or more independent clauses and at least one subordinate clause.

EXAMPLES

The band (S) played (V) at a dance, and Ray (S) was pulled (V) into a line dance that (S) was starting (V).

To his surprise, he (S) was (V) good at line dancing; afterward, he (S) joined (V) in whenever he (S) got (V) the chance.

Exercise 6 **Classifying Sentences According to Structure**

Classify each of the following sentences as *simple, compound, complex,* or *compound-complex.* Be sure that you can identify all subordinate and independent clauses.

Learning for Life *Continued on pp. 111–113*

Writing a Business Letter. Tell students that one's writing can be an ambassador creating a first impression. For example, prospective employers read letters of application, and college admissions officers read essays as part of the selection process.

Creating a good first impression in writing requires clarity of thought. Dependent clauses connect additional information and clarify main and supporting ideas.

To demonstrate, you may want to invite guest speakers to your class to reinforce the

EXAMPLE 1. The Iroquois are American Indian peoples originally from New York State.

1. *simple*

1. Members of the Iroquois—which include the Mohawk, Oneida, Onondaga, Cayuga, Tuscarora, and Seneca—have an ancient history of storytelling. 1. cx.
2. In the early days, professional storytellers went from house to house, and they were paid for their storytelling with small gifts. 2. cd.
3. Most of what is known today about Iroquois folk tales comes from the Senecas, whose stories have been written down by historians. 3. cx.
4. Some of the most popular stories are about a creature who is hairless except for one strip of fur down his back. 4. cx.
5. He is so huge that his back can be seen above the trees. 5. cx.
6. He eats people; because he cannot be killed in any ordinary way, he is especially frightening. 6. cd.-cx.
7. The tales about this creature are even more frightening than are the ones about Stone Coat, who has skin like stone. 7. cx.
8. Fortunately, Stone Coat is not very smart, and many of the folk tales tell of ways that the Iroquois outsmart him. 8. cd.-cx.
9. There are also tales about the Whirlwinds, who usually appear as bodiless heads with fiery eyes; in some stories, the Whirlwinds eat sticks and rocks when they cannot catch people. 9. cd.-cx.
10. Other Iroquois stories tell about the adventures of Elk, Partridge, Skunk, and Rattlesnake. 10. s.

Oral Practice

Classifying Sentences According to Structure

Read each of the following sentences aloud, and classify it as *simple, compound, complex,* or *compound-complex.*

EXAMPLE 1. In all the world, there is only one art museum for children's art, and it is located in Norway.

1. *compound*

1. This museum is the International Museum of Children's Art, which occupies a big, old house in Oslo. 1. cx.
2. The walls are covered from top to bottom with brilliantly colored creations by young artists up to age seventeen. 2. s.

PRACTICE

GRAMMAR

Using Clauses

Activity. To provide students with more practice using clauses, you might divide the class into groups of three or six and give each group identical sets of cards with the following subordinate clauses:

1. whom I trust
2. if the concert is canceled
3. who won the race
4. that you bought
5. until the bell rings
6. where the treasure is hidden

Have each team write as many sentences as possible with the clauses in three minutes. Award a point for each correct sentence. You may wish to continue the game by having each team write clauses of their own on cards and give the cards to another team. Again, give the teams a time limit to write sentences with the clauses.

Oral Practice

DISTRIBUTED REVIEW

Have students find the simple subject and verb in sentences 2, 4, and 8.

2. walls—are covered
4. few—depict; most—express
8. Mr. Goldin—has hung

importance of clear, concise writing. Possible guests could include a college admissions officer, the editor of the local newspaper, or a business executive. Ask them to talk about what impresses them most about a piece of writing.

Then, assign each student to write a letter of application for a job or for school or camp admission. Tell students they must use the development on the following page.

Extension

Sentence Structure

Activity. To emphasize the concept that sentence structure should vary for different audiences, have students work in groups to revise the simple sentences often found in children's books. You may wish to provide a stack of these books for students or ask students in advance to bring the books.

Divide the class into groups of four. Tell the students they will be revising the sentences in a children's book for an older audience. First, have the group read the book and identify sentence types. Then, have them decide what type of audience they want to address—middle school, high school, or adult.

Then, assign each group member specific pages. Remind students to use a combination of simple, compound, complex, and compound-complex sentences. Once each student has a draft of his or her pages, the group should revise it for added variety if necessary. Students may want to number their sentences and use a four-column chart to record the sentence numbers of each type of sentence used.

EXAMPLE

SIMPLE	COMPD	COMPX	CC
1, 7	2, 5	3, 4	6

You may want to ask volunteers from each group to read aloud both versions of their stories and allow the class to make suggestions for further changes.

MEETING THE CHALLENGE

Flip through a book that you enjoy, and find five examples each of simple, compound, complex, and compound-complex sentences. Write the sentences down on a sheet of paper along with the title of the book and the page number on which each sentence appears.

ANSWER
Sentences will vary, but students should have written down twenty sentences, five each of simple, compound, complex, and compound-complex sentences.

3. Many of the 100,000 works, which come from 150 countries, deal with objects from nature, but a few, like the bicycle sculpture on the previous page, focus on manufactured objects. 3. cd.-cx.
4. Of course, a few of the paintings depict troubles or problems, but most of the works express happiness and energy. 4. cd.
5. Rafael Goldin, the museum's director, says a child's first meeting with exhibited art is very important. 5. cx.
6. Children visit the museum, and they "see that a museum can mean joy and color." 6. cd.-cx.
7. "If their first visit is to a boring, dusty museum, children will always associate museums with *dusty* and *boring*." 7. cx.
8. Mr. Goldin has even hung some of the paintings at toddlers' eye level to encourage each young visitor's own personal relationship with art. 8. s.
9. Young visitors are very excited when they learn that all the artwork was created by children, and they are often inspired to start painting. 9. cd.-cx.
10. Wouldn't it be great if there were a museum like that here? 10. cx.

Review B Identifying and Classifying Subordinate Clauses

Identify the subordinate clause or clauses in each of the following sentences. Tell whether each clause is used as an *adjective*, an *adverb*, or a *noun*. If a clause is used as an adjective or an adverb, write the word or words the clause modifies. If a clause is used as a noun, write *subj.* for subject, *d.o.* for direct object, *i.o.* for indirect object, *p.n.* for predicate nominative, or *o.p.* for object of a preposition.

EXAMPLES
1. When our science teacher described insect-eating plants, we listened with amazement.
   1. *When our science teacher described insect-eating plants—adverb—listened*
2. What we heard sounded like science fiction.
   2. *What we heard—noun—subj.*

1. Plants that eat insects usually live in swampy areas. 1. adj.
2. Because the soil in these regions lacks nutrients, these plants do not get enough nitrogen through their roots. 2. adv.
3. The nitrogen that these plants need comes from the protein in the bodies of insects. 3. adj.
4. How these plants catch their food is interesting. 4. n.—subj.
5. A pitcher plant's sweet scent appeals to whatever insect is nearby. 5. n.—o.p.

112 Chapter 4 The Clause

Learning for Life *Continued from p. 111*

DEVELOPMENT OF LETTER	
Paragraph 1	Introduce self, giving other background
Paragraph 2	Announce goal and means of achieving it
Paragraphs 3 and 4	Outline and support qualifications
Paragraph 5	Summarize desires and thank recipient

6. The insect thinks that it will find food inside the plant. 6. n.—d.o.
7. What happens instead is that the insect drowns in the plant's digestive juices. 7. n.—subj./n.—p.n.
8. The Venus' flytrap shown on the preceding page has what looks like small bear traps at the ends of its stalks. 8. n.—d.o.
9. When a trap is open, an insect can wander in and spring the trap. 9. adv.
10. The insect is then digested by the plant in a process that can take several days. 10. adj.

Review C **Classifying Subordinate Clauses**

Classify each of the following italicized clauses as an *adjective*, an *adverb*, or a *noun clause.* Be prepared to explain your answers.

EXAMPLES [1] *Until our class visited the county courthouse,* we had imagined [2] *that most court cases were like the ones on TV.*

1. *adverb*
2. *noun*

[1] *As we left the courtroom,* we thought about the men [2] *who had been on trial.* [3] *Although they had not committed a serious crime,* they had broken the law. The law says [4] *that removing sand from our local beach is illegal.* A police officer caught the men [5] *when they could not move their truck,* [6] *which had become stuck in the sand.* [7] *After the judge had read the law to them,* the men claimed [8] *that they had never heard of that law.* The judge, who reminded them [9] *that ignorance of the law is no excuse,* fined each man one hundred dollars. The men promised [10] *that they would not take any more beach sand.*

HELP—In the examples in Review C, the first italicized clause is an adverb clause that modifies the verb phrase *had imagined*. The second italicized clause is a noun clause that acts as a direct object of the verb phrase *had imagined*.

1. adj. 2. adv.
3. adv.
4. n.
5. adv.
6. adj. 7. adv.
8. n.
9. n.
10. n.

Review D **Rewriting a Paragraph to Include a Variety of Sentence Structures**

You and a partner are working together on an essay about life in the 1800s. While researching the topic, the two of you discover a diary written by a young woman named Barbara Sneyd. You and your partner have made copies of Sneyd's paintings and have recorded information about her life. Your job is to rewrite the paragraph on the next page to improve its style. You will need to vary the sentence structure, and you may want to add or delete details to improve the organization. Write at least one sentence with each kind of structure: *simple, compound, complex,* and *compound-complex.* Be prepared to identify the structure of each sentence you write.

GRAMMAR

You might want students to work in small groups to brainstorm material for their letters. Once students have created their first drafts, you could allow them to share their drafts with their groups for input.

Students should make revisions, proofread, and present a final draft for publication. They can publish the letters either by sending them to a prospective interviewer or by posting them on the class bulletin board.

GRAMMAR

Review D **Rewriting a Paragraph to Include a Variety of Sentence Structures**

POSSIBLE ANSWERS

Barbara Sneyd lived more than one hundred years ago *(simple)*. Her wealthy family lived in the English countryside, and they loved to ride and hunt *(compound)*. Barbara had a governess, and although the governess kept her very busy studying, Barbara did have time to pursue her greatest passion, which was riding *(compound-complex)*. Barbara's mother encouraged her to keep a diary about her life *(simple)*. When Barbara was fourteen, she started her diary *(complex)*. It took the form of a sketchbook, and in it she recorded her family's life *(compound)*. She painted many small pictures of her family's activities: fishing, visiting, and picnicking *(simple)*. Barbara was also a keen observer of nature; she drew and painted her family's horses and pets and the flowers from the garden, as well as many small landscapes of the countryside around her home *(compound)*. Above all, her diary is full of paintings of horses, which she loved *(complex)*. If you want to see what her paintings look like, some pictures from her diary are shown on this page *(complex)*.

Barbara Sneyd lived more than one hundred years ago. Her home was in the English countryside. She came from a wealthy family. Her family loved to ride and hunt. Barbara had a governess. The governess kept Barbara very busy studying. Barbara did have time to pursue her greatest passion. Her greatest passion was riding. Her mother encouraged her to keep a diary. The diary would be about Barbara's life. Barbara started the diary. She was fourteen. It took the form of a sketchbook. In it she recorded her family's life. She painted many small pictures of her family's activities. They went fishing, visiting, and picnicking. Barbara was also a keen observer of nature. She drew and painted her family's horses and pets and the flowers from the garden. She painted many small landscapes. The landscapes showed the countryside around her home. Above all, her diary is full of paintings of horses. She loved horses. You may want to see what her paintings look like. Some pictures from her diary are shown on this page.

Numerals in brackets refer to rules tested by the items in the Chapter Review.

Chapter Review

A. Identifying Clauses

Identify each italicized clause in the following sentences as independent or subordinate.

1. The fire started *because someone did not smother a campfire.*
2. The family *that bought our house* is moving in next week.
3. Did you know *that Dr. Joel is the new ambassador to Lebanon*?
4. Mr. Kim will buy the store *if the bank lends him the money.*
5. According to Ms. Garza, our math teacher, *the binary system is important to know.*
6. *Wherever Maggie goes,* her poodle Jack follows.
7. *She won the golf match* because she had practiced diligently.
8. *Whatever you decide* is fine with me.
9. *I saw the job advertised in the school paper* and decided to apply for it.
10. We were proud *that you conceded defeat so graciously.*

1. [4c]
2. [4c]
3. [4c]
4. [4c]
5. [4b]
6. [4c]
7. [4b]
8. [4c]
9. [4b]
10. [4c]

B. Identifying and Classifying Subordinate Clauses

Identify the subordinate clause in each of the following sentences. Tell whether each clause is used as an *adjective,* an *adverb,* or a *noun.*

11. Emily Dickinson, who was born in 1830 in Amherst, Massachusetts, was a great American poet.
12. She appeared to lead a fairly normal life until she became a recluse in her family's home.
13. There she wrote poems that literary critics now call "great American poetry."
14. Unfortunately, only a few of Dickinson's poems were published while she was alive.
15. After she died in 1886, her other poems were published.
16. I think everyone should read at least some of Dickinson's poetry.
17. Dickinson is a poet whose work I now read often.
18. The poems I have just finished reading are "A Narrow Fellow in the Grass" and "Apparently with No Surprise."

11. adj. [4c, d]
12. adv. [4c, e]
13. adj. [4c, d]
14. adv. [4c, e]
15. adv. [4c, e]
16. n. [4c, f]
17. adj. [4c, d]
18. adj. [4c, d]

ASSESSING

Monitoring Progress

Chapter Review. To assess student progress, you may want to compare the types of items missed on the **Diagnostic Preview** to those missed on the **Chapter Review.** You may want to work out specific goals for mastering essential information with individual students who are still having difficulty.

GRAMMAR

RESOURCES

The Clause

Review

- *Language & Sentence Skills Practice,* pp. 104–107

Assessment

- *Holt Handbook Chapter Tests with Answer Key,* pp. 7–8, 52

19. adv. [4c, e]
20. n. [4c, f]

19. The rhythms of Dickinson's poems are best appreciated when you read the poems aloud.
20. Whatever I read by Emily Dickinson surprises and inspires me.

C. Classifying Sentences According to Structure and Identifying Independent and Subordinate Clauses

Classify each of the following sentences as *simple, compound, complex,* or *compound-complex.* Identify all subordinate and independent clauses.

21. s. [4g(1), b]
22. cd. [4g(2), b]
23. cd. [4g(2), b]
24. cx. [4g(3), b, c]
25. cx. [4g(3), b, c]
26. cd.-cx. [4g(4), b, c]
27. s. [4g(1), b]
28. cd. [4g(2), b]
29. cd.-cx. [4g(4), b, c]
30. cd. [4g(2), b]
31. s. [4g(1), b]
32. cd.-cx. [4g(4), b, c]
33. cx. [4g(3), b, c]
34. cd. [4g(2), b]
35. cd.-cx. [4g(4), b, c]

21. After eating and drinking, the elephants galloped through the wheat field.
22. Mr. Chisholm wanted to go bowling, but Mrs. Chisholm preferred the dinner theater.
23. Ten steps up the dark staircase, the twins lost their nerve; dinner at home suddenly seemed much more appealing.
24. Kenzuo insisted that the bullet train was the best way to get to Osaka after midnight.
25. When the travelers arrived at the inn, the innkeeper greeted them.
26. Dr. Bourgeois knew that singing loudly would only irritate others, so he decided to keep his high spirits to himself.
27. Preparing to eat, the dog spotted itself in the mirror.
28. Mom always wanted to live in New Mexico, but Dad was too used to living in North Carolina to move.
29. Before the concert began, the first violinist leaned forward to tie his shoe; this innocent action set off a whole chain of unlikely events.
30. Tom Bell is Angela's favorite actor, but Sally likes Ricky Blake.
31. Washing the car, Benito paused to admire the vintage biplane flying overhead.
32. Joseph had worked hard for straight A's on his exams, and when the results came in, he discovered that his hard work had paid off.
33. When the crocodile approached, the heron flew away.
34. Arnie carefully lined up the pieces on the chessboard; however, Dario's foot caught the edge of the board, and both board and pieces flew into the air.
35. We had hoped that being subtle would be enough, and, indeed, for a while this tactic seemed to be working; but as the day wore on, we slowly realized that a bolder approach was needed.

36. President Kennedy was assassinated in Dallas on November 22, 1963.

37. Charles argued that a picnic lunch was the best idea.

38. Professor Chan showed his class his slides of the Great Wall of China, and he used the slides later as the basis for a lecture on Genghis Khan.

39. After the cyclists rounded the bend, the Swiss champion Michel Neibergall took the lead.

40. When the crows descended on the barren field, the field mice scurried for shelter.

36. s. [4g(1), b]
37. cx. [4g(3), b, c]
38. cd. [4g(2), b]
39. cx. [4g(3), b, c]
40. cx. [4g(3), b, c]

Writing Application

Using Sentence Variety in Postcards

Sentence Structures You are writing postcards about your summer activities, such as baseball or soccer camp, computer camp, or cheerleading camp. Write a brief note telling your six-year-old cousin about a few experiences that you think he or she would find interesting. Write another note to an adult friend or relative about your experiences. Use sentence structure and language that are appropriate to each reader.

Prewriting If you have been to a summer camp, make a list of experiences that you could describe. If you haven't been to camp, list activities that you enjoy during the summer.

Writing As you write your first draft, make sure to include details that would interest your different audiences. Show the relationships between your details by using a variety of subordinate adjective, adverb, and noun clauses.

Revising Read your notes to a classmate, without telling which note is to your cousin and which is to your adult friend or relative. If your classmate can't tell which note is to which person, you should revise your language, information, and sentence structures.

Publishing Check to be sure that all your sentences are complete sentences. Pay special attention to the use of commas to separate clauses. You may want to post your notes on a class bulletin board or create a Web page for them.

Reference Note

For more about using **commas,** see page 271.

GRAMMAR

APPLICATION

Writing Application

Prewriting Tip. Because students will be writing for two different audiences, you may suggest that they create two separate prewriting lists. Remind them that the experiences that interest a six-year-old sister may not be the experiences they want to share with an adult friend or relative.

Prewriting Tip. Depending on their familiarity with summer camps, students might create extensive lists in the prewriting stage. Tell them that they must narrow their lists to fit the length of their letters. Limiting a broad topic requires analysis. Remind students that they must keep their audience and purpose in mind when narrowing their topics.

Scoring Rubric. While you will want to pay particular attention to students' use of appropriate language and sentence structure, you will also want to evaluate overall writing performance. You may want to give a split score to indicate development and clarity of the composition as well as grammar skills.

CHAPTER

5

INTRODUCING THE CHAPTER

- This chapter offers a review of subject-verb agreement and pronoun-antecedent agreement, with special emphasis on the compound subject and other agreement problems.
- The chapter concludes with a **Chapter Review** including a **Writing Application** feature that asks students to write a description using correct subject-verb agreement.
- For help in integrating the chapter with writing assignments, use the **Teaching Strands** chart on pp. T24–T25.

CHAPTER

5

Agreement

Subject and Verb, Pronoun and Antecedent

Diagnostic Preview

A. Proofreading Sentences for Subject-Verb and Pronoun-Antecedent Agreement

Each of the following sentences contains an error in agreement. Identify each incorrect verb or pronoun, and supply the correct form.

EXAMPLE 1. Rochelle Richardson, one of our city's former mayors, live next door to me.

1. *live—lives*

Numerals in brackets refer to rules tested by the items in the Diagnostic Preview.

1. was [5k, c]
2. his or her [5t(1), s]
3. is [5d, c]
4. her [5t(1), s]
5. has [5d]
6. their [5t(2)]
7. give [5i]
8. are [5m, g]
9. has [5q]
10. it [5z]

1. When the truck overturned, a herd of cattle were set free on the expressway.
2. The teacher reminded everyone to sharpen their pencil.
3. Not one of our tomato plants are producing any fruit, but the green beans seem to be thriving.
4. Has each of the girls memorized their part?
5. Everybody have been talking about the class picnic ever since you thought of the idea.
6. Both of the finalists played his or her best.
7. Many of their experiments have failed, but neither Dr. Jenkins nor his assistants ever gives up hope.
8. There is a brush, a comb, and a mirror on the dresser top.
9. Many a sailor have perished when his or her ship ran aground on that reef.
10. Read *Little Women* and write a plot summary about them.

CHAPTER RESOURCES

Internet

- Web resources: go.hrw.com

Practice & Review

- *Language & Sentence Skills Practice,* pp. 112–132
- *Language & Sentence Skills Practice Answer Key,* pp. 53–61

Application & Enrichment

- *Language & Sentence Skills Practice,* pp. 111, 133–136
- *Language & Sentence Skills Practice Answer Key,* pp. 53, 61

B. Proofreading Sentences for Subject-Verb and Pronoun-Antecedent Agreement

Most of the following sentences contain at least one agreement error. For each error, identify the incorrect verb or pronoun and supply the correct form. If the sentence is already correct, write *C*.

EXAMPLE 1. Filming an animal in its natural surroundings present many problems.

1. *present—presents*

11. One problem is that the filmmaker, in most cases, have to get quite close to the animal.
12. Ten yards often make the difference between a good scene and no scene at all.
13. A zoom lens or a telephoto lens are generally used, but even then, getting good photographs can be very difficult.
14. Before filming, the crew usually take turns watching the animal for weeks to learn its habits and find good vantage points for taking pictures.
15. In addition, the filmmaker and the crew uses every trick of the trade in filming wild animals.
16. For example, *Foxes at Night* were almost certainly not filmed at night!
17. "Nighttime" films are generally made during daylight hours, when there is plenty of natural light.
18. Later, all of the daytime footage are darkened through the use of filters.
19. Also, many of the animals used in a nature film has been trained or partially tamed.
20. For example, if a filmmaker or a member of the crew take care of a bird from the moment it hatches, it will instinctively follow them.
21. The photographer can then easily take close-up pictures of the bird after it matures.
22. In many films, scenes of animals giving birth and raising its young are filmed in a studio, not in the wild.
23. Photographers get good footage by building a den where he or she can film the baby animals through a window beside the nest.
24. This film, along with footage taken in the natural habitat, are then skillfully edited.
25. As a result, few of the viewers ever suspect that the film shown to him or her has been shot indoors.

11. has [5c]
12. makes [5n]
13. is [5h]
14. C [5k, s(1)]
15. use [5g]
16. was [5p]
17. C [5b(2), m]
18. is [5f]
19. have [5e, c]
20. takes / him or her [5h, s(1)]
21. C [5b(1), s(1)]
22. their [5s(2)]
23. they [5s(2)]
24. is [5c]
25. them [5t(2)]

USAGE

ASSESSING

Entry-Level Assessment

Diagnostic Preview. The **Diagnostic Preview** requires students to understand and use correct subject-verb and pronoun-antecedent agreement. Item numbers 2, 4, 6, and 10 in Part A and 20, 22, 23, and 25 in Part B have pronoun errors. If students miss all or most of these, you may want to emphasize the **Agreement of Pronoun and Antecedent** section.

PRETEACHING

Lesson Starter

Motivation. Encourage student interest in the chapter by assigning an ongoing project to find agreement bloopers. Tell students to watch for agreement errors in magazines, newspapers, books, advertisements, television shows, movies, and conversations. Students should keep a notebook of the errors, including corrected or edited versions. Allow students a few minutes per week to share errors, or select bloopers for display on the bulletin board.

Differentiating Instruction

- *Developmental Language & Sentence Skills Guided Practice,* pp. 61–68
- *Developmental Language & Sentence Skills Guided Practice Teacher's Notes and Answer Key,* p. 16

Assessment

- *Holt Handbook Chapter Tests with Answer Key,* pp. 9–10, 52

Number
Rule 5a *(p. 120)*

OBJECTIVE

- To classify nouns and pronouns by number

DIFFERENTIATING INSTRUCTION

English-Language Learners

Cantonese and Vietnamese. The plural *–s* ending is often one of the last aspects of English to be mastered by speakers of Cantonese and Vietnamese. Neither language generally uses a plural form of a noun, relying instead on other features in the sentence: *one book, two book.* Also, Cantonese speakers may have difficulty pronouncing the consonant cluster that results from the plural *–s* ending because Cantonese words follow a consonant-vowel-consonant-vowel pattern.

To practice forming plurals, ask students to list the items in pictures: one table, two chairs, and so on. Make a card with a large *S* on it to hold up as a prompt when students leave off the plural *–s.*

Similarly, the *–s* ending on third-person singular verbs will often be left off by speakers of these languages because of the pronunciation difficulty, not because they don't know the rules for subject-verb agreement.

Exercise 1 Classifying Nouns and Pronouns by Number

ANSWERS

1. pl.
2. pl.
3. pl.
4. sing.
5. sing.
6. sing.
7. pl.
8. sing.
9. sing.
10. pl.

USAGE

Number

Number is the form a word takes to indicate whether the word is singular or plural.

5a. A word that refers to one person, place, thing, or idea is *singular* in number. A word that refers to more than one is *plural* in number.

Singular	Plural
student	students
princess	princesses
child	children
tooth	teeth
it	they
himself	themselves
berry	berries
deer	deer

Exercise 1 Classifying Nouns and Pronouns by Number

Identify each italicized word as either *singular* or *plural.*

EXAMPLE As a child, the girl in the **[1]** *photograph* was sure she was not very good at anything.

1. *singular*

She was overshadowed by the other [1] *children* in her family, especially by her older sister Madge, who wrote [2] *stories* and plays. Lonely and full of self-doubt, the girl surrounded herself with imaginary [3] *companions.* [4] *Everything* changed, though, when she caught influenza and became restless during her recovery. Her mother brought her a [5] *notebook* and suggested that, like Madge, she might write a story. After practicing on short stories, she decided to tackle a detective [6] *novel.* [7] "*They* are very difficult to do," said Madge. "I don't think you could write one." Madge was wrong: The young author was Agatha Christie, who became the most successful mystery [8] *writer* in history. Her mystery novels and story collections have sold many millions of copies in [9] *English* and in at least sixty other [10] *languages.*

RESOURCES

Number

Practice

- *Language & Sentence Skills Practice,* p. 112

Agreement of Subject and Verb

5b. **A verb should agree in number with its subject.**

(1) Singular subjects take singular verbs.

EXAMPLES **He washes** the dishes. [The singular verb *washes* agrees with the singular subject *He.*]

A **girl** in my neighborhood **plays** in the band. [The singular subject *girl* takes the singular verb *plays.*]

(2) Plural subjects take plural verbs.

EXAMPLES **They wash** the dishes.

Several **girls** in my neighborhood **play** in the band.

In the examples above, the verbs agree in number with their subjects. Like the single-word verbs above, verb phrases also agree with their subjects. However, in a verb phrase, only the first helping (auxiliary) verb changes its form to agree with a singular or plural subject.

EXAMPLES **He has been washing** the dishes.

They have been washing the dishes.

A **girl** in my neighborhood **was playing** in the band.

Several **girls** in my neighborhood **were playing** in the band.

NOTE Generally, nouns ending in *–s* are plural (*friends, girls*), but verbs ending in *–s* are generally singular (*sees, hears*).

5c. **The number of the subject usually is not determined by a word in a phrase or clause following the subject.**

EXAMPLES The apartments **across the street** do not have balconies. [*Do have* agrees with *apartments,* not *street.*]

The planes **pulling up to the gate** were purchased by a movie company. [*Were purchased* agrees with *planes,* not *gate.*]

Eli, **one of my friends,** was late. [*Was* agrees with *Eli,* not *friends.*]

The movie **that I saw two weeks ago** was reviewed in today's paper. [*Was reviewed* agrees with *movie,* not *weeks.*]

Reference Note

For more about **helping verbs,** see page 19.

Reference Note

For guidelines on **forming plurals of nouns,** see page 367.

Reference Note

For more about **phrases,** see Chapter 3. For more about **clauses,** see Chapter 4. For examples of **subjects whose number is determined by a phrase following the subject,** see page 124.

Agreement of Subject and Verb

Rules 5b–f *(pp. 121–126)*

OBJECTIVES

- To identify verbs that agree in number with their subjects
- To identify subjects and choose verbs that agree in number
- To choose verbs with the correct number

DIRECT TEACHING

Modeling and Demonstration

Agreement of Subject and Verb. Model how to identify verbs that agree in number with their subjects by using the example *A girl in my neighborhood was playing in the band.* First, ask what the subject is. [*girl*] Next, ask whether this subject is singular or plural. [*singular*] Then, ask which word or word group functions as the verb. [*was playing*] Ask whether this verb phrase is singular or plural. [*singular*] Explain that singular subjects take singular verbs, and that plural subjects take plural verbs. Also, point out that in a verb phrase, the first helping verb, in this case *was,* agrees with the subject in number. Now, have a volunteer use another example from this chapter to demonstrate how to determine subject-verb agreement.

RESOURCES

Agreement of Subject and Verb

Practice

- *Language & Sentence Skills Practice,* pp. 113–116

Differentiating Instruction

- *Developmental Language & Sentence Skills,* pp. 61–64

Exercise 2

DISTRIBUTED REVIEW
For a review of **Chapters 3** and **4**, have students find the following items in sentences 1, 4, 5, 6, and 7.

1. a noun clause [*how noodles are prepared*]

4. an infinitive phrase [*to prevent sticking*]

5. an adverb clause [*After the noodles have dried a little*]

6. a prepositional phrase [*from either wheat flour, called* udon, *or buckwheat flour, called* soba]

7. two past participles [*cooked, mixed*]

USAGE

RETEACHING

Subject-Verb Agreement

To demonstrate to students that they may naturally recognize correct subject-verb agreement, you might put the following nonsense sentences on the chalkboard and ask students to select the correct "verb."

1. The shink (grimp, grimps) the vork. [*grimps*]

2. The shinks (grimp, grimps) the vork. [*grimp*]

Then, ask students to explain how they chose their "verbs." [*Students may say that plural nouns and singular third-person verbs commonly end in –s.*]

NOTE *As well as, along with, together with,* and *in addition to* are compound prepositions. Words in phrases beginning with compound prepositions do not affect the number of the subject or verb.

EXAMPLE **Anne,** together with her cousins, **is** backpacking in Nevada.

Exercise 2 Identifying Verbs That Agree in Number with Their Subjects

For each of the following sentences, choose the verb in parentheses that agrees with the subject.

EXAMPLE **1.** Did you know that people in Japan frequently (*eat, eats*) noodles?

1. eat

1. These pictures (*show, shows*) how noodles are prepared.
2. First, the noodle maker (*roll, rolls*) out the dough as thin as possible.
3. Then, the cook (*slice, slices*) the folded layers.
4. Next, the strands of noodles (*is, are*) separated and dusted with flour to prevent sticking.
5. After the noodles have dried a little, they (*go, goes*) into boiling water or broth to cook.
6. The Japanese (*enjoy, enjoys*) noodles made from either wheat flour, called *udon,* or buckwheat flour, called *soba.*
7. A dish of cooked noodles mixed with sauce, broth, fish, or vegetables (*makes, make*) a popular lunch.
8. Noodle shops all over Japan (*serves, serve*) a variety of noodle dishes.
9. These shops often (*resemble, resembles*) fast-food restaurants in the United States.
10. For lunch or a snack, customers at a noodle shop (*order, orders*) noodles with their favorite toppings.

MINI-LESSON Mechanics

Forming Plurals. As a quick review, you may want to remind students of common ways plural nouns are formed in English:

- add –*s* (car, cars)
- add –*es* (fox, foxes)
- change letters in the word (woman, women)
- keep the same form (sheep, sheep)

Ask students to write in their journals examples of each type of plural form.

Exercise 3 **Identifying Subjects and Verbs That Agree in Number**

Identify the subject of each verb in parentheses in the following paragraph. Then, choose the form of the verb that agrees with the subject.

EXAMPLE Units of measure sometimes **[1]** (*causes, cause*) confusion.

1. Units—cause

Confusion among shoppers **[1]** (*is, are*) understandable because the traditional system for indicating quantities **[2]** (*makes, make*) shopping a guessing game. For example, the quantity printed on yogurt containers **[3]** (*is, are*) the number of ounces in a container. A shopper on the lookout for bargains **[4]** (*does, do*) not know whether liquid or solid measure is indicated. In addition, different brands of juice **[5]** (*shows, show*) the same quantity in different ways. A can labeled "twenty-four ounces" **[6]** (*contains, contain*) the same quantity as a can labeled "one pint eight ounces." Shoppers' confusion over such labeling, along with rising prices, **[7]** (*is, are*) a matter of concern to consumer groups. These groups believe that the metric system, in use in European countries, **[8]** (*clears, clear*) up most of the confusion. The units in the metric system **[9]** (*has, have*) fixed relationships to one another. As a result, consumer groups in this country **[10]** (*continues, continue*) to advocate our adopting this system of measurement.

Exercise 4 **Choosing Verbs with the Correct Number**

Each of the following sentences contains an italicized pair of verbs in parentheses. From each pair, choose the form of the verb that agrees with its subject.

EXAMPLE **1.** Of all numbers, the number 12 (*is, are*) one of the most versatile.

1. is

1. The even division of 12 by 1, 2, 3, 4, and 6 (*is, are*) possible.

2. Curiously, the sum of these five divisors (*is, are*) a square, 16; and their product is 144, which is the square of 12 itself.

3. When the Greek philosopher Plato devised his ideal state, the system of weights and measures (*were, was*) based on the number 12 because it could be evenly divided in so many ways.

4. To this day, many quantities in our lives (*involve, involves*) the number 12.

EXAMPLES

1. alphabet (alphabets)

2. box (boxes)

3. man (men)

4. Chinese (Chinese)

Students may want to use their words in a rhyme or a sentence.

PRACTICE

Guided and Independent

Exercises You may wish to use **Exercise 3** as guided practice. Then, have students complete **Exercise 4** as independent practice.

HOMEWORK

DIFFERENTIATING INSTRUCTION

English-Language Learners

Japanese and Korean. In these languages, objects often appear before their verbs. For example, the English sentence "Mary sees the boys" might be ordered "Boys Mary sees" or "Mary boys sees." To help students avoid making the verb agree with the object, you might request that students write most sentences in subject-verb-object order.

Advanced Learners

Students may be interested to learn that many of the forms that were once used to show number, tense, person, and gender were dropped as Old English evolved into Modern English. In addition to the pronouns that became *I*, *we*, and *you*, there were once forms used to refer to only two people: *wit* (we two) and *git* (pronounced *yit*, "you two").

Special Education Students

To reinforce subject-verb agreement, you might have students color-code sentence parts in sentences they copy or write themselves. For example, students might use yellow for subjects and blue for verbs. To help students focus on endings, have them indicate *–s* endings on nouns and verbs by using red. Remind them that if both the subject and the verb end in *–s*, something is probably wrong.

USAGE

5. The number of months in a year, inches in a foot, and items in a dozen (*is, are*) 12.
6. In our courts of law, 12 members of a jury (*decides, decide*) a defendant's guilt or innocence.
7. Each player in a game of checkers (*begin, begins*) with 12 pieces.
8. In bowling, 12 consecutive strikes (*give, gives*) you a perfect game.
9. The number of black pentagons on a soccer ball (*equal, equals*) the number of buttons on a push-button telephone—12.
10. Samuel Clemens even used this number as his pen name—the riverboat slang for 2 fathoms, or 12 feet, (*are, is*) *mark twain*!

TIPS & TRICKS

The words *one, thing,* and *body* are singular, and so are the indefinite pronouns that contain these words.

EXAMPLES

Is [any]**one** late?

[Every]**body was** welcome.

[No]**thing has** been lost.

5d. The following indefinite pronouns are singular: *anybody, anyone, anything, each, either, everybody, everyone, everything, neither, nobody, no one, nothing, one, somebody, someone,* and *something.*

EXAMPLES **Each** of the athletes **runs** effortlessly.

Neither of the women **is** ready to start.

Someone was waving a large flag.

Does everyone who signed up **enjoy** playing tennis?

5e. The following indefinite pronouns are plural: *both, few, many,* and *several.*

EXAMPLES **Were both** of the games **postponed**?

Few that I know of **have qualified.**

Several of the runners **are exercising.**

5f. The indefinite pronouns *all, any, more, most, none,* and *some* may be singular or plural, depending on their meaning in a sentence.

These pronouns are singular when they refer to a singular word and plural when they refer to a plural word.

EXAMPLES **Some** of the test **is** hard. [*Some* refers to the singular noun *test.*]

Some of the questions **are** easy. [*Some* refers to the plural noun *questions.*]

All of the exhibit **is** open to the public.

All of the paintings **are** on display.

MEETING THE CHALLENGE

Authors must write clear and informative descriptions to truly immerse a reader into the world of the book. Imagine that you are writing a description of a place or person you love. Write a brief paragraph of ten sentences describing this person or place. Be precise in your description, and use at least one indefinite pronoun in each sentence. Be sure to check for proper subject-verb agreement.

ANSWER
Sentences will vary.

DIRECT TEACHING

Indefinite Pronouns

To help students learn when the pronouns listed in **Rule 5f** are singular and when they are plural, divide the class into groups of three and have each group contribute six prepositional phrases beginning with *of*. Then, have groups trade phrases and make complete sentences by inserting the pronouns *some*, *all*, *more*, *most*, *any*, and *none* before the *of* phrases and using the pronouns as subjects. Have groups trade sentences to check for correct agreement.

MINI-LESSON Grammar

Prepositional Phrases. Familiarity with prepositional phrases should help simplify subject-verb agreement for students. Refer students to the list of prepositions on p. 28, and remind them that a prepositional phrase includes a preposition, a noun or pronoun as an object, and any modifiers of that object. Use the following example to illustrate that the verb must agree with the subject—not the object of the preposition.

subj. prep. obj. v.
This bag [of old clothes] is heavy.

Most of his routine **sounds** familiar.
Most of his jokes **sound** familiar.

Was any of the feedback positive?
Were any of the reviews positive?

The rice was eaten. **None is** left.
The potatoes were eaten. **None are** left.

More of the class **is** going to the archaeological dig.
More of the students **are** going to the archaeological dig.

Exercise 5 Identifying Subjects and Verbs That Agree in Number

Identify the subject of each verb in parentheses. Then, choose the form of the verb that agrees with that subject.

EXAMPLE
1. Several of the kittens (*has, have*) been adopted.
1. *Several—have*

1. Each of the comedians (*tries, try*) to outdo the other.
2. Somebody on the bus (*was, were*) whistling.
3. (*Is, Are*) all of the apples spoiled?
4. Neither of these books (*has, have*) an index.
5. (*Do, Does*) everybody in the class have a pencil?
6. Few of these jobs (*sounds, sound*) challenging.
7. (*Is, Are*) more of the vendors in the market?
8. She said that no one in the office (*leaves, leave*) early.
9. Both of her parents (*has, have*) offered us a ride.
10. (*Do, Does*) most of those CDs belong to her?

Review A Proofreading a Paragraph for Subject-Verb Agreement

Identify the agreement errors in the following paragraph. Then, supply the correct form of each incorrect verb.

EXAMPLE
[1] On weekends, I often goes with my mother to antique shops.
1. *goes—go*

[1] Until recently, this hunt for old things were very boring. [2] Then one day I noticed that a dusty shoe box full of antique postcards were sitting near me on a counter. [3] Soon I was flipping through the cards, and before you knows it, I had decided to start a

TIPS & TRICKS

Some of the words listed in **Rule 5d** can also be used as adjectives or as parts of correlative conjunctions: *each, either, neither, one*. Used as these parts of speech, such words cannot function as subjects.

Reference Note

For more information about **adjectives,** see page 10. For more about **correlative conjunctions,** see page 32.

Reference Note

For more information about **indefinite pronouns,** see page 9. For information on distinguishing **indefinite pronouns from adjectives,** see page 11.

USAGE

DIFFERENTIATING INSTRUCTION

Learners Having Difficulty

To help students avoid making the verb agree with the object of a preposition rather than with the subject, you might ask them to use removable adhesive strips to cover prepositional phrases in sentences 1, 2, 4–6, 8, and 9 of **Exercise 5.** Remind them to find the subject by starting with the verb and asking *who* or *what* is doing the action.

Ask students to locate a piece of their own writing and highlight all prepositional phrases to determine whether such phrases have interfered with subject-verb agreement. Have students make any necessary corrections.

For additional information and practice, refer students to **Chapter 1: Parts of Speech Overview** and **Chapter 3: The Phrase.**

Review A Proofreading a Paragraph for Subject-Verb Agreement

ANSWERS

1. were—was
2. were—was
3. knows—know

Review A **Proofreading a Paragraph for Subject-Verb Agreement**

ANSWERS continued

4. is—are
5. has—have
6. glows—glow
7. shows—show
8. are—is
9. are—is
10. was—were

USAGE

The Compound Subject

Rules 5g–i *(pp. 126–128)*

OBJECTIVES

- To read aloud sentences with correct subject-verb agreement
- To choose correct verb forms in sentences with compound subjects

EXTENSION

Relating to Literature

If your literature book contains Toni Cade Bambara's short story "My Delicate Heart Condition," have students look at the sixth sentence in the third paragraph. In her list of food vendors she passed, Bambara uses a number of conjunctions in close succession. Ask students to explain why the author might have chosen this construction. [*It makes the sentence sound like conversation, emphasizes the number of food vendors she passed, and creates a rhythmic pace.*] Ask students to read the sentence without the conjunctions, as though the items in the list were joined with commas, and explain how the effect changed. [*The rhythm is slower because the commas call for pauses.*]

postcard collection! [**4**] The cards in my collection is very precious to me. [**5**] Because I am interested in American history, I has chosen to specialize in cards showing American Indians. [**6**] On one of my cards, the flames of a campfire glows in front of several Plains Indian tepees under a colorful sunset. [**7**] Most of the postcards in my collection shows pictures of Native American leaders and warriors. [**8**] On my favorite card, a Navajo mother wrapped in beautiful blankets are posing with her baby on her back. [**9**] Collecting postcards are not an expensive hobby either. [**10**] Many of my cards was priced at a dollar or less.

The Compound Subject

A ***compound subject*** consists of two or more subjects that are joined by a conjunction and that have the same verb.

Reference Note

For more information about **compound subjects,** see page 52.

5g. Subjects joined by *and* generally take a plural verb.

The following compound subjects joined by *and* name more than one person, place, thing, or idea and take plural verbs.

EXAMPLES **George Lucas** and **Steven Spielberg make** movies. [Two persons make movies.]

Rhyme, rhythm, and **imagery help** poets express their feelings. [Three things help.]

Compound subjects that name only one person, thing, place, or idea take a singular verb.

EXAMPLES My **pen pal and best friend is** my cousin. [One person is my best friend and pen pal.]

Broccoli and melted cheese makes a tasty dish. [The one combination makes a dish.]

5h. Singular subjects joined by *or* or *nor* take a singular verb. Plural subjects joined by *or* or *nor* take a plural verb.

EXAMPLES After dinner, either **Anne** or **Tony loads** the dishwasher. [Anne loads the dishwasher *or* Tony loads the dishwasher.]

Neither the **coach** nor the **principal is** happy with the team's performance. [Neither *one* is happy.]

Either the **boys** or their **sisters take** the garbage out.

Neither the **dogs** nor the **cats come** when we call them.

RESOURCES

The Compound Subject

Practice

- *Language & Sentence Skills Practice,* pp. 117–118

Differentiating Instruction

- *Developmental Language & Sentence Skills,* pp. 61–62

5i. When a singular subject and a plural subject are joined by *or* or *nor*, the verb agrees with the subject nearer the verb.

ACCEPTABLE Neither the children nor their **mother was** ready for the trip.

ACCEPTABLE Neither the mother nor her **children were** ready for the trip.

STYLE TIP

Constructions like those shown with Rule 5i can sound awkward. Try rephrasing sentences to avoid such awkward constructions.

EXAMPLES

The **children were** not ready for the trip, and neither **was** their **mother.**

or

The **mother was** not ready for the trip, and neither **were** her **children.**

Oral Practice 1 Using Verbs That Agree in Number with Their Subjects

Read the following sentences aloud, stressing the italicized words.

1. The *books* on that shelf *need* dusting.
2. A *carton* of duck eggs *is* in the refrigerator.
3. *Tina and Betty are* first cousins once removed.
4. *Playing* games *or listening* to old records *is* an enjoyable way to spend a rainy Saturday.
5. *Several* of these insects *eat* through wood.
6. Every *one* of you *has* met my friend Phil.
7. Neither the *twins nor Greg enjoys* listening to that kind of music.
8. Both *Mr. and Mrs. Chen agree* to be chaperons for our spring dance.

Exercise 6 Choosing Verbs That Agree in Number with Their Subjects

Choose the correct form of the verb in parentheses in each of the following sentences.

EXAMPLE 1. In August, eager players and their fans (*looks, look*) forward to the start of football season.

1. look

1. The coach and the player (*was, were*) surprised by the referee's call.
2. (*Is, Are*) Drew or Virgil going out for the pass?
3. Neither the quarterback nor the wide receiver (*hear, hears*) the referee's whistle.
4. The marching band or the pep squad (*has, have*) already performed.
5. (*Do, Does*) Christopher and Alexander enjoy football as much as Rachel does?
6. Either Albert or Selena (*leads, lead*) the student fight song.
7. The drum major and student council president (*is, are*) my older sister Janet.
8. The principal, the band director, and the gymnastics coach (*was, were*) proud of the half-time show.

DIFFERENTIATING INSTRUCTION

Learners Having Difficulty

Students who have trouble with compound subjects and their verbs should not be introduced to the finer points of compound subject-verb agreement until they have mastered the basics. Have students do **Oral Practice 1** as a group. Ask them whether any of the verbs sounded strange to them as they said them. If so, ask students to read these sentences again, omitting any prepositional phrases.

Special Education Students

For **Exercise 6**, you might encourage students to make stick-figure diagrams to indicate how many people are mentioned in the subject of each sentence. (If no specific number is indicated, have students draw three figures.) Students should draw the stick figures with conjunctions placed appropriately between them. If the sentence contains a singular and a plural subject joined by *or* or *nor*, have students cross out the stick figure or figures representing the noun farther from the verb. Then, have students choose the correct verb and write it in the appropriate place in the diagram.

EXAMPLE

Either the boys or Jo (is, are) ordering fruit cups.

boys **or** **Jo** **is.**

Other Problems in Agreement

Rules 5j–r *(pp. 128–134)*

OBJECTIVES

- To use *doesn't* and *don't* correctly in sentences
- To write sentences with collective nouns
- To read aloud sentences with correct subject-verb agreement
- To identify the subjects of sentences and choose verbs that agree in number with their subjects

USAGE

DIFFERENTIATING INSTRUCTION

Learners Having Difficulty

Since **Rules 5j–r** each address a different aspect of agreement, you may want to discuss each rule individually as it applies to the class's writing or speech activities during the school year. The fact that titles of books, poems, and stories are treated as singular, for instance, may be mentioned when students prepare for literary-analysis assignments or as they write book reports.

9. Neither the coach nor the players (*has, have*) ever won a state championship game.
10. (*Was, Were*) the announcer or the referees prepared for the triumphant fans to rush the field?

Review B **Revising Sentences for Subject-Verb Agreement**

Revise each of the following sentences according to the directions given in parentheses. Change the verb in the sentence to agree with the subject as necessary.

EXAMPLE 1. The teachers have finished grading the tests. (Change *The teachers* to *Each of the teachers.*)

1. Each of the teachers has finished grading the tests.

1. My aunt is planning a trip to Nairobi National Park in Kenya. (Change *aunt* to *aunts.*) — 1. aunts are
2. Have Yoko and Juan already seen that movie? (Change *and* to *or.*) — 2. Has / or
3. Nobody on the team plans to attend the award ceremonies. (Change *Nobody* to *Many.*) — 3. Many / plan
4. My grandmother, as well as my mother and aunts, raises tropical fish to earn extra money. (Change *grandmother* to *grandparents.*) — 4. grandparents / raise
5. Most of the food for the party is in the refrigerator. (Change *food* to *salads.*) — 5. salads / are
6. Neither the librarian nor the aides have found the missing book. (Change *Neither the librarian nor the aides* to *Neither the aides nor the librarian.*) — 6. aides / librarian has
7. Black bean soup and a tossed salad make an inexpensive meal. (Change *Black bean soup and a tossed salad* to *Macaroni and cheese.*) — 7. Macaroni and cheese makes
8. Some of my friends take the bus to school. (Change *Some* to *One.*) — 8. One / takes
9. Few of the reporter's questions were answered in detail. (Change *Few* to *Neither.*) — 9. Neither / was
10. The puppy playing with my sisters is two months old. (Change *puppy* to *puppies* and *sisters* to *sister.*) — 10. puppies / sister are

Other Problems in Agreement

5j. **The contractions *don't* and *doesn't* should agree with their subjects.**

The word *don't* is the contraction of *do not.* Use *don't* with all plural subjects and with the pronouns *I* and *you.*

RESOURCES

Other Problems in Agreement

Practice

- *Language & Sentence Skills Practice,* pp. 119–124

EXAMPLES I **don't** know. They **don't** give up.
You **don't** say. **Don't** these shrink?
We **don't** want to. Apathetic people **don't** care.

The word *doesn't* is the contraction of *does not.* Use *doesn't* with all singular subjects except the pronouns *I* and *you.*

EXAMPLES He **doesn't** know. One **doesn't** give up.
She **doesn't** say. This **doesn't** shrink.
It **doesn't** want to. **Doesn't** Donna care?

STYLE TIP

Many people consider contractions informal. Therefore, it is generally best not to use contractions in formal speaking and writing.

Exercise 7 Using *Doesn't* and *Don't* Correctly

Write the correct form (*doesn't* or *don't*) for each of the following sentences.

EXAMPLE 1. _____ that bouquet of roses look great?
1. Doesn't

1. This apple _____ taste sweet. 1. doesn't
2. _____ he want to see the game? 2. Doesn't
3. These _____ impress me. 3. don't
4. One of the players _____ plan to go. 4. doesn't
5. _____ Jason and Tanya like the new band uniforms? 5. Don't
6. You and she _____ have time to play computer games now. 6. don't
7. The engine in that old pickup _____ start in winter. 7. doesn't
8. Tonio asked why we _____ want to go mountain biking. 8. don't
9. _____ several of those in the front window cost more than these in the fruit cart? 9. Don't
10. The international children's chorus is so marvelous that their new fans _____ want to leave the theater. 10. don't

5k. A collective noun may be either singular or plural, depending on its meaning in a sentence.

The singular form of a ***collective noun*** names a group of persons or things.

Reference Note

For more information about **collective nouns,** see page 5.

Collective Nouns				
army	class	family	group	public
assembly	club	fleet	herd	swarm
audience	committee	flock	jury	team

DIRECT TEACHING

Modeling and Demonstration

Other Problems in Agreement. Model how to identify correct subject-verb agreement by using the examples *The class have completed their projects,* and *The class has elected its officers.* First, ask what the subject of the first sentence is. [*class*] Then, ask whether *class* is singular or plural. [*plural*] Explain that the collective noun *class* is thought of as individuals in this sentence, so it takes the plural verb *have.* Next, ask whether the subject of the second sentence is singular or plural. [*singular*] Point out that although a class has more than one member, the collective noun *class* takes a singular verb, in this case *has,* when it refers to the group as a single unit. Now, have a volunteer use another example from this chapter to demonstrate how to identify correct subject-verb agreement.

USAGE

Learning for Life

Continued on pp. 130–131

Writing a Business Letter. Although informal usage is acceptable in casual conversation, students must be able to write according to the rules of standard, formal usage when they need to make a good impression. Agreement errors are particularly noticeable, so written communication, especially letters of application, must be drafted carefully. To review agreement while building skills for real-life situations, have each student compose a letter for a job application.

USAGE

Differentiating Instruction

Special Education Students

Allow students to choose five nouns from a list like the following one, and have students use the nouns as subjects with both singular and plural verbs in oral sentences. Next, students should write these sentences and reread them. Then, students can highlight singular verbs in one color and plural verbs in another.

army	committee	herd
assembly	family	jury
audience	fleet	public
class	flock	swarm
club	group	team

Exercise 8 Writing Sentences with Collective Nouns

ANSWERS

Sentences will vary. Here are some possibilities:

1. The club meets every Monday. The club are wearing their new T-shirts.
2. The team is ready to play. The team are comparing their statistics for the past season.
3. The audience has shown its approval by clapping. The audience have read their programs.
4. The flock is making its way south for the winter. The flock already have their winter feathers.
5. The modern family has its challenges. The family have finished their chores.

Use a plural verb with a collective noun when the noun refers to the individual parts or members of the group. Use a singular verb when the noun refers to the group as a unit.

EXAMPLES The class **have completed** their projects. [*Class* is thought of as individuals.]

The class **has elected** its officers. [*Class* is thought of as a unit.]

Notice in the examples above that any pronoun referring to a collective noun has the same number as the noun. In the first example, *their* refers to *class.* In the second example, *its* refers to *class.*

Reference Note

See page 139 for more about **pronoun-antecedent agreement** with **collective nouns.**

Exercise 8 Writing Sentences with Collective Nouns

Select five collective nouns, and write five pairs of sentences that show clearly how the nouns you choose may be singular or plural.

EXAMPLE 1. *The jury is ready.*
The jury are still arguing among themselves.

5l. A verb agrees with its subject, but not necessarily with a predicate nominative.

EXAMPLES The marching **bands** (S) **are** the main attraction (PN).

The main **attraction** (S) **is** the marching bands (PN).

5m. When the subject follows the verb, find the subject and make sure that the verb agrees with it.

The subject generally follows the verb in questions and in sentences that begin with *here* and *there.*

EXAMPLES Here **is** a **list** of addresses.

Here **are** two **lists** of addresses.

There **is** my **notebook.**

There **are** my **notebooks.**

Where **is Heather**? Where **is Chris**?

Where **are Heather** and **Chris**?

TIPS & TRICKS

To find the subject in a sentence in which the subject follows the verb, rearrange the sentence.

EXAMPLES

A **list** of addresses **is** here.

My **notebooks are** there.

Heather and **Chris are** where?

Learning for Life 

Continued from p. 129

Enlist the help of guidance counselors for sample job applications. Then, suggest that students brainstorm in small groups about what to include in their letters. [*They might begin by introducing themselves and then outlining the reasons they believe they would be suitable candidates for employment.*]

After students have written their letters, pair them to work on identifying subjects

Contractions such as *here's, where's, how's,* and *what's* include the singular verb *is.* Use these contractions only with singular subjects.

NONSTANDARD There's some facts on that topic in a chart.
STANDARD There **are** some **facts** on that topic in a chart.
STANDARD There**'s** a **chart** with some facts on that topic.

5n. An expression of an amount (a measurement, a percentage, or a fraction, for example) may be singular or plural, depending on how it is used.

A word or phrase stating an amount is singular when the amount is thought of as a unit.

EXAMPLES **Thirty dollars is** too much for a concert ticket.

Two hours is a long time to wait.

Sometimes, however, the amount is thought of as individual pieces or parts. If so, a plural verb is used.

EXAMPLES **Five dollars were scattered** on the desk.

Two hours—one before school and one after—**are** all I have for practice.

A fraction or a percentage is singular when it refers to a singular word and plural when it refers to a plural word.

EXAMPLES **Three fourths** of the pizza **is** gone.

Of these songs, **three fourths are** new.

5o. Some nouns that are plural in form take singular verbs.

EXAMPLES **Politics is** a controversial topic.

The **news** of the nominee **was** a surprise.

Rickets is a serious health problem in some countries.

NOTE Some nouns that end in *–s* take a plural verb even when they refer to a single item.

EXAMPLES The **scissors need** to be sharpened.

Were these **pants** on sale?

The **Olympics are** on television.

Reference Note

For more on **contractions,** see page 335.

Reference Note

For a discussion of **standard and nonstandard English,** see page 223.

HELP

If you do not know whether a noun that is plural in form is singular or plural in meaning, look up the word in a dictionary.

DIRECT TEACHING

Correcting Misconceptions

Singular Subjects. Because words that appear to be plural but take singular verbs can be troublesome, you might want to have the class brainstorm a list of such words. [*Examples include* mathematics, economics, physics, measles, genetics, *and* blues.]

Then, you might assign small groups of students to create worksheets for the class to practice using these words. Encourage students to study exercises in this book as examples for writing the practice exercises. Students might choose to create a paragraph for revision or a multiple-choice format.

Have students evaluate their material and check for errors, but review the worksheets before groups copy and distribute them.

Plural Forms with Singular Meanings

Mnemonics. You might reinforce the note following **Rule 5o** by asking students what the examples *scissors* and *pants* have in common. [*They are pairs.*] In a short brainstorming session, ask students to suggest tricks they could use for remembering these exceptions. [*For example, "Pairs are plural."*] Ask students if they can think of other examples of pairs to test their new memory device(s).

USAGE

and verbs and editing their letters for correctness and effectiveness. Encourage students to examine their usage, especially of verbs, very carefully; they should strive for variety and clarity.

When students have completed their editing, they should type their final drafts and file them for later use.

5p. **Even when plural in form, the title of a creative work (such as a book, song, film, or painting), the name of an organization, or the name of a country or city generally takes a singular verb.**

EXAMPLES ***The Souls of Black Folk* is** often **cited** as a classic of African American literature. [one book]

"Greensleeves" is an old English folk song. [one piece of music]

The United Nations was founded in 1945. [one organization]

White Plains is home to several colleges. [one city]

Review C Using Titles That Agree with Verbs in Number

Terence and Janeese are at the video rental store deciding what movies they will rent for the weekend. In the following sentences, wherever *TITLE* appears, supply the name of a movie of your choice. Then, choose the correct form of the verb to complete each sentence.

Movie titles will vary.

EXAMPLE 1. Look, Terence. TITLE (*is, are*) supposed to be very funny.

1. Horse Feathers—is

1. Terence: According to LaShonda, TITLE and TITLE (*is, are*) very exciting.
2. Janeese: Well, TITLE or TITLE (*sounds, sound*) more interesting to me. Let's ask the clerk.
3. Terence: Sir, (*is, are*) TITLE in stock?
4. Clerk: I'm afraid not, but TITLE (*entertain, entertains*) almost everyone, and you might enjoy it.
5. Terence: Janeese, TITLE (*is, are*) a fairly recent movie, but TITLE (*are, is*) an old-timer.
6. Janeese: Well, I like animated films, and TITLE (*fit, fits*) that category.
7. Clerk: If you ask me, TITLE (*beat, beats*) every other film we have, but someone just rented my last copy.
8. Janeese: Both TITLE and TITLE (*are, is*) good, but I've seen each of them twice.
9. Terence: (*Isn't, Aren't*) TITLE any good? I'm surprised.
10. Janeese: All right, here's my vote. TITLE (*is, are*) tonight's movie, and either TITLE or TITLE (*is, are*) the movie for Saturday night's party.

CONTENT-AREA CONNECTIONS

Science

Foreign Plurals 2. Many terms in science, such as *data*, *amoeba*, *genus*, and *bacteria*, come from Latin. Because the endings of these words may be different from English endings, students may have trouble determining whether the words are singular or plural. Have students scan their science books for words that may cause difficulty and make lists of singular and plural words that pose potential problems.

5q. Subjects preceded by *every* or *many a* take singular verbs.

EXAMPLES **Every** homeowner and storekeeper **has joined** the cleanup drive sponsored by the town council.

Many a litterbug **was surprised** by the stiff fines.

5r. When the relative pronoun *that, which,* or *who* is the subject of an adjective clause, the verb in the adjective clause agrees with the word to which the relative pronoun refers.

EXAMPLES This is the store **that has** the discount sale. [*That* refers to the singular noun *store.*]

London, **which is** the capital of England, is the largest city in Europe. [*Which* refers to the singular noun *London.*]

The Garcias, **who live** next door, are going with us to the lake. [*Who* refers to the plural noun *Garcias.*]

Reference Note

For more about **relative pronouns,** see page 8. For more about **adjective clauses,** see page 101.

Oral Practice 2 Using Subject-Verb Agreement

Read each of the following sentences aloud, stressing the italicized words.

1. Of the inhabitants, *two thirds are* registered to vote.
2. *Many a* writer and scholar *has* puzzled over that problem.
3. *Is economics* taught at your high school?
4. *Are* there any green *apples* in that basket?
5. *Romeo and Juliet has* been made into a ballet, a Broadway musical, and several movies.
6. *Two weeks is* more than enough time to write a report.
7. My *family is* planning to hold its reunion in October.
8. My *family are* planning their schedules now.

Exercise 9 Identifying Subjects and Verbs That Agree in Number

Identify the subject of each verb in parentheses. Then, choose the form of the verb that agrees with the subject.

EXAMPLE 1. (*Do, Does*) Meals on Wheels deliver in your neighborhood?

1. Meals on Wheels—Does

1. The class (*has, have*) chosen titles for their original plays.
2. First prize (*was, were*) two tickets to Hawaii.

Agreement of Subject and Verb 133

3. Three quarters of the movie (*was, were*) over when we arrived at the theater.
4. Rattlesnakes (*was, were*) the topic of last week's meeting of the hiking club.
5. (*Has, Have*) every student in the class memorized a poem to present for the oral interpretation contest?
6. *Crime and Punishment* (*is, are*) a world-famous novel.
7. Two thirds of the missing books (*was, were*) returned to the downtown branch of the library.
8. Mathematics (*is, are*) an important part of many everyday activities.
9. Where (*is, are*) the paragraphs you wrote?
10. Four weeks (*is, are*) enough time to rehearse the play.

Review D Identifying Verbs That Have the Correct Number

Choose the correct form of the verb in parentheses in each of the following sentences.

EXAMPLE 1. Fifty pesos (*was, were*) a great price for that carving.
1. *was*

1. Mumps (*is, are*) a common childhood disease that causes swelling in glands in the neck.
2. Politics (*is, are*) always a popular subject both to debate and to study at college.
3. Not one of the ushers (*know, knows*) where the lounge is.
4. The team (*is, are*) on a winning streak.
5. Carol, as well as Inés, (*write, writes*) a weekly column for the *East High Record.*
6. "Beauty and the Beast" (*is, are*) a folk tale that exists in many different cultures.
7. Ten pounds (*is, are*) too much weight for a young child to carry in a backpack.
8. It is difficult to concentrate when there (*is, are*) radios and stereos blasting away.
9. (*Has, Have*) either of you read the book or seen the movie version of *To Kill a Mockingbird*?
10. In most situation comedies, there (*is, are*) a very wise character, a very foolish character, and a very lovable character.

134 Agreement

Agreement of Pronoun and Antecedent

A pronoun usually refers to a noun or another pronoun that comes before it. The word that a pronoun refers to is called its ***antecedent.***

5s. A pronoun should agree in number and gender with its antecedent.

(1) A pronoun that refers to a singular antecedent is singular in number.

EXAMPLES **Daniel Defoe** wrote **his** first book at the age of fifty-nine.

The **elephant** is a long-lived animal. **It** grows **its** tusks at maturity.

(2) A pronoun that refers to a plural antecedent is plural in number.

EXAMPLES Reliable **cars** make **their** owners happy.

We walk **our** dogs daily.

A few singular pronouns have forms that indicate the gender of the antecedent. Masculine pronouns refer to males; feminine pronouns refer to females. Neuter pronouns refer to places, things, ideas, and, often, to animals.

Masculine	Feminine	Neuter
he	she	it
him	her	it
his	hers	its
himself	herself	itself

Often, when the antecedent of a personal pronoun is another kind of pronoun, a word in a phrase following the antecedent will help to determine gender.

EXAMPLES **One** of the **women** designs **her** own costumes.

Each of the **boys** rode **his** bicycle to school.

Neither of the **kittens** has opened **its** eyes yet.

Reference Note

For a further discussion of **antecedents,** see page 6.

Agreement of Pronoun and Antecedent

Rules 5s–z *(pp. 135–140)*

OBJECTIVE

- **To identify antecedents and write pronouns that agree with them**

DIRECT TEACHING

Modeling and Demonstration

Agreement of Pronoun and Antecedent. Model how a pronoun's gender and number must agree with the noun or pronoun to which it refers by using the example *Daniel Defoe wrote his first book at the age of fifty-nine.* First, ask which word or words are pronouns. [*his*] Next, ask whether this pronoun refers to a noun in the sentence. [*yes;* Daniel Defoe] Then, ask what the gender and number of this noun is. [*masculine, singular*] Ask whether the pronoun has the same gender and number. [*yes*] Point out that pronouns and their antecedents must agree in number and gender. Now, have a volunteer use another example from this chapter to demonstrate how to choose pronouns that agree with their antecedents.

USAGE

RESOURCES

Agreement of Pronoun and Antecedent

Practice

- *Language & Sentence Skills Practice,* pp. 125–129

Differentiating Instruction

- *Developmental Language & Sentence Skills,* pp. 65–68

USAGE

Differentiating Instruction

Learners Having Difficulty

To help students focus on singular indefinite pronouns, write these three lists on the chalkboard and ask students to tell what the words in each list have in common. [*The words in the first list all contain* one; *the words in the second list all contain* body; *and the words in the third list all contain* thing.]

LIST 1	LIST 2	LIST 3
one	everybody	nothing
everyone	somebody	everything
anyone	nobody	anything
someone	anybody	something
no one		

You might want to have students work in pairs to write sentences using each word in the list. Once students have written their sentences, they might want to compose five-sentence worksheets for their classmates to use as practice. Students may want to use a multiple-choice format, giving both singular and plural verb choices.

Reteaching

Indefinite Pronouns

To help students remember that pronouns referring to singular indefinite pronouns must also be singular, encourage students to read compound indefinite pronouns as though they were two separate words with the word *single* between the two parts. For example, encourage students to think of *everybody* as *every single body* to help them recognize that *body* is singular and thus other pronouns referring to *body* must also be singular.

HELP

In many cases you can avoid the awkward *his or her* construction by rephrasing the sentence and using the plural form of the pronoun or by substituting an article (*a, an,* or *the*).

EXAMPLES

The **passengers** will be shown where **they** can check in.

A **person** should choose **a** college carefully.

STYLE TIP

In informal conversation, plural personal pronouns are often used to refer to singular antecedents that can be either masculine or feminine. Such usage is becoming increasingly common in writing. However, you should avoid such usage in formal writing and speaking.

INFORMAL

Everybody has packed their lunch in an insulated cooler.

FORMAL

Everybody has packed **his or her** lunch in an insulated cooler.

When a singular antecedent may be either masculine or feminine, use both the masculine and the feminine forms, connected by *or*.

EXAMPLES **Each passenger** will be shown where **he or she** can check in.

A **person** should choose **his or her** college carefully.

If you talk on the phone with **someone** you don't know well, speak clearly to **him or her.**

5t. Some indefinite pronouns are singular, and some are plural. Other indefinite pronouns can be either singular or plural, depending on their meaning in a sentence.

(1) Use a singular pronoun to refer to *anybody, anyone, anything, each, either, everybody, everyone, everything, neither, nobody, no one, nothing, one, somebody, someone,* or *something.*

EXAMPLES **Either** of the girls can bring **her** CD player.

Neither of the workmen forgot **his** tool belt.

Did **each** of the mares recognize **her** own foal?

Someone left **his or her** hat on the field.

One of the parakeets escaped from **its** cage.

NOTE Sometimes the meaning of *everyone* or *everybody* is clearly plural. In informal situations, the plural pronoun should be used.

CONFUSING Everyone laughed when he or she saw the clowns.

INFORMAL **Everyone** laughed when **they** saw the clowns.

In formal situations, it is best to revise the sentence so that it is both clear and grammatically correct.

FORMAL The **audience** laughed when **they** saw the clowns.

(2) Use a plural pronoun to refer to *both, few, many,* and *several.*

EXAMPLES **Both** of the sisters recited **their** lines.

Few of the animals willingly leave **their** natural habitat.

Many of the volunteers shared **their** coats with the flood victims.

Several of the audience were late getting to **their** seats.

(3) **The indefinite pronouns *all, any, more, most, none,* and *some* may be singular or plural, depending on their meaning in a sentence.**

EXAMPLES **All** of the water has melted; **it** is pooling in the valley.

All of the streams are full; **they** are rushing torrents.

Most of her cooking tastes good. In fact, **it** is delicious.

Most of the dishes she cooks taste good. **They** contain unusual spices.

5u. **Use a singular pronoun to refer to two or more singular antecedents joined by *or* or *nor.***

EXAMPLES Neither **Richard nor Bob** distinguished **himself** in the finals.

Paula or Janet will present **her** views on the subject.

5v. **Use a plural pronoun to refer to two or more antecedents joined by *and.***

EXAMPLES **Mona and Janet** left early because **they** had to be home before ten o'clock.

Mom and Dad celebrated **their** twentieth wedding anniversary yesterday.

5w. **The number of a relative pronoun (such as *who, which,* or *that*) is determined by its antecedent.**

EXAMPLES Aretha is one **friend who** always keeps **her** word. [*Who* refers to the singular noun *friend.* Therefore, the singular form *her* is used to agree with *who.*]

Many who volunteer **their** time find the experience rewarding. [*Who* refers to the plural pronoun *Many.* Therefore, the plural form *their* is used to agree with *who.*]

Review E Identifying Antecedents and Writing Pronouns

Each of the sentences on the following page contains a blank where a pronoun should be. Complete each sentence by inserting at least one pronoun that agrees with its antecedent. Identify the antecedent.

EXAMPLE 1. Carmen and Tina said that _____ thought my idea was sensible.

1. they—Carmen and Tina

STYLE TIP

Sentences like those shown under **Rule 5u** can sound awkward if the antecedents are of different genders. If a sentence sounds awkward, revise it to avoid the problem.

AWKWARD
Ben or Maya will read his or her report.

REVISED
Ben will read **his** report, or **Maya** will read **hers.**

Reference Note

For more information on **relative pronouns in adjective clauses,** see page 101.

Differentiating Instruction

English-Language Learners

General Strategies. You may want to have students relate pronoun-antecedent agreement in English to agreement in their native languages by asking them how pronouns are used in those languages. Ask whether the pronouns indicate gender or number. If someone mentions that in Spanish it is possible to identify the gender of a group (as in *ellos hablan,* "the males speak," or *ellas hablan,* "the females speak"), note that in English the pronoun *they* is used for both males and females in the third-person plural.

USAGE

Extension

Critical Thinking

Analysis. You might ask students to think about how pronoun-antecedent agreement compares to subject-verb agreement. They might consider what factors make a pronoun agree with its antecedent. [*for all personal pronouns: person and number; for third-person singular pronouns: gender*] Then, ask what factors are considered in making a subject agree with its verb. [*person and number*]

Extension

Critical Thinking

Metacognition. As a concluding activity and review, ask students to make a chart listing their own most frequent or noticeable agreement errors.

SAMPLE CHART

INCORRECT	CORRECT
There's two buildings.	There are two buildings.

Then, ask them to formulate a plan for eliminating errors. [*For example:* To find the true subject, look after the verb when an introductory *there* is used.]

Differentiating Instruction

Learners Having Difficulty

So that students can keep track of their progress, you might suggest that they count and record the number of times per day or week they make their most frequent mistakes. Then, they can chart their progress for a chosen length of time. Students might use a simple tick chart to tally their errors.

DAY	M	T	W	TH	F	WKLY TOTAL
Errors	////	//	////	///	/	~~////~~ ~~////~~ ////

After students have collected their data, they can plot their progress with a bar or line graph.

USAGE

1. Please give me Ronald's address so that I can send ____ a letter. 1. him
2. The uniform company finally sent Jerome and Ken the shirts that ____ had ordered. 2. they
3. Claire or Ida will go to the nursing home early so that ____ can help the residents into the lounge. 3. she
4. Several of the volunteers contributed ____ own money to buy the shelter a new van. 4. their
5. Did each of the contestants answer ____ questions correctly? 5. his or her
6. Both of the girls packed ____ suitcases carefully for the trip to Canada and Alaska. 6. their
7. Every car at the service center had ____ oil changed. 7. its
8. Neither of the women withdrew ____ job application. 8. her
9. Anyone can belong to the International Students Association if ____ is interested. 9. he or she
10. Neither the coaches nor the players blamed ____ for the loss. 10. themselves

HELP— Some sentences in Review F may contain more than one error in agreement.

Review F Proofreading Sentences for Pronoun-Antecedent Agreement

Many of the following sentences contain errors in agreement between pronouns and their antecedents. Identify each of these errors, and give the form of the pronoun that agrees with its antecedent. If a sentence is already correct, write *C.*

EXAMPLE 1. All of us need to choose a topic for his or her reports.

1. his or her—our

1. George has chosen Walt Disney as the subject of his report. 1. C
2. Several others in our class have also submitted ~~his or her~~ topics. 2. their
3. Dominic, one of the Perrone twins, has chosen Alfred Hitchcock as ~~their~~ subject. 3. his
4. Neither George nor Dominic will have difficulty finding material for ~~their~~ report. 4. his
5. Each of these moviemakers has left ~~their~~ mark on the world. 5. his
6. Either Minnie or Sue offered ~~their~~ help with proofreading. 6. her
7. Each of the boys refused politely, saying that ~~they~~ would proofread the report on ~~their~~ own. 7. he / his
8. Does everyone, including George and Dominic, know that ~~they~~ must assemble facts, not opinions? 8. he or she
9. Neither George nor Dominic should forget to include amusing anecdotes about ~~their~~ subject. 9. his
10. Nobody likes to discover that ~~they~~ just read a dull report about an interesting subject. 10. he or she

5x. **A collective noun is singular when it refers to the group as a unit and plural when it refers to the individual members of the group.**

EXAMPLES The **pride** of lions is hunting **its** prey on the savanna. [*Pride* is thought of as a unit.]

The **pride** of lions are licking **their** chops in anticipation. [*Pride* is thought of as separate individuals.]

NOTE Sometimes the number of a collective noun depends on the meaning the writer intends.

EXAMPLES The swim **team** proudly displayed **their** trophies. [The members of the team displayed individual trophies.]

The swim **team** proudly displayed **its** trophy. [The team as a whole displayed a shared trophy.]

Reference Note

For information on **subject-verb agreement** with **collective nouns,** see page 129. For a list of **collective nouns,** see page 5.

5y. **An expression of an amount (a measurement, a percentage, or a fraction, for example) may be singular or plural, depending on how it is used.**

A word or phrase stating an amount is singular when the amount is thought of as a unit.

EXAMPLES **Ten minutes** isn't long; **it** will go by quickly.

Here is **five dollars.** Is **it** enough?

Sometimes, however, the amount is thought of as individual pieces or parts. If so, a plural pronoun is used.

EXAMPLES **Ten** of the twenty minutes were wasted; we spent **them** arguing.

Five dollars were counterfeit, weren't **they**?

A fraction or a percentage is singular when it refers to a singular word and plural when it refers to a plural word.

EXAMPLES **One third** of the total is yours. Would you like **it** in ones?

One third of the birds have left. Are **they** migrating?

5z. **Singular pronouns are used to refer to some nouns that are plural in form.**

EXAMPLES Aunt Jean rarely watches the **news** because she finds **it** depressing.

USAGE

Agreement of Pronoun and Antecedent 139

The **United States** celebrated **its** bicentennial in 1976.

After Chad finished reading ***Mules and Men,*** he wrote a report on **it.**

Future Farmers of America meets tomorrow to plan **its** convention.

Marble Falls is in Texas; **it** is north of San Antonio and Blanco.

NOTE Plural pronouns are used to refer to some nouns that end in *–s* but that refer to a single item.

EXAMPLES I'll buy these **pants** because **they** fit better and are a better value than **those.**

If you're looking for the **scissors,** you'll find **them** in the third drawer on the left.

Review G Agreement of Pronoun and Antecedent

Some of the following sentences contain errors in pronoun-antecedent agreement. Identify each incorrect pronoun, and give the pronoun that agrees with its antecedent. If a sentence is already correct, write *C.*

EXAMPLE **1.** Several people in the neighborhood have expressed his or her views.

1. his or her—their

1. they
2. C
3. its
4. it
5. its
6. his or her
7. C
8. his or her
9. they're
10. is

1. The school finally sent Michael and Kathryn the results of the tests ~~he or she~~ had taken.
2. On the Serengeti Plain, a cheetah enjoys its freedom.
3. After World War II, the United States gave most of ~~their~~ foreign aid to help Europe rebuild.
4. Five percent of the profit will be donated, won't ~~they~~?
5. The U.S. Olympic team won ~~their~~ third gold medal.
6. A person with a health problem should always select the best doctor for ~~their~~ needs.
7. During *ferragosto,* or August holiday, the Italian Parliament takes its recess.
8. Each of the mimes gave ~~their~~ impression of a chimney sweep.
9. I like the way the pants look; also, at that price, ~~it's~~ a great bargain.
10. *War and Peace* ~~are~~ the most famous of Leo Tolstoy's works.

USAGE

EXTENSION

Relating to Literature

If your literature book includes "The Necklace" by Guy de Maupassant, you might use the selection to point out the literary use of masculine and feminine pronouns. This short story, which explores the relationship between a husband and wife, emphasizes the use of personal pronouns over names. Ask students why the author might have chosen to use pronouns so extensively. [*The use of* he *and* she *emphasizes the main characters' viewpoints, presenting a nineteenth-century version of "he said, she said"; eliminating most of the proper names makes the story universal but also personal.*]

Numerals in brackets refer to rules tested by the items in the Chapter Review.

Chapter Review

A. Identifying Verbs that Agree in Number with Their Subjects

For each of the following sentences, choose the correct form of the verb in parentheses.

1. (*Doesn't, Don't*) she know when she'll be back? — 1. [5j]
2. Most of my jewelry (*was, were*) lost in the fire. — 2. [5f]
3. For better or for worse, politics (*play, plays*) an important part in all our lives. — 3. [5o]
4. Many ideas in her book (*requires, require*) a great deal of thought. — 4. [5b(2), c]
5. (*Has, Have*) Lisa and Haruo been paid for their work? — 5. [5m, g]
6. (*Is, Are*) everybody finished with the project? — 6. [5m, d]
7. Neither the president nor the vice-president (*goes, go*) to every meeting. — 7. [5h]
8. There (*has, have*) been many accidents at that intersection. — 8. [5m]
9. Three fourths of the apartments (*was, were*) rented before the building was completed. — 9. [5n]
10. Our class president, with the help of several others, usually (*sets, set*) the agenda for the meeting. — 10. [5c]
11. Nobody here (*has, have*) the correct time. — 11. [5d]
12. A herd of cattle (*is, are*) by the river. — 12. [5k, c]
13. Some of Pat's nacho recipes (*contains, contain*) very hot spices. — 13. [5f]
14. One of the owners (*work, works*) at the store on weekends. — 14. [5d, c]
15. Physics (*is, are*) a challenging and fascinating subject. — 15. [5o]
16. Where (*do, does*) the scissors go? — 16. [5m, o]
17. The main attraction in the parade (*is, are*) the student floats. — 17. [5l]
18. Van Gogh's *The Potato Eaters* (*show, shows*) a Dutch farm family at dinner. — 18. [5p]
19. If two thirds of the people (*vote, votes*) for the measure, it will become law. — 19. [5n]
20. Here (*is, are*) a new football and a helmet for your birthday. — 20. [5m, g]

B. Proofreading Sentences for Subject-Verb Agreement

Each of the following sentences contains an error in agreement. Identify each incorrect verb, and supply the correct form.

21. Every man and woman were questioned by the police. — 21. was [5q]

ASSESSING

Monitoring Progress

Chapter Review. To assess student progress, you may want to compare the types of items missed on the **Diagnostic Preview** to those missed on the **Chapter Review.** You may want to work out specific goals for mastering essential information with individual students who are still having difficulty.

USAGE

RESOURCES

Agreement

Review

- *Language & Sentence Skills Practice*, pp. 130–132

Assessment

- *Holt Handbook Chapter Tests with Answer Key*, pp. 9–10, 52

22. was [5k, c]
23. has [5d, c]
24. are [5f]
25. doesn't [5j]
26. is [5f]
27. was [5d, c]
28. has [5q]
29. has [5d]
30. are [5i]

22. The pile of papers were scattered by the wind.
23. Each of the girls have her own tennis balls.
24. Some of the sheep from that flock is lost.
25. Your explanation don't really help that much.
26. Most of the poetry are in English.
27. Each of the students were happy the exam was over.
28. Many a student have been grateful for being in Ms. Makowski's history class.
29. Someone have my umbrella.
30. Either Bill or his uncles is waiting downstairs.

C. Identifying Antecedents and Writing Pronouns

Each of the following sentences contains a blank where a pronoun should be. Complete each sentence by writing a pronoun that agrees with its antecedent. Identify the antecedent.

31. they [5v]
32. him [5s(1)]
33. its [5s(1)]
34. his [5s(1)]
35. she [5u, s]
36. they [5v]
37. his [5t(1), s]
38. their [5t(2)]
39. their [5v]
40. herself [5u]

31. Uncle Harry and Aunt Nell said that ____ would be happy to contribute to the silent auction.
32. Can I have Trevor's phone number, so that I can tell ____ about the ceremony?
33. Every horse in the stable had ____ own bucket of oats.
34. Louis Pasteur, the great French scientist, made ____ first scientific discovery at the age of twenty-six.
35. Teresa or Sandra will go to the airport early so that ____ will be sure to meet Jorge's plane.
36. Patsy and Debbie will be late because ____ forgot the appointment.
37. Neither of the men changed ____ mind on the issue.
38. Because of the strike, several of the drivers had to change ____ own oil.
39. Both Henry James and his brother William became famous through ____ writings.
40. Neither Marie nor Delilah blamed ____ for the mistake.

D. Proofreading a Paragraph for Subject-Verb and Pronoun-Antecedent Agreement

For each error in the following paragraph, identify the incorrect verb or pronoun and supply the correct form.

USAGE

[**41**] CDs of popular music ~~is~~ getting very expensive. [**42**] The economics of this situation ~~have~~ hit young people right in the wallet! [**43**] Few ~~has~~ enough money to buy all the best new songs. [**44**] A teenager will have to use ~~their~~ brain if ~~they want~~ to save money in the music store. [**45**] Several of my friends buy an audiotape instead of a CD if ~~he or she~~ want to save a little money. [**46**] Danny, one of my best friends, ~~take~~ another approach. [**47**] His favorite group ~~are~~ The Avengers, and he tapes every new Avengers song straight off the radio. [**48**] He ~~don't~~ have to pay for anything but the blank tape. [**49**] Copying tapes is perfectly legal if all the music you record ~~are~~ just for your own use. [**50**] Kristi and Selena, two of my friends, save as much as four or five dollars a tape by buying ~~her~~ tapes on sale.

41. are [5c]
42. has [5o, c]
43. have [5e]
44. his or her / he or she wants [5s(1), h]
45. they [5t(2)]
46. takes [5c]
47. is [5k, l, p]
48. doesn't [5j]
49. is [5b(1)]
50. their [5v]

Writing Application

Using Agreement in a Paragraph

Subject-Verb Agreement During Career Day, the school counselor asks you to write a paragraph beginning with this statement: "People I know work at a variety of jobs." Using subjects and verbs that agree, describe the jobs of three people you know.

Prewriting Start by listing at least three people you know who have different kinds of jobs. Think of action verbs that describe what these people do. For example, instead of saying "Mrs. Ruíz is a chemistry teacher," say "Mrs. Ruíz teaches chemistry."

Writing As you write your first draft, be sure to include some details that clearly show how the jobs differ from one another.

Revising Check your rough draft to be sure that the examples you have chosen show a variety of jobs. If not, you may want to replace some examples or add new ones. Make sure each job is described vividly.

Publishing Identify the subjects and verbs in each sentence, and be sure that they agree. Read your paragraph aloud to help you recognize any errors in usage, spelling, and punctuation. Be sure that you have capitalized all proper names. Your class might photocopy and display their paragraphs during Career Day. With the permission of the people you wrote about, your class could also prepare a job information directory.

APPLICATION

Writing Application

Prewriting Tip. Making a list of differences might be a good way for students to prepare descriptions that clearly define each job. Some possible areas of difference are location, clientele/patrons, finished product, co-workers, amount of travel involved, and amount of time worked.

Prewriting Tip. To help students think of details for their paragraphs, have them respond to the following questions for each person they describe.

1. What job does the person do?
2. How does he or she do the job?
3. What kinds of tools does he or she use?
4. Where does he or she work?

Scoring Rubric. While you will want to pay particular attention to students' use of subject-verb agreement, you will also want to evaluate the students' overall writing performance. You may want to give a split score to indicate development and clarity of the composition as well as usage skills.

Chapter Review 143

CHAPTER

▼

INTRODUCING THE CHAPTER

- The first part of this chapter covers the principal parts of verbs, concentrating on the correct use of regular and irregular verbs. The second part deals with tense and tense consistency. The third explains active and passive voice, six troublesome verbs, and mood.
- The chapter concludes with a **Chapter Review** including a **Writing Application** feature that asks students to write instructions using verbs correctly.
- For help in integrating this chapter with writing assignments, see the **Teaching Strands** chart on pp. T24–T25.

CHAPTER

Using Verbs Correctly

Principal Parts, Tense, Voice, Mood

Diagnostic Preview

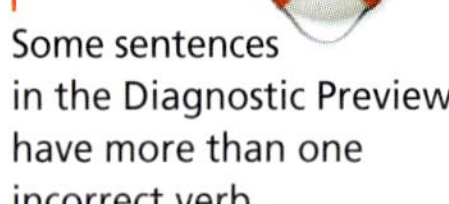

HELP

Some sentences in the Diagnostic Preview have more than one incorrect verb.

Numerals in brackets refer to rules tested by the items in the Diagnostic Preview.

1. asked/said *or* ask/say [6f, b]
2. sitting/spotted [6i, f, b]
3. folded/hopped [6f, b]
4. saw [6a, c, e(2)]
5. lying [6h]
6. reached [6f, b]
7. C [6f, d, e(2), c, b]
8. took [6c]

Proofreading Sentences for Correct Verb Forms

Read the following sentences. If a sentence contains an incorrect or awkward verb form, write the correct form or revise the sentence. If a sentence is already correct, write *C.*

EXAMPLES

1. I have always wanted a pet.

1. C

2. As a child, I use to dream about having a dog or cat.

2. used

1. Every time I ~~ask~~ my parents, they ~~said~~, "No, not in an apartment."
2. One day last year, I was ~~setting~~ on the front steps reading the newspaper when I ~~spot~~ an ad for a female ferret.
3. Deciding to investigate, I ~~fold~~ the paper, ~~hop~~ on my bike, and rode to the pet shop that had placed the ad.
4. When I walked into the store, I ~~seen~~ the ferret right away.
5. She was ~~laying~~ in a cardboard box on top of the counter.
6. I told the owner I wanted to hold her, and he ~~reaches~~ into the box.
7. When he withdrew his hand, the ferret was holding on to his finger with what looked like very sharp teeth.
8. I cautiously reached out and ~~taked~~ the ferret's hindquarters in my cupped hands.

CHAPTER RESOURCES

Internet
- Web resources: go.hrw.com

go.hrw.com

Practice & Review
- *Language & Sentence Skills Practice,* pp. 138–158
- *Language & Sentence Skills Practice Answer Key,* pp. 62–69

Application & Enrichment
- *Language & Sentence Skills Practice,* pp. 137, 159–162
- *Language & Sentence Skills Practice Answer Key,* pp. 62, 69–70

9. The rest of her long body poured slowly into my hands until she was sitting on her haunches.
10. She looked up at me and suddenly ~~clamps~~ her teeth onto my thumb.
11. The ferret ~~done~~ it to show me who was boss.
12. I should have ~~knowed~~ then that my troubles had just ~~began~~.
13. I ran all the way home and persuaded my parents to let me keep the ferret on a trial basis.
14. I had already ~~give~~ her a name—Ferris the Ferret—and I ~~lose~~ no time rushing back to the pet shop.
15. When I ~~come~~ home with Ferris, I ~~sit~~ a dish of cat food in front of her.
16. She stuck her snout into the dish and ate greedily.
17. After she had ~~went~~ into each room in the apartment, she ~~choosed~~ the top of the TV as her special place.
18. When my parents objected, I made a cardboard house with two entry holes and set it in a corner of my bedroom.
19. Ferris sniffed around her new home; then she ~~goes~~ in and ~~laid~~ down for a nap.
20. For the next few days, Ferris spent her time either napping or nipping.
21. She always ~~attackted~~ me when I least expected it.
22. Once, as she ~~lies~~ on my desk while I ~~am~~ studying, she suddenly locked her teeth onto my earlobe.
23. I was so startled that I ~~jump~~ up quickly, and Ferris wound up ~~laying~~ on the floor with a look that ~~makes~~ me feel guilty.
24. The next day the bad news was ~~gave~~ to me by my parents: Ferris had to go back to the pet shop.
25. I no longer want a pet ferret, but I have ~~wrote~~ to the local zoo-keeper to ask about snakes.

9. C [6f, d, e(2), b, i]
10. clamped [6f,b]
11. did [6a, c, e(2)]
12. known/begun [6c, a, e(5)]
13. C [6f, d, e(2), c, b]
14. given/lost [6a, c, f, d, e(2, 5)]
15. came/set [6f, c, i]
16. C [6f, d, e(2), c]
17. gone/chose [6a, c, d, e(5, 2)]
18. C [6f, b, c, i, d, e(2)]
19. went/lay [6f, c, h]
20. C [6c, d, e(2)]
21. attacked [6b]
22. lay/was [6f, h, c]
23. jumped/lying/made [6f, b, h, c]
24. given [6a, c, g]
25. written [6a, c, d, e(4)]

The Principal Parts of Verbs

The four basic forms of a verb are called the ***principal parts*** of the verb.

6a. The four principal parts of a verb are the *base form,* the *present participle,* the *past,* and the *past participle.*

The principal parts of the verb *ring,* for example, are *ring* (base form), *ringing* (present participle), *rang* (past), and *rung* (past participle). These principal parts are used to form all of the different verb tenses.

HELP—
Some teachers refer to the base form as the *infinitive.* Follow your teacher's directions when labeling this form.

USAGE

ASSESSING

Entry-Level Assessment

Diagnostic Preview. While many students at this level will know the principal parts of common irregular verbs, some will still have difficulty with troublesome verbs such as *lie* and *lay.* You may want to have students who are unable to demonstrate mastery read the definitions of the troublesome verbs and work the exercises together. Even though students may show mastery on the preview, they may make verb errors in their writing. If students have this problem, encourage them to circle all the verbs in their sentences when proofreading and to check each one for appropriate tense, consistency, and form.

TEACHING TIP

Diagnostic Preview. You may wish to accept answers in either the active or passive voice for sentence 24.

Differentiating Instruction

- *Developmental Language & Sentence Skills Guided Practice,* pp. 69–82
- *Developmental Language & Sentence Skills Guided Practice Teacher's Notes and Answer Key,* pp. 17–18

Assessment

- *Holt Handbook Chapter Tests with Answer Key,* pp. 11–12, 52

PRETEACHING

Lesson Starter

Motivating. Ask students to name the three basic forms of water: solid (ice), liquid, and gas (steam). Briefly discuss how the forms are all water yet are very different.

Explain that verbs also have different forms. Each form has a specific use or purpose. To illustrate the four basic verb forms, write the following sentences on the chalkboard:

I *study.*
He *is studying.*
She *studied.*
They *have studied.*

Invite students to suggest other examples of things that have various forms.

Regular Verbs

Rule 6b *(pp. 146–147)*

OBJECTIVE

- To pronounce the past and past participle forms of regular verbs correctly

DIFFERENTIATING INSTRUCTION

English-Language Learners

Spanish. Remind Spanish speakers that the English present participle suffix *–ing* is equivalent to the Spanish *–ando* and *–iendo* (e.g., *hablando,* "speaking," from *hablar* "to speak" and *comiendo,* "eating," from *comer* "to eat") and that the English past participle suffix *–(e)d* is equivalent to the Spanish *–ado* and *–ido* (e.g., *marcado,* "marked," and *adquirido,* "acquired"). In English and in Spanish, the past participle can also be used as an adjective.

EXAMPLES The bells **ring** every day. The bells **rang** at noon.
The bells **are ringing** now. The bells **have rung** already.

Notice that the tenses made from the present participle and past participle contain helping verbs, such as *am, is, are, has,* and *have.*

Reference Note

For more about how **participles and helping verbs** work together, see page 77.

Regular Verbs

6b. **A *regular verb* forms its past and past participle by adding *–d* or *–ed* to the base form.**

Base Form	Present Participle	Past	Past Participle
ask	[is] asking	asked	[have] asked
use	[is] using	used	[have] used
suppose	[is] supposing	supposed	[have] supposed
risk	[is] risking	risked	[have] risked

The words *is* and *have* are included in the preceding chart because helping verbs are used with the present participle and past participle to form some tenses.

NOTE The present participle of most regular verbs ending in *–e* drops the *–e* before adding *–ing.*

EXAMPLE smile + ing = smil**ing**

Reference Note

See page 363 for more on **spelling words when adding suffixes.**

One common error in the use of the past and the past participle forms is to leave off the *–d* or *–ed* ending.

NONSTANDARD We use to play soccer.
STANDARD We **used** to play soccer.

NONSTANDARD She was suppose to come home early.
STANDARD She was **supposed** to come home early.

Another common error is to misspell or mispronounce verbs.

NONSTANDARD We were attackted by mosquitoes.
STANDARD We were **attacked** by mosquitoes.

STYLE TIP

A few regular verbs have an alternate past form ending in *–t.* For example, the past form of *burn* is *burned* or *burnt.* Both forms are correct.

RESOURCES

The Principal Parts of Verbs and Regular Verbs

Practice

- *Language & Sentence Skills Practice,* pp. 138–139

Differentiating Instruction

- *Developmental Language & Sentence Skills,* pp. 69–70

Oral Practice 1 **Pronouncing the Past and Past Participle Forms of Regular Verbs Correctly**

Read each sentence aloud, stressing the italicized verb.

1. Aunt Rosie *used* to do needlepoint.
2. What has *happened* to your bicycle?
3. Several people were *drowned* in the flood.
4. The agents *risked* their lives.
5. Aren't you *supposed* to sing?
6. The game was well *advertised.*
7. The critics *praised* Amy Tan's new book.
8. He *carried* the suitcases to the car.

Irregular Verbs

6c. An *irregular verb* forms its past and past participle in some other way than by adding *–d* or *–ed.*

An irregular verb forms its past and past participle in one of these ways:

- changing consonants
- changing vowels
- changing vowels *and* consonants
- making no change at all

	Base Form	Past	Past Participle
Consonant Change	bend	bent	[have] bent
	send	sent	[have] sent
Vowel Change	sing	sang	[have] sung
	begin	began	[have] begun
Vowel and Consonant Change	catch	caught	[have] caught
	go	went	[have] gone
	fly	flew	[have] flown
No Change	set	set	[have] set
	burst	burst	[have] burst

"When I say 'runned,' you know I mean 'ran.' Let's not quibble."

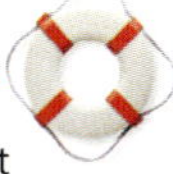
HELP If you are not sure about the principal parts of a verb, look in a dictionary, which lists the principal parts of irregular verbs. If no principal parts are listed, the verb is regular.

RESOURCES

Irregular Verbs

Practice

- *Language & Sentence Skills Practice,* pp. 140–144

Differentiating Instruction

- *Developmental Language & Sentence Skills,* pp. 71–72

USAGE

Irregular Verbs

Rule 6c *(pp. 147–156)*

OBJECTIVES

- To pronounce the past and past participle forms of irregular verbs correctly
- To write the past and past participle forms of irregular verbs
- To identify the correct forms of irregular verbs in sentences

PRACTICE

Irregular Verbs

To show students how irregular verbs can be misused, you might ask students to work in pairs to write a brief conversation between a preschooler and an adult. Have pairs use the verb forms each speaker might be expected to use. Students might use the following format to organize their examples.

BASE FORM	CHILD'S FORM	STANDARD FORM
catch	catched	caught
see	seed	saw
go	goed	went

Ask volunteers to read their conversations aloud.

USAGE

Extension

Critical Thinking

Analysis. To conclude the Practice activity described on p. 147, ask students why they think young children just learning English regularize irregular verbs. [*Students might say that young children acquire language through listening and form generalizations based in part on the number of times they have heard a particular pattern; some may add that children form conclusions about usage rules but don't understand the exceptions and apply the rules to all situations. Some might even recognize that young learners are testing their use of language by constant practice and feedback from others.*]

Direct Teaching

Modeling and Demonstration

Regular and Irregular Verbs. Model how to identify regular and irregular verbs by using the example verbs *suppose* and *begin.* First, ask whether *suppose* takes either *–d* or *–ed* to form the past tense. [*yes, –d*] Then, ask what the principal parts of *suppose* are. [*supposed, (is) supposing, supposed, (have) supposed*] Ask whether *suppose* is regular or irregular. [*regular*] Next, ask whether *begin* takes either *–d* or *–ed* to form the past tense. [*no*] Ask what the principal parts of *begin* are. [*begin, (is) beginning, began, (have) begun*] Then, ask, whether *begin* is regular or irregular. [*irregular*] Now, have a volunteer use other examples from this chapter to demonstrate how to identify regular and irregular verbs.

Reference Note

For more about **standard and nonstandard English,** see page 223.

NOTE Since most English verbs are regular, people sometimes try to make irregular verbs follow the regular pattern. However, such words as *throwed, knowed, shrinked,* and *choosed* are considered nonstandard.

Principal Parts of Common Irregular Verbs

Base Form	Present Participle	Past	Past Participle
become	[is] becoming	became	[have] become
begin	[is] beginning	began	[have] begun
blow	[is] blowing	blew	[have] blown
break	[is] breaking	broke	[have] broken
bring	[is] bringing	brought	[have] brought
build	[is] building	built	[have] built
burst	[is] bursting	burst	[have] burst
buy	[is] buying	bought	[have] bought
choose	[is] choosing	chose	[have] chosen
come	[is] coming	came	[have] come
cost	[is] costing	cost	[have] cost
cut	[is] cutting	cut	[have] cut
do	[is] doing	did	[have] done
draw	[is] drawing	drew	[have] drawn
drink	[is] drinking	drank	[have] drunk
drive	[is] driving	drove	[have] driven
eat	[is] eating	ate	[have] eaten
fall	[is] falling	fell	[have] fallen
feel	[is] feeling	felt	[have] felt
fight	[is] fighting	fought	[have] fought
find	[is] finding	found	[have] found
fly	[is] flying	flew	[have] flown
freeze	[is] freezing	froze	[have] frozen
get	[is] getting	got	[have] gotten *or* got
give	[is] giving	gave	[have] given
go	[is] going	went	[have] gone
grow	[is] growing	grew	[have] grown

Principal Parts of Common Irregular Verbs

Base Form	Present Participle	Past	Past Participle
have	[is] having	had	[have] had
hear	[is] hearing	heard	[have] heard
hide	[is] hiding	hid	[have] hidden *or* hid
hit	[is] hitting	hit	[have] hit
hold	[is] holding	held	[have] held
keep	[is] keeping	kept	[have] kept
know	[is] knowing	knew	[have] known
lead	[is] leading	led	[have] led
leave	[is] leaving	left	[have] left
let	[is] letting	let	[have] let
light	[is] lighting	lighted *or* lit	[have] lighted *or* lit
lose	[is] losing	lost	[have] lost
make	[is] making	made	[have] made
put	[is] putting	put	[have] put
read	[is] reading	read	[have] read
ride	[is] riding	rode	[have] ridden
ring	[is] ringing	rang	[have] rung
run	[is] running	ran	[have] run
say	[is] saying	said	[have] said
see	[is] seeing	saw	[have] seen
seek	[is] seeking	sought	[have] sought
shake	[is] shaking	shook	[have] shaken
sing	[is] singing	sang	[have] sung
sink	[is] sinking	sank *or* sunk	[have] sunk
slide	[is] sliding	slid	[have] slid
speak	[is] speaking	spoke	[have] spoken
spend	[is] spending	spent	[have] spent
stand	[is] standing	stood	[have] stood
steal	[is] stealing	stole	[have] stolen
sting	[is] stinging	stung	[have] stung
strike	[is] striking	struck	[have] struck *or* stricken

(continued)

STYLE TIP

Some verbs have two correct past or past participle forms. However, these forms are not always interchangeable.

EXAMPLES

I **shone** the flashlight into the woods. [*Shined* would also be correct.]

I **shined** my shoes. [*Shone* would be incorrect in this usage.]

If you are unsure about which past participle form to use, check an up-to-date dictionary.

DIFFERENTIATING INSTRUCTION

English-Language Learners

General Strategies. Reassure students that many people have trouble conjugating irregular verbs because the past and past participle may often look and sound quite different from their base forms. Reinforce the principal parts of irregular verbs through oral practice. Encourage students to use a dictionary or the **Principal Parts of Common Irregular Verbs** chart when they are unsure of any irregular verb form.

CONTENT-AREA CONNECTIONS

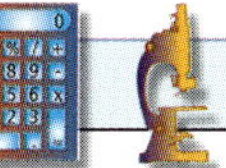

History

Historical Research. Work with a history teacher to coordinate a writing project based on historical research. Assign students to work in pairs to write brief narratives about a particular historical event they have studied. Have one student write a present-tense eyewitness account of the event while the second student writes a past-tense account. Read the samples to the class, and allow students to compare and contrast the effect of the pieces. [*The present-tense account may make them feel as though they are there while the past-tense account may add the authority time brings to a perspective on history.*]

Differentiating Instruction

Learners Having Difficulty

A visual approach might help students remember the principal parts of irregular verbs. Provide each student with four colors of paper. Designate a specific color for each principal part (for example, purple for base form, orange for past). Have each student choose an irregular verb and write four sentences on the correct colored paper, one for each of the four principal parts of the verb. Then, have students make mobiles with the sentence strips. Hang the mobiles around the room as reminders of the correct use of irregular verbs.

USAGE

(continued)

Principal Parts of Common Irregular Verbs

Base Form	Present Participle	Past	Past Participle
swim	[is] swimming	swam	[have] swum
take	[is] taking	took	[have] taken
teach	[is] teaching	taught	[have] taught
tear	[is] tearing	tore	[have] torn
tell	[is] telling	told	[have] told
think	[is] thinking	thought	[have] thought
throw	[is] throwing	threw	[have] thrown
wear	[is] wearing	wore	[have] worn
win	[is] winning	won	[have] won
write	[is] writing	wrote	[have] written

HELP

To avoid nonstandard usage, include a form of *be* with the present participle and a form of *have* with the past participle. Say *do, is doing, did, have done,* for example, or *see, is seeing, saw, have seen.*

NONSTANDARD
We already seen that program.

STANDARD
We **have** already **seen** that program.

When the present participle and past participle forms are used as verbs in sentences, they require helping verbs.

Helping Verb	+	Present Participle	=	Verb Phrase
forms of *be*	+	taking walking going	=	am taking was walking have been going

Helping Verb	+	Past Participle	=	Verb Phrase
forms of *have*	+	taken walked gone	=	have taken has walked had gone

NOTE Sometimes a past participle is used with a form of *be: was chosen, are known, is seen.* This use of the verb is called the ***passive voice.***

Reference Note

For more about **passive voice,** see page 163.

Oral Practice 2 Using the Past and Past Participle Forms of Irregular Verbs Correctly

Read each of the following sentences aloud, stressing the italicized verbs.

1. *Have* you *begun* the research for your report?
2. Last week we *saw* a video about Alexander the Great.
3. The bell *rang*, and the door *burst* open.
4. I *have known* her since the first grade.
5. He *brought* his rock collection to school.
6. They *fought* to rescue the survivors.
7. Elizabeth *has written* a short article for the school newspaper.
8. She *has given* us her permission.

Exercise 1 Writing the Past and Past Participle Forms of Irregular Verbs

Change each of the following verb forms. If the base form is given, change it to the past form. If the past form is given, change it to the past participle. Use *have* before the past participle form.

EXAMPLES 1. eat 2. took
1. ate *2. have taken*

1. do	5. went	9. blew	13. drink	17. ran
2. began	6. know	10. bring	14. froze	18. ring
3. see	7. spoke	11. choose	15. drove	19. fell
4. rode	8. stole	12. broke	16. sang	20. swim

Exercise 2 Identifying Correct Forms of Irregular Verbs

Choose the correct form of the verb in parentheses in each of the following sentences.

EXAMPLE 1. Mai's parents (*telled, told*) her about their journey in a boat from South Vietnam to Malaysia.
1. told

1. They (*rode, rid*) in a crowded boat like the one you see in the picture on the next page.
2. Along with many other people, Mai's parents (*chose, choosed*) to make such a journey rather than stay in South Vietnam after the Vietnam War ended.

Oral Practice 2

DISTRIBUTED REVIEW
Have students find the following constructions in **Oral Practice 2.**

1. the direct object of an infinitive [sentence 6—*survivors*]
2. an indirect object [sentence 8—*us*]

Exercise 1 Writing the Past and Past Participle Forms of Irregular Verbs

ANSWERS
1. did
2. have begun
3. saw
4. have ridden
5. have gone
6. knew
7. have spoken
8. have stolen
9. have blown
10. brought
11. chose
12. have broken
13. drank
14. have frozen
15. have driven
16. have sung
17. have run
18. rang
19. have fallen
20. swam

USAGE

PRACTICE

Guided and Independent

Exercise 1 You may wish to use the first ten items in **Exercise 1** as guided practice. Then, have students complete the exercise as independent practice. HOMEWORK

3. These refugees (*came, come*) to be called boat people.
4. Mai's parents abandoned their home after the South Vietnamese capital, Saigon, had (*fell, fallen*) to North Vietnamese forces.
5. The people on the boat (*brang, brought*) few possessions or supplies.
6. After they had (*drank, drunk*) what little water was on board, they went thirsty.
7. Mai's father said the people had (*ate, eaten*) all the food in a few days.
8. When another boat of refugees had (*sank, sunk*), its passengers crowded onto Mai's parents' boat.
9. They spent many days and nights on the ocean before they (*saw, seen*) land again.
10. Then it (*took, taked*) months for Mai's parents to be moved from Malaysian refugee camps to the United States.

Exercise 3 Identifying Correct Forms of Irregular Verbs

For each sentence in the following paragraph, choose the correct form of the verb in parentheses.

EXAMPLE I just **[1]** (*wrote, written*) to my Russian pen pal!

1. wrote

Joining the Russian-American pen-pal club Druzhba is one of the most interesting things I have ever [1] (*did, done*). The founder of the club [2] (*chose, chosen*) the name *Druzhba* because it means "friendship" in Russian. This club has [3] (*given, gave*) American and Russian students the chance to become friends. I [4] (*began, begun*) to write to my pen pal Vanya last September. His reply to my first letter [5] (*took, taken*) weeks to get to me. I wish it could have [6] (*flew, flown*) here faster from the other side of the globe. In his letters, Vanya has often [7] (*written, wrote*) about his daily life, his family, and his thoughts and feelings. We have [8] (*become, became*) good friends through our letters even though we have never [9] (*spoke, spoken*) to each other. Reading each other's essays in the club newsletter has also [10] (*brung, brought*) us closer together.

CONTENT-AREA CONNECTIONS

Multidisciplinary

World Languages. Involve students in the study of irregular verbs by drawing on their prior knowledge; ask them for examples of irregular verbs in other languages. Record their responses in a graphic organizer like the one on the right.

LANGUAGE	VERB	ENGLISH EQUIVALENT

Social Studies. To encourage further practice and real-world application, work with

Review A Writing the Past and Past Participle Forms of Verbs

For each of the following sentences, write the correct past or past participle form of the verb given.

EXAMPLE 1. run Yesterday we ____ around the track twice.
1. *ran*

1. *sing* Boyz II Men ____ last night. **1.** sang
2. *burst* The car suddenly ____ into flames. **2.** burst
3. *drink* Yesterday they ____ juice with their tossed salads and turkey sandwiches. **3.** drank
4. *use* He ____ to camp out every summer. **4.** used
5. *do* They ____ their best to repair the damage caused by the very large hail. **5.** did
6. *give* Grandma has ____ us some old photos. **6.** given
7. *risk* The detective ____ her life. **7.** risked
8. *ring* My alarm ____ at six o'clock. **8.** rang
9. *speak* Toni has not ____ to me since our argument. **9.** spoken
10. *fall* A tree has ____ across the highway. **10.** fallen

BORN LOSER reprinted by permission of Newspaper Enterprise Association, Inc.

Review B Writing the Past and Past Participle Forms of Verbs

Write the correct past or past participle form of each italicized verb in the following paragraph.

EXAMPLE All my life I have **[1]** (*know*) that I must make my own choices.
1. *known*

I have never [1] (*choose*) to be on a sports team because I am not a very athletic person. Some people are surprised because my brother and sister have [2] (*drive*) themselves very hard and have [3] (*become*) excellent athletes. For example, my brother, Emilio, [4] (*break*) three swimming records this year alone. He has [5] (*swim*) better than anyone else in our school. He also [6] (*go*) out for tennis and track this year. My sister, Elena, is only a junior, but she has already [7] (*run*) the 100-meter dash faster than any senior girl. I [8] (*use*) to think I wanted to follow in my brother's and sister's footsteps, but now I have [9] (*take*) a different path in life. My English teacher just [10] (*give*) me a chance to lead the debating team, and I am going to grab it!

DIFFERENTIATING INSTRUCTION

Learners Having Difficulty

A game of Verb-down will reinforce students' knowledge of past and past-participle forms of irregular verbs and give students practice hearing the correct forms. Divide the class into two teams. Use the present-tense form of a verb in a question, and then have a player rephrase the question and answer it by using the past and past-participle forms correctly in two sentences. [*Teacher: Do you write letters often? Student: Do I write letters often? I* wrote *one last week. I* have written *many letters.*]

If a student succeeds, he or she then poses a question for the other team. If the student misses, the original question goes to the other team.

USAGE

Review B Writing the Past and Past Participle Forms of Verbs

ANSWERS

1. chosen
2. driven
3. become
4. broke
5. swum
6. went
7. run
8. used
9. taken
10. gave

other teachers to help students find pen pals in other countries. Students and teachers should work out a list of questions to ask pen pals about their cultures. As students begin their correspondence, choose a particular editing focus, such as irregular verb forms, for students to concentrate on each week when writing and editing their letters.

Art. Students might like to paint or draw illustrations for postcards to send to their pen pals; others might use magazine clippings.

USAGE

RETEACHING

Irregular Verbs

If students have difficulty remembering irregular verb forms, try an oral, interactive approach. Divide the class into groups of three. Have each group make flashcards of the verbs listed in the **Common Irregular Verbs** chart. Next, group members should shuffle the cards and randomly choose five each. Each group member then presents his or her verbs to the group, giving the four principal parts of the verb and categorizing the formation of its past and past participle as changing vowels, changing consonants, changing vowels and consonants, or making no change. Group members shuffle the cards again and work together to write three sentences using the past or past participle of three randomly chosen verbs. Have groups share their sentences with the class.

Review D

DISTRIBUTED REVIEW

Have students find the following items.

1. an appositive phrase [*the mule (between 6 and 7)*]
2. a reflexive pronoun [*myself (between 9 and 10)*]

Review C Writing the Past and Past Participle Forms of Verbs

Write the correct past or past participle form of the verb given for each of the following sentences.

EXAMPLES
1. *go* We ____ to the Ozark Mountains.
   1. went
2. *swim* I have never ____ in an ocean.
   2. swum

1. *throw* Kerry should have ____ the ball to Lee, who could have tagged the runner out. [1. thrown]
2. *freeze* Has the water ____ yet? [2. frozen]
3. *write* Theo has ____ me a long letter. [3. written]
4. *see* Have you ____ that actor in person? [4. seen]
5. *sing* The tenors have ____ in Rome, Paris, and New York. [5. sung]
6. *throw* I finally ____ my old running shoes away and bought a new pair at the mall. [6. threw]
7. *drown* No one has ever ____ in this lake. [7. drowned]
8. *give* Taro ____ me a bowl of miso soup. [8. gave]
9. *blow* The strong wind this afternoon ____ down our tree-house in the backyard. [9. blew]
10. *take* I have already ____ a picture of you, Molly. [10. taken]

Review D Writing the Past and Past Participle Forms of Verbs

Write the correct past or past participle form of each of the ten italicized verbs in the following paragraph.

EXAMPLE Have you ever **[1]** (*take*) a trip to the country?
1. taken

We have always [1] (*spend*) summer vacations at Uncle Dan's farm in Vermont. We [2] (*do*) the most relaxing things there last year! We [3] (*swim*) in the millpond and [4] (*eat*) watermelon on the back porch. A few times, we [5] (*ride*) our bikes into town to get groceries. We also [6] (*take*) turns riding Horace, the mule. I have [7] (*fall*) off Horace twice, but I have never [8] (*break*) any bones. Both times, I [9] (*come*) down in a pile of soft hay. Then I dusted myself off and [10] (*climb*) on again.

1. spent
2. did
3. swam
4. ate
5. rode
6. took
7. fallen
8. broken
9. came
10. climbed

Review E Proofreading Sentences for Correct Verb Forms

Some of the following sentences contain an incorrect verb form. If a verb form is wrong, write the correct form. If the sentence is already correct, write *C.*

EXAMPLE 1. Marian Anderson sung her way out of poverty.

1. sang

1. She went on to earn fame and the Medal of Freedom. 1. C
2. Can you tell from this picture that she ~~use~~ to sing classical music? 2. used
3. In 1955, Marian Anderson ~~become~~ the first African American singer to perform with the Metropolitan Opera in New York City. 3. became
4. She performed in concerts and operas all over the world, but she ~~begun~~ her career as a child singing hymns in church. 4. began
5. Anderson, who was from a poor Philadelphia family, was awarded a scholarship to study music in Europe. 5. C
6. European audiences soon ~~taked~~ notice of her. 6. took
7. Audiences admired her determination and courage. 7. C
8. In 1939, Anderson was not permitted to sing at a hall in Washington, D.C., so she ~~give~~ a free concert, attended by 75,000 people, at the Lincoln Memorial. 8. gave
9. In the 1950s, the U.S. government ~~choosed~~ her to go on a goodwill tour of Asia and to be a United Nations delegate. 9. chose
10. Anderson ~~writed~~ of her experiences in her autobiography, *My Lord, What a Morning.* 10. wrote

Review F Proofreading a Paragraph for Correct Verb Forms

The following paragraph contains ten incorrect verb forms. If a verb form is wrong, write the correct form. If a sentence is already correct, write *C.*

EXAMPLE [1] A Confederate search party had went out to get boots for their soldiers and saddles for their horses.

1. had gone

[1] By chance, the search party ~~runned~~ into the Union cavalry. [2] It is not clear who ~~attackted~~ first, but a battle ~~begun~~ near

1. ran
2. attacked/began

DIFFERENTIATING INSTRUCTION

Advanced Learners

Add interest to **Review E** by having students find recordings of Anderson's singing to share with the class.

You might ask students to read **Review F,** do a statistical comparison of the impact of the losses on each army, and present the results. Encourage them to use bar or pie graphs of the numbers to show the relative significance of the 45,000 deaths.

3. went
4. C
5. burst
6. climbed/flew
7. drove
8. come/fallen

Gettysburg, Pennsylvania, on July 1, 1863. [3] The fighting ~~goed~~ on for three days. [4] First one side and then the other got the upper hand. [5] Shells ~~bursted~~ in the air, and cannonballs whistled in all directions. [6] At one point, some Confederate soldiers ~~clumb~~ to the top of Cemetery Ridge, and their flag ~~flown~~ there a brief time. [7] However, the Union army ~~drived~~ them back. [8] By the time the battle had ~~came~~ to an end, 20,000 Union soldiers and 25,000 Confederate soldiers had ~~fell~~.

Tense

6d. **The *tense* of a verb indicates the time of the action or of the state of being expressed by the verb.**

The tenses are formed from the verb's principal parts. Verbs in English have the six tenses shown on the following time line:

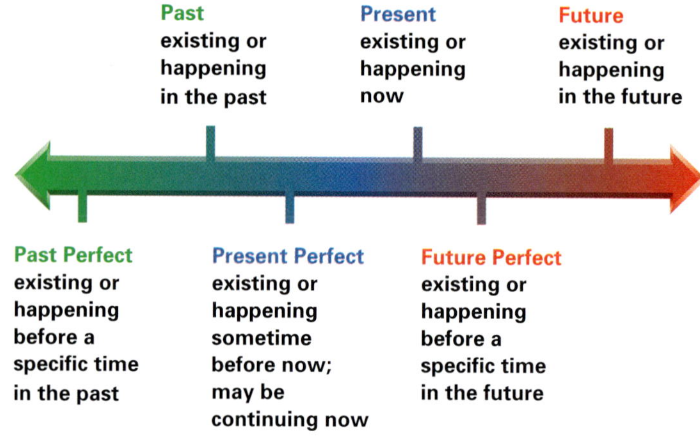

EXAMPLES

Max **has worked** [present perfect] all summer, and now he **has** [present] enough money to buy a bicycle.

The chorus **had practiced** [past perfect] for weeks before they **sang** [past] in public last night.

The surgeon **will have reviewed** [future perfect] the test results by next Friday, and she **will decide** [future] whether or not to operate then.

USAGE

Tense

Rules 6d–f *(pp. 156–162)*

OBJECTIVES

- To identify and explain the use of tenses in sentences
- To change verbs in sentences from one tense to another
- To proofread a paragraph to make verb tenses consistent

DIFFERENTIATING INSTRUCTION

English-Language Learners

General Strategies. Use the question "Have you ever _____?" to introduce present perfect tense. Have students work in pairs to ask and answer the following questions or others like them.

1. Have you ever studied Chinese? [*I have never studied Chinese.*]
2. Has he ever been to Europe? [*He has been to Europe.*]
3. Have you ever slept outside? [*I have never slept outside.*]
4. Have you ever seen a flamingo? [*I have seen a flamingo at a bird preserve.*]
5. Has she ever had the mumps? [*She has had the mumps.*]

Have students continue the question-answer session using the same format. Rhythmic repetition is a key method of language acquisition and will help English-language learners fix this construction in their minds.

RESOURCES

Tense

Practice

- *Language & Sentence Skills Practice,* pp. 145–147

Differentiating Instruction

- *Developmental Language & Sentence Skills,* pp. 73–78

Conjugation of the Verb *Give* in the Active Voice

Present Tense	
Singular	**Plural**
I give	we give
you give	you give
he, she, *or* it gives	they give

Past Tense	
Singular	**Plural**
I gave	we gave
you gave	you gave
he, she, *or* it gave	they gave

Future Tense	
Singular	**Plural**
I will (shall) give	we will (shall) give
you will (shall) give	you will (shall) give
he, she, *or* it will (shall) give	they will (shall) give

Present Perfect Tense	
Singular	**Plural**
I have given	we have given
you have given	you have given
he, she, *or* it has given	they have given

Past Perfect Tense	
Singular	**Plural**
I had given	we had given
you had given	you had given
he, she, *or* it had given	they had given

Future Perfect Tense	
Singular	**Plural**
I will (shall) have given	we will (shall) have given
you will (shall) have given	you will (shall) have given
he, she, *or* it will (shall) have given	they will (shall) have given

Reference Note

See page 164 for a **conjugation of *give* in the passive voice.**

STYLE TIP

Traditionally, the helping verbs *shall* and *will* were used differently. Now, however, *shall* can be used almost interchangeably with *will.*

EXTENSION

Critical Thinking

Analysis. To help students realize that there are strong similarities and differences among verb forms in various languages, you might ask them to provide textbooks of the languages they speak or are studying. Then, group students according to languages. Ask groups to examine verbs in various languages and to draw conclusions about language and verb tense. [*Students will probably notice that many languages use the same general verb tenses and forms, and some will point out cognates—words that are recognizable to speakers and readers of other, usually related, languages.*]

Relating to Literature

To show students how a skilled writer uses the present tense effectively, you might refer them to "Salvador Late or Early" by Sandra Cisneros if the selection is included in their literature books. Call on members of the class to read the passage aloud, substituting past-tense verbs. Then, ask students why they think Cisneros chose to use present-tense verbs. [*Present tense gives a sense of immediacy.*]

USAGE

CONTENT-AREA CONNECTIONS

World Languages

Translating Verb Tenses. So that students can draw on prior knowledge of other languages and so that they can see similarities among languages, ask them to work in small groups to create charts showing translations of common English verbs in **progressive** and **emphatic** forms. Students may ask world language teachers for input. Have students post the charts on the bulletin board.

Extension

Relating to Literature

If students' literature books include "The Scarlet Ibis," by James Hurst, help make students aware of the use of tenses by reading aloud the first two paragraphs. Have students listen for shifts in verb tense, and then discuss the effect of the shift from past tense in the first paragraph to present tense in the second paragraph. [*The past-tense description creates intrigue, foreboding, and suspense. The switch to present tense in the second paragraph changes the setting and places the reader with the writer in the present.*]

USAGE

The Progressive Form

Each of the six tenses has an additional form called the ***progressive form,*** which expresses continuing action. It consists of a form of the verb *be* plus the present participle of a verb. The progressive is not a separate tense but an additional form of each of the six tenses.

PRESENT PROGRESSIVE	am, are, is giving
PAST PROGRESSIVE	was, were giving
FUTURE PROGRESSIVE	will (shall) be giving
PRESENT PERFECT PROGRESSIVE	has, have been giving
PAST PERFECT PROGRESSIVE	had been giving
FUTURE PERFECT PROGRESSIVE	will (shall) have been giving

NOTE The ***emphatic form*** of a verb is used to show emphasis. The emphatic form consists of the present or past tense of *do* with the base form of the main verb.

PRESENT EMPHATIC	Although the grass is green, the lawn **does need** watering.
PAST EMPHATIC	The writer endured many setbacks in his career, yet he **did** finally **become** famous.

STYLE  TIP

The emphatic form is also used in questions and negative statements. These uses do not place special emphasis on the verb.

QUESTION
Why **do** bears hibernate?

NEGATIVE STATEMENT
If the car **does**n't [does not] start, check the battery.

6e. Each of the six tenses has its own special uses.

(1) The *present tense* is used mainly to express an action or a state of being that is occurring now.

EXAMPLES The new jet **has** two engines.

Leotie **belongs** to the Latin Club.

They **are decorating** the gym. [progressive form]

The present tense is also used

- to show a customary or habitual action or state of being
- to express a general truth—something that is always true
- to make historical events seem current (such use is called the ***historical present***)
- to discuss a literary work (such use is called the ***literary present***)
- to express future time

Learning for Life 

Continued on pp. 159–161

Eyewitness news. For this activity, tell students they are reporters for the *Good News Gazette,* a local magazine that reports on positive happenings. Their assignment is to write brief eyewitness reports about true or imagined good-news events in their neighborhood or school. Because using proper tense sequence is necessary to relate an event accurately, students should be particularly careful in their choice of verb forms.

You may want to share the following model with students.

EXAMPLES We **recycle** newspapers, glass, and aluminum cans. [customary actions]

The sun **sets** in the west. [general truth]

In 1905, Albert Einstein **makes** history when he **proposes** his theory of relativity. [historical present]

In *David Copperfield,* Dickens **shows** us the extremes of Victorian life. [literary present]

Finals **begin** next week. [future time]

(2) The *past tense* is used to express an action or state of being that occurred in the past but that is not occurring now.

EXAMPLES They **looked** for seashells.

The manatees **were swimming** in the canal. [progressive form]

NOTE A past action or state of being may also be shown with the past form *used*, plus *to,* plus the base form of the main verb.

EXAMPLE Chicago **used to be** the second-largest U.S. city.

(3) The *future tense* is used to express an action or a state of being that will occur. It is formed with *will* or *shall* and the main verb's base form.

EXAMPLES **Shall** we **set** the table?

The new model cars **will arrive** soon.

They **will be selling** them soon. [progressive form]

NOTE A future action or state of being may also be shown in other ways.

EXAMPLES We **are going to make** our own Mardi Gras costumes.

The president **holds** a press conference **next Monday.**

(4) The *present perfect tense* is used to express an action or a state of being that occurred at some indefinite time in the past. It is formed with the helping verb *have* or *has.*

EXAMPLES The Mendozas **have invited** us over for a cookout.

The Red Cross **has been delivering** medical supplies. [progressive form]

USAGE

Rerun Returns

After a frantic hour of searching, Ms. Rachel Bowen of 12345 Tabby Trail was reunited with her five-month-old kitten, Rerun. Ms. Bowen reported that Rerun had disappeared while conducting his daily survey of the butterfly population.

Ms. Bowen combed the area, interviewing children and peering down rabbit holes. Back in her yard, she was relieved to hear Rerun's distant mew, but she could not see him. Ms. Bowen searched in the nearby

DIRECT TEACHING

Verb Tense Forms

Activity. To help students practice the use of verb tense forms, divide the class into small groups, providing each group with a tape recorder and a sentence that begins a narrative. [*For example,* As I stumbled down the dark path, I heard footsteps behind me.] Have the first student in each group record the sentence provided, and then have each subsequent student record a sentence to further the story. Once the group has completed the story, have members play the tape back. Have a student list each verb in the story. The others should take turns identifying and justifying the choice of the verb tense. Allow students to rerecord the tape to replace inappropriate verbs with appropriate ones. Have each group play the revised tape for the class.

USAGE

NOTE Do not use the present perfect tense to express a specific time in the past. Instead, use the past tense.

NONSTANDARD We have seen that movie last Saturday. [*Last Saturday* indicates a specific time in the past.]

STANDARD We **saw** that movie last Saturday.

The present perfect tense is also used to express an action or a state of being that began in the past and continues into the present.

EXAMPLES Li Hua **has taken** violin lessons for eight years.

We **have been living** in Amarillo since early 1998. [progressive form]

(5) The *past perfect tense* is used to express an action or a state of being that was completed in the past before some other past action or event. It is formed with the helping verb *had.*

EXAMPLES Once the judges **had viewed** the paintings, they announced the winners. [The viewing occurred before the announcing.]

By the time that the Spanish conquistadors arrived, that redwood **had been growing** for three centuries. [progressive form]

(6) The *future perfect tense* is used to express an action or a state of being that will be completed in the future before some other future occurrence. It is formed with the helping verbs *will have* or *shall have.*

EXAMPLES By the time Mom returns, I **will have done** my chores. [The doing will be completed before the returning.]

In August, Aaron **will have been taking** Hebrew lessons for two years. [progressive form]

HELP

In the examples for Exercise 4, the first sentence expresses customary action and the second sentence expresses action that is happening right now.

Exercise 4 Explaining the Uses of Tenses in Sentences

Each item on the next page contains two correct sentences. Identify the tense or tenses used in each sentence. Be prepared to explain the meanings of the two sentences in each pair.

EXAMPLE 1. a. For breakfast she eats a bagel and some cereal.
b. For breakfast she is eating a bagel and some cereal.

1. a. present
b. present progressive

Learning for Life

Continued from p. 159

garage and in the peach tree. Finally, she looked up and discovered Rerun asleep in the rain gutter, his chin resting on the roof's edge, his plume of a tail floating above the oleander bush.

Ms. Bowen retrieved a stepladder for the rescue. When she returned, she found Rerun happily jumping off the peach tree. On the ground, he arched his back, flexed his claws, and raced at high speed after a grasshopper.

Ms. Bowen said, "The insect population

1. **a.** You will put down your pencils when the bell rings.
   b. You will have put down your pencils when the bell rings.
2. **a.** He worked at the gas station in the summertime.
   b. He has worked at the gas station in the summertime.
3. **a.** What caused the computer to crash?
   b. What has been causing the computer to crash?
4. **a.** When I arrived, Morton left.
   b. When I arrived, Morton had left.
5. **a.** Shelley was working on her bicycle.
   b. Shelley had been working on her bicycle when we arrived.

Exercise 5 Using the Different Tenses of Verbs in Sentences

Change the tense of the verb in each of the following sentences to the tense indicated in parentheses.

EXAMPLE 1. Maria always goes home at five o'clock. (*past*)
1. *went*

1. The quick, graceful otter swam to the edge of the pool. (*present perfect*) — 1. has swum
2. Our class will read Shakespeare's *Much Ado About Nothing.* (*future progressive*) — 2. will be reading
3. Before the concert, the orchestra practices the new pieces. (*past perfect*) — 3. had practiced
4. The guests will be arriving at the train station. (*present perfect progressive*) — 4. have been arriving
5. By then, I will solve the riddle. (*future perfect*) — 5. will have solved
6. The three sisters regularly meet for lunch. (*past*) — 6. met
7. The new computers have been working fine for three weeks. (*past perfect progressive*) — 7. had been working
8. Wasps were entering the house through the torn screen. (*present*) — 8. enter
9. The lawn mower has started after all! (*past emphatic*) — 9. did start
10. We reset the clocks for daylight saving time. (*future*) — 10. will reset

Consistency of Tense

6f. **Do not change needlessly from one tense to another.**

When describing events that occur at the same time, use verbs in the same tense. When describing events that occur at different times, use different tenses to show the order of events clearly.

Exercise 4 Explaining the Uses of Tenses in Sentences

ANSWERS

1. **a.** future / present
   b. future perfect / present
2. **a.** past
   b. present perfect
3. **a.** past
   b. present perfect progressive
4. **a.** past / past
   b. past / past perfect
5. **a.** past progressive
   b. past perfect progressive

USAGE

DIFFERENTIATING INSTRUCTION

Special Education Students

You might want to have all instructions read aloud and the terms and concepts explained. You might also want to limit the number of tenses the students deal with at one time.

For **Exercise 5,** provide students with a three-column list including the specified tenses, the base forms of the words, and a blank space for writing the required form. Allow students to consult the textbook and, with a helper, to fill in the blanks with the appropriate forms.

You might want to provide colored markers and let students choose a specific color to highlight each tense.

will be safe for at least two weeks. Rerun is grounded."

Students can compile their issue of the *Good News Gazette*, or volunteers could read their features aloud.

USAGE

TEACHING TIP

Exercise 6 Some students may be confused by the verbals in **Exercise 6** (*to study; fishing; going; fishing; Getting; to be; beginning; to form*). You may want to review the three kinds of verbals—participles, gerunds, and infinitives—and tell students to focus on verbs rather than verbals as they do this exercise.

Exercise 6 Proofreading a Paragraph to Make the Tenses of the Verbs Consistent

ANSWERS

Answers will depend on whether students decide to use present or past tense in their revisions.

	Present Tense	Past Tense
1.	C	was, had planned
2.	is	C
3.	drops	C
4.	C	dashed, ran, called
5.	wants	was
6.	C	had been thinking
7.	C	became, could, was
8.	know	saw, were
9.	C	rained
10.	are	C

NONSTANDARD Cara fielded the ball and throws the runner out. [*Fielded* is past tense; *throws* is present tense.]

STANDARD Cara **fielded** the ball and **threw** the runner out. [*Fielded* and *threw* are both past tense.]

STANDARD Cara **fields** the ball and **throws** the runner out. [*Fields* and *throws* are both present tense.]

NONSTANDARD She stands on the mound and will stare at the batter. [*Stands* is present tense; *will stare* is future tense.]

STANDARD She **stands** on the mound and **stares** at the batter. [*Stands* and *stares* are both present tense.]

STANDARD She **will stand** on the mound and **stare** at the batter. [*Will stand* and *stare* are both future tense.]

NONSTANDARD The batter wished that he practiced more before the game. [Because the action of practicing was completed before the action of wishing, the verb should be *had practiced,* not *practiced*.]

STANDARD The batter **wished** that he **had practiced** more before the game.

HELP For the paragraph in Exercise 6, either the present tense or the past tense can be used correctly.

Exercise 6 Proofreading a Paragraph to Make the Tenses of the Verbs Consistent

Proofread the following paragraph, looking for needless changes of verb tense. Choose whether to rewrite the paragraph in the present or past tense. Then, change the verbs to make the tenses consistent.

EXAMPLE **[1]** It all started as soon as I come home from school.

1. *It all started as soon as I came home from school.*

or

It all starts as soon as I come home from school.

[1] I am in my room, and I have planned to study for two hours. [2] It was about five o'clock in the afternoon. [3] To my surprise, Nancy Meng dropped by. [4] She dashes into the house, runs up the stairs, and calls my name. [5] What she wanted is a fishing companion. [6] All week she has been thinking about going fishing. [7] Getting my fishing gear together, I become excited and can almost see the fish fighting over which one is to be my first catch of the day. [8] On our way out to the lake, we see clouds beginning to form, and we knew we are in for trouble. [9] It rains all right—for the whole weekend. [10] The fish were safe for another week.

Active and Passive Voice

6g. **A verb in the *active voice* expresses an action done by its subject. A verb in the *passive voice* expresses an action done to its subject.**

ACTIVE VOICE	The coach **instructed** us. [The subject, *coach,* performs the action.]
PASSIVE VOICE	We **were instructed** by the coach. [The subject, *We,* receives the action.]
ACTIVE VOICE	**Did** Brandon **score** the winning touchdown? [The subject, *Brandon,* performs the action.]
PASSIVE VOICE	**Was** the winning touchdown **scored** by Brandon? [The subject, *touchdown,* receives the action.]

Compare the following related sentences:

ACTIVE The author (S) **provides** helpful diagrams (O).

PASSIVE Helpful diagrams (S) **are provided** by the author.

In these two sentences, the object of the active sentence is the subject of the passive one. The subject of the active sentence is expressed in a prepositional phrase in the passive sentence. Note that this phrase can be omitted.

PASSIVE Helpful diagrams **are provided.**

In a passive sentence, the verb phrase includes a form of *be* and the past participle of the main verb. Other helping verbs may also be included.

ACTIVE The tutor (S) **is helping** Sharon (O).

PASSIVE Sharon (S) **is being helped** by the tutor.

ACTIVE Someone (S) **has erased** the tapes (O).

PASSIVE The tapes (S) **have been erased.**

The chart on the following page shows the conjugation of the verb *give* in the passive voice.

Reference Note

For more information on **helping verbs,** see page 14.

Reference Note

For the **conjugation of the verb *give* in the active voice,** see page 157.

Active and Passive Voice

Rule 6g *(pp. 163–166)*

OBJECTIVES

- To identify active and passive voice in sentences
- To revise sentences in the passive voice to make them active voice

DIFFERENTIATING INSTRUCTION

English-Language Learners

Hmong. Hmong relies primarily upon the active voice, so the distinction in English between the active and passive voice may pose both translation difficulties and writing challenges for some Hmong speakers. Remind students of the purpose of the passive voice—to stress the object of a verb's action—and offer translation assistance when necessary.

USAGE

RESOURCES

Active and Passive Voice

Practice

- *Language & Sentence Skills Practice,* pp. 148–149

Differentiating Instruction

- *Developmental Language & Sentence Skills,* pp. 79–80

Differentiating Instruction

English-Language Learners

General Strategies. Because of the many helping verbs that must be correctly sequenced, some students have difficulty forming the passive voice. Using the conjugation of the verb *give* as a model (p. 164), you might want to have them practice changing active-voice transitive verbs to the passive voice.

In addition, give students newspaper articles and ask them to highlight any passive forms. Then, have them identify the receiver of the action, performer of the action (if any), and verb tense.

Extension

Critical Thinking

Evaluating. After students have edited their writing to eliminate the unnecessary use of passive voice, ask them for their conclusions about the effectiveness of changing some verbs to the active voice. [*Sometimes the writer's purpose or message requires the passive voice; the doer of the action may be unknown or unnecessary. Using active voice often makes the writing direct and succinct.*]

USAGE

Conjugation of the Verb *Give* in the Passive Voice

Singular	Plural
Present Tense	
I am given	we are given
you are given	you are given
he, she, *or* it is given	they are given
Past Tense	
I was given	we were given
you were given	you were given
he, she, *or* it was given	they were given
Future Tense	
I will (shall) be given	we will (shall) be given
you will (shall) be given	you will (shall) be given
he, she, *or* it will (shall) be given	they will (shall) be given
Present Perfect Tense	
I have been given	we have been given
you have been given	you have been given
he, she, *or* it has been given	they have been given
Past Perfect Tense	
I had been given	we had been given
you had been given	you had been given
he, she, *or* it had been given	they had been given
Future Perfect Tense	
I will (shall) have been given	we will (shall) have been given
you will (shall) have been given	you will (shall) have been given
he, she, *or* it will (shall) have been given	they will (shall) have been given

NOTE The progressive forms of the passive voice exist for all six tenses. However, the use of *be* or *been* with *being* is extremely awkward—*give,* for example, in the passive future perfect is *will (shall) have been being given.* Consequently, the progressive form of the passive voice is generally used only in the present and past tenses.

Using the Passive Voice

Although the passive voice is not any less correct than the active voice, it is less direct, less forceful, and less concise. In general, you should avoid using the passive voice. First, it generally requires more words to express a thought than the active voice does. Consequently, the passive voice can result in awkward writing. Second, the performer of the action in a passive voice construction is revealed indirectly or not at all. As a result, a sentence written in the passive voice can sound weak. Compare the following pairs of sentences.

PASSIVE The ball **was hit** over the outfield fence by Jody.
ACTIVE Jody **hit** the ball over the outfield fence.

PASSIVE The totals for the new budget **were** carefully **checked.**
ACTIVE The club treasurer carefully **checked** the totals for the new budget.

The passive voice is useful, however, in situations such as the following ones:

(1) when you do not know the performer of the action

EXAMPLES Over three thousand roses **were planted.**

Are the peaches **being harvested** on schedule?

(2) when you do not want to reveal the performer of the action

EXAMPLES Charges **were brought** against the vandals.

Many large donations to the building fund **have been made.**

(3) when you want to emphasize the receiver of the action

EXAMPLES Jacques Chirac **was elected** president of France in 1995.

These remarkable fossils **were found** nearby.

MEETING THE CHALLENGE

Mystery writers sometimes use the passive voice to relate information about a crime without revealing who performed the action. Write a one-page "mini-mystery" of your own in which you make use of the passive voice to describe an event while keeping the doer a secret. Try to include some clues in your story, and then see whether your classmates can solve the mystery.

ANSWER
Mini-mysteries will vary; students should make use of the passive voice.

COMPUTER TIP 

Some software programs can identify and highlight verbs in the passive voice. If you use such a program, keep in mind that it can't tell why you used the passive voice. If you did so for a particular reason, you may want to leave the verb in the passive voice.

USAGE

Active and Passive Voice 165

APPLICATION

Relating to Writing

To have students examine voice in their own writing, ask each of them to find a piece of his or her narrative writing. Next, have them label the voice of each verb. Then, as in **Exercise 8,** have them change passive-voice verbs to active-voice verbs if appropriate.

USAGE

Exercise 8 Using Verbs in the Active Voice and the Passive Voice

ANSWERS

2. Initially, only farm children joined 4-H clubs.
5. Members often exhibit projects at county fairs.
7. Many 4-H members attend summer camps.
8. Our club plans community projects yearly.
10. Participation in 4-H helps many young people.

Exercise 7 Identifying Active and Passive Voice

For each of the following sentences, tell whether the verb is in the *active* or *passive* voice.

EXAMPLE 1. In the morning, I am awakened by the alarm clock.
1. passive

1. The newest CD by my favorite group was not reviewed by most music critics. 1. passive
2. The student body elects the council president. 2. active
3. Angelo's courageous act of putting out the fire in the basement prevented a tragedy. 3. active
4. W. C. Handy composed the famous jazz classic "St. Louis Blues." 4. active
5. Your generous contribution to help the homeless is greatly appreciated. 5. passive
6. The half-time show at the state championship was performed by the band from Millersville. 6. passive
7. This afternoon the baby stood up by himself. 7. active
8. Was Mr. Yañez awarded the trophy? 8. passive
9. I don't understand this math problem. 9. active
10. Brian has been appointed captain of the basketball team. 10. passive

Exercise 8 Using Verbs in the Active Voice and the Passive Voice

Identify the verb in each of the following sentences as either *active* or *passive*. Then, revise each sentence that is in the passive voice so that it is in active voice.

EXAMPLE 1. My 4-H project was just completed.
1. passive; I just completed my 4-H project.

1. For my project I grew vegetables in containers. 1. active
2. Initially, 4-H clubs were joined only by farm children. 2. passive
3. Their projects focused on crops and livestock. 3. active
4. Later projects, such as personal safety and career studies, interested young people in the city. 4. active
5. Projects are often exhibited by members at county fairs. 5. passive
6. The 4-H club members also learn about good citizenship. 6. active
7. Summer camps are attended by many 4-H members. 7. passive
8. Community projects are planned by our club yearly. 8. passive
9. The city appreciated our tree-planting project. 9. active
10. Many young people are helped by participation in 4-H. 10. passive

Six Troublesome Verbs

Lie and *Lay*

6h. The verb *lie* means "to rest," "to recline," or "to remain in a lying position." *Lie* does not take an object. The verb *lay* means "to put" or "to place (something somewhere)." *Lay* generally takes an object.

Principal Parts of *Lie* and *Lay*			
Base Form	**Present Participle**	**Past**	**Past Participle**
lie	[is] lying	lay	[have] lain
lay	[is] laying	laid	[have] laid

EXAMPLES **Lie** down if you don't feel well.
Lay those books down.

Lambert **lay** on the lounge chair.
Lambert **laid** the towel on the lounge chair.

He **had lain** on the couch too long.
He **had laid** the newspaper on the couch.

Exercise 9 Choosing the Correct Forms of *Lie* and *Lay*

Write the correct form of *lie* or *lay* for the blank in each of the following sentences.

EXAMPLE 1. Jennifer _____ the flowers on the table and looked for a vase.
1. laid

1. He _____ the report aside and called for order. 1. laid
2. Alma will _____ down for a siesta. 2. lie
3. She has _____ on the couch all morning, watching those silly cartoons and eating cereal. 3. lain
4. The baby was _____ quietly in the nurse's arms. 4. lying
5. Is that today's paper _____ in the mud? 5. lying
6. I have _____ the shoes near the fire to dry, and I hung my wet clothes in the garage. 6. laid
7. _____ down, Spot. 7. Lie
8. The lace had _____ in the trunk for years before we explored Grandmother's attic. 8. lain

Reference Note

For more about **objects of verbs,** see page 59.

HELP

The verb *lie* can also mean "to tell an untruth." Used in this way, *lie* still does not take an object. The past and past participle forms of this meaning of *lie* are *lied* and *[have] lied.*

Six Troublesome Verbs

Rules 6h–j *(pp. 167–171)*

OBJECTIVE

- To complete sentences by writing the correct forms of *lie* and *lay, sit* and *set,* and *rise* and *raise*

DIFFERENTIATING INSTRUCTION

Learners Having Difficulty

To help students remember the difference between *lie* and *lay,* you might have them write five sentences using forms of *lie* and five using forms of *lay* and illustrate the sentences with stick figures. Then, have students label each sentence either "resting" or "putting."

EXTENSION

Critical Thinking

Analysis. Challenge students to examine the sentences in **Exercises 9, 10,** and **11** and determine what *lie, sit,* and *rise* all have in common. [*All three are used as intransitive verbs and therefore do not take direct objects.*]

Then, ask what *lay, set,* and *raise* have in common. [*All three are used as transitive verbs, requiring direct objects to complete a thought.*]

USAGE

RESOURCES

Six Troublesome Verbs

Practice

- *Language & Sentence Skills Practice,* pp. 150–153

Differentiating Instruction

- *Developmental Language & Sentence Skills,* pp. 81–82

DIRECT TEACHING

Modeling and Demonstration

Six Confusing Verbs. Model how to use the verbs *sit* and *set* correctly by using the examples *I will sit on the porch swing* and *I will set the cushion on the porch swing.* First, ask whether a word in the first sentence receives the action. [*no*] The verb *sit* takes no direct object; *sit* is correct here because there is no direct object in the sentence. Next, ask whether a word in the second sentence receives the action. [*yes;* cushion] *Set* does take a direct object; therefore, *set* is correct here. Now, have a volunteer use other examples from this chapter to demonstrate how to determine correct use of the other confusing verbs.

USAGE

TEACHING TIP

Mnemonics. To help students choose the correct forms of *sit* and *set,* suggest that they use the following mnemonic sentence:

> *I sit* with an *i;* I *set* the book on the *edge* with an *e.*

You may also want to demonstrate the actions as you say the sentences.

HELP—You may know that the word *set* has more meanings than the two given here. Check in a dictionary to see if the meaning you intend requires an object.

EXAMPLE
We watched silently as the sun **set.** [Here, *set* does not take an object.]

9. Our cat ____ in the sun whenever it can. 9. lies
10. After reading for almost three hours, I ____ back and rested my head on the cushions. 10. lay

Sit and *Set*

6i. The verb *sit* means "to rest in an upright, seated position." *Sit* seldom takes an object. The verb *set* means "to put" or "to place (something somewhere)." *Set* generally takes an object.

Principal Parts of *Sit* and *Set*			
Base Form	Present Participle	Past	Past Participle
sit	[is] sitting	sat	[have] sat
set	[is] setting	set	[have] set

EXAMPLES **Sit** down.
Set it down.

The cups **sat** on the tray.
I **set** the cups there.

How long **has** it **sat** on the bench?
She **had set** the picnic basket on the bench.

Exercise 10 Writing the Forms of *Sit* and *Set*

Write the correct form of *sit* or *set* for the blank in each of the following sentences.

EXAMPLE 1. Will you ____ with me, Josh?
1. sit

1. Please ____ here, Mrs. Brown. 1. sit
2. Have you ____ the seedlings in the sun? 2. set
3. We were ____ in the park during the Fourth of July fireworks display. 3. sitting
4. Someone has already ____ the kettle on the stove. 4. set
5. Grandpa is busily ____ several varieties of tomato plants in the vegetable garden. 5. setting
6. At the concert, Keith ____ near Isabelle. 6. sat
7. Mrs. Levine ____ the menorah on the mantel and asked Rachel to light the first candle. 7. set

8. They were _____ on the rocks, watching the surfers who were riding the large waves. 8. sitting
9. We had _____ still for almost an hour. 9. sat
10. Have you ever _____ on the beach at sundown and waited for the stars to come out? 10. sat

Rise and *Raise*

6j. The verb *rise* means "to go in an upward direction." *Rise* does not take an object. The verb *raise* means "to move (something) in an upward direction." *Raise* generally takes an object.

Principal Parts of *Rise* and *Raise*			
Base Form	**Present Participle**	**Past**	**Past Participle**
rise	[is] rising	rose	[have] risen
raise	[is] raising	raised	[have] raised

EXAMPLES She **rises** early.
She **raises** that question.

The price of cereal **rose.**
The store **raised** prices.

The lakes **have risen** since the spring rains.
The rains **have raised** the water level.

HELP—
The verb *raise* has definitions other than the one given here. Another common definition is "to grow" or "to bring to maturity."

EXAMPLES
They **raise** cotton.
He **raises** cattle.

Notice that both of these uses also take an object.

Exercise 11 Writing the Forms of *Rise* and *Raise*

Write the correct form of *rise* or *raise* for the blank in each of the following sentences.

EXAMPLE 1. The river has been _____ rapidly since noon.
1. rising

1. Please _____ and face the audience; then, begin your oral interpretation of the poem. 1. rise
2. After the speech, the reporters _____ several questions that the senator refused to answer. 2. raised
3. Will the governor _____ sales tax again this year, or will he wait until after the election? 3. raise
4. The price of fuel has _____ steadily. 4. risen
5. Let's get there before the curtain _____. 5. rises

Differentiating Instruction

English-Language Learners

General Strategies. Some students might have difficulty distinguishing the vowel differences in the troublesome verbs. To focus on these differences, you may want to write numbered verbs on the chalkboard and pronounce them in random order.

1—lie, **2**—lay, **3**—sit,
4—set, **5**—rise, **6**—raise

Have students identify by number which verb they hear. Then, pair English-language learners with English-proficient speakers who can give feedback on pronunciation as students read aloud the forms of the troublesome verbs in the exercises in this section.

USAGE

Teaching Tip

Mnemonics. Tell students that one trick for remembering *rise* and *raise* is to memorize the sentence "All *rise* and *raise* the window."

Reteaching

Six Confusing Verbs

Activity. If students have difficulty with these troublesome verbs, try a peer-teaching approach. Divide the class into groups of three. Have each group member study a different pair of the six confusing verbs in the lesson and present an explanation of the differences between the two verbs to the group. Students' explanations should include strategies for using the verbs correctly and example sentences. Group members should then work together to write a paragraph in which all six of the verbs are used correctly. Invite a group spokesperson to read his or her group's paragraph to the class.

6. Jerry and Alexander, two of the stagehands, will _____ the curtain for each act. 6. raise
7. The bread has _____ beautifully. 7. risen
8. The moon _____ and slipped behind a cloud, but there was still plenty of light for us to find our way home. 8. rose
9. The candidate _____ to address her supporters. 9. rose
10. The children _____ their flag for Cinco de Mayo. 10. raised

Review G Identifying the Correct Forms of *Lie* and *Lay, Sit* and *Set,* and *Rise* and *Raise*

Choose the correct verb in parentheses in each of the following sentences.

EXAMPLE 1. The number of immigrants coming to the United States (*rose, raised*) steadily during the late 1800s and early 1900s.

1. rose

1. The Hungarian mother shown below (*sat, set*) with her children for this picture around 1910.
2. They were among thousands of immigrant families who (*sat, set*) their baggage on American soil for the first time at the immigration station on Ellis Island in New York Harbor.
3. (*Lying, Laying*) down was often impossible on the crowded ships that brought these immigrants to the United States.
4. Most immigrants were thankful to be able to (*lie, lay*) their few belongings on the deck and think of the future.
5. Their hopes for new lives must have (*risen, raised*) as they drew closer to the United States.
6. The history book (*lying, laying*) on my desk states that eleven million immigrants came to the United States between 1870 and 1899.
7. (*Sit, Set*) down and read more about the immigrants who came from Germany, Ireland, Great Britain, Scandinavia, and the Netherlands in the early 1800s.
8. After 1890, the number of immigrants from Austria-Hungary, Italy, Russia, Poland, and Greece (*rose, raised*).
9. Many United States citizens were (*rising, raising*) concerns that there would not be enough jobs for everyone in the country.

The Granger Collection, New York

USAGE

DIFFERENTIATING INSTRUCTION

Learners Having Difficulty

As a review strategy after student papers for **Review G** have been corrected, you might ask students who had trouble distinguishing between any two verbs to pantomime the action of the correct verb.

CONTENT-AREA CONNECTIONS

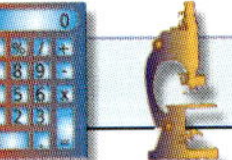

Art

Illustrating Verb Forms. To depict the correct forms of easily confused verbs in **Review G,** you may wish to assign each student to draw images related to the correct and incorrect verb forms in an assigned sentence. For example, for sentence 1 a student would illustrate *mother sat* and *mother set.* After discussing the drawings, display them where students can refer to them or have students create a booklet of the illustrations.

10. However, we know now that immigrant workers helped the country to (*rise, raise*) to new industrial heights.

Mood

6k. *Mood* is the form a verb takes to indicate the attitude of the person using the verb.

(1) The *indicative mood* is used to express a fact, an opinion, or a question.

EXAMPLES Seamus Heaney **is** the Irish poet who **won** the Nobel Prize in literature in 1995.

I **think** he **is** the best of the poets featured in this book.

Have you **read** the poem, Anita?

(2) The *imperative mood* is used to express a direct command or request.

EXAMPLES **Halt!** [command]

Please **write** your answers on a separate sheet of paper. [request]

(3) The *subjunctive mood* is used to express a suggestion, a necessity, a condition contrary to fact, or a wish.

EXAMPLES Gerald suggested that we **be** ready to board the train. [suggestion]

It is essential that all of the delegates **be** available for questions. [necessity]

If I **were** you, I would call them immediately. [condition contrary to fact]

Leilani wishes she **were** scuba diving off the Yucatán peninsula. [wish]

PEANUTS reprinted by permission of United Feature Syndicate, Inc.

Review H **Identifying the Mood of Verbs**

For each of the sentences on the following page, identify the mood of the italicized verb as *indicative, imperative,* or *subjunctive.*

EXAMPLE **1.** Ferryboats *sail* frequently between Calais, France, and Dover, England.

1. indicative

Mood

Rule 6k *(pp. 171–172)*

OBJECTIVE

- **To identify the mood of verbs as indicative, imperative, or subjunctive**

DIFFERENTIATING INSTRUCTION

Advanced Learners

Challenge students to write a dialogue between a coach and a player using the three moods. Before students begin writing, have them brainstorm which situations are suited to each mood. [*Imperative mood is used for commands: "Joe, replace Jones at forward." Indicative mood is used for straightforward conversation: "The game will begin at 7:30." Subjunctive indicates, among other things, the conditional: "If the field were dry, the players wouldn't get so muddy."*]

RESOURCES

Mood

Practice

- *Language & Sentence Skills Practice,* p. 154

USAGE

1. imp.
2. ind.
3. ind.
4. sub.
5. imp.
6. sub.
7. ind.
8. ind.
9. imp.
10. sub.

1. Please *hold* your applause until after all of the presentations.
2. La Paz, in Bolivia, *is* the world's highest capital city.
3. Female marsupials *carry* their young in pouches.
4. Is it necessary that he *rehearse* tonight?
5. *Take* out the trash immediately, Paul!
6. If I *were* you, I would not swim in that lake.
7. How much interest *does* State Bank *pay* on savings accounts and checking accounts?
8. Angela *intends* to continue her work at the humane society after school.
9. Mr. Guzman, please *consider* postponing the practice until next week.
10. For rust to form, it is essential that four atoms of solid iron and three molecules of oxygen *be* present.

Review I Identifying Correct Uses of Verbs

From each pair of words in parentheses, choose the correct item.

EXAMPLE [1] Look at this great old photograph that Grandma has just (*gave, given*) me.
1. *given*

Grandma told me that the Pop Corn King [1] (*been, was*) her grandfather and, consequently, my great-great-grandfather. This warmhearted man [2] (*took, taken*) Grandma and her sister into his home after their parents had [3] (*drowned, drownded*) in a flood. He would sometimes let the girls [4] (*sit, set*) in the driver's seat with him. The photograph was [5] (*maked, made*) in 1914 in the resort town of Petoskey, Michigan. During the summer, my great-great-granddad [6] (*use, used*) to drive through the streets in the late afternoon. He [7] (*rang, rung*) a bell, and children [8] (*run, ran*) out to buy treats just as kids do today. Look—the popcorn [9] (*cost, costed*) only five cents! The last time I [10] (*buyed, bought*) popcorn at the movies, I paid $3.75!

Chapter Review

A. Identifying Correct Forms of Verbs

If a sentence contains an incorrect verb form, write the correct form. If a sentence is already correct, write *C.*

1. That car breaked the land speed record.
2. Grandfather walks around the park every morning when he lived in Madrid.
3. The crocodile ran across the marsh and slips into the water.
4. Are the bells of Sant' Angelo rung every day at sunset?
5. After Lourdes had drove two hours, she stopped for a break.
6. Grandpa has swam across Santa Rosa Sound.
7. Our dog Pippa likes to set in the doorway and watch the traffic.
8. Will the bread raise faster in the oven or on the table?
9. Uncle Ben brung us a giant jigsaw puzzle of the Mojave Desert.
10. I could have sworn that the Green Bay Packers won the Super Bowl that year.
11. Carmilla's blouse was stained, but she knowed how to get the stain out.
12. Lilly has drunk two glasses of milk and still wants more.
13. Toucans fly by the window, and a cool breeze blew from the gulf.
14. Last night, Dr. Madison talks about the new laser operation.
15. The dogs are laying under the porch.
16. The curtains raised at the beginning of the first act.
17. She has apparently choosed the color blue.
18. The heron waits for the fish before it caught it.
19. We laid the tools down and had lunch.
20. It's a good thing that truck hasn't broke down—it was certainly an expensive investment.

B. Identifying Active and Passive Voice

For each of the following sentences, tell whether the verb is in the *active* or *passive* voice.

21. The United States president is elected every four years by a majority of electoral votes.

Numerals in brackets refer to rules tested by the items in the Chapter Review.

1. broke [6c]
2. walked [6f, b]
3. runs/slips *or* ran/slipped [6f, c, b]
4. C [6c, d, e(1)]
5. driven [6a, c, d, e(5)]
6. swum [6a, c, d, e(4)]
7. sit [6i]
8. rise [6j]
9. brought [6c]
10. C [6c]
11. knew [6c]
12. C [6c, d, e(4, 1)]
13. flew/blew *or* fly/blows [6f, c]
14. talked[6b, d, e(2)]
15. lying [6h]
16. rose [6j]
17. chosen [6c]
18. waited/caught *or* waits/catches [6f, b, c]
19. C [6h, d, e(2)]
20. broken [6a, c, d, e(4)]
21. passive [6g]

ASSESSING

Monitoring Progress

Chapter Review. To assess students' progress, you may want to compare the types of items missed on the **Diagnostic Preview** to those missed on the **Chapter Review.** If students have not made significant progress, you could refer them to **Chapter 17: Correcting Common Errors, Exercises 10–13** for additional practice.

USAGE

RESOURCES

Using Verbs Correctly

Review

- *Language & Sentence Skills Practice,* pp. 155–158

Assessment

- *Holt Handbook Chapter Tests with Answer Key,* pp. 11–12, 52

USAGE

22. active [6g]
23. passive [6g]
24. passive [6g]
25. active [6g]
26. passive [6g]
27. active [6g]
28. passive [6g]
29. active [6g]
30. passive [6g]

22. Yesterday the fawn ate its first full meal.
23. Was Oscar told the news beforehand?
24. The Veterans of Foreign Wars banquet was well attended.
25. Jenny speaks French and Arabic as well as English.
26. Was Ruth Lopez appointed goodwill ambassador by the secretary-general?
27. Most early British racing cars had superchargers.
28. The best songs in the show were performed by a husband-and-wife duet from San Marcos, Texas.
29. Our club sponsors a variety of community projects.
30. Large numbers of elephants are herded into different areas of the park in order to preserve the foliage.

C. Proofreading a Paragraph for Correct Verb Forms

The following paragraph contains errors in verb usage. If a verb form is wrong, write the correct form. If a sentence is already correct, write *C.*

31. blew [6c]
32. fallen [6e(5), c]
33. C [6c, d, e(2)]
34. eaten [6a, c, e(5)]
35. C [6f, c, d, e(2)]
36. came [6f, c]
37. known [6c]
38. went [6f, c]
39. frozen [6c, e(5)]
40. brought [6c]

[31] Last night the wind ~~blowed~~ for hours during the snowstorm. **[32]** When Libby and I looked outside in the morning, at least a foot of snow had ~~fell~~. **[33]** Instead of a brown, lifeless yard, we saw a glittering fantasy world. **[34]** Never in our lives had we ~~ate~~ our cereal as fast as we did that morning! **[35]** We quickly put on our parkas and ran out the door to build a snow fort. **[36]** Mom, smiling, ~~come~~ outside, too. **[37]** We should have ~~knowed~~ she would start a snowball fight! **[38]** Before we could get our revenge, Mom ~~goes~~ back into the house to warm up. **[39]** Soon afterward, our feet felt as if they had ~~freezed~~ solid. **[40]** When we were finally back inside, Mom ~~brung~~ us hot apple cider as a peace offering.

D. Identifying the Correct Forms of Six Troublesome Verbs

Choose the correct verb in parentheses for each of the following sentences.

41. [6j]

41. Their hopes (*raised, rose*) when the sun broke through and shone on the city below.

42. Please (*set, sit*) the orchid next to the rhododendron in the greenhouse.
43. Tim (*sat, set*) in the old armchair and recalled long summer evenings from his childhood.
44. Was that you I saw (*laying, lying*) in the hammock a minute ago?
45. (*Lay, Lie*) that magazine down, and listen to what I have to say!
46. The cadets stood at attention as the color sergeant (*rose, raised*) the flag.
47. The mythical phoenix is a bird that (*rises, raises*) from its own ashes.
48. He has a cold, so he has (*laid, lain*) on the couch most of the afternoon.
49. The seals were (*laying, lying*) on the beach.
50. He has (*sat, set*) his tools on the workbench.

42. [6i]
43. [6i]
44. [6h]
45. [6h]
46. [6j]
47. [6j]
48. [6h]
49. [6h]
50. [6i]

Writing Application

Using Verbs in Instructions

Verb Tense You have been asked to teach your eight-year-old brother to make his own after-school snack. Write instructions for making a nutritious treat. Use correct verb tense so that your directions are easy to follow.

Prewriting You will need to choose a snack that a child would be able to make and would enjoy. You may want to list all of the steps first and then go back and number them in order.

Writing As you write your first draft, think about how to define or clarify words that an eight-year-old might not know. Make sure that your verb tenses show the sequence of the steps.

Revising Ask a friend or young child you know to act out your instructions. Revise any steps that confuse your assistant. Add words that indicate chronological order (such as *first, second, then,* and *next*).

Publishing Check to be sure your verb tenses are correct. Use your textbook or a dictionary to check the spelling of the verbs in your instructions. Pay special attention to irregular verbs. Your class may decide to make its own snack cookbook to share with elementary school students or your local parent-teacher organization.

APPLICATION

Writing Application

Prewriting Tip. Remind students that as they write instructions, they will have to analyze their audience's knowledge and vocabulary. For instance, if the instructions on a box of cake mix are read to a five-year-old who has never made a cake, the phrase "add one egg" might need explanation. Without the added directions to crack open the egg, the child might lay the egg, shell and all, on top of the mix.

Scoring Rubric. While you will want to pay particular attention to students' correct use of verb tense, you will also want to evaluate overall writing performance. You may want to give a split score to assess development and clarity of the composition as well as usage skills.

CHAPTER 7

INTRODUCING THE CHAPTER

- This chapter discusses the correct use of pronouns within sentences. The first section focuses on the uses of the nominative, objective, and possessive cases. The second section addresses common pronoun problems. A brief final section introduces the concept of clear pronoun reference.
- The chapter closes with a **Chapter Review** including a **Writing Application** feature that asks students to write a magazine article that uses a variety of pronouns as subjects, predicate nominatives, direct objects, indirect objects, and objects of prepositions.
- For help in integrating this chapter with writing assignments, use the **Teaching Strands** chart on pp. T24–T25.

CHAPTER 7

Using Pronouns Correctly

Nominative and Objective Uses; Clear Reference

Diagnostic Preview

A. Correcting Pronoun Forms

Identify each incorrectly used pronoun in the following sentences. Then, write the correct form of that pronoun. If a sentence is already correct, write *C*.

Numerals in brackets refer to rules tested by the items in the Diagnostic Preview.

1. us [7i,f]
2. her [7f]
3. C [7h,b]
4. she [7c]
5. I [7j, b]
6. me [7d]
7. C [7b]

EXAMPLE 1. Excuse me, Rhonda, but this arrangement is strictly between Carl and I.

1. I—me

1. The author spoke to we history students about Slavic culture in Eastern Europe.
2. During the Olympic trials every diver except she received a low score from the judges.
3. The instructor, who seemed nervous during the show, was proud of Lani's performance.
4. It couldn't have been her.
5. Van is more energetic than me.
6. Rick couldn't spot Maura and I in the huge crowd at the state fairgrounds.
7. Tyrone and he are playing backgammon at Regina's house this afternoon.

CHAPTER RESOURCES

Internet

- Web resources: go.hrw.com

Practice & Review

- *Language & Sentence Skills Practice,* pp. 164–184
- *Language & Sentence Skills Practice Answer Key,* pp. 71–77

Application & Enrichment

- *Language & Sentence Skills Practice,* pp. 163, 185–188
- *Language & Sentence Skills Practice Answer Key,* pp. 71, 77–78

8. Laura gave he and Edwin a beautiful poem that she had written about friendship.
9. Angie's neighbors, Mrs. Brandt and he, helped plant the trees for Arbor Day.
10. Whomever can possibly take her place?

8. him [7e]
9. C [7i, b]
10. Whoever [7h,b]

B. Proofreading a Paragraph for Correct Pronoun Forms

Some of the sentences in the following paragraph contain pronouns that have been used incorrectly. Identify each incorrectly used pronoun. Then, write the correct form of that pronoun. If a sentence is already correct, write *C*.

EXAMPLE [1] To Velma and I, Dizzy Dean is one of the greatest baseball players of all time.

1. I—me

[11] We think there never has been another baseball player like him. [12] Fans still talk about he and his teammates. [13] Dean pitched for the St. Louis Cardinals, to who his fastball was a great help, especially in the 1934 World Series. [14] Dean was such a character that his fans never knew what crazy notion might come to he during games. [15] He had a real confidence about him, too. [16] According to one famous story about Dean, whom was also known for his quips, he once said, "Tain't braggin' if you kin really do it!" [17] When Dean became a sportscaster, him and his informal speech appealed to fans. [18] He liked his fans, and they liked him. [19] A big honor for he was being elected to baseball's Hall of Fame. [20] Us fans can go to the Dizzy Dean Museum in Jackson, Mississippi, to find out more about Dean's career.

11. C [7b, f]
12. him [7f]
13. whom [7h,f]
14. him [7f]
15. C [7b, f]
16. who [7h, b]
17. he [7b]
18. C [7b, d]
19. him [7f]
20. We [7i, b]

Case

7a. *Case* is the form that a noun or pronoun takes to show its relationship to other words in a sentence.

In English, there are three cases: *nominative, objective,* and *possessive.* Choosing the correct case form for a noun is usually simple because the form remains the same in the nominative and objective cases.

NOMINATIVE My **dentist** has opened a new practice in the office building next to the mall.

OBJECTIVE The receptionist who works for my **dentist** recently graduated from junior college.

USAGE

ASSESSING

Entry-Level Assessment

Diagnostic Preview. By ninth grade, many students will be able to use pronouns correctly as subjects and objects if the subjects and objects are not compound. Compile data on your class's common mistakes on the preview to use as a guide for instruction.

Students who make few errors on the preview may still make errors in written work. You might ask these students to focus on the **Special Pronoun Problems** section.

PRETEACHING

Lesson Starter

Motivating. Introduce pronoun forms by introducing yourself to the class, asking for a book, and noting possession of the book. Emphasize the pronouns: *I* am Mrs. Smith. Please hand *me* that book. This is *his* book.

Then ask students to identify the function of each pronoun you have used. [*subject; indirect object; shows ownership*] Point out that the pronouns you have used are examples of the subject form, object form, and possessive form of pronouns.

Differentiating Instruction

- *Developmental Language & Sentence Skills Guided Practice,* pp. 83–92
- *Developmental Language & Sentence Skills Guided Practice Teacher's Notes and Answer Key,* pp. 19–20

Assessment

- *Holt Handbook Chapter Tests with Answer Key,* pp. 13–14, 52

USAGE

DIFFERENTIATING INSTRUCTION

English-Language Learners

Spanish. In Spanish, *su* can mean *your*, *his*, *her*, *its*, or *their*, and *suyo* can mean *yours*, *his*, *hers*, or *theirs*. The possessive pronouns *su* and *suyo* agree in gender and/or number with the thing possessed, not with the possessor. Therefore, Spanish speakers may be tempted to say "her class" and "hers classes." To help your students distinguish between the possessive pronouns that can be used to modify nouns [*my*, *our*, and so on] and those that can be used only as pronouns [*mine*, *ours*, and so on], use template sentences such as "This is ____ apartment." and "This apartment is ____."

The Nominative Case

Rules 7b, c *(pp. 178–180)*

OBJECTIVES

- To read aloud sentences containing pronouns used as subjects
- To identify pronouns used as subjects
- To read aloud sentences containing pronouns used as predicate nominatives
- To identify correct nominative case pronouns and their use as subjects or predicate nominatives in sentences

BORN LOSER reprinted by permission of Newspaper Enterprise Association, Inc.

Only in the possessive case does a noun change its form, usually by adding an apostrophe and an *s*.

POSSESSIVE My **dentist's** business is thriving.

Personal pronouns, however, have distinct case forms. In the following example, the pronouns in boldface type all refer to the same person. They have different forms because of their different uses.

EXAMPLE **I** [nominative] forgot to bring **my** [possessive] notebook with **me** [objective].

The Case Forms of Personal Pronouns

Personal Pronouns			
	Nominative Case	Objective Case	Possessive Case
Singular			
First Person	I	me	my, mine
Second Person	you	you	your, yours
Third Person	he, she, it	him, her, it	his, her, hers, its
Plural			
First Person	we	us	our, ours
Second Person	you	you	your, yours
Third Person	they	them	their, theirs

Notice that *you* and *it* have the same form in the nominative and the objective cases. All other personal pronouns have different nominative and objective forms.

The Nominative Case

Nominative case pronouns—*I, you, he, she, it, we,* and *they*—are used as subjects of verbs and as predicate nominatives.

7b. The subject of a verb should be in the nominative case.

EXAMPLES **I** told Phillip that **we** would win. [*I* is the subject of *told; we* is the subject of *would win.*]

Were **Renata** and **he** on time? [*Renata* and *he* are the compound subject of *were.*]

Reference Note

For more about the **subjects of verbs,** see page 44.

RESOURCES

Case and The Nominative Case

Practice

- *Language & Sentence Skills Practice,* pp. 164–167

Differentiating Instruction

- *Developmental Language & Sentence Skills,* pp. 83–84

Oral Practice 1 Using Pronouns as Subjects

Read the following sentences aloud, stressing the italicized pronouns.

1. *He* and *I* agree that lacrosse is the most exciting game *we*'ve ever played.
2. *They* and their friends enjoyed the field trip.
3. Will Sue Ann and *she* enter the art contest?
4. Our teacher and *we* are glad that *he* and *she* are returning from their vacation soon.
5. *He* and *she* said that *we* were responsible for counting the ballots and posting the results.
6. Where are *they* and my parents?
7. Will *you* and *he* help us with the book sale?
8. When are *you* and *I* going to Arizona?

HELP

To choose the correct pronoun forms in a compound subject, try each pronoun separately with the verb.

EXAMPLE

(*She, Her*) and (*they, them*) answered the ad.

[*She answered* or *Her answered? They answered* or *Them answered?*]

She and **they** answered the ad.

Exercise 1 Identifying Pronouns Used as Subjects

The following paragraph contains ten pairs of pronouns in parentheses. For each pair, choose the correct pronoun to use as a subject.

EXAMPLE **[1]** (*They, Them*) may be the most famous husband and wife scientist team ever.

1. They

Although Marie and Pierre Curie were both brilliant physicists, [1] (*she, her*) is better known than her husband is today. In fact, [2] (*I, me*) was genuinely surprised to learn that [3] (*them, they*), along with another scientist, shared the Nobel Prize in physics in 1903. [4] (*We, Us*) tend to remember only Marie primarily because [5] (*her, she*) was the first woman to win a Nobel Prize. During their life together, Marie Curie always felt that [6] (*her, she*) and Pierre were a team. Working in a small laboratory in Paris, [7] (*they, them*) didn't have room for independent research. Before his death in 1906, [8] (*them, they*) collaborated on almost every project. In 1911, [9] (*she, her*) was again honored by the Nobel committee when [10] (*she, her*) was awarded the prize in chemistry.

MINI-LESSON Usage *Continued on p. 180*

Using *You*. Students often use the indefinite *you* in writing. Sometimes the *you* is an inexact substitute for the indefinite pronoun *one* or for *a person*, and sometimes it is an avoidance of a first-person pronoun like *I*, *me*, *we*, or *us*. Remind students that in formal writing, second-person pronouns are used only when a writer addresses the reader directly, as in commands and directions.

Use the following examples to illustrate vague uses of *you*.

USAGE

DIFFERENTIATING INSTRUCTION

Special Education Students

For further practice with pronouns used as subjects, have students work with a helper to change declarative sentences in **Oral Practice 1** into questions (for example, "Do he and I agree that lacrosse is the most exciting game we've ever played?") and questions into statements (for example, "Sue Ann and she will enter the art contest").

English-Language Learners

Spanish. In some languages, including Spanish, a pronoun used as a subject is understood; person and number are conveyed by the verb ending. The pronoun is stated only for clarification or stress. Emphasize that in English a pronoun used as a subject is stated unless the sentence is a command or request with an understood *you*, such as "Open the window."

DIRECT TEACHING

Modeling and Demonstration

The Forms of Personal Pronouns. Model how forms of personal pronouns are used in a sentence by using the example *She had to turn the box on its end to get it into her car.* First, ask which words are pronouns. [*She, its, it, her*] Ask how *She* is used in this sentence. [*as a subject*] Ask how *her* and *its* are used. [*to show possession*] Then, ask how *it* is used. [*as a direct object*] *She* is in the nominative form, *her* and *its* are in the possessive form, and *it* is the object form. Point out that a pronoun takes different forms depending on how it is used in a sentence. Now, have a volunteer use another example from this chapter to demonstrate how to identify the form of a pronoun.

USAGE

EXTENSION

Relating to Literature

If Abraham Lincoln's speech "With a Task Before Me" is available, you might use the speech to emphasize how personal pronouns in the first person are used. Have students find all the first-person pronouns and classify them by case. Students could use a chart like the following to present their findings:

SENTENCE NUMBER	PRONOUN	CASE
1.	my	possessive

DIRECT TEACHING

Correcting Misconceptions

Pronouns in Compound Constructions. Students may mistakenly combine cases in compound constructions. To test for correct case forms in compound constructions, have students use each pronoun alone in the sentence. (For example, in **Exercise 2**, sentence 2, students would say "She will move to San Miguel" and "He will move to San Miguel.") Remind them that when trying this trick, they may need to change the verb form to agree with a singular subject. (For example, in **Exercise 2**, sentence 4, "You and I are . . ." would become "I am . . .")

Reference Note

For more information about **predicate nominatives,** see page 58.

STYLE TIP

Widespread usage has made such expressions as *It's me, That's him,* or *Could it have been her?* acceptable in informal conversation and writing. Avoid using them in formal speaking and in your written work unless you are writing notes, informal dialogue, or friendly letters.

STYLE TIP

Sometimes pronouns such as *I, he, she, we,* and *they* sound awkward when used as parts of a compound subject or a compound predicate nominative. In such cases, it is a good idea to revise the sentence.

AWKWARD
She and we are going to the concert.

BETTER
We are going to the concert with **her.**

7c. A predicate nominative should be in the nominative case.

A ***predicate nominative*** is a word or word group in the predicate that identifies the subject or refers to it. A predicate nominative is connected to its subject by a linking verb. A pronoun used as a predicate nominative generally follows a form of the verb *be* or a phrase ending in *be* or *been.*

EXAMPLES This is **he.**

Did you know that the pitcher was **she**?

Oral Practice 2 Using Pronouns as Predicate Nominatives

Read the following sentences aloud, stressing the italicized pronouns.

1. Do you know whether it was *he*?
2. I thought it was *they.*
3. The winner of the marathon is *she.*
4. The ones you saw dancing were not *we.*
5. Can the valedictorian be *she*?
6. The first ones to arrive were *he* and *she.*
7. Do you think it may have been *they*?
8. The best speakers are *she* and *I.*

Exercise 2 Identifying Pronouns Used as Subjects and Predicate Nominatives

Identify the correct pronoun in parentheses for each of the following sentences. Then, give its use in the sentence—as a *subject* or *predicate nominative.*

EXAMPLE 1. If the phone rings, it will probably be (*she, her*).
1. she—predicate nominative

1. How did you know the guest speakers were (*they, them*)? **1.** p.n.
2. (*She, Her*) and (*he, him*) will move to San Miguel. **2.** sub./sub.
3. Open the door! It is (*I, me*)! **3.** p.n.
4. You and (*me, I*) are the only candidates left. **4.** sub.
5. It was wonderful to hear that the winner was (*he, him*). **5.** p.n.
6. (*Us, We*) and (*them, they*) will meet at five o'clock. **6.** sub./sub.
7. That man looked a little like Harry, but it was not (*he, him*) after all. **7.** p.n.
8. Believe it or not, (*she, her*) was on the radio this morning. **8.** sub.
9. Yes, the one in costume was really (*she, her*)! **9.** p.n.
10. You and (*we, us*) were the first visitors. **10.** sub.

MINI-LESSON Usage *Continued from p. 179*

1. Sunny weather may make you feel optimistic. [*Revision: Sunny weather may make people feel optimistic.*]
2. My mother always offers you fresh fruit. [*Revision: My mother always offers me fresh fruit.*]

The Objective Case

Objective case pronouns—*me, you, him, her, it, us,* and *them*—are used as direct objects, indirect objects, and objects of prepositions.

7d. A direct object should be in the objective case.

A ***direct object*** is a noun, pronoun, or word group that tells who or what receives the action of the verb or shows the result of the action.

EXAMPLES Phil called **her** last night. [*Her* tells *whom* Phil called.]

We still don't know what caused **them.** [*Them* shows the results of the action caused.]

Oral Practice 3 Using Pronouns as Direct Objects

Read the following sentences aloud, stressing the italicized pronouns.

1. They saw Liang and *me* at the fair.
2. Julia said that she recognized *him* and *me* at once.
3. Has anyone called *her* or *him* lately?
4. They took *us* to the reggae concert.
5. Alicia often visits Charlene and *her.*
6. A dog chased *her* and *me* out of the yard.
7. Within a few hours, the search party found Duane and *him.*
8. Did you ask *them* or *us*?

Exercise 3 Choosing Pronouns Used as Direct Objects

For each item below, write an appropriate pronoun in the objective case. Use a variety of pronouns. Do not use *you* or *it.* Answers will vary.

EXAMPLE 1. Have you told _____ yet?
1. him

1. I found Nina and _____ in the library. **1.** her
2. Will you help _____ or _____ with their homework? **2.** us/them
3. Sylvia Chu drove Candy and _____ to the movies. **3.** me
4. We all watched Aaron and _____ as they ran the marathon. **4.** him
5. These gloves fit both Carl and _____. **5.** me
6. Did you tell _____ about the picnic? **6.** them
7. If you don't call _____, I will. **7.** her
8. The realtor showed _____ and _____ the apartment. **8.** her/me
9. That solution suits _____. **9.** us
10. The doctor cured _____. **10.** him

Reference Note

For more about the different types of **objects,** see page 59.

STYLE TIP

When the object is compound, try each pronoun separately with the verb. All parts of the compound must be correct for the sentence to be correct.

EXAMPLE

Phil's call surprised (*she, her*) and (*I, me*). [*Phil's call surprised she* or *Phil's call surprised her? It surprised I* or *It surprised me?*]

Phil's call surprised **her** and **me.**

MEETING THE CHALLENGE

To keep from confusing their readers, news reporters need to keep their pronouns straight when writing a story. Write a short news report in which you relate the details of an interesting event or crime. Use personal pronouns in the appropriate cases, and try to use at least four different pronoun forms.

ANSWER
News reports will vary.

The Objective Case and the Possessive Case

Rules 7d–g *(pp. 181–187)*

OBJECTIVES

- To read aloud sentences containing pronouns used as direct and indirect objects
- To complete sentences by supplying appropriate pronouns as direct and indirect objects

USAGE

DIRECT TEACHING

Modeling and Demonstration

The Object Form. Model how a pronoun takes the object form when it is the direct object of a verb by using the example *The teacher thanked me for cleaning the chalkboard.* First, ask which word or words in this sentence are pronouns. [*me*] Then, ask how this pronoun is used in the sentence. [*as the direct object of the verb*] The forms of the pronoun *I* include the subject forms: *I, we;* the object forms: *me, us;* and the possessive forms: *my/mine,* and *our/ours.* Ask which form is used in the sentence. [*object form*] Now, have a volunteer use another example from this chapter to demonstrate how to identify the object form of a pronoun.

RESOURCES

The Objective Case and the Possessive Case

Practice

- *Language & Sentence Skills Practice,* pp. 168–173

Differentiating Instruction

- *Developmental Language & Sentence Skills,* pp. 85–86

DIFFERENTIATING INSTRUCTION

English-Language Learners

Spanish. Spanish uses three different objective forms for third-person pronouns: one for direct objects, another for indirect objects, and a third for objects of prepositions. Tell students that in English, the objective case pronouns are the same for all kinds of objects. Provide simple cloze activities for practice.

EXAMPLES

1. Mother gave _____ a book. [*him, her, them*]
2. Mother called _____ to dinner. [*him, her, them*]
3. Mother gave the book to _____. [*him, her, them*]

Learners Having Difficulty

For further oral practice with indirect objects, have students reword the sentences in **Oral Practice 4** to change the indirect objects to objects of prepositions. (For example, sentence 1 becomes "Mrs. Petratos offered delicious moussaka to them.")

APPLICATION

Objective Case

Activity. To help students become more familiar with objective case pronouns, divide the class into small groups and have them find examples of objective case pronouns in newspapers, magazines, and books. Provide poster board and markers for students to use to list labeled examples and the source of each example.

USAGE

TIPS & TRICKS

Generally, the indirect object comes between the verb and the direct object.

EXAMPLES

Grandma knitted **us** sweaters.

We gave **climbing the cliff** our full attention.

7e. An indirect object should be in the objective case.

An ***indirect object*** is a noun, pronoun, or word group that appears in sentences containing direct objects. An indirect object tells *to whom* or *to what* or *for whom* or *for what* the action of the verb is done.

EXAMPLES Molly made **me** a tape. [*Me* tells *for whom* the tape was made.]

The puppies were muddy, so we gave **them** a bath. [*Them* tells *to what* we gave a bath.]

NOTE Indirect objects do not follow prepositions. If a preposition such as *to* or *for* precedes an object, the object is an object of a preposition.

Oral Practice 4 Using Pronouns as Indirect Objects

Read the following sentences aloud, stressing the italicized pronouns.

1. Mrs. Petratos offered *them* delicious moussaka.
2. Show Yolanda and *her* your snapshots of Chicago.
3. Sara made Dad and *me* mittens and matching scarves.
4. Send Tom and *him* your new address.
5. My parents told *her* and *me* the news.
6. Mrs. Morita gave *him* and *her* applications.
7. Tell Willie and *them* the story that you told Erin and *me.*
8. The judges awarded *us* the trophy.

Exercise 4 Writing Pronouns Used as Indirect Objects

For each item below, write an appropriate pronoun in the objective case. Use a variety of pronouns. Do not use *you* or *it.* Answers will vary.

EXAMPLE 1. The teacher gave _____ their homework assignments.
1. them

1. Hassan asked _____ the most difficult question. (1. them)
2. Alex baked _____ a loaf of banana bread. (2. her)
3. The teacher handed _____ and _____ the homework assignments. (3. him/me)
4. Linda threw _____ the ball. (4. me)
5. Mr. Young has never told _____ and _____ the real story. (5. her/him)
6. Writing stories gives _____ great pleasure. (6. us)
7. We brought _____ T-shirts from California. (7. them)
8. Mr. Cruz sent _____ a pen as a graduation gift. (8. her)
9. My little sister gave _____ an animal carved out of soap. (9. him)
10. Lee's cousin knitted _____ a sweater. (10. him)

Review A Identifying Correct Forms of Pronouns

Identify the correct pronoun in parentheses for each of the following sentences. Then, give its use in the sentence—as a *subject, predicate nominative, direct object,* or *indirect object.*

EXAMPLE 1. Brian and (*I, me*) visited the computer fair.
1. *I—subject*

1. A guide showed (*we, us*) the latest in technology. 1. i.o.
2. She told Brian and (*I, me*) some interesting facts about software. 2. i.o.
3. In a short time, we had surprised (*she, her*) and several bystanders with our new computer game. 3. d.o.
4. The new computer aces were (*we, us*)! 4. p.n.
5. Another guide showed Brian and (*I, me*) all kinds of robotic machines. 5. i.o.
6. The guide said that (*he, him*) and his twin sister were going to dance with two robots. 6. sub.
7. The crowd and (*they, them*) seemed to enjoy the performance. 7. sub.
8. One robot reached out and touched (*us, we*) with a metal hand. 8. d.o.
9. Brian and (*I, me*) asked our guides how the machines worked. 9. sub.
10. (*They, Them*) patiently explained the control panels. 10. sub.

7f. An object of a preposition should be in the objective case.

A noun or pronoun that follows a preposition is called the ***object of a preposition.*** Together, a preposition, its object, and any modifiers of that object make up a prepositional phrase.

EXAMPLES with **me** before **her** next to **them**
for **us** behind **him** instead of **me**

NOTE Many people use incorrect pronoun forms with prepositions. You may have heard phrases like *between he and they* and *for you and I.* These phrases are incorrect. The pronouns are objects of a preposition and should be in the objective case: *between him and them, for you and me.*

EXAMPLES The coaches rode in a bus in front of **us.**

She is always very polite to **him** and **me.**

May I play soccer with **you** and **them**?

Between **you** and **me,** I am worried about **them.**

Reference Note

For a **list of common prepositions,** see page 28.

TIPS & TRICKS

To determine the correct pronoun form when the object of a preposition is compound, try each pronoun separately in the prepositional phrase.

EXAMPLE
The company sent a letter to (*she, her*) and (*I, me*).
[*To she or to her? To I or to me?*]
The company sent a letter to **her** and **me.**

Review A

DISTRIBUTED REVIEW

To review concepts taught earlier, ask students to find examples of the following items and write down the example and the number of the sentence in which the example appears.

1. past perfect tense verb [3. *had surprised*]
2. two infinitives [6. *to dance,* 7. *to enjoy*]
3. the object of an infinitive [7. *performance*]
4. noun clause [6. *that he and his twin sister were going to dance with two robots,* 9. *how the machines worked*]

USAGE

EXTENSION

Relating to Literature

If your literature book includes Langston Hughes's poem "Dream Deferred," also known as "Harlem," read it to the class and ask students to consider how Hughes uses the pronoun *it* in the poem. [*The pronoun clearly refers to the dream in the first line of the poem. Repetition of dream in lines 2, 6, 9, and 11 would lessen that word's impact.* It *is not only concise but also unstressed, allowing the stress to fall on the important words that follow the pronoun: "dry up," "stink," "sags," and "explode."*]

MINI-LESSON Grammar

What Is a Preposition? You might need to remind students that a preposition is a word used to show the relationship of a noun or a pronoun to some other word in the sentence. Have students refer to **Chapter 1: Parts of Speech Overview,** for examples of commonly used prepositions. Then, ask students to use the following prepositions in phrases.

1. beyond [*beyond the horizon*]
2. before [*before Sunday*]
3. until [*until bedtime*]

Review B Proofreading a Paragraph for Correct Pronoun Forms

ANSWERS

1. me—I; us—C
2. You—C; us—we
3. we—us
4. Her—She; we—us
5. her—she
6. they—them; they—C

USAGE

Review B Proofreading a Paragraph for Correct Pronoun Forms

Identify the ten personal pronouns in the following paragraph. If a pronoun is incorrect, write the correct form. If a pronoun is already correct, write *C*.

EXAMPLE **[1]** She thinks all of we should have the experience of working at a store checkout counter.

1. She—C; we—us

[1] Mrs. Jenkins, the home economics teacher that Tricia and me admire, told us all about the Universal Product Code (UPC) yesterday. [2] You and us have seen the black-striped UPC symbols on nearly everything that is for sale. [3] Mrs. Jenkins patiently showed the other classes and we how to interpret the numerals on the UPC. [4] Her explained to we that the first digit identifies the product, the next several digits stand for the manufacturer, the next few digits tell things about the product (such as color and size), and the last digit is a check number that tells the computer if another digit is incorrect. [5] Tricia said that Gregory and her found the lesson especially interesting. [6] The two of they had used the code when they worked as clerks in a store last summer.

The Possessive Case

7g. The personal pronouns in the possessive case—*my, mine, your, yours, his, her, hers, its, our, ours, their, theirs*—are used to show ownership or possession.

(1) The possessive pronouns *mine, yours, his, hers, its, ours,* and *theirs* are used as parts of a sentence in the same ways in which the pronouns in the nominative and the objective cases are used.

SUBJECT	Your car and **mine** need tune-ups.
PREDICATE NOMINATIVE	This backpack is **hers.**
DIRECT OBJECT	We finished **ours** yesterday.
INDIRECT OBJECT	Ms. Kwan gave **theirs** a quick review.
OBJECT OF PREPOSITION	Next to **yours,** my Siamese cat looks puny.

(2) The possessive pronouns *my, your, his, her, its, our,* and *their* are used as adjectives before nouns.

EXAMPLES **My** alarm clock is broken.

Do you know **their** address?

NOTE Some authorities prefer to call these possessive forms adjectives. Follow your teacher's instructions regarding these words.

Generally, a noun or pronoun preceding a gerund should be in the possessive case.

EXAMPLES We were all thrilled by **Ken's** scoring in the top 5 percent. [*Ken's* modifies the gerund *scoring*. Whose scoring? *Ken's* scoring.]

We were all thrilled by **his** scoring in the top 5 percent. [Whose scoring? *His* scoring.]

Reference Note

For more about **gerunds,** see page 81.

Review C Identifying Correct Forms of Pronouns

Choose the correct pronoun from each pair given in parentheses in the following paragraph.

EXAMPLE My cousin Felicia showed **[1]** (*I, me*) some photographs of buildings designed by I. M. Pei.

1. me

Felicia, who is studying architecture, told [**1**] (*I, me*) a little about Pei. [**2**] (*He, Him*) is a famous American architect who was born in China. In 1935, [**3**] (*him, he*) came to the United States to study, and in 1954, [**4**] the government granted (*he, him*) citizenship. Pei's reputation grew quickly, and by the 1960s many people easily recognized the structures [**5**] (*he, him*) designed. His buildings, such as the East

APPLICATION

Case Forms

To review case forms, you could create a cube with the following words written on each of the six sides: *first-person nominative, first-person objective, first-person possessive, third-person nominative, third-person objective,* and *third-person possessive.*

Tell students they will compose a story based on a beginning you will give them. Each person will have a chance to roll the cube and to add a sentence using the form required in either singular or plural form.

You may want to use one of the following beginnings:

- As the swirling whirlpool threatened to suck the child into its inky depths, . . .
- Eyes squinting, cameras focused, the group saw the first lion. . . .

You may want to record students' stories for future use.

USAGE

PRACTICE

Guided and Independent

Reviews You may want to have students complete **Review C** as guided practice and **Review D** as independent practice.

HOMEWORK

MINI-LESSON Usage

Point of View. Point out that pronoun forms indicate point of view in writing. A piece written in the first-person point of view uses *I, we, me,* or *us,* whereas third person uses *he, she, they, him, her,* or *them.* Tell students that they should choose the point of view they find most comfortable and appropriate in their writing, but that they must be careful to use point of view correctly.

TEACHING TIP

Review D Remind students that pronouns in a compound construction must be in the same case. For example, *him and I* can never be a correct compound since *him* is objective case and *I* is nominative case. Before students begin **Review D,** write columns headed "Nominative" and "Objective" on the chalkboard, and ask students to help you fill in the chart. Allow them to use the chart as they choose the pronouns for **Review D.**

USAGE

DRABBLE reprinted by permission of United Feature Syndicate, Inc.

Building of the National Gallery of Art in Washington, D.C., are quite distinctive; consequently, many people greatly admire [6] (*they, them*). [7] (*Him, His*) being in charge of numerous projects in the United States, Europe, and Canada earned Pei an international reputation. Did you know that the architect of the glass pyramids at the Louvre is [8] (*him, he*)? Felicia doesn't like the pyramids because [9] (*they, them*) look so different from the buildings that surround them. However, I think that design of [10] (*him, his*) is a work of art.

Review D Identifying Correct Pronoun Forms

For each of the following sentences, choose the correct pronoun in parentheses. Then, give its use in the sentence—as a *subject, predicate nominative, direct object, indirect object,* or *object of the preposition.*

EXAMPLE 1. Did Alva or (*she, her*) leave a message?
1. *she—subject*

1. The pranksters were (*they, them*). **1.** p.n. **2.** sub./sub.
2. (*He, Him*) and (*I, me*) are working on a special science project.
3. Is that package for Mom or (*I, me*)? **3.** o.p.
4. No one saw Otis or (*I, me*) behind the door. **4.** d.o.
5. I hope that you and (*she, her*) will be on time. **5.** sub.
6. The teacher gave Rosa and (*I, me*) extra math homework. **6.** i.o.
7. That's (*he, him*) on the red bicycle. **7.** p.n.
8. Between you and (*I, me*), I like your plan better. **8.** o.p.
9. When are your parents and (*they, them*) coming home? **9.** sub.
10. Everyone in the class except (*she, her*) and (*I, me*) had read the selection from the *Mahabharata.* **10.** o.p./o.p.

Review E Identifying Correct Pronoun Forms

For each sentence in the following paragraph, choose the correct pronoun in parentheses. Then, give its use in the sentence—as a *subject, predicate nominative, direct object, indirect object,* or *object of the preposition.*

EXAMPLE You may not know **[1]** (*they, them*) by name, but you may remember the actors Ossie Davis and Ruby Dee from movies or television shows.
1. *them—direct object*

For many years, the actors Ossie Davis and Ruby Dee have entertained [1] (*we, us*) with their talented performances. My friend Elvin and [2] (*me, I*) really admire both of [3] (*they, them*). Did you know that [4] (*they, them*) have been married since 1948? When Davis worked on Broadway, [5] (*he, him*) wrote and starred in *Purlie Victorious*, and critics gave [6] (*he, him*) great reviews. In addition, [7] (*him, he*) has appeared on the TV show *Evening Shade*. One of the stars of the movie *The Jackie Robinson Story* was [8] (*she, her*). What Elvin and [9] (*me, I*) admire most about Davis and Dee is that [10] (*them, they*) are fine performers who actively support civil rights and other humanitarian causes.

1. d.o.
2. sub.
3. o.p.
4. sub.
5. sub.
6. i.o.
7. sub.
8. p.n.
9. sub.
10. sub.

Special Pronoun Problems

Who and *Whom*

Nominative Case		Objective Case	
who	whoever	whom	whomever

7h. The use of *who* or *whom* in a subordinate clause depends on how the pronoun functions in the clause.

When you are choosing between *who* and *whom* in a subordinate clause, follow these steps:

STEP 1 Find the subordinate clause.

STEP 2 Decide how the pronoun is used in the clause—as a subject, a predicate nominative, a direct or indirect object, or an object of a preposition.

STEP 3 Determine the case of the pronoun according to the rules of formal standard English.

STEP 4 Select the correct form of the pronoun.

EXAMPLE Do you know (*who, whom*) she is?

STEP 1 The subordinate clause is (*who, whom*) *she is.*

STEP 2 The pronoun (*who, whom*) is the predicate nominative: *she is* (*who, whom*).

STEP 3 As a predicate nominative, the pronoun is in the nominative case.

STEP 4 The nominative form is *who.*

ANSWER Do you know **who** she is?

STYLE  TIP

In informal English, the use of *whom* is becoming less common. In fact, when you are in informal situations, you may correctly begin any question with *who* regardless of the grammar of the sentence. In formal English, however, you should distinguish between *who* and *whom.*

Reference Note

For information on **subordinate clauses,** see page 99.

STYLE  TIP

Frequently, *whom* in subordinate clauses is omitted, but its use is understood.

EXAMPLE
The people (whom) you imitate are your role models.

Leaving out *whom* tends to make writing sound informal. In formal situations, it is generally better to include *whom.*

Special Pronoun Problems

Rules 7h–k *(pp. 187–194)*

OBJECTIVES

- To read aloud sentences containing *who* and *whom*
- To choose correct usage of *who* and *whom* in clauses and to identify their functions within the clauses
- To identify the correct forms of pronouns used as appositives
- To complete incomplete clauses using the correct pronoun forms and to tell how pronouns are used in clauses
- To correct inexact pronoun references

USAGE

RESOURCES

Special Pronoun Problems

Practice

- *Language & Sentence Skills Practice,* pp. 174–180

Differentiating Instruction

- *Developmental Language & Sentence Skills,* pp. 87–92

USAGE

Differentiating Instruction

Advanced Learners

After stressing that words outside the clause do not affect the case of the pronoun in the clause, point out that this rule is similar to that of math expressions in which the operation inside the parentheses is not affected by operations outside it until the operation in parentheses has been completed. Write the following simple equation on the chalkboard to demonstrate your point: $2(10 \times 2)$. Remind students that they would do the operation in parentheses first and then multiply that number by 2.

Learners Having Difficulty

If students have trouble distinguishing between *who* and *whom,* suggest that they reword clauses like those in **Oral Practice 5** to make statements using *he* or *she* in place of *who,* and *him* or *her* in place of *whom.* (For example, in sentence 1, students would say, "You met him yesterday." For sentence 2, they would say, "He lives next door to us.") Students may want to reorder the words; for example, *him you met yesterday* would become *you met him yesterday.*

English-Language Learners

General Strategies. Because many languages do not distinguish between *who* and *whom,* English-language learners may not have a context for this concept. You may want to have students practice with *who/whom* using the method explained above.

TIPS & TRICKS

If you are not sure whether to use *who* or *whom* in a sentence, try the following test. Omit everything but the subordinate clause; then, substitute a nominative case pronoun such as *he, she,* or *they* for *who* or substitute an objective case pronoun such as *him, her,* or *them* for *whom.* If the nominative case pronoun is correct, use *who.* If the objective case pronoun is correct, use *whom.*

EXAMPLE
The coach will help anyone (*who, whom*) tries hard. [*He tries hard* or *Him tries hard? He tries hard* is correct.]

The coach will help anyone **who** tries hard.

In the example on the previous page, the entire clause *who she is* is used as a direct object of the verb *do know.* However, the way the pronoun is used within the clause—as a predicate nominative—is what determines the correct case form.

EXAMPLE Susan B. Anthony, about (*who, whom*) Sam reported, championed women's right to vote.

STEP 1 The subordinate clause is *about* (*who, whom*) *Sam reported.*

STEP 2 The subject is *Sam,* and the verb is *reported.* The pronoun is the object of the preposition *about: Sam reported about* (*who, whom*).

STEP 3 The object of a preposition is in the objective case.

STEP 4 The objective form is *whom.*

ANSWER Susan B. Anthony, about **whom** Sam reported, championed women's right to vote.

Oral Practice 5 Using the Pronouns *Who* and *Whom* in Subordinate Clauses

Read each of the following sentences aloud, stressing the italicized pronouns.

1. Take this book to Eric, *whom* you met yesterday.
2. Mr. Cohen is the man *who* lives next door to us.
3. Can you tell me *who* they are?
4. Toni Morrison is an author *whom* many readers admire.
5. *Whom* Mona finally voted for is a secret.
6. The coach will penalize anyone *who* misses the bus.
7. *Whoever* wins the race will get a prize.
8. The woman to *whom* I was speaking is conducting a survey of people who ride the bus.

Exercise 5 Classifying Pronouns Used in Subordinate Clauses and Identifying Correct Forms

For each of the following sentences, choose the correct pronoun in parentheses. Then, give its use in the subordinate clause—as a *subject, predicate nominative, direct object, indirect object,* or *object of a preposition.*

EXAMPLE 1. I know (*who, whom*) you are.
1. who—predicate nominative

1. Mrs. James, (*who, whom*) I work for, owns a pet shop in the mall and a feed store in our town. 1. o.p.

2. Is there anyone here (*who*, *whom*) needs a bus pass? 2. sub.
3. She is the only one (*who*, *whom*) everybody trusts. 3. d.o.
4. Both of the women (*who*, *whom*) ran for seats on the city council were elected. 4. sub.
5. I helped Mr. Thompson, (*who*, *whom*) was painting his garage and shingling his porch roof. 5. sub.
6. Eileen couldn't guess (*who*, *whom*) the secret agent was. 6. p.n.
7. It was Octavio Paz (*who*, *whom*) won the Nobel Prize in literature in 1990. 7. sub.
8. Her grandmother, to (*who*, *whom*) she sent the flowers, won the over-fifty division of the marathon. 8. o.p.
9. The person (*who*, *whom*) you gave the daisies is none other than my long-lost twin! 9. i.o.
10. Shirley Chisholm, (*who*, *whom*) we are studying in history class, was the first African American woman elected to Congress. 10. d.o.

Appositives

7i. A pronoun used as an appositive is in the same case as the word to which it refers.

An ***appositive*** is a noun or pronoun placed next to another noun or pronoun to identify or describe it.

EXAMPLES The winners—**he, she,** and **I**—thanked the committee. [The pronouns are in the nominative case because they are used as appositives of the subject, *winners*.]

The teacher introduced the speakers, Laura and **me.** [The pronoun is in the objective case because it is used as an appositive of the direct object, *speakers*.]

NOTE Sometimes a pronoun is followed by an appositive that indentifies or describes the pronoun. The case of the pronoun is not affected by the appositive.

EXAMPLES **We** soloists will rehearse next week. [The pronoun is in the nominative case because it is the subject of the sentence. The appositive *soloists* identifies *We*.]

Give **us** girls a turn to bat. [The pronoun is in the objective case because it is the indirect object of the verb *Give*. The appositive *girls* identifies *us*.]

Reference Note

For more about **appositives,** see page 89.

To determine the correct form for a pronoun used with an appositive or as an appositive, read the sentence with only the pronoun.

EXAMPLE
(*We, Us*) scouts offered to help. [*We offered to help or Us offered to help? We offered to help* is correct.]
We scouts offered to help.

USAGE

Reteaching

Appositives

If students have difficulty deciding which case pronoun to use when the pronoun is followed by an appositive, tell them to drop the appositive and read the sentence aloud.

For example, sentence 1 in **Exercise 6** would become *The coach showed (we, us) the new uniforms.* Ask students how the pronoun is used in the sentence. (*indirect object*) Then, ask which pronoun they would choose. [us]

CONTENT-AREA CONNECTIONS

Art/Science

Appostion. To connect apposition to other curriculums, have interested students inform the class about apposition in art and provide examples (for example, the juxtaposition of visual elements, as in a stained-glass window). Students might also investigate apposition in connection to biology (for example, the accumulation of layers next to each other, as in the case of cell walls). Encourage students to check the *Oxford English Dictionary* (*OED*) to find more cross-curricular links to *appositive.*

Exercise 6

DISTRIBUTED REVIEW

To review pronoun functions, have students name the sentence parts the appositive pronouns identify or describe in sentences 2, 3, 6, and 8.

2. subject

3. object of preposition

6. direct object

8. predicate nominative

USAGE

PRACTICE

Guided and Independent

Reviews You may want to have students complete **Review F** as guided practice and **Review G** as independent practice.

HOMEWORK

Exercise 6 Identifying Correct Pronoun Forms as Appositives and with Appositives

For each of the following sentences, give the correct form of the pronoun in parentheses.

EXAMPLE **1.** The principal named the winners, Julia and (*I, me*).

1. me

1. The coach showed (*we, us*) girls the new uniforms.
2. Our friends, (*she, her*) and Lucas, made the refreshments.
3. All of the class saw it except three people—Floyd, Ada, and (*I, me*).
4. Mrs. López hired (*we, us*) boys for the summer.
5. (*We, Us*) girls are excellent chess players.
6. Kiole listed her three favorite actors: Leonardo DiCaprio, Cuba Gooding, Jr., and (*he, him*).
7. Come to the game with (*we, us*) hometown fans, and you'll have a better time.
8. The best singers in school may be the quartet, Ellen and (*they, them*).
9. I want to go to the concert with two friends, Iola and (*he, him*).
10. The librarian gave the best readers, Craig and (*I, me*), two books by our favorite authors.

Review F Identifying Correct Pronoun Forms

For each of the following sentences, choose the correct pronoun in parentheses. Then, give its use in the sentence—as a *subject, predicate nominative, direct object, indirect object, object of a preposition* or an *appositive.*

EXAMPLE **1.** The cyclist gave (*we, us*) a smile as she rode past.

1. us—indirect object

1. sub. — 1. Students (*who, whom*) want to help organize the Kamehameha Day celebration should speak to Kai or me.
2. sub. — 2. Give these magazines to (*whoever, whomever*) wants them.
3. sub./sub. — 3. Don't (*they, them*) know that (*we, us*) students do our best?
4. app. — 4. The candidates, Ralph and (*he, him*), will speak at the rally tomorrow.
5. p.n. — 5. The Earth Day planners from our community are (*they, them*).
6. sub. — 6. Len and (*I, me*) had planned to watch the laser light show together.
7. i.o. — 7. Will you pass (*I, me*) the dictionary, please?
8. d.o./sub. — 8. Celine Dion, (*who, whom*) I saw in concert, sings many songs that (*I, me*) like.

Learning for Life

Continued on pp. 191–192

Speaking on the Telephone. Remind students that it is important to make a good impression when answering the phone, particularly in a professional situation. Emphasize that one way to create a good telephone impression is to use correct pronoun forms.

Copy onto the chalkboard the following beginnings of phone conversations, and ask pairs of volunteers to read them aloud.

1. #1 Hello.
#2 Is Leah there?
#1 This is she.

9. It would be a great help to (*we, us*) beginners if (*they, them*) would give us more time.

10. Visiting Australia is an exciting opportunity for Clay and (*she, her*).

9. o.p./sub.

10. o.p.

Review G Identifying Correct Pronoun Forms

Choose the correct pronoun from each pair in parentheses in the following paragraph.

EXAMPLE **[1]** My sister Angela is one of many women in our society (*who, whom*) use makeup.

1. who

The use of makeup to enhance beauty has a longer history than most of [**1**] (*we, us*) might imagine. In fact, [**2**] (*we, us*) cosmetic historians must look back to ancient times for the origins of makeup. For example, heavy, black eye makeup was worn by the ancient Egyptians, [**3**] (*who, whom*) originally used it as protection from reflected sunlight. It was they [**4**] (*who, whom*) first lined their eyes with a dark liquid called *kohl,* which [**5**] (*they, them*) applied with a small wooden or ivory stick. During the reign of Queen Nefertiti, [**6**] (*she, her*) and her noblewomen used not only *kohl* but other cosmetics as well. To [**7**] (*they, them*), dark, heavily made-up eyes and red lips were the marks of beauty. European nobles in the Middle Ages and the Renaissance wanted to emphasize their pale skin, so [**8**] (*them, they*) dusted their faces with chalk-white powder. It was Queen Elizabeth I, an English monarch, [**9**] (*who, whom*) set this style in her court. Although we might think that [**10**] (*them, they*) look strange today, both Nefertiti and Queen Elizabeth I were fashionable in their times.

2. #1 Hello.
#2 May I please speak with Paul?
#1 Who is speaking, please?

3. #1 Hello.
#2 Is Mrs. Tays there?
#1 Yes, she is. May I say who is calling?

Then, have students incorporate lines like the ones listed into a conversation about one of the following situations.

- You are a volunteer answering phones at a care facility for senior citizens.

USAGE

USAGE

TEACHING TIP

Exercise 7 Students' answers may include the following possibilities, which are grammatical but illogical.

1. Justin throws a football better than he throws me.

2. The story mystified him as much as we did.

14. Do you like cantaloupe as much as you like her?

16. When you serve dessert, don't serve yourself more than he serves you.

The Pronoun in an Incomplete Construction

7j. After *than* and *as* introducing an incomplete construction, use the form of the pronoun that would be correct if the construction were completed.

Notice how pronouns change the meaning of sentences with incomplete constructions.

EXAMPLES Everyone knows that you like Jolene much better than **I** [like Jolene].

Everyone knows that you like Jolene much better than [you like] **me.**

Did you help Ira as well as **they** [helped Ira]?

Did you help Ira as well as [you helped] **them**?

HELP Some items in Exercise 7 may have more than one correct answer, but you need to give only one.

1. than I do—sub.
2. as it mystified us—obj.
3. than he is—sub.
4. as we have—sub.
5. than she has—sub. *or* than we have known her—obj.
6. than he is—sub.
7. as I did—sub.
8. than they do—sub. *or* than I like them—obj.
9. than we are—sub.
10. as she is—sub.
11. than they were—sub.
12. than I am—sub.
13. than he has—sub.

Exercise 7 Completing Incomplete Constructions and Classifying Pronoun Forms

Beginning with *than* or *as,* write the understood clause for each sentence, using the correct form of the pronoun. Then, tell whether the pronoun in the completed clause is a *subject* or an *object.*

EXAMPLE 1. Did the noise bother you as much as (*she, her*).

1. as the noise bothered her—object

or Answers may vary slightly.

as she bothered you—subject

1. Justin throws a football better than (*I, me*).
2. The story mystified him as much as (*we, us*).
3. Is your sister older than (*he, him*)?
4. Have they studied as long as (*we, us*)?
5. We have known him longer than (*she, her*).
6. Are you more creative than (*he, him*)?
7. Did you read as much as (*I, me*)?
8. I like René better than (*they, them*).
9. Many people are less fortunate than (*we, us*).
10. Are you as optimistic as (*she, her*)?
11. After winning the city championship, there were no girls happier than (*they, them*).
12. When did you become taller than (*I, me*)?
13. Mary has collected more coins than (*he, him*).

Learning for Life

Continued from p. 191

- You are taking phone orders at a restaurant.
- You are acting as an office receptionist.

Record conversations, and allow peers to review the use of pronouns.

14. Do you like cantaloupe as much as (*she, her*)?
15. This label says the toy is not safe for a child as young as (*he, him*).
16. When you serve dessert, don't serve yourself more than (*he, him*).
17. Can he really play saxophone as well as (*I, me*)?
18. To win the contest, you must do as many sit-ups as (*she, her*).
19. I'm shocked that you gave her a nicer card than (*I, me*)!
20. Daniel doesn't visit his relatives as often as (*she, her*).

14. as she does—sub.
15. as he is—sub.
16. than you serve him—obj.
17. as I can—sub.
18. as she does—sub.
19. than I did—sub. *or* than you gave me—obj.
20. as she does—sub. *or* as he visits her—obj.

Clear Pronoun Reference

7k. A pronoun should refer clearly to its antecedent.

(1) An *ambiguous reference* occurs when any one of two or more words can be a pronoun's antecedent.

AMBIGUOUS My uncle called my brother after he won the marathon. [Who won the marathon, my uncle or my brother?]

CLEAR After my brother won the marathon, my uncle called him.

CLEAR After my uncle won the marathon, he called my brother.

(2) A *general reference* is the use of a pronoun that refers to a general idea rather than to a specific antecedent.

The pronouns commonly found in general-reference errors are *it, that, this, such,* and *which.*

GENERAL The ski jumper faces tough competition and a grueling schedule, but she says that doesn't worry her.

CLEAR The ski jumper faces tough competition and a grueling schedule, but she says these problems don't worry her.

(3) A *weak reference* occurs when a pronoun refers to an antecedent that has been suggested but not expressed.

WEAK Paul likes many of the photographs I have taken; he thinks I should choose this as my profession.

CLEAR Paul likes many of the photographs I have taken; he thinks I should choose photography as my profession.

(4) An *indefinite reference* is the use of a pronoun that refers to no particular person or thing and that is unnecessary to the meaning of the sentence.

INDEFINITE In the book it explains how cells divide.

CLEAR The book explains how cells divide.

EXTENSION

Pronoun Reference

Activity. Have students work in small groups to prepare and present a lesson on clear pronoun reference. Have them brainstorm how to present the material. Then, have each person choose a specific role to play in the teaching process. Possible roles include *administrative,* such as arranging for a student or group of students to tutor, setting up a time and place to teach the lesson, and getting permissions needed; *creative,* such as preparing materials, which might include pantomimes, worksheets, charts, or cartoons for the lesson; *instructional,* such as giving and evaluating the lesson; *media,* such as making a video or audiotape of the lesson or material to be used in instruction; and *reporting,* such as preparing and delivering an oral report on the experience or preparing a written report for a school or classroom newspaper.

USAGE

Exercise 8 Correcting Inexact Pronoun References

ANSWERS

Possible answers are given.

1. Meals on Wheels can help when older persons, people with disabilities, and people who are ill cannot prepare meals for themselves.
2. Meals on Wheels is an organization that arranges to have meals delivered to people's homes.
3. Because the nonprofit organization Meals on Wheels has a limited budget, it relies on volunteers.
4. Many businesses, churches, clubs, and organizations supply volunteers and contribute money.
5. People who receive services provided by Meals on Wheels usually help to pay for these services, but contributions are voluntary and based on a person's ability to pay.
6. In addition to delivering meals, some Meals on Wheels organizations offer clients a variety of other services.
7. Grocery shopping is a service provided to clients by volunteers who purchase and then deliver groceries.
8. When some clients have appointments and errands to run, they depend on volunteers for rides.
9. To lift clients' spirits, some volunteers regularly call clients on the phone; other volunteers help clients by performing minor home safety repairs.
10. Since volunteers not only provide needed services but also often form personal bonds with their clients, you may want to volunteer at a local Meals on Wheels.

USAGE

STYLE TIP

Familiar expressions such as *it is raining, it seems as though . . .,* and *it's early* are correct even though they contain inexact pronoun references.

Exercise 8 Correcting Inexact Pronoun References

Revise each of the following sentences, correcting each inexact pronoun reference.

EXAMPLE 1. Have you ever been physically unable to prepare a meal for yourself? That can be a serious problem.

1. *Being physically unable to prepare a meal for yourself can be a serious problem.*

1. Older persons, people with disabilities, and people who are ill sometimes cannot prepare meals for themselves, which is when Meals on Wheels can help.
2. Meals on Wheels is an organization in which they arrange to have meals delivered to people's homes.
3. Because it is a nonprofit organization, Meals on Wheels has a limited budget, which is why it relies on volunteers.
4. Many businesses, churches, clubs, and organizations supply volunteers, and they contribute money.
5. People who receive services provided by Meals on Wheels usually help to pay for these services, but it's voluntary and based on a person's ability to pay.
6. In some Meals on Wheels organizations, they offer clients a variety of other services in addition to delivering meals.
7. Grocery shopping is a service provided to clients by volunteers who purchase and then deliver them.
8. Some clients depend on volunteers for rides when they have appointments and errands to run.
9. To lift their spirits, some volunteers regularly call clients on the phone; other volunteers help clients by performing minor home safety repairs.
10. Volunteers not only provide needed services but also often form personal bonds with their clients; that is why you may want to volunteer at a local Meals on Wheels.

Chapter Review

A. Identifying Correct Forms of Pronouns

For each of the following sentences, choose the correct form of the pronoun or pronouns in parentheses.

Numerals in brackets refer to rules tested by the items in the Chapter Review.

1. [7b]
2. [7h, f]
3. [7d]
4. [7j, b]
5. [7i, b]
6. [7f]
7. [7h, b]
8. [7e]
9. [7c]
10. [7j, f]
11. [7h, f]
12. [7b]
13. [7f]
14. [7c]
15. [7f]
16. [7h, d]
17. [7d]
18. [7d]
19. [7f]
20. [7c]

1. Janell and (*I, me*) painted the room together.
2. Alan, for (*who, whom*) I did the typing, said that he would pay me on Friday.
3. The young Amish couple drove us and (*they, them*) into town in a horse-drawn buggy.
4. Carolyn has been playing the guitar longer than (*she, her*).
5. The last two people to arrive, Tranh and (*me, I*), had trouble finding the skating rink.
6. Hector wrote this song for you and (*I, me*).
7. The winner is (*whoever, whomever*) finishes first.
8. Ellis was worried about his project, but Ms. Atkinson gave (*he, him*) an A.
9. Was the winner of the race (*he, him*) or Aaron?
10. The pictures of the Grand Canyon made a greater impression on the Rileys than on (*we, us*).
11. To (*who, whom*) did you speak?
12. Schuyler and (*she, her*) will lead the group singalong.
13. Imagine my surprise when I saw Todd Franklin sitting behind Kenan and (*I, me*) in the theater.
14. The most productive employees at the plant were (*they, them*).
15. He was going to have dinner with (*her and me, she and I*), but fog delayed his departure from New York.
16. The prince knew precisely (*who, whom*) to appoint as his chamberlain.
17. Stanislas and Tina were at a Pulaski Day parade in Chicago, and I saw (*they, them*) there on the television news.
18. The ferret, annoyed at being woken up, bit (*she, her*) on the arm.
19. Why don't you come to the play with Carrie and (*I, me*)?
20. The first one to arrive was (*she, her*).

ASSESSING

Monitoring Progress

Chapter Review. To assess student progress, you may want to compare the types of items missed on the **Diagnostic Preview** to those missed on the **Chapter Review.** If students have not made significant progress, you may want to refer them to **Chapter 17: Correcting Common Errors, Exercises 14, 15,** and **16** for additional practice.

USAGE

RESOURCES

Using Pronouns Correctly

Review

- *Language & Sentence Skills Practice,* pp. 181–184

Assessment

- *Holt Handbook Chapter Tests with Answer Key,* pp. 13–14, 52

Chapter Review

B. Proofreading a Paragraph for Correct Pronoun Forms

ANSWERS

21. me—I
22. C
23. me—I
24. me—I
25. Us—We
26. me—I
27. whom—who
28. C
29. whom—who
30. I—me

USAGE

B. Proofreading a Paragraph for Correct Pronoun Forms

Some of the sentences in the following paragraph contain a pronoun that has been used incorrectly. If a pronoun is incorrect, write the correct form. If the sentence is already correct, write *C*.

21. [7j, b]
22. [7i, f]
23. [7b]
24. [7j, b]
25. [7i, b]
26. [7b]
27. [7h, b]
28. [7b]
29. [7h, b]
30. [7f]

[21] Do you grow as many plants as me? **[22]** Nowadays, scientists are hard at work trying to develop blue roses for us plant enthusiasts. **[23]** My science teacher, Ms. Phillips, and me wonder whether they can do so. **[24]** She doubts even more than me that breeding a blue rose is possible. **[25]** Us modern rose-lovers have never seen a blue rose. **[26]** However, Ms. Phillips and me learned that an Arab agriculturist in the thirteenth century once grew one. **[27]** For centuries, rose breeders whom have tried to produce the legendary blue rose have failed. **[28]** Some genetic engineers that I read about are working on this project now. **[29]** Scientists aren't sure whom would buy a blue rose. **[30]** Still, like you and I, they can't resist a challenge.

C. Identifying Pronouns Used as Subjects and Objects

For each of the following sentences, give the correct form of the pronoun or pronouns in parentheses. Then, tell whether each pronoun is in *nominative* case or *objective* case.

31. obj. [7i, f]
32. obj. [7e]
33. nom. [7i, b]
34. obj. [7i, f]
35. nom. [7i, b]
36. nom. [7i, b]
37. obj. [7i, e]
38. obj. [7i, e]
39. obj. [7i, d]
40. obj. [7d]

31. Dr. Schultz sang to the birthday brothers, Otto and (*I, me*).
32. Ms. Vlatkin showed (*we, us*) how to dance a *pas de deux.*
33. (*Him and her, He and she*), the brother-and-sister team, were the first archaeologists present at the opening of the royal tomb.
34. They went on the trip with their cousins, Jin-Hua and (*he, him*).
35. The last remaining contestants—(*she and they, her and them*)—walked in silence to the podium.
36. (*We, Us*) students at King High are very proud of our football team.
37. The teacher gave the best students, (*her and him, she and he*), a commendation.
38. I thought they should give (*we, us*) junior actors a chance to shine.
39. Rosa mentioned her favorite Tejano musicians, Emilio, David Lee Garza, and (*he, him*).
40. With regard to the Garcia twins, Blair said the best way to tell (*they, them*) apart was to make them laugh.

D. Correcting Unclear Pronoun Reference

Revise each of the following sentences, correcting each unclear pronoun reference.

41. Sally called Carla while she was doing her homework.
42. The ship's captain explained to the passenger the meaning of the announcement he had just made.
43. Police Sergeant Molloy's daily assignments involve hard work and a certain amount of risk, but he claims that it doesn't bother him.
44. Jill is impressed by Jeff's track-and-field records. She thinks he should do it professionally.
45. On the radio it said that afternoon thunderstorms were likely.

41. [7k(1)]
42. [7k(1)]
43. [7k(2)]
44. [7k(3)]
45. [7k(4)]

Writing Application

Using Pronouns in a Magazine Article

Using Correct Case Forms You and three of your friends are planetary explorers. Write a magazine article about your exploration of Mars. Use a variety of pronouns as subjects, predicate nominatives, direct objects, indirect objects, and objects of prepositions.

Prewriting To get started, jot down what you know about space travel and astronomy. You could get additional ideas from books and magazine articles about Mars. Think of things that a person might see or do while exploring that planet.

Writing As you write your first draft, be sure to include details that draw your reader into the story.

Revising Ask a classmate to read your story. Should you add or delete any details? Using your classmate's suggestions, revise your story to make it clearer and more entertaining.

Publishing Do your pronouns clearly show who did what? As you check over the grammar, spelling, and punctuation of your story, make sure that all of your pronouns are in the correct case. With your teacher's permission, you may want to post the story on your class bulletin board or create a Web page for it on the Internet.

Chapter Review

D. Correcting Unclear Pronoun Reference

POSSIBLE ANSWERS

41. While Carla was doing her homework, Sally called her.
42. After the ship's captain made an announcement, he explained its meaning to the passenger.
43. Police Sergeant Molloy claims that the hard work and certain amount of risk involved in his daily assignments don't bother him.
44. Jill is impressed by Jeff's track-and-field records and thinks he should become a professional athlete.
45. The radio announcer said that afternoon thunderstorms were likely.

USAGE

APPLICATION

Writing Application

Tip. To help students get a feeling for the writing style used in travel magazines, you might want to have students look at such publications before they begin writing.

Scoring Rubric. While you will want to pay particular attention to students' use of pronouns, you will also want to evaluate the students' overall writing performance. You may want to give a split score to indicate development and clarity of the composition as well as usage skills.

CHAPTER

8

INTRODUCING THE CHAPTER

- The first part of the chapter describes one-word, phrase, and clause modifiers. Eight troublesome modifiers and the positive, comparative, and superlative degrees of comparison are discussed as are dangling and misplaced modifiers.
- The chapter closes with a **Chapter Review** including a **Writing Application** feature that asks students to write a restaurant review using modifiers correctly.
- For help in integrating this chapter with writing assignments, use the **Teaching Strands** chart on pp. T24–T25.

CHAPTER

Using Modifiers Correctly

Comparison and Placement

Diagnostic Preview

HELP

A sentence in the Diagnostic Preview may contain more than one error.

Numerals in brackets refer to rules tested by the items in the Diagnostic Preview.

1. [8i]
2. [8j]
3. [8g]
4. [8i]
5. [8j]

A. Correcting Modifiers

The following sentences contain dangling modifiers, misplaced modifiers, and mistakes in comparisons. Revise each sentence so that it is clear and correct.

EXAMPLE **1.** When traveling through Scotland, I discovered that stories about monsters were more popular than any kind of story.

1. When traveling through Scotland, I discovered that stories about monsters were more popular than any other kind of story.

1. Having received a great deal of publicity, I had already read several articles about the so-called Loch Ness monster.
2. One article described how a young veterinary student spotted the monster who was named Arthur Grant.
3. While cycling on a road near the shore of Loch Ness one day, Grant came upon the most strangest creature he had ever seen.
4. Cycling closer, the monster took a leap and plunged into the lake.
5. Numerous theories have been discussed about the origin and identity of the monster in the local newspapers.

CHAPTER RESOURCES

Internet

- Web resources: go.hrw.com

Practice & Review

- *Language & Sentence Skills Practice,* pp. 190–213
- *Language & Sentence Skills Practice Answer Key,* pp. 79–87

Application & Enrichment

- *Language & Sentence Skills Practice,* pp. 189, 214–217
- *Language & Sentence Skills Practice Answer Key,* pp. 79, 87–88

6. Of all the proposed theories, the better and more fascinating one was that the monster must be a freshwater species of sea serpent.
7. Having found a huge, dead creature on the shore of the lake in 1942, the mystery of the monster was thought to be solved finally.
8. One famous photograph of the monster has recently been revealed to be a hoax that seemed to confirm the creature's existence.
9. Skeptical, stories about the Loch Ness monster have always struck some people as unbelievable.
10. However, reported sightings of the monster have continued, perhaps more than of any mysterious creature.

6. [8e]
7. [8i]
8. [8j]
9. [8j]
10. [8j, f, h]

B. Using Modifiers Correctly in Sentences

Most of the following sentences have mistakes in the use of modifiers. Revise each incorrect sentence to correct these errors. If a sentence is already correct, write *C.*

EXAMPLE 1. In the United States, is the use of solar energy more commoner than the use of geothermal energy?

1. In the United States, is the use of solar energy more common than the use of geothermal energy?

HELP — Although some sentences in Part B of the Diagnostic Preview can be correctly revised in more than one way, you need to give only one revision.

11. Kay has a better understanding of both solar and geothermal energy than anyone I know.
12. Yoko isn't sure she agrees with me, but I have talked with Kay more than Yoko.
13. Kay thinks that, of the two, solar energy is the best method for generating power.
14. She claims that the energy from the sun will soon be easier to harness than geothermal energy.
15. Arguing that the sun's energy could also be less expensive to use, Kay says that more research into solar energy is needed.
16. Yoko disagrees and thinks that geothermal energy would provide more cheaper power than solar energy.
17. She told me that for centuries people in other countries have been using geothermal energy, such as Iceland and Japan.
18. However, she added that geothermal energy is less well known than any source of power in our country.
19. Although infrequently used in the United States, Yoko feels that geothermal energy has already proven itself to be safe and efficient.
20. Unconvinced, both points of view seem to me to offer promising new sources of energy.

11. [8f]
12. [8h]
13. [8e]
14. [8d, e, h]
15. [8i, j, d]
16. [8g]
17. [8j]
18. [8f]
19. [8j]
20. [8i]

USAGE

ASSESSING

Entry-Level Assessment

Diagnostic Preview. You may wish to compile data on your class's most common mistakes on the preview and use this information as a guide for instruction and for establishing a set of individual goals each student could use as guidelines when proofreading his or her writing assignments.

Diagnostic Preview: Part A

POSSIBLE ANSWERS

1. I had already read several articles about the so-called Loch Ness monster, which had received a great deal of publicity.
2. One article described how Arthur Grant, a young veterinary student, spotted the monster.
3. . . . the strangest creature . . .
4. As Grant cycled closer, the monster . . .
5. The local newspapers have discussed numerous theories about the . . .
6. Of all the proposed theories, the best and most fascinating one . . .
7. When a huge, dead creature was found on the shore of the lake in 1942, . . .

Differentiating Instruction

- *Developmental Language & Sentence Skills Guided Practice,* pp. 93–98
- *Developmental Language & Sentence Skills Guided Practice Teacher's Notes and Answer Key,* p. 21

Assessment

- *Holt Handbook Chapter Tests with Answer Key,* pp. 15–16, 52

Diagnostic Preview: Part A

POSSIBLE ANSWERS continued

8. One famous photograph that seemed to confirm the creature's existence has recently been revealed to be a hoax.
9. Stories about the Loch Ness monster have always struck some skeptical people as unbelievable.
10. However, reported sightings of the monster have continued, perhaps more than of any other mysterious creature.

Diagnostic Preview: Part B

POSSIBLE ANSWERS

11. . . . than anyone else I know.
12. Yoko may not agree with Kay, but I have talked with Kay more than Yoko has.
13. Kay thinks that, of the two, solar energy is a better method for generating power.
14. C
15. C
16. Yoko disagrees and thinks that geothermal energy would provide cheaper power than solar energy.
17. She told me that for centuries people in other countries, such as Iceland and Japan, . . .
18. However, she added that geothermal energy is less well known than any other . . .
19. Yoko feels that geothermal energy, although infrequently used in the United States, has already proven . . .
20. Although I am unconvinced of which plan is better, . . .

What Is a Modifier?

Rules 8a–c *(pp. 200–203)*

OBJECTIVE

- **To determine whether words, phrases, and clauses are modifiers**

Reference Note

For more about **adjectives,** see page 10. For more about **adverbs,** see page 21.

What Is a Modifier?

A ***modifier*** is a word or word group that makes the meaning of another word or word group more specific. The two kinds of modifiers are *adjectives* and *adverbs.*

One-Word Modifiers

Adjectives

8a. An adjective makes the meaning of a noun or pronoun more specific.

EXAMPLES

Samia gave a **broad** smile. [The adjective *broad* makes the meaning of the noun *smile* more specific.]

Only she knows the answer. [The adjective *only* makes the meaning of the pronoun *she* more specific.]

The sweater is **soft** and **warm.** [The adjectives *soft* and *warm* make the meaning of the noun *sweater* more specific.]

Isn't he a **well-mannered** boy? [The compound adjective *well-mannered* makes the meaning of the noun *boy* more specific.]

Adverbs

8b. An adverb makes the meaning of a verb, an adjective, or another adverb more specific.

EXAMPLES

Samia grinned **broadly.** [The adverb *broadly* makes the meaning of the verb *grinned* more specific.]

Sometimes I wonder about the future. [The adverb *sometimes* makes the meaning of the verb *wonder* more specific.]

The dog is **very** hungry. [The adverb *very* makes the meaning of the adjective *hungry* more specific.]

The alarm rang **surprisingly** loudly. [The adverb *surprisingly* makes the meaning of the adverb *loudly* more specific.]

Adjective or Adverb?

While many adverbs end in *–ly,* others do not. Furthermore, not all words with the *–ly* ending are adverbs. Some adjectives also end in *–ly.*

RESOURCES

What Is a Modifier?

Practice

- *Language & Sentence Skills Practice, pp.* 190–198

Therefore, you can't tell whether a word is an adjective or an adverb simply by looking for the *–ly* ending. To decide whether a word is an adjective or an adverb, determine how the word is used in the sentence.

Adverbs Not Ending in *–ly*		
broadcast **soon**	return **home**	run **loose**
not sleepy	stand **here**	**very** happy

Adjectives Ending in *–ly*		
elderly people	**only** child	**silly** behavior
curly hair	**holy** building	**lonely** person

Some words can be used as either adjectives or adverbs.

Adjectives	Adverbs
She is an **only** child.	She has **only** one brother.
Tina has a **fast** car.	The car goes **fast.**
We caught the **last** train.	We left **last.**

8c. If a word in the predicate modifies the subject of the verb, use the adjective form. If it modifies the verb, use the adverb form.

ADJECTIVE The gazelles were **graceful.** [*Graceful* modifies *gazelles.*]

ADVERB The gazelles moved **gracefully.** [*Gracefully* modifies *moved.*]

ADJECTIVE The boy grew **tall.** [*Tall* modifies *boy.*]

ADVERB The boy grew **quickly.** [*Quickly* modifies *grew.*]

Phrases Used as Modifiers

Like one-word modifiers, phrases can also be used as adjectives and adverbs.

EXAMPLES It was time **for celebration.** [The prepositional phrase *for celebration* acts as an adjective that modifies the noun *time.*]

Uprooting trees and bushes, the tornado swept across the Panhandle. [The participial phrase *Uprooting trees and bushes* acts as an adjective that modifies the noun *tornado.*]

Reference Note

For more about **subjects** and **predicates,** see page 42.

Reference Note

For more about different **kinds of phrases,** see page 70.

PRETEACHING

Lesson Starter

Motivating. To help students understand how adjectives modify words, consider using the following demonstration. First, identify for the class objects in the classroom, using only nouns such as "desk, flag, chair." Then, ask students to modify those nouns by using descriptive words called adjectives: "*metal* desk, *American* flag, *swivel* chair." Next, ask them to use phrases to modify the words: "desk *in the front of the room,* flag *with stars and stripes,* chair *leaning against the wall.*" Finally, ask students to use adjective clauses to modify the nouns: "desk *which I chose,* flag *which we salute,* chair *which will be replaced.*" Invite students to repeat this exercise by describing the school cafeteria, gymnasium, or library.

USAGE

DIRECT TEACHING

Modeling and Demonstration

One-Word Modifiers. Model how to identify adjectives and adverbs by using the examples *Does Stephen know the secret combination?* and *The car backfired loudly.* First, ask which word in the first sentence specifies what kind of *combination.* [*secret*] Then, ask what part of speech *combination* is. [*noun*] Point out that since adjectives describe nouns, *secret* is an adjective. Next, ask which word in the second example describes how the car backfired. [*loudly*] Then, ask what part of speech *backfired* is. [*verb*] Since adverbs describe verbs, *loudly* is an adverb. Now, have a volunteer use another example from this chapter to demonstrate how to identify adjectives and adverbs.

CONTENT-AREA CONNECTIONS

Math

Numbers as Modifiers. Point out to your students that modifiers have algebraic equivalents. For example, in $3x$, 3 is equivalent to the modifier and x is equivalent to the word modified.

Differentiating Instruction

Learners Having Difficulty

To help students visualize phrases and clauses used as modifiers, have them create captions using these forms. Provide students with magazines from which to cut pictures, and have them work in pairs to find and mount on construction paper pictures that illustrate adjective or adverb phrases or clauses. Then, have them add appropriate captions labeling the adjective or adverb phrases and clauses. ["Sitting in the car, *she made herself comfortable." (participial phrase)* or "By the door, *she paused and smiled." (adverbial prepositional phrase)*] Post the labeled pictures on the bulletin board.

USAGE

Professor Martinez is the one **to ask.** [The infinitive phrase *to ask* acts as an adjective that modifies the pronoun *one*.]

Ray is becoming quite good **at soccer.** [The prepositional phrase *at soccer* acts as an adverb that modifies the adjective *good*.]

Walk **with care on icy pavements.** [The prepositional phrases *with care* and *on icy pavements* act as adverbs that modify the verb *Walk*.]

The guide spoke slowly enough **to be understood.** [The infinitive phrase *to be understood* acts as an adverb that modifies the adverb *enough*.]

Clauses Used as Modifiers

Like words and phrases, clauses can also be used as adjectives and adverbs.

Reference Note

For more about **clauses,** see Chapter 4.

EXAMPLES Vermeer is the painter **that I like best.** [The adjective clause *that I like best* modifies the noun *painter*.]

Before Toni left for work, she took the dog for a walk. [The adverb clause *Before Toni left for work* modifies the verb *took*.]

Exercise 1 Identifying Modifiers

Identify the italicized word or word group in each of the following sentences as a *modifier* or *not a modifier.* M *or* Not M

EXAMPLES 1. Rudyard Kipling, *who was born in India,* wrote a wonderful story about a brave mongoose.

1. *modifier*

2. The mongoose's *name* was Rikki-tikki-tavi.

2. *not a modifier*

1. Rikki-tikki was adopted by a *very* kind family. 1. M
2. The family fed him meat and bananas and *boiled* eggs. 2. M
3. *Like all mongooses,* Rikki-tikki was always curious. 3. M
4. While exploring the garden, he *heard* Darzee and his wife, the tailorbirds, crying in their nest. 4. Not M
5. One of their babies had fallen out *of the nest* and been eaten by a cobra. 5. M
6. Rikki-tikki had to protect his family and friends *against the snakes.* 6. M

MINI-LESSON Grammar *Continued on pp. 203–204*

What Is a Clause? Quickly review the following definitions:

- A **clause** is a group of words that contains a subject and a verb and that is used as a sentence or as part of a sentence.
- An **independent clause** expresses a complete thought and can stand alone as a sentence.
- A **subordinate clause** does not communicate a complete thought even though it has a subject and a verb; it cannot stand

7. Mongooses and snakes are *natural* enemies. **7.** M

8. Rikki-tikki overheard *two* cobras planning to kill the family. **8.** M

9. He attacked the first cobra *while it was waiting for the father to come into the room.* **9.** M

10. The second *cobra* dragged Rikki-tikki down a hole in the ground, but Rikki-tikki killed the snake and came out alive. **10.** Not M

Eight Troublesome Modifiers

Bad and *Badly*

Bad is an adjective. In most uses, *badly* is an adverb.

ADJECTIVE The dog was **bad.**

ADVERB The dog behaved **badly.**

Remember that a word that modifies the subject of a verb should be in adjective form.

NONSTANDARD The stew tasted badly.

STANDARD The stew tasted **bad.**

NOTE In informal situations, *bad* or *badly* is acceptable after *feel.*

INFORMAL He feels **badly** about the incident.

FORMAL He feels **bad** about the incident.

Good and *Well*

Good is an adjective. It should not be used to modify a verb.

NONSTANDARD He speaks Italian good.

STANDARD He speaks Italian **well.**

STANDARD His Italian sounds **good.** [*Good* is an adjective that modifies the noun *Italian.*]

Well may be used either as an adjective or as an adverb. As an adjective, *well* has two meanings: "in good health" and "satisfactory."

EXAMPLES John is **well.** [John is in good health.]

All is **well.** [All is satisfactory.]

As an adverb, *well* means "capably."

EXAMPLE They did **well** in the tryouts.

Eight Troublesome Modifiers

(pp. 203–204)

USAGE

DIFFERENTIATING INSTRUCTION

English-Language Learners

Romance Languages. Point out that the English *–ly* suffix is equivalent to the Spanish and Portuguese *–mente* suffix and the French *–ment.* All of these endings convert adjectives to adverbs.

Learners Having Difficulty

You may want to place students in pairs to create illustrations of adjectives and adverbs. Assign one student to illustrate the four troublesome adjectives and the other to illustrate the four troublesome adverbs. Then, have students label their illustrations with the appropriate word and part of speech. When they have finished, have them compare their drawings and discuss whether or not the same illustrations could be used for adjectives as for adverbs.

alone as a sentence.

- An **adjective clause** is a subordinate clause used to modify a noun or pronoun; it tells *what kind* or *which one* and starts with a relative pronoun like *who, whom, whose, which,* or *that* or occasionally the relative adverbs *where* or *when.*
- An **adverb clause** is a subordinate clause used to modify a verb, adjective, or adverb; it tells *why, where, when, how*

USAGE

DIRECT TEACHING

Modeling and Demonstration

Special Problems in Using Modifiers. Model how to use the modifiers *good* and *well* correctly by using the examples *The farmers had a good crop this year* and *The day started well.* First, ask what the modifier *good* describes in the first sentence. [*crop*] Then, ask what part of speech *crop* is. [*noun*] Point out that since *good* is an adjective, it is used to modify the noun. Next, ask what the modifier *well* describes in the second sentence. [*started*] Then, ask what part of speech *started* is. [*verb*] Point out that since *well* is an adverb, it is used to modify the verb. Adverbs also can be used to modify adjectives and other adverbs, but they cannot be used to modify nouns. Now, have a volunteer use other examples from this chapter to demonstrate how to identify the correct use of *good* and *well.*

Correcting Misconceptions

Linking Verbs. Students may have difficulty choosing correct modifiers because they often mistakenly believe that a modifier after a linking verb modifies that verb. Make sure that students understand that a linking verb is followed by an adjective rather than an adverb because the adjective modifies the subject of the verb, not the verb itself.

Slow and *Slowly*

Slow is used as both an adjective and an adverb.

EXAMPLES We took a **slow** drive through the countryside. [*Slow* is an adjective modifying the noun *drive.*]

Go **slow.** [*Slow* is an adverb modifying the verb *Go.*]

Slowly is an adverb. In most adverb uses, it is better to use *slowly* than to use *slow.*

EXAMPLES The train **slowly** came to a stop.

Drive **slowly** on slippery roads.

Real and *Really*

Real is an adjective meaning "actual" or "genuine." *Really* is an adverb meaning "actually" or "truly." Although *real* is commonly used as an adverb meaning "very" in everyday situations, avoid using it as an adverb in formal speaking and writing.

INFORMAL He batted real well in the game.

FORMAL He batted **really** well in the game.

HELP — A sentence in Exercise 2 may contain more than one error.

Exercise 2 Revising Sentences with Modifier Errors

Most of the following sentences contain at least one error in modifier usage. If a sentence contains an error, revise the sentence with the correct modifier. If a sentence is already correct, write *C.*

EXAMPLE 1. The ball was thrown so bad it went over the fence.

1. The ball was thrown so badly it went over the fence.

1. You have done very ~~good~~ today, Marcia. 1. well
2. The nurse shark was moving very ~~slow~~ over the seabed. 2. slowly
3. The fireworks exploded with a ~~real~~ loud bang. 3. really
4. The team did not play badly, but they lost anyway. 4. C
5. James thinks that Jakob Dylan is a ~~well~~ singer. 5. good
6. The box was not damaged too ~~bad~~ when it fell. 6. badly
7. The turtle is very ~~slowly~~ on land, but it is much faster underwater. 7. slow
8. Is that really Sammy Sosa's autograph? 8. C
9. Even if your day is going ~~bad~~, getting angry at me will not help. 9. badly
10. Slowly but surely, the fawn improved until it could run ~~real good~~. 10. really well

Grammar ***Continued from p. 203***

much, or *to what extent* and begins with a subordinating conjunction like *after, although, because, if, when,* and *where* (for more examples, see the **Common Subordinating Conjunctions** chart on p. 105).

For more information and examples, see p. 99.

Comparison of Modifiers

8d. Modifiers change form to show comparison.

There are three degrees of comparison: *positive, comparative,* and *superlative.*

Positive	Comparative	Superlative
young	younger	youngest
fearful	more fearful	most fearful
rapidly	more rapidly	most rapidly
good	better	best

Regular Comparison

(1) Most one-syllable modifiers form the comparative degree by adding *–er* and the superlative degree by adding *–est.*

Positive	Comparative	Superlative
large	larger	largest
deep	deeper	deepest

(2) Two-syllable modifiers may form the comparative degree by adding *–er* or by using *more.* They may form the superlative degree by adding *–est* or by using *most.*

Positive	Comparative	Superlative
wealthy	wealthier	wealthiest
lovely	lovelier	loveliest
rapid	more rapid	most rapid
softly	more softly	most softly
common	commoner *or* more common	commonest *or* most common

Reference Note

For guidelines on **how to spell comparative and superlative forms** correctly, see page 363.

STYLE TIP

Most two-syllable modifiers can form their comparative and superlative forms either way. If adding *–er* or *–est* makes a word sound awkward, use *more* or *most* instead.

AWKWARD frugaler
BETTER more frugal
AWKWARD rapidest
BETTER most rapid

Comparison of Modifiers

Rule 8d *(pp. 205–208)*

OBJECTIVES

- To form and write comparative and superlative forms of given words
- To use the correct comparative and superlative forms of words
- To proofread sentences for correct comparative and superlative forms of modifiers

USAGE

PRACTICE

Relating to Literature

The poem "The Girl Who Loved the Sky" by Anita Endrezze will give students extra practice with comparative and superlative forms. Go through the poem line by line, asking students to identify the modifiers and record the appropriate forms using a three-column organizer similar to the following one.

POSITIVE	COMPARATIVE	SUPERLATIVE
yellowed	more yellowed	most yellowed
big	bigger	biggest

RESOURCES

Comparison of Modifiers

Practice

- *Language & Sentence Skills Practice,* pp. 199–202

Differentiating Instruction

- *Developmental Language & Sentence Skills,* pp. 93–94

USAGE

Exercise 3 **Writing Comparative and Superlative Forms**

POSSIBLE ANSWERS

1. faster, fastest
2. sooner, soonest
3. happier, happiest
4. more careful, most careful
5. simpler, simplest
6. hazier, haziest
7. safer, safest
8. more wisely, most wisely
9. calmer, calmest
10. prettier, prettiest

RETEACHING

Comparative and Superlative Forms

Activity. To make students aware of the common use of comparative and superlative modifiers, involve them in a sports commentary. Provide or have students bring to class pictures of sports events such as swim team competitions, track meets, or basketball games. Have students work in pairs to prepare an oral presentation for the class; one student can hold up a picture while the other plays the role of a sports announcer, providing a commentary using comparative- and superlative-degree words to describe the sports event. Then, have partners reverse roles.

Exercise 3 **Writing Comparative and Superlative Forms**

Write the comparative and superlative forms of the following words.

EXAMPLE 1. bright
1. brighter, brightest

1. fast
2. soon
3. happy
4. careful
5. simple
6. hazy
7. safe
8. wisely
9. calm
10. pretty

(3) **Modifiers that have three or more syllables form the comparative degree by using *more* and the superlative degree by using *most.***

Positive	Comparative	Superlative
energetic	more energetic	most energetic
significantly	more significantly	most significantly

(4) **To show a decrease in the qualities they express, modifiers form the comparative degree by using *less* and the superlative degree by using *least.***

Positive	Comparative	Superlative
helpful	less helpful	least helpful
frequently	less frequently	least frequently

STYLE TIP

The word *little* also has regular comparative and superlative forms: *littler, littlest.* These forms are used to describe physical size (the **littlest** puppy). The forms *less* and *least* are used to describe an amount (**less** homework).

Irregular Comparison

The comparative and superlative degrees of some modifiers are irregular in form.

Positive	Comparative	Superlative
bad	worse	worst
good/well	better	best
many/much	more	most
far	further/farther	furthest/farthest
little	less	least

NOTE Do not add *–er / –est* or *more / most* to irregularly compared forms. For example, use *worse,* not *worser* or *more worse.*

CONTENT-AREA CONNECTIONS

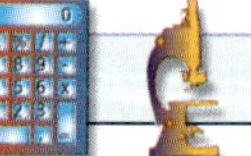

World Languages

Translations of Irregular Comparisons. Ask your students for equivalents in other languages of each of the words in the table under **Irregular Comparison.** Have students write responses on the chalkboard using the table as a guide; ask the students who offer the examples if the forms are regular or irregular.

Exercise 4 Using Comparative and Superlative Forms

In the blank in each of the following sentences, write the correct form of the modifier in italics.

EXAMPLE *little* 1. Both pairs of jeans are on sale, but I will buy the ____ expensive pair.

1. less

1. *well* I can skate ____ now than I could last year.
2. *many* She caught the ____ fish of anyone in our group that day.
3. *bad* That is the ____ movie I have ever seen.
4. *much* We have ____ homework today than we had all last week.
5. *good* Felicia has the ____ attendance record of anyone.
6. *many* Are there ____ plays than poems in your literature book?
7. *good* Tyrone is the ____ pitcher on our baseball team this year.
8. *much* Of the three groups of volunteers, our group cleaned up the ____ litter.
9. *bad* My notebook looks ____ than Joshua's.
10. *little* I have ____ time to finish than he does.

Oral Practice Identifying Comparative and Superlative Forms

Read the following modifiers aloud, and give the comparative and superlative forms of each. Do not include decreasing comparisons.

EXAMPLE 1. meaningful

1. more meaningful, most meaningful

1. bad	6. loose	11. far	16. much
2. good	7. well	12. special	17. unlikely
3. early	8. noisy	13. happily	18. elaborate
4. many	9. patiently	14. eager	19. quiet
5. fuzzy	10. graceful	15. sleepy	20. rich

HELP

A dictionary will tell you when a word forms its comparative or superlative form in some way other than by adding *–er* / *–est* or *more* / *most*. Look in a dictionary if you are not sure whether a word has irregular comparative or superlative forms or whether you need to change the spelling of a word before adding *–er* or *–est*.

Exercise 5 Proofreading Sentences for Correct Comparative and Superlative Forms

Identify the comparative and superlative modifiers in the following sentences. If the form of a modifier is incorrect or awkward, write the correct form. If the form is already correct, write *C*.

Exercise 4 Using Comparative and Superlative Forms

POSSIBLE ANSWERS

1. better
2. most
3. worst
4. more
5. best
6. more
7. best
8. most
9. worse
10. less

Oral Practice Writing Comparative and Superlative Forms

POSSIBLE ANSWERS

1. worse, worst
2. better, best
3. earlier, earliest
4. more, most
5. fuzzier, fuzziest
6. looser, loosest
7. better, best
8. noisier, noisiest
9. more patiently, most patiently
10. more graceful, most graceful
11. farther, farthest; further, furthest
12. more special, most special
13. more happily, most happily
14. more eager, most eager
15. sleepier, sleepiest
16. more, most
17. more unlikely, most unlikely
18. more elaborate, most elaborate
19. quieter, quietest
20. richer, richest

USAGE

PRACTICE

Guided and Independent

Exercise You may want to have students complete **Exercise 4** as independent practice after doing the **Oral Practice.** HOMEWORK

USAGE

Differentiating Instruction

English-Language Learners

Vietnamese. The comparative forms used in English—*more than* or adjective+*er than* and the form *(not) as . . . as*—are expressed differently in Vietnamese and must be learned and practiced.

The comparison in Vietnamese follows the pattern noun+adjective+*more than*+noun being compared, as in *Mr. Nguyen old more than Mr. Tran.* Students may use such constructions in English and may prefer the *more*+ adjective form to the adjective+*er* form. Students need to practice making comparisons in formal and informal class situations.

Julio is taller than Maria.

Which story was more exciting?

Use of Comparative and Superlative Forms

Rules 8e–h *(pp. 208–212)*

OBJECTIVES

- To identify and correct comparative and superlative forms of modifiers in sentences
- To revise faulty comparisons for logic and clarity
- To revise sentences to eliminate double comparisons
- To rewrite sentences to correct unclear comparisons

EXAMPLE 1. The Romany make up one of Europe's interestingest cultures.

1. interestingest—most interesting

1. The Romany, also known as Gypsies, are ~~commonlier~~ found in Eastern Europe than anywhere else in the world. 1. more commonly
2. Although most Romany live in Romania, Hungary, and other European countries, the culture of the Romany suggests that they migrated to Europe from other lands. 2. C
3. The ~~bestest~~ theory about the origin of the Romany is that they came from India. 3. best
4. As this photograph shows, the Romany wear some of their ~~colorfulest~~ traditional clothing for their celebrations. 4. most colorful
5. They also brighten their lives with the ~~most wild~~ violin music they can play. 5. wildest
6. On the move ~~frequentlier~~ than most other Europeans, they used to travel in brightly painted wagons. 6. more frequently
7. The Romany usually live in groups, with the largest groups consisting of several hundred families. 7. C
8. The ~~most high~~ law in Romany society is the *kris,* a system of rules based on the religious beliefs of the Romany. 8. highest
9. The Romany generally earn their living as migrant agricultural workers and, less frequently, as entertainers. 9. C
10. Although change has come ~~slowlier~~ to these wanderers than to most other ethnic groups in Europe, some Romany now are living in settled communities. 10. more slowly

STYLE TIP

In informal situations and in standard expressions, people sometimes use the superlative degree in comparing two things: *Put your best foot forward.* Generally, however, you should use the comparative degree in formal situations when you are comparing two things.

Use of Comparative and Superlative Forms

8e. **Use the comparative degree when comparing two things. Use the superlative degree when comparing more than two.**

COMPARATIVE Writing mysteries seems **more challenging** than writing nonfiction.

In my opinion, Dorothy L. Sayers is a **better** writer than Agatha Christie.

RESOURCES

Use of Comparative and Superlative Forms

Practice

- *Language & Sentence Skills Practice,* pp. 203–205

SUPERLATIVE Writing a mystery story is the **most challenging** assignment I've had so far.

This is the **best** Sherlock Holmes story that I have ever read.

Exercise 6 Identifying Correct Comparative and Superlative Forms

Identify the comparative and superlative modifiers in the following sentences. If the form of a modifier is incorrect, write the correct form. If the form is correct for the number of items compared, write *C*.

EXAMPLE **1.** Nina's report on American Indian star legends was the more interesting report in the class.

1. most interesting

1. Although Nina and I both researched our reports carefully, her report was the ~~most thorough~~ one of the two.
2. The American Indian stories about the stars and the sky are more diverse than the Norse myths, in my opinion.
3. Nina told several stories; I found the myth that she told about the cluster of stars known as the Pleiades to be the ~~more fascinating~~.
4. The ~~stranger~~ tale, which is from the Monache Indian people of central California, tells how a little girl and six women who wouldn't give up eating onions became the Pleiades.
5. The scariest of the tales is the Skidi Pawnee myth about six brothers and an adopted sister who fight the Rolling Skull.
6. That story was the ~~longer~~ legend that Nina told, and Frank said it was the ~~more interesting~~.
7. Of all the earthly creatures in the stories Nina told, Coyote is perhaps the ~~more important~~.
8. In fact, in some stories people often play a ~~least important~~ role than Coyote plays.
9. I told Nina that, compared with my report, hers was ~~the best~~.
10. She said that telling the stories was easier than finding them.

1. more thorough
2. C
3. most fascinating
4. strangest
5. C
6. longest most interesting
7. most important
8. less important
9. better
10. C

8f. Include the word *other* or *else* when comparing one member of a group with the rest of the group.

NONSTANDARD Juan is more considerate than any boy in his school. [Juan is a boy in his school, and he cannot be more considerate than himself. The word *other* should be added.]

STANDARD Juan is more considerate than any **other** boy in his school.

Reference Note

For a discussion of **standard and nonstandard English,** see page 223.

USAGE

Exercise 6

DISTRIBUTED REVIEW

Have students find the following items in sentences 1, 2, and 5 in **Exercise 6.**

1. an adverb clause [*Although Nina and I both researched our reports carefully*]

2. compound objects of a preposition [*stars, sky*]

5. a subordinate clause [*who fight the Rolling Skull*]

DIFFERENTIATING INSTRUCTION

English-Language Learners

General Strategies. Because many languages use only one form to show comparisons, you may need to explain to English-language learners that English may differ from their first languages by having a special form for comparing more than two items.

Learners Having Difficulty

So that students can understand the thought process involved in choosing between the comparative and superlative forms, discuss **Exercise 6** sentence by sentence, asking students to point out the number of people or things compared in each sentence. Remind students that the number of people or things being compared determines whether the comparative (two) or the superlative (more than two) form is used.

Differentiating Instruction

Learners Having Difficulty

Have students work in small groups to complete **Exercise 7** orally. Tell them to read each sentence aloud as it is written and then to read it again, making the necessary corrections.

NONSTANDARD Dana arrived earlier than anyone. [*Anyone* includes all people, and Dana is a person. Since she cannot arrive earlier than herself, *else* should be added.]

STANDARD Dana arrived earlier than anyone **else.**

Exercise 7 Correcting Faulty Comparisons

Correct each of the following sentences by adding either *other* or *else* to make the comparison logical and clear.

EXAMPLE 1. Rodney spells better than anyone in his class.

1. Rodney spells better than anyone else in his class.

1. Today has been colder than any day this year. — 1. other
2. Kumiko eats more slowly than anybody in this cafeteria. — 2. else
3. Flying is faster than any type of travel. — 3. other
4. My sunflowers grew taller than any flowers I planted this year. — 4. other
5. Luís enjoys swimming more than anyone in his family. — 5. else
6. Dad bought that sedan because it gets better mileage than any car. — 6. other
7. This hot-and-sour soup is spicier than any soup I've ever tasted. — 7. other
8. Does Renee study harder than anyone? — 8. else
9. Whales are bigger than any animals. — 9. other
10. In my opinion, cycling is more fun than any type of exercise. — 10. other

8g. Avoid using double comparisons.

A ***double comparison*** is incorrect because it contains both *–er* and *more* (*less*) or *–est* and *most* (*least*).

NONSTANDARD She is more funnier than he.

STANDARD She is **funnier** than he.

NONSTANDARD It was the least cloudiest night of the year.

STANDARD It was the **least cloudy** night of the year.

Exercise 8 Revising Modifiers to Correct Double Comparisons

Write each incorrect modifier in the following sentences. Then, correct the double comparison by crossing out the unnecessary part.

EXAMPLE 1. Today is more colder than yesterday.

1. ~~more~~ colder

1. That is the ~~most~~ softest sweater I have ever had.
2. You seem to be trying ~~more~~ harder in school this year.

MEETING THE CHALLENGE

A *haiku* is an unrhymed Japanese poem of three lines consisting of five syllables, seven syllables, and five syllables, respectively. Write a *haiku* in which each line contains the same modifier used in a different degree: positive, comparative, or superlative. You can include these degrees in any order to suit the meaning of your poem.

Answer

Haiku will vary but should have a modifier used in different degrees in each of the three lines.

Learning for Life

Continued on pp. 211–212

Personal Marketing. Tell students that one life skill they must learn is to market themselves. They will need to "sell" themselves to employers, organizations, and colleges.

Explain to students that during an application process they may be asked to answer questions in a way that they might consider to be bragging. Encourage them to see that those interviewing them are trying to get

3. Is she the least tired~~est~~ runner on the team?
4. Illustrations help make the explanations ~~more~~ clearer to the readers.
5. Georgia is ~~more~~ larger in area than any other state east of the Mississippi.
6. We had the ~~most~~ best basketball team in our division.
7. The first day of winter is the ~~most~~ shortest day of the year.
8. Parrots are ~~more~~ smarter than other birds.
9. Cynthia's room is much less clean~~er~~ than John's.
10. Did you know that Rome is one of the ~~most~~ oldest capitals in the world?

8h. Be sure your comparisons are clear.

UNCLEAR Weeds in the lawn are harder to get rid of than the garden. [This sentence incorrectly compares weeds to a garden.]

CLEAR Weeds in the lawn are harder to get rid of than **weeds in** the garden.

UNCLEAR Is the skin of the rhinoceros harder than the alligator?

CLEAR Is the skin of the rhinoceros harder than **the skin of** the alligator?

or

Is the skin of the rhinoceros harder than the **alligator's?**

Both parts of an incomplete comparison should be stated if there is any chance of misunderstanding.

UNCLEAR Theresa called Greg more than Maria.

CLEAR Theresa called Greg more than Maria **did.**

CLEAR Theresa called Greg more than **she called** Maria.

Exercise 9 Correcting Unclear Comparisons

Rewrite the following sentences to correct unclear comparisons.

EXAMPLE 1. The annual rainfall in Seattle is higher than London.

1. The annual rainfall in Seattle is higher than that in London.

1. A kangaroo's jump is higher than a rabbit.
2. The power of that truck's engine is greater than a sports car.
3. In those days, the Pottstown Panthers' winning streak was longer than the Lindale Lions.
4. Is a baboon's grip stronger than a human?

HELP — Although some sentences in Exercise 9 may be correctly revised in more than one way, you need to give only one revision for each sentence.

USAGE

EXTENSION

Critical Thinking

Challenge students to explain why the comparative degree is sometimes used instead of the superlative degree. For example, a realtor with a listing of hundreds of houses for sale may say "This is one of our better homes." After many years of leading a high school football team, a coach might say, "He was one of our better quarterbacks." [*Possible responses may include that the superlative degree has been overused and the comparative now sounds stronger or that the comparative suggests a modest reaction or uses the power of understatement.*]

Relating to Literature

If students' textbooks contain O. Henry's story "The Gift of the Magi," have students study the final paragraph and discuss the effect of O. Henry's repeated use of forms of the adjective *wise* as he comments on the "foolish" young people. [*O. Henry plays with words and uses comparison and repetition poetically in this paragraph.*]

Exercise 9 Correcting Unclear Comparisons

POSSIBLE ANSWERS

1. . . . than a rabbit's.
2. . . . than a sports car's.
3. . . . than that of the Lindale Lions.
4. . . . than a human's?

clear information to form an opinion about their abilities. Provide the following prompt. *What skills and accomplishments qualify you for this opening? Provide specific examples to support your position.*

Tell students to think of a job interview, college application, and so forth. Then, ask students to prepare an answer using specific adjectives and adverbs, particularly ones in the comparative and superlative

Exercise 9 **Correcting Unclear Comparisons**

POSSIBLE ANSWERS continued

5. . . . as Juan's.
6. . . . than those in Venice, California.
7. . . . than Houston's.
8. . . . than those in the Costellos' house.
9. . . . than those of the ibex.
10. . . . Jessica's.

Review A **Correcting Modifiers in a Paragraph**

POSSIBLE ANSWERS

1. . . . as one of their strongest symbols . . .
2. C
3. . . . some of the better-known countries . . .
4. . . . a better symbol . . .
5. . . . the more practical choice . . .
6. . . . the better choice of the two.
7. While eagles are not larger than all other . . . [*More effective* can also be *most effective*.]
8. . . . than the turkey's.
9. The eagle's wings are also stronger and very wide.
10. . . . the eagle is more beautiful, too.

USAGE

5. Tony's bike is as new and gleaming as Juan.
6. The canals in Venice, Italy, are wider than Venice, California.
7. Rome's climate is milder than Houston.
8. Our new windows are bigger than the Costellos' house.
9. The kudu's horns are longer than the ibex.
10. Pat's assignments are usually better written than Jessica.

Review A Correcting Modifiers in a Paragraph

Identify and correct the incorrect comparative and superlative forms in each sentence in the following paragraph. Some sentences contain more than one incorrect or unclear comparison. If a sentence is already correct, write *C*.

EXAMPLE **[1]** Eagles are widely regarded as more majestic than any bird in the world.

1. *Eagles are widely regarded as more majestic than any other bird in the world.*

[1] Many cultures have revered the eagle as one of their most strongest symbols of bravery and power. [2] In fact, the eagle seems to be the most popular bird used as a national symbol. [3] Mexico, Austria, and Egypt are some of the more best-known countries with eagles on their national flags. [4] In the United States, early colonial leaders thought that the bald eagle would be a more better symbol for their new country than the turkey. [5] Benjamin Franklin had argued that the turkey was the most practical choice of the two birds, but he was outvoted. [6] I think most people would agree that the eagle is the best choice of the two. [7] While eagles are not more larger than all birds, they are among the more effective hunters and fliers. [8] As you can see from these pictures, the eagle's sharp beak and long claws are more powerful than the turkey. [9] The eagle's wings are also more strong and very wide. [10] I think the eagle is beautifuller, too.

Learning for Life  ***Continued from p. 211***

degrees. A student might write, "My typing skills have improved greatly over the last year since I have spent more hours than ever using my computer, both to write better school compositions and to research material for personal and academic reasons."

Next, assign students to write answers and present them in a peer-editing session. Then they may type a formal copy or prepare an audiotape or videotape of their response.

Dangling Modifiers

8i. **Avoid using dangling modifiers.**

A modifying word, phrase, or clause that does not clearly and sensibly modify a word or a word group in a sentence is a ***dangling modifier.***

DANGLING Together, the litter along the highway was picked up, bagged, and hauled away. [Was the litter together?]

CORRECT Together, we picked up, bagged, and hauled away the litter along the highway.

DANGLING Time seemed to stand still, watching the sunset and listening to the cicadas. [Was time watching and listening?]

CORRECT Time seemed to stand still as we watched the sunset and listened to the cicadas.

When a modifying participial or infinitive phrase comes at the beginning of a sentence, the phrase is followed by a comma. Immediately after that comma should come the word or word group that the phrase modifies.

DANGLING Jogging in the park, a rabbit peered at me from the underbrush. [Was the rabbit jogging?]

CORRECT Jogging in the park, **I** saw a rabbit peering at me from the underbrush.

DANGLING Listening closely, distant thunder could be detected. [Was the thunder listening?]

CORRECT Listening closely, **she** could detect distant thunder.

DANGLING To master a musical instrument, practice or natural talent is usually needed. [Is practice or talent mastering an instrument?]

CORRECT To master a musical instrument, **a musician** usually needs practice or natural talent.

DANGLING Even when equipped with the best gear, the rock cliff was difficult to climb. [Was the rock cliff equipped?]

CORRECT Even when equipped with the best gear, **the mountaineers** had difficulty climbing the rock cliff.

A sentence may appear to have a dangling modifier when *you* is the understood subject. In such cases, the modifier is not dangling; instead, it is modifying the understood subject.

EXAMPLE To find the correct spelling, (you) look up the word.

Reference Note

For more information on **participial phrases,** see page 79. For more information on **infinitive phrases,** see page 86.

Reference Note

For more about the **understood subject,** see page 51.

Dangling Modifiers

Rule 8i *(pp. 213–215)*

OBJECTIVES

- To write sentences with introductory modifiers
- To revise sentences by correcting dangling modifiers

DIRECT TEACHING

Modeling and Demonstration

Placement of Modifiers. Model how the placement of a modifier can change the meaning of a sentence by using the example *The diplomat from Australia gave a speech for the visitors.* First, ask what the prepositional phrase *from Australia* modifies. [*diplomat*] Point out that *from Australia* immediately follows the noun it describes. Move the phrase to the beginning of the sentence and ask what word it modifies. [*gave*] Point out that moving the phrase changes the meaning of the sentence. Then, move the phrase to the end of the sentence and ask what word it modifies. [*visitors*] The phrase immediately follows the noun it modifies. Now, have a volunteer use another example from this chapter to demonstrate how the placement of a modifier can change the meaning of a sentence.

USAGE

RESOURCES

Dangling Modifiers

Practice

- *Language & Sentence Skills Practice,* p. 206

Differentiating Instruction

- *Developmental Language & Sentence Skills,* pp. 95–96

Exercise 10 Writing Sentences with Introductory Modifiers

POSSIBLE ANSWERS

1. Leaping from branch to branch, the squirrel entertained us.
2. Yawning, JoAnn stretched.
3. While eating our lunch, we watched a fashion show.
4. Surrounded by the cheering crowd, the athlete waved.
5. To make sure he wouldn't be late, Lance set three alarms.
6. Alone, Melanie walked through the storm.
7. Following Leila's example, Jason searched the Internet for information.
8. Not wanting to wake them up, Jon tiptoed past the kittens.
9. Having filled out the forms, Mother mailed the family's tax return.
10. To solve this riddle, the children thought and thought.

USAGE

Exercise 10 Writing Sentences with Introductory Modifiers

Write complete sentences that begin with the following introductory modifiers.

EXAMPLE 1. Having solved one problem,

1. *Having solved one problem, Joe Harris found that another awaited him.*

1. Leaping from branch to branch,
2. Yawning,
3. While eating our lunch,
4. Surrounded by the cheering crowd,
5. To make sure he wouldn't be late,
6. Alone,
7. Following Leila's example,
8. Not wanting to wake them up,
9. Having filled out the forms,
10. To solve this riddle,

Correcting Dangling Modifiers

To correct a dangling modifier, rearrange the words in the sentence and add or change words to make the meaning logical and clear.

DANGLING While lighting the birthday candles, the cake started to crumble.

CORRECT While **I was** lighting the birthday candles, the cake started to crumble.

or

While lighting the birthday candles, **I noticed** the cake **starting** to crumble.

DANGLING To become a physicist, years of study and research are required.

CORRECT To become a physicist, **you** must spend years studying and doing research.

or

If you want to become a physicist, **you** must spend years studying and doing research.

or

If a person wants to become a physicist, **he or she** must spend years studying and doing research.

Exercise 11 Correcting Dangling Modifiers

Most of the following sentences contain dangling modifiers. If a sentence has a dangling modifier, revise the sentence to correct it. If a sentence is already correct, write *C*. Answers may vary.

EXAMPLE 1. While mopping the kitchen, my baby brother woke up from his nap.

1. *While I was mopping the kitchen, my baby brother woke up from his nap.*

1. Walking through the gate, the swimming pool is on the right.
2. Lost, the small village was a welcome sight.
3. To earn money, Mom suggested shoveling snow for our neighbors.
4. After studying hard, a long walk can be refreshing.
5. Walking in the woods, listening to the singing birds is enjoyable.
6. To understand a sentence, even little words can be important.
7. To become a great athlete, you need dedication and self-discipline.
8. Standing on the beach, a school of dolphins suddenly appeared.
9. After winning the last game of the season, the celebration lasted nearly all night.
10. Tired and sore, the job was finally finished.

1. As you walk
2. I welcomed the sight of
3. that I earn money by
4. he finds that
5. I enjoy
6. remember that
7. C
8. As we were
9. players celebrated
10. we finally finished

Misplaced Modifiers

8j. Avoid using misplaced modifiers.

A word, phrase, or clause that seems to modify the wrong word or word group in a sentence is a ***misplaced modifier.*** Place modifying words, phrases, and clauses as near as possible to the words they modify.

MISPLACED My cousin's dog was chasing the geese, yapping and barking.
CORRECT **Yapping and barking,** my cousin's dog was chasing the geese.

MISPLACED I read about the bank robbers who were captured in this morning's paper.
CORRECT I read **in this morning's paper** about the bank robbers who were captured.

MISPLACED Blackened beyond recognition, even the birds refused to eat the toast.
CORRECT Even the birds refused to eat the toast **blackened beyond recognition.**

STYLE TIP

Be sure to place modifiers correctly to show clearly the meaning you intend.

EXAMPLES
Only Uncle Jim sells bikes. [Uncle Jim, not anybody else, sells bikes.]

Uncle Jim **only** sells bikes. [Uncle Jim sells bikes; he does not repair them.]

Uncle Jim sells **only** bikes. [Uncle Jim does not sell cars or motorcycles.]

RETEACHING

Dangling Modifiers

If students have difficulty visualizing the errors in **Exercise 11,** try another approach. Have students in small groups create graphic aids that help the class visualize the errors in **Exercise 11.** Assign each group a sentence. Have students brainstorm what to include in their illustration and how to produce it. [*Students might use computer graphics, create cartoons, make collages, draw or paint, or pantomime or act out the sentence with props.*] Students may divide tasks so that one person gives directions, another gathers necessary materials, and a third creates the actual illustration.

USAGE

Misplaced Modifiers

Rule 8j *(pp. 215–218)*

OBJECTIVES

- To revise sentences by correcting misplaced modifiers
- To revise sentences by correcting misplaced clauses

RESOURCES

Misplaced Modifiers

Practice

- *Language & Sentence Skills Practice,* pp. 207–209

Differentiating Instruction

- *Developmental Language & Sentence Skills,* pp. 97–98

DIFFERENTIATING INSTRUCTION

Learners Having Difficulty

Before students begin **Exercise 12,** remind them that unlike dangling modifiers, misplaced modifiers do modify a word in the sentence. It might be helpful for students to ask themselves what the phrase or clause modifies or to sketch the image created by both the properly placed and the misplaced modifiers.

USAGE

Review B Correcting Dangling and Misplaced Modifiers

POSSIBLE ANSWERS

1. Seeing the tremendous force of Niagara Falls was awe inspiring.
2. When reading about the falls, I was impressed by many facts.
3. We discovered that Goat Island separates the two principal parts of the falls.
4. Most visitors admire both sets of falls, the Horseshoe Falls and the American Falls, which form the border between Canada and the United States.
5. While we were climbing the tower, Niagara Falls, shown on the next page, looked magnificent.
6. Because we were trying to see and do everything around Niagara Falls, the days passed quickly.

Answers may vary.

1. with Uncle Saburo
2. With my binoculars
3. When I was
4. roses
5. From my sister,
6. in the attic
7. patiently
8. in a tank at the aquarium
9. Watching TV,
10. children

Exercise 12 Correcting Misplaced Modifiers

Revise the following sentences to correct misplaced modifiers. In revising a sentence, be sure not to misplace another modifier.

EXAMPLE 1. The security guard was watching for the arrival of the armored car through the window.

1. *The security guard was watching through the window for the arrival of the armored car.*

1. Michiko went outside to trim the bonsai trees ~~with Uncle Saburo.~~
2. I could see the scouts marching over the hill ~~with my binoculars.~~
3. As a child, my grandfather taught me how to make tortillas.
4. One advertiser handed ~~out roses to~~ customers with dollar bills pinned to them.
5. I borrowed a radio ~~from my sister~~ with a weather band.
6. Did you find any of the hats your mother used to wear ~~in the attic?~~
7. Our cat waited on the porch for us to come home ~~patiently.~~
8. ~~In a tank at the aquarium,~~ we watched the seals play.
9. She ate two peaches and a plate of strawberries ~~watching TV.~~
10. We gave the boxes of cereal ~~to the children~~ with prizes inside.

Review B Correcting Dangling and Misplaced Modifiers

Most of the following sentences contain dangling or misplaced modifiers. If a sentence is incorrect, revise it. If a sentence is already correct, write *C.*

EXAMPLE 1. Only the American Falls are slightly higher than the Horseshoe Falls.

1. *The American Falls are only slightly higher than the Horseshoe Falls.*

1. Arriving at Niagara Falls, the sight of nature's tremendous force was awe inspiring.
2. When reading about the falls, many facts impressed me.
3. Separated by Goat Island, we discovered that the falls are in two principal parts.
4. Forming the border between Canada and the United States, most visitors admire both the Horseshoe Falls and the American Falls.
5. While climbing the tower, Niagara Falls, shown on the next page, looked magnificent to us.
6. Trying to see and do everything around Niagara Falls, the days passed quickly.

7. While riding in a tour boat called the *Maid of the Mist,* the spray from the base of the falls drenched us.
8. Roaring constantly, an awesome amount of power is generated.
9. After walking through Queen Victoria Park, a hearty lunch at the restaurant was refreshing.
10. To see the waterfalls at their most beautiful, a visit at night—when they are illuminated—was recommended by the tour guide.

Misplaced Clause Modifiers

Adjective clauses should be placed near the words they modify.

MISPLACED There is a car in the garage that has no windshield.
CORRECT In the garage, there is a car **that has no windshield.**

MISPLACED The money and tickets are still in my wallet that I meant to return to you.
CORRECT The money and tickets **that I meant to return to you** are still in my wallet.

Reference Note

For more information on **adjective clauses,** see page 101.

Exercise 13 Correcting Misplaced Clauses

Revise each of the following sentences by placing the misplaced clause near the word it modifies.

EXAMPLE 1. Alejandro searched the sand dunes for shells, which were deserted.
1. Alejandro searched the sand dunes, which were deserted, for shells.

1. Birds are kept away by scarecrows, many of which eat seeds.
2. The disabled truck is now blocking the overpass that suddenly went out of control.
3. There was a bird in the tree that had a strange-looking beak.
4. A huge dog chased me as I rode my bicycle that was growling and barking loudly.
5. An old log sat in the fireplace that was covered with moss.

1. , many of which eat seeds,
2. that suddenly went out of control
3. In the tree
4. chased me as I rode my bicycle
5. sat in the fireplace

Review B Correcting Dangling and Misplaced Modifiers

POSSIBLE ANSWERS continued

7. While riding in a tour boat called the *Maid of the Mist,* we were drenched by the spray from the base of the falls.
8. Roaring constantly, the falls generate an awesome amount of power.
9. After walking through Queen Victoria Park, we enjoyed a hearty lunch at the restaurant.
10. A guide recommended that we visit the waterfalls at night to see them when they are illuminated and at their most beautiful.

USAGE

RETEACHING

Misplaced and Dangling Modifiers

To offer an alternative to using logical thought processes and memorization, you might suggest that students use their imaginations. For each sentence in **Exercise 13** and **Review C,** ask students what images are evoked by the mistakes in modification. [*For example, Exercise 13, sentence 1, might inspire the image of scarecrows eating seeds; sentence 2 might suggest thoughts of overpasses out of control.*]

PRACTICE

Guided and Independent

Exercise You may wish to use **Exercise 13** as guided practice. Then, have students complete **Review C** as independent practice.

HOMEWORK

USAGE

Review C **Correcting Dangling and Misplaced Modifiers**

POSSIBLE ANSWERS

1. Awakening from a nap, I saw the island of Puerto Rico through my airplane window.
2. Our guide was waiting inside the baggage-claim area to take us to our hotel.
3. To understand the guide's presentation, we found some knowledge of both Spanish and English helpful.
4. Driving along the Panoramic Route, we saw breathtaking scenery!
5. We stopped for lunch at a roadside stall made from palm branches.
6. To hungry people, the spicy rice and beans was delicious.
7. From a young boy, we bought a souvenir rock decorated with island scenes.
8. Look at that strange fish that is puffing up in the water!
9. Anxious to shower and unpack, we stopped next at our hotel room.
10. To fully appreciate all the island had to offer, we needed more time.

6. At the post office
7. On our shelves
8. was standing at the bus stop
9. , on a ferry
10. Behind the shed

6. We thanked the clerk ~~at the post office~~ that had helped us with our overseas packages.
7. There are several books ~~on our shelves~~ that were written by Rolando Hinojosa-Smith.
8. A boy ~~was standing at the bus stop~~ that looked remarkably like my cousin.
9. She crossed the river ~~on a ferry~~, which was more than a mile wide.
10. There is a flower garden ~~behind the shed~~ that is planted with prize-winning dahlias.

Review C Correcting Dangling and Misplaced Modifiers

Revise each of the following sentences by correcting the placement of a modifier or by rephrasing the sentence.

EXAMPLE 1. Feeling nervous about flying, the twin-engine plane looked small but dependable.

1. *Feeling nervous about flying, we thought the twin-engine plane looked small but dependable.*

1. Awakening from a nap, the island of Puerto Rico came into view through my airplane window.
2. Our guide was waiting to take us to our hotel inside the baggage-claim area.
3. To understand the guide's presentation, some knowledge of both Spanish and English proved to be helpful.
4. Driving along the Panoramic Route, the scenery was breathtaking!
5. We stopped for lunch at a stall along the road that was made from palm branches.
6. Hungry, the spicy rice and beans was delicious.
7. We bought a souvenir rock from a young boy that was decorated with island scenes.
8. Look at that strange fish in the water that is puffing up!
9. Anxious to shower and unpack, our hotel room was the next stop.
10. To fully appreciate all the island had to offer, more time was needed.

Numerals and terms in brackets refer to rules and concepts tested by the items in the Chapter Review.

1. M [Modifier]
2. M [Modifier]
3. Not M [Modifier]
4. M [Modifier]
5. Not M [Modifier]
6. M [Modifier]
7. M [Modifier]
8. M [Modifier]
9. Not M [Modifier]
10. M [Modifier]

Chapter Review

A. Identifying Modifiers

Identify the italicized word or word group in each of the following sentences as a *modifier* or *not a modifier.* M *or* Not M

1. Sammy Sosa is a *natural* baseball talent.
2. The elephant ambled *out of the trees* into the clearing.
3. Two well-known Mexican *authors* are Carlos Fuentes and Octavio Paz.
4. Austin, Texas, is a *pleasant* place to live.
5. As Stan *entered* the house, the cat dashed under the bed.
6. Amrit the waiter is a *very* helpful person, don't you think?
7. Jean-Marc joined the resistance to fight *against the enemy.*
8. The group Los Lobos is *well established* as a major force in the Latino music world.
9. Chi *fed* the three horses in the stables.
10. Gustav Mahler was a *gifted* Austrian composer and conductor.

11. [8i]
12. [8i]
13. [8j]
14. [8j]
15. [8j]
16. [8i]
17. [8j]
18. [8i]
19. [8i]
20. [8j]

B. Correcting Dangling and Misplaced Modifiers

For each of the following sentences, identify the dangling or misplaced modifier and revise the sentence to correct the error.

11. Growing up in a big family, that family movie rings true to me.
12. To paint landscapes, patience and a steady hand are helpful.
13. Almost hidden under the pile of old books, Janelle saw the letter.
14. In different parts of the world I read about unusual customs.
15. A tree was almost destroyed by a bulldozer that was two hundred years old.
16. Jogging in the park, it was a sunny day.
17. The convicts were caught by the police trying to escape from jail.
18. Rushing out the door, Ben's homework was left on the table.
19. When told of the potential threat, nothing was done.
20. The mayor pledged she would build more roads at the political rally.

ASSESSING

Monitoring Progress

Chapter Review. To assess student progress, you may want to compare the types of items missed on the **Diagnostic Preview** to those missed on the **Chapter Review.** If students have not made significant progress, you may want to refer them to **Chapter 17: Correcting Common Errors, Exercises 17–19** and **21–23** for additional practice.

USAGE

Chapter Review

B. Correcting Dangling and Misplaced Modifiers

POSSIBLE ANSWERS

11. Because I grew up in a big family, I find that family movie rings true.
12. To paint landscapes, one needs patience and a steady hand.
13. Janelle saw the letter that was almost hidden under the pile of old books.
14. I read about unusual customs from different parts of the world.
15. A two-hundred-year-old tree was almost destroyed by a bulldozer.
16. The team jogged in the park on a sunny day.
17. The police caught the convicts trying to escape from jail.
18. Rushing out the door, Ben left his homework on the table.
19. Although the potential threat was reported, nothing was done.
20. At the political rally, the mayor pledged she would build more roads.

RESOURCES

Using Modifiers Correctly

Review

- *Language & Sentence Skills Practice,* pp. 210–213

Assessment

- *Holt Handbook Chapter Tests with Answer Key,* pp. 15–16, 52

USAGE

C. Identifying Correct Comparative and Superlative Forms and Revising Faulty Comparisons

Identify the comparative and superlative modifiers in the following sentences. If the form of the modifier is incorrect, write the correct form. If the form is already correct, write *C*. Add words to sentences in which a faulty or unclear comparison is made.

21. easier [8g]
22. C [8d, e]
23. other [8f]
24. worse [8g]
25. more [8e]
26. most [8d]
27. C [8d, e, h]
28. C [8d, e]
29. best [8e]
30. else [8f]
31. deeper [8d]
32. less [8e]
33. better [8g]
34. longer [8g]
35. more [8d]
36. C [8d, e, h]
37. else [8f]
38. C [8d, e]
39. worse [*bad, badly;* 8d]
40. the tree in / yard [8h]

21. Which plan is ~~more easier~~ to follow, his or hers?

22. My bowling was worse than usual last night.

23. This paella is more delicious than any dish I've ever eaten.

24. His problem is ~~more worse~~ than yours.

25. I like both shirts, but I think I like this one ~~the most~~.

26. That was one of the interesting~~est~~ movies he's seen.

27. The tomatoes from our garden taste sweeter than those from the store.

28. This is the nicest surprise I've ever had!

29. Which route is ~~better~~—upstream, downstream, or overland?

30. The sun is brighter than anything in our solar system.

31. The water in the pond was ~~more deep~~ than Nicky expected.

32. Arnie is the ~~least~~ helpful of the two brothers.

33. Doesn't Granddad feel ~~more better~~ now that he's rested?

34. Did you know that the Nile is ~~more longer~~ than any other river in the world?

35. When Marcos was five, he was careful~~ler~~ than he is now.

36. Which do you like better—Theseus Flatow's older or more recent music?

37. Ken completed the exercise faster than anyone.

38. The last problem is the most complicated one in the entire exercise.

39. Jesse is feeling ~~more badly~~ about the accident today than he did yesterday.

40. The tree in our yard is bigger than our neighbors.

D. Correcting Misplaced Clause Modifiers

Revise each of the following sentences by placing the misplaced clause near the word it modifies.

41. [8j]

41. There is a magazine on the table that has no cover.

Chapter Review

D. Correcting Misplaced Clause Modifiers

POSSIBLE ANSWERS

41. On the table is a magazine that has no cover.
42. The test papers that I want to hand in to Mr. Saenz are still in my locker.
43. In that display case is a vase that was made during the Ming dynasty.
44. In the street was a Dalmatian that had a silver collar.
45. The young chestnut mare that just won the steeplechase is drinking water.
46. We called the helpful lady at the nursing home.
47. Tom looked for dents on the cars on the dealer's lot.
48. A trailer covered with rust sat in the empty field.
49. There is a five-thousand-year-old mummy in the museum.
50. A woman that I thought was my friend Fran was running along the lake.

42. The test papers are still in my locker that I want to hand in to Mr. Saenz.
43. There is a vase in that display case that was made during the Ming dynasty.
44. There was a Dalmatian in the street that had a silver collar.
45. The young chestnut mare is drinking water that just won the steeplechase.
46. We called the lady at the nursing home that had been so helpful.
47. Tom inspected the cars for dents, which were on the dealer's lot.
48. A trailer sat in the empty field that was covered with rust.
49. There is a mummy in the museum that is five thousand years old.
50. A woman was running along the lake that I thought was my friend Fran.

42.–50. [8j]

Writing Application

Using Modifiers in a Restaurant Review

Comparative and Superlative Forms As the restaurant critic for *Good Food* magazine, you always give a year-end summary of the best restaurants and their foods. Discuss your choices in a paragraph in which you use five comparative and five superlative forms of both adjectives and adverbs.

Prewriting Using either real or imaginary restaurants, make a list of several places and their best dishes. Think of some ways to compare the restaurants (food, atmosphere, service, price).

Writing As you write your first draft, use your list to help you make accurate comparisons.

Revising Read your paragraph to a classmate to see if your comparisons are clearly stated. Revise any comparisons that are confusing.

Publishing As you correct any mistakes in spelling, grammar, and punctuation, pay special attention to the spelling of comparative and superlative forms made by adding *–er* and *–est.* You and your classmates could prepare a *Good Food* newcomer's guide to local restaurants. Decide how you want the guide to look. Then, type the guide and make photocopies or input the guide on a computer and print it out.

Reference Note

For information about **spelling words with suffixes,** see page 363.

USAGE

APPLICATION

Writing Application

Prewriting Tip. You may wish to bring in newspaper and magazine reviews of local restaurants for students to study and use as resources.

Scoring Rubric. While you will want to pay particular attention to students' use of comparative and superlative modifiers, you will also want to evaluate students' overall writing performance. You may want to give a split score to indicate development and clarity of the composition as well as usage skills.

CHAPTER

9

INTRODUCING THE CHAPTER

- This chapter addresses common usage problems in students' speech and writing.
- The chapter closes with a **Chapter Review** including a **Writing Application** feature that asks students to write a letter to the school board telling why students should or should not be required to wear uniforms.
- For help in integrating this chapter with writing assignments, use the **Teaching Strands** chart on pp. T24–T25.

CHAPTER

A Glossary of Usage

Common Usage Problems

Terms in brackets refer to concepts tested by the items in the Diagnostic Preview.

1. teaches [*learn, teach*]
2. have [*could of*]
3. anywhere [*anyways*]
4. take [*bring, take*]
5. fewer [*fewer, less*]
6. Besides [*beside, besides*]
7. who [*which, that, who; could of*]
8. affects/than [*affect, effect; than, then*]
9. [*he, she, they; at*]
10. anything/unless [double negative; *without, unless*]
11. can [double negative]
12. these [*kind, sort, type*]
13. burst [*bust, busted*]

Diagnostic Preview

Correcting Errors in Standard Usage

Each of the sentences in the following passage contains at least one error in formal, standard usage. Revise the passage, correcting all such errors.

EXAMPLE **[1]** Everyone accept him joined this here club.

1. *Everyone except him joined this club.*

Some answers may vary.

[1] Our school has a hiking club that ~~learns~~ us how to appreciate nature. [2] Our club usually goes to parks that we might not ~~of~~ discovered by ourselves. [3] We go hiking ~~anywheres~~ that can be reached by bus in a few hours. [4] Before we go, we decide what to ~~bring~~ with us. [5] The ~~less~~ things that we have to carry, the better off we are. [6] ~~Beside~~ water, a hat, and a jacket, little else is needed. [7] Those ~~which~~ pack too much soon wish they hadn't ~~of~~. [8] After all, a ten-mile hike ~~effects~~ you differently when you are weighted down ~~then~~ when you are not.

[9] Our adviser, Mr. Graham, ~~he~~ knows where all the best hiking areas are ~~at~~. [10] He always tells us that we won't see ~~nothing~~ interesting ~~without~~ we're willing to exert ourselves. [11] We ~~can't~~ hardly keep up with him once he starts walking.

[12] We go on ~~this~~ sorts of walks because we enjoy them. [13] Although we sometimes think our lungs will ~~bust~~, everyone wants

CHAPTER RESOURCES

Internet

- Web resources: go.hrw.com

Practice & Review

- *Language & Sentence Skills Practice*, pp. 219–228
- *Language & Sentence Skills Practice Answer Key*, pp. 89–93

Application & Enrichment

- *Language & Sentence Skills Practice*, pp. 218, 229, 230–231, 232
- *Language & Sentence Skills Practice Answer Key*, pp. 89, 94

to keep up with the others. [14] The real reward is when we see an unusual sight, like a fawn, a family of otters, a panoramic view, and etc. [15] Than we're sure that all of our time spent outdoors ain't been wasted. [16] We also except nature like it is and do not try to change it none. [17] When we find bottles or cans in the woods, we get upset with people who can't seem to go anywheres without leaving some mark.

[18] Everyone in the club feels the same way, so we're going to start an cleanup campaign. [19] People ought to enjoy being inside of a park without busting or changing anything there. [20] We'd rather have more hikers enjoying the wilderness and less people destroying nature.

14. seeing [*when, where; and etc.*]
15. Then/hasn't [*than, then; ain't*]
16. accept/as/any [*accept, except; like, as;* double negative]
17. anywhere [*anyways*]
18. a [*a, an*]
19. breaking [*of; bust, busted*]
20. fewer [*fewer, less*]

About the Glossary

This chapter provides a compact glossary of common problems in English usage. A ***glossary*** is an alphabetical list of special terms or expressions with definitions, explanations, and examples. You will notice that some examples in this glossary are labeled *nonstandard, standard, formal,* or *informal.*

The label ***nonstandard*** identifies usage that is suitable only in the most casual speaking situations and in writing that attempts to re-create casual speech. ***Standard*** English is language that is grammatically correct and appropriate in formal and informal situations. ***Formal*** identifies usage that is appropriate in serious speaking and writing situations (such as in speeches and in compositions for school). The label ***informal*** indicates standard usage common in conversation and in everyday writing such as personal letters. In doing the exercises in this chapter, be sure to use only standard English.

The following are examples of formal and informal English.

Formal	Informal
angry	steamed
unpleasant	yucky
agreeable	cool
very impressive	totally awesome
accelerate	step on it

HELP

The word *diction* is often used to refer to word choice. Your choice of words affects the tone and clarity of what you say and write. When you know which usages are formal, informal, standard, and nonstandard, you can choose diction that is appropriate to any audience.

Reference Note

For a list of **words often confused,** see page 374. Use the **index** at the back of the book to find discussions of other usage problems.

Differentiating Instruction

- *Developmental Language & Sentence Skills,* pp. 99–104
- *Developmental Language & Sentence Skills Guided Practice Teacher's Notes and Answer Key,* p. 22

Assessment

- *Holt Handbook Chapter Tests with Answer Key,* pp. 17–18, 52

USAGE

ASSESSING

Entry-Level Assessment

Diagnostic Preview. Many of the errors covered here are problems commonly addressed in the revision and proofreading stages of the writing process. For this reason, you may want to administer the preview before students proofread the final drafts of their first compositions and base your instructional strategies on the preview results.

You may want to administer this diagnostic tool every few months, using the results as a guide to student progress and as an aid to setting proofreading and editing goals.

PRETEACHING

Lesson Starter

Motivating. Start the chapter by having each student complete the sentence "The usage mistake I make the most is . . ." Refer students who need ideas to the glossary entries in boldface type.

Have students work in small groups, creating mnemonics to help eliminate their errors. [*Example: I can* accept *help with anything* except *prepositions.*] Finally, have each person write his or her most common mistake and mnemonic on a classroom chart.

As an alternative motivator, you may want to have students draw and compile cartoons of the most common mistakes and create a scrapbook or a Web site.

Usage: *A, An—Good, Well*

(pp. 224–230)

OBJECTIVES

- To choose the correct word from given pairs in sentences
- To proofread sentences to correct common usage problems

USAGE

DIRECT TEACHING

Modeling and Demonstration

Bring, Take. Model how to identify and correct errors by using the model *After you take the car to the service station, please bring home a newspaper.* First, ask whether the person taking the car to the service station is going away or coming back. [*going away*] Point out that *take* means to "go away, carrying something." Next, ask whether the person bringing a newspaper home is going away or coming back. [*coming back*] Note that *bring* means to "come back, carrying something." Suggest that students might choose the correct word by remembering that *bring* begins with a *b* for "back," and *take* begins with a *t* for "to." Finally, have a volunteer use another example from this chapter to demonstrate how to identify correct usage.

Reference Note

For more about **articles**, see page 12.

a, an These ***indefinite articles*** refer to one of a general group. Use *a* before words beginning with a consonant sound; use *an* before words beginning with a vowel sound.

EXAMPLES We saw **a** blue jay and **an** owl.

A hawk flew over us **an** hour ago. [*An* is used before *hour* because *hour* begins with a vowel sound.]

This is **a** one-way street. [*A* is used before *one-way* because *one-way* begins with a consonant sound.]

accept, except *Accept* is a verb that means "to receive." *Except* may be either a verb or a preposition. As a verb, *except* means "to leave out" or "to omit." As a preposition, it means "excluding."

EXAMPLES I couldn't **accept** such a valuable gift!

Why should they be **excepted** from the test?

No one in my class **except** me has been to Moscow.

affect, effect *Affect* is a verb meaning "to influence." *Effect* used as a verb means "to bring about" or "to accomplish." Used as a noun, *effect* means "the result of some action."

EXAMPLES The bright colors **affect** how the patients feel.

The treatment will **effect** a cure for the disease.

The bright colors have a beneficial **effect** on the patients.

ain't Avoid using this word in speaking or in writing; it is nonstandard English.

all the farther, all the faster This expression is used in some parts of the country to mean "as far as" or "as fast as."

NONSTANDARD This is all the faster I can go.

STANDARD This is **as fast as** I can go.

all right See page 375.

a lot Do not write the expression *a lot* as one word. It should be written as two words.

EXAMPLE I have **a lot** of homework tonight.

among See **between, among.**

STYLE TIP

The expression *a lot* is overused. Try replacing *a lot* with a more descriptive, specific word or phrase.

EXAMPLES

mountains of homework

four subjects' worth of homework

RESOURCES

Usage: *A, An—Good, Well*

Practice

- *Language & Sentence Skills Practice,* pp. 219–220

Differentiating Instruction

- *Developmental Language & Sentence Skills,* pp. 99–102

and etc. *Etc.* is an abbreviation of the Latin phrase *et cetera,* meaning "and other things." Thus, *and etc.* means "and and other things." Do not use *and* with *etc.*

EXAMPLE We'll need paint, brushes, thinner, some rags, **etc.** [not *and etc.*]

anyways, anywheres, everywheres, nowheres, somewheres Use these words without a final *s.*

EXAMPLE That bird is described **somewhere** [not *somewheres*] in this book.

as See **like, as.**

as if See **like, as if, as though.**

at Do not use *at* after *where.*

NONSTANDARD This is where I live at.
STANDARD This is **where** I live.

bad, badly See page 203.

because See **reason . . . because.**

beside, besides *Beside* is a preposition that means "by the side of" someone or something. *Besides* as a preposition means "in addition to." As an adverb, *besides* means "moreover."

EXAMPLES Sit **beside** me on the couch.

Besides songs and dances, the show featured several comedy sketches.

It's too late to rent a movie. **Besides,** I'm sleepy.

between, among Use *between* when you are referring to two things at a time, even if they are part of a group consisting of more than two. Use *among* when you are thinking of a group rather than of separate individuals.

EXAMPLES Take the seat **between** Alicia and Noreen in the third row.

On the map, the boundaries **between** all seven counties are drawn in red. [Although there are more than two counties, each boundary lies between only two.]

Among our graduates are several prominent authors.

There was some confusion **among** the jurors about the defendant's testimony. [The jurors are thought of as a group.]

COMPUTER TIP

The spellchecker on a computer will usually catch misspelled words such as *anywheres* and *nowheres.* The grammar checker may catch errors such as double negatives. However, in the case of words often confused, such as *than* and *then* and *between* and *among,* a computer program may not be able to help. You will have to check your work yourself for correct usage.

DIFFERENTIATING INSTRUCTION

Special Education Students

Students may benefit from visualizing the difference between words like *beside* and *besides, between* and *among.* Discuss the meanings with students, and have them draw stick-figure sketches for these words, or have a helper draw sketches based on student directions. You may want to continue this technique throughout the chapter.

English-Language Learners

Spanish. Students who speak Spanish may need further explanation of the difference between *between* and *among* because one word (*entre*) is used for both prepositions in Spanish.

Cantonese. Cantonese does not use the equivalent of the English articles *a, an,* or *the.* Also, Cantonese-speaking students may find the concepts of countable/uncountable and definite/indefinite difficult to grasp. Students may either omit articles *(I like book),* add articles unnecessarily *(She goes to the school every morning),* or confuse the two main types of articles *(Please lend me the pen and the piece of paper).*

Articles are unstressed in English and difficult to hear for those whose language does not use articles. When introducing nouns, use the article with the noun: *This is* **a** *noun, and this is* **an** *adjective.* Also, have students practice the definite *the* by using it to point to specific items.

Teacher: *Which book do you want?*

Student: ***The** one with the red cover.*

USAGE

MINI-LESSON Grammar

The Parts of Speech. Because the glossary entries refer to parts of speech without explanation, you may want to review each part of speech as it appears in the glossary. (See **Chapter 1: Parts of Speech Overview.**)

For practice, have students identify the parts of speech of often-confused pairs such as *accept* (verb), *except* (verb; preposition); and *affect* (verb), *effect* (noun; verb).

DIFFERENTIATING INSTRUCTION

Learners Having Difficulty

To personalize the glossary entries, place students in groups of four and have each student create an exercise item based on one glossary entry. (You may wish to have students use the items in the **Oral Practice** on pp. 226–227 as models.) Then, have the group members work together to find the correct answers. Have students repeat this process several times. Then, have them compile their items into a practice test to share with other groups.

Tell students to use the following memory aids to determine the correct use of *bring* and *take*: ***bring** it **to*** and ***take** it **away*** or *to **bring** something when you **come*** and ***take** it when you **go**.*

Oral Practice

DISTRIBUTED REVIEW

To reinforce what students have learned about the parts of speech, ask them to identify the part of speech of the correct answers in sentences 3, 9, and 10.

3. noun

9. preposition

10. verb

USAGE

borrow, lend, loan *Borrow* means "to take [something] temporarily." *Lend* means "to give [something] temporarily." *Loan,* a noun in formal language, is sometimes used in place of *lend* in informal speech.

EXAMPLES Tadzio **borrowed** a copy of *O Pioneers!* from the library.

I try not to forget to return things people **lend** me.

Could you **loan** me a dollar? [informal]

bring, take *Bring* means "to come carrying something." *Take* means "to go carrying something." Think of *bring* as related to *come, take* as related to *go.*

EXAMPLES **Bring** that box over here.

Now **take** it down to the basement.

bust, busted Avoid using these words as verbs. Use a form of either *burst* or *break* or *catch* or *arrest.*

EXAMPLES Even the hard freeze didn't **burst** [not *bust*] the pipes.

When aircraft **break** [not *bust*] the sound barrier, a sonic boom results.

Molly **caught** [not *busted*] Mr. Whiskers nibbling her tuna sandwich.

Did the police **arrest** [not *bust*] a suspect in the burglary?

Oral Practice **Solving Common Usage Problems**

Read each of the following sentences aloud, and identify the correct word or words in parentheses, according to standard usage.

EXAMPLE **1.** Everyone seemed greatly (*affected, effected*) by her speech on animal rights.

1. affected

1. There was complete agreement (*between, among*) the members of the council.
2. Is that (*all the farther, as far as*) you were able to hike?
3. The (*affects, effects*) of lasers on surgical procedures have been remarkable.
4. My schedule includes English, math, science, (*etc., and etc.*)
5. The boiler (*busted, burst*) and flooded the cellar.

6. Liza promised to (*bring, take*) me the new cassette when she comes to visit.
7. I don't know where it (*is, is at*).
8. Please (*bring, take*) this note to the manager's office when you go.
9. (*Beside, Besides*) my aunts and uncles, all my cousins are coming to our family reunion.
10. Ms. Yu (*accepted, excepted*) my excuse for being late.

Exercise 1 Proofreading Sentences for Standard Usage

The following sentences contain errors in standard English usage. Identify the error or errors you find in each sentence. Then, write the correct usage. If a sentence is already correct, write *C.*

EXAMPLE
1. It isn't pretty, but the fossilized skull in the picture below has caused alot of talk in the scientific world.
   1. *alot—a lot*

1. Discussions between various groups of scholars focus on what killed the dinosaurs.
2. Some scientists believe an asteroid hit earth and wiped out the dinosaurs, but others think there was a severe climate change where the dinosaurs lived at.
3. Even if we don't know why the dinosaurs disappeared, most of us enjoy looking at dinosaur fossils in museums, in exhibitions, on TV, and etc.
4. The San Juan, Argentina, area is one of the best places anywheres to find dinosaur fossils.
5. In 1988, the biologist Paul Sereno's discovery there busted the old record for the most ancient dinosaur remains.
6. On a expedition with some of his students from the University of Chicago, Sereno found the oldest dinosaur fossils unearthed up to that time.
7. Besides being in good shape, Sereno's herrerasaurus fossil doesn't even look its age.
8. In fact, the 230-million-year-old skeleton was amazingly complete accept for the hind limbs.

Exercise 1 Proofreading Sentences for Standard Usage

ANSWERS

1. between—among
2. lived at—lived
3. and etc.—etc.
4. anywheres—anywhere
5. busted—broke
6. a—an
7. C
8. accept—except

USAGE

Exercise 1 **Proofreading Sentences for Standard Usage**

ANSWERS continued

9. ain't—isn't
10. effected—affected

DIFFERENTIATING INSTRUCTION

English-Language Learners

Spanish. You may want to point out to your Spanish-speaking students that *good* and *well* are the English equivalents of *bueno* and *bien,* respectively.

Also, when discussing the problems writers have with *had of* and *would of,* you may need to give more attention to Spanish speakers because Spanish does not have as many helping verbs as English does.

General Strategies. English-language learners usually make different kinds of mistakes than native speakers of English. However, if your students have been in the United States for a number of years, they may have acquired some of the language forms they hear in their environment. These may include nonstandard forms such as *He don't* and *I don't want none.* Explain to students that the language they hear may not be appropriate for formal, academic work. Point out that both native and non-native speakers of English need to learn standard English to be successful in school and workplace settings.

USAGE

9. That quality of find certainly ain't ordinary.
10. Sereno and his herrerasaurus have effected the work of biologists and dinosaur-lovers everywhere.

can, may Use *can* to express ability. Use *may* to express possibility or permission.

EXAMPLES **Can** you speak German? [ability]

Pedro **may** join us at the restaurant. [possibility]

May I be excused? [permission]

could of Do not write *of* with the helping verb *could.* Write *could have.* Also avoid *had of, ought to of, should of, would of, might of,* and *must of.*

EXAMPLE Diane **could have** [not *could of*] telephoned us.

discover, invent *Discover* means "to be the first to find, see, or learn about something that already exists." *Invent* means "to be the first to do or make something."

EXAMPLES Who **discovered** those fossil dinosaur eggs?

Robert Wilhelm Bunsen, for whom the Bunsen burner is named, **invented** the spectroscope.

STYLE TIP

Many people consider contractions informal. Therefore, it is usually best to avoid using them in formal writing and speech.

Reference Note

For more information about **formal** and **informal English,** see page 223.

don't, doesn't *Don't* is the contraction of *do not. Doesn't* is the contraction of *does not.* Use *doesn't,* not *don't,* with *he, she, it, this,* and singular nouns.

EXAMPLES It **doesn't** [not *don't*] matter.

The trains **don't** [not *doesn't*] stop at this station.

effect See **affect, effect.**

everywheres See **anyways,** etc.

fewer, less *Fewer* is used with plural words. *Less* is used with singular words. *Fewer* tells "how many"; *less* tells "how much."

EXAMPLES **Fewer** students have enrolled this semester.

Therefore, there will be **less** competition.

good, well *Good* is an adjective. Do not use *good* to modify a verb; use *well,* an adverb.

NONSTANDARD Tiger Woods played good.

STANDARD Tiger Woods played **well.**

MINI-LESSON Grammar

Definitions. You may want to review with students the following definitions.

- **contraction:** shortened form of a word or group of words
- **apostrophe:** symbol used to indicate where letters have been omitted or to form the possessive case (see p. 327)

While *well* is usually an adverb, it is also used as an adjective to mean "healthy."

EXAMPLE She does not feel **well.**

NOTE *Feel good* and *feel well* mean different things. *Feel good* means "to feel happy or pleased." *Feel well* simply means "to feel healthy."

EXAMPLES Compliments make you feel **good.**

Do dogs and cats really eat grass when they don't feel **well**?

Exercise 2 Solving Common Usage Problems

For each sentence, choose the correct word in parentheses, according to standard usage.

EXAMPLE 1. Today people are using (*fewer, less*) salt than they did years ago.

1. *less*

1. You should (*of, have*) written sooner.
2. Who (*discovered, invented*) what makes fireflies glow?
3. (*Don't, Doesn't*) Otis know that we're planning to leave in five minutes?
4. I usually do (*good, well*) on that kind of test.
5. Our doctor advised my uncle to eat (*fewer, less*) eggs.
6. He (*don't, doesn't*) look angry to me.
7. If I had known, I might (*of, have*) helped you with your project.
8. We had (*fewer, less*) snowstorms this year than last.
9. (*Can, May*) I please be excused now?
10. Whoever (*discovered, invented*) the escalator must have been ingenious.

Review A Solving Common Usage Problems

Most of the following sentences contain errors in standard usage. If a sentence contains an error in standard usage, write the correct form. If a sentence is already correct, write *C*.

EXAMPLE 1. Don't anyone know when this game will start?

1. *Doesn't*

1. Perhaps I should of called before visiting you.
2. Who discovered the cellular phone system?

1. have
2. invented

• **helping verb:** verb form that precedes the main verb in a verb phrase and that may indicate tense—all forms of *be* plus *do, has, have, had, shall, will, can,* etc. (see p. 14)

Differentiating Instruction

Learners Having Difficulty

Mnemonics. Show students the following examples to distinguish between the uses of *good* and *well.*

They didn't feel **well** digging the well. (adj.)

They dug a **good** well. (adj.)

They dug the well **well.** (adv.)

They did a **good** job on the well. (adj.)

USAGE

Practice

Correct Usage

Activity. As preparation for **Reviews A** and **B,** have students play Usage Baseball. Divide the class into two teams. Set up four chairs in a diamond formation, each chair representing a base. As each batter sits at home plate, ask him or her to compose a sentence using one of the chapter's problem words, chosen from a list on the chalkboard. Have the other team judge each sentence by reading the entry that applies to it. A student whose sentence is correct moves to first base; students proceed from base to base with each correct answer given. If the sentence is incorrect, the student is out. After the first team has three outs, send the second team to bat. As a word is used, put a check by it. Students will not be allowed to reuse a word until all other words have been used.

3. affecting
4. C
5. fewer
6. C
7. effect
8. accept
9. C
10. take

3. The beautiful weather is ~~effecting~~ my powers of concentration.
4. We can't decide between this movie and that one.
5. That box contains ~~less~~ cookies than this one.
6. We felt good because practice went so well.
7. What ~~affect~~ did the quiz have on your grade?
8. Why won't you ~~except~~ my help?
9. We stood beside the lake and watched the swans.
10. Did you ~~bring~~ flowers to your aunt when you went to visit her in her new home?

Review B Solving Common Usage Problems

Choose the word or expression in parentheses that is correct according to standard usage.

EXAMPLE Alvin Ailey significantly **[1]** (*affected, effected*) modern dance in America.

1. *affected*

Alvin Ailey [1] (*could of, could have*) just dreamed of being a famous choreographer; instead, he formed [2] (*a, an*) interracial dance company that is known all over the world. Ailey started his dance company with [3] (*less, fewer*) than ten dancers in New York City in 1958. Today, the Alvin Ailey American Dance Theater has a very [4] (*good, well*) reputation [5] (*between, among*) modern-dance lovers [6] (*everywhere, everywheres*). Ailey also ran a dance school and [7] (*discovered, invented*) many fine young dancers there. [8] (*Beside, Besides*) teaching, he choreographed operas, television specials, and numerous ballets. The scene shown to the left is from Ailey's ballet *Revelations*, an energetic and emotional celebration of the cultural heritage of African Americans. During his lifetime, Ailey [9] (*accepted, excepted*) much praise, countless compliments, numerous rave reviews, [10] (*and etc., etc.*), for his creativity.

had of See **could of.**

had ought, hadn't ought Unlike other verbs, *ought* is not used with *had.*

NONSTANDARD Lee had ought to plan better; he hadn't ought to leave his packing until the last minute.
STANDARD Lee **ought** to plan better; he **ought not** to leave his packing until the last minute.
STANDARD Lee **should** plan better; he **shouldn't** leave his packing until the last minute.

hardly, scarcely See **The Double Negative** (page 237).

he, she, they Do not use an unnecessary pronoun after the subject of a clause or a sentence. This error is called a ***double subject.***

NONSTANDARD My mother she grows organic vegetables.
STANDARD My mother grows organic vegetables.

hisself, theirself, theirselves Avoid using these nonstandard forms.

EXAMPLE He bought **himself** [not *hisself*] a new notebook.

invent See **discover, invent.**

its, it's See page 379.

kind, sort, type The words *this, that, these,* and *those* should always agree in number with the words *kind, sort,* and *type.*

EXAMPLE **This kind** of wrench is more versatile than **those** other **kinds.**

kind of, sort of In formal situations, avoid using *kind of* for the adverb *somewhat* or *rather.*

INFORMAL We are kind of anxious to know our grades.
FORMAL We are **somewhat** [or **rather**] anxious to know our grades.

learn, teach *Learn* means "to acquire knowledge." *Teach* means "to instruct" or "to show how."

EXAMPLE Some of our coaches **teach** classes in gymnastics, where young gymnasts can **learn** many techniques.

leave, let *Leave* means "to go away" or "to depart from." *Let* means "to allow" or "to permit."

Usage: *Had of—Ought to of*
(pp. 231–233)

OBJECTIVE

- To choose the correct word from given pairs in sentences

USAGE

DIRECT TEACHING

Modeling and Demonstration

Its, It's—Them. Model how to identify correct usage of commonly misused words by using the example *The raccoon washed its face in the shallows of the stream.* First, ask what *its* means in this sentence. [*the raccoon's*] Next, ask whether *its* is the correct word here. [*yes*] Then, ask whether *it's* could be used instead of *its* here. [*no*] Point out that *its* is a possessive pronoun and that *it's* is a contraction meaning *it is.* Now, have a volunteer use another example from this chapter to demonstrate how to identify correct usage of commonly misused words.

EXTENSION

Relating to Literature

Explain to students that informal and nonstandard English can be used as valuable writing tools to create vivid characters. The short story "Blues Ain't No Mockin Bird" by Toni Cade Bambara exemplifies the craft of writing dialect. If your literature text includes this selection, ask students to identify at least five examples of dialect and to show how its use characterizes the speaker.

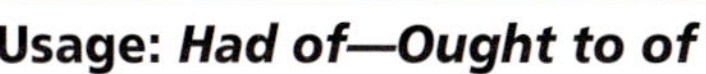
RESOURCES

Usage: *Had of—Ought to of*

Practice

- *Language & Sentence Skills Practice,* p. 221

Differentiating Instruction

- *Developmental Language & Sentence Skills,* pp. 101–102

Extension

Relating to Writing

Suggest to your students that just as a person's appearance makes an impression on others, so does one's language. Whether written or spoken, language affects the image an individual projects.

Ask your students to work in pairs to write paragraphs describing the appearance of a real or fictitious character. Have them write their descriptions in a dialect that is indicative of the character's background. Remind students that dialect involves differences in both usage and pronunciation.

Reteaching

Correct Usage

Activity. If students have difficulty absorbing the differences between pairs of words, reinforce correct usage with a game of Sentence Sense. Compose twelve short sentences of four words each, using *good, well, affect, effect, bring, take, discover, invent, fewer, less, among,* or *between* in each sentence. Write each word of the sentences on a separate note card, and shuffle the cards.

Form groups of three or four students, and give each group an equal number of cards. Tell students that they are to use their cards to form four-word sentences. They can trade cards with other groups. The game ends when each group has composed three sentences.

USAGE

NONSTANDARD Just leave him walk in the rain if he wants.
STANDARD Just **let** him walk in the rain if he wants.
STANDARD **Leave** the dishes for tomorrow, and we'll take a walk.

lend, loan See **borrow, lend, loan.**

less See **fewer, less.**

lie, lay See page 167.

like, as In informal English, the preposition *like* is often used as a conjunction meaning "as." In formal English, use *like* to introduce a prepositional phrase, and use *as* to introduce a subordinate clause.

EXAMPLES She looks **like** her sister. [The preposition *like* introduces the phrase *like her sister.*]

We should do **as** our coach recommends. [The clause *as our coach recommends* is introduced by the conjunction *as.*]

Reference Note

For more information about **prepositional phrases,** see Chapter 3. For more about **subordinate clauses,** see Chapter 4.

like, as if, as though In formal written English, *like* should not be used for the compound conjunctions *as if* or *as though.*

INFORMAL Scamp looks like he's been in the swamp again.
FORMAL Scamp looks **as though** he has been in the swamp again.

may See **can, may.**

might of, must of See **could of.**

no, none, nothing See **The Double Negative** (page 237).

nowheres See **anyways,** etc.

of Do not use *of* with prepositions such as *inside, off,* or *outside.*

EXAMPLES He fell **off** [not *off of*] the ladder **outside** [not *outside of*] the garage.

What's **inside** [not *inside of*] that box?

ought to of See **could of.**

Exercise 3 Solving Common Usage Problems

For each sentence, choose the correct word or words in parentheses, according to formal, standard usage.

EXAMPLE 1. I (*had ought, ought*) to write my report on the Chinese inventions of paper and printing.

1. ought

Mini-Lesson Grammar

Terminology. Subordinating conjunctions that introduce adverb clauses sometimes have two words (*as if, as though*). Have students use *as, if,* and *though* in sentences alone and then use *as if* and *as though* as subordinating conjunctions in sentences. Ask students to explain the difference between the words as they have used them. [As *is used in comparisons,* if *is used in conditional statements, and* though *is used to show contrast.* As if *and* as though *are used to compare things with possible or imaginary situations.*]

1. The report must be on ancient Chinese history, (*like, as*) my teacher directed.
2. For (*this, these*) kind of report, I should start with the information that the Chinese invented paper as we know it early in the second century A.D.
3. If I (*had of, had*) seen them make paper by soaking, drying, and flattening mulberry bark, I would have been amazed.
4. (*The Chinese they, The Chinese*) didn't have the technology to mass-produce paper for another four hundred years.
5. By A.D. 200, the Chinese were using paper for writing and painting (*like, as if*) they always had done so.
6. I (*hadn't ought, ought not*) to forget that the Chinese also used paper for making umbrellas, fans, and lanterns.
7. In addition to (*this, these*) sorts of uses, the Chinese were using paper money by the seventh century.
8. You could have knocked me (*off of, off*) my chair when I learned that the Chinese were printing by A.D. 600—some eight hundred years before the invention of modern printing in Germany.
9. (*Leave, Let*) me tell you about how they used wooden blocks with characters carved on them for printing.
10. By the tenth century, the Chinese had (*learned, taught*) themselves how to print entire books with wooden blocks and had invented movable type.

reason . . . because In formal situations, do not use the construction *reason . . . because.* Instead, use *reason . . . that.*

INFORMAL The reason for his victory is because he knew what the voters wanted.

FORMAL The **reason** for his victory is **that** he knew what the voters wanted.

rise, raise See page 169.

sit, set See page 168.

some, somewhat In formal situations, do not use *some* for the adverb *somewhat.*

INFORMAL I've neglected the garden some.

FORMAL I've neglected the garden **somewhat.**

sort See **kind,** etc.

Exercise 3

DISTRIBUTED REVIEW

Have students find the items indicated for the following sentences in **Exercise 3.**

1. adverb clause [*as . . . directed*]
3. gerunds used as the objects of a preposition [*soaking, drying,* and *flattening*]

   noun used as the direct object of gerunds [*bark*]
4. infinitive phrase including a direct object [*to mass-produce paper*]
5. adverb clause [*as if . . . so*]
7. prepositional phrase with a compound preposition [*In addition to these sorts of uses*]

USAGE

Usage: *Reason . . . because—Your, You're*

(pp. 233–237)

OBJECTIVE

- **To choose the correct word from given pairs in sentences**

RESOURCES

Usage: *Reason...because—Your, You're*

Practice

- *Language & Sentence Skills Practice,* pp. 222–223

Differentiating Instruction

- *Developmental Language & Sentence Skills,* pp. 103–104

A Glossary of Usage 233

DIFFERENTIATING INSTRUCTION

Learners Having Difficulty

Mnemonics. To help students distinguish between *than* and *then,* suggest the following "equation": *then = when.*

RETEACHING

USAGE

Correct Usage

Activity. If students have difficulty with the concept of standard English, reteach the concept with a game. Have pairs of students create two sets of flashcards. In one set of flashcards, words and groups of words from this section should be used correctly in sentences. The backs of these cards should be labeled *Standard English.* In the second set of cards, the words, groups of words, and nonstandard constructions (such as *theirselves*) should be used in sentences that do not conform to standard English. The backs of these cards should be labeled *Nonstandard English* and, below the label, should have corrected versions of the nonstandard sentences. Have students shuffle the flashcards and then take turns quizzing each other with the cards, alternating roles after each card. Students should tell whether each sentence uses standard English and correct any sentence written in nonstandard English.

TECHNOLOGY TIP

Remind students that a spellchecker will not help them distinguish between words like *than* and *then.* As long as the word is spelled correctly, the program will accept it, even if it is not used correctly.

supposed to, suppose to Do not leave off the *d* when you write *supposed to.*

EXAMPLE I am **supposed to** [not *suppose to*] clean my room.

take See **bring, take.**

teach See **learn, teach.**

than, then Do not confuse these words. *Than* is a subordinating conjunction used in comparisons; *then* is an adverb meaning *next* or *at that time.*

EXAMPLES Algebra is easier **than** I thought it would be.

Read the directions; **then,** follow each step.

their, there, they're See page 382.

them *Them* should not be used as an adjective. Use *those.*

EXAMPLE I like **those** [not *them*] jeans, don't you?

this here, that there The words *here* and *there* are unnecessary after *this* and *that.*

EXAMPLE I'm buying **this** [not *this here*] cassette instead of **that** [not *that there*] one.

this kind, sort, type See **kind,** etc.

try and, try to Use *try to,* not *try and.*

EXAMPLE We will **try to** [not *try and*] be on time.

type See **kind,** etc.

used to, use to Do not leave off the *d* when you write *used to.*

EXAMPLE I **used to** [not *use to*] play badminton, but now I don't have time.

way, ways Use *way,* not *ways,* in referring to a distance.

EXAMPLE We hiked a long **way** [not *ways*].

well See **good, well.**

what Do not use *what* for *that* to introduce an adjective clause.

EXAMPLE The part of the car **that** [not *what*] lets the wheels turn at different speeds is called the differential gear.

Learning for Life

Continued on pp. 235–236

Formal and Informal English. Because students must be able to use English in ways ranging from formal business communications to the slang of their peers, they must be flexible.

Lead students to realize that word choice, expressions, and structure are all part of varying styles. You might start with a discussion on the following types of English students hear or read.

when, where In formal situations, do not use *when* or *where* to begin a definition.

INFORMAL In botany, a "sport" is when a plant is abnormal or has mutated in some way.

FORMAL In botany, a "sport" is a plant **that is** abnormal or **that has** mutated in some way.

where Do not use *where* for *that* to introduce a noun clause.

EXAMPLE I read in this magazine **that** [not *where*] Carol Clay is a champion parachutist.

which, that, who The relative pronoun *who* refers to people only; *which* refers to things only; *that* refers to either people or things.

EXAMPLES Here is the man **who** will install the new carpet. [person]

We decided to replace our old carpet, **which** we have had for nearly ten years. [thing]

The dealer is a person **that** stands behind all of her products. [person]

It is the kind of carpet **that** will wear well. [thing]

without, unless Do not use the preposition *without* in place of the conjunction *unless.*

EXAMPLE A rattlesnake won't strike you **unless** [not *without*] you surprise or threaten it.

would of See **could of.**

your, you're *Your* is a possessive form of *you. You're* is the contraction of *you are.*

EXAMPLES Is that **your** bike?

I hope **you're** going to the party.

Exercise 4 Solving Common Usage Problems

For each sentence, choose the correct word or words in parentheses, according to formal, standard usage.

EXAMPLE **1.** (*That, That there*) motorcycle belongs to my cousin.

1. That

1. Don't use more paper (*than, then*) you need.
2. (*Them, Those*) dogs have impressive pedigrees.

EXTENSION

Critical Thinking

Metacognition. As a form of self-evaluation, have students record the following statements in their grammar logs and evaluate each statement as *rarely, sometimes,* or *often.*

- I know when and how to use formal English.
- I recognize my own usage errors and work to correct them.
- I use language to communicate with others rather than to distinguish myself from them.
- I find myself being misunderstood by my elders.

After students have completed their logs, ask them to write one rubric to help them develop their language usage. [*Possible answers: Is my language appropriate to my audience? Does my language aid or inhibit communication?*]

USAGE

PRACTICE

Guided and Independent

Exercise You may wish to have the class work through **Exercise 4** as guided practice and **Review C** as independent practice.

HOMEWORK

- **Formal English:** used in formal business letters, reports, and documents
- **Informal English:** used in conversation, personal letters and e-mails
- **Slang:** special words used by a group or subculture

After the discussion, have students form groups of three, one student for each category: formal, informal, and slang.

Differentiating Instruction

Advanced Learners

Activity. Have interested students create a proofreading exercise similar to **Review C.** Have students in small groups brainstorm topics for the exercise. Then, have students create a list of glossary items that need to be emphasized and divide the items among the group members. Finally, individual students should research a part of the chosen topic and create exercise sentences including the assigned items.

Review the groups' materials, and suggest revisions before distributing copies to the class.

USAGE

Review C Correcting Usage Errors

ANSWERS

1. like—as though [*or* as if]
2. alot—a lot
3. who—which
4. might of—might have
5. historians they—historians [*or* Those historians they—They]
6. some—somewhat
7. without—unless

---

3. Manuel prefers (*this, these*) kind of skateboard.
4. It is only a short (*way, ways*) to the video store.
5. Tricia relaxed (*some, somewhat*) after she began to speak.
6. On the news, I heard (*where, that*) the game was called off because of rain.
7. Please set the books on (*your, you're*) desk.
8. Is she the player (*who, which*) is favored by most to win at Wimbledon this year?
9. He would not have released the report (*without, unless*) he had first verified his sources.
10. The reason we've requested your help is (*that, because*) you know the grounds better than we do.

HELP 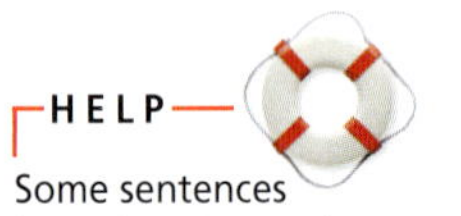

Some sentences in Review C contain more than one error.

Review C Correcting Usage Errors

Identify each usage problem that you find in the sentences in the following paragraph. Then, write the usage that is correct according to formal, standard usage. If a sentence is already correct, write *C*.

EXAMPLE [1] The legendary statue, the Sphinx at Giza in Egypt, would of weathered away completely if it had not been rescued by modern technology.

1. *would of—would have*

[1] Some famous monuments, such as the Eiffel Tower, don't look like they need any restoration. [2] However, monuments older than the Eiffel Tower, like Egypt's Sphinx, often need alot of care. [3] The Sphinx, who has the head of a human and the body of a lion, was built around 4500 B.C. [4] Some historians think the Sphinx, shown below, might of been built at the same time as the pyramid of King Khafre, which stands beside it. [5] Those historians they believe the Sphinx's face is a portrait of Khafre. [6] The Sphinx was suffering some from old age, exposure, and bad restoration attempts, so Egyptian museum officials began a major renewal project in 1990. [7] Scientists knew that the world eventually would lose that famous statue without restoration was begun immediately. [8] Workers

Learning for Life 

Continued from p. 235

Have each student who chose the formal category offer three short examples of formal English. Then, have the group compose sentences equivalent in meaning using the other two types of English.

Finally, have each group share their favorite examples orally with the class. You might ask students proficient in videotape technology to record the groups' presentations.

dismantled many stones, set new ones in their places, and than added natural mortar to let them stones breathe. [**9**] Workers also stabilized the water table under the mammoth Sphinx, which towers sixty-six feet above the desert sands. [**10**] These kind of restorations will help to preserve the Sphinx against the harmful affects of wind, rain, and sand for many years to come.

Review D Correcting Usage Errors

Revise each of the following sentences, correcting the error or errors in usage. Answers may vary.

EXAMPLE **1.** I saw on the news where the mayor doesn't plan to run for re-election.

1. I saw on the news that the mayor doesn't plan to run for re-election.

1. Optimism is ~~when a person~~ look on the bright side.
2. Luanne was ~~suppose~~ to buy a birthday card for Jo.
3. Take this rake and ~~them~~ seedlings to Mae ~~like~~ I asked.
4. I would ~~of~~ begun my report sooner ~~then~~ I did if I had known it would need this much research.
5. I heard ~~where~~ people will not be allowed back in the concert hall after intermission ~~without~~ they show their tickets.
6. The tire came off ~~of~~ the truck and rolled a long ~~ways~~ away.
7. Heather Ruiz has promised to ~~learn~~ us karate.
8. The people ~~which~~ witnessed the crime ~~hadn't ought~~ to have left before the police arrived.
9. Did Thomas Edison ~~discover~~ the lightbulb?
10. Is it safe to ~~leave~~ the dog to run around the park without a leash?

1. a tendency to
2. supposed
3. those/as
4. have/than
5. that/unless
6. way
7. teach
8. who/ought not
9. invent
10. let

The Double Negative

In a ***double negative,*** two or more negative words are used when one is sufficient. Do not use double negatives in formal writing and speaking.

hardly, scarcely The words *hardly* and *scarcely* convey a negative meaning. They should not be used with another negative word.

EXAMPLES I **can** [not *can't*] **hardly** turn the key in the lock.

We **have** [not *haven't*] **scarcely** enough time.

"Dropping out of school never done me no harm."

© Jim Unger, distributed by United Media, 1998.

Review C **Correcting Usage Errors**

ANSWERS continued

8. than—then; them—those
9. C
10. These kind—These kinds; affects—effects

USAGE

The Double Negative
(pp. 237–238)

OBJECTIVE

- To revise sentences by correcting errors in double negatives

RESOURCES

The Double Negative

Practice

- *Language & Sentence Skills Practice,* p. 224

Differentiating Instruction

- *Developmental Language & Sentence Skills,* pp. 103–104

Differentiating Instruction

English-Language Learners

General Strategies. Tell students that some languages, such as French and Spanish, use two or more words to express the negative. Because the use of double and sometimes triple negatives to indicate one negative idea is common in these languages, you will need to work closely with French- or Spanish-speaking students to help them avoid double negatives in their English usage.

USAGE

Nonsexist Language

(pp. 238–240)

OBJECTIVE

- To rewrite sentences to avoid gender-specific and awkward expressions

MEETING THE CHALLENGE

Write a short dialogue of ten lines in which the two people speaking use nonstandard English. Then, go back and rewrite the dialogue, changing the nonstandard usage to standard English usage.

ANSWER
Dialogues will have two versions: one with nonstandard English usage and another with standard English usage.

HELP

Although two revisions are shown for the example in Exercise 5, you need to give only one for each sentence.

no, nothing, none Do not use these words with another negative word.

NONSTANDARD	That answer doesn't make no sense.
STANDARD	That answer **doesn't make any** sense.
STANDARD	That answer **makes no** sense.
NONSTANDARD	The field trip won't cost us nothing.
STANDARD	The field trip **won't cost** us **anything.**
STANDARD	The field trip **will cost** us **nothing.**
NONSTANDARD	We wanted grapes, but there weren't none.
STANDARD	We wanted grapes, but there **weren't any.**
STANDARD	We wanted grapes, but there **were none.**

Exercise 5 Correcting Double Negatives

Revise each of the following sentences, correcting the usage errors. Answers may vary.

EXAMPLE **1.** It doesn't make no difference to me.

1. It makes no difference to me.

or

It doesn't make any difference to me.

1. Rachel didn't say ~~nothing~~ to him. **1.** anything
2. There ~~isn't~~ hardly anything left to eat. **2.** is
3. I haven't borrowed ~~no~~ books from the library this week. **3.** any
4. Laura ~~couldn't~~ hardly make herself heard. **4.** could
5. What you're saying doesn't make ~~no~~ sense to me. **5.** any
6. By the time we wrote for tickets, there weren't ~~none~~ available. **6.** any
7. Hasn't ~~no one~~ in the class read *And Now Miguel*? **7.** anyone
8. There ~~wasn't~~ scarcely enough water to keep the fish alive. **8.** was
9. Didn't you ~~never~~ say ~~nothing~~ about the noise? **9.** ever/anything
10. I haven't ~~never~~ told ~~no one~~ about our discovery. **10.** ever/anyone

Nonsexist Language

Nonsexist language is language that applies to people in general, both male and female. For example, the nonsexist terms *humanity, human beings,* and *people* can substitute for the gender-specific term *mankind.*

In the past, many skills and occupations were generally closed to either men or women. Expressions like *seamstress, stewardess,* and

RESOURCES

Nonsexist Language

Practice

- *Language & Sentence Skills Practice,* p. 225

mailman reflect those limitations. Since most jobs can now be held by both men and women, language is adjusting to reflect this change.

When you are referring generally to people, it is best to use nonsexist expressions rather than gender-specific ones. Below are some widely used nonsexist terms that you can use to replace the gender-specific ones.

Gender-specific	Nonsexist
businessman	executive, businessperson
chairman	chairperson, chair
deliveryman	delivery person
fireman	firefighter
foreman	supervisor
housewife	homemaker
mailman	mail carrier
man-made	synthetic, manufactured
manpower	workers, human resources
May the best man win!	May the best person win!
policeman	police officer
salesman	salesperson, salesclerk
seamstress	needleworker
steward, stewardess	flight attendant
watchman	security guard

If the antecedent of a pronoun may be either masculine or feminine, use both masculine and feminine pronouns to refer to it.

EXAMPLES **Anyone** who wants to enter the poster contest should bring **his or her** entry to Room 21 by Friday.

Any student may bring a poster with **him or her** to Room 21.

You can often avoid the awkward *his or her* construction (or the alternative *his/her*) by substituting an article (*a, an,* or *the*) for the construction. You can also rephrase the sentence, using the plural forms of both the pronoun and its antecedent.

EXAMPLES Any interested **student** may submit **a** poster.

All interested **students** may submit **their** posters.

STYLE  TIP

You can make similar revisions to avoid using the awkward expressions *s/he* and *wo/man.*

EXTENSION

Nonsexist Language

Assign students to work in small groups to investigate nonsexist language. Provide students with recent magazines, newspapers, catalogues, or brochures. Have each student skim one of the samples, looking for examples of both gender-specific and nonsexist language. Have students share their examples with the class. If possible, have students investigate thirty-year-old copies of similar publications and pool their findings to compile charts showing examples of changes in language usage. Students could also compare language in a current sitcom with that from a 1950s or 1960s sitcom like *The Andy Griffith Show, I Love Lucy,* or *Father Knows Best.*

USAGE

CONTENT-AREA CONNECTIONS

Math. Have students consider the use of double negatives in mathematical terms. Ask a volunteer to determine the value of x in the following problem:

$$x = 6 - (-4)$$

[*The answer is x = 10. When a double negative appears in such an equation, the numbers are added rather than subtracted.*] Explain that the effect in English is the same as in mathematics: The redundancy of the two negatives creates a positive.

USAGE

Exercise 6 Using Nonsexist Language

Rewrite each of the following sentences to avoid using gender-specific terms and awkward expressions. Answers may vary.

EXAMPLE 1. An airline stewardess works hard to keep her passengers comfortable.

1. Flight attendants work hard to keep their passengers comfortable.

1. The project was short of ~~manpower~~, so the management hired more staff.
2. A three-alarm fire broke out in the factory, and the ~~firemen~~ were soon on the scene.
3. Whether or not ~~s/he gets~~ a commission depends on how persuasive ~~each salesman is~~.
4. May the best ~~wo/man~~ win!
5. Our dog growls when it sees a delivery ~~man~~ and barks loudly at every ~~mailman~~.
6. Being a ~~policeman~~ is a demanding job.
7. Did you hear that Susan was elected ~~chairman~~ of the board?
8. The ~~foreman~~ of the crew will distribute the helmets.
9. When Aunt Tina and Uncle Lewis had a baby, Aunt Tina decided to become a ~~housewife~~.
10. Some ~~man-made~~ medicines are considerably cheaper than natural medicines.

1. workers
2. firefighters
3. salespeople get/ they are
4. person
5. person/mail carrier
6. police officer
7. chairperson
8. supervisor
9. homemaker
10. synthetic

Terms in brackets refer to concepts tested by the items in the Chapter Review.

1. doesn't [*don't, doesn't*]
2. let [*leave, let*]
3. outside [*of*]
4. well [*good, well*]
5. C [*beside, besides*]
6. fewer [*fewer, less*]
7. C [*don't, doesn't; kind, sort, type*]
8. that [*where*]
9. as though (*or* as if) [*like, as if, as though*]
10. have [*could of*]

11. [*like, as*]
12. [*when, where*]
13. [*don't, doesn't; good, well*]
14. [double negative, *a lot*]
15. [*like, as*]
16. [*fewer, less*]
17. [*learn, teach*]
18. [*he, she, they*]
19. [double negative]
20. [*between, among*]

Chapter Review

A. Correcting Errors in Standard Usage

For each of the following sentences, identify and correct the error or errors in usage. If a sentence is already correct, write *C.*

1. Why ~~don't~~ Guadalupe try out for the team?
2. Please ~~leave~~ Mike solve the problem by himself.
3. The ball can't go ~~outside of~~ the boundary lines.
4. You are playing ~~good~~ now that you practice every day.
5. We sat beside the lake and fished.
6. Every spring we see ~~less~~ bluebirds than the year before.
7. Tyrone doesn't like this kind of frosting.
8. I read ~~where~~ another royal wedding is taking place.
9. Terry looked ~~like~~ she needed a rest after the relay.
10. They wouldn't ~~of~~ missed going to the mountains.

B. Proofreading a Paragraph for Standard Usage

For each sentence in the following paragraph, identify and correct the error or errors in standard English usage. If a sentence is already correct, write *C.*

[11] Please bring me a dictionary so that I can look up what *left-handed* means, like I started to do earlier. [12] Left-handedness is where the person uses the left hand more than the right hand. [13] It don't matter which hand a person mainly uses because a left-hander functions just as good as a right-hander does. [14] Being left-handed couldn't hardly be a handicap; alot of clever people have been left-handed. [15] For example, artists like Leonardo da Vinci and Michelangelo Buonarroti were left-handed. [16] Of course, less people are left-handed than right-handed. [17] Many scientists learn their students the theory that left-handedness is determined by which side of the brain is dominant. [18] Some scientists they say that the left side of the brain is more dominant in a right-handed person. [19] They also say that the right side of the brain is more dominant in a left-handed person, but there isn't nobody who knows for sure. [20] Discussions on this subject between various groups of scientists will probably continue into the distant future.

ASSESSING

Monitoring Progress

Chapter Review. To assess student progress, you may want to compare the types of items missed on the **Diagnostic Preview** to those missed on the **Chapter Review.** If students have not made significant progress, you may want to refer them to **Chapter 17: Correcting Common Errors, Exercises 19, 23, 24, 37,** and **38** for additional practice.

USAGE

Chapter Review

B. Proofreading a Paragraph for Standard Usage

ANSWERS

11. like—as
12. is where—occurs when [answers will vary]
13. don't—doesn't; good—well
14. couldn't hardly—could hardly [*or* couldn't]; alot—a lot
15. C
16. less—fewer
17. learn—teach
18. scientists they—scientists
19. isn't nobody—isn't anybody [*or* is nobody]
20. between—among

RESOURCES

A Glossary of Usage

Review

- *Language & Sentence Skills Practice,* pp. 226–228

Assessment

- *Holt Handbook Chapter Tests with Answer Key,* pp. 17–18, 52

USAGE

C. Solving Common Usage Problems

For each sentence, choose the correct word in parentheses, according to formal, standard usage.

21. [*anyways*]
22. [double negative]
23. [*bust, busted*]
24. [*discover, invent*]
25. [*anyways*]
26. [*fewer, less*]
27. [*affect, effect*]
28. [double negative]
29. [*discover, invent*]
30. [*could of*]
31. [*good, well*]
32. [*fewer, less*]
33. [*way, ways*]
34. [*between, among*]
35. [*accept, except*]
36. [*leave, let*]
37. [*where*]
38. [*which, that, who*]
39. [*without, unless*]
40. [*borrow, lend, loan*]

21. I looked for the library book all over the house, but I couldn't find it (*anywheres, anywhere*).

22. The deer searched the ground for food, but there wasn't (*none, any*).

23. When the temperature dropped to zero, we worried that the pipes might (*bust, burst*).

24. In the 1820s and '30s, the French scientists Louis Daguerre and Nicéphore Niépce (*discovered, invented*) photography.

25. That airline's slogan is "We fly (*everywhere, everywheres*)."

26. Dr. Mendez advised me to eat (*less, fewer*) sweets.

27. What (*affect, effect*) did the good news have on her?

28. However much you try to outrun a tornado, it doesn't make (*no, any*) difference; the best idea is to seek shelter immediately.

29. Who (*discovered, invented*) what a comet's tail is made of, Kai?

30. Nick admitted that he (*should of, should have*) told his family what time he was planning to come home.

31. "If you study hard now, you will be more confident later, and you will do (*good, well*) on the final," declared Ms. Echevarria.

32. Although it has (*fewer, less*) options than the car advertised, that car on the lot is a better deal, overall.

33. From New Orleans to Los Angeles is quite a long (*ways, way*).

34. That orchestra has a top-notch reputation (*between, among*) music lovers worldwide.

35. The author (*accepted, excepted*) the award with the grace that had long been characteristic of her.

36. Mother asked Simon to (*leave, let*) her read her book in peace.

37. I heard (*where, that*) today's discounts are the best ever.

38. Is Belle the singer (*which, that*) had that TV special last week?

39. It's hard to imagine how ice got onto the moon (*without, unless*) there had once been water there.

40. Could you (*lend, loan*) me your book?

D. Using Nonsexist Language

Rewrite each of the following sentences to avoid gender-specific terms and awkward expressions. Answers may vary.

41. The ~~foreman~~ issued her first work order of the day.
42. May the best ~~man~~ win!
43. Caroline's friend was ~~an airline stewardess~~.
44. Only the very courageous need apply to be ~~firemen~~.
45. Three of the ~~salesmen~~ were under twenty-five.
46. The space shuttle is the most useful ~~man-made~~ device ever.
47. The ~~deliverymen~~ for that company wear brown shorts.
48. My next-door neighbor was a first-rate ~~seamstress~~.
49. Fewer women become ~~housewives~~ these days than in the past.
50. The computer plant is advertising for a ~~watchman~~, I hear.

41.–50. [Nonsexist Language]
41. supervisor
42. person
43. a flight attendant
44. firefighters
45. salespeople
46. manufactured
47. delivery people
48. needleworker
49. homemakers
50. security guard

Writing Application

Writing a Business Letter

Using Formal, Standard English After reading studies showing the benefits of school uniforms, the school board in your district has proposed requiring students to wear uniforms. One study found that schools that require uniforms experience less violence. Another study concluded that students who wore uniforms made better grades. Write a letter to the school board, telling why your district should or should not require students to wear uniforms.

Prewriting If you already have an opinion about school uniforms, jot down some reasons to support your view. If you are undecided, you may want to make two lists—one pro and one con. Give several reasons to support each position. Then, choose the more persuasive side.

Writing As you write your first draft, keep focused on your topic. Choose only the best reasons from your list, and expand on these.

Revising Add, delete, or rearrange details to support your argument. Also, see that the tone and word choice of your letter conform to the standards of a polite business letter.

Publishing Proofread your paper for any errors in spelling and punctuation. Then, use the glossary entries in this chapter to correct common usage errors. You and your classmates may wish to have a debate on the school uniform issue. You might also like to post your letter on the class bulletin board or Web page.

APPLICATION

Writing Application

Prewriting Tip. Because the aim of this letter is persuasive, students will need to analyze their audience for its beliefs and interests. Then students can decide what types of support are necessary to convince their readers.

Writing Tip. The writing assignment gives students practice in adapting language to suit a particular audience. Reinforce the necessity for formal language when a writer wants to be taken seriously, and review the proper form for a business letter.

Scoring Rubric. While you will want to pay particular attention to students' use of appropriate language, you will also want to evaluate overall writing performance. You may want to give a split score to indicate development and clarity of the composition as well as usage skills.

CHAPTER

10

INTRODUCING THE CHAPTER

- This chapter presents the basic rules of capitalization. Some of the material is in the form of notes and examples that are given after the rules. While students are studying the examples in the textbook, they may wish to develop their own examples.
- The chapter closes with a **Chapter Review** including a **Writing Application** feature that asks students to write a paragraph about a foreign city and its attractions. Students should use correct capitalization.
- You may want to refer students to this chapter throughout the year, especially when they are in the proofreading stage of a writing assignment.
- For help in integrating this chapter with writing assignments, use the **Teaching Strands** chart on pp. T24–T25.

CHAPTER

10

Capital Letters

The Rules for Capitalization

Diagnostic Preview

A. Correcting Sentences That Contain Errors in Capitalization

Correct the errors in capitalization in the following sentences by capitalizing or lowercasing letters as needed. If a sentence contains no errors, write *C.*

Numerals in brackets refer to rules tested by the items in the Diagnostic Preview.

1. [10f(8)]
2. C [10a, h(2), g]
3. [10f(9)]
4. [10f(5)]
5. C [10a, f(3)]
6. [10f(5), f, f(4)]
7. [10f(6, 3, 7)]
8. [10f(8)]
9. [10g, h(3)]

EXAMPLE 1. My Aunt and I visited the White house in Washington, D.C.

1. aunt, House

1. Val's new schwinn bike had a flat tire.
2. My father is taking a course in public speaking.
3. The atmosphere on venus is one hundred times denser than the atmosphere on earth.
4. Has your favorite team ever won the rose bowl?
5. The opossum can be found as far south as Argentina and as far north as Canada.
6. For our Spring project, our Club raised money for the American heart association.
7. The maya of the Yucatán peninsula worshiped nature Gods such as chac, a god of rain, and Itzamná, a sky god.
8. My uncle Scott works at Apex hardware store.
9. In drama 2, we staged a production of Denise Chávez's *The flying tortilla Man.*

CHAPTER RESOURCES

Internet

- Web resources: go.hrw.com

go.hrw.com

Practice & Review

- *Language & Sentence Skills Practice,* pp. 234–249
- *Language & Sentence Skills Practice Answer Key,* pp. 95–102

Application & Enrichment

- *Language & Sentence Skills Practice,* pp. 233, 250, 251–252, 253
- *Language & Sentence Skills Practice Answer Key,* pp. 95, 102–103

10. The U.S. senate and the house of representatives may pass a bill into law, but the president can veto it.
11. Mr. Williams is a Reporter for United Press international.
12. We went to Sea World over easter vacation.
13. Both rabbi Frankel and reverend Stone organized aid for the many victims of the fire.
14. The Winter Games of the 1998 olympics were held in Nagano, Japan.
15. Michelangelo's *The creation of the World* and *The Last Judgment* are paintings that depict scenes from the bible.

10. (*or* President) [10f(4), h(1)]
11. [10f, f(4)]
12. [10f(5, 7)]
13. [10h(1)]
14. [10f(5)]
15. [10h(3), f(7)]

B. Correcting Capitalization Errors in a Paragraph

Correct the errors in capitalization in the following paragraph by capitalizing or lowercasing letters as needed. If a sentence contains no errors, write *C.*

EXAMPLE **[1]** A gentle elephant named jumbo was once the largest, most popular captive animal in the World.
1. Jumbo, world

[**16**] When p. t. barnum bought Jumbo in 1882, the elephant had already become a star with the London royal circus. [**17**] All of england protested the sale when the unhappy elephant refused to board the ship for New York city. [**18**] however, even queen Victoria and the Prince of wales could not prevent Jumbo's going, since the sale had been completed. [**19**] Jumbo's Trainer, Matthew Scott, kept the elephant content on the journey across the atlantic ocean. [**20**] In april, the new addition to the Show arrived in New York, and the 13,500-pound Star marched up broadway to the cheers of a huge crowd. [**21**] Soon Jumbo-mania swept across the United States. [**22**] The elephant was so popular that his name became a common word in the english language—*jumbo,* meaning "extra large." [**23**] He died tragically on September 15, 1885, in the canadian town of St. Thomas, Ontario. [**24**] The big-hearted giant, seeing a train bearing down on a baby elephant, pushed the youngster to safety but could not save himself. [**25**] To keep Jumbo's memory alive, Barnum donated the skeleton of his beloved elephant to the American Museum of natural history.

16. [10f(2, 1, 4)]
17. [10f(3)]
18. [10a, h(1), f(3)]
19. [10f, f(3)]
20. [10f(5), f, f(3)]
21. C [10a, f(1, 3)]
22. [10f(6)]
23. [10f(3)]
24. C [10a, f]
25. [10f(4)]

ASSESSING

Entry-Level Assessment

Diagnostic Preview. The **Diagnostic Preview** contains two parts. **Part A** asks students to correct capitalization errors in sentences. **Part B** checks the students' ability to proofread a paragraph for correct capitalization. After identifying problem areas, have students make lists of their particular problems to use as checklists when they revise their writing assignments.

MECHANICS

Differentiating Instruction

- *Developmental Language & Sentence Skills,* pp. 105–118
- *Developmental Language & Sentence Skills Guided Practice Teacher's Notes and Answer Key,* pp. 23–26

Assessment

- *Holt Handbook Chapter Tests with Answer Key,* pp. 19–20, 52

Capitalizing First Words, *I*, and *O*

Rules 10a–e *(pp. 246–247)*

OBJECTIVES

- To capitalize the first words of sentences in a paragraph and to add appropriate end marks
- To correct capitalization errors in sentences

PRETEACHING

Lesson Starter

Motivating. To illustrate that the placement of capital letters is vital to effective communication, write the following pairs of sentences on the chalkboard for volunteers to explain.

1. Won't we need that heavy-duty jack at Cecil's Garage to lift my father's Bronco? [*Won't we need the equipment at Cecil's auto repair shop to lift my father's car?*]

Won't we need that heavy-duty Jack at Cecil's garage to lift my father's bronco? [*Won't we need the strong person named Jack at a garage owned by Cecil to lift my father's horse?*]

2. Some Friends in south Dakota are getting together to watch the orange bowl. [*Some Quakers in the southern part of a place named Dakota are congregating to watch a bowl with oranges in it (or to watch an orange bowling or an orange-colored bowl).*]

Some friends in South Dakota are getting together to watch the Orange Bowl. [*Some friends in the state of South Dakota are congregating to watch a football game.*]

MECHANICS

Using Capital Letters Correctly

A capital letter at the beginning of a word is an important signal to the reader. A capital letter may indicate the beginning of a sentence and also may mark a significant difference in meaning, such as the difference between *may* (as in *you may*) and *May* (as in *May 3, 2002*).

STYLE TIP

Some professional writers do not follow the rules shown in this chapter. When you are quoting a person, use capital letters as they are used in the source of the quotation.

10a. **Capitalize the first word in every sentence.**

EXAMPLES **T**he world of computers has its own vocabulary. **C**omputer equipment is called *hardware,* and the programs are called *software.*

Exercise 1 **Capitalizing Sentences in a Paragraph**

Rewrite the following paragraph. Capitalize the ten words that should begin with a capital letter. Add the appropriate punctuation mark to the end of each sentence.

EXAMPLE **1.** what are some new developments in science

1. What are some new developments in science?

work has begun on a new kind of laser radar. this instrument would be especially useful for people with visual impairments. how does the radar work? a laser device that is small enough to fit onto an eyeglass frame emits invisible infrared light beams. when the light strikes an object, it bounces back to a receiver placed in the wearer's ear. the receiver, in turn, sounds a small tone. with this sort of device, the person can "hear" any object nearby. the device is very promising. in fact, it may one day replace the cane or the guide dog as an aid for people who are blind. there are few better examples of how beneficial laser research can be.

10b. **Traditionally, the first word of a line of poetry is capitalized.**

EXAMPLES **A** bird came down the walk:
He did not know I saw;
He bit an angleworm in halves
And ate the fellow, raw.

Emily Dickinson, "A Bird Came Down the Walk"

10c. **Capitalize the first word of a directly quoted sentence.**

EXAMPLE Eduardo wondered, "**W**here did I put my backpack?"

Reference Note

For more information on using **capital letters in quotations,** see page 315.

RESOURCES

Capitalizing First Words, *I*, and *O*

Practice

- *Language & Sentence Skills Practice,* p. 234

Differentiating Instruction

- *Developmental Language & Sentence Skills,* pp. 105–106

10d. **Capitalize the first word in both the salutation and the closing of a letter.**

EXAMPLES **D**ear Service Manager: **S**incerely,

Dear Amy, **Y**ours truly,

10e. **Capitalize the pronoun *I* and the interjection *O*.**

Although it is rarely used, *O* is always capitalized. Generally, it is reserved for invocations and is followed by the name of the person or thing being addressed. You will more often use the interjection *oh*, which is generally not capitalized unless it is the first word in a sentence.

EXAMPLES "Exult **O** shores! and ring **O** bells!" is a line from Walt Whitman's poem "**O** Captain! My Captain!"

The play was a hit, but **o**h, how nervous I was!

Oh, I forgot my book.

BORN LOSER reprinted by permission of Newspaper Enterprise Association, Inc.

Exercise 2 Correcting Capitalization Errors in Sentences

Correct the errors in capitalization in the following sentences. If a sentence contains no errors, write *C*.

EXAMPLE 1. in "Jazz Fantasia," the speaker tells the Musicians, "Go to it, o jazzmen."

1. In, musicians, O

1. yesterday i learned two psalms that begin, "Bless the Lord, o my soul."
2. Ms. Jones asked, "can anyone name the author of that poem?"
3. I haven't decided, but Oh, how I'd like to be an astronaut!
4. "you must be careful of the coral snake," said the guide, "because it is the most poisonous snake in our region."
5. In the poem "The Fool's Prayer," the jester pleads, "O Lord, be merciful to me, a fool!" 5. C
6. do you know that the fifth of May is a Mexican American holiday?
7. most trucks have rear-wheel drive.
8. Two days ago—oh, such a short time!—I left without a care. 8. C
9. The car stopped suddenly, and Oh, was i glad for my seat belt!
10. My favorite verses from that scene are

    see how she leans her cheek upon her hand!
    oh, that i were a glove upon that hand,
    that i might touch that cheek!

DIRECT TEACHING

Modeling and Demonstration

Proper Nouns and Proper Adjectives. Model how to proofread sentences for correct capitalization by using the example *Charles Dickens lived during the victorian era.* First, explain that a proper noun names a particular person, place, thing, or idea, and that a proper adjective is an adjective formed from a proper noun. Next, ask if there are any proper adjectives in the example. [*yes;* victorian] Ask if this adjective needs to be capitalized. [*yes;* Victorian] Point out that proper adjectives should be capitalized like proper nouns. Now, have a volunteer use another example from this chapter to demonstrate how to proofread for correct capitalization.

DIFFERENTIATING INSTRUCTION

English-Language Learners

Spanish. Spanish-speaking students may need extra help with the first part of **Rule 10e** because the first-person pronoun is not capitalized in Spanish.

Proper Nouns and Proper Adjectives

Rules 10f, g *(pp. 248–257)*

OBJECTIVES

- To recognize the correct use of capital letters in sentences
- To write sentences using correct capitalization
- To correct the capitalization of words and phrases

DIRECT TEACHING

Correcting Misconceptions

Capitalizing Direction Words. Students may mistakenly capitalize words indicating direction, such as *north* and *south.* It may help students understand the difference between words used to indicate direction and the same words used to indicate a section of the country by telling them that an article (*a*, *an*, or *the*) will be used before a section of the country, such as *the Wild West.* If there is no article, there should be no capital letter.

DIFFERENTIATING INSTRUCTION

English-Language Learners

Spanish. Because names of nationalities, races and peoples, days of the week, and months of the year are not capitalized in Spanish, you may wish to give Spanish-speaking students extra practice in these areas.

MECHANICS

Reference Note

For more about **common** and **proper nouns,** see page 3. For a discussion of **proper adjectives,** see page 11.

HELP

Proper nouns and proper adjectives sometimes lose their capitals through frequent usage.

EXAMPLES
watt **t**itanic **s**andwich

To find out whether a noun should be capitalized, check in a dictionary. The dictionary will tell you whether a word should always be capitalized or whether it should be capitalized only in certain uses.

COMPUTER TIP

The spellings of personal names can challenge even the best spellchecking software. However, you may be able to customize your spellchecker. If your software allows, add to it any names that you use frequently but have difficulty spelling or capitalizing.

10f. Capitalize proper nouns and proper adjectives.

A ***common noun*** names any one of a group of persons, places, things, or ideas. A ***proper noun*** names a particular person, place, thing, or idea. A ***proper adjective*** is an adjective formed from a proper noun.

Proper nouns are capitalized. Common nouns are generally not capitalized unless they

- begin a sentence
  or
- begin a direct quotation
  or
- are part of a title

Common Nouns	Proper Nouns	Proper Adjectives
a **p**atriot	**T**homas **J**efferson	**J**effersonian ideals
a **c**ountry	**T**urkey	**T**urkish border
a **q**ueen	**Q**ueen **E**lizabeth	**E**lizabethan drama
a **r**eligion	**I**slam	**I**slamic beliefs
a **r**egion	the **S**outhwest	**S**outhwestern cooking

In proper nouns of more than one word, do not capitalize

- short prepositions (generally, ones with fewer than five letters, such as *in*, *on*, and *with*)
- articles (*a, an, the*)
- coordinating conjunctions (*and, but, for, nor, or, so, yet*)
- the sign of the infinitive (*to*)

EXAMPLES Mary, Queen **o**f Scots

Eric **t**he Red

*Romeo **and** Juliet*

"Writing **t**o Persuade"

(1) Capitalize the names of persons and animals.

Given Names	**A**lana	**M**ark	**L**a**V**erne
Surnames	**D**iaz	**C**ollins	**W**illiams
Animals	**T**rigger	**S**ocks	**R**over

RESOURCES

Proper Nouns and Proper Adjectives

Practice

- *Language & Sentence Skills Practice,* pp. 235–243

Differentiating Instruction

- *Developmental Language & Sentence Skills,* pp. 107–116

NOTE For names having more than one part, capitalization may vary.

EXAMPLES **D**e **V**ere — **d**e **l**a **G**arza — **M**c**G**regor — **O'L**eary — **I**bn-**K**haldun — **v**on **B**raun

Always check the spelling of such a name with the person who has that name, or look in a reference source.

(2) Capitalize initials in names and abbreviations that come before or after names.

EXAMPLES **A. E.** Roosevelt — Lewis **F.** Powell, **Jr.** — **Sr.** Gomez — **Ms.** Sonstein — Sabra Santos, **M.D.** — **Dr.** Alan Berg

(3) Capitalize geographical names.

Type of Name	Examples	
Towns and Cities	**P**ortland **D**etroit	**M**exico **C**ity **R**io de **J**aneiro
Counties, Townships, and Provinces	**K**ane **C**ounty **H**ayes **T**ownship **P**lum **B**orough	**E**ast **B**aton **R**ouge **P**arish **Q**uebec **P**rovince **W**illiamson **C**ounty
States	**I**owa **M**issouri	**A**laska **N**orth **C**arolina
Countries	**E**l **S**alvador **N**ew **Z**ealand	**U**nited **A**rab **E**mirates **S**witzerland
Continents	**A**sia	**S**outh **A**merica
Islands	**W**ake **I**sland the **W**est **I**ndies	the **I**sle of **P**alms the **F**lorida **K**eys
Mountains	**M**ount **A**rarat **H**imalayas	the **A**lps the **M**ount of **O**lives
Bodies of Water	**I**ndian **O**cean **A**driatic **S**ea	**R**ed **R**iver **L**ake of the **W**oods

(continued)

Reference Note

For more about **capitalizing titles used with names,** see Rule 10h(1). For information on **punctuating abbreviations** that come before or after names, see page 267.

Reference Note

Abbreviations of the names of states are capitalized. See page 268 for more about **using and punctuating such abbreviations.**

STYLE  **TIP**

Words such as *north, west,* and *southeast* are not capitalized when they indicate direction.

EXAMPLES
farther **n**orth
traveling **s**outheast

However, these words are capitalized when they name a particular region.

EXAMPLES
states in the **N**orthwest
driving in the **S**outh

Differentiating Instruction

English-Language Learners

General Strategies. Students might not realize that certain words in English are proper nouns. Select names that are well known to the students for practice. Include the names of classmates, school personnel, local parks, teams, and malls, as well as major global geographical names.

Spanish. Students may need practice capitalizing street and highway names since these names are not capitalized in Spanish, except at the beginning of a line.

MECHANICS

Mini-Lesson Mechanics

Punctuation and Abbreviations. Remind students that abbreviations usually end with periods. Ask students to volunteer examples of each of the following:

Titles: [*Mr. Brown*]
Personal Names: [*A. J. Foyt*]
Times of Day: [*7:00 A.M.*]
Years: [*A.D. 1776*]
Addresses: [*500 Tamerine Tr.*]

Differentiating Instruction

Advanced Learners

Have students interview speakers of other languages to find out how capitalization rules differ from language to language. Ask students to report their findings to the class. Students might post their findings on the school's Web site.

MECHANICS

Exercise 3

DISTRIBUTED REVIEW

To review phrases and sentence parts, have students find the following items: two-word prepositional phrases [3. *in Oregon*, 8. *of Mexico*, 9. *of California*]; a three-word predicate nominative [4. *1614 Robin Street*].

Reference Note

In addresses, abbreviations such as *St., Blvd., Ave., Dr.,* and *Ln.* are capitalized. For information about **punctuating abbreviations,** see page 267.

STYLE  TIP

Since *rio* is Spanish for "river," *Rio de la Plata River* is redundant. Use only *Rio de la Plata.*

Other terms to watch for are

- *sierra,* Spanish for "mountain range" [Use only *Sierra Nevada,* not *Sierra Nevada Mountains.*]
- *yama,* Japanese for "mountain" [Use only *Fujiyama* or *Mount Fuji,* not *Mount Fujiyama.*]
- *sahara,* Arabic for "desert" [Use only *Sahara,* not *Sahara Desert.*]
- *gobi,* Mongolian for "desert" [Use only *Gobi,* not *Gobi Desert.*]

(continued)

Type of Name	Examples	
Parks and Forests	**C**leburne **S**tate **P**ark the **E**verglades **N**ational **P**ark	**P**almetto **S**tate **P**ark **O**uachita **N**ational **F**orest
Regions	the **W**est the **S**outheast	**G**reat **P**lains **C**orn **B**elt
Other Geographical Names	**S**inai **P**eninsula **C**arlsbad **C**averns	**H**arding **I**cefield **B**ryce **C**anyon
Roads, Streets, and Highways	**S**tate **R**oad 17 **I**nterstate 787	**M**o-**P**ac **E**xpressway **W**est **F**irst **S**treet

NOTE In a street name that is a hyphenated number, the second word begins with a lowercase letter.

EXAMPLE Twenty-**s**econd Street

Words like *city, island, river, street,* and *park* are capitalized when they are part of a name. When words like these are not part of a proper name, they are common nouns and are not capitalized.

Common Nouns	Proper Nouns
life in a big **c**ity	life in **N**ew **Y**ork **C**ity
the **r**iver	the **S**pokane **R**iver
a small **i**sland	**L**iberty **I**sland
on a narrow **s**treet	on **S**tate **S**treet

Exercise 3 Recognizing the Correct Use of Capital Letters

Write the letter of the correctly capitalized sentence in each of the following pairs.

EXAMPLE
1. **a.** Drive Northeast until you get to New Haven.
   b. Drive northeast until you get to New Haven.

1. b

Learning for Life

Finding a Pen Pal. Have students practice capitalization by writing personal ads for pen pals. The following template offers a possible wording:

Are you looking for a pen pal from _________ who belongs to the _________? Do you like listening to _________ and _________? Do you want to travel to _________ to see the _________? If so, then we should be pen pals! Write _________ at _________.

1. a. We went canoeing on the Ohio river.
   (b.) We went canoeing on the Ohio River.
2. a. I read the article on south America.
   (b.) I read the article on South America.
3. (a.) Farewell Bend State Park is in Oregon.
   b. Farewell Bend State park is in Oregon.
4. (a.) Her address is 1614 Robin Street.
   b. Her address is 1614 Robin street.
5. a. I will be at Forty-Second Street and Park Avenue.
   (b.) I will be at Forty-second Street and Park Avenue.
6. (a.) The North Sea is east of Great Britain.
   b. The North sea is East of great Britain.
7. a. Atlanta is a fast-growing City in the south.
   (b.) Atlanta is a fast-growing city in the South.
8. a. Pensacola is on the gulf of Mexico.
   (b.) Pensacola is on the Gulf of Mexico.
9. (a.) The Hawaiian Islands are southwest of California.
   b. The Hawaiian islands are Southwest of California.
10. a. Laredo is on the Mexican Border in Webb county.
    (b.) Laredo is on the Mexican border in Webb County.

(4) Capitalize the names of organizations, teams, government bodies, and institutions.

Type of Name	Examples	
Organizations	**U**nited **N**ations	**B**oy **S**couts of **A**merica
	National **W**eather **S**ervice	**M**illersville **O**rchid **S**ociety
Teams	**G**reen **B**ay **P**ackers	**R**iver **C**ity **A**llstars
	Golden **S**tate **W**arriors	**L**ady **L**obos
		Pitt **P**anthers
Government Bodies	**C**ongress	**P**eace **C**orps
	Federal **T**rade **C**ommission	**S**tate **D**epartment
		Austin **C**ity **C**ouncil
Institutions	**S**mithsonian **I**nstitution	**N**ew **C**ollege
		North **H**igh **S**chool
	Stanford **U**niversity	**B**ellevue **H**ospital

STYLE  TIP

The names of organizations, businesses, and government bodies are often abbreviated to a series of capital letters.

EXAMPLES

National **O**rganization for **W**omen — **NOW**

American **T**elephone & **T**elegraph — **AT&T**

National **S**cience **F**oundation — **NSF**

Usually the letters in such abbreviations are not followed by periods, but always check an up-to-date dictionary or other reliable source to be sure.

MECHANICS

EXTENSION

Critical Thinking

Analysis. To give students practice in analyzing capitalization rules, assign two capitalization rules to each student. Then, ask students to find examples of the use of each rule in newspapers or magazines. While searching for their examples, students might find uses that contradict the capitalization rules they have learned. You may wish to explain that newspapers and magazines often use their own styles, which may differ from standard use.

Tell students who prefer to write free-form ads to include five of the following items in the ad: name or initials, titles, city and state where you live, names of organizations and teams to which you belong, institutions you have attended, and awards you have received.

Students could publish ads on student Web pages, in publications of official pen pal organizations, or in student newspapers.

RETEACHING

Capitalization

If students have difficulty knowing when to capitalize the name of an organization, team, government body, institution, historical event and period, special event, or holiday, have them work in pairs to plan a short article that would include three of these problem areas and make a list of proper nouns, properly capitalized, that they would include.

Oral Practice **Creating Sentences Using Lowercase and Capital Letters**

POSSIBLE ANSWERS

1. During flood season, we can see the raging **river** from the cabin window.
2. The scouts went canoeing on the **Ohio River**.
3. Art club members will stay in a **hotel** when they visit Fort Worth to see the Picasso exhibit.
4. My grandparents once visited the **Ritz Hotel** in London.
5. On which **street** do the Deans live now?
6. My brother plays baseball at the field on **First Street**.
7. The band will play a **march** before Friday's football game.
8. Grandfather's favorite composer is John Philip Sousa, the "**March** King."
9. Because the baseball field faces **west**, fans sometimes see the sun set during the game.
10. When we studied the **West** in geography, we learned that California is known not only for the gold rush, but also for agricultural products.

MECHANICS

NOTE Do not capitalize words such as *democratic, republican,* or *socialist* when they refer to principles or forms of government. Capitalize these words when they refer to specific political parties.

EXAMPLES The new regime promises to institute **d**emocratic reforms.

The **D**emocratic candidate will debate the **R**epublican candidate tonight.

The word *party* in the name of a political party may be capitalized or not; either way is correct. Be consistent in the use of the word throughout a particular piece of writing.

EXAMPLES Libertarian **p**arty *or* **P**arty

Federalist **p**arty *or* **P**arty

(5) Capitalize the names of historical events and periods, special events, holidays, and other calendar items.

Type of Name	Examples	
Historical Events and Periods	**F**rench **R**evolution **A**ge of **R**eason	**W**orld **W**ar II **B**attle of **B**ritain
Special Events	**S**pecial **O**lympics **P**arents' **D**ay	**G**ulf **C**oast **T**rack-and-**F**ield **C**hampionship
Holidays and Other Calendar Items	**T**hursday **D**ecember **N**ew **Y**ear's **D**ay	**V**alentine's **D**ay **L**abor **D**ay **A**ugust

NOTE Do not capitalize the name of a season unless it is personified ("Here is **S**pring in her green dress!") or used in the name of a special event (**F**all **F**estival, **S**pring **J**ubilee).

Oral Practice **Creating Sentences Using Lowercase and Capital Letters**

Correctly use each of the following words in a sentence spoken aloud.

EXAMPLE 1. river

1. *The river is rising.*

1. river	**3.** hotel	**5.** street	**7.** march	**9.** west
2. River	**4.** Hotel	**6.** Street	**8.** March	**10.** West

CONTENT-AREA CONNECTIONS

Geography/Art

Planning a Cruise. Have students plan a cruise to a location they have studied. Suggest that students draw ornamental maps including geographic names that are correctly capitalized.

(6) Capitalize the names of nationalities, races, and peoples.

EXAMPLES Canadian, Korean, Caucasian, Asian, Kurds, Zulu, Seminole

(7) Capitalize the names of religions and their followers, holy days and celebrations, sacred writings, and specific deities.

Type of Name	Examples		
Religions and Followers	Judaism Buddhism	Muslim Taoist	Baptist Quaker
Holy Days and Celebrations	Lent Diwali	Passover Epiphany	Ramadan Rosh Hashanah
Sacred Writings	Bible Talmud	Upanishads Deuteronomy	Koran Dead Sea Scrolls
Specific Deities	Allah	Brahma	God

NOTE The words *god* and *goddess* are not capitalized when they refer to the deities of ancient mythology. However, the names of specific mythological gods and goddesses are capitalized.

EXAMPLE The Greek poet paid tribute to the **g**od **Z**eus.

(8) Capitalize the names of businesses and the brand names of business products.

BUSINESSES Motorola, Inc., Bank of America, Sam's Shoes

BRAND NAMES Formica, Chevrolet, Ace, Kleenex, Whirlpool

NOTE Do not capitalize a common noun that follows a brand name: Formica **c**ountertop, Chevrolet **v**an, Ace **b**andage.

(9) Capitalize the names of planets, stars, constellations, and other heavenly bodies.

Type of Name	Examples		
Planets and Other Heavenly Bodies	Saturn the Milky Way	Orion Vega	Jupiter Proxima Centauri

STYLE TIP

The words *black* and *white* may or may not be capitalized when they refer to races. However, within a particular piece of writing, be consistent in the way you capitalize these words.

STYLE TIP

In some writings, you may notice that pronouns referring to deities are always capitalized as a sign of respect. In other cases, writers capitalize such pronouns only to prevent confusion.

EXAMPLE

The Lord called upon Moses to lead **H**is people out of Egypt. [*His* is capitalized to show that it refers to *the Lord*, not *Moses*.]

STYLE TIP

The word *earth* is not capitalized unless it is used along with the names of other heavenly bodies that are capitalized. The words *sun* and *moon* generally are not capitalized.

DIFFERENTIATING INSTRUCTION

Learners Having Difficulty

Tell students they will work in groups to create stories using proper nouns and proper adjectives. Have each student prepare three slips of paper, each slip indicating a type of name from one of the twelve numbered subrules of **Rule 10f**. (For example, a slip might read *a dog's name, a street name,* or *a state.*)

Place students in groups of five. Have each student draw one of the prepared slips of paper and write for the story a sentence using the type of word indicated on the slip. (For example, for the word type *state*, the sentence might be *When I lived in Rhode Island, I joined a club.*) Have students add to the story until all of the slips have been drawn. Groups should record their narratives on audiotape to play for the class.

HELP

The proper names of vehicles such as boats or cars generally are capitalized: **B**lue **B**ird [boat], **M**ustang [car].

(10) Capitalize the names of ships, trains, aircraft, and spacecraft.

Type of Name	Examples		
Ships, Trains, Aircraft, and Spacecraft	***A**rgo*	***Y**ankee **C**lipper*	***C**olumbia*
	***S**putnik*	***F**lying **S**cotsman*	***T**hunder **B**ird*

(11) Capitalize the names of awards, memorials, and monuments.

Type of Name	Examples	
Awards, Memorials, and Monuments	**N**obel **P**rize	**L**incoln **M**emorial
	Silver **S**tar	**T**omb of the **U**nknown **S**oldier

(12) Capitalize the names of particular buildings and other structures.

Type of Name	Examples		
Buildings and Other Structures	**T**ower of **L**ondon	**P**laza **H**otel	**S**hasta **D**am
	Golden **G**ate **B**ridge	the **A**lamo	**G**reat **W**all of **C**hina
		Fort **K**nox	

NOTE Generally, do not capitalize words like *hotel, theater, college, high school,* and *courthouse* unless they are part of a proper name.

EXAMPLES		
	Jackson **H**igh **S**chool	a **h**igh **s**chool principal
	Copley Square **H**otel	a **h**otel in Boston
	Fox **T**heater	a **t**heater in Dallas
	Victoria County **C**ourthouse	a **c**ourthouse hallway

PRACTICE

Guided and Independent

Exercise 4 You may want to use the first ten items of **Exercise 4** as guided practice and the second ten as independent practice.

HOMEWORK

Exercise 4 Correcting the Capitalization of Words and Phrases

Correct the following words and phrases, using capital letters as needed.

EXAMPLE
1. a methodist minister
1. *a Methodist minister*

1. somewhere between mars and jupiter
2. a shopping center on twenty-third street

3. lafayette park in tallahassee, florida
4. some wheaties cereal
5. jefferson racquet club
6. harvard university
7. at the new jewish synagogue
8. on memorial day
9. an african american
10. the sinking of the *lusitania*
11. making easter baskets for the children
12. a visit to the washington monument
13. seeing venus through a telescope
14. reading a passage from the koran
15. flying in the *spruce goose*
16. to the ritz hotel
17. stories about the Egyptian god ra
18. a hammer from Ridgeway hardware store
19. passed by a dodge minivan
20. taking pictures of the eiffel tower

Review A Identifying and Correcting Errors in Capitalization

Correct the capitalization errors in each of the following sentences by capitalizing and lowercasing letters as needed.

EXAMPLE 1. The earliest African American Folk tales have their roots in africa.

1. folk, Africa

1. Africans who first came to the americas enjoyed folk tales that blended their own african songs with stories they heard here.
2. Before the civil war, African Americans created new tales that reflected their experiences as Slaves and their desire for Freedom.
3. Many of these tales are about Animals, especially the small but clever character named brer rabbit.
4. Zora neale hurston collected a number of these animal stories and published them in *Mules and Men.*
5. Brer rabbit, a character that was especially popular in the south in the 1800s, constantly plays tricks on brer fox and brer wolf.
6. In some later tales, the main Character isn't a rabbit but a slave, john, who outsmarts the slave owner.

DIFFERENTIATING INSTRUCTION

Special Education Students

Because it contains so many errors, **Review A** may be overwhelming to students. Set specific tasks such as "Find and correct errors in place names." Have students work on the exercise with a helper—one error at a time—until all the rules that apply have been covered.

MECHANICS

7. The author virginia hamilton, winner of the newbery medal and the national book award, tells other tales in *The People Could Fly: American Black Folktales.*
8. Both the title of that Book and the Painting on its cover refer to another popular kind of black folk tale that developed during the years of slavery.
9. Can you tell that the People on the book's cover are flying above the Earth?
10. "The People Could Fly" is one of many fantasy tales about enslaved people who use Magic Powers to fly away from their troubles.

10g. **Do not capitalize the names of school subjects, except the names of language classes or course names that contain a number.**

EXAMPLES This year I am taking **g**eometry, **E**nglish, **c**ivics, **D**rafting **I**, and a **f**oreign **l**anguage. Next year I plan to take **A**merican **g**overnment, **E**nglish, **t**rigonometry, **B**iology **I**, and **S**panish.

HELP — Do not capitalize the class names *freshman, sophomore, junior,* or *senior* unless they are part of a proper noun.

EXAMPLES
All **f**reshmen should meet after school to discuss the **F**reshman-**S**ophomore **B**anquet.

Review B Correcting Capitalization Errors in Sentences

Correct the following sentences by changing lowercase letters to capital letters as needed.

EXAMPLE 1. mi kyung's mother told us that buddhism and confucianism have a long history in korea.
1. Mi Kyung's mother told us that Buddhism and Confucianism have a long history in Korea.

1. in tuesday's class, mrs. garcía explained that the diameter of earth is only 405 miles greater than that of venus.
2. this year's freshmen will be required to take more courses in english, science, and math than prior freshmen at briarwood county high school were.
3. in chicago we visited soldier field and the museum of science and industry, which are known all over the world.
4. Aboard the space shuttle *columbia* in january 1986, franklin Chang-Díaz became the first astronaut to send a message in spanish back to earth.
5. are latin and biology the most helpful courses for someone planning to go into medicine?
6. after i went to the mall and the hardware store, i stopped at quik mart on twenty-second street.

DIFFERENTIATING INSTRUCTION

English-Language Learners

General Strategies. For an exercise such as **Review B,** students might benefit from knowing the number of errors in each sentence. They can use the process of elimination to find the proper nouns more easily.

Spanish. In Spanish, proper adjectives are not capitalized. Names of languages are not capitalized except as part of a course title.

MECHANICS

7. we vacationed in the west, stopping to see pikes peak and to go camping and fishing in colorado.
8. in kentucky, one of the border states between the north and the south, you can visit mammoth cave, churchill downs, and the lincoln birthplace national historic site.
9. after labor day last fall, the columbus youth fellowship sponsored a softball tournament at maxwell field.
10. augustus saint-gaudens, a great sculptor who came to the united states from ireland as a child, portrayed abraham lincoln as a tall, serious man standing with his head bowed.

10h. Capitalize titles.

(1) Capitalize a person's title when the title comes before the person's name.

EXAMPLES		
	President Kennedy	**M**r. Nakamura
	Dr. Dooley	**F**riar Tuck
	Professor Simmons	**P**rincipal Phillips
	Mrs. Robinson	**L**ady Jane Grey

Generally, a title that is used alone or following a person's name is not capitalized, especially if the title is preceded by *a* or *the.*

EXAMPLES We saw the **m**ayor at the park.

Daniel Inouye was first elected **s**enator in 1962.

Who was the **q**ueen of England during the Victorian Age?

Titles used alone in direct address, however, generally are capitalized.

EXAMPLES Well, **D**octor, what is your diagnosis?

There's a message for you, **A**dmiral.

Good morning, **M**a'am [or ***m****a'am*].

(2) Capitalize a word showing a family relationship when the word is used before or in place of a person's name, unless the word follows a possessive noun or pronoun.

EXAMPLES **U**ncle Jack, **C**ousin Joshua, **G**randfather,
my **u**ncle Jack, your **c**ousin Joshua, Kim's **g**randfather

Reference Note

For information about **capitalizing** and **punctuating abbreviations,** see pages 249 and 267.

STYLE  TIP

For special emphasis or clarity, writers sometimes capitalize a title used alone or following a person's name.

EXAMPLES

Many young people admire the **M**ayor.

How did the **S**enator vote on this issue?

At the ceremony, the **Q**ueen knighted Paul McCartney.

Titles

Rule 10h *(pp. 257–260)*

OBJECTIVE

- **To correct capitalization errors, including errors in titles**

DIFFERENTIATING INSTRUCTION

English-Language Learners

General Strategies. You may need to explain the term *title* to students. Before you begin your explanation, be sure students understand that this word is used for both people and documents. Drawing a stick figure, a book, and a painting on the chalkboard may help students see how each has a title. (For example, you may write *Dr. Rodriguez* under the stick figure, *Great Expectations* under the book, and *Mona Lisa* under the painting.)

Spanish. The titles of persons are not capitalized before a name in Spanish unless the title is abbreviated. Words showing family relationships also are not capitalized, even when they are used before or in place of a person's name.

With the exception of names and other words normally capitalized, only the first word of a title is capitalized in Spanish (for example, *Cien años de soledad*, or *One Hundred Years of Solitude*, by Gabriel García Márquez).

RESOURCES

Titles

Practice

- *Language & Sentence Skills Practice,* pp. 244–246

Differentiating Instruction

- *Developmental Language & Sentence Skills,* pp. 117–118

MECHANICS

Extension

Relating to Writing

Have students imagine that they have created works like the ones listed on the chart on pp. 258 and 259. Have each student name his or her imagined work, correctly punctuate the title, and write a brief synopsis or description of the work. [*comic strip: "Dogwood"—canine hero is noted for his eating habits and his adventures in space; song: "Cloudy Weekend"—a hip-hop lament about Saturday plans threatened by storms; computer game: "Space Angel"—the object is for angels to reach heaven without being grounded during an intergalactic war.*]

Reference Note

For information on using **italics with titles,** see page 312. For information on using **quotation marks with titles,** see page 320.

HELP

The official title of a book is found on the title page. The official title of a newspaper or other periodical is found on the masthead, which usually appears on the editorial page or the table of contents.

MEETING THE CHALLENGE

Write a one-page biography about your favorite author, artist, filmmaker, or songwriter. Mention at least five titles by your subject, being careful to use proper capitalization. (Also, make sure that the titles are properly italicized or placed in quotation marks.)

Answer

Biographies will vary but should contain at least five properly capitalized titles.

(3) Capitalize the first and last words and all important words in titles and subtitles.

Unimportant words in a title include

- articles: *a, an, the*
- short prepositions (fewer than five letters): *of, to, for, from, in, over*
- coordinating conjunctions: *and, but, for, nor, or, so, yet*
- the sign of the infinitive: *to*

NOTE Capitalize an article (*a, an,* or *the*) at the beginning of a title or subtitle only if it is the first word of the official title or subtitle.

EXAMPLES "An Ancient Gesture" — the *Saturday Review*

The Miami Herald — the *Houston Chronicle*

A Christmas Carol — the *Odyssey*

Type of Name	Examples	
Books	*The Sea Around Us* *Ultimate Visual Dictionary*	*Nisei Daughter* *Island of the Blue Dolphins*
Chapters and Other Parts of Books	"The Circulatory System" "Lesson 5: Manifest Destiny"	Chapter 11 "Unit 3: Poetry"
Periodicals	*The New York Times*	the *Hispanic Review*
Poems	"Woman Work" "Mending Wall"	*The Song of Hiawatha*
Stories	"The Pit and the Pendulum"	"Raymond's Run" "The Eclipse"
Historical Documents	Treaty of Paris The Declaration of Independence	Magna Carta The Emancipation Proclamation
Movies and Videos	*It's a Wonderful Life* *Willy Wonka and the Chocolate Factory*	*Fly Away Home* *Yoga: Beginners' Level*

MINI-LESSON Grammar

Using Prepositions. Before students attempt to capitalize titles that include prepositions, you may wish to review prepositions. Then, give students a list of prepositions. For each preposition, have students write a title including that preposition and using correct capitalization. Students may use actual titles or make up their own.

Type of Name	Examples	
Television and Radio Programs	*Ancient Mysteries*	*60 Minutes*
	Meet the Press	*All Things Considered*
	Law and Order	*Sesame Street*
Plays	*The Three Sisters*	*A Doll's House*
Works of Art	*The Rebel Slave*	*La Primavera*
Musical Works	"The Flight of the Bumblebee"	*Liverpool Oratorio*
		Sweeney Todd
Audiotapes and CDs	*Romantic Adagio*	*Blue*
	Left of the Middle	*This Fire*
	Dos Mundos	*Ray of Light*
Computer Games and Video Games	Sonic the Hedgehog	Sim City
	Logical Journey	Frogger
	Legend of Zelda	X-Men
Cartoons and Comic Strips	*Jump Start*	*Dilbert*
	For Better or Worse	*Daria*
	Scooby Doo	*Peanuts*

Review C Correcting Capitalization Errors

If the capitalization in a word group below is incorrect, rewrite it correctly. If a word group contains no errors, write *C.*

EXAMPLE 1. watched the classic movie *casablanca*

1. watched the classic movie Casablanca

1. mayor Cartwright
2. "Home on The Range"
3. the *Reader's Digest* 3. C
4. visiting Yosemite national park
5. the president of the United States 5. C (*or* President)
6. was a hindu priest
7. saying hello to grandma higgins
8. my Cousin's parents
9. N. Scott Momaday won the Pulitzer Prize. 9. C
10. *the Mystery of Edwin Drood*

[Sample answers: *as*—"I Wandered Lonely as a Cloud"; *before*—"With a Task Before Me"; *of*—"The Gift of the Magi," "The Cask of Amontillado," The Diary of a Young Girl; *on*—"Southbound on the Freeway"; *behind*—"The History Behind the Ballad"]

Differentiating Instruction

Learners Having Difficulty

As an alternative review, give students copies of different kinds of application forms, such as those for jobs, schools, and driver's licenses, to fill out using correct capitalization. Point out that correct capitalization and standard usage will often be important to the people evaluating these types of applications.

Practice

Guided and Independent

Reviews You may wish to have students complete **Review C** as guided practice and **Review D** as independent practice.

HOMEWORK

MECHANICS

Review D Correcting Capitalization Errors in Paragraphs

Correct the sentences in the following paragraphs by capitalizing or lowercasing letters as needed. If a sentence is already correct, write *C*.

EXAMPLE [1] Louis armstrong was one of america's most gifted Jazz Vocalists and Performers.

1. *Louis Armstrong was one of America's most gifted jazz vocalists and performers.*

1. C

16. C

[1] In social studies last week, we learned all about Louis Armstrong. [2] Nicknamed "satchmo," Armstrong was born in poverty in new Orleans in august 1901. [3] He learned to play the Cornet, a kind of small trumpet, while serving a sentence for delinquency. [4] While growing up, he also played the trumpet on the paddleboats that sailed on the Mississippi river.

[5] In 1922, his favorite bandleader, king Oliver, asked him to play second trumpet in a band in chicago. [6] King Oliver's band was called the creole jazz band. [7] While performing with the Creole Jazz band, Armstrong was coached by the band's classically trained pianist, Lil hardin, who became mrs. Armstrong in 1924. [8] Armstrong soon left Oliver and joined the Fletcher henderson band in New York city.

[9] Louis Armstrong soon established himself as a great Trumpeter and Vocalist. [10] One of his innovations was scat, a vocal technique in which a Musician's rhythmic, wordless voice imitates the sound of instruments. [11] This technique first appeared in recordings such as "Heebie jeebies," issued under the band name hot Five. [12] The scat technique was later imitated by other famous african american singers such as ella Fitzgerald and Al jarreau.

[13] As a Composer, Armstrong was known for such classic jazz songs as "dippermouth blues" and "Wild Man Blues." [14] Armstrong's outgoing personality and Style attracted new audiences to jazz. [15] By the Mid-1930's, Armstrong had become a popular entertainer. [16] He retained his brilliance as a jazz trumpeter, however. [17] After world war II, he formed a series of small bands. [18] When the U.S. state department made Armstrong a goodwill ambassador, it honored his worldwide reputation as a generous and well-liked personality. [19] In his capacity as Ambassador, he traveled widely around the world. [20] Louis Armstrong died at his home in queens, New York, in July 1971.

MECHANICS

CONTENT-AREA CONNECTIONS

Music

Capitalizing Song Lyrics. To review capitalization, have each student listen to a favorite song and write down the lyrics of one verse, focusing on capitalizing words correctly. Then, ask students to list which capitalization rules they used for each line.

Numerals in brackets refer to rules tested by the items in the Chapter Review.

1. *or* C [10h(1)]
2. [10h(3)]
3. C [10a, f(3)]
4. [10f(6), f]
5. [10f, f(7)]
6. [10f(3)]
7. [10h(2)]
8. [10h(3)]
9. [10f]
10. [10f(4, 3)]
11. [10f(3)]
12. [10f(5, 4)]
13. [10h(3)]
14. [10f(5, 7)]
15. [10f(4)]
16. [10f(3)]
17. C [10a, f(5, 6)]

Chapter Review

A. Correcting Sentences That Contain Errors in Capitalization

Most of the following sentences contain at least one error in capitalization. Write each sentence, capitalizing or lowercasing letters where necessary. If a sentence is already correct, write *C*.

1. The only U.S. President who was never elected was Gerald Ford.
2. The program was titled *Animals of the serengeti plain.*
3. Would you say that the South and the Northeast are the regions of the United States with the most distinctive accents?
4. Although the wheel was unknown to the inca people, their Empire contained many miles of roads.
5. Students at a yeshiva, or Jewish Seminary, study the torah.
6. The highest peak in the alps is Mont Blanc, on the French-italian border, or so I'm told.
7. I later learned that uncle Steve had been taking three courses in night school.
8. Henri Matisse's early paintings include *A glimpse of Notre Dame in the late afternoon* and *Green stripe.*
9. My aunt Terry is an Editor at a large textbook Publishing Company in Texas.
10. The united nations building is on the east River in New York city.
11. The letter was mistakenly delivered to 1408 West Twenty-third Street instead of 1408 east Twenty-third Street.
12. Uncle Matt served in the Vietnam war before he studied medicine at Iowa state university.
13. While recovering from surgery, Mr. Gomez watched *Good morning, America* every day on television.
14. What is the date of easter Sunday this year?
15. The woman from the U.S. department of labor was sent to our community hospital when she became sick.
16. The *Queen Elizabeth 2* was delayed by serious storms while crossing the Atlantic ocean.
17. Last Thursday, July 4, we Americans celebrated Independence Day.

ASSESSING

Monitoring Progress

Chapter Review. To assess student progress, you may want to compare the types of items missed on the **Diagnostic Preview** to those missed on the **Chapter Review.** If students have not made significant progress, you may want to refer them to **Chapter 17: Correcting Common Errors, Exercises 26, 27,** and **28** for additional practice.

MECHANICS

RESOURCES

Capital Letters

Review

- *Language & Sentence Skills Practice,* pp. 247–249

Assessment

- *Holt Handbook Chapter Tests with Answer Key,* pp. 19–20, 52

18. [10h(3)]
19. [10h(1)]
20. [10f(5, 7)]

18. The tenor sang "America the beautiful" at the dedication of the new monument.

19. Did you know, professor, that the *Mona Lisa* will be shown this year at the Metropolitan Museum of Art?

20. On Thanksgiving day, my family thanks god for many blessings.

B. Correcting Errors in Capitalization

Correct the errors in capitalization in the following paragraph by capitalizing or lowercasing words as needed.

21. [10a]
22. [10f]
23. [10f]
24. [10f(3)]
25. [10f(4), h(1), f]
26. [10f]
27. [10f]
28. [10h(1)]
29. [10f(4)]
30. [10f]

[21] almost everybody has heard of pasteurization, but how many people know what it is, or who originated it? **[22]** The French Chemist Louis Pasteur developed the process, which involves destroying disease-causing microorganisms by applying heat. **[23]** That was only one of many accomplishments of this Scientific Genius. **[24]** Born in 1822 in a small town in Eastern France, he made his first scientific discovery at the age of 26. **[25]** As his reputation grew, he was elected to the academy of Scientists in Paris and named Director of Scientific studies at one of the Capital City's most prestigious schools. **[26]** Pasteur's discovery that Microorganisms can cause disease led to recognition of the importance of vaccination. **[27]** The Great Scientist developed vaccines for rabies, anthrax, and a form of Cholera found in farmyard fowl. **[28]** Thanks to the support of emperor Napoleon III, a special laboratory was created for Pasteur. **[29]** In 1874, the French parliament granted him a lifetime stipend, and the Pasteur institute was inaugurated in Paris a few years before he died. **[30]** His discoveries were crucial, but perhaps Pasteur's greatest contribution to Science was his new way of looking at things.

C. Proofreading for Correct Capitalization

Correct the following word groups, using capital letters as needed.

31. [10f(3)]
32. [10f(6)]
33. [10f(10)]
34. [10f(12)]
35. [10f(5, 7)]

31. the cities of san miguel and cuernavaca

32. an irish american

33. the great ship *titanic*

34. at the hotel bristol

35. on christmas day

MECHANICS

36. a call from uncle Ernesto
37. smith and garcia, inc.
38. gulf of mexico
39. southwest texas state university
40. whoever won the nobel prize
41. driving a dodge colt
42. zilker park in austin, texas
43. sarge's deli on third avenue
44. on labor day
45. the greek god apollo

36. [10h(2)]
37. [10f(8)]
38. [10f(3)]
39. [10f(4)]
40. [10f(11)]
41. [10f(8)]
42. [10f(3)]
43. [10h(8, 3)]
44. [10f(5)]
45. [10f(6), (7)]

Writing Application

Using Capital Letters Correctly in a Paragraph

Proper Nouns Your school's language club plans to publish a booklet about foreign cities that most interest students. Write a paragraph telling about one city and its major attractions.

Prewriting Choose a foreign city that interests you, and jot down the reasons you find it interesting. You may want to gather some information about it from encyclopedias, travel books or brochures, and magazine or newspaper articles. Make a list of the city's major attractions.

Writing As you write your first draft, be sure to include information about the city's location and historical or cultural importance.

Revising Ask a friend who is unfamiliar with the city to read your paragraph. Does the information you have presented make your friend want to visit the city? Add or delete details to make your writing more interesting and informative.

Publishing Be sure that you have correctly capitalized geographical names and the names of businesses, institutions, places, and events. Pay particular attention to the spelling of foreign words. With your teacher's permission, post your paragraph on the class bulletin board or Web page.

APPLICATION

Writing Application

Prewriting Tip. You may wish to have students brainstorm for cities about which they would like to write. Some students might want to make up cities or places to visit. Encourage students to use their imaginations and to include details to describe each place fully to give the reader a clear picture of what the city is like.

Prewriting Tip. To help students decide which city to choose, have them analyze and evaluate other students' traveling interests. The booklet should contain information about cities that have attractions of interest to other teenagers. You may want to suggest to students that they poll their peers outside class to decide which cities would be appropriate to include in the booklet.

Scoring Rubric. While you will want to pay particular attention to students' use of capitalization, you will also want to evaluate overall writing performance. You may want to give a split score to indicate development and clarity of the composition as well as skill in capitalization.

CHAPTER 11

INTRODUCING THE CHAPTER

- This chapter discusses the rules for punctuating sentences with end marks and commas. The first two sections present the use of end marks in sentences classified according to purpose and the use of periods with abbreviations.
- The third section explains the use of commas in series, independent clauses, and with introductory and interrupting elements. It also explains conventional uses of commas.
- The chapter concludes with a **Chapter Review** including a **Writing Application** feature that asks students to write directions using commas correctly.
- For help in integrating the chapter with writing assignments, use the **Teaching Strands** chart on pp. T24–T25.

CHAPTER 11

Punctuation

End Marks, Abbreviations, and Commas

Diagnostic Preview

Correcting Sentences by Adding Periods, Question Marks, Exclamation Points, and Commas

Write the following paragraphs, adding periods, question marks, exclamation points, and commas where necessary.

Optional commas are underscored.

EXAMPLE **[1]** Computers therefore are not my cup of tea

1. Computers, therefore, are not my cup of tea.

Numerals in brackets refer to rules tested by the items in the Diagnostic Preview.

1. [11i(4), a]
2. [11i(3), g, a]
3. Ph.D. *or* PhD [11j(1), e, k(3), a]
4. [11j(1), f, a]
5. [11f(2), a]
6. [11g, a]
7. [11e, h, a]
8. [11i(3), a]
9. [11h, a]
10. ! *or* . [11c *or* a]
11. [11i(2), a]
12. [11 f, a]

[1] Although TV commercials tell you otherwise, computers are not for everyone. [2] One day in the showroom of a computer store, I stared at a personal computer for more than half an hour, but I was still unable to locate the on-off switch. [3] The demonstrator, Pearl Rangely, PhD., tried her best to be helpful. [4] A computer consultant, she quickly explained the functions of various switches, buttons, and boxes. [5] She pressed keys, she flashed words on the screen, and she pushed around the mouse very quickly. [6] I was confused and puzzled and frustrated, yet I was also fascinated.

[7] Dr. Rangely, who had often encountered confused consumers before, told me that I had a "terminal" phobia. [8] With a frown, I asked her what that meant. [9] She replied, grinning broadly, that it was the fear that bits and bytes can actually bite. [10] What a comedian she was! [11] Totally disenchanted, I left the store.

[12] I headed straight for the library to check out everything that I could find about computers: books, magazines, catalogs, and pamphlets.

CHAPTER RESOURCES

Internet

- Web resources: go.hrw.com

go.hrw.com

Practice & Review

- *Language & Sentence Skills Practice,* pp. 255–271
- *Language & Sentence Skills Practice Answer Key,* pp. 104–111

Application & Enrichment

- *Language & Sentence Skills Practice,* pp. 254, 272, 273–274, 275
- *Language & Sentence Skills Practice Answer Key,* pp. 104, 111–112

[13] For example, I read *The Soul of a New Machine*, a fascinating book written by Tracy Kidder. [14] When I had finished the book, I knew about input, output, high-level languages, and debugging. [15] Armed with this knowledge, I confidently returned to the store on Friday, March 13. [16] Well, the same demonstrator was there, smiling like a Cheshire cat. [17] I rattled off several technical questions that I think must have surprised her. [18] By the end of a single afternoon, Dr. Rangely had taught me something about every computer in the store. [19] I left, however, without asking one simple, embarrassing question. [20] Could you please tell me where the on-off switch is?

13. [11j(3,1), a]
14. [11i(4), f, a]
15. [11i(2), k(1), a]
16. [11i(1), h, a]
17. [11a]
18. [11i(3), e, a]
19. [11j(3), f(3), a]
20. [11b]

End Marks

Sentences

End marks—periods, question marks, and exclamation points—are used to indicate the purpose of a sentence.

11a. **A statement (or declarative sentence) is followed by a period.**

EXAMPLES Nancy López won the golf tournament.

What Balboa saw below was the Pacific Ocean.

Flora wondered who had already gone.

NOTE Notice in the third example that a declarative sentence containing an indirect question is followed by a period. (An ***indirect question*** is one that does not use the speaker's exact words.) Be sure to distinguish between a declarative sentence that contains an indirect question and an interrogative sentence, which asks a direct question.

INDIRECT QUESTION I wondered what makes that sound. [declarative]
DIRECT QUESTION What makes that sound? [interrogative]

11b. **A question (or interrogative sentence) is followed by a question mark.**

EXAMPLES Do you know American Sign Language?

Why don't you ask Eileen?

Who wrote this note? Did you?

STYLE TIP

As you speak, the tone and pitch of your voice, the pauses in your speech, and the gestures and expressions you use all help make your meaning clear. In writing, marks of punctuation, such as end marks and commas, show readers where these verbal and nonverbal cues occur.

Punctuation alone won't clarify the meaning of a confusing sentence, however. If you have trouble punctuating a sentence, check to see whether rewording it would help express your meaning more clearly.

Reference Note

For information about how **sentences** are **classified according to purpose,** see Chapter 2.

Differentiating Instruction

- *Developmental Language & Sentence Skills,* pp. 119–128
- *Developmental Language & Sentence Skills Guided Practice Teacher's Notes and Answer Key,* pp. 27–28

Assessment

- *Holt Handbook Chapter Tests with Answer Key,* pp. 21–22, 52

ASSESSING

Entry-Level Assessment

Diagnostic Preview. Although your ninth-graders may not have trouble with end marks, the results of the **Diagnostic Preview** may indicate a need to review the comma rules in this chapter. You may want to have each student make a chart including the rules he or she has not mastered. Students may refer to their charts as guides to areas for additional study and for problem areas to target when proofreading writing assignments.

MECHANICS

End Marks

Rules 11a–d *(pp. 265–267)*

OBJECTIVE

- **To correct sentences by adding end marks and to identify kinds of sentences**

PRETEACHING

Lesson Starter

Prior Knowledge. Divide students into small groups, and ask each group to compose a statement, a question, an exclamation, and a command, punctuating each sentence correctly. Have students write their sentences on a transparency or on the chalkboard, and have a group spokesperson explain to the class the reasons why each punctuation mark is used.

Differentiating Instruction

English-Language Learners

General Strategies. Because the question mark takes different forms in languages other than English, students may make punctuation errors when writing in English. For example, Spanish uses an inverted question mark at the beginning of a question (¿Where is Bill?); Greek uses a semicolon to indicate a question (Where is Bill;).

You may want to ask students to give all of their writing assignments one proofreading pass just to check the punctuation of questions.

Hmong. In Hmong, interrogatives often are indicated by the inclusion of the word *puas,* meaning "what," within the body of a sentence rather than through the use of end punctuation. Therefore, some Hmong speakers will use periods where question marks are appropriate or will include the word *what* inappropriately within their sentences. Remind students of the differences between declarative, imperative, and interrogative sentences, and point out that written English, in part, relies upon end punctuation to determine those sentence functions.

MECHANICS

Extension

Critical Thinking

Analysis. Students may be aware that publications sometimes customize punctuation rules. Have students use periodicals, particularly advertisements, to find sentences ending in exclamation points. Students should contribute their samples to a class list. Ask the class to use **Rules 11c** and **11d** to analyze sentences and to form generalizations about the current commercial use of exclamations and imperative sentences.

STYLE  TIP

Sometimes declarative and interrogative sentences show such strong feeling that they are more like exclamations than like statements or questions. In such cases, an exclamation point should be used instead of a period or a question mark.

EXAMPLES
Here comes the bus!
Can't you speak up!

STYLE  TIP

An interjection is generally set off from the rest of the sentence by a comma or an exclamation point.

EXAMPLES
Well, I guess so.
Ouch! That hurt.

Reference Note

For more about **interjections,** see page 33.

STYLE  TIP

Sometimes a command or request is expressed as if it were a question. The meaning, however, may be imperative, in which case a period or exclamation point is used.

EXAMPLES
May I say a few words now.
Will you leave me alone!

A direct question may have the same word order as a declarative sentence. Since it is a question, it is followed by a question mark.

EXAMPLES You know American Sign Language?
You're not asking Eileen?

11c. An exclamation (or exclamatory sentence) is followed by an exclamation point.

EXAMPLES Hurrah! The rain stopped!
Ouch!
Look out!

11d. A command or request (or imperative sentence) is followed by either a period or an exclamation point.

When an imperative sentence makes a request, it is generally followed by a period. When an imperative sentence expresses a strong command, an exclamation point is generally used.

EXAMPLES Please answer my question. [request]
Turn off your radio. [command]
Answer me right now! [strong command]

Exercise 1 Using Periods, Question Marks, and Exclamation Points

Write the following sentences, adding periods, question marks, and exclamation points where they are needed. Identify each sentence as *declarative, imperative, interrogative,* or *exclamatory.*

EXAMPLE 1. Are you familiar with lacrosse, a field game
1. Are you familiar with lacrosse, a field game?—interrogative

1. Do you know how to play lacrosse? 1. int.
2. On TV last night there was a segment on teams playing lacrosse. 2. dec.
3. What a rough sport lacrosse must be! 3. exc.
4. Did you know that North American Indians developed this game? 4. int.
5. Before Columbus came to the Americas in A.D. 1492, the Iroquois were playing lacrosse in what is now upper New York State and Canada. 5. dec.
6. Do you realize that this makes lacrosse the oldest organized sport in America? 6. int.

RESOURCES

End Marks

Practice

- *Language & Sentence Skills Practice,* p. 255

Differentiating Instruction

- *Developmental Language & Sentence Skills,* pp. 119–120

7. Lacrosse is played by two opposing teams. 7. dec.
8. Use a stick to catch, carry, and throw the ball. 8. imp.
9. The name of the game comes from *la crosse,* French for a bishop's staff, which the lacrosse stick resembles. 9. dec.
10. Lacrosse is especially popular in Canada, the British Isles, and Australia, and it is played in the United States, too. 10. dec.

Abbreviations

11e. Use a period after certain abbreviations.

An ***abbreviation*** is a shortened form of a word or word group. Notice how periods are used with abbreviations in the examples in this part of the chapter.

Personal Names

Abbreviate given names only if the person is most commonly known by the abbreviated form of the name.

EXAMPLES Ida **B.** Wells **T. H.** White **M.F.K.** Fisher

Titles

(1) Abbreviate social titles whether used before the full name or before the last name alone.

EXAMPLES **Mr.** Tom Evans **Ms.** Jody Aiello **Mrs.** Dupont
Sr. (Señor) Cadenas **Sra.** (Señora) Garza **Dr.** O'Nolan

(2) You may abbreviate civil and military titles used before full names or before initials and last names. Spell such titles out before last names used alone.

EXAMPLES **Sen.** Kay Bailey Hutchison **Senator** Hutchison
Prof. E. M. Makowski **Professor** Makowski
Brig. Gen. Norman Schwarzkopf **Brigadier General** Schwarzkopf

(3) Abbreviate titles and academic degrees that follow proper names.

EXAMPLES Hank Williams, **Jr.** Peter Garcia, **M.D.**

STYLE TIP

Only a few abbreviations are appropriate in the text of a formal paper written for a general audience. In tables, notes, and bibliographies, abbreviations are used more freely in order to save space.

STYLE TIP

Leave a space between two initials, but not between three or more.

HELP

If a statement ends with an abbreviation, do not use an additional period as an end mark. However, do use a question mark or an exclamation point if one is needed.

EXAMPLES
Mrs. Tavares just received her Ph.D.
When did she receive her Ph.D.?

Abbreviations

Rule 11e *(pp. 267–271)*

OBJECTIVE

- To correct errors in the use of abbreviations in sentences

DIRECT TEACHING

End Marks and Abbreviations

Activity. To teach students to use end marks and abbreviations, try a team game. Divide the class into five teams. Specify a sentence type and a specific abbreviation to be used in that sentence. You could combine the following types:

Sentence Type	Abbreviation
statement	personal name
question	title with name
exclamation	state
request	address
command	organization/ company
	time
	unit of measure

Team members may confer for thirty seconds; then, each team must send a member to the chalkboard to write the sentence. Give a point each for the correct sentence type, end mark, and abbreviation. Continue the game by having every student take a turn at the chalkboard.

MECHANICS

RESOURCES

Abbreviations

Practice

- *Language & Sentence Skills Practice,* pp. 256–259

Differentiating Instruction

- *Developmental Language & Sentence Skills,* pp. 119–120

Extension

Abbreviations

Tell students they will be creating an abbreviation game based on a television game show. Assign small groups of writers to investigate an assigned category, such as military titles or sports abbreviations.

Writing groups will each develop ten questions, such as "What is the abbreviation for *General*?" or "What does the acronym *scuba* stand for?" (For help developing questions and answers, refer students to a dictionary of acronyms and abbreviations, if available.)

Once questions have been created, assign values of 10, 20, 30, 40, or 50 points, depending on difficulty. Then, choose three contestants, a moderator to read the questions, and a judge with the answers. Allow a set of contestants to play the game for ten minutes; then, introduce a new set of contestants. Allow the game to continue until all students have had a chance to play and all questions have been asked.

After students have created their games, ask them to consider the following questions:

Which abbreviation seemed most difficult? Why?

What did I learn through the process of forming questions?

MECHANICS

NOTE Do not include the titles *Mr., Mrs., Ms.,* or *Dr.* when you use a professional title or degree after a name.

EXAMPLE **Dr.** Joan West *or* Joan West, **M.D.** [*not* Dr. Joan West, M.D.]

Agencies and Organizations

An ***acronym*** is a word formed from the first (or first few) letters of a series of words. Acronyms are written without periods. After spelling out the first use of the names of agencies and organizations, abbreviate these names and other things commonly known by their acronyms.

EXAMPLE My older sister works for the **National Institute of Mental Health (NIMH).** She is compiling data for one of **NIMH**'s behavioral studies.

AMA American Medical Association
HUD (Department of) Housing and Urban Development
CPU Central Processing Unit
RAM random-access memory
USAF United States Air Force
UN United Nations
NEA National Endowment for the Arts
FM Frequency Modulation

NOTE A few acronyms, such as *radar, laser,* and *sonar,* are now considered common nouns. They do not need to be spelled out on first use and are no longer capitalized. When you're not sure whether an acronym should be capitalized, look it up in a recent dictionary.

Geographical Terms

In text, spell out names of states and other political units whether they stand alone or follow other geographical terms. Abbreviate such names in tables, notes, and bibliographies.

TEXT On our vacation to Canada, we visited Victoria, the capital of British Columbia.

CHART

London, U.K.	Tucson, Ariz.
Victoria, B.C.	Fresno, Calif.

268 Punctuation

FOOTNOTE [3]The Public Library in Annaville, Mich., has an entire collection of Smyth's folios.

BIBLIOGRAPHY ENTRY "The Last Hurrah." Editorial. *Star-Ledger* [Newark, N.J.] 29 Aug. 1991: 30.

NOTE Include the traditional abbreviation for the District of Columbia, *D.C.*, with the city name *Washington* to distinguish it from the state of Washington.

In text, spell out every word in an address. Such words may be abbreviated in letter and envelope addresses and in tables and notes.

TEXT We live at 413 West Maple Street.

ENVELOPE 413 **W.** Maple **St.**

NOTE Two-letter state abbreviations without periods are used only when the ZIP Code is included.

EXAMPLE Cincinnati, **OH** 45233

Time

Abbreviate the frequently used era designations A.D. and B.C. The abbreviation A.D. stands for the Latin phrase *anno Domini*, meaning "in the year of the Lord." It is used with dates in the Christian era. When used with a specific year number, A.D. precedes the number. When used with the name of a century, it follows the name.

EXAMPLES In **A.D.** 476, the last Western Roman emperor, Romulus Augustulus, was overthrown by Germanic tribes.

The legends of King Arthur may be based on the life of a real British leader of the sixth century **A.D.**

The abbreviation B.C., which stands for "before Christ," is used for dates before the Christian era. It follows either a specific year number or the name of a century.

EXAMPLES Homer's epic poem the *Iliad* was probably composed between 800 and 700 **B.C.**

The poem describes battles that probably occurred around the twelfth century **B.C.**

STYLE TIP

In your reading, you may come across the abbreviations *C.E.* and *B.C.E.* These abbreviations stand for *Common Era* and *Before Common Era.* These terms are sometimes used in place of *A.D.* and *B.C.*, respectively, and are written after the date.

EXAMPLES
752 **C.E.**
1550 **B.C.E.**

DIFFERENTIATING INSTRUCTION

Advanced Learners

Even the ancient Egyptians used abbreviations. The hieroglyphic for the first sound in a word could stand for the word itself.

Abbreviations were common in ancient Greek and Latin. One two-thousand-year-old Latin abbreviation, INRI, which stands for *Iesus Nazarenus Rex Iudaeorum* (Jesus of Nazareth, King of the Jews), is still familiar today. Similarly, the Latin abbreviations *A.D. (anno Domini,* "the year of our Lord"); *e.g.* (*exempli gratia,* "for the sake of example"); and *i.e.* (*id est,* "that is") were used by medieval scribes and are still used today.

For a medieval scribe, abbreviations helped conserve the valuable parchment on which texts were written. Then, as now, abbreviations saved time and effort.

STYLE TIP

Do not use the words *morning, afternoon,* or *evening* with numerals followed by *A.M.* or *P.M.*

INCORRECT
The next bus for Roanoke leaves at 1:30 P.M. in the afternoon.

CORRECT
The next bus for Roanoke leaves at **1:30 P.M.** (or **one-thirty in the afternoon**).

In regular text, spell out the names of months and days whether they appear alone or in dates. Both types of names may be abbreviated in tables, notes, and bibliographies.

TEXT Please join us on Thursday, March 21, to celebrate Grandma and Grandpa's anniversary.

NOTE Thurs**.**, Mar**.** 21

Abbreviate the designations for the two halves of the day measured by clock time. The abbreviation *A.M.* stands for the Latin phrase *ante meridiem,* meaning "before noon." The abbreviation *P.M.* stands for *post meridiem,* meaning "after noon." Both abbreviations follow the numerals designating the specific time.

EXAMPLE My mom works four days a week, from 8:00 **A.M.** until 6:00 **P.M.**

Units of Measurement

Abbreviations for units of measurement are usually written without periods. However, do use a period with the abbreviation for *inch* (*in.*) to prevent confusing it with the word *in*.

EXAMPLES mm, kg, ml, tsp, doz, yd, ft, lb

In regular text, spell out the names of units of measurement whether they stand alone or follow a spelled-out number or a numeral. Such names may be abbreviated in tables and notes when they follow a numeral.

TEXT The speed limit here is fifty-five **miles per hour** [not *mph*].

The cubicle measured ten **feet** [not *ft*] by twelve.

TABLE

1 **tsp** pepper	97° **F**
12 **ft** 6 **in.**	2 **oz** flour

Exercise 2 Using Abbreviations

Rewrite the following sentences, correcting errors in the use of abbreviations. Answers may vary.

EXAMPLE **1.** Hillary Clinton was born in Chicago, IL.
1. Hillary Clinton was born in Chicago, Illinois.

1. The flight for Montevideo departs at 11:15 A.M. ~~in the morning.~~

MECHANICS

2. Julius Caesar was assassinated in the Roman Forum in B.C. 44.
3. Harun ar-Rashid, whose reign is associated with the Arabian Nights, ruled as caliph of Baghdad from 786 to 809 A.D..
4. The Mississippi River flows from Lake Itasca, MN, all the way to the Gulf of Mexico at Port Eads, LA. 4. Minnesota/Louisiana
5. I will be leaving soon to visit Mr. Nugent on Elm St. in New Paltz, NY. 5. Street/New York
6. The Fbi. is the chief investigative branch of the U.S. Department of Justice. 6. FBI
7. The keynote speaker was Dr. Matthew Villareal, Ph.D.
8. We will meet at 4:00 P.M..
9. I wrote "56 in." in the blank labeled "height."
10. G. Washington was the first president of the United States. 10. George

Review A Correcting Sentences by Adding Periods, Question Marks, and Exclamation Points

Write the following sentences, adding periods, question marks, and exclamation points as needed.

EXAMPLE 1. Does Josh come from Chicago
1. Does Josh come from Chicago?

1. What a great car that is!
2. Whose car is that?
3. We asked who owned that car.
4. Roman troops invaded Britain in 54 B.C. 4. [*or* BC]
5. By A.D. 809, Baghdad was already an important city. 5. [*or* AD]
6. Dr. Edward Jenner gave the first vaccination against smallpox in 1796.
7. Why do so many children enjoy using computers?
8. Please explain why so many children enjoy using computers.
9. When did Alan Keyes run for president?
10. Terrific! Here's another coin for my collection. 10. [*or* !]

Commas

If you fail to use necessary commas, you may confuse your reader.

CONFUSING The friends I have invited are Ruth Ann Jerry Lee Derrick Martha and Julie. [How many friends?]

CLEAR The friends I have invited are Ruth Ann, Jerry Lee, Derrick, Martha, and Julie. [five friends]

MECHANICS

Commas

Rules 11f–l *(pp. 271–290)*

OBJECTIVES

- To correct sentences and write by using commas in series
- To correct sentences by adding commas between independent clauses
- To use commas correctly in sentences with nonessential and essential clauses
- To use commas correctly in sentences with participial phrases
- To use commas correctly in sentences with introductory elements
- To use commas correctly in sentences with appositives and appositive phrases
- To use commas correctly in sentences with words used in direct address
- To use commas correctly in sentences with parenthetical expressions

MECHANICS

DIRECT TEACHING

Modeling and Demonstration

Commas. Model how to proofread sentences for correct use of commas by using the example *All my relatives friends classmates and teachers came to the performance.* Ask if there is a series of three or more items in the sentence. [*yes;* relatives, friends, classmates, teachers] Next, ask if all the items in the series are joined by *and*, *or*, or *nor*. [*no*] Therefore, the items in the series *relatives, friends, classmates, teachers* need to be separated by commas. Now, have a volunteer use another example from this chapter to demonstrate how to proofread sentences for correct use of commas.

Items in a Series

11f. Use commas to separate items in a series.

Notice in the following examples that the number of commas in a series is one fewer than the number of items in the series.

EXAMPLES All my cousins**,** aunts**,** and uncles came to our family reunion. [words in a series]

The children played in the yard**,** at the playground**,** and by the pond. [phrases in a series]

Those who had flown to the reunion**,** who had driven many miles**,** or who had even taken time off from their jobs were glad that they had made the effort to be there. [subordinate clauses in a series]

STYLE TIP

Because using the final comma is never wrong, some writers prefer always to use the comma before the *and* in a series. Follow your teacher's instructions on this point.

When the last two items in a series are joined by *and*, the comma before the *and* is sometimes omitted if the comma is not necessary to make the meaning clear.

CLEAR WITH COMMA OMITTED	The salad contained lettuce, tomatoes, onions, cucumbers, carrots and radishes.
NOT CLEAR WITH COMMA OMITTED	Our school newspaper has editors for news, sports, humor, features and art. [How many editors are there, four or five? Does one person serve as a features and art editor, or is an editor needed for each job?]
CLEAR WITH COMMA INCLUDED	Our school newspaper has editors for news, sports, humor, features**,** and art. [five editors]

NOTE Some words—such as *bread and butter, rod and reel, table and chairs*—are used in pairs and may be considered one item in a series.

EXAMPLE Our collection includes pop, reggae, mariachi, **rhythm and blues,** and hip-hop music.

(1) If all items in a series are joined by *and, or,* or *nor,* do not use commas to separate them.

EXAMPLES I need tacks **and** nails **and** a hammer.

Sam **or** Carlos **or** Yolanda will be able to baby-sit tomorrow.

Neither horses **nor** elephants **nor** giraffes are carnivorous.

RESOURCES

Commas

Practice

- *Language & Sentence Skills Practice,* pp. 260–268

Differentiating Instruction

- *Developmental Language & Sentence Skills,* pp. 121–128

(2) **Short independent clauses may be separated by commas.**

EXAMPLE The engine roared, the wheels spun, and a cloud of dust swirled behind the sports car.

NOTE Sentences that contain more than one independent clause are ***compound*** or ***compound-complex sentences.***

COMPOUND The Wilsons grow organic vegetables, and they sell them at the farmers' market.

COMPOUND-COMPLEX When the weather is bad, the dog hides under the bed, and the cat retreats to my closet.

(3) **Use commas to separate two or more adjectives preceding a noun.**

EXAMPLE Are you going to that hot, crowded, noisy mall?

When the last adjective in a series is thought of as part of the noun, the comma before the adjective is omitted.

EXAMPLES I study in our small **dining room.**

Let's have our picnic under that lovely, shady **fruit tree.**

Compound nouns like *dining room* and *fruit tree* are considered single units—the two words act as one part of speech.

NOTE If one of the words modifies another modifier, do not separate those two words with a comma.

EXAMPLE Do you like this **dark blue** sweater?

Exercise 3 Correcting Sentences by Adding Commas

Write each series in the following sentences, adding commas where needed. Optional commas are underscored.

EXAMPLE **1.** Rita plays soccer volleyball and softball.

1. soccer, volleyball, and softball

1. Dr. Charles Drew worked as a surgeon, developed new ways of storing blood, and was the first director of the Red Cross blood bank program.
2. I am going to take English, science, social studies, and algebra.
3. The loud, insistent smoke alarm woke us just before dawn.

Reference Note

Independent clauses in a series can be separated by semicolons. For more about this use of **semicolons,** see page 298.

Reference Note

For more information about **compound** and **compound-complex sentences,** see page 109.

Reference Note

For more information on **compound nouns,** see page 4.

Differentiating Instruction

Learners Having Difficulty

Students will probably be familiar with the use of commas to separate single-word items in a series, but they may not be familiar with commas used to separate phrases or clauses in a series. You may want to review **Chapter 3: The Phrase** and **Chapter 4: The Clause** and to give additional examples of phrases and clauses in series.

Special Education Students

Students with processing problems may have difficulty if many new concepts are introduced at one time. Be prepared to spend ample time on each rule before proceeding to the next one.

English-Language Learners

Spanish. A comma is not used in Spanish after the penultimate item in a series.

Reteaching

Correct Use of Commas

Activity. If students have trouble punctuating adjectives in a series, try using an activity. Have students divide a piece of paper into six slips by folding and tearing. Tell them to write a different adjective on each slip of paper. Collect the slips, shuffle them, and redistribute them. Each student will receive six slips of paper. Tell students to create and carefully punctuate two sentences using three adjectives from the slips for each sentence. Have several volunteers write their sentences on the chalkboard, and have the other students check the punctuation.

Differentiating Instruction

Learners Having Difficulty

Hold a team race to help reinforce the use of commas in a series of words or phrases. Give teams of four students five minutes to write sentences with commas in series. To help them begin, list the following examples on the chalkboard.

Word Series

- Red, gold, and blue were her colors.
- She was tall, gentle, and graceful.

Phrase Series

- The water flowed over the tub, onto the floor, and under the door.
- Counting the money, writing checks, and making deposits took four hours.

Award a point for each correct use of a comma in a series.

MECHANICS

Exercise 4 Using Commas Correctly in Series

ANSWERS

Individual sentences will vary, but answers must follow the style requested.

TIPS & TRICKS

When two or more adjectives precede a noun, you can use two tests to determine whether the last adjective and the noun form a unit.

TEST 1
Insert the word *and* between the adjectives. If *and* fits sensibly between the adjectives, use a comma.

EXAMPLE
A juicy, tangy apple makes a good snack.
[*Juicy and tangy* makes sense, so the comma is correct.]

TEST 2
Change the order of the adjectives. If the order of the adjectives can be reversed sensibly, use a comma.

EXAMPLE
The quiet, polite girl sat next to her mother.
[*Polite, quiet girl* makes sense, so the comma is correct.]

4. Please pass those delicious blueberry pancakes, the margarine, and the syrup.
5. My twin sister can run faster, jump higher, and do more push-ups than I can.
6. Where is the nearest store that sells newspapers, magazines, and paperbacks?
7. Horns tooted, tires screeched, a whistle blew, and sirens wailed.
8. Steel is made from iron, other metals, and small amounts of carbon.
9. The clown wore a long, blue raincoat; big, red plastic gloves; and floppy, yellow tennis shoes.
10. Robert Browning says that youth is good, that middle age is better, and that old age is best.

Exercise 4 Using Commas Correctly in Series

Your school's new counselor wants to get to know the students better. He has developed the following personality questionnaire, and today he has given a copy to all the students in your class. Answer each question by writing a sentence that includes a series of words, phrases, or clauses. Use commas where needed in each series.

EXAMPLE 1. What do you consider your most outstanding traits?
1. *I am considerate, thoughtful, and loyal.*

Personality Questionnaire

1. What do you consider your most outstanding traits?
2. What qualities do you admire most in a person?
3. Who are the people who have influenced you most?
4. What are your favorite hobbies?
5. What famous people would you like to meet?
6. What countries would you most like to visit?
7. For what reasons do you attend school?
8. What are your favorite subjects in school?
9. What things about the world would you most like to change?
10. What goals do you hope to achieve during the next ten years?

Independent Clauses

11g. Use a comma before *and, but, for, nor, or, so,* or *yet* when it joins independent clauses.

EXAMPLES Hector pressed the button, **and** the engine started up.

She would never argue, **nor** would she complain to anyone.

Are you going to the football game, **or** do you have other plans for Saturday?

He is an accomplished actor, **yet** he's very modest.

Do not be misled by compound verbs, which can make a sentence look like a compound sentence.

SIMPLE SENTENCE Mara **cleared** the table and **did** the dishes. [one subject with a compound verb]

COMPOUND SENTENCE **Mara cleared the table,** and **Roland did the dishes.** [two independent clauses]

NOTE The comma joining two independent clauses is sometimes omitted before *and, but, or,* or *nor* when the independent clauses are very short and when there is no possibility of misunderstanding.

CLEAR The dog barked and the cat meowed.

AWKWARD Bill bathed the dog and the cat hid under the bed. [confusing without comma]

CLEAR Bill bathed the dog, and the cat hid under the bed.

Exercise 5 Correcting Sentences by Adding Commas Between Independent Clauses

Where a comma should be used, write the word preceding the comma, the comma, and the conjunction following it. If a sentence is already correct, write *C.*

EXAMPLE 1. Accident-related injuries are common and many of these injuries can be prevented.

1. common, and

1. It is important to know first aid, for an accident can happen at almost any time.
2. More than 83,000 people in the United States die in accidents each year, and many millions are injured.

Reference Note

For more about **compound sentences,** see page 109. For information on **compound subjects** and **compound verbs,** see page 52.

STYLE TIP

For clarity, some writers prefer always to use the comma before a conjunction joining independent clauses. Follow your teacher's instructions on this point.

DIRECT TEACHING

Correcting Misconceptions

Compound Sentences. Some students may think that the word *then* is a conjunction and that adding a comma before *then* will make a correct compound sentence. Explain that the following sentence is not standard English. *We ate lunch, then we played soccer.* Explain that to correct the sentence they must add an *and. We ate lunch, and then we played soccer.*

English-Language Learners

General Strategies. Because comma usage differs from language to language, students may use commas between sentences where a comma and a conjunction or a period is used in English. For example, students might write "The rain was falling steadily, it looked like the game would be called off." Explain to students that such sentences are considered run-on sentences in English. Students should proofread separately for commas used in this manner and then either replace the comma with a period and capitalize the first word of the second sentence; add an appropriate conjunction after the comma; replace the comma with a semicolon; or replace the comma with a semicolon, conjunctive adverb, and comma.

Learners Having Difficulty

Have students create original sentences with the same structure and elements as those in **Exercise 5.** Next, have students check each other's work for correct punctuation, marking their partners' sentences as correct (C) or questionable (?). Finally, allow the class as a whole to discuss sentences marked with a question mark.

3. Many household products can cause illness or even death but are often stored where small children can reach them. 3. C
4. Biking accidents are common wherever cars and bicycles use the same road, so many communities have provided bicycle lanes.
5. Car accidents are the leading cause of childhood fatalities, but seat belts have saved many lives.
6. Everyone should know what to do in case of fire, and different escape routes should be tested.
7. If you need to escape a fire, you should stay close to the floor and be very cautious about opening doors. 7. C
8. Holding your breath, keep low and protected behind a door when opening it, for a blast of superheated air can be fatal.
9. An injured person should not get up, nor should liquid be given to someone who is unconscious.
10. Always have someone with you when you swim, or you may find yourself without help when you need it.

Nonessential Clauses and Phrases

11h. Use commas to set off nonessential subordinate clauses and nonessential participial phrases.

A ***nonessential*** (or ***nonrestrictive***) clause or participial phrase adds information that is not necessary to the main idea in the sentence.

NONESSENTIAL CLAUSES

Eileen Murray, **who is at the top of her class,** wants to go to medical school.

Texas, **which has the most farms of any state in this country,** produces one fourth of our oil.

NONESSENTIAL PHRASES

Tim Ricardo, **hoping to make the swim team,** practiced every day.

The Lord of the Rings, **written by J.R.R. Tolkien,** has been translated into many languages.

Omitting each boldface clause or phrase in the preceding examples does not change the main idea of the sentence.

EXAMPLES

Eileen Murray wants to go to medical school.

Texas produces one fourth of our oil.

Tim Ricardo practiced every day.

The Lord of the Rings has been translated into many languages.

Reference Note

For more information about **subordinate clauses,** see page 99. For more about **participial phrases,** see page 79.

MECHANICS

DIRECT TEACHING

Modeling and Demonstration

Nonessential Clauses and Phrases. Model how to proofread sentences for correct use of commas by using the example *Eileen Murray who is at the top of her class wants to go to medical school.* First, ask whether the clause *who is at the top of her class* is an essential or nonessential clause. [*nonessential*] Point out that the meaning of the sentence is not changed if the nonessential clause is omitted. [*Eileen Murray wants to go to medical school.*] Next, ask if the clause *who is at the top of her class* should be set off by commas. [*yes*] Explain that commas should be used to set off nonessential clauses. Now, have a volunteer use another example from this chapter to demonstrate how to proofread sentences for correct use of commas.

DIFFERENTIATING INSTRUCTION

Advanced Learners

To give students more practice analyzing subordinate clauses, write the following sentence on the chalkboard and ask students to determine whether or not the underlined clause should be set off with commas. Tell students to be prepared to explain their answers.

> Washington which is the only state named after a president shares a border with Canada. [*commas; the clause is nonessential*]

Next, have students write similar sentences, using essential and nonessential clauses without commas. Have pairs of students exchange papers, adding required punctuation. Ask students to write some examples on the chalkboard and to explain why the clause is essential or nonessential.

When a clause or phrase is necessary to the meaning of a sentence—that is, when it tells *which one(s)*—the clause or phrase is ***essential*** (or ***restrictive***), and commas are not used.

Notice how the meaning of each of the following sentences changes when the essential clause or phrase is omitted.

ESSENTIAL CLAUSE All students **whose names are on that list** must report to Ms. Washington this afternoon. [All students must report to Ms. Washington this afternoon.]

ESSENTIAL PHRASE A Ming vase **displayed in the museum** was once owned by Chiang Kai-shek. [A Ming vase was once owned by Chiang Kai-shek.]

"SURE I GOT ALL THE PUNCTUATION: COMMA, COMMA, PERIOD, PERIOD, QUESTION MARK, COMMA, SEMI-COLON, COMMA, EXCLAMATION POINT, PERIOD..."

Depending on the writer's meaning, a participial phrase or clause may be either essential or nonessential. Including or omitting commas tells the reader how the clause or phrase relates to the main idea of the sentence.

NONESSENTIAL CLAUSE LaWanda's brother, who is a senior, works part time at the mall. [LaWanda has only one brother. He works at the mall.]

ESSENTIAL CLAUSE LaWanda's brother who is a senior works part time at the mall. [LaWanda has more than one brother. The one who is a senior works at the mall.]

NOTE An adjective clause beginning with *that* is usually essential.

EXAMPLE Was Hank Aaron the first major league baseball player **that** broke Babe Ruth's home run record?

Exercise 6 Correcting Sentences with Essential and Nonessential Clauses by Adding or Deleting Commas

The following sentences contain essential and nonessential clauses. Add or delete commas as necessary to punctuate each of these clauses correctly. If a sentence is already correct, write *C*.

EXAMPLE 1. My mother who is a Celtics fan has season tickets.

1. My mother, who is a Celtics fan, has season tickets.

MECHANICS

CONTENT-AREA CONNECTIONS

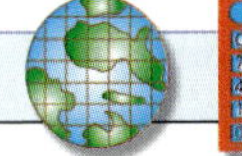

Math

Percentages. This exercise will give students practice working with percentages while also reviewing comma **Rules 11f–i.** Assign students to choose a ten-sentence-long passage from a short story or novel to analyze comma usage. Next, have students track how each comma in the passage is used. For example, students might list the rules simply by their number and place a mark next to each rule every time it is used, as in the following example:

22f	22g	22h	22i
////	///	/	///

Continued on p. 278

MEETING THE CHALLENGE

Write a one-page short story on any topic you like. In your story, use two nonessential subordinate clauses and three nonessential participial phrases. Be sure to punctuate the phrases and clauses correctly.

ANSWERS
Short stories will vary but should have two nonessential subordinate clauses and three nonessential participial phrases, each correctly punctuated with commas.

1. *Jump Start*, which is my favorite comic strip, makes me think as well as laugh.
2. Ms. Lopez, who teaches social studies and gym, will leave at the end of the year.
3. The amusement rides that are the most exciting may be the most dangerous. 3. C
4. Many of the first Spanish settlements in California were founded by Father Junípero Serra, who liked to take long walks between them.
5. People, who carry credit cards, should keep a record of their account numbers at home.
6. Amy Kwan, who is our class president, plans to go to Yale after she graduates from high school.
7. A town like Cottonwood, which has a population of five thousand, seems ideal to me.
8. All dogs that pass the obedience test get a reward; those that don't pass get to take the test again later. 8. C
9. Have you tried this pemmican, which my mother made from an old Cree recipe?
10. "The Gift of the Magi" is a story, in which the two main characters, who are deeply in love, make sacrifices in order to buy gifts for each other.

Exercise 7 Correcting Sentences with Participial Phrases by Adding or Deleting Commas

Add or delete commas as necessary to punctuate the following sentences correctly. If a sentence is already correctly punctuated, write *C*.

EXAMPLE 1. Our dog startled by the noise began to bark.
1. Our dog, startled by the noise, began to bark.

1. People, visiting the reservation, will be barred from burial sites, which are considered holy by American Indians.
2. Players breaking training will be dismissed from the team. 2. C
3. Students, planning to go on the field trip, should bring their lunches.
4. When Tony, holding up a parsnip, asked whether parsnips are related to carrots, I said, "Well, they certainly look alike."
5. Joe told me that kudzu, introduced into the United States in the 1800s, now grows in much of the South.
6. Elizabeth Blackwell, completing her medical studies in 1849, became the first female doctor in the United States.

CONTENT-AREA CONNECTIONS

Continued from p. 277
Then, students can divide the number of times a specific rule is used by the total number of commas to determine the percentage of times a specific comma rule is illustrated in the passage. After students complete their calculations, ask volunteers to share their findings. Ask if anyone can propose a generalization about comma usage based on this exercise.

MECHANICS

7. Pressure and heat acting on the remains of plants and animals turn those remains into gas or oil or coal. 7. C
8. Every child, registering for school for the first time, must present evidence of certain vaccinations.
9. The astronauts living in the space station studied the effects of weightlessness. 9. C
10. Windsor Castle, built during the reigns of Henry III and Edward III, stands twenty-one miles west of London.

Review B Correcting Sentences with Nonessential Clauses and Participial Phrases by Adding Commas

Some of the following sentences contain clauses and phrases that need to be set off by commas. If a sentence is incorrect, add the necessary comma or commas. If a sentence is already correctly punctuated, write *C*.

EXAMPLE 1. Hanukkah which is also called the Feast of Lights is a major Jewish celebration.

1. Hanukkah, which is also called the Feast of Lights, is a major Jewish celebration.

1. The picture on this page shows a part of the Hanukkah celebration that is very beautiful. 1. C
2. The girl, following an ancient custom, is lighting the menorah.
3. The menorah, which is an eight-branched candlestick, symbolizes the original festival.
4. Hanukkah, which means "dedication," celebrates the rededication of the Temple of Jerusalem in 165 B.C.
5. This event followed the Jewish people's victory over Syria, which was led by a pagan king. 5. C
6. During the first Hanukkah, according to traditional lore, the Jews had a one-day supply of lamp oil that lasted for eight days. 6. C
7. Today, celebrating the memory of this miraculous event, modern Jews light one candle on the menorah each day of the eight-day festival.
8. Hanukkah starts on the twenty-fifth day of the Hebrew month of Kislev, which is usually in December on the Gregorian calendar.

Differentiating Instruction

Learners Having Difficulty

Auditory Learners. Have students work in groups of three on **Review B.** Students should rotate to a new position with each sentence. Have one student read each sentence aloud while another student writes it, adding commas where necessary. The third student then checks the sentences against the rules to see if each comma is in the right place.

English-Language Learners

Russian. In Russian, almost all subordinate clauses are set off by commas, even if the clauses are essential. For example, "I wonder, who is playing that trombone. Maybe it's the radio, that I am hearing." Tell students to avoid putting commas around essential clauses.

Differentiating Instruction

Learners Having Difficulty

Allow students to work in pairs to complete **Review C,** but require them to cite the rule number that applies to each answer.

MECHANICS

9. The festival, celebrated all over the world, is a time of feasting, gift giving, and happiness.
10. During Hanukkah, children play a game with a dreidel, which is a four-sided toy that is like a top.

Review C **Correcting Sentences by Adding Commas**

Add commas where they are needed in the following sentences. If a sentence does not require any commas, write *C.*

Optional commas are underscored.

EXAMPLE
1. The emu is a large flightless bird from Australia.
1. *The emu is a large, flightless bird from Australia.*

1. The students sold crafts, used books, and baked goods at the bazaar.
2. John Wayne, whose real name was Marion Morrison, won an Academy Award for *True Grit.*
3. Add flour, mix the ingredients, and stir the batter.
4. People who come to the game early will be allowed to take pictures of the players. 4. C
5. *Exiles,* written by James Joyce, will be performed by the Grantville Community Players and will run for three weeks.
6. The float in the homecoming parade was covered with large, pink rose petals and small, silvery spangles.
7. Members of the committee met for three hours, but they still have not chosen a theme for the dance.
8. Helium, which is used by balloonists, deep-sea divers, and welders, is an inert gas.
9. An eclipse that occurs when the earth prevents the sun's light from reflecting off the moon is called a lunar eclipse. 9. C
10. In one month our little town was hit by a tornado and a flood and a fire, yet we managed to survive.

Introductory Elements

11i. Use commas after certain introductory elements.

(1) Use a comma to set off a mild exclamation such as *well, oh,* or *why* at the beginning of a sentence. Other introductory words such as *yes* and *no* are also set off with commas.

EXAMPLES **Why,** you're Andy's brother, aren't you?

Yes, she's going to the cafeteria.

(2) Use a comma after an introductory participial phrase.

EXAMPLES **Switching on a flashlight,** the ranger led the way down the path to the caves.

Disappointed by the high prices, we made up a new gift list.

Given a choice, I would rather work in the yard early in the morning.

(3) Use a comma after two or more introductory prepositional phrases or after a long one.

EXAMPLES **Near the door to the garage,** you will find hooks for the car keys.

Inside the fence at the far end of her property, she built a potting shed.

By the time they had finished, the boys were exhausted.

NOTE One short introductory prepositional phrase does not require a comma unless the comma is necessary to make the meaning clear.

EXAMPLES **At our house** we share all the work.

At our house, plants grow best in the sunny, bright kitchen. [The comma is necessary to avoid reading *house plants.*]

(4) Use a comma after an introductory adverb clause.

EXAMPLES **After Andrés Segovia had played his last guitar concert,** the audience applauded for more than fifteen minutes.

If you see smoke, you know there is a fire.

NOTE An adverb clause in the middle or at the end of a sentence is generally not set off by a comma.

EXAMPLES Miranda, please remember to phone me **when you get home this evening.** [No comma is necessary between *me* and *when.*]

We stayed a long time **because we were having fun.** [No comma is necessary between *time* and *because.*]

Reference Note

For information on **participial phrases,** see page 79. For information on **prepositional phrases,** see page 70.

Reference Note

For information on **adverb clauses,** see page 104.

RETEACHING

Introductory Elements

If students have difficulty knowing when to place commas, try an auditory approach. Assign students to small groups, and tell group members to have a conversation using sentences that start with an introductory element. Tell them they will naturally have slight pauses in their spoken sentences where commas would be if the sentences were written. You might encourage the conversation by offering pictures or topics such as "A Day at a Theme Park," "An Aquarium Tour," or "My Most Exciting or Enlightening Experience." Have students speak in the order in which they are seated so that all of them speak an equal number of times. You might want to tape-record the conversations and play the tape for the class to analyze where the pauses occur that signify places where commas would be in written sentences.

MECHANICS

Differentiating Instruction

Learners Having Difficulty

To help students visualize specific comma usage rules, show examples in three columns on the chalkboard. Label the columns "Nonessential Clause," "Introductory Element," and "Interrupter." Then, help students write their own examples. Ask volunteers to put their sentences in the proper columns. For example:

NONESSENTIAL CLAUSE	INTRODUCTORY ELEMENT	INTERRUPTER
Nico, who passed the test, was exempt from the course.	Before he could get to the gym, the rainstorm began.	Charlie, my neighbor, will soon be moving.

Exercise 8 Correcting Sentences with Introductory Elements by Adding Commas

Add commas where they are needed after introductory elements in the following sentences. If a sentence is already correct, write *C.*

EXAMPLE 1. When Marco Polo visited China in the thirteenth century he found an advanced civilization.

1. When Marco Polo visited China in the thirteenth century, he found an advanced civilization.

1. Although there was a great deal of poverty in China, the ruling classes lived in splendor.
2. Valuing cleanliness, Chinese rulers took baths every day. 2. C
3. Instead of using coins as currency, the Chinese used paper money.
4. After marrying, a Chinese woman usually lived in her mother-in-law's home.
5. After one Chinese emperor had died, he was buried with more than eight thousand statues of servants and horses.
6. Respected by their descendants, elderly people were highly honored.
7. Built around 200 B.C., the main part of the Great Wall of China is about four thousand miles long.
8. Why, until modern freeways were built, the Great Wall was the world's longest construction.
9. In the picture on this page, you can see that Asian landscapes look different from those created by Western artists.
10. In Asian art, people are often very small and are usually shown in harmony with nature. 10. [*or* C]

Interrupters

11j. Use commas to set off elements that interrupt the sentence.

Two commas are used around an interrupting element—one before and one after.

EXAMPLES His guitar, **according to him,** once belonged to Bo Diddley.

Mr. Gonzales, **my civics teacher,** encouraged me to enter my essay in the contest.

Sometimes an "interrupter" comes at the beginning or at the end of a sentence. In such cases, only one comma is needed.

EXAMPLES **Nevertheless,** you must go with me.

I need the money**, Josh.**

(1) Nonessential appositives and nonessential appositive phrases should be set off with commas.

Reference Note

For more information on **appositives** and **appositive phrases,** see page 89.

A ***nonessential*** (or ***nonrestrictive***) ***appositive*** or ***appositive phrase*** provides information that is unnecessary to the basic meaning of the sentence.

EXAMPLES Their new parrot**, Mina,** is very gentle. [The sentence means the same thing without the appositive.]

Elizabeth Peña**, my favorite actress,** stars in the movie I rented. [The sentence means the same thing without the appositive phrase.]

An ***essential*** (or ***restrictive***) ***appositive*** or ***appositive phrase*** adds information that makes the noun or pronoun it identifies more specific.

EXAMPLES My friend **Tamisha** lost her wallet. [The writer has more than one friend. *Tamisha* identifies which friend. The meaning of the sentence changes without the appositive.]

He recited the second stanza of "Childhood" by the poet **Margaret Walker.** [The appositive *Margaret Walker* identifies which poet.]

We **art club members** made the decorations. [The appositive phrase *art club members* explains who is meant by *We.*]

Exercise 9 Correcting Sentences with Appositives and Appositive Phrases by Adding Commas

Correctly use commas to punctuate the appositives in the following sentences. If a sentence needs no commas, write *C*.

EXAMPLE 1. My cousin consulted Dr. Moniz an allergy specialist about the harmful effects of pollution.

1. My cousin consulted Dr. Moniz, an allergy specialist, about the harmful effects of pollution.

1. *Ecology,* an obscure word forty years ago, is now a popular term.
2. The word *ecology* comes from *oikos,* the Greek word meaning "house." 2. C

Exercise 9

DISTRIBUTED REVIEW

To help students see the relationship between appositives and adjective clauses, have them rewrite sentences 1, 7, and 10, changing the appositives into adjective clauses.

1. *Ecology,* which was an obscure word forty years ago, is now a popular term.
7. She and many of her friends attended Earth Day, which is a festival devoted to ecology.
10. The mayor, who was a member of the audience, promised to appoint a committee to study the problem.

MECHANICS

3. Ecology is the study of an enormous "house," the world of all living things.
4. Ecologists study the bond of a living organism to its environment, the place in which it lives.
5. Humans, one kind of living organism, affect their environment in both beneficial and harmful ways.
6. My twin sister, Margaret Anne, is worried about the future of the environment.
7. She and many of her friends attended Earth Day, a festival devoted to ecology.
8. An amateur photographer, my cousin prepared a slide show on soil erosion in Grant Park.
9. One of many displays at the Earth Day Festival, my cousin's presentation attracted wide attention and won a prize.
10. The mayor, a member of the audience, promised to appoint a committee to study the problem.

(2) Words used in direct address are set off by commas.

EXAMPLES **Linda,** you know the rules.

I did that exercise last night, **Ms. Ryan.**

Sir, are these your keys?

Your room, **Bernice,** needs cleaning.

Oral Practice Correcting Sentences with Words in Direct Address by Adding Commas

Read the following sentences aloud, and say where commas are needed.

EXAMPLE **1.** Annabella when will you be at the station?

1. Annabella, when will you be at the station?

1. Dad, why can't I go to the movies tonight?
2. As soon as you're ready, Virginia, we'll leave.
3. Yes, Mom, I washed the dishes.
4. What we need, Mayor Wilson, is more playgrounds.
5. Will you answer the last question, Jim?
6. Rex, fetch the ball!
7. I think, ma'am, that my piano playing has improved this year.

MECHANICS

Differentiating Instruction

Special Education Students

Have students work with helpers to use the sentences in **Oral Practice** as a pattern for their own sentences. Have the helper create a sentence modeled on sentence 1. [*Mom, may I go to the homecoming game tomorrow?*] Then, have students create their own versions of sentence 1 and state them orally to their helpers. Students should also tell what punctuation is needed. After students have created several sentences based on sentence 1, have them write or dictate their own versions of three more of the sentences in **Oral Practice.**

8. We left some for you, Bella.
9. José, how far from here is the teen recreation center that has the heated swimming pool?
10. May I help you with the gardening, Grandma?

(3) Parenthetical expressions are set off by commas.

Parenthetical expressions are side remarks that add information or relate ideas.

Commonly Used Parenthetical Expressions		
after all	generally speaking	nevertheless
at any rate	however	of course
consequently	I believe	on the contrary
for example	in the first place	on the other hand
for instance	moreover	therefore

EXAMPLES **Of course,** I am glad that he called me about the extra movie tickets.

She is, **in fact,** a dentist.

You should try out for quarterback, **in my opinion.**

Some expressions may be used either parenthetically or not parenthetically. Do not set them off with commas unless they're truly parenthetical.

EXAMPLES Sandra will, **I think,** enjoy the program. [parenthetical]

I think Sandra will enjoy the program. [not parenthetical]

However, Phuong Vu finished her report on time. [parenthetical]

However did Phuong Vu finish her report on time? [not parenthetical—similar to "How did she finish?"]

To tell the truth, he tries. [parenthetical]

He tries **to tell the truth.** [not parenthetical]

After all, we've been through this situation before. [parenthetical]

After all we've been through, we need a vacation. [not parenthetical]

Reference Note

For information on using **parentheses** and **dashes** to set off parenthetical expressions, see Chapter 15.

MECHANICS

MINI-LESSON Mechanics

Parenthetical Expressions. To help students use commas with parenthetical expressions, have them choose favorite pieces of writing from their portfolios and exchange papers with partners. Next, have each student choose a parenthetical expression from the list on this page and rewrite a sentence from his or her partner's paper, including the expression and proper punctuation. Finally, ask students to return the sample sentences to the original authors and to explain why they chose particular parenthetical expressions.

EXTENSION

Critical Thinking

Metacognition. To help students analyze the processes they use in working **Exercise 10,** first have them complete the exercise. Then, randomly assign two sentences from the exercise to each student. Have students explain in their Language Logs how they selected the punctuation they used. After students have written their analyses, ask for volunteers to read explanations of their processes, and allow others to offer alternative processes.

NOTE A contrasting expression introduced by *not* is parenthetical and should be set off by commas.

EXAMPLES The divisor, **not the dividend,** is the bottom number of a fraction.

The coach and I believe the winner of the long jump will be Rachel, **not her.**

Exercise 10 Correcting Sentences with Parenthetical Expressions by Adding Commas

Correctly punctuate the parenthetical expressions in the following sentences.

EXAMPLE **1.** In my opinion my little sister Iona has great taste in music.

1. In my opinion, my little sister Iona has great taste in music.

1. For instance, her favorite collection of songs is called *Gift of the Tortoise.*
2. Performed, I believe, by Ladysmith Black Mambazo, the lyrics of the songs are a blend of English and Zulu words and phrases.
3. The South African performers, in fact, sing a cappella (without musical instruments accompanying them).
4. Not surprisingly, their powerful style of music is known by millions of people worldwide.
5. Fudugazi, by the way, is the storytelling tortoise who explains the meaning of the songs.
6. By listening to the song "Finger Dance," Iona has learned, believe it or not, to count to five in Zulu.
7. She has not yet learned to sing any of her favorite songs in Zulu, however.
8. Of course, our whole family enjoys listening to these lovely South African songs.
9. The spirited music and moving sound effects, moreover, seem to transport us to a faraway land and culture.
10. Everyone should, I think, follow Fudugazi's advice: "There is magic in these songs; close your eyes and listen, and you will feel the magic, too!"

FAMILY/COMMUNITY ACTIVITY

Continued on pp. 287–288

Writing Letters to Public Figures. To give students practice with the comma rules covered in this chapter, ask them to write letters about issues important to them. Allow the class to brainstorm possible important issues [*pollution, curfews, summer jobs, teenage smoking, and so forth*] and possible public figures who could address these issues.

Then, assign students to small groups that share a common issue, and have members discuss specifically what they want to achieve or request. Students may discover that there

Conventional Uses of Commas

11k. **Use commas in certain conventional situations.**

(1) **Use commas to separate items in dates and addresses.**

EXAMPLES After Tuesday, November 23, 2001, address all orders to Emeryville, CA 94608.

Please send your cards by November 23, 2000, to 7856 Hidalgo Way, Emeryville, CA 94608.

Notice that no comma divides the month and day (November 23) or the house number and the street name (7856 Hidalgo Way) because each is considered one item. Also, the ZIP Code is not separated from the abbreviation of the state by a comma (Emeryville, CA 94608).

NOTE Commas are not needed if the day precedes the month or if only the month and year are given.

EXAMPLES President Bill Clinton took office on **20 January 1993.**

Hurricane Andrew hit southern Florida in **August 1992.**

(2) **Use a comma after the salutation of a personal letter and after the closing of any letter.**

EXAMPLES Dear Mr. Arpajian, Sincerely yours,

My dear Anna, Yours very truly,

(3) **Use commas to set off abbreviations such as *Jr.*, *Sr.*, or *M.D.* when they follow persons' names.**

EXAMPLES Please welcome Allen Davis, Sr.

Carol Ferrara, M.D., is our family physician.

HELP — Use a colon after the salutation of a business letter.

EXAMPLE
Dear Service Manager:

Reference Note

For more about using **colons,** see page 303.

Review D Correcting Sentences by Adding Commas

Add commas where they are needed in the following sentences. If a sentence is already correct, write *C.*

EXAMPLE 1. On July 14 1789 the people of Paris stormed the Bastille.
1. On July 14, 1789, the people of Paris stormed the Bastille.

1. Please address the envelope to Ms. Marybeth Correio, 1255 S.E. 56th Street, Bellevue, WA 98006.

DIFFERENTIATING INSTRUCTION

Learners Having Difficulty

To illustrate two common uses of commas, write the following sentence on the chalkboard:

Halley's comet could be seen in the night sky on November 30 1835 in the town of Florida Missouri the birthplace of Samuel Clemens.

After students have read the sentence, ask them whether they spotted any mistakes. Have volunteers use colored chalk to insert commas in the proper places. Then, ask other students to explain why these commas were included in the text.

[Halley's comet could be seen in the night sky on November 30, 1835, in the town of Florida, Missouri, the birthplace of Samuel Clemens.]

MECHANICS

are several aspects of the problem they would like to deal with and that a variety of people might be able to help them. If so, have the group divide the topic and the people to be addressed so that each student has a topic and a person to address.

Otherwise, more than one student could write a letter to the same public figure.

Next, have each student write and share with the group a rough draft of his or her letter. Once the content of each letter has been evaluated and revised, ask students to

2. Sources claim that on April 6, 1909, Matthew Henson, assistant to Commander Robert E. Peary, reached the North Pole.
3. I glanced quickly at the end of the letter, which read, "Very sincerely yours, Alice Ems, Ph.D."
4. The Constitution of the United States was signed on September 17, 1787, eleven years after the adoption of the Declaration of Independence on July 4, 1776.
5. Did you go on a field trip to the desert in March or April of 1999? 5. C
6. We used to live in Monterey, but now we live at 100 Robin Road, Austin, Texas.
7. Tony, watch out for that spider.
8. My grandmother, a Russian, learned English late in life.
9. That man is the governor, by the way.
10. The gauchos crossed the hot, windy, vast expanse of the pampas.

Unnecessary Commas

11l. Do not use unnecessary commas.

Have a reason for every comma and other mark of punctuation that you use. When there is no rule requiring punctuation and when the meaning of the sentence is clear without it, do not insert any punctuation mark.

INCORRECT My friend, Jessica, said she would feed my cat, and my dog while I'm away, but now, she tells me, she will be too busy.

CORRECT My friend Jessica said she would feed my cat and my dog while I'm away, but now she tells me she will be too busy.

Review E Correcting Sentences by Adding Commas

For each of the following sentences, write all the words that should be followed by a comma. Place a comma after each of these words.

EXAMPLE **1.** Yes Phyllis I know that you want to transfer to Bayside the high school that has the best volleyball team in the city.

1. Yes, Phyllis, Bayside,

Optional commas are underscored.

1. Scuttling across the dirt road, the large, hairy spider, a tarantula, terrified Steve, Ellen, and me.
2. Whitney, not Don, won first prize.
3. German shepherds are often trained as guide dogs; other breeds that have also been trained include Labrador retrievers, golden retrievers, and Doberman pinschers.

MECHANICS

Extension

Relating to Literature

As a review of punctuation usage, have students select a poem with commas—like "American Hero," "Lucinda Matlock," or "The Road Not Taken"—from their literature anthology. Assign students to work in small groups based on their choice of poem, and have them analyze the poem's punctuation. Students should suggest a punctuation rule to apply to each comma used in the poem. (You may want to tell students that since writing poetry is a highly creative activity, poets may sometimes ignore standard comma use.) Have groups share their poems and their analyses with the class.

Practice

Guided and Independent

Review E You may wish to use the first ten items in **Review E** as guided practice. Then, have students complete the review as independent practice.

FAMILY/COMMUNITY ACTIVITY

Continued from p. 287

create double-spaced copies and to write beneath the commas the numbers of the rules that apply to each comma they used. Then, have students get input from other group members. After you have reviewed their work and students have written their final drafts, have them send their letters.

4. According to her official birth certificate, Mary Elizabeth was born September 7, 1976, in Juneau, Alaska, but she does not remember much of the city.
5. Angela and Jennifer, are you both planning to write poems to enter in the contest?
6. All entries for the essay-writing competition should be submitted no later than Friday to Essay Contest, 716 North Cliff Drive, Salt Lake City, UT 84103.
7. The best time to plant flower seeds, of course, is just before a rainy season, not in the middle of a hot, dry summer.
8. Our next-door neighbor, Ms. Allen, manages two large apartment buildings downtown.
9. As a matter of fact, most horses can run four miles without having to stop.
10. The Comanches, like some other nomadic American Indians, once traveled throughout the states of Kansas, New Mexico, Texas, and Oklahoma.
11. My favorite story, "The Most Dangerous Game," was written back in 1924.
12. Even though I ran quickly around the base of the tree, the squirrel always stayed on the opposite side of the tree from me.
13. We planted irises because they are perennials, flowers that bloom year after year.
14. One of Cleopatra's Needles, famous stone pillars from ancient Egypt, stands in Central Park in New York City, New York.
15. In April 1976, a fifth-grader in Newburgh, New York, released a helium balloon; it was found in Strathaven, Scotland, on the other side of the Atlantic Ocean two days later.
16. Danny's father just bought a 1967 Ford Mustang with green, white, and red stripes on the sides.
17. Before we begin reading *The Odyssey*, we will see a movie about ancient Greece.
18. Mount Waialeale, Hawaii, receives an average of 460 inches of rain each year, making it the rainiest place in the world.
19. A light frost was on the ground, the leaves were falling, the air was cool, and the wind was blowing stronger; autumn had arrived overnight.
20. The performance of our school's spring musical has been sold out for weeks, but those of us who helped build the set will get free tickets.

MECHANICS

Commas 289

MECHANICS

Review F Adding End Marks and Commas

Add end marks and commas where they are needed in each sentence in the following paragraph.

EXAMPLE **[1]** As you can see from the map below Cabeza de Vaca explored areas in North America and South America

1. *As you can see from the map below, Cabeza de Vaca explored areas in North America and South America.*

[1] Did you know that Álvar Núñez Cabeza de Vaca a Spanish explorer participated in two trips to this region [2] To tell the truth neither trip ended successfully [3] In the summer of 1527 he was treasurer of an expedition that was sent to conquer and colonize Florida [4] However the invasion didn't work out as planned and he was one of a handful of survivors [5] These men intended to sail to Mexico but their ship wrecked off the coast of Texas [6] What an unlucky expedition that was [7] Cabeza de Vaca was captured by a native people but he later escaped and wandered through Texas and Mexico for eight years [8] He tells about his Florida expedition in the book *Naufragios* which has the Spanish word for "shipwrecks" as its title. [9] In 1541 this adventurer led an expedition to South America and he became governor of Paraguay [10] When the colonists revolted Cabeza de Vaca returned to Spain under arrest but he was later pardoned.

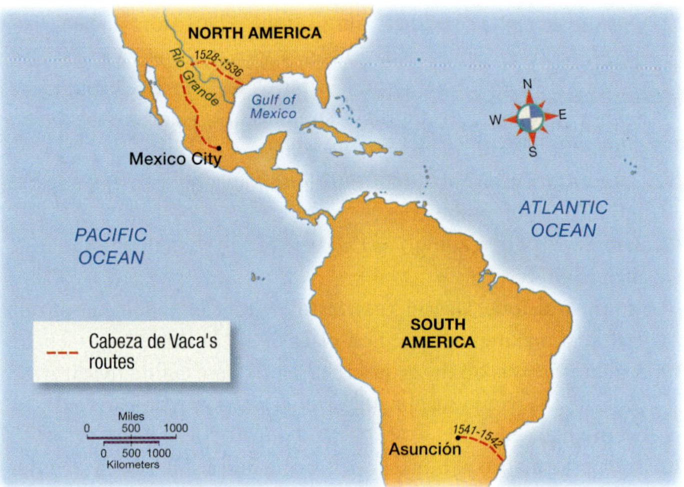

290 Punctuation

Chapter Review

A. Correcting Sentences by Adding End Marks and Commas

Numerals in brackets refer to rules tested by the items in the Chapter Review.

1. [11j(1), a]
2. [11i(1), a]
3. [11k(3), e, b]
4. [11h, a]
5. [11j(3), d]
6. [11g, k(1), a]
7. [11f, b]
8. [11f(3), c]
9. [11e, i(4), a]
10. [11j(2), d]
11. [11i(4)]
12. [11j(1), a]
13. [11k(1), e, d]
14. [11j(3), a]
15. [11i(2), a]
16. [11g, a]
17. [11c, a]
18. [11h, a]
19. [11i(3), a]
20. [11j(2), a]

Most of the following sentences contain errors in the use of end marks and commas. Write each sentence, adding end marks and commas where needed. If no additional punctuation is needed, write *C.*

Optional commas are underscored.

1. She says tae kwon do, a Korean martial art, improves concentration.
2. Well, that's the last time that I'll ever ride in one of those taxis.
3. Is the card addressed to Robert Danieli, Jr., or to Robert Danieli?
4. The batter, hoping to advance the runners, laid down a perfect bunt.
5. Use light colors, by the way, to make a small room seem larger.
6. We used to live in Lansing, but now we live at 457 Cleveland Road, Huntsville, Alabama.
7. Did you ask Joe to bring the forks, plates, and cups to the picnic?
8. What an interesting, enjoyable book that is!
9. When we complained to Mrs. Finch about the remark, she apologized to us.
10. Reva, look out for that pothole in the road. 10. [*or* . . . road!]
11. If the worn tire had not been replaced, it could have caused an accident.
12. The green flag, the signal to begin the race, was seen by thousands.
13. Send your application to Box 36, New York, N.Y., before June 30, 2003.
14. Your homework, of course, must be finished before you go hiking.
15. Sitting on their front porch, my grandparents talk to the children who pass.
16. We looked after our neighbors' dog while they toured Canada for two weeks, and they offered to feed our cat next Thanksgiving.
17. Wow! this movie is exciting. 17. [*or* . . . exciting!]
18. People watching the parade were sitting on curbs and standing on sidewalks. 18. C
19. At the convenience store on the corner, my sister bought juice.
20. Désirée, I would like to know your secret for a beautiful complexion.

ASSESSING

Monitoring Progress

Chapter Review. To assess student progress, you may want to compare the types of items missed on the **Diagnostic Preview** to those missed on the **Chapter Review.** If students have not made significant progress, you may want to refer them to **Chapter 17: Correcting Common Errors, Exercises 29** and **30,** for additional practice.

MECHANICS

RESOURCES

Punctuation

Review

- *Language & Sentence Skills Practice,* pp. 269–271

Assessment

- *Holt Handbook Chapter Tests with Answer Key,* pp. 21–22, 52

B. Using Periods, Commas, Question Marks, and Exclamation Points

Add commas, periods, question marks, and exclamation points where needed in the following sentences. Identify each sentence as *declarative*, *imperative*, *interrogative*, or *exclamatory*.

Optional commas are underscored.

21. Did the author Willa Cather write about life on the prairie?
22. Angelo had cereal, a muffin, a boiled egg, and toast for breakfast.
23. How long did that project take?
24. Well, wouldn't hearing Domingo sing be worth the trip?
25. Oh boy, what a great idea! 25. [*or* Oh boy! What . . .]
26. Students, sign up in the office if you are going on the field trip.
27. You will find the test on my desk, which is near the bookcase.
28. Rita wants to invite Ingrid, Ingrid's cousin, and their friend Jamila.
29. My younger sister, who will be twelve, wants to have a birthday party.
30. Turn down the radio.

21. int. [11b]
22. dec. [11f, a]
23. int. [11b]
24. int. [11b]
25. exc. [11i(1), c]
26. imp. [11d]
27. dec. [11h, a]
28. dec. [11f, a]
29. dec. [11h, a]
30. [*or* radio!] imp. [11d]

C. Using Abbreviations

Rewrite the following sentences, correcting errors in the use of abbreviations. Answers may vary.

31. The guest of honor was Dr. Steve Welch, ~~M. D~~.
32. ~~Maj. Gen.~~ McCambridge, the base commander, was on TV.
33. This statue was probably sculpted between B.C. 500 and 400.
34. At 9:35 A.M. ~~in the morning~~, the race started.
35. Following family custom, Samuel Brandt, ~~Junior~~, named his first-born son Samuel Brandt III.
36. The interns working in the ~~ER~~ enjoyed the challenges and the unpredictability of life in an ~~emergency room~~.
37. In 1271 A.D., the Italian adventurer Marco Polo left Venice on his long voyage to China.
38. My parents spent their early years in Wilmington, ~~DE~~, and Miami, ~~FL~~.
39. The explorers set up camp in what would later become Seattle, ~~Wash~~.
40. The speeding car was clocked at seventy-five ~~m.p.h~~.

31. [11e]
32. Major General [11e]
33. [11e]
34. [11e]
35. Jr. [11e]
36. emergency room / ER. [11e]
37. [11e]
38. Delaware / Florida [11e]
39. Washington [11e]
40. miles per hour [11e]

MECHANICS

D. Proofreading a Paragraph for End Marks and Commas

In the following paragraph, insert end marks and commas as needed.

[41] As I took photos last Saturday with an instant camera, I became increasingly curious about the origin of this type of camera. [42] Being the persistent seeker after knowledge that I am, how could I not spend time the next day researching the topic? [43] The results of my research, needless to say, were quite interesting. [44] Apparently, Edwin Land's daughter once asked him why a camera couldn't immediately produce pictures. [45] Land, who had taught himself physics, quickly worked out the basic principles and design of an instant camera. [46] What a tremendous achievement that was! [47] He became head of Polaroid Corp., and that company produced the first Polaroid Land camera in 1948. [48] Did you know that Land later made important contributions to the study of lasers and color vision? [49] Land died on March 1, 1991. [50] Among his honors were the Presidential Medal of Freedom and, of course, the National Medal of Science.

41. [11i(4), a]
42. [11i(2), b]
43. [11j(3), a]
44. [11j(3), a]
45. [11h, a]
46. [11c]
47. [*or* Corporation] [11e, g, a]
48. [11b]
49. [11k(1), a]
50. [11j(3), a]

Writing Application

Writing Clear Directions

Using Commas A friend asks you for directions from your school to a particular destination. In your instructions, use commas to separate items in a series, to join independent clauses, to set off an introductory adverb clause, to set off a noun of direct address, and to separate items in an address.

Prewriting Choose a destination (real or imagined), and then outline on paper the way to get there.

Writing As you write your first draft, concentrate on making the directions clear and easy to follow.

Revising Read your directions to be sure they are arranged in a logical order. Check to see that you have used commas in the five ways specified in the instructions for this writing activity.

Publishing Proofread your directions for correct grammar and punctuation. You and your classmates may want to collect your directions into a newcomers' guide for new students at your school.

APPLICATION

MECHANICS

Writing Application

Writing Tip. This activity involves many concepts. Students will have to use what they know about writing imperative sentences. Also, organization is important because students will have to specify actual steps that follow a prescribed order.

Scoring Rubric. While you will want to pay particular attention to students' use of commas, you will also want to evaluate overall writing performance. You may want to give a split score to assess development and clarity of the composition as well as mechanics skills.

Chapter Review 293

CHAPTER 12

INTRODUCING THE CHAPTER

- This chapter begins with rules for using semicolons to join independent clauses and to separate items in a series. **Exercises 1** and **2** and **Reviews A** and **B** provide practice using semicolons in various situations. A discussion of correct colon use follows, and **Exercise 3** provides practice using colons.
- The chapter closes with a **Chapter Review** including a **Writing Application** feature that asks students to write a short letter, using business-letter style.
- For help integrating the chapter with writing assignments, see the **Teaching Strands** chart on pp. T24–T25.

CHAPTER

12 Punctuation

Semicolons and Colons

Diagnostic Preview

A. Correcting Sentences by Adding Semicolons and Colons

For the following sentences, write each word or numeral that should be followed by a semicolon or colon, and then insert the missing semicolon or colon. If a sentence is already correct, write *C*.

EXAMPLE 1. Someday, robots may do many simple household chores, wash windows, answer the telephone, make repairs, and serve dinner.

1. chores:

1. I didn't go to the game last night, instead, I took care of my baby brother, Carl.
2. The band members will perform at the civic center on Tuesday, January 15, at the Kiwanis Club on Saturday, January 19, and at the Oak Nursing Home on Friday, January 25.
3. For the lesson on figures of speech, we had to find examples of similes, metaphors, personification, and hyperbole.
4. Dr. Enríquez has traveled to rain forests in many parts of the world, Borneo, Brazil, Costa Rica, and Sri Lanka.
5. The first Spaniards who settled in America built forts, missions, and pueblos, evidence of Spanish influence on American architecture can be found throughout the Southwest.

Numerals in brackets refer to rules tested by the items in the Diagnostic Preview.

1. night; [12b]
2. 15;/19; [12d]
3. C [12e(1)]
4. world: [12e(1)]
5. pueblos; [12a]

CHAPTER RESOURCES

Internet

- Web resources: go.hrw.com

go.hrw.com

Practice & Review

- *Language & Sentence Skills Practice,* pp. 277–285
- *Language & Sentence Skills Practice Answer Key,* pp. 113–118

Application & Enrichment

- *Language & Sentence Skills Practice,* pp. 276, 286, 287–288, 289
- *Language & Sentence Skills Practice Answer Key,* pp. 113, 118–119

6. The Tower of Babel, as described in Genesis 11 1–9, resembled a ziggurat, or terraced pyramid.
7. Erica seldom misses a football playoff on TV, last Saturday, for example, she watched the NFC championship game from noon to 3 00 P.M.
8. I invited Peggy, Josefina, and Sonya, and Beth, Errol, and Randy are coming too.
9. My brother doesn't like many TV shows; instead of watching TV, he prefers to read books.
10. The events for the annual Ironman Triathlon, which is held in Hawaii and is open to men and to women, are as follows, swimming in the ocean 2.4 miles, bicycling 112 miles, and running 26.2 miles.

6. 11:1–9 [12f(2)]
7. TV; / 3:00 [12a, f(1)]
8. Sonya; [12c]
9. C [12a]
10. follows: [12e(1)]

B. Proofreading a Letter for Correct Use of Semicolons and Colons

Find the ten places where a semicolon or a colon should be used in the following letter. Write each word or number that should be followed by a semicolon or a colon; then, add the necessary punctuation mark.

EXAMPLE [1] Last summer we stayed home during summer vacation, this summer we took a trip in the car.
1. *vacation;*

290 Eureka Street
Dallas, TX 76012

August 15, 2001

Director
California Department of Parks and Recreation
Box 2390
Sacramento, CA 95811

[11] Dear Sir or Madam,

[12] While on vacation this summer, my family and I visited the following states Washington, Oregon, and California. [13] We wanted you to know that we especially enjoyed our stay in California, we learned a lot and are planning to return soon.

[14] What we liked best was visiting the Spanish missions in the Los Angeles area they gave us a real sense of history. [15] My favorite places were Mission San Fernando Rey de España, located in Mission Hills, Mission San Gabriel Arcangel, located in San Gabriel, and El Pueblo de Los Angeles. [16] The Old Plaza Church, Nuestra Señora la

11. Madam: [12f(3)]
12. states: 12e(1)]
13. California; [12a]
14. area; [12a]
15. Hills; / Gabriel; [12d]

ASSESSING

Entry-Level Assessment

Diagnostic Preview. The results of the **Diagnostic Preview** will identify students who have mastered the use of semicolons and colons, as well as those who need a rule-by-rule explanation of the chapter.

Even students who do well on the preview may need to pay attention to the correct use of semicolons and colons in their writing. Students may wish to set goals for proofreading for semicolon and colon use in their essays to vary sentence style.

MECHANICS

PRETEACHING

Lesson Starter

Background Information. Imagine that a writer could decide that a semicolon looked attractive between a subject and verb or that a word processor ran out of commas. Centuries ago there were no standardized punctuation rules: Writers used punctuation at will, and typesetters punctuated sentences based on the type available in their typecases.

Regularization of printing and punctuation began in Italy in the 1400s and 1500s. The consistent use of specific symbols by an Italian printer, Aldus Manutius, was one origin of the systematic punctuation used in languages today.

Differentiating Instruction

- *Developmental Language & Sentence Skills,* pp. 129–132
- *Developmental Language & Sentence Skills Guided Practice Teacher's Notes and Answer Key,* pp. 29–30

Assessment

- *Holt Handbook Chapter Tests with Answer Key,* pp. 23–24, 52

Semicolons

Rules 12a–d *(pp. 296–303)*

OBJECTIVE

- To correct sentences by adding semicolons between independent clauses

DIRECT TEACHING

Modeling and Demonstration

Semicolons. Model how to use semicolons correctly with the example *June sat with Tony, Pat, and me, and Josh sat with Flora, Zack, and Geraldo.* First, ask if there are two independent clauses here. [*yes*] Next, ask if the two clauses are joined by a coordinating conjunction. [*yes;* and] Then, ask if the sentence is clear. [*no*] Point out that the words *and Josh,* which begin the second independent clause, might appear to be part of the series *Tony, Pat, and me,* which ends the first clause. Explain that independent clauses joined by a coordinating conjunction usually do not need a semicolon, but here one is needed after *me* in order to clarify where one clause ends and the next begins. Now, have a volunteer use another example from the chapter to demonstrate how to use semicolons correctly.

RETEACHING

Semicolons

To illustrate the need for a variety of punctuation marks, introduce the following activity. Draw on the chalkboard the following traffic signs: an octagonal stop sign, a triangular yield sign, and a round railroad-crossing sign. Have students imagine the confusion that would result from placing *yield* on an octagonal sign.

Then, write a period, a comma, and a semicolon on the chalkboard. Explain

(continued)

MECHANICS

16. wonderful; / 5:00 [12a, f(1)]
17. great; [12a]
18. Francisco; [12b]

Reina de Los Angeles, which dates from 1822, was especially wonderful, we stayed there from noon to 500 P.M., when the mission closed.

[17] Our stay in California was great, we hope to return next summer when we will have more time. [18] I would like to visit some of the missions around San Francisco therefore, I would appreciate it if you could send me some information on that area. Thank you very much.

Yours truly,

Angie Barnes

Angie Barnes

STYLE TIP

Use a semicolon to join independent clauses only if the ideas in the clauses are closely related.

INCORRECT
Josh wants to go to Venezuela; Elaine wants to swim.

CORRECT
Josh wants to go to Venezuela; Elaine wants to go to Paraguay.

Reference Note

For information on **simple and compound sentences,** see page 109.

Semicolons

12a. Use a semicolon between independent clauses that are closely related in meaning if they are not joined by *and, but, for, nor, or, so,* or *yet.*

Notice in the following pairs of examples that the semicolon takes the place of the comma and the conjunction joining the independent clauses.

EXAMPLES
First, I had a sandwich and a glass of milk, **and** then I called you for the homework assignment.
First, I had a sandwich and a glass of milk; then I called you for the homework assignment.

Patty likes to act, **but** her sister gets stage fright.
Patty likes to act; her sister gets stage fright.

Similarly, a semicolon can take the place of a period to join two or more clauses that are closely related.

EXAMPLES
Manuel looked out at the downpour. Then he put on his raincoat and boots. [two simple sentences]
Manuel looked out at the downpour; then he put on his raincoat and boots. [one compound sentence]

Rain soaked the earth. Plants became green. Fragrant flowers bloomed. [three simple sentences]
Rain soaked the earth; plants became green; fragrant flowers bloomed. [one compound sentence]

RESOURCES

Semicolons

Practice

- *Language & Sentence Skills Practice,* pp. 277–279

Differentiating Instruction

- *Developmental Language & Sentence Skills,* pp. 129–130

Exercise 1 Correcting Sentences by Adding Semicolons Between Independent Clauses

Indicate where a semicolon should be placed in each of the following sentences. In some instances, you may prefer to use a period. Be prepared to explain your choice. Answers may vary.

EXAMPLE
1. Great earthquakes usually begin gently only one or two slight shocks move the earth.
1. *Great earthquakes usually begin gently; only one or two slight shocks move the earth.*

1. Pressure builds along faults, or cracks, in the earth's crust; the weight of this pressure causes earthquakes.
2. The San Andreas fault, shown here, extends nearly the entire length of California; earthquakes often occur all along this fault.
3. During an earthquake, huge chunks of the earth's crust begin to move. The San Francisco earthquake of 1906, pictured here, was one of the most destructive earthquakes recorded in history.
4. Energy released during an earthquake is tremendous; it can equal the explosive force of 180 metric tons of TNT.
5. Scientists study the force of earthquakes; they measure this force on a scale of numbers called the Richter scale.
6. An earthquake measuring less than 5 on the Richter scale is not serious; more than 1,000 earthquakes measuring 2 or less occur daily.
7. In 1906, one of the most powerful earthquakes in history occurred in the Pacific Ocean near Ecuador; it measured 8.9 on the Richter scale.
8. Tidal waves are a dangerous result of earthquakes; geologists use the Japanese word *tsunami* for these destructive ocean waves.
9. Predicting when earthquakes will occur is not yet possible; predicting where they will occur is somewhat more certain.
10. Earthquakes seem to strike in a regular time sequence; in California, for example, a major earthquake usually occurs every fifty to one hundred years.

HELP In the example for Exercise 1, a semicolon is used because the two independent clauses are closely related.

to students that these signals—each with a specific meaning—help the reader to interpret written information. Use the following sentence to illustrate these marks at work. Discuss with students the function of each mark.

Aunt Edna invited Uncle Brian, her oldest brother; Aunt Sophia, Brian's wife; and Cousin Tillie, a respected artist, to the reunion; however, Tillie was unable to attend because of a gallery opening.

Differentiating Instruction

English-Language Learners

Spanish. Spanish punctuation rules do not require that the independent clauses joined by a semicolon be closely related. You may want to define what is meant by "closely related" in **Rule 12a** on p. 296 and use the sentences in **Exercise 1** as examples. (In *1, 2, 4, 5, 7, 8,* and *9,* the second clause gives additional or more specific information; in *3, 6,* and *10,* the second clause provides examples; and in *4* and *7,* it adds more specific information.)

Advanced Learners

Divide the class into groups of three to search for semicolons in professional writing. Assign each member of the group to find semicolons in one specified source: a novel, a magazine article, or a technical manual.

When students have completed their searches, have them give brief oral reports describing where semicolons are found, how they are used, and what effect is created by using the semicolons.

MECHANICS

Content-Area Connections

Music

Noting Punctuation. When printers first began to standardize punctuation, one authority compared punctuation marks to musical symbols, equating a period with a whole rest, a colon with a dotted half rest, a semicolon with a half rest, and a comma with a quarter rest.

Direct Teaching

Correcting Misconceptions

Compound Sentences. Some students may think that using a comma between two independent clauses is adequate punctuation. For example, they may write *We finished the history test, then we watched a video about the Alamo.* Explain that to correct the sentence they may replace the comma with a semicolon. *We finished the history test; then we watched a video about the Alamo.*

Extension

Critical Thinking

Metacognition. As students become more comfortable with the use of semicolons, ask them to record in their writing logs how they distinguish between the use of commas and semicolons. [*Some students may say they go by the rules; others may say they consider what types of things are being joined and what the relationships are between the things being linked.*]

Differentiating Instruction

Learners Having Difficulty

Visual Learners. Have students create a bulletin board display or poster as an aid to remembering semicolon rules. Students may want to work in small groups to develop sentences as examples for each rule, using oversized and brightly colored semicolons and drawing illustrations for the sentences.

MECHANICS

12b. Use a semicolon between independent clauses joined by a conjunctive adverb or transitional expression.

EXAMPLES Emma felt shy**;** **however,** she soon made some new friends.

My bird does unusual tricks**;** **for example,** he rings a bell and says "Wow."

Commonly Used Conjunctive Adverbs			
accordingly	furthermore	meanwhile	otherwise
also	however	moreover	still
besides	indeed	nevertheless	then
consequently	instead	next	therefore

Commonly Used Transitional Expressions			
as a result	for instance	in fact	on the other hand
for example	in addition	that is	in other words

Notice in the examples under Rule 12b that the conjunctive adverb and the transitional expression are preceded by semicolons and followed by commas.

NOTE When a conjunctive adverb or transitional expression appears within one of the clauses and not between clauses, it is usually punctuated as an interrupter (set off by commas). The two clauses are still separated by a semicolon.

EXAMPLES Our student council voted to have a Crazy Clothes Day**;** the principal**,** **however,** vetoed the idea.

That quilt is quite old**;** it is**,** **in fact,** filled with cotton, not polyester, batting.

12c. A semicolon (rather than a comma) may be needed to separate independent clauses joined by a coordinating conjunction when the clauses contain commas.

CONFUSING Alana, Eric, and Kim voted for her, and Scott, Roland, and Vanessa voted for Jason.

CLEAR Alana, Eric, and Kim voted for her**;** and Scott, Roland, and Vanessa voted for Jason.

STYLE TIP

Use a semicolon between clauses joined by a coordinating conjunction only when a semicolon is needed to prevent misreading, as in the examples of confusing sentences given for Rule 12c. If a sentence is clear without a semicolon, don't add one just because the clauses contain commas.

EXAMPLE

Lana, you are the best musician I know**,** and you're a great dancer, too. [clear without semicolon]

Mini-Lesson Grammar

Identifying Independent Clauses. Students may need a review of independent clauses in order to see clearly where these clauses should be punctuated. Remind students that an independent clause includes a subject and a verb and expresses a complete thought. Refer students to **Chapter 2: Parts of a Sentence** and **Chapter 4: The Clause.**

Ask students to identify independent clauses in each of the following sentences and to add a semicolon between the clauses.

CONFUSING Scanning the horizon for the source of the whirring sound, Pedro saw a huge, green cloud traveling in his direction, and, suddenly recognizing what it was, he knew that the crops soon would be eaten by a horde of grasshoppers.

CLEAR Scanning the horizon for the source of the whirring sound, Pedro saw a huge, green cloud traveling in his direction; and, suddenly recognizing what it was, he knew that the crops soon would be eaten by a horde of grasshoppers.

Exercise 2 Correcting Sentences by Adding Semicolons Between Independent Clauses

Write each word that should be followed by a semicolon in the following sentences and add the semicolon. In some cases, you may prefer to use a period. Be prepared to explain your choice. Answers may vary.

EXAMPLE 1. Cape Cod is only one of many attractions in Massachusetts, Boston and the Berkshires are also worth visiting.

1. *Massachusetts;*

1. My mother and I sometimes go to Massachusetts in late summer; however, last year we went in July.
2. We visit Cape Cod once a year; my grandparents live there, so we always have a place to stay.
3. I miss my friends and sometimes find the yearly trip to Cape Cod boring. Besides, my cousins in Massachusetts are all older than I am.
4. To my great surprise, we had a very good time last year; we even did some sightseeing in Boston, Plymouth, and Marblehead.
5. One hot day my mother, my grandparents, and I went to the beach; and my grandfather, the most active man I know, immediately went down to the water for a swim.
6. My grandfather loves the water and is a strong swimmer; nevertheless, because the currents are strong and tricky, we worried when we saw that he was swimming out farther and farther.
7. Grandpa, to our great relief, finally turned around and swam back to shore; he was astonished that we had been worried about him.
8. While he was in the water, Mom had gathered driftwood, dug a shallow pit in the sand, and built a fire in it; and Grandma had put lobster, corn, and potatoes on the coals.
9. By the time we had finished eating, it was quite late; consequently, everyone else on the beach had gone home.
10. We didn't leave for home right away; instead, we spent the evening watching the darkening ocean, listening to the whispering waves, and watching the stars come out.

HELP

In the example for Exercise 2, a semicolon is used because the independent clauses are closely related.

Exercise 2

DISTRIBUTED REVIEW

Have students identify by sentence number the following constructions: a sentence with three independent clauses [2]; a compound-complex sentence including a *that* clause used as a direct object [6]; a compound-complex sentence beginning with an adverb clause [8]; a compound sentence including a series of participial phrases [10]; five sentences with independent clauses joined by conjunctive adverbs [1, 3, 6, 9, 10].

PRACTICE

Guided and Independent

Exercise You may wish to have students complete **Exercise 2** as guided practice and **Review A** as independent practice.

HOMEWORK

MECHANICS

1. I recently visited Savannah, Georgia, it was the first city established in the original thirteenth colony. [*I . . . Georgia; it . . . colony.*]
2. Georgia was originally a debtors' colony, it gave people who could never hope to get out of debt in their homeland a second chance. [*Georgia . . . colony; it . . . chance.*]

DIFFERENTIATING INSTRUCTION

Learners Having Difficulty

You may wish to pair students to work on **Review A.** To give students help on where to place semicolons, instruct pairs to identify the subjects and verbs of all independent clauses before they think about where to place the semicolons. Then, have students use the list on p. 298 to identify conjunctive adverbs. Also, have students identify any series of items in which the items contain commas.

MECHANICS

12d. Use a semicolon between items in a series if the items contain commas.

EXAMPLES I would like to introduce Mrs. Boyce, our mayor; Mr. Bell, her secretary; Ms. Lincoln, the editor of our newspaper; and Mr. Quinn, our guest of honor.

The Photography Club will meet on Wednesday, September 12; Wednesday, September 19; and Tuesday, September 25.

Review A Correcting Sentences by Adding Semicolons

Write each word or numeral that should be followed by a semicolon in the following sentences and add the semicolon. If a sentence needs no semicolons, write *C*.

EXAMPLE 1. Tina likes playing basketball, I prefer hockey.
1. basketball;

1. The first passenger jet was Britain's *Comet*, first flown in 1949; it had some problems at first but later became a quite popular plane.

2. C
2. On our trip to Paris, my sister wanted to visit the Louvre, but I was more interested in the Eiffel Tower.
3. Africa's kingdoms included Mali, on the Niger River; Benin, in what is now Nigeria; and Mwanamutapa, in southern Africa.
4. Formerly, most cars had carburetors; the newer models have fuel injectors.
5. Many words in modern Japanese come from English; for instance, the word *doonatsu* comes from *doughnut*.
6. The Incas planted crops, such as corn; they domesticated animals, such as the llama; and they developed crafts, such as weaving.
7. Many scientists believe that one of the elephant's closest living relatives is not a large animal at all; surprisingly, it is a small rodentlike creature called the hyrax.
8. Mrs. Gillis said that we could write about Dekanawidah, the Huron founder of the Iroquois League; Mansa Musa, the Muslim emperor of Mali; or Tamerlane, the Mongol conqueror of the Ottoman Turks.
9. Most of Grandmother's belongings were packed away in the attic; however, Mother discovered another suitcase in the cellar, and there were things locked up in the safe-deposit box, too.

10. C
10. In the fifteenth century, the kings of France, England, and Spain grew stronger as they unified their lands.

Oral Practice Correcting Sentences by Adding Semicolons

Most of the following sentences contain an error in the use of semicolons. Read each sentence aloud. Then, say where a semicolon should be added. If a sentence is already correct, say "correct."

EXAMPLE **1.** The largest animal in the world today is the blue whale the largest blue whale ever caught measured slightly more than 112.5 feet and weighed about 170 tons.

1. whale; the

1. Each of the more than seventy-five species of whales is different; however, all whales migrate with the seasons.
2. Whales, which are warmblooded marine mammals, are divided into two main families; these families are the toothed whales (the larger family) and the toothless whales.
3. The biggest toothed whale, the sperm whale, hunts giant squid along the bottom of the ocean; like all toothed whales, it uses its teeth for catching food, not chewing it.
4. The sperm whale is a record holder in the animal kingdom; it has the largest brain and the thickest skin. 4. C
5. Other species of whales include the gray whale, which is probably the best-known toothless whale; the Baird's beaked whale, which is also called the giant bottlenose whale; the bowhead whale, which is also known as the arctic whale; and the killer whale, which is also called *orca.*

MECHANICS

Semicolons 301

6. Whales take very full, deep breaths; consequently, they can dive almost a mile below the surface of the ocean and remain underwater for more than an hour at a time.
7. Some whale species exhibit remarkable social behavior; for example, members of a group may stay with a wounded animal or even support it in the water. 7. C
8. During the past 250 years, whalers have nearly wiped out many species of whales; the whaling industry continues to threaten those species that have managed to survive.
9. Several countries, including the United States, have banned the killing of certain whale species; but the blue whale, which is close to extinction, remains an endangered species. 9. C
10. Whale-watching cruises originated with the public's growing concern over the survival of whales; today whalewatching attracts as many as 350,000 people a year.

Review B Correcting Sentences by Adding Semicolons

Most of the following sentences need at least one semicolon. For each incorrectly punctuated sentence, write the word preceding each missing semicolon, the semicolon, and the word following the semicolon. If a sentence needs no semicolon, write *C.*

EXAMPLE 1. American Indian pottery fascinates me, whenever I can, I watch potters like this woman at the Tigua (pronounced TEE-wah) Indian Reservation and Pueblo in El Paso, Texas.

1. *me; whenever*

1. I could have watched for hours as this artist painted designs on the vases; however, I knew that the rest of my family was eager to see more of the reservation.
2. There is much to see there, and they were determined to see it all! 2. C
3. The Tiguas have a large adobe visitors center, where they display their arts and crafts and have dance demonstrations; and my younger brothers, Jaime and Lucas, ran all around it. 3. [*or* C]
4. Of course, we had to sample the Tigua specialties at the restaurant; otherwise, we would have missed a unique experience.
5. I've eaten American Indian dishes in Phoenix, Arizona; Muskogee, Oklahoma; and Taos, New Mexico; but the food at the Tigua Reservation was my favorite.
6. I especially enjoyed the *gorditas,* which are a little like tacos; the bread, which was fresh out of the oven; and the chili, which was very spicy.

MECHANICS

DIFFERENTIATING INSTRUCTION

Learners Having Difficulty

You may want to try the following activity to give students additional practice using semicolons. First, assign students to small groups and distribute to each group slips of paper containing words or phrases from one sentence in **Review B.** Next, have groups rearrange the words to form a sentence and add the proper punctuation. Ask students to explain why they arranged the sentence parts and used the punctuation as they did. Repeat the process with other sentences until students are comfortable with using semicolons.

7. After lunch, a guide told us that the community was established in 1682 by Tiguas who were displaced from northern New Mexico; he said the reservation is the oldest inhabited community in Texas today.
8. The Tiguas are especially proud of their mission; they certainly should be.
9. Now known as the Ysleta Mission, it is a beautiful restored building; we enjoyed seeing it.
10. It is the oldest mission in Texas; moreover, it is one of the oldest in all of North America.

7. C

Colons

12e. Use a colon to mean "note what follows."

(1) Use a colon before a list of items, especially after expressions like *the following* and *as follows.*

EXAMPLES You will need to bring **the following equipment:** a sleeping bag, a warm sweater, and extra socks.

Additional supplies are **as follows:** a toothbrush, toothpaste, a change of clothes, and a pillow.

Sometimes the items that follow a colon are used as appositives. If a word is followed by a list of appositives, the colon makes the sentence clear.

EXAMPLES At the air base we saw three signs: To Norway, To Paris, and To Lisbon.

You need to shop for several items: brown shoelaces, a quart of milk, and five or six carrots.

Reference Note

For more on **appositives** and **appositive phrases,** see page 89.

Colons

Rules 12e, f *(pp. 303–306)*

OBJECTIVE

- To correct sentences by adding colons

MECHANICS

Colons

Practice

- *Language & Sentence Skills Practice,* pp. 280–282

Differentiating Instruction

- *Developmental Language & Sentence Skills,* pp. 131–132

Direct Teaching

Colons

Activity. Introduce colon usage by offering students a list of activities such as making chili, shopping for groceries, preparing for a camping trip, and so forth. Have each student choose an activity, and form groups based on their choices. Each group should complete the model statement below, adding the proper punctuation.

To ________________, we will need the following items ____________.

Be sure students add a colon after *the following items*.

MECHANICS

NOTE Do not use a colon between a verb and its complements or between a preposition and its objects.

INCORRECT Additional supplies are: a toothbrush and toothpaste, a change of clothes, a towel, a pillow, and an air mattress.

CORRECT Additional supplies are a toothbrush and toothpaste, a change of clothes, a towel, a pillow, and an air mattress.

INCORRECT You need to shop for: brown shoelaces, a quart of milk, and five or six carrots.

CORRECT You need to shop for brown shoelaces, a quart of milk, and five or six carrots.

Reference Note

For more about using **long quotations,** see page 318.

(2) Use a colon before a long, formal statement or a long quotation.

EXAMPLE Horace Mann had this to say**:** "Do not think of knocking out another person's brains because he differs in opinion from you. It would be as rational to knock yourself on the head because you differ from yourself ten years ago."

(3) Use a colon between independent clauses when the second clause explains or restates the idea of the first.

EXAMPLE Thomas Jefferson had many talents**:** He was a writer, a politician, an architect, and an inventor.

NOTE The first word of a sentence following a colon is capitalized.

EXAMPLE Lois felt that she had done something worthwhile**: S**he had designed and sewn her first quilt.

HELP

Use a comma after the salutation of a personal letter.

EXAMPLES
Dear Kim**,**
Dear Uncle Remy**,**

12f. Use a colon in certain conventional situations.

(1) Use a colon between the hour and the minute.

EXAMPLES 10**:**30 A.M. 6**:**30 P.M.

(2) Use a colon between the chapter and the verse in Biblical references and between titles and subtitles.

EXAMPLES Exodus 1**:**6–14 *Whales***:** *Giants of the Sea*

(3) Use a colon after the salutation of a business letter.

EXAMPLES Dear Ms. González**:** Dear Dr. Fenton**:** Dear Sir or Madam**:** To Whom It May Concern**:**

Learning for Life

Continued on pp. 305–306

Using Colons Correctly. Many schools require students to use book covers for textbooks, and many businesses pay for these covers by placing ads on them. Make arrangements with local businesses to have students work with them to write and design these ads. You might have students work in pairs with one member responsible for the final wording of the ad and the other in charge of generating artwork.

Exercise 3 Correcting Sentences by Adding Colons

Correct the following sentences by adding necessary colons. If a sentence does not need a colon, write *C.*

EXAMPLE 1. When I came into class at 9 15 A.M., everyone was writing an essay based on this West African proverb "To know nothing is bad; to learn nothing is worse."

1. When I came into class at 9:15 A.M., everyone was writing an essay based on this West African proverb: "To know nothing is bad; to learn nothing is worse."

1. Last summer I read "Choices:A Tribute to Dr. Martin Luther King, Jr.," by Alice Walker.
2. Mrs. Hughes named the three students who had completed extra projects:Marshall, Helena, and Regina.
3. At the festival we bought tacos and refried beans. 3. C
4. The qualities she likes most in a person are as follows:reliability, a good sense of humor, and willingness to work.
5. Learn to spell the following new words:*aneurysm, fluoroscope, peregrination,* and *serendipity.*
6. An enduring statement of loyalty, found in Ruth 1:16, begins as follows:"Entreat me not to leave thee or to return from following after thee, for whither thou goest, I will go."
7. The desk was littered with papers, pencils, paperback books, food wrappers, and dirty socks. 7. C
8. From 8:00 A.M. until 6:00 P.M., Mr. Brooks sells brushes, brooms, and cleaning products.
9. Alone in the house at night, I heard some scary sounds:the creaking of a board, the scratching of tree branches against a window, and the hissing of steam in the radiator.
10. Tomorrow's test will include the punctuation marks that we have studied so far:commas, semicolons, and colons.

DILBERT reprinted by permission of United Feature Syndicate, Inc.

COMPUTER TIP

Some software programs can evaluate your writing for common errors in the use of end marks, commas, semicolons, and colons. Such grammar-checking programs can help you proofread your drafts.

MEETING THE CHALLENGE

Create a recipe listing ingredients and directions. You may wish to create a recipe for your favorite dish or for an abstract idea, such as happiness or success.Write the recipe directions in complete sentences. Correctly use at least one colon and at least three semicolons in your directions.

ANSWER
Directions will vary but should include at least one colon and three semicolons.

DIFFERENTIATING INSTRUCTION

English-Language Learners

General Strategies. Using a formula might make students more comfortable with the phrases *as follows* and *the following.*

1. SUBJECT + LINKING VERB + *as follows* + list

   Supplies are as follows: tent, tent pegs, and a camp stove.

2. SUBJECT + VERB + *the following* + OBJECT + list

   You should bring the following supplies: flour, eggs, milk, and baking powder.

Spanish. The colon is frequently used in Spanish to introduce quotations. Explain that in English, colons are used to introduce only long, formal quotations or explanatory statements.

Learners Having Difficulty

Some students might confuse the colon and the semicolon. Tell students to think of a colon as a signal or pointer to what follows it and a semicolon as a means to separate thoughts to avoid confusion.

MECHANICS

PRACTICE

Guided and Independent

Exercise You may wish to have students complete **Exercise 3** as guided practice and **Review C** as independent practice.

HOMEWORK

Emphasize that students must brainstorm and work out their ideas together.

Supply students with catalogs, brochures, and magazines to use to determine how colons are used in advertising. [*Colons might precede a list of services, an address, or a quotation. Colons might also divide units of time in business hours.*] Then, have students, with their parents' or guardians' written permission, meet with an advertiser

Review C Correcting Sentences by Adding Semicolons and Colons

Correct the following sentences, using semicolons and colons where they are needed.

EXAMPLE 1. We didn't have time to go to Michigan, instead, we went to New Mexico.

1. We didn't have time to go to Michigan; instead, we went to New Mexico.

1. A small, windowless log cabin stood against the rail fence; directly behind it ran a muddy stream.
2. Because the club has run out of funds, the following supplies must be brought from home: pencils, erasers, paper, and envelopes.
3. Other jobs take too much time; for example, if I worked in a store, I probably would have to work most nights.
4. I enjoy the following hobbies: fly-fishing, reading, and riding my bike.
5. American cowhands used the ten-gallon hat as protection from the sun and as a dipper for water; the leather chaps they wore served as protection from thorny bushes.
6. A rabbi, a Lutheran minister, and a Catholic priest discussed their interpretations of Isaiah 2:2 and 5:26.
7. In his speech Dr. Fujikawa quoted from several poets: Rudyard Kipling, David McCord, and Nikki Giovanni.
8. Sojourner Truth, a former slave, could neither read nor write; however, this accomplished woman spoke eloquently against slavery and for women's rights.
9. From 1853 to 1865, the United States had three presidents: Franklin Pierce, a Democrat from New Hampshire; James Buchanan, a Democrat from Pennsylvania; and Abraham Lincoln, a Republican from Illinois.
10. From 12:30 to 1:00 P.M., I was so nervous that I could not sit still; I paced up and down, swinging my arms and taking deep breaths, while I rehearsed my lines in my mind.

Learning for Life 

Continued from p. 305

to discuss the advertiser's needs and the students' ideas.

Once students have created a mock-up of the cover, have them offer it to the advertiser for input and approval. When the advertiser and students have reached an agreement, students should create the final book cover.

MECHANICS

12

Chapter Review

A. Correcting Sentences by Adding Semicolons Between Independent Clauses

The following sentences are missing semicolons. Write each sentence, adding semicolons where needed.

1. Irma likes cats; her sister is allergic to them.
2. First I cleaned my room; then I called the movie theater to find out the time of the next show.
3. Two of the world's longest railway tunnels are in Italy; moreover, one of the longest motor-traffic tunnels is also located there.
4. My brother Manuel enjoys cooking; I prefer eating.
5. Marty decided to invite Adam, Oliver, and Dorian; and Don, Guy, and Sarah would be there, too.
6. On our first trip to Houston, I wanted to see the Astrodome; my little brother wanted to visit the Johnson Space Center.
7. Tim and Maria often spend Christmas at home; however, this year they are going to visit Maria's family in Guanajuato.
8. The popular names of certain animals are misleading; for example, the koala bear is not really a bear.
9. French and Spanish were Charlotte's most difficult subjects; accordingly, she gave them more time than any of her other subjects at school.
10. The teacher settled the argument; he told us we each had to give a presentation.

B. Correcting Sentences by Adding Colons

Correct the following sentences by adding necessary colons. If a sentence is already correct, write *C*.

11. You will need to bring the following equipment: a hammer, a screwdriver, and safety goggles.
12. At the crossroads we saw three signs: To Quebec, To Montreal, and To Ottawa.
13. We need to shop for several items: salad greens, milk, and a loaf of bread.

HELP — In Part A of the Chapter Review, you may need to delete some commas and replace them with semicolons.

Numerals in brackets refer to rules tested by the items in the Chapter Review.

1. [12a]
2. [12b]
3. [12b]
4. [12a]
5. [12c]
6. [12a]
7. [12b]
8. [12b]
9. [12b]
10. [12a]
11. [12e(1)]
12. [12e(1)]
13. [12e(1)]

ASSESSING

Monitoring Progress

Chapter Review. To assess student progress, you may want to compare the types of items missed on the **Diagnostic Preview** to those missed on the **Chapter Review.** If students have not made significant progress, you may want to refer them to **Chapter 17: Correcting Common Errors, Exercises 31** and **32,** for additional practice.

MECHANICS

RESOURCES

Punctuation

Review

- *Language & Sentence Skills Practice,* pp. 283–285

Assessment

- *Holt Handbook Chapter Tests with Answer Key,* pp. 23–24, 52

14. [12f(2)]
15. [12f(1)]
16. [12e(1)]
17. C [12e(1)]
18. [12e]
19. [12e(1)]
20. [12f(1)]

14. Exodus 1:6–14 is my favorite passage in the Old Testament.

15. The corner store is open from 6:00 A.M. until 11:00 P.M.

16. Last year I read the following novels: *David Copperfield,* by Charles Dickens; *The Joy Luck Club,* by Amy Tan; and *Bel-Ami,* by Guy de Maupassant.

17. The desert floor was strewn with rocks, pebbles, tumbleweed, and mineral shards.

18. This evening's program will focus on what we have discussed so far: the changes in the West over the last two centuries.

19. Especially challenging were the following spelling words: *fluorescent, dissuade, annotate,* and *fortuitous.*

20. At 11:45 A.M. the flight to Mexico City, Bogotá, Brasilia, and Buenos Aires will depart from Gate 2.

C. Proofreading for Correct Use of Semicolons and Colons

The following advertisement contains errors in the use of semicolons and colons. Write the word or number preceding the error, and add the needed punctuation mark.

HELP

In Part C of the Chapter Review, you may need to delete some commas and replace them with semicolons and colons.

21. [12b]
22. [12a]
23. [12a]
24. [12b]
25. [12a]
26. [12b]
27. [12e(3), f(1)]
28. [12d]
29. [12a]
30. [12e]

[21] Your pet probably loves to watch TV; therefore, it should have the best in quality entertainment. **[22]** Forcing your dog or cat to watch only what humans watch is not only boring for the pet; it is somewhat inconsiderate on your part. **[23]** Buy your faithful friend the new *Rockin' and Rollin' Pets* video; it will change your pet's life. **[24]** No dog or cat will be bored with this movie; on the contrary, Fidos and Tabbies everywhere have been sitting up and taking notice. **[25]** With this video, your pet will get the exciting, up-to-date entertainment it has been craving; as a concerned owner, you will feel good about what your pet is watching. **[26]** Science has proven that dogs and cats like the movement and music on television; moreover, they like human contact while watching TV. **[27]** Ask yourself this question: Are you thinking about your pet's happiness when you turn on the set at 7:00 or 8:00 in the evening? **[28]** Do you think your pet really likes to watch situation comedies, which are about families it doesn't know; movies, which are too long; and news programs, which are too serious? **[29]** You already know the answer; order your pet a *Rockin' and Rollin' Pets* video today! **[30]** To place your order, call the following toll-free number: 1-000-PET-ROCK.

308 Punctuation

Writing Application

Punctuating a Business Letter

Semicolons and Colons You have volunteered to order the items that the members of your school band will sell to raise money for road trips. Write a short letter to order these items.

Prewriting First, decide what kinds of items to sell (for example, ballpoint pens, dried fruit, candles, or book covers) and how many to order. Also, decide on each item's price and make up a name and address for the company from which you will purchase the items.

Writing As you write your first draft, try to keep the body of your letter short and to the point.

Revising Be sure that you have followed the correct form for a business letter. Make sure that you have included all the information necessary for the order.

Publishing Check that you have used a colon after the salutation and before the list of items that you are ordering. Slowly read your letter, focusing on spelling and punctuation. Have you capitalized all proper names, company names, addresses, and brand names? You may want to put your letter-writing abilities to use for your school band or for another school or community organization that holds fund-raisers.

APPLICATION

Writing Application

Tip. You may wish to brainstorm with students what constitutes a formal tone. [*Students may mention a formal vocabulary, excluding slang and contractions, as well as a serious, businesslike approach.*] This writing application offers students the chance to apply their knowledge of colon usage as well as any fund-raising experience they might have had for school and community clubs and activities.

Scoring Rubric. While you will want to pay particular attention to students' use of colons, you will also want to evaluate overall writing performance. You may want to give a split score to indicate development and clarity of the composition as well as mechanics skills.

MECHANICS

CHAPTER 13

▼

INTRODUCING THE CHAPTER

- The first part of the chapter explains the use of italics for titles, names of vehicles, words and letters referred to as such, and foreign words. The second part explains the use of quotation marks for dialogue, quoted material, and titles.
- The material in this chapter will be of use to students as they write literary analyses, reviews of TV programs, personal narratives, and stories.
- The chapter closes with a **Chapter Review** including a **Writing Application** feature that asks students to write a dialogue in which characters tell a story, either fact or fiction, through a conversation. Students must use quotation marks correctly.
- For help in integrating this chapter with writing assignments, use the **Teaching Strands** chart on pp. T24–T25.

CHAPTER 13

Punctuation

Italics and Quotation Marks

Diagnostic Preview

A. Correcting Sentences by Adding Underlining (Italics) and Quotation Marks

Add underlining (italics) and quotation marks where they are needed in each of the following sentences.

EXAMPLE 1. Don't forget your umbrella, said Jody. I read in the Sun Times that it's going to rain today.

1. *"Don't forget your umbrella," said Jody. "I read in the* _Sun Times_ *that it's going to rain today."*

Numerals in brackets refer to rules tested by the items in the Diagnostic Preview.

1. [13d, h(1), a]
2. [13d, b, h(1)]
3. [13d, h(2)]
4. [13a, l]
5. [13d, c, h(1)]
6. [13c]

1. "My grandmother asked me which one I wanted for my birthday," Laura said, "a subscription to _Time_ or one to _Popular Mechanics_."
2. "Welcome aboard the _Elissa_," said the skipper. "It was built in the 1800s, but it has been restored and is still a seaworthy ship."
3. Emerson once said, "The only way to have a friend is to be one"; I think he's right.
4. In the book _The Complete Essays of Mark Twain_, you'll find an essay titled "Taming the Bicycle."
5. Jennifer said, "I never can remember how many _c_'s and _s_'s the word _necessary_ has."
6. Beth finally figured out that when Tranh used the Vietnamese phrase _không biết_, he was telling her that he didn't understand.

CHAPTER RESOURCES

Internet

- Web resources: go.hrw.com

go.hrw.com

Practice & Review

- *Language & Sentence Skills Practice,* pp. 291–302
- *Language & Sentence Skills Practice Answer Key,* pp. 120–125

Application & Enrichment

- *Language & Sentence Skills Practice,* pp. 290, 303, 304–305, 306
- *Language & Sentence Skills Practice Answer Key,* pp. 120, 126–127

7. "The 18 on her uniform looks like a 13," Earl said.
8. Alexandra replied, "I'm surprised you watched Gone with the Wind. Two days ago you said, 'I don't want to see the movie until I've read the book.' "
9. Every week the whole family gathered in front of the television to watch 7th Heaven.
10. The Beatles' song "Yesterday" has been a favorite of several generations.

7. [13d, c, h(1)]
8. [13d, a, k, h(1)]
9. [13a]
10. [13l]

B. Correcting Paragraphs of Dialogue by Adding Underlining (Italics) and Quotation Marks

The following dialogue contains errors in the use of underlining (italics) and quotation marks. Correct these errors by adding appropriate marks of punctuation. If a sentence is already correct, write *C.*

EXAMPLES **[1]** I thought the poetry unit in English class would be dull, Ella said, but it's not. **[2]** We're studying Langston Hughes, and he's great!

1. "I thought the poetry unit in English class would be dull," Ella said, "but it's not. 2. We're studying Langston Hughes, and he's great!"

[11] "Oh, I've heard of him," Chet said. [12] "Didn't he write a poem called 'The Dream Keeper'?"

[13] "Yes, that's one of my favorites," Ella said. [14] "An entire book of his poems is called The Dream Keeper, too. [15] Another one of his best-known poems is called 'Dreams.' "

[16] "I guess he dreamed a lot," Chet replied.

[17] Ella said, "He did much more than that! [18] Mrs. Berry told us that Langston Hughes traveled extensively. [19] For a time, he was on the crew of a steamer that sailed around Africa and Europe. [20] In fact, one of his autobiographies is called The Big Sea."

11. [13d, h(1)]
12. [13d, l, h(3)]
13. [13d, h(1)]
14. [13d, a]
15. [13l, h(1), d]
16. [13d, h(1)]
17. [13d]
18. C [13d]
19. C [13d]
20. [13a, d, h(1)]

HELP

In Part B of the Diagnostic Preview, each error in the use of quotation marks involves a pair of single or double quotation marks.

Italics

Italic letters slant to the right, *like this.* When writing or typing, indicate italics by underlining. If your composition were to be printed, the typesetter would set the underlined words in italics. For example, if you typed the sentence

```
Helen Keller wrote The Story of My Life.
```

it would be printed like this:

Helen Keller wrote *The Story of My Life.*

ASSESSING

Entry-Level Assessment

Diagnostic Preview. Since the concepts in this chapter pertain specifically to writing, you may want to use this preview to assess students' knowledge of punctuating direct and indirect quotations and titles before students are given writing assignments requiring these skills.

PRETEACHING

Lesson Starter

Motivating. Newspapers and magazines may have their own house styles regarding punctuation of titles. For example, some publications use quotation marks rather than italics for movie titles.

Have students research the punctuation of titles in various newspapers and magazines from your school library. Suggest that students look at art, music, and film reviews to find examples of titles. Ask volunteers to share their findings with the class.

Differentiating Instruction

- *Developmental Language & Sentence Skills,* pp. 133–138
- *Developmental Language & Sentence Skills Guided Practice Teacher's Notes and Answer Key,* pp. 31–33

Assessment

- *Holt Handbook Chapter Tests with Answer Key,* pp. 25–26, 52

Italics

Rules 13a–c *(pp. 311–314)*

OBJECTIVE

- To correct sentences by adding underlining (italics)

DIRECT TEACHING

Modeling and Demonstration

Italics. Model how to identify words that should be underlined (italicized) by using the example *I am reading John Knowles's A Separate Peace.* First, ask what *A Separate Peace* is. [*title of a book*] Next, ask if this title should be underlined (italicized). [*yes*] Then, ask if *A* is part of the book's title. [*yes*] Point out that when *A* is part of the title it should also be underlined (italicized). Now, have a volunteer use another example from this chapter to demonstrate how to use underlining (italics) correctly.

DIFFERENTIATING INSTRUCTION

English-Language Learners

General Strategies. You may need to clarify the difference between the terms *underlining* and *italics.* Explain that italics are used in publishing and can now be easily produced on word processors, and underlining is used to indicate italics when writing by hand or on a typewriter. Direct students to examples of italics in the text and reproduce some sample titles on the chalkboard using underlining.

MECHANICS

COMPUTER TIP

If you use a personal computer, you can probably set words in italics yourself. Most word-processing software and many printers are capable of producing italic type.

Reference Note

For information on **capitalizing titles,** see page 258.

STYLE TIP

Chapter headings and titles of magazine articles, short poems, short stories, short musical compositions, and individual episodes of TV shows should be placed in quotation marks, not italicized.

HELP

Generally, the title of an entire work (book, magazine, TV series) is italicized, while the title of a part (chapter, article, episode) is enclosed in quotation marks.

Reference Note

See page 314 for more about using **quotation marks.**

13a. **Use italics (underlining) for titles and subtitles of books, periodicals, long poems, plays, films, television series, long musical works and recordings, and works of art.**

Type of Title	Examples
Books	*Vanity Fair: A Novel Without a Hero*
Periodicals	*Seventeen, The New York Times*
Long Poems	*Evangeline, Beowulf*
Plays	*The Piano Lesson, King Lear*
Films	*Casablanca, Harvey*
Television Series	*60 Minutes, Home Improvement*
Long Musical Works and Recordings	*The Magic Flute, Sinfonia Antarctica, The Three Tenors, Dos Mundos*
Works of Art	*The Thinker, Birth of Venus*

The words *a, an,* and *the* written before a title are italicized only when they are part of the title. The official title of a book appears on the title page. The official title of a newspaper or other periodical appears on the masthead, which is usually found on the editorial page or the table of contents.

EXAMPLES I am reading John Knowles's ***A*** *Separate Peace.*

An *Incomplete Education* is a book that tries to summarize everything you should have learned in college.

My parents subscribe to ***The*** *Wall Street Journal* and **the** *Atlantic.*

NOTE A long poem is one that is long enough to be published as a separate volume. Such poems are usually divided into titled or numbered sections, such as cantos, parts, or books. Long musical compositions include operas, symphonies, ballets, oratorios, and concertos.

EXAMPLES In my report on Coleridge, I plan to quote from the seventh stanza of ***The Rime of the Ancient Mariner.***

At her recital, she will play a selection from ***Swan Lake.***

RESOURCES

Italics

Practice

- *Language & Sentence Skills Practice,* pp. 291–293

Differentiating Instruction

- *Developmental Language & Sentence Skills,* pp. 133–134

13b. **Use underlining (italics) for the names of ships, trains, aircraft, and spacecraft.**

Type of Name	Examples
Ships	*Titanic, Queen Elizabeth 2*
Trains	*Orient Express, City of New Orleans*
Aircraft and Spacecraft	*Spirit of Saint Louis, Apollo 1*

13c. **Use italics (underlining) for words, letters, symbols, and numerals referred to as such and for foreign words that are not yet a part of the English vocabulary.**

EXAMPLES The word ***Mississippi*** has four ***s***'s and four ***i***'s.

The ***8*** on that license plate looks like an ***&.***

The ***corrido,*** a fast-paced ballad, evolved from a musical form brought to the Americas by early Spanish explorers and settlers.

NOTE English has borrowed many words from other languages. Once such words are considered a part of the English vocabulary, they are no longer italicized.

EXAMPLES

amoeba (Greek)	judo (Japanese)
boss (Dutch)	kibbutz (Modern Hebrew)
canyon (Spanish)	okra (West African)
chimpanzee (Bantu)	résumé (French)
chipmunk (Algonquian)	vermicelli (Italian)

HELP If you are not sure whether to italicize a word of foreign origin, look in a recently published dictionary to see if the word is italicized there.

DIRECT TEACHING

Correcting Misconceptions

Italics. Students may mistakenly believe that all numerals, symbols, and letters used in a sentence should be in italics. To help students remember to italicize only words, letters, and numerals referred to as such, encourage them to look for phrases like *the word, the letter,* or *the numeral* before a word, letter, or numeral. If one of these expressions is present, or could be added without changing the meaning of the sentence, then the word, letter, or numerals should be italicized or underlined.

MECHANICS

Exercise 1

DISTRIBUTED REVIEW
Have students identify sentences 1, 3, 9, and 10 as simple, compound, complex, or compound-complex. [1. *complex,* 3. *simple,* 9. *compound,* 10. *compound-complex*]

MECHANICS

Quotation Marks

Rules 13d–l *(pp. 314–322)*

OBJECTIVES

- To rewrite sentences, using direct and indirect quotations correctly
- To correct sentences by adding quotation marks for titles

Exercise 1 **Correcting Sentences by Adding Underlining (Italics)**

Rewrite the following sentences. Then, underline all the words and word groups that should be italicized.

EXAMPLE 1. We gave Mom a subscription to Working Woman.
1. We gave Mom a subscription to <u>Working Woman</u>.

1. Jason named his ship <u>Argo</u> because Argos had built it.
2. The motto of the United States Marine Corps is <u>Semper Fidelis</u>, which means "always faithful."
3. Have you read the novel <u>Great Expectations</u> by Charles Dickens?
4. When I spelled <u>occurrence</u> with one <u>r</u>, I was eliminated from the spelling contest.
5. The Gilbert and Sullivan comic opera <u>The Mikado</u> and the Puccini opera <u>Madama Butterfly</u> are both set in Japan.
6. Shari asked if she could borrow my copy of <u>Sports Illustrated</u>.
7. Mrs. Hopkins said that if she had to describe me in one word, the word would be <u>loquacious</u>.
8. My grandmother, who grew up in Chicago, still subscribes to the <u>Chicago Tribune</u>.
9. My favorite painting is Georgia O'Keeffe's <u>Black Iris</u>; my favorite sculpture is Constantin Brancusi's <u>Bird in Space</u>.
10. My parents own a set of the <u>Encyclopaedia Britannica</u>; and my aunt, who lives within walking distance of us, just bought a set of <u>The World Book Encyclopedia</u>.

Quotation Marks

13d. **Use quotation marks to enclose a *direct quotation*—a person's exact words.**

EXAMPLES Melanie said, "This car is making a very strange noise."
"Maybe we should pull over," suggested Amy.

Always be sure to place quotation marks at both the beginning and the end of a direct quotation.

INCORRECT She shouted, "We can win, team!
CORRECT She shouted, "We can win, team!"

Do not use quotation marks for an ***indirect quotation***—a rewording of a direct quotation.

RESOURCES

Quotation Marks

Practice

- *Language & Sentence Skills Practice,* pp. 294–299

Differentiating Instruction

- *Developmental Language & Sentence Skills,* pp. 135–138

DIRECT QUOTATION Stephanie said, "I'm going to wash the car." [the speaker's exact words]

INDIRECT QUOTATION Stephanie said that she was going to wash the car. [not the speaker's exact words]

An interrupting expression is not a part of a quotation and therefore should not be inside quotation marks.

INCORRECT "Let's sit here, Ann whispered, not way down there."

CORRECT "Let's sit here," Ann whispered, "not way down there."

When two or more sentences by the same speaker are quoted together, use only one set of quotation marks.

INCORRECT Brennan said, "I like to sit close to the screen." "The sound is better there."

CORRECT Brennan said, "I like to sit close to the screen. The sound is better there."

13e. A direct quotation generally begins with a capital letter.

EXAMPLES Explaining the lever, Archimedes said, "**G**ive me a place to stand, and I can move the world."

Miss Pérez answered, "**T**he rest of the chapter, of course." [Although this quotation is not a sentence, it is Miss Pérez's complete remark.]

Reference Note

For more about **capitalizing quotations,** see page 246.

NOTE If the direct quotation is obviously a fragment of the original quotation, it may begin with a lowercase letter.

EXAMPLE Are our ideals, as Scott says, mere "**s**tatues of snow" that soon melt? [The quotation is obviously only a part of Scott's remark.]

13f. When an interrupting expression divides a quoted sentence into two parts, the second part begins with a lowercase letter.

EXAMPLES "I wish," she said, "**t**hat we went to the same school."

"I know," I answered, "**b**ut at least we are friends."

If the second part of a quotation is a new sentence, a period (not a comma) follows the interrupting expression, and the second part begins with a capital letter.

EXAMPLE "I requested an interview," the reporter said. "**S**he told me she was too busy."

Direct Teaching

Modeling and Demonstration

Quotation Marks. To model how to use quotation marks, write on a transparency *Melanie said, This car is making a very strange noise.* First, ask if the example contains the speaker's exact words. [*yes*] Explain that this is a direct quotation, and therefore the speaker's words should be enclosed in quotation marks. Then, ask where the quotation marks should be placed. [before *This* and after *noise*] Insert the quotation marks in the appropriate places on the transparency. Explain that *this* should be capitalized since a direct quotation generally begins with a capital letter, and point out that the period after *noise* should be placed inside the closing quotation marks. Now, have a volunteer use another example from this chapter to demonstrate how to use quotation marks correctly.

MECHANICS

Extension

Activity. Divide the class into groups of three or four. Have each group role-play real or imaginary situations in which they have been displeased consumers. Then, have group members collaborate on writing a complaint letter to a consumer protection agency or a newspaper consumer column, using both direct and indirect quotations in describing the transaction.

DIFFERENTIATING INSTRUCTION

English-Language Learners

Spanish. Quotation marks in Spanish look like this: « ». However, dashes rather than quotation marks are often used to indicate dialogue in Spanish. The style would look like the following:

—No —he said—, I don't believe it.

—¿Why not? —she asked.

Periods and commas are placed outside the closing quotation marks or dashes.

Vietnamese. The Vietnamese language also uses dashes or « » to indicate direct speech. If your students have learned to write in Vietnamese, ask which form of quotation marks they usually use, and show them how the marks correspond with English quotation marks. These students may also place some punctuation marks outside the closing quotation marks when the whole sentence is not being quoted.

MECHANICS

13g. A direct quotation can be set off from the rest of a sentence by a comma, a question mark, or an exclamation point, but not by a period.

EXAMPLES Delores explained**,** "You know how much I like chicken**,**" as she passed her plate for more.

"When will we be leaving**?**" asked Tony.

The plumber shouted**,** "Turn off that faucet**!**" when the water started gushing out of the pipe.

13h. When used with quotation marks, other marks of punctuation are placed according to the following rules:

(1) Commas and periods are placed inside closing quotation marks.

EXAMPLES "I haven't seen the movie**,"** remarked Jeannette, "but I understand that it's excellent**."**

(2) Semicolons and colons are placed outside closing quotation marks.

EXAMPLES Socrates once said, "As for me, all I know is that I know nothing**";** I wonder why everyone thinks he was such a wise man.

The following actresses were nominated for the award for "best performance in a leading role**":** Helen Hunt, Meryl Streep, Cher, and Jodie Foster.

(3) Question marks and exclamation points are placed inside the closing quotation marks if the quotation itself is a question or an exclamation; otherwise, they are placed outside.

EXAMPLES "Is it too cold in here**?"** the manager asked as I shivered.

"Yes**!"** I answered. "Please turn down the air conditioner**!"**

Can you explain the saying "Penny wise, pound foolish**"?**

It's not an insult to be called a "bookworm**"!**

NOTE When both a sentence and the quotation at the end of that sentence are questions or exclamations, only one question mark or exclamation point is used. It goes inside the closing quotation marks.

EXAMPLE Did Elizabeth Barrett Browning write the poem that begins with "How do I love thee**?"**

CONTENT-AREA CONNECTIONS

History

Dialogue. Have students choose two historical figures from a period they have studied and compose a dialogue between them using direct quotations. Students might use figures from different periods. For example, Joan of Arc could talk to Eleanor Roosevelt, or Napoleon could converse with Richard Nixon.

Exercise 2 Writing Sentences with Direct and Indirect Quotations

If a sentence contains a direct quotation, change it to an indirect quotation. If a sentence contains an indirect quotation, change it to a direct quotation. Make sure your answers are correctly punctuated.

EXAMPLES

1. "Where should we go for vacation?" asked my mother.
   1. *My mother asked where we should go for vacation.*
2. My little brother Jason said that he wanted to see castles like the ones in the brochures.
   2. *My little brother Jason said, "I want to see castles like the ones in the brochures."*

1. When we planned our trip to England, Mom said, "Our stops should include some castles."
2. Our tour book says that Colchester Castle, begun in 1076, is a good place to start.
3. Jason asked whether the castles were haunted.
4. "No," said Mom, "and, besides, we'll stay close together."
5. In England, Jason told Mom that he wanted to swim in a moat.
6. "Warwick Castle," said our guide, "is one of the most beautiful."
7. "One of its towers," he went on to say, "was built in 1066."
8. The guide said that the castle contains many works of art.
9. "I like the collection of suits of armor best," said Jason.
10. "Is it still the home of the Earls of Warwick?" I asked.

13i. When you write dialogue (a conversation), begin a new paragraph every time the speaker changes.

EXAMPLE

"What's that?" Sally demanded impatiently.

Luisa seemed surprised. "What's what?"

"That thing, what you got in your hand."

"Oh this . . ." and she held it up for Sally to inspect. "A present."

"A what?"

"A present I picked up."

"Oh." Sally moved her eyes to the house. "Looks like his place burned down. What d'you find inside?"

"Just this," Luisa said, gazing blankly at the house.

"What d'you want that for?"

Ron Arias, "El Mago"

STYLE  **TIP**

In dialogue, a paragraph may be only one line long and may consist of one or more sentence fragments.

Exercise 2 Writing Sentences with Direct and Indirect Quotations

POSSIBLE ANSWERS

1. When we planned our trip to England, Mom said that our stops should include some castles.
2. Our tour book says, "Colchester Castle, begun in 1076, is a good place to start."
3. Jason asked, "Are the castles haunted?"
4. Mom said that they weren't but that we would stay close together.
5. In England, Jason told Mom, "I want to swim in a moat."
6. Our guide said that Warwick Castle is one of the most beautiful.
7. He went on to say that one of its towers had been built in 1066.
8. The guide said, "The castle contains many works of art."
9. Jason said that he liked the collection of suits of armor best.
10. I asked whether it was still the home of the Earls of Warwick.

DIFFERENTIATING INSTRUCTION

Learners Having Difficulty

Give students additional practice with using commas, periods, semicolons, and colons with quotation marks by using sentences cut into strips. First, form small groups of students and give each group a sentence to punctuate based on one of the subrules from **Rule 13h** on p. 316. Give all groups punctuation marks on separate pieces of paper, and have them place the punctuation marks correctly in the sentence. After giving students a few minutes to discuss their sentences, ask a spokesperson from each group to share the sentence with the class by writing it on a transparency.

EXTENSION

Critical Thinking

Metacognition. First, tell or read a brief joke in which two characters speak to each other, and instruct students to transcribe your words. Next, ask students to punctuate the dialogue. Then, ask students the question "Where did you place the quotation marks, and how did you know to place them there?" Encourage students to refer to specific rules they have learned for punctuating dialogue with quotation marks.

MECHANICS

MEETING THE CHALLENGE

"Funniest movie of the summer!" Whenever a new movie debuts, critics give it their mark of approval or disapproval. Clip two or three ads for movies out of a newspaper or magazine. You likely will see many quotation marks in the ads. In a brief paragraph, tell how these quotation marks are used. What do the quotations contribute to the ad? Now, using correct punctuation, create your own ads for movies you have seen. Share your ads with classmates.

ANSWERS

Paragraphs may point out that the use of quotations from critics adds authority to their comments and provides testimonials vouching for the movie. Students' ads will vary but should be correctly punctuated.

13j. **When a quoted passage consists of more than one paragraph, put quotation marks at the beginning of each paragraph and at the end of the entire passage. Do not put quotation marks after any paragraph but the last.**

EXAMPLE "At nine o'clock this morning someone entered the Mill Bank by the back entrance, broke through two thick steel doors guarding the bank's vault, and escaped with sixteen bars of gold.

"No arrests have been made, but state police are confident the case will be solved within a few days."

NOTE A long passage (not dialogue) quoted from a book or another printed source is usually set off from the rest of the text. The entire passage is usually indented and double-spaced. When a quoted passage has been set off in one of these ways, no quotation marks are necessary.

EXAMPLE In his autobiography The Interesting Narrative of the Life of Olaudah Equiano, or Gustavus Vassa, the African, Olaudah Equiano describes encountering African languages other than his own:

> From the time I left my own nation I always found somebody that understood me till I came to the sea coast. The languages of different nations did not totally differ, nor were they so copious as those of the Europeans, particularly the English. They were therefore easily learned; and while I was journeying thus through Africa, I acquired two or three different tongues.

13k. **Use single quotation marks to enclose a quotation within a quotation.**

EXAMPLES Annoyed, Becky snapped, "Don't tell me, 'That's not the way to do it.'"

My uncle said, "Remember the words of Chief Joseph: 'I have heard talk and talk, but nothing is done. Good words do not last long unless they amount to something.' This is good advice."

Tiffany exclaimed, "How dare you say, 'Yuck!'"

Review A Correcting Sentences by Adding Quotation Marks for Dialogue

Correct each of the following passages, adding quotation marks where necessary. Remember to begin a new paragraph each time the speaker changes. Carets indicate paragraph breaks.

EXAMPLE 1. Is Rio de Janeiro the capital of Brazil, asked Linda, or is Brasília?

1. *"Is Rio de Janeiro the capital of Brazil," asked Linda, "or is Brasília?"*

1. "Race-car driver Janet Guthrie," said Chet, reading from his notes, "is a trained physicist who has spent many years working at an aircraft corporation."
2. "Who shot that ball?" Coach Larsen wanted to know. ^"I did," came the reply from the small, frail-looking player. ^"Good shot," said the coach, "but always remember to follow your shot to the basket." ^"I tried, but I was screened," the player explained.
3. "The *Brownsville Beacon*," the editorial began, "will never support a candidate who tells the taxpayers, 'Vote for me, and I will cut taxes.' The reason is simple. Taxes, just like everything else in this inflationary society, must increase. Any candidate who thinks otherwise is either a fool or a liar."
4. In the interview, the candidate said, "I am a very hospitable person." ^"Yes," her husband agreed, "Ralph Waldo Emerson must have been thinking of you when he said, 'Happy is the house that shelters a friend.'"

Differentiating Instruction

Special Education Students

For **Review A,** provide students with strips of paper, each containing a word or phrase from sentence 1, and with self-adhesive squares containing marks of punctuation. Have students physically arrange the parts of the sentence and the punctuation. Then, have them work with a helper to continue this process for the rest of the exercise.

MECHANICS

Learning for Life

Continued on pp. 320–321

Writing a Review. Lead students in a brief discussion of popular music or current television programs. Point out that commenting on artistic work is something they will continue to do throughout life, whether in newspaper columns, in letters to the editor, in e-mail correspondence, or in lunch table conversation.

Allow students to work in small groups to create a four-point rating scale for

Reteaching

Italics and Quotations Marks

To help students review, have a helper prepare an index card for each type of item listed in **Rules 13a–c** and **13l.** For example, one card might say *name of a submarine,* while another might read *television show episode.* Divide the class into two teams, designating one team as *X* and the other as *O,* and draw a tic-tac-toe grid on the chalkboard. Have each team in turn draw a card and identify the correct punctuation for the item (italics or quotation marks). The correct answer earns the team a mark on the tic-tac-toe grid. When the stack has been completed, shuffle the cards and repeat the process. Play continues until one team has made three of its marks in a row.

MECHANICS

Reference Note

Remember that the **titles of long poems and long musical works are italicized,** not enclosed in quotation marks. See the examples on page 312.

13l. Use quotation marks to enclose titles and subtitles of articles, essays, short stories, poems, songs, individual episodes of TV series, and chapters and other parts of books and periodicals.

Type of Title	Examples
Articles	"What Teenagers Need to Know About Diets" "Satellites That Serve Us"
Essays	"Charley in Yellowstone" "An Apartment in Moscow"
Short Stories	"The Man to Send Rain Clouds" "The Pit and the Pendulum"
Poems	"Fog" "Incident" "The End of My Journey"
Songs	"The Ballad of Gregorio Cortez" "Peace Train"
Episodes of TV Series	"The Sure Thing" "Monarch in Waiting"
Chapters and Other Parts of Books and Periodicals	"Life in the First Settlements" "The Talk of the Town"

NOTE When titles listed in 13l appear within quotations, use single quotation marks.

EXAMPLE "Did Thomas Hardy write 'The Dynasts'?" asked Terri.

Oral Practice Correcting Sentences by Adding Quotation Marks for Titles

Read each of the following sentences aloud, and tell which word or word group should be enclosed in quotation marks. If a sentence is already correctly punctuated, say *correct.*

EXAMPLE **1.** Did O. Henry write the story The Last Leaf?
1. Did O. Henry write the story "The Last Leaf"?

1. That address to the United Nations can be found in our literature book, in the chapter titled "Essays and Speeches."

2. One popular Old English riddle song is "Scarborough Fair."

Learning for Life 

Continued from p. 319

evaluating a television series or a musical work. Groups should come up with at least three or four valid criteria on which to rate the work.

Then, have students choose a favorite TV series or CD to review for a friend. Tell students their work will be evaluated based on clear support of the criteria they have chosen and on the correct use of quotation marks and italics. For review, students

3. Have you read the story Split Cherry Tree by Jesse Stuart?
4. Which Eve Merriam poem is that, Cheers or How to Eat a Poem?
5. Have you read Fran Lebowitz's essay Tips for Teens?
6. One of Pat Mora's poems about being bilingual and bicultural is titled Legal Alien.
7. I read Kurt Vonnegut's short story "Harrison Bergeron" last week. 7. C
8. In his essay Misspelling, Charles Kuralt examines some of the difficulties people have with spelling.
9. Fiona said, "My favorite Irish ballad is Cliffs of Dooneen."
10. The whole class enjoyed reading Naomi Shihab Nye's poem Daily.

Review B **Correcting Sentences by Adding Underlining (Italics) and Quotation Marks**

Write the following sentences, adding underlining (italics) and quotation marks where needed.

EXAMPLE 1. Please turn to the chapter titled A Walk in the Highlands.
1. *Please turn to the chapter titled "A Walk in the Highlands."*

1. The Bay Area Youth Theater is presenting Bernard Shaw's play Major Barbara.
2. Tyrone announced that he is going to sing Some Enchanted Evening from the musical South Pacific.
3. I have tickets to the opera Carmen, said Karen, and I would like you to be my guest.
4. Does the Swahili word kwa heri mean the same thing that the Spanish word adiós does?
5. My favorite story by Sir Arthur Conan Doyle is The Adventure of the Dying Detective, which is included in the anthology The Complete Sherlock Holmes.
6. Ms. Loudon said, I enjoyed your report on Ernest Hemingway. Remember, however, that the name Ernest is spelled without an a.
7. In her review of The King and I, the drama critic for the Los Angeles Times commented, This production is an excellent revival of a play that never seems to wear thin.
8. In my paper, which I titled The Hispanic Soldier in Vietnam, I cited several passages from Luis Valdez's play The Buck Private.
9. Mrs. Howard asked, In the play Julius Caesar, who said, This was the noblest Roman of them all? Which Roman was being described?
10. Have you read Hannah Armstrong, one of the poems in the Spoon River Anthology by Edgar Lee Masters?

DIFFERENTIATING INSTRUCTION

Learners Having Difficulty

Before students begin **Review B,** list the following guidelines on the chalkboard:

1. Look for words that are a direct quotation. Copy the sentence, inserting quotation marks and paying attention to where other punctuation marks should go.
2. Look for words and letters used as such, and for foreign words.
3. Look for words that are titles. Decide what the title refers to (a book, a newspaper, and so forth). Use clues in the sentence to help you. If the item is a long work, then it should be underlined (italicized). If it is a shorter work, then use quotation marks.

Advanced Learners

Have students create a guide on the use of italics and quotation marks for titles, to be used as a quick reference when completing writing assignments.

To start, suggest that students brainstorm a list of items to add to the list in the textbook. Have students list all items in alphabetical order and label each item as requiring either italics or quotation marks. Students may lay out and print the guides on a computer or decorate and illustrate their guides by hand.

PRACTICE

Guided and Independent

Reviews You may wish to have students complete **Review B** as guided practice and **Review C** as independent practice.

HOMEWORK

should also check for the correct use of capital letters and commas.

Have students offer their reviews for publication in a classroom or school newspaper or for posting on a classroom or all-school Web page.

EXTENSION

Relating to Literature

If your literature textbook contains the selection "The Fifty-First Dragon" by Heywood Broun, have students read it as a review of dialogue. This story can be used to demonstrate several points, including how tone can be achieved by placement of dialogue tags. Have students refer to the conversation between the dragon and Gawaine. Ask them to note the differences in how the quotations are attributed to the dragon and to Gawaine. [*The dragon's comments are attributed with interrupting expressions. Gawaine's are attributed at the ends of his speeches.*] Then, ask what effects the use of interrupting expressions has. [*It gives the effect of the dragon toying with Gawaine. It makes the reader wait a little longer for the full development of the dragon's thoughts, thereby increasing suspense.*] Suggest that students consider the effects of their dialogue tags as they write their dialogues.

MECHANICS

Review C **Correcting Paragraphs by Adding Underlining (Italics) and Quotation Marks**

Correct the following paragraphs by adding underlining (italics) and quotation marks where necessary.

EXAMPLE **[1]** Are all of these books by or about Benjamin Franklin? asked Bonnie Lou.

1. *"Are all of these books by or about Benjamin Franklin?" asked Bonnie Lou.*

[1] "Yes, Bonnie Lou," Mr. Reyes answered. **[2]** "There's even one, Ben and Me by Robert Lawson, that's a biography written from the point of view of Amos, Franklin's pet mouse."

[3] "This one, The Many Lives of Benjamin Franklin by Mary Pope Osborne, sounds really interesting," said Jasmine.

[4] "It is," Mr. Reyes said. **[5]** "That's exactly what we're going to talk about today—the many lives of this early American genius. **[6]** Who can tell me about one of them?"

[7] "He invented electricity, didn't he?" asked Liam.

[8] "Well, he didn't invent electricity," corrected Mr. Reyes, "but his experiments proved that lightning is a form of electricity."

[9] "Franklin," he continued, "also helped draft some of our important historical documents, and he was a diplomat, a printer, and a publisher. **[10]** Franklin's writings, especially his Autobiography and Poor Richard's Almanack, have given us many well-known sayings."

Numerals in brackets refer to rules tested by the items in the Chapter Review.

1. [13l]
2. [13l, a]
3. [13a]
4. [13a, l]
5. [13a]
6. [13a]
7. [13a]
8. [13l]
9. [13c]
10. [13b]
11. [13a]
12. [13a]
13. [*or* "yes"] [13c]
14. [13d, h(3)]
15. [13a]
16. [13c]
17. [13d, h(1), a]

Chapter Review

A. Correcting Sentences by Adding Underlining (Italics) and Quotation Marks

The following sentences contain errors in the use of underlining (italics) and quotation marks. Write each sentence, adding underlining and quotation marks where needed.

1. The concert ended with a stirring rendition of "The Stars and Stripes Forever."
2. "There's Still Gold in Them Thar Hills," an article in Discover, describes attempts to mine low-grade gold deposits on Quartz Mountain in California.
3. Mozart's opera The Magic Flute is being performed tonight.
4. The fifth episode in the TV series The African Americans is titled "The Harlem Renaissance."
5. I Am Joaquín is an epic poem about Mexican American culture.
6. As a baby sitter I have read the children's book The Pokey Little Puppy at least a dozen times.
7. The journalist Horace Greeley founded the New York Tribune, an influential newspaper.
8. Although the poem "When You Are Old" has three stanzas, it contains only one sentence.
9. The word recommended has two m's but only one c.
10. Robert Fulton's steamboat, Claremont, was the first one that could be operated without losing money.
11. My father always swore by Newsweek, but Mother preferred U.S. News & World Report.
12. In his novel David Copperfield, Dickens draws a vivid picture of Victorian life.
13. In Spanish, sí means yes; in French, si is also used to mean yes, but only in answer to a negative statement.
14. Tim asked, "What time did they say they would be here?"
15. Usually, they read the Daily News on Sundays.
16. Those b's look like 6's.
17. "I didn't think I would be able to sit through an opera," said Brittany, "but I really enjoyed Hansel and Gretel."

ASSESSING

Monitoring Progress

Chapter Review. To assess student progress, you may want to compare the types of items missed on the **Diagnostic Preview** to those missed on the **Chapter Review.** If students have not made significant progress, you may want to refer them to **Chapter 17: Correcting Common Errors, Exercises 32** and **33,** for additional practice.

MECHANICS

RESOURCES

Punctuation

Review

- *Language & Sentence Skills Practice,* pp. 300–302

Assessment

- *Holt Handbook Chapter Tests with Answer Key,* pp. 25–26, 52

18. [13a]
19. [13d, c, h(3)]
20. [13a]

18. On Mondays during football season, the entire family watches *Monday Night Football* on television.

19. "How many *m*'s and *t*'s does the word *committee* have?" asked Betty.

20. One of Kathryn's favorite novels is *Martin Chuzzlewit* by Charles Dickens.

B. Punctuating Dialogue by Adding Quotation Marks

The following dialogue contains errors in the use of quotation marks. Write each sentence, adding quotation marks where needed.

21. [13d, h(1)]
22. [13d, h(3)]
23. [13d, h(1)]
24. [13d, h(3)]
25. [13d, h(3), h(1)]
26. [13d, h(1), k, h(3)]
27. [13d, h(1)]
28. [13d, h(1)]
29. [13d, h(3)]
30. [13d, h(1), k, h(3)]

[21] "Before our field trip begins," continued Mrs. Garcia, "be sure that you have a notebook and a collection kit."

[22] "Will we need binoculars?" asked Melvin.

[23] "Leave your binoculars at home," answered Mrs. Garcia. "Your ears will be more helpful than your eyes on this trip."

[24] "What will we be able to hear out there?" asked Arnold.

[25] "What a question!" exclaimed Felicia. "This time of year, you can hear all sorts of sounds."

[26] "I hope that we hear and see some birds," said Koko. "Didn't someone once say, 'The birds warble sweet in the springtime'?"

[27] "When," asked James, "do we eat lunch? My mom packed my favorite kinds of sandwiches."

[28] "Don't worry," said Mrs. Garcia. "Most birds are quiet at midday. We can have our lunch then."

[29] Ruth Ann said, "Mrs. Garcia, would you believe that I don't know one birdcall from another?"

[30] "That's all right, Ruth Ann," laughed Mrs. Garcia. "Some birds call out their own names. For example, the bobolink repeats its name: 'Bob-o-link! Bob-o-link!'"

C. Correcting Paragraphs by Adding Underlining (Italics) and Quotation Marks

The following paragraph contains errors in the use of underlining (italics) and quotation marks. Write each sentence, adding underlining and quotation marks where necessary. Be sure to start a new paragraph each time the speaker changes. Carets indicate paragraph breaks.

31. [13d, h(1), h(3)]

[31] "As most of you probably know," said Mr. Sundaresan, our geography teacher, "Everest, on the border of Tibet and Nepal, is the

MECHANICS

324 Punctuation

world's highest mountain; does anyone know the name of the world's second-highest peak? Yes, Elaine? [32] It's K2. [33] Yes, said Mr. Sundaresan, impressed. How did you know? [34] Well, said Elaine, for Christmas my parents gave me a book called K2: Challenging the Sky by Roberto Mantovani. I just finished reading it last night. [35] Very good, said Mr. Sundaresan. Now can anyone tell me the name of the highest mountain in Europe? I'll give you a hint: It's not in Switzerland. Elaine's hand shot up again. [36] Isn't it Mont Blanc, on the border of France and Italy? she asked. [37] Quite right, said Mr. Sundaresan. May I ask how you knew that? [38] For my birthday I got a copy of The Alps and Their People by Susan Bullen. It's a really interesting book. [39] Well, have you read any books on the Rockies, Elaine? asked Mr. Sundaresan. [40] As a matter of fact, I just started reading The Rockies by David Muench, and before you ask, I can tell you that Mount Elbert is the highest peak in the Rockies!

32. [13i, d, h(1)]
33. [13i, d, h(1), h(3)]
34. [13i, d, h(1), a]
35. [13i, d, h(1)]
36. [13i, d, h(3)]
37. [13i, d, h(1), h(3)]
38. [13i, d, a, h(1)]
39. [13i, d, h(3)]
40. [13i, d, a, h(3)]

Writing Application

Writing a Dialogue

Using Quotation Marks Write a page of dialogue in which characters tell a story, either fact or fiction, through a conversation.

Prewriting Decide on a story and a few characters to tell it. You could retell a favorite anecdote, report the exact words of an amusing conversation, or write an imaginary interview with a famous person.

Writing As you write your first draft, think about making the characters sound different from one another.

Revising First, ask a classmate to read your dialogue. Revise any parts that are unclear or uninteresting to your reader. Be sure that you have begun a new paragraph every time the speaker changes. Also, check that you have followed the rules for punctuating direct quotations and quotations with interrupting expressions.

Publishing Read through your dialogue again, this time concentrating on correcting errors in grammar, spelling, and punctuation. You and your classmates may want to work in small groups to present your dialogues to the class.

APPLICATION

Writing Application

Prewriting Tip. Characterization—making characters sound different from one another—requires the use of a variety of elements. Choose a few lines of dialogue from a short story in which the characterization is clear, such as Truman Capote's "A Christmas Memory" or Toni Cade Bambara's "Blues Ain't No Mockin Bird." Have students analyze the dialogue. They might point out that the use of formal or informal speech, slang, or dialect can create a distinct style; sentence length can convey information about mood or personality; and the length and placement of dialogue tags can contribute to the emotional tone of the situations and characters.

Writing Tip. This activity encourages students to try out some of the many variations possible in constructing dialogue. Students may have to refer to the rules repeatedly, so you may want to hand out a summary sheet of rules from the textbook.

Scoring Rubric. While you will want to pay particular attention to students' use of italics and quotation marks, you will also want to evaluate overall writing performance. You may want to give a split score to indicate development and clarity of the composition as well as mechanics skills.

CHAPTER

14

INTRODUCING THE CHAPTER

- The first part of this chapter explains the use of apostrophes to form the possessive case of nouns and covers the absence of apostrophes in possessive personal pronouns. The second part of the chapter discusses the use of apostrophes to form contractions and plurals.
- The chapter closes with a **Writing Application** feature that asks students to write a paragraph using possessive nouns, plural nouns, indefinite pronouns, and the possessive case correctly.
- For help in integrating this chapter with writing assignments, use the **Teaching Strands** chart on pp. T24–T25.

CHAPTER 14

Punctuation

Apostrophes

Diagnostic Preview

Revising Sentences in a Journal Entry by Using Apostrophes Correctly

In the following journal entry, Josh often incorrectly uses contractions and possessive forms. Write the correct form of each incorrect word or expression used.

EXAMPLE **[1]** Im still working on todays assignment.

1. I'm; today's

[**1**] Ive just finished tonights homework. [**2**] Writing a composition is usually two hours hard work for me, but Im pleased with this one. [**3**] Ill read it over in the morning to make sure that my handwritings legible. [**4**] My teacher has trouble reading my *ds, ts,* and *os.* [**5**] He also objects to my overuse of *ands* and *sos.* [**6**] If theres an error, Ill have to revise my composition. [**7**] Thats one good reason for being careful, isnt it?

[**8**] My compositions title is "The Reign of Animals." [**9**] Moms friend suggested that I call it "Whose in Charge Here?" [**10**] My familys love for animals is well known in the neighborhood and among our friends'. [**11**] At the moment were owned by two inside cats; three outside cats; our resident dog, Pepper; and a visiting dog we call Hugo.

[**12**] During Peppers walks, Im usually followed by at least one other dog. [**13**] Some owners care of their dogs never seems to go beyond feeding them. [**14**] The city councils decision to fine owners'

Numerals in brackets refer to rules tested by the items in the Diagnostic Preview.

1. I've/tonight's [14g, a]
2. hours'/I'm [14b, g]
3. I'll/handwriting's [14g]
4. *d*'s/*t*'s/*o*'s [14h]
5. *and*'s/*so*'s [14h]
6. there's/I'll [14g]
7. That's/isn't [14g]
8. composition's [14a]
9. Mom's/Who's [14a, c, g]
10. family's/friends [14a, b]
11. we're [14g]
12. Pepper's/I'm [14a, g]
13. owners' [14b]
14. council's/owners/their [14a, b, c]

CHAPTER RESOURCES

Internet

- Web resources: go.hrw.com

go.hrw.com

Practice & Review

- *Language & Sentence Skills Practice,* pp. 308–318
- *Language & Sentence Skills Practice Answer Key,* pp. 128–131

Application & Enrichment

- *Language & Sentence Skills Practice,* pp. 307, 319, 320–321, 322
- *Language & Sentence Skills Practice Answer Key,* pp. 128, 131–132

who let they're dogs run loose makes sense. [15] Hugos a huge dog who's always wandering loose in my neighborhood. [16] We took him in several times after hed narrowly escaped being hit by a car. [17] In fact, Hugos and Peppers feeding dishes sit side by side in our kitchen.

[18] Peter, our senior cat, who was once one of our neighborhoods strays, isnt about to run from anyones dog. [19] At times weve seen him safeguarding other cats of ours' by running in front of them and staring down an approaching dog and it's owner. [20] Our dogs and cats different personalities never cease to fascinate me.

15. Hugo's [14g]
16. he'd [14g]
17. Hugo's/Pepper's [14f]
18. neighborhood's/ isn't/anyone's [14a, g, d]
19. we've/ours/its [14g, c]
20. dogs'/cats' [14b]

Possessive Case

The ***possessive case*** of a noun or pronoun shows ownership or possession.

EXAMPLES **Larry's** friend Dana uses a wheelchair.

You need a good **night's** sleep.

Can I count on **their** votes?

I appreciate **your** waiting so long.

14a. To form the possessive case of most singular nouns, add an apostrophe and an *s.*

EXAMPLES	
Yuki**'s** problem	a bus**'s** wheel
the mayor**'s** desk	this evening**'s** paper
Mrs. Ross**'s** job	a dollar**'s** worth

NOTE For a proper name ending in *s,* add only an apostrophe if the name has two or more syllables and if the addition of *'s* would make the name awkward to pronounce.

EXAMPLES	
Ulysses' plan	**West Indies'** export
Mrs. Rawlings' car	**Texas'** governor

For a singular common noun ending in *s,* add both an apostrophe and an *s* if the added *s* is pronounced as a separate syllable.

EXAMPLES	
the actress**'s** costumes	the dress**'s** sleeves
the class**'s** teacher	a platypus**'s** tail

MECHANICS

Assessing

Entry-Level Assessment

Diagnostic Preview. You may wish to use the **Diagnostic Preview** to determine the problems students might have using apostrophes. Give this test when students are assigned to write descriptive essays or personal narratives using contractions in dialogue or possessives in descriptions such as *sister's hair* or *brothers' favorite activities.*

Possessive Case

Rules 14a–f *(pp. 327–335)*

OBJECTIVES

- To form the possessive case of singular and plural nouns
- To revise phrases by forming the possessive case of nouns
- To identify correct forms of pronouns
- To revise phrases by using the possessive case

Differentiating Instruction

- *Developmental Language & Sentence Skills,* pp. 139–140
- *Developmental Language & Sentence Skills Guided Practice Teacher's Notes and Answer Key,* p. 34

Assessment

- *Holt Handbook Chapter Tests with Answer Key,* pp. 27–28, 52

PRETEACHING

Lesson Starter

Motivating. Tell students that they are going to work as a class to create a conversation. Begin the conversation with an opener like "I can't believe that Ray's cat . . . ," and call on students at random to build the conversation by each adding a sentence that includes a contraction, a possessive phrase, or both. Point out to students how common such constructions are in everyday conversation.

PRACTICE

Exercise 1 **Using Apostrophes to Form the Possessive Case of Singular Nouns**

POSSIBLE ANSWERS

1. baby's bottle
2. uncle's house
3. year's events
4. cent's worth
5. class's problem
6. Terry's friend
7. Ellen's plans
8. mouse's cheese
9. Mr. Chan's daughter
10. Miss Reynolds' car
11. plane's wings
12. boss's secretary
13. child's game
14. Ms. Sanchez's son
15. horse's mane
16. Paris's cafés
17. system's problem
18. judge's robe
19. Mr. Jones's car
20. synagogue's location

MECHANICS

Exercise 1 **Using Apostrophes to Form the Possessive Case of Singular Nouns**

Form the possessive case of each of the following nouns. After each possessive word, give an appropriate noun.

EXAMPLE 1. Teresa
1. *Teresa's pencil*

1. baby	**8.** mouse	**15.** horse
2. uncle	**9.** Mr. Chan	**16.** Paris
3. year	**10.** Miss Reynolds	**17.** system
4. cent	**11.** plane	**18.** judge
5. class	**12.** boss	**19.** Mr. Jones
6. Terry	**13.** child	**20.** synagogue
7. Ellen	**14.** Ms. Sanchez	

14b. **To form the possessive case of a plural noun ending in *s*, add only the apostrophe.**

EXAMPLES two birds' feathers — all three cousins' vacation
the Garzas' patio — the Girl Scouts' uniforms

Although most plural nouns end in *s*, some are irregular. To form the possessive case of a plural noun that does not end in *s*, add an apostrophe and *s*.

Reference Note
For more examples of **irregular plurals,** see page 368.

EXAMPLES children's shoes — those deer's food

Exercise 2 **Forming the Possessive Case of Plural Nouns**

Form the possessive case of each of the following plural nouns.

EXAMPLE 1. knives
1. *knives'*

1. men	**8.** cattle	**15.** runners
2. cats	**9.** mice	**16.** attorneys
3. teachers	**10.** parents	**17.** allies
4. enemies	**11.** the Smiths	**18.** friends
5. princesses	**12.** sheep	**19.** women
6. dollars	**13.** wives	**20.** bats
7. elves	**14.** O'Gradys	

1. men's
2. cats'
3. teachers'
4. enemies'
5. princesses'
6. dollars'
7. elves'
8. cattle's
9. mice's
10. parents'
11. the Smiths'
12. sheep's
13. wives'
14. O'Gradys'
15. runners'
16. attorneys'
17. allies'
18. friends'
19. women's
20. bats'

RESOURCES

Possessive Case

Practice

- *Language & Sentence Skills Practice,* pp. 308–311

Differentiating Instruction

- *Developmental Language & Sentence Skills,* pp. 139–140

Exercise 3 Revising Phrases by Forming the Possessive Case of Nouns

Revise the following phrases by using the possessive case.

EXAMPLE 1. the parties for seniors
1. the seniors' parties

1. prizes for winners
2. manners for teenagers
3. yokes of oxen
4. duties of nurses
5. names of players
6. suits for women
7. ideas of inventors
8. medals for veterans
9. routines for dancers
10. roles for actresses

NOTE In general, you should not use an apostrophe to form the plural of a noun.

INCORRECT Two player's left their gym suits on the locker room floor.

CORRECT Two **players** left their gym suits on the locker room floor. [plural]

CORRECT Two **players'** gym suits were left on the locker room floor. [The apostrophe shows that the gym suits belong to the two players.]

Review A Recognizing Correct Forms of Nouns

Choose the correct form of each noun in parentheses in the following paragraph.

EXAMPLES Several **[1]** (*photographs, photograph's*) taken by *Voyagers 1* and *2* were combined into the illustration on the next page to show a few of **[2]** (*Saturns, Saturn's*) many satellites.
1. photographs
2. Saturn's

At least eighteen natural satellites, or celestial [1] (*bodies, body's*), revolve around the planet Saturn. Seven of our solar [2] (*systems, system's*) nine planets have satellites, but Saturn and Jupiter have the most. [3] (*Scientists, Scientists'*) figures on the true number of [4] (*satellites, satellite's*) vary, and new space [5] (*probes, probe's*) sometimes reveal more satellites. Two [6] (*planets, planets'*), Earth and Pluto, have only one satellite each. Of course, you are already familiar with our

Exercise 3 Revising Phrases by Forming the Possessive Case of Nouns

ANSWERS

1. winners' prizes
2. teenagers' manners
3. oxen's yokes
4. nurses' duties
5. players' names
6. women's suits
7. inventors' ideas
8. veterans' medals
9. dancers' routines
10. actresses' roles

DIFFERENTIATING INSTRUCTION

MECHANICS

Learners Having Difficulty

To personalize the use of possessive case, have students use possessive case nouns and pronouns to describe objects in their immediate surroundings. To begin, have each student write three items that belong to other students in the classroom and three things that are shared by two people. Then, have students write the name of the owner or owners in front of each object listed, using apostrophes correctly. You may want to offer models like the following:

Maija's backpack
winner's prize
his sweater
Tina and Jed's teacher

MINI-LESSON Mechanics

Plurals. Before students create plural possessive forms, you may want to review with them how to form plurals. Provide a list of words like the following, and ask students to give the plural form of each word.

watch	[*watches*]	tax	[*taxes*]
potato	[*potatoes*]	woman	[*women*]

Refer students to **Chapter 16: Spelling,** for rules and examples for forming plurals.

Possessive Case 329

Differentiating Instruction

English-Language Learners

Spanish. Spanish has a possessive form for pronouns but not for nouns; therefore, students may be confused about the use of apostrophes. For example, in Spanish, "his book" would be translated as *su libro,* but "Javier's book" would be translated as *el libro de Javier* ("the book of Javier"). You may want to give students a series of statements to change by using the possessive form of the noun. An example is "This book belongs to José. It is ____________ book." (*José's*)

Cantonese and Vietnamese. Cantonese and Vietnamese form possessives with a construction more like the English *wheel of the bus* than *Mike's car.* That, combined with the lack of *s* sounds at the ends of words in both languages and the consonant clusters produced by the possessive *–s* in English, may cause speakers of Cantonese and Vietnamese to have difficulty recognizing and pronouncing possessives. Discuss the meaning of the possessive with the students. Illustrate with objects in the classroom, if necessary. Reinforce pronunciation of the possessive *–s* by prompting students with a card with *'s* on it.

Direct Teaching

Correcting Misconceptions

Plural Possessives. Many students habitually add an apostrophe and an *s* to form the plural possessive of all nouns. After all, apostrophes are commonly used incorrectly on signs and in ad copy, and *student's, students,* and *students',* for example, all sound alike. Remind students that the plural form does not change when the possessive ending is added; they should form the plural of a noun first, and then add the possessive ending.

MECHANICS

own [7] (*planets, planet's*) satellite, the moon. As you can see from this illustration, [8] (*satellite's, satellites'*) sizes and features vary greatly. Titan, a satellite of Saturn, is the largest of that [9] (*planets, planet's*) satellites. Another of [10] (*Saturns, Saturn's*) satellites, Mimas, has a crater that covers about one third of its diameter.

14c. **Possessive personal pronouns do not require an apostrophe.**

Reference Note

For more about **using pronouns correctly,** see Chapter 7.

Possessive Personal Pronouns	
Singular	**Plural**
my, mine	our, ours
your, yours	your, yours
his, her, hers, its	their, theirs

My, your, her, its, our, and *their* are used before nouns or pronouns. *Mine, yours, hers, ours,* and *theirs,* on the other hand, are not used before a noun or pronoun; they are used as subjects, subject complements, or objects in sentences. *His* may be used in either way.

EXAMPLES		
	Lee has **your** sweater.	Lee has a sweater of **yours.**
	That is **your** watch.	That watch is **yours.**
	Her idea was wonderful.	**Hers** was the best idea.
	This is **our** plant.	This plant is **ours.**
	There is **his** CD.	There is a CD of **his.**

Reference Note

For more about ***whose, its,*** and ***their,*** see pages 384, 379, and 382.

NOTE The possessive form of *who* is *whose,* not *who's.* Similarly, do not write *it's* for *its,* or *they're* for *their.*

EXAMPLES **Whose** [not *Who's*] book is this?

Its [not *It's*] cover is torn.

Is that **their** [not *they're*] copy?

Exercise 4 Choosing Correct Forms of Possessive Personal Pronouns

Choose the correct pronoun in parentheses in each of the following sentences.

EXAMPLE 1. Ralph Ellison, (*who's, whose*) book *Invisible Man* won a National Book Award, studied music at Tuskegee Institute.

1. *whose*

1. Did you know, Sumi, that two poems of (*yours, yours'*) have been chosen for the literary magazine?
2. When I first read that book, I was surprised by the high quality of (*its, it's*) artwork.
3. (*Hers, Her's*) is the bicycle with the reflectors on (*its, it's*) fenders.
4. Eudora Welty, (*who's, whose*) short stories often involve eccentric characters, is my favorite writer.
5. "The trophy is (*ours, our's*)!" shouted the captain as the *Flying S* crossed the finish line.
6. (*Theirs, Theirs'*) is the only house with blue shutters.
7. Penny and Carla worked as gardeners this summer and saved (*their, they're*) money for a ski trip.
8. The students (*who's, whose*) names are called should report backstage.
9. (*Their, They're*) schedule calls for a test on Tuesday.
10. (*Who's, Whose*) signature is this?

14d. Indefinite pronouns in the possessive case require an apostrophe and *s*.

EXAMPLES nobody**'s** wishes another**'s** viewpoint
someone**'s** license neither**'s** school

Exercise 5 Choosing Correct Forms of Possessive Pronouns

Choose the correct pronoun in parentheses in each of the following sentences.

EXAMPLE 1. That Mozart CD is (*hers, her's*).

1. *hers*

1. (*No ones, No one's*) guess was correct.
2. (*Ours, Our's*) works better than (*theirs, their's*).
3. (*Who's, Whose*) game is that?

Reference Note

For a list of **indefinite pronouns,** see page 9.

HELP

For the expressions *everyone else* and *nobody else,* the correct possessives are *everyone else's* and *nobody else's.*

Exercise 4

DISTRIBUTED REVIEW

Have students find the following constructions in the designated sentences: sentence 1—a direct address [*Sumi*]; sentence 4—a predicate nominative [*writer*]; sentence 7—a compound verb [*worked, saved*]

RETEACHING

Apostrophes

Activity. If students have difficulty using the possessive forms correctly, try a hands-on approach. Prepare a list of singular and plural nouns and pronouns (for example, *student*, *seniors*, *it*, *our*, *Paula and Li*) and a list of possible possessions (for example, *diamonds, video collection*, *best-selling novel*). Cut each list into strips that each contain one noun, pronoun, or possession, and form one stack of noun and pronoun strips and a second stack of the possible possessions strips. Then, have each student draw one strip from each of the two stacks and create a possessive phrase by adding an apostrophe or apostrophe and an *s* where needed. (*Possible answers: student's diamonds, seniors' video collection.*) You may wish to have volunteers write their combinations on the chalkboard and have the class check for accurate apostrophe placement.

Review B **Writing the Singular, Plural, and Possessive Forms of Nouns**

POSSIBLE ANSWERS

1. friend, friend's house, friends, friends' houses
2. typist, typist's desk, typists, typists' desks
3. bicycle, bicycle's tire, bicycles, bicycles' tires
4. referee, referee's whistle, referees, referees' whistles
5. sheep, sheep's nose, sheep, sheep's noses
6. woman, woman's dress, women, women's dresses
7. penny, penny's date, pennies, pennies' dates
8. dress, dress's collar, dresses, dresses' collars
9. musician, musician's fee, musicians, musicians' fees
10. lioness, lioness's cub, lionesses, lionesses' cubs
11. actor, actor's part, actors, actors' parts
12. mechanic, mechanic's car, mechanics, mechanics' cars
13. deer, deer's tail, deer, deer's tails, *or* deers, deers' tails
14. artist, artist's easel, artists, artists' easels
15. purse, purse's strap, purses, purses' straps
16. man, man's shirt, men, men's shirts
17. truck, truck's headlights, trucks, trucks' headlights
18. dish, dish's pattern, dishes, dishes' patterns
19. window, window's shape, windows, windows' shapes
20. mouse, mouse's ear, mice, mice's ears

MECHANICS

4. (*Theirs, Their's*) is the best frozen yogurt in town.
5. Your car needs to have (*its, it's*) oil changed.
6. It wasn't (*anyone's, anyones'*) fault that we missed the bus.
7. (*Her's, Hers*) is the best project in the Science Fair.
8. (*Someones, Someone's, Someones'*) choir robe was left on the bus.
9. (*Everybodys, Everybody's, Everybodys'*) morale suffered.
10. That dog of (*their's, theirs*) should be on a leash.

Reference Note

For information on **forming the plurals of nouns,** see Chapter 16.

Review B Writing the Singular, Plural, and Possessive Forms of Nouns

On a piece of paper, make four columns headed *Singular, Singular Possessive, Plural,* and *Plural Possessive.* Write each of those forms of the following nouns. Add a suitable noun to follow each word in the possessive case. If you do not know how to spell a plural form, use a dictionary.

EXAMPLE

	Singular	Singular Possessive	Plural	Plural Possessive
1.	*dog*	*dog's owner*	*dogs*	*dogs' owners*

1. friend	**6.** woman	**11.** actor	**16.** man
2. typist	**7.** penny	**12.** mechanic	**17.** truck
3. bicycle	**8.** dress	**13.** deer	**18.** dish
4. referee	**9.** musician	**14.** artist	**19.** window
5. sheep	**10.** lioness	**15.** purse	**20.** mouse

Review C Correcting the Forms of Nouns and Pronouns

Identify and correct the ten incorrect possessive forms in the following paragraph.

EXAMPLE **[1]** The women shown in these photographs welcomed us to the Shaker village of Pleasant Hill, Kentucky, during our history class' field trip last spring.

1. class's

1. women's
2. village's
3. their
4. Shakers'/its
5. Everyone's
6. children's

[**1**] As you can see, the style of the ~~womens~~ dresses is quite old. [**2**] In fact, the ~~villages~~ history goes back to 1806. [**3**] That was the year that the religious group known as the Shakers founded ~~they're~~ own community. [**4**] We learned that the ~~Shaker's~~ lively way of dancing gave the group ~~it's~~ name. [**5**] ~~Everyones~~ life in the Shaker village was supposed to be orderly, simple, and productive. [**6**] This basic harmony was true of even the ~~childrens'~~ routines. [**7**] During the ~~days~~ tour of the village, we saw several people practicing Shaker crafts. [**8**] One guide of ~~our's~~

told us that the Shakers invented the common clothespin and the flat broom and designed useful furniture and boxes. [**9**] I enjoyed visiting the gardens and the Centre Family House and imagining what a ~~Shakers~~' life must have been like.

7. day's
8. ours
9. Shaker's

14e. Generally, in compound words, names of organizations and businesses, and words showing joint possession, only the last word is possessive in form.

COMPOUND WORDS	community **board's** meeting
	vice-president's contract
	her brother-in-**law's** gifts
ORGANIZATIONS	the Museum of **Art's** budget
	United **Fund's** drive
BUSINESSES	Berkeley Milk **Company's** trucks
JOINT POSSESSION	Peggy and **Lisa's** tent [The tent belongs to both Peggy and Lisa.]
	children and **parents'** concerns [The children and the parents have the same concerns.]

When one of the words showing joint possession is a pronoun, both words should be possessive in form.

EXAMPLE **Peggy's** and **my** tent [not *Peggy and my tent*]

STYLE TIP

Use a phrase beginning with *of* or *for* to avoid awkward possessive forms.

AWKWARD
the Society for the Prevention of Cruelty to Animals' advertisement

BETTER
the advertisement **for** the Society for the Prevention of Cruelty to Animals

PRACTICE

Guided and Independent

Reviews You may wish to have students complete **Review B** as guided practice and **Review C** as independent practice.

HOMEWORK

MECHANICS

CONTENT-AREA CONNECTIONS

Science

Research. As a short research project that will give students a chance to practice using the possessive case while also learning about important achievements, challenge students to research and create short reports on mathematical or scientific concepts that bear their discoverers' names in the possessive case. One example is Bernoulli's principle, which explains how the speed of a fluid affects its pressure. Students should create short written versions of their research, and volunteers may want to explain their findings to the class.

Exercise 6 **Using the Possessive Case**

ANSWERS

1. Sylvia's and Eric's tickets
2. the FBI's investigation
3. Gwen and Carlos's duet
4. the master sergeant's uniform
5. the Grand Canyon's history
6. Isabel's and my job
7. the Acme Life Insurance Company's agent
8. my uncle's and our tractors
9. the Sales Department's award
10. her mother-in-law's and her cousin's businesses

MECHANICS

Reference Note

For more about **acronyms** see page 268.

NOTE The possessive of an acronym (NASA, DOS) or an abbreviation (CIA, CBS) is formed by adding an apostrophe and *s.*

EXAMPLES NASA**'s** latest space probe

CBS**'s** hit television series

14f. When two or more persons possess something individually, each of their names is possessive in form.

EXAMPLES **Mrs. Martin's** and **Mrs. Blair's** cars [the cars of two different women]

Asha's and **Daniella's** tennis rackets [individual, not joint, possession]

Exercise 6 Using the Possessive Case

Use the possessive case to rewrite the following word groups.

EXAMPLE 1. the book owned by Natalie and Stan

1. *Natalie and Stan's book*

1. the ticket of Sylvia and the ticket of Eric
2. an investigation by the FBI
3. the duet of Gwen and Carlos
4. a uniform belonging to the master sergeant
5. the history of the Grand Canyon
6. the job shared by Isabel and me
7. an agent for the Acme Life Insurance Company
8. one tractor belonging to my uncle and one to us
9. the award received by the Sales Department
10. the business of her mother-in-law and the business of her cousin

Review D Identifying Words That Require Apostrophes

Identify the ten words requiring apostrophes in the following paragraph. Then, write the words, inserting the apostrophes.

EXAMPLE [1] Have you ever heard of the U.S. Patent Offices Hall of Fame for inventors?

1. *Offices—Office's*

1. Fame's

[1] The Hall of Fames members, who are both American and foreign, include many people that you've probably heard of as well as some you haven't. [2] Vladimir Kosma Zworykin's picture tube helped

CONTENT-AREA CONNECTIONS

Social Studies

Report on a Person. Refer students to any social studies report they have written about a person, and ask them to check for the correct use of apostrophes. If students do not have an essay to check, ask them to write two paragraphs about the accomplishments of their favorite role model and then check for the correct use of apostrophes.

lead to ~~televisions~~ development. [3] Charles Richard Drew changed ~~peoples~~ lives all over the world with his work on blood plasma in transfusions. [4] Luther ~~Burbanks~~ accomplishment was the development of more than eight hundred new plant varieties. [5] Heart ~~patients~~ pacemakers were invented by Wilson Greatbatch. [6] You'll probably recognize such famous inventors as the Ford Motor ~~Companys~~ founder, Henry Ford. [7] Of course, Thomas ~~Edisons~~ and Alexander Graham ~~Bells~~ achievements assured their enduring fame. [8] No ~~ones~~ pleasure is greater than mine that Orville and Wilbur ~~Wrights~~ invention of the airplane landed them in such good company, too.

2. television's
3. people's
4. Burbank's
5. patients'
6. Company's
7. Edison's/Bell's
8. one's/Wright's

Contractions

14g. Use an apostrophe to show where letters, numerals, or words have been omitted in a contraction.

A ***contraction*** is a shortened form of a word, a group of words, or a numeral. The apostrophes in contractions indicate where letters, numerals, or words have been left out.

EXAMPLES		
	who is . . . who**'s**	I am . . . I**'m**
	1991 . . . **'91**	you are . . . you**'re**
	of the clock . . . **o'**clock	we had . . . we**'d**
	let us . . . let**'s**	she has . . . she**'s**
	she will . . . she**'ll**	I had . . . I**'d**
	Bill is . . . Bill**'s**	we have . . . we**'ve**

Ordinarily, the word *not* is shortened to *n't* and added to a verb without any change in the spelling of the verb.

EXAMPLES		
	is not . . . is**n't**	were not . . . were**n't**
	are not . . . are**n't**	has not . . . has**n't**
	does not . . . does**n't**	have not . . . have**n't**
	do not . . . do**n't**	had not . . . had**n't**
	did not . . . did**n't**	would not . . . would**n't**
EXCEPTIONS	will not . . . wo**n't**	cannot . . . ca**n't**

STYLE  **TIP**

Many people consider contractions informal. Therefore, it is usually best to avoid using them in formal writing and speech.

INFORMAL
The Founding Fathers couldn't foresee the mobility of modern life.

FORMAL
The Founding Fathers **could not** foresee the mobility of modern life.

Contractions

Rule 14g *(pp. 335–337)*

OBJECTIVE

- To correct sentences by using apostrophes for contractions

DIRECT TEACHING

Modeling and Demonstration

Contractions. Model how to distinguish contractions from possessive pronouns by using the following examples: *Who is at bat? Whose bat is that? It is roaring. Listen to its roar.* First, ask if *Who is,* in the first sentence, can be made into a contraction. [*yes;* Who's] Next, ask if *Whose,* in the second sentence, can be made into a contraction. [*no*] Explain that *whose* is a possessive pronoun and should not be confused with the contraction *who's.* Then, ask if *It is,* in the third example, can be made into a contraction. [*yes;* it's] Ask if *its,* in the fourth sentence, should also have an apostrophe. [*no*] Point out that *its* is a possessive pronoun and should not be confused with the contraction *it's* meaning *it is.* Now, have a volunteer use another example from this chapter to demonstrate how to distinguish contractions from possessive pronouns.

MECHANICS

RESOURCES

Contractions

Practice

- *Language & Sentence Skills Practice,* p. 312

Differentiating Instruction

- *Developmental Language & Sentence Skills,* p. 140

Extension

Relating to Literature

You may want to assign parts to students and have them read aloud dialogue from a short story such as Daphne du Maurier's "The Birds." Ask students why the author used contractions. [*Contractions make dialogue sound natural because they are informal and conversational.*]

Then, have students re-read the dialogue, replacing all contractions with complete words. Discuss with students what effect removing the contractions has on the dialogue. [*Removing contractions may cause the language to sound stilted and unnatural.*]

MECHANICS

Differentiating Instruction

English-Language Learners

Spanish. Because Spanish has no written contracted verb forms, you may wish to use a visual aid to show students how contractions are formed. Write the following groups of words on the chalkboard.

is not she will let us

Then, cross out the *o* in *not* and cover the *o* with an index card on which you have written a large apostrophe. Do the same for the *wi* in *will* and for the *u* in *us*. Emphasize that when the apostrophe is added, the pronunciation of the words changes: *isn't*, *she'll*, and *let's*. Have students work in small groups to practice forming and pronouncing other contractions.

Hmong. Hmong speakers may find contractions confusing because written Hmong does not use apostrophes. Remind students that English uses apostrophes in contractions to indicate missing letters. Students should practice forming contractions: *Do not, don't; I am, I'm.*

Meeting the Challenge

Writers sometimes have trouble with the following pairs of words: *it's/its, they're/their, who's/whose,* and *you're/your. It's, they're, who's,* and *you're* all have apostrophes and are contractions (of *it is/has, they are, who is/has,* and *you are*). Possessive pronouns make up the other set. How can writers remember which word to use at which time? For each pair of words, write a sentence to help you distinguish between the two words. For example, for *it's/its*, you could write "It's time to feed the puppy its food." Share your four sentences with your classmates.

Answer
Sentences will vary, but students should use each word correctly.

Do not confuse contractions with possessive pronouns.

Contractions	Possessive Pronouns
Who's at bat? [Who is]	**Whose** bat is that?
It's roaring. [It is]	Listen to **its** roar.
You're too busy. [You are]	**Your** friend is busy.
There's a kite. [There is]	That kite is **theirs.**
They're tall trees. [They are]	**Their** trees are tall.

Exercise 7 Correcting Sentences by Using Apostrophes for Contractions

Write each incorrect contraction in the following sentences, adding an apostrophe as necessary. If a sentence is already correct, write *C.*

EXAMPLE 1. Hes pleased by his promotion.
1. He's

1. "~~Youve~~ changed," she said. 1. You've
2. World War II ended in ~~45~~. 2. '45
3. ~~Whos~~ coming to the party? 3. Who's
4. "The ~~stores~~ about to close," said the clerk. 4. store's
5. Several stores were closed because of the storm. 5. C
6. ~~Well~~ have to try to make it there on time. 6. We'll
7. Whose telescope is that, Richard? 7. C
8. She gets up at 6 ~~oclock~~. 8. o'clock
9. ~~Im~~ very glad to meet you. 9. I'm
10. Don't you play chess? 10. C

Oral Practice Recognizing the Correct Use of Apostrophes

Read aloud each sentence in the following paragraph, and say which choice in parentheses is correct.

EXAMPLE [1] (*Your, You're*) likely to see fiesta scenes like the one on the next page in Mexican American communities across the United States each year on September 16.
1. You're

[1] (*It's, Its*) a day of celebration that includes parades, speeches, music, and, as you can see, even colorful folk dances. Of course, [2] (*theirs, there's*) plenty of food, including stacks of tortillas and bowls of beans and soup. [3] (*Who's, Whose*) to say how late the merry-making will last? [4] (*It's, Its*) a joyful holiday of fun, but everyone remembers [5] (*it's, its*) importance, too. Mexican Americans know that

Family/Community Activity

Meeting Minutes. Writing the minutes for a meeting should allow students to use possessives and contractions. Ask students to take minutes for a real or imagined student or community organization using a specified number of possessives and contractions. Students should post or distribute minutes for input from classmates.

[6] (*they're, their*) celebrating the beginning of Mexico's rebellion to gain independence from Spain. On September 16, 1810, Father Miguel Hidalgo y Costilla gathered his forces for the rebellion and uttered [7] (*it's, its*) first battle cry. Father Hidalgo, [8] (*who's, whose*) parish was in west central Mexico, led an army across the country. If [9] (*your, you're*) in Mexico City on the eve of September 16, you can hear the president of Mexico ring what is believed to be the bell that Hidalgo rang to summon his people for [10] (*they're, their*) historic march.

Plurals

14h. **To prevent confusion, use an apostrophe and an *s* to form the plurals of lowercase letters, some capital letters, numerals, symbols, and some words that are referred to as words.**

EXAMPLES Grandma always tells me to mind my *p*'**s** and *q*'**s**.

I got A'**s** on both tests I took last week. [An apostrophe is used because without one the plural spells the word *As*.]

The *1*'**s** in this exercise look like *l*'**s**.

Two different Web site addresses began with ##'**s** and ended with *.com*'**s**.

His *hi*'**s** are always cheerful. [An apostrophe is used because without one the plural spells the word *his*.]

STYLE TIP

Many writers add only *s* when forming the kinds of plurals listed in Rule 14h. However, using both an apostrophe and *s* is not wrong and may be necessary to make your meaning clear. Therefore, it is a good idea always to include the apostrophe.

Exercise 8 Forming Plurals by Using Apostrophes

Use an apostrophe to form the plural of each of the italicized items in the following word groups.

EXAMPLE 1. margins filled with *?*

1. *?'s*

1. *s* that look like *f*
2. to put *U* at the end
3. two *r* and two *s*
4. adding columns of *$* and *%*

Reference Note

For more information on **forming these kinds of plurals,** see page 371.

1. *s's/f's* 2. *U's* 3. *r's/s's* 4. *$'s/%'s*

DIFFERENTIATING INSTRUCTION

Advanced Learners

You may wish to have students write short poems using possessive case/contraction homonyms such as *their/they're, whose/who's,* and *your/you're.* Students may wish to keep copies of their poems in their writing logs for quick reference. You may want to write the following example on the chalkboard.

You're too smart to give up
Your dreams.
They're there to give you
Their guidance.
Who's going to reach your dreams
If not you?
Whose dreams will you reach
If not your own?

Plurals

Rule 14h *(pp. 337–338)*

OBJECTIVE

- To form the plurals of letters used as letters and words used as words

DIFFERENTIATING INSTRUCTION

Learners Having Difficulty

You may wish to simplify **Exercise 8** by giving students options from which to choose. For example, write the following choices on the chalkboard:

a. *s's* that look like *f's*

b. *ss* that look like *fs*

Do the same for the remainder of the exercise, and then have students discuss the correct answers.

MECHANICS

RESOURCES

Plurals

Practice

- *Language & Sentence Skills Practice,* p. 313

Differentiating Instruction

- *Developmental Language & Sentence Skills,* p. 140

Differentiating Instruction

Learners Having Difficulty

The eight categories of rules in this chapter for the use of apostrophes might be displayed on the border of an octagon as a review for students or as a memory device to include in their notebooks. In the following example, the rule categories are written on the inside of the border; students should add examples on the outside of the border.

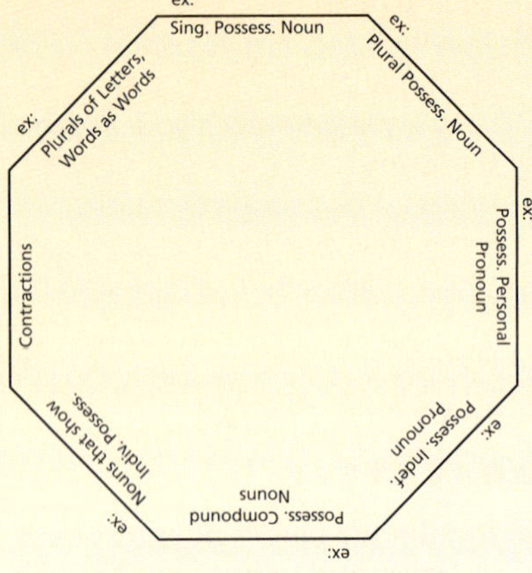

Students might work in pairs to come up with appropriate examples for each rule.

5. *q's/g's* 6. *C's/B's* 7. *his's/its's* 8. *her's/their's* 9. *i's/t's* 10. *I's*

5. these *q* or *g*
6. all *C* and *B*
7. replace all the *his* with *its*
8. too many *her* and *their*
9. your *i* and your *t*
10. two *I* in the sentence

HELP You may need to change the spelling of some words in Review F.

Review E Using Apostrophes Correctly

Add or delete apostrophes as needed in the following sentences.

EXAMPLE 1. Summers here, but because of air conditioning its more bearable than it used to be.

1. Summer's; it's

1. Dont you wonder when people started cooling they're homes with air conditioning? **1.** Don't/their
2. Air cooling isnt a new practice; in fact, in ancient Rome, wet grass mat's were hung over window's to cool incoming air by evaporation. **2.** isn't/mats/windows
3. In the early sixteenth century, one of the greatest Italian artist's and engineer's, Leonardo da Vinci, built historys first mechanical fan. **3.** artists/engineers/history's
4. The British scientist David B. Reid's air-ventilation system's were installed in the British House of Commons in 1838. **4.** systems
5. However, modern technique's of air conditioning werent invented until the early twentieth century in Buffalo, New York. **5.** techniques/weren't
6. One of Buffalos most famous citizen's, Willis Carrier, who's name is still on many air conditioners, invented the first air-conditioning unit in 1902. **6.** Buffalo's/citizens/whose
7. By 1928, the technologys' rapid development had produced the first fully air-conditioned office building, the Milam Building in San Antonio, Texas. **7.** technology's
8. Wasnt Texas—where in summer the temperature can reach 90 degrees by eleven oclock in the morning—a logical place to have the first air-conditioned office building? **8.** Wasn't /o'clock
9. By the late 1950's, more and more homes' had window air conditioner's, and smaller unit's for motor vehicle's were becoming increasingly common. **9.** homes/conditioners/units/vehicles
10. Arent you glad air conditioning is so common nowaday's? **10.** Aren't/nowadays

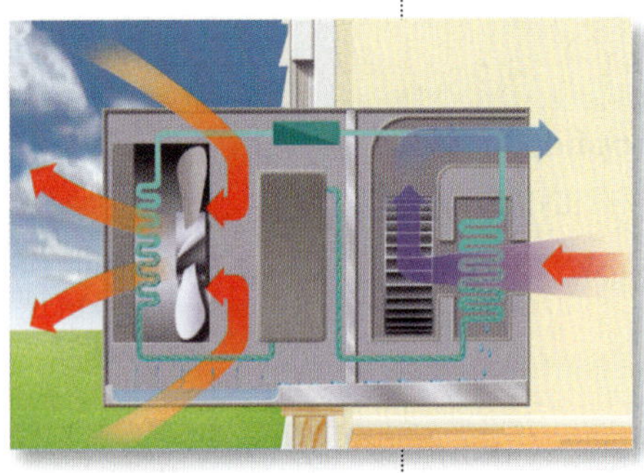

Chapter Review

Numerals in brackets refer to rules tested by the items in the Chapter Review.

1. its [14c]
2. elders/tribe's [14b,a]
3. We're/centuries [14g, b]
4. There's/their [14g, c]
5. Spain's/years [14b]
6. Peruvians' [14a]
7. Someone's/ weren't [14d, g]
8. one's/characters [14d, b]
9. Store's/systems [14e, b]
10. whose/Hard-wick's/ store's [14c, a]

A. Correcting Sentences by Using Apostrophes Correctly

In the following sentences, apostrophes are either missing or incorrectly used. Write the correct form of each incorrect word. In some cases, an apostrophe must be added or deleted; in others, the spelling of the word also must be changed.

1. Ancient peoples felt that writing had a magic power of it's own.
2. Writing was practiced by the elders' of a tribe to preserve the tribes lore as well as its laws.
3. Were not sure when or how writing began, but we do know that it existed several century's before 3000 B.C.
4. Theres plenty of evidence that people communicated through they're drawings long before they had a system of writing.
5. Spain and France's wonderful cave drawings were painted more than thirty thousand year's ago.
6. The ancient Peruvians message system was a complicated arrangement of knots.
7. Someones research has shown that *W*'s and *J*'s werent used in English writing until the late Middle Ages.
8. In China, ones mastery of basic reading depends on learning one thousand character's.
9. Hardwick Book Stores window display features early system's of writing, such as cuneiform.
10. Bess and Robert, who's reports were on the history of writing, asked one of Mr. Hardwicks clerks for permission to examine the stores display.

B. Proofreading a Paragraph for Correct Use of Apostrophes

The following paragraph contains errors in the use of apostrophes. For each sentence, write the correct form of each incorrect word.

11. years' [14b]
12. Napoleon's [14a]

[11] Despite many years work, scholars were not able to decipher hieroglyphics until the early nineteenth century. **[12]** In 1799, one of Napoleons soldiers serving in Egypt discovered a stone tablet. **[13]** The

ASSESSING

Monitoring Progress

Chapter Review. To assess student progress, you may want to compare the types of items missed on the **Diagnostic Preview** to those missed on the **Chapter Review.** If students have not made significant progress, you may want to refer them to **Chapter 17: Correcting Common Errors, Exercise 34,** for additional practice.

MECHANICS

RESOURCES

Punctuation

Review

- *Language & Sentence Skills Practice,* pp. 316–318

Assessment

- *Holt Handbook Chapter Tests with Answer Key,* pp. 27–28, 52

13. Europeans [14b]
14. tablet's/languages [14a, b]
15. experts' [14b]
16. Their/names [14c, b]
17. wasn't [14g]
18. scholar's [14a]
19. stone's [14a]
20. doors [14b]

tablet came to be known as the Rosetta Stone after the town in which it was found: Rashid, which European's called Rosetta. [14] The tablets surface was inscribed in three ancient language's: Greek, Egyptian hieroglyphics, and Coptic, a language derived from ancient Egyptian. [15] The experts translations of the Greek text revealed that the same information had been written in all three languages in 196 B.C. [16] They're next step was to use their knowledge of Greek and Coptic to identify how names' of specific people and places were written in hieroglyphics. [17] It wasnt until 1822, however, that a Frenchman named Jean-François Champollion deciphered the ancient Egyptians' writing. [18] Following another scholars' theory that hieroglyphic symbols represent sounds, Champollion figured out which symbols represent which sounds. [19] He also established that the stones' hieroglyphics were a translation from the Greek—not, as had been thought, the other way around. [20] Though many door's remained to be opened, a key to ancient Egyptian history had been found.

Chapter Review

C. Using Apostrophes to Form Possessive Nouns

POSSIBLE ANSWERS

21. Humble Oil Company's profits
22. buffalo's horns
23. anything's effect
24. geese's feathers
25. Lori's backpack
26. Massachusetts' capital
27. Northern Ireland's linen mills
28. bishops' robes
29. NBC's programs
30. mosque's ceiling

MECHANICS

21. [14e]
22. [14a]
23. [14d]
24. [14b]
25. [14a]
26. [14a]
27. [14a, e]
28. [14b]
29. [14e]
30. [14a]

C. Using Apostrophes to Form Possessive Nouns

Write the possessive form for each of the following nouns. After each possessive word, give an appropriate noun.

21. Humble Oil Company
22. buffalo
23. anything
24. geese
25. Lori
26. Massachusetts
27. Northern Ireland
28. bishops
29. NBC
30. mosque

31. Haven't/refrigerators [14g, b]
32. Romans' [14b]
33. cellars/pits[14b]
34. Didn't/India's/Egypt's [14g, f, a]

D. Using Apostrophes Correctly

The following sentences contain errors in the use of apostrophes. Write each incorrect word or expression, adding or deleting apostrophes where needed. You may need to change the spelling as well.

31. Havent you ever wondered when the first refrigerator's were used?
32. Wealthy Romans main method of refrigeration was to cool food in snow cellars.
33. Snow cellar's were pit's dug in the ground, insulated with straw, and filled with snow and ice.
34. Didnt ancient India and Egypts' cooling techniques include using evaporative cooling to freeze perishable products?

35. Evaporative cooling means placing water in shallow ~~tray's~~ and using the ice ~~thats~~ formed during rapid evaporation.

36. In the sixteenth century, ~~Italians'~~ discovered that a mixture of water and potassium nitrate could be used to cool bottled liquids.

37. During the 1850's, Ferdinand Carré, a French inventor, developed the ~~worlds'~~ first absorption system using ammonia.

38. Absorption ~~system's~~ use the direct application of heat to initiate the refrigeration cycle by changing ~~refrigerant's~~ from liquid to gas and back again.

39. Another system that produces refrigeration is compression, in which ~~compressor's~~ are used to bring about refrigeration cycles.

40. In 1876, the scientific world learned the name of Carl von Linde, a German engineer ~~who's~~ compression system using ammonia was the foundation of modern refrigeration.

35. trays/that's [14b]
36. Italians [14b]
37. world's [14a]
38. systems/refrigerants [14b]
39. compressors [14b]
40. whose [14c]

Writing Application

Using Apostrophes in a Paragraph

Possessive Case Write a paragraph about the musical preferences of one or more family members or friends. Use at least two singular possessive nouns, two plural possessive nouns, and one indefinite pronoun in the possessive case.

Prewriting First, make a list of family members or friends, and beside each name write what you know about that person's musical tastes. If you are not sure about someone's preferences, ask him or her.

Writing As you write your first draft, think about ways of organizing your information by type of music, age of listener, and so on.

Revising Ask a family member or friend to read your paragraph. Is it clear whose preferences are discussed? Are the preferences accurately expressed?

Publishing Check your placement of apostrophes. As you read through your paragraph, correct errors in spelling, grammar, and punctuation. With the permission of the person or persons whose musical tastes you have discussed in your paragraph, post your piece on a class bulletin board, or use it as a basis for a class discussion.

APPLICATION

Writing Application

Prewriting Tip. Remind students to apply their knowledge of correct possessive forms to their writing. If they want to describe their friend Juan's taste in music, then they must use the singular possessive. If they are describing several friends' CD collections, then they must use plural nouns.

Writing Tip. This writing assignment gives students practice using singular possessive nouns, plural nouns, and indefinite pronouns in the possessive case. You may want to write **Rules 14a**, **14b**, **14c**, and **14d** on the chalkboard for students to refer to as they develop and proofread their paragraphs.

Scoring Rubric. While you will want to pay particular attention to students' punctuation of possessive nouns and indefinite pronouns, you will also want to evaluate overall writing performance. You may want to give a split score to indicate development and clarity of the composition as well as mechanics skills.

Chapter Review 341

CHAPTER

15

INTRODUCING THE CHAPTER

- The punctuation marks taught in this chapter—hyphens, dashes, parentheses, brackets, and ellipsis points—differ from one another in the frequency with which they are used, even by professional writers. Ninth-graders are probably familiar with parentheses and the use of hyphens to divide words into syllables, but the other marks may be new to them. Students may need to be reminded of the rules for brackets, ellipsis points, and parentheses when they proofread research papers.
- The chapter closes with a **Chapter Review** including a **Writing Application** feature that asks students to write a three-paragraph report using hyphens, dashes, parentheses, brackets, and ellipsis points.
- For help integrating this chapter with writing assignments, see the **Teaching Strands** chart on pp. T24–T25.

CHAPTER

15

Punctuation

Hyphens, Dashes, Parentheses, Brackets, Ellipsis Points

Diagnostic Preview

A. Using Hyphens, Dashes, and Parentheses

Use hyphens, dashes, and parentheses to punctuate the following sentences. Do not add commas to these sentences.

Answers may vary.

EXAMPLE 1. Henry Viscardi he founded the National Center for Disability Services dedicated his life to creating opportunities for people who have disabilities.

1. Henry Viscardi—he founded the National Center for Disability Services—dedicated his life to creating opportunities for people who have disabilities.

HELP—If there are multiple ways to correct a sentence, give only one.

Numerals in brackets refer to rules tested by the items in the Diagnostic Preview.

1. hyp. / hyp. [15b]
2. hyp. / par. / par. / hyp. [15b, e, f, c]
3. par. / par. [15e]
4. hyp. / dash / hyp. / dash [15c, e, f]
5. dash / dash / hyp. [15e, f, c]
6. dash / dash [15e, f]
7. hyp. / dash [15c, g]
8. dash [15f]

1. The soup was three fourths water and one fourth vegetables.
2. Twenty six students most of them from the advanced math class represented our school at the all state chess match.
3. The Battle of Bunker Hill June 17, 1775 damaged the confidence of the British.
4. The ex treasurer of our club he's an extremely self confident person is now running for class president.
5. My sister she lives in Boston now is studying pre Columbian art.
6. If you have ever dreamed of finding buried treasure and who hasn't? your search could begin on Padre Island.
7. George Grinnell was a self taught expert on the American West and helped negotiate treaties with three American Indian peoples the Blackfoot, the Cheyenne, and the Pawnee.
8. Aunt Jo murmured, "Please turn out the" and then fell asleep.

CHAPTER RESOURCES

Internet

- Web resources: go.hrw.com

go.hrw.com

Practice & Review

- *Language & Sentence Skills Practice,* pp. 324–334
- *Language & Sentence Skills Practice Answer Key,* pp. 133–136

Application & Enrichment

- *Language & Sentence Skills Practice,* pp. 323, 335, 336–337, 338
- *Language & Sentence Skills Practice Answer Key,* pp. 133, 137–138

9. Rachel Carson was working for the U.S. Fish and Wildlife Service created in 1940 when she first recognized the threat of pesticides.
10. Her book *Silent Spring* copyright 1962 alerted the public to the dangers of environmental pollution.

9. par. / par. [15e]
10. par. / par. [15e]

B. Using Hyphens, Dashes, Brackets, and Parentheses

Use hyphens, dashes, brackets, and parentheses to punctuate the following sentences. If a sentence is already correct, write *C*. Do not add commas.

EXAMPLE 1. There are several countries Senegal, Gambia, Guinea, Guinea-Bissau, Sierra Leone, and Liberia along the west-central coast of Africa.

1. *There are several countries—Senegal, Gambia, Guinea, Guinea-Bissau, Sierra Leone, and Liberia—along the west-central coast of Africa.*

11. Liberia's history its founding, that is is unique.
12. Liberia was settled in pre Civil War days by freed slaves from the United States.
13. An antislavery group known as the American Colonization Society it was officially chartered by the U.S. Congress started sending freed slaves to a colony in Africa in 1822.
14. Twenty five years later, the colonists how proud they must have been! declared Liberia independent.
15. They named their capital Monrovia in honor of President James Monroe in office 1817–1825.
16. They also modeled their country's constitution and government not surprisingly on those of the United States.
17. The first president of Liberia, Joseph Jenkins Roberts (he originally served for eight years 1848–1856 and again during an economic crisis 1872–1876), was born in Virginia.
18. Roberts began his political career as an aide to the colonial governor, Thomas H. Buchanan a white member of the American Colonization Society.
19. During Liberia's early years, the United States provided financial aid.
20. However, the U.S. government didn't officially recognize Liberia until President Lincoln's administration 1862.

11. dash / dash [15f]
12. hyp. [15c]
13. dash / dash [15e, f]
14. hyp. / dash / dash [15b, e, f]
15. par. / par. [15e]
16. dash / dash [15f]
17. br. / br. / br. / br. [15i]
18. par. / par. [15e]
19. C [15a]
20. par. / par. [15e]

MECHANICS

ASSESSING

Entry-Level Assessment

Diagnostic Preview. You may want to use the **Diagnostic Preview** to assess students' knowledge of the use of hyphens, dashes, brackets, and parentheses. Students could tally the number of errors in each of the four categories to determine which rules and exercises need attention.

PRETEACHING

Lesson Starter

Motivating. Explain to students that although the punctuation marks covered in this chapter are not the most common, they are needed to communicate effectively in some writing situations. To illustrate the confusion caused by missing punctuation, copy the following sentences on the chalkboard, omitting the new marks of punctuation. Ask volunteers to try to clarify the sentences by indicating where a punctuation mark

(continued)

Differentiating Instruction

- *Developmental Language & Sentence Skills,* pp. 141–144
- *Developmental Language & Sentence Skills Guided Practice Teacher's Notes and Answer Key,* pp. 35–36

Assessment

- *Holt Handbook Chapter Tests with Answer Key,* pp. 29–30, 52

should occur. Then, insert hyphens, dashes, parentheses, brackets, and ellipses for the class.

1. "Well, I think . . . no, I really don't know," he admitted.
2. The *Journal* reported on commencement ceremonies:

   "On Friday evening valedictorian Tamara Larken addressed the audience: 'I am pleased to speak on behalf of my classmates [the Ratcliffe High School Class of 2001].'"
3. Lana Kelly, my neighbor, just celebrated her twenty-first birthday.
4. They will meet us at the movie (the one about a sinking ship).
5. I think I'll stop—oh, excuse me, Mary—right here.

MECHANICS

Hyphens

Rules 15a–d *(pp. 344–347)*

OBJECTIVES

- **To use hyphens to divide words at the ends of lines**
- **To hyphenate words correctly in sentences**

DIFFERENTIATING INSTRUCTION

English-Language Learners

Cantonese and Vietnamese. All Cantonese and Vietnamese languages are monosyllabic. The concept of dividing words into syllables may be new to your students. They will need help with the rules for determining syllables. Cantonese and Vietnamese speakers will also tend to pronounce English words with a break after every syllable, as if each were a separate word. This pronunciation results in a very choppy sound. They will benefit from practice in blending syllables and from practice with the stress system of English that makes some syllables shorter than others.

HELP

If you need to divide a word and are not sure about its syllables, looking it up in a dictionary may help. Many dictionaries show how to break words into syllables.

Hyphens

Word Division

15a. **Use a hyphen to divide a word at the end of a line.**

EXAMPLE The new governor's victory celebration will be organized by her campaign committee.

When you divide a word at the end of a line, keep in mind the following rules:

(1) Do not divide a one-syllable word.

INCORRECT The line of people waiting to buy tickets stretched halfway down the block.

CORRECT The line of people waiting to buy tickets stretched
halfway down the block.

CORRECT The line of people waiting to buy tickets
stretched halfway down the block.

(2) Divide a word only between syllables.

INCORRECT The stars Betelgeuse and Rigel are in the constellation known as Orion.

CORRECT The stars Betelgeuse and Rigel are in the constellation known as Orion.

CORRECT The stars Betelgeuse and Rigel are in the constellation known as Orion.

(3) A word containing double consonants usually may be divided between those two consonants.

EXAMPLES con-nect drum-mer

(4) Divide a word with a prefix or a suffix between the prefix and the base word (or root) or between the base word and the suffix.

EXAMPLES pre-judge post-pone half-back
fall-ing frag-ment con-fusion

(5) Divide an already hyphenated word only at a hyphen.

INCORRECT The speaker this morning is my mother-in-law.

CORRECT The speaker this morning is my mother-
in-law.

RESOURCES

Hyphens

Practice

- *Language & Sentence Skills Practice,* pp. 324–326

Differentiating Instruction

- *Developmental Language & Sentence Skills,* pp. 141–142

(6) Do not divide a word so that one letter stands alone.

INCORRECT The utility company built a new turbine to generate e-lectricity.

CORRECT The utility company built a new turbine to generate elec-tricity.

Exercise 1 Using Hyphens to Divide Words at the Ends of Lines

Write each of the following words, using hyphens to indicate where the word may be divided at the end of a line. If a word should not be divided, write *one-syllable word*.

Carets indicate where hyphens could be placed to divide each word correctly.

EXAMPLES 1. thoroughly 2. cooked

1. *thor-ough-ly* 2. *one-syllable word*

1. Olym^pics
2. li^brary
3. fourth 3. o.s.w.
4. un^changed
5. im^po^lite
6. to^mor^row
7. breathe 7. o.s.w.
8. cor^po^ra^tion
9. through 9. o.s.w.
10. merry-^go-^round

Compound Words

Some compound words are hyphenated (*red-hot*); some are written as one word (*redhead*); and some are written as two or more words (*red tape*). Whenever you need to know whether a word is hyphenated, look it up in a current dictionary.

15b. Use a hyphen with compound numbers from *twenty-one* to *ninety-nine* and with fractions used as modifiers.

EXAMPLES **seventy-six** trombones

three-quarters cup [but *three quarters* of a cup]

15c. Use a hyphen with the prefixes *ex–*, *self–*, *all–*, and *great–*; with the suffixes *–elect* and *–free*; and with all prefixes before a proper noun or proper adjective.

EXAMPLES			
	ex-coach	**great-**aunt	**mid-**July
	self-made	president-**elect**	**pro-**American
	all-star	fat-**free**	**pre-**Columbian

HELP

If you are uncertain of the proper syllabication of the words in Exercise 1, check a dictionary that shows how to break words into syllables.

Word breaks are based on Webster's New World College Dictionary, Third Edition.

STYLE TIP

The prefix *half–* often requires a hyphen, as in *half-life, half-moon,* and *half-truth.* However, sometimes *half* is used without a hyphen, either as a part of a single word (*halftone, halfway, halfback*) or as a separate word (*half shell, half pint, half note*). If you are not sure how to spell a word containing *half,* look up the word in a dictionary.

TEACHING TIP

Exercise 1 Answers may vary according to the dictionaries used. Some dictionaries recommend, for the sake of style, that words not be broken at the end of a line between certain syllables. For example, the vertical lines in the first, second, fifth, and tenth words indicate places where the words should not be divided at the ends of lines, according to *Webster's New World College Dictionary,* Third Edition.

DIRECT TEACHING

Correcting Misconceptions

Prefixes. As students learn to recognize and understand the meanings of prefixes and root words, they may mistakenly apply **Rule 15a(4)** to all words with prefixes. Point out to students that the syllabication of words often depends on pronunciation and that two words with the same prefix and root may be divided differently.

EXAMPLES

pre•judge	prej•u•dice
re•cog•ni•zance	rec•og•nize
pre•pare	prep•a•ra•tion
pro•ject	proj•ect

DIRECT TEACHING

Modeling and Demonstration

Hyphens. Model how to use hyphens correctly by using the example *My great grandfather is ninety nine years old.* First, ask if there are any numbers in this sentence. [*yes;* ninety-nine] Explain that compound numbers from *twenty-one* to *ninety-nine* should be punctuated with hyphens. Next, ask if any other words in this sentence need hyphens. [*yes;* great-grandfather] Point out that hyphens should be used with the prefixes *ex–, self–, all–,* and *great–* and with the suffixes *–elect* and *–free.* Now, have a volunteer use another example from this chapter to demonstrate how to use hyphens correctly.

MECHANICS

TEACHING TIP

Exercise 2 The compound proper adjective in sentence 2 may cause difficulty for some students. Explain that compound proper nouns used as proper adjectives, such as the *United States,* are not confusing when left open and should not be hyphenated.

PRACTICE

Guided and Independent

Exercise You may wish to have students complete **Oral Practice** on page 346 before doing **Exercise 2** as independent practice.

HOMEWORK

HELP — If you are unsure about whether a compound adjective is hyphenated, look up the word in a current dictionary.

15d. Hyphenate a compound adjective when it precedes the noun it modifies.

EXAMPLES a **well-written** book [but *a book that is well written*]

a **small-town** boy [but *a boy from a small town*]

Do not use a hyphen if one of the modifiers is an adverb that ends in *–ly.*

EXAMPLE a **bitterly cold** day

NOTE Some compound adjectives are always hyphenated, whether they precede or follow the nouns they modify.

EXAMPLES a **brand-new** shirt

a shirt that is **brand-new**

a **down-to-earth** person

a person who is **down-to-earth**

Exercise 2 Hyphenating Words Correctly

Insert hyphens in the words that should be hyphenated in the following sentences. If a sentence is already correct, write *C.*

EXAMPLE 1. The world famous speaker was very well informed.

1. *The world-famous speaker was very well informed.*

Carets indicate where hyphens should be inserted.

1. The ex^governor presented the all^American trophy at the competition.
2. Until 1959, the United States flag had forty^eight stars.
3. In twenty^five days my great^grandparents will celebrate their seventy^fifth wedding anniversary; about three fourths of the family will attend the celebration.
4. The ex^ambassador's lecture focused on the post^Napoleonic era.
5. He added one^half teaspoon of sugar^free vanilla extract to the mixture and set the timer for thirty^five minutes.
6. A documentary called "The Self^Improvement Culture" was on TV last night.
7. Herman's new mountain bike was very up^to^date.
8. Well^designed buildings have clearly marked fire escapes.
9. Sally has always been very down-to-earth. 9. C
10. The President^elect gathered his Cabinet to discuss future policy.

Oral Practice Identifying the Correct Use of Hyphens

You have just received the following e-mail message from your friend Eduardo. His computer is acting up and putting in hyphens that are not supposed to be there. Read each numbered item aloud, and list words containing incorrectly used hyphens and words containing correctly used ones. Hyphens used incorrectly are circled.

EXAMPLE [1] My brother-in-law says that the early-bird catches the worm.

Incorrect	Correct
early-bird	*brother-in-law*

Hey there!

[1] So, how have you-been? [2] I can't believe it's mid-April. [3] I've really been running myself ragged with home-work, club-meetings, sports, and ninety-nine other things. [4] You wouldn'-t believe how busy I've been!

[5] I've got a role in our spring-play. [6] It's not a big role, but I'm part of an all-star cast. [7] We're doing *Our Town*. [8] I am managing the props, too.

[9] Enclosed is a good recipe that I used last week to make pop-corn topping. [10] I'm president-elect of the foreign language-club, and it was once again my turn to host the monthly meeting. [11] Thirty-three members came to my house on Friday (we have a total of fifty-one members). [12] Of course, I served refreshments, and every-one loved this topping.

[13] Recipe for Mexican Popcorn Topping: In a small bowl, mix one-fourth cup of chili-powder and one-half teaspoon of salt. Then, add one-teaspoon each of garlic powder, cilantro, and cumin. [14] (Those last two are herbs.) [15] Sprinkle mixture over plain-popcorn.

Take care, and write soon.

Eduardo

Oral Practice

DISTRIBUTED REVIEW

Have students find examples of the following items and give the sentence number in which each was found.

- a reflexive pronoun [3. *myself*]
- an adjective clause [9. *that I used last week to make popcorn topping*]
- two infinitive phrases [9. *to make popcorn topping;* 10. *to host the monthly meeting*]

EXTENSION

Relating to Literature

The poet E. E. Cummings uses hyphens to create images in his poem "in Just-." If the poem is available, ask students to read it and to notice the ways Cummings uses hyphens to link words and, therefore, images. Ask them what the images "Just-spring," "mud-luscious," and "puddle-wonderful" bring to mind. [*Students may visualize "Just-spring" as a miniseason at the very beginning of spring when winter is still hanging on, creating mud puddles from melting snow and allowing children a place to splash and squish and celebrate the wonder of spring.*]

Parentheses

Rule 15e *(pp. 348–349)*

OBJECTIVE

- To use parentheses to set off parenthetical elements in sentences

DIFFERENTIATING INSTRUCTION

English-Language Learners

General Strategies. In their native languages, some students may use a feature called the topic-comment subject, or double subject. For example, the construction "My mother, she. . ." includes a topic (*mother*) and a comment (*she. . .*). Students who use this feature may have trouble telling the difference between the topic-comment subject and a parenthetical element. These students may need individual help in editing their papers to eliminate the topic-comment feature. Point out that students may choose to use either the topic or the subject of the comment to write a clear, complete sentence.

MECHANICS

PRACTICE

Parentheses

Activity. Have students work in small groups to write sentences with parentheses. Have groups exchange sentences to evaluate each other's use of parenthetical information. The groups that wrote the sentences should rewrite overloaded sentences to make them smooth without losing any of the information in the parentheses.

STYLE  TIP

Commas, parentheses, and dashes are all used to set off parenthetical information, but they affect meaning differently. Commas separate elements, usually without emphasizing them. Parentheses indicate that the information they contain is of minor importance. Dashes set off parenthetical information abruptly, emphasizing it. Choose your punctuation according to the meaning you intend.

STYLE  TIP

Too many parenthetical expressions in a piece of writing can distract the reader from the main idea. Keep your meaning clear by limiting the number of parenthetical expressions you use.

Parentheses

15e. Use parentheses to enclose material that is added to a sentence but is not considered to be of major importance.

Notice in the following examples that parenthetical material may be omitted without changing the basic meaning and construction of the sentence.

EXAMPLES During the Middle Ages **(**from about A.D. 500 to A.D. 1500**)**, both Moors and Vikings invaded parts of Europe.

The music of Liszt **(**always a favorite of mine**)** was quite popular in the nineteenth century.

Material enclosed in parentheses may range from a single word to a short sentence. A short sentence in parentheses may stand by itself or be contained within another sentence.

Use punctuation marks within the parentheses when the punctuation belongs to the parenthetical matter. Do not use punctuation within the parentheses if such punctuation belongs to the sentence as a whole.

EXAMPLES Fill in the application carefully. **(**Use a pen**.)**

That old house **(**it was built at the turn of the century**)** may soon become a landmark.

After we ate dinner **(**we had leftovers again**),** we went to the mall.

Exercise 3 Using Parentheses Correctly

Use parentheses to set off the parenthetical elements in the following sentences. Carets indicate where parentheses should be inserted.

EXAMPLE 1. A fly-specked calendar it was five years out-of-date hung on the kitchen wall.

1. A fly-specked calendar (it was five years out-of-date) hung on the kitchen wall.

1. I have read all the *Oz* books that I own^a considerable number^.
2. Edna St. Vincent Millay^1892–1950^began writing poetry as a child.
3. In 1850, California entered the Union as a free state^read more about free states in Chapter 5^.
4. Gwendolyn Brooks^her first book was *A Street in Bronzeville*^has received high praise from critics.

RESOURCES

Parentheses

Practice

- *Language & Sentence Skills Practice*, p. 327

Differentiating Instruction

- *Developmental Language & Sentence Skills*, pp. 143–144

5. Killer whales they're the ones with the black-and-white markings often migrate more than one thousand miles annually.
6. We arrived in Poland through the port city of Gdańsk called Danzig in German.
7. The black rat scientific name *Rattus rattus* is found on every continent.
8. During the French Revolution and the Terror 1789–1793 France underwent dramatic changes.
9. Paulo Coelho born 1947 is a bestselling Brazilian author.
10. The cooking of New Mexico my home state is rich and varied.

Dashes

Sometimes words, phrases, and sentences are used ***parenthetically;*** that is, they break into the main thought of a sentence.

EXAMPLES The penguin, **however,** has swum away.

Her worry **(how could she explain the mix-up?)** kept her up all night.

Most parenthetical elements are set off by commas or parentheses. Sometimes, however, parenthetical elements are such an interruption that a stronger mark is needed. In such cases, a dash is used.

15f. **Use a dash to indicate an abrupt break in thought or speech or an unfinished statement or question.**

EXAMPLES There are a thousand reasons—well, not a thousand, but many—that we should go.

Our dog—he's a long-haired dachshund—is too affectionate to be a good watchdog.

"Why—why can't I come, too?" Janet asked hesitatingly.

"You're being—" Tina began and then stopped.

15g. **Use a dash to indicate *namely, that is,* or *in other words* or to otherwise introduce an explanation.**

EXAMPLES I know what we could get Mom for her birthday—a new photo album. [namely]

She could put all those loose pictures—the ones she's taken since Christmas—in it. [that is]

NOTE Either a dash or a colon is acceptable in the first example above.

STYLE  TIP

Do not overuse dashes. When you evaluate your writing, check to see that you have not used dashes carelessly for commas, semicolons, and end marks. Saving dashes for instances in which they are most appropriate will make them more effective.

COMPUTER TIP 

When you use a word processor, you can type two hyphens to make a dash. Do not leave a space before, between, or after the hyphens. When you write by hand, use an unbroken line about as long as two hyphens.

Reference Note

For information on using **colons,** see page 303.

Dashes, Ellipsis Points, and Brackets

Rules 15f–i *(pp. 349–354)*

OBJECTIVE

- **To insert dashes, ellipsis points, and brackets into the appropriate places in sentences**

DIRECT TEACHING

Modeling and Demonstration

Dashes. Model how to insert dashes correctly by using the example *I know what we could get Mom for her birthday, a new photo album.* First, ask what purpose the phrase *a new photo album* serves in the sentence. [*an explanation of what we could get Mom for her birthday*] Then, ask if the comma after birthday is the appropriate punctuation. [*no*] Ask what should replace the comma. [*a dash*] Explain that a dash should be used to indicate *namely, that is,* or *in other words* or to introduce an explanation. Now, have a volunteer use another example from this chapter to demonstrate how to insert dashes correctly.

MECHANICS

RESOURCES

Dashes, Ellipsis Points, and Brackets

Practice

- *Language & Sentence Skills Practice,* pp. 328–331

Differentiating Instruction

- *Developmental Language & Sentence Skills,* pp. 141–144

TECHNOLOGY TIP

Standard keyboards for computers and typewriters do not have a key for dashes. On a typewriter, dashes are keyed by using two hyphens without any spacing before, between, or after them. Some word-processing programs automatically change two hyphens to a dash. Others may use a combination of the shift key and another key in addition to the hyphen key to create a dash. (Users should check manuals for exact keys for particular software.) Remind students to proofread for the correct use of hyphens and dashes in their writing.

EXTENSION

Relating to Listening and Speaking

Explain to students that interrupting a train of thought with a parenthetical element may be more common in casual conversation than in formal writing. To make students aware of oral pauses indicating abrupt breaks or unfinished thoughts, have students read the examples in this section aloud. Then, have pairs of students create a conversation including breaks in the train of thought.

Suggested topics:

- talking while watching a basketball game
- talking to a friend on the phone in the presence of a parent who wants the line cleared
- talking to a supermarket checker while soothing an impatient child

MECHANICS

MEETING THE CHALLENGE

Writers sometimes set off asides in sentences with dashes; other times they use parentheses. Each punctuation mark assigns a slightly different emphasis to the words set off. Which type of mark makes the words stand out? Which mark pushes them into the background? Write one sentence that contains words that are set off. Punctuate it first with parentheses, then with dashes. Read both sentences aloud. What effect does the punctuation have on meaning? Finally, try using commas to set off the words. Do commas work? Why or why not?

ANSWERS
Sentences and observations will vary.

HELP

Although some sentences in Review B can be corrected in more than one way, you need to give only one revision for each.

Exercise 4 Inserting Dashes in Sentences

Insert dashes where they are appropriate in the following sentences.
Carets indicate where dashes should be inserted.

EXAMPLE
1. The winner is but I don't want to give it away yet.
   1. The winner is—but I don't want to give it away yet.
2. It was an exciting game Brazil had taken the lead, but Italy scored in overtime.
   2. It was an exciting game—Brazil had taken the lead, but Italy scored in overtime.

1. Tom said, "I'd like to thank^" and then blushed and sat down.
2. We were surprised^in fact, amazed^to learn that the game had been called off.
3. The valedictorian^that is, the student with the highest average^will be given a scholarship.
4. She remembered what she wanted to tell them^the plane was leaving at seven, not eight.
5. My brother's engagement^it's been kept a secret till now^will be announced Sunday.
6. The ancient Mediterranean seafaring cultures^the Phoenician, the Greek, and the Roman^all used versions of the trireme, a ship driven by three rows of oars.
7. The truth is^and I'm sure you realize this^we have no way of getting to the airport.
8. The manager of the restaurant^I can't remember his name^said he would reserve a table for us.
9. Because Maria^she's the one who accompanies us^will be away next week, choral practice will be postponed until the following week.
10. Very few carmakers^three, to be precise^offer models exclusively with full-time all-wheel drive.

Review A Using Hyphens, Dashes, and Parentheses Correctly

Rewrite each of the following sentences, inserting hyphens, dashes, and parentheses where they are needed. If a sentence is already correct, write *C.* Answers may vary.

EXAMPLE
1. State flags you can tell by looking at those shown on the next page are as different as the states themselves.
   1. State flags—you can tell by looking at those shown on the next page—are as different as the states themselves.

MINI-LESSON Mechanics

Parenthetical Expressions. Remind students that parenthetical expressions as they have studied them in relationship to commas are usually restricted to a set list of words or phrases that provide emphasis or transition (see p. 285).

To review this concept, ask students to add commas to the following sentences:

Karen is in fact already on her way to Chicago. [*Karen is, in fact, already on her way to Chicago.*]

1. I think the shield on the Oklahoma flag reflects that state's pre^ statehood years as the territorial home of the Osage, the Cherokee, and other American Indian peoples. 1. hyp.
2. "What kind of tree is in the center of the South Carolina flag?" Emilio asked. "Is it^oh, it's a palmetto." 2. dash
3. Two goddesses^Ceres, or the goddess of agriculture, and Liberty^are in the center of New Jersey's flag. 3. par. / par.
4. On the Colorado flag, one third of the background is white and the rest is blue. 4. C
5. Arkansas^by the way, a major diamond-producing state^has a large diamond on its flag. 5. par. / par.
6. An ancient Pueblo symbol of the all^important sun is on New Mexico's flag. 6. hyp.
7. The Union Jack of the United Kingdom^look closely^is on a corner of the Hawaiian flag. 7. dash / dash
8. "The Texas flag is red, white, and blue and contains one lone star because^" Megan said before she was interrupted. 8. dash
9. Blue is a dominant color in forty^one state flags. 9. hyp.
10. Only one state flag^Washington's^has a green background. 10. dash / dash

Review B Using Hyphens, Dashes, and Parentheses Correctly

Insert hyphens, dashes, and parentheses where they are needed in the following sentences. Do not add commas. If a sentence is already correct, write *C*. Answers may vary.

EXAMPLE 1. You might be able to tell from the photograph on the next page that the Comanche chief Quanah Parker 1845–1911 was a man of strong character.

1. *You might be able to tell from the photograph on the next page that the Comanche chief Quanah Parker (1845–1911) was a man of strong character.*

PRACTICE

Guided and Independent

Reviews You may wish to have students complete **Review A** as guided practice and **Review B** as independent practice.

DIFFERENTIATING INSTRUCTION

Learners Having Difficulty

To help students with **Review B,** suggest that they work through the exercise three times, looking for one mark of punctuation each time. Suggest that students use this method whenever they proofread for punctuation mistakes.

MECHANICS

Rich Williams deserved the raise in my opinion. [*Rich Williams deserved the raise, in my opinion.*]

To tell the truth I do not know. [*To tell the truth, I do not know.*]

1. Parker^can you tell this from the photograph?^was both a great war chief and a great peace chief. 1. dash / dash
2. He was the son of a Comanche tribal leader and a young woman ^Cynthia Ann Parker^who was captured during a raid on a Texas homestead. 2. par. / par.
3. In the 1870s, Parker himself led a band of Comanche warriors in the Texas Panhandle. 3. C
4. Parker surrendered with his band^the Quahadi^in 1875; they were the last Comanches on the southern plains to surrender. 4. par. / par.
5. After surrendering, Parker became a prosperous rancher^quite a change of lifestyle^and even owned railroad stock. 5. dash / dash
6. In fact, he embodied the ideal of the self^made man. 6. hyp.
7. Parker encouraged his people to learn modern ways and to farm. 7. C
8. Parker guided the Comanches^his title was principal chief^dur^ing difficult times after the war ended. 8. par. / par. / hyp.
9. In later years, he went to Washington, D.C., and^this fact may surprise you^became a friend of President Theodore Roosevelt. 9. dash / dash
10. The Texas city called Quanah^a Comanche word meaning "sweet smelling"^was named after this chief. 10. par. / par.

Ellipsis Points

15h. Use ellipsis points (. . .) to mark omissions from quoted materials and pauses in a written passage.

ORIGINAL The streetlights along Toole Street, which meandered downhill from the Language Academy to the town, were already lit and twinkled mistily through the trees. Standing at the gates were small groups of students, clustered together according to nationality. As Myles passed by, he could not help overhearing intense conversation in Spanish, German, and Japanese; all of his students had momentarily abandoned English in the urgency of deciding where to go for the weekend and how to get there.

(1) When you omit words from the middle of a sentence, use three spaced ellipsis points.

EXAMPLE The streetlights along Toole Street . . . were already lit and twinkled mistily through the trees.

NOTE Be sure to include a space before the first ellipsis point and after the last one.

EXTENSION

Relating to Writing

Because ellipsis points are often used in connection with quoted material in research papers, you may want to teach this section while students are working on any writing assignment in which they would use portions of quoted material. If students have completed research assignments, ask them to work in small groups to examine quoted passages in each other's papers. Assign the group to rewrite passages, eliminating unnecessary parts of the quotations by using ellipsis points.

MECHANICS

Learning for Life 

Continued on pp. 353–354

Creating a Newsletter. Tell students they will be responsible for creating a classroom newsletter in which they will use the types of punctuation they have learned in this chapter, as well as reviewing marks studied in previous chapters.

To prepare students, provide samples of newsletters or ask a newsletter editor to speak to the class about the process involved. Suggest that the expert relate an

(2) When you omit words at the beginning of a sentence within a quoted passage, keep the previous sentence's end punctuation and follow it with the ellipsis points.

EXAMPLE Standing at the gates were small groups of students, clustered together according to nationality. . . . [A]ll of his students had momentarily abandoned English in the urgency of deciding where to go for the weekend and how to get there.

NOTE Be sure not to begin a quoted passage with ellipsis points.

(3) When you omit words at the end of a sentence within a quoted passage, keep the sentence's end punctuation and follow it with the ellipsis points.

EXAMPLE Standing at the gates were small groups of students. . . . As Myles passed by, he could not help overhearing intense conversation in Spanish, German, and Japanese; all of his students had momentarily abandoned English in the urgency of deciding where to go for the weekend and how to get there.

(4) When you omit one or more complete sentences from a quoted passage, keep the previous sentence's end punctuation and follow it with the ellipsis points.

EXAMPLE The streetlights along Toole Street, which meandered downhill from the Language Academy to the town, were already lit and twinkled mistily through the trees. . . . As Myles passed by, he could not help overhearing intense conversation in Spanish, German, and Japanese; all of his students had momentarily abandoned English in the urgency of deciding where to go for the weekend and how to get there.

(5) To show that a full line or more of poetry has been omitted, use an entire line of spaced periods.

ORIGINAL
Half a league, half a league,
Half a league onward,
All in the valley of Death
Rode the six hundred.
"Forward the Light Brigade!
Charge for the guns!" he said.
Into the valley of Death
Rode the six hundred.

Alfred, Lord Tennyson,
"The Charge of the Light Brigade"

HELP—Notice in the example to the left that the *a* beginning *all* has been capitalized because it begins the sentence following the ellipsis points. Brackets are used around the *A* to show that it was not capitalized in the original passage.

Differentiating Instruction

Advanced Learners

Have small groups of students brainstorm ways punctuation marks and musical notations are similar. To get them started, ask what punctuation mark might correspond to a musical rest. [*Students might suggest either a comma or a period.*]

anecdote about a misunderstanding created by incorrect punctuation.

Then, brainstorm with students what topics they might include in the newsletter and what punctuation is required for specific needs. (For example, ellipsis points might be used in a long quotation from the principal praising the class for a service project, while brackets or parentheses might be used in schedules.)

Reteaching

Dashes, Parentheses, Brackets, and Ellipses

If students are still uncomfortable using these marks of punctuation, offer them hands-on experience. Assign students to groups of four or five based on their choice of a preferred area of study, such as math or social studies. Then, explain that they will look through textbooks or reference books on their chosen subject to find uses of parentheses, dashes, ellipses, and brackets. Before students look for examples, have them brainstorm possible uses of these punctuation marks. Assign groups to prepare their examples for a bulletin board display. [*Hints: Students may find that brackets and parentheses are used in algebraic equations and scientific formulas and in literature or social studies books for biographical information or for dates of historical periods. Ellipses are used generally in any text to indicate material that is left out of a quotation.*]

MECHANICS

WITH OMISSION

Half a league, half a league,
Half a league onward,
. . . .
Into the valley of Death
Rode the six hundred.

Notice that the line of periods is as long as the line above it.

(6) To indicate a pause in dialogue, use three spaced ellipsis points with a space before the first point and a space after the last point.

EXAMPLE "Well, I could . . . I can't honestly say," he hedged.

Brackets

15i. Use brackets to enclose an explanation within quoted or parenthetical material.

EXAMPLES In her acceptance speech, the star said: "I am honored by this award [the Oscar], and I want to thank my parents and everybody who worked with me." [The words are enclosed in brackets to show that they have been inserted into the quotation and are not the exact words of the speaker.]

The growth of the Irish economy in recent years is a great success story. (See page 15 [Graph 1A] for a time line.)

Exercise 5 **Using Ellipsis Points and Brackets Correctly**

Revise the following sentences, using ellipsis points and brackets correctly.

EXAMPLE 1. Franklin said, "That cat just . . . . . flew up to the top of the refrigerator!"

1. Franklin said, "That cat just . . . flew up to the top of the refrigerator!"

1. br. / br.
2. ell. . . .
3. br. / br.
4. br. / br.
5. ell. . . .

1. At the committee meeting, Judy said, "We have to make this (the Homecoming Dance) the most memorable event of the year."
2. "I . . I can't believe she would have said that!" Aaron exclaimed.
3. The levels of photosynthesis activity varied drastically with the different cycles of light and darkness. (See page 347 (Chart 17D) for details.)
4. "Do you really believe they have a chance to win the (Stanley) Cup this year?" asked Martin skeptically.
5. "But . . . . . then how can we be sure it's true?" Carla asked.

Learning for Life

Continued from p. 353

After students have worked individually to write an article, place them in small groups to proofread each other's work. Finally, groups may staple individual articles together to make a class newsletter or produce the newsletter, complete with graphics and illustrations, by using a desktop-publishing program. Students may decide that they want to continue publishing a newsletter for a group or club.

15

Chapter Review

Numerals in brackets refer to rules tested by the items in the Chapter Review.

1. d.n.d. [15a(1)]
2. [15a(2)]
3. [15a(4)]
4. [15a(2, 4)]
5. [15a(5)]
6. [15a(2)]
7. [15a(2)]
8. [15a(2)]
9. d.n.d. [15a(6)]
10. d.n.d. [15a(1)]

A. Using Hyphens to Divide Words at the Ends of Lines

Write each of the following words, using a hyphen to indicate where the word may be divided at the end of a line. If a word should not be divided, write *do not divide.*

Carets indicate where a hyphen should be used.

1. baked
2. com^plete
3. in^put
4. un^ex^pect^ed
5. yo^-yo
6. ba^gel
7. thor^ough
8. di^vide
9. away
10. whale

B. Using Hyphens, Dashes, and Parentheses Correctly

Use hyphens, dashes, and parentheses to punctuate the following sentences. Do not add commas to these sentences.

HELP

Some sentences in Part B may be correctly punctuated in more than one way, but you need to give only one answer per item.

11. hyp. [15b]
12. dash [15f]
13. hyp. / hyp. [15c]
14. dash/dash [15e, f]
15. dash / dash [15f]
16. par. / par. [15e, f]
17. hyp. / hyp. / [15b, d]
18. hyp. [15c]
19. par. / par. [15e]
20. dash/dash [15e, f]

Answers may vary.

11. Yuri, our Russian exchange student, will be twenty^one on the first of September this year.
12. "That sounds like^" gasped Jeff as he dashed for the window.
13. A former all^state quarterback, our coach insists that there is no such thing as a self^made star.
14. A dog^I think it was a poodle^jumped into the lake.
15. The Historical Society^the local members, that is^will conduct a tour of the harbor.
16. My sister Patricia^she is in college now^wants to be a marine biologist.
17. This recipe for savory bread calls for one and one^half cups of whole^wheat flour.
18. At the auction someone bid one thousand dollars for a pre^Revolutionary desk.
19. The Inca empire flourished during the reign of the emperor Pachacuti^1438–1471^.
20. Next month^of course, I'll write you before then^we're going on an overnight trip.

ASSESSING

Monitoring Progress

Chapter Review. To assess student progress, you may want to compare the types of items missed on the **Diagnostic Preview** to those missed on the **Chapter Review.** You may want to work out specific goals for mastering essential information with individual students who are still having difficulty.

MECHANICS

RESOURCES

Punctuation

Review

- *Language & Sentence Skills Practice,* pp. 332–334

Assessment

- *Holt Handbook Chapter Tests with Answer Key,* pp. 29–30, 52

21. par. / par. [15e]
22. dash / dash [15e, f]
23. hyp. [15a(2)]
24. dash / dash [15e, f]
25. par. / hyp. / par. [15e, f, c]
26 hyp. [15c, a(5)]
27. hyp. [15b]
28. par. / par. [15e]
29. dash [15f]
30. dash / dash [15e, f]
31. hyp. [15c]
32. par. / par. [15e, f]
33. dash / dash [15e, f]
34. hyp. / hyp. [15c, b]
35. par. / par. [15e]
36. par. / par. / hyp. [15e, b]
37. hyp. [15c]
38. dash / dash [15e, f]
39. par. / par. [15e, f]
40. dash [15g]

21. John F. Kennedy 1917–1963 was the first Roman Catholic president of the United States.
22. Four of our former classmates yes, Beth was among them traveled to Australia with the U.S. athletes.
23. My grandparents will celebrate their fiftieth wedding anni versary on the third of October.
24. My friend Juan he went back to Puerto Rico has always wanted to be a veterinarian.
25. Linda Wing she is the ex champion will award the trophies.
26. Doing homework and seeing their improvement raised their self esteem.
27. Add exactly one half tablespoon of sugar to that recipe.
28. Napoleon's reign as emperor of France 1804–1815 was marked by great achievements and great setbacks.
29. "You don't mean to" exclaimed Renata.
30. The Friends of Silesia the Midwestern chapter, of course will have their annual dinner in Chicago this year.
31. Four players have been chosen for the state's all star team.
32. Beth I don't know her last name plays the lead role in the play.
33. She said wearily she often sounded weary "I'll go tomorrow."
34. By mid January twenty four inches of snow had fallen.
35. Mr. Brandt our neighbor of twelve years moved back to Germany after that country's reunification.
36. Franklin D. Roosevelt 1882–1945 was the thirty second president.
37. The ex governor of Kansas will speak at the reception.
38. Blake Ricky Blake, I mean was waiting for me downstairs.
39. Reggae music I heard it in the West Indies is popular here.
40. We all grew up in the same town Boise, Idaho.

HELP

Some sentences in Part C may be correctly punctutated in more than one way, but you need to give only one answer for each item.

41. dash / dash / dash [15e, f]
42. ell. . . . [15h(6)]

C. Using Hyphens, Dashes, Parentheses, Ellipsis Points, and Brackets Correctly

Correctly use hyphens, dashes, parentheses, ellipsis points, and brackets where needed in the following sentences. If a sentence is already correct, write *C.* Answers may vary.

41. The Italian flag red, white, and green is similar in design to the French tricolor flag red, white, and blue.
42. "Well, I'll try . . . . or maybe not," she stammered.

MECHANICS

43. The large building on the corner of Elm Street is the headquarters of the organization.

44. The Battle of Verdun February–July 1916 was a crucial French victory over the Germans in World War I.

45. In Mexico, San Miguel de Allende population approximately 80,000 is a popular destination for American artists and retirees.

46. See page 100 Map 2 for a more detailed look at the developing military situation.

47. "My goodness!" exclaimed Grandpa. "Isn't that the?" and he hurriedly consulted his program.

48. The museum's preColumbian artifacts are well worth seeing.

49. I can think of dozens of people well, maybe not dozens, but quite a few who would agree with me.

50. Lorenzo Da Ponte was the man who wrote the libretto for Mozart's opera *Don Giovanni* and later and this came as a surprise to me taught Italian in New York City.

43. C [15e]
44. par. / par. [15e]
45. par. / par. [15e]
46. par. / br. / br. / par. [15e, i]
47. dash [15f]
48. hyp. [15c]
49. dash / dash [15e, f]
50. dash / dash [15f]

Writing Application

Writing a Report

Using Punctuation Write a short report of no more than three paragraphs on your favorite author. Use at least three of the five elements of punctuation (hyphens, dashes, parentheses, ellipsis points, and brackets) discussed in this chapter.

Prewriting First, gather biographical information on your chosen author. Include any details you find interesting or unusual.

Writing As you write your first draft, think about how you plan to organize your information: by type of writing (fiction, nonfiction, poetry) or chronologically; or you could focus on a particular story, novel, or poem. Compare your draft to other short treatments of the author.

Revising Read through your draft. Is the organization clear? If not, add, cut, or rearrange information to make it clearer.

Publishing Proofread your essay for errors in grammar, spelling, and punctuation. You and your classmates may want to post the finished report on the class bulletin board or on a school Web page.

APPLICATION

Writing Application

Prewriting Tip. Before students can begin writing their reports, they must synthesize the information they have gathered into an orderly format. For example, students must decide what to use from their research. Remind students that the main idea must go in the first paragraph and the other material they use should support the main idea.

Writing Tip. Before students begin their prewriting, you may want to have them brainstorm a list of authors to consider.

Scoring Rubric. While you will want to pay particular attention to students' use of punctuation marks, you will also want to evaluate the students' overall writing performance. You may want to give a split score to indicate development and clarity of the composition as well as mechanics skills.

CHAPTER

16

INTRODUCING THE CHAPTER

- The purpose of this chapter is to give students rules and techniques to improve their spelling skills. The chapter covers Good **Spelling Habits, Spelling Rules, 75 Commonly Misspelled Words,** and **300 Spelling Words.**
- The chapter closes with a **Chapter Review** including a **Writing Application** feature that asks students to write a letter to a volleyball coach using words from the spelling lists and from the lists of words that are often confused.
- For help in integrating this chapter with writing assignments, use the **Teaching Strands** chart on pp. T24–T25.

CHAPTER 16

Spelling

Improving Your Spelling

Diagnostic Preview

A. Choosing Correct Spelling

Numerals and terms in brackets refer to rules tested by the items in the Diagnostic Preview.

1. [*passed, past; threw through*]
2. [*principal, principle; their, there, they're*]
3. [*lead, led, lead; stationary, stationery*]
4. [*peace, piece; quiet, quite*]
5. [*who's, whose; formally, formerly*]
6. [*all together, altogether; complement, compliment*]
7. [*coarse, course; choose, chose*]

Choose the correct word from the pair in parentheses.

EXAMPLE **1.** I was very careful not to (*brake, break*) the vase.

1. break

1. After the Paris-Lyon high-speed train (*past, passed*) the waving onlookers and raced (*threw, through*) the tunnel, it reached a maximum speed of more than 180 miles per hour.
2. When the new (*principle, principal*) talked to her staff, she tried to get (*there, their, they're*) honest opinions.
3. The auctioneer (*led, lead*) the bidding on the original White House (*stationary, stationery*) on which was written President Roosevelt's actual signature.
4. Cuenca, near Madrid, is a lovely old town that is known for its (*piece, peace*) and (*quite, quiet*).
5. My aunt (*who's, whose*) picture appeared in yesterday's paper was (*formerly, formally*) a vice-president at First State Bank.
6. (*Altogether, All together*), the guitar music, the songs, and the aroma of *pan dulce* were a wonderful (*compliment, complement*) to the relaxed atmosphere.
7. Of (*course, coarse*), I found it nearly impossible to (*choose, chose*) between those two movies.

CHAPTER RESOURCES

Internet

- Web resources: go.hrw.com

go.hrw.com

Practice & Review

- *Language & Sentence Skills Practice,* pp. 340–365
- *Language & Sentence Skills Practice Answer Key,* pp. 139–146

Application & Enrichment

- *Language & Sentence Skills Practice,* pp. 339, 366, 367–368, 369
- *Language & Sentence Skills Practice Answer Key,* pp. 139, 146–147

8. I took a (*plain, plane*) to Houston, and I visited family members who live (*there, their, they're*).
9. Although (*its, it's*) smaller than both Geneva and Zurich, Bern is the (*capital, capitol*) of Switzerland.
10. The new British (*council, consul, counsel*) and her husband returned to the embassy after having coffee and (*desert, dessert*) with the emir.

8. [*plane, plain; their, there, they're*]
9. [*its, it's; capital, capitol*]
10. [*consul, council, counsel; desert, dessert*]

B. Proofreading a Paragraph for Spelling Errors

Identify any misspelled or misused words in the following paragraph, and then write the words correctly. If all the words in a sentence are already correct, write *C*.

EXAMPLE **[1]** I have read about Santa Fe, but I have never been their.
1. their—there

[11] Santa Fe, New Mexico, is an all together charming and unusual city. **[12]** It is not only the capitol of the state but also a major tourist center. **[13]** The city lies in the north-central part of New Mexico at a hieght of about 7,000 feet and enjoys outstanding whether year-round. **[14]** The altitude sometimes has a bad affect on first-time visitors. **[15]** They are adviced not to exert themselves for the first day or so. **[16]** Santa Fe is one of the oldest citys in the United States. **[17]** It was founded in 1610 as the seat of government of the Spanish colony of New Mexico. **[18]** In 1912, New Mexico joined the United States as the 47th state. **[19]** I think the food in Santa Fe is awsome. **[20]** I suggest sampleing Southwestern cuisine, some of which is very spicy.

11. altogether [*all together, altogether*]
12. capital [*capital, capitol*]
13. height/weather [16c; *weather, whether*]
14. effect [*affect, effect*]
15. advised [*advice, advise*]
16. cities [16m(2)]
17. C [16a]
18. forty-seventh [16p]
19. awesome [16h]
20. sampling [16g]

Good Spelling Habits

16a. **To learn the spelling of a word, pronounce it, study it, and write it.**

(1) **Pronounce words carefully.**

Mispronunciation can lead to misspelling. For instance, if you say *mis • chē • vē • əs* instead of *mis • chə • vəs,* you will be more likely to spell the word incorrectly.

- First, make sure that you know how to pronounce the word correctly, and then practice saying it.

HELP

If you are not sure how to pronounce a word, look in a dictionary. In the dictionary, you will usually find the pronunciation given in parentheses after the word. The information in parentheses generally shows the sounds used, the syllable breaks, and any accented syllables. A guide to the pronunciation symbols is usually found at the front of the dictionary.

ASSESSING

Entry-Level Assessment

Diagnostic Preview. You may want to use the **Diagnostic Preview** to help students develop personal goals to master spelling rules. Encourage students to refer to the rules in this chapter and to the lists of spelling words as they proofread their writing assignments throughout the year.

PRETEACHING

Lesson Starter

Motivating. One of the most difficult aspects of English spelling is the prevalence of words with silent letters. For example, *a* is silent in the word *head; b* is silent in the word *numb;* and the first *c* is silent in the word *science.*

Have students work in groups of four or five to locate words with silent letters from the **300 Spelling Words** list. Groups should record all the words with silent letters that they find and circle the silent letter or letters in each word.

Differentiating Instruction

- *Developmental Language & Sentence Skills,* pp. 145–156
- *Developmental Language & Sentence Skills Guided Practice Teacher's Notes and Answer Key,* pp. 37–38

Assessment

- *Holt Handbook Chapter Tests with Answer Key,* pp. 31–32, 52

RESOURCES

Good Spelling Habits

Practice

- *Language & Sentence Skills Practice,* p. 340

Good Spelling Habits

Rule 16a *(pp. 359–361)*

OBJECTIVES

- To pronounce spelling words correctly
- To spell by syllables using a dictionary
- To spell commonly misspelled words containing silent letters correctly

DIFFERENTIATING INSTRUCTION

Special Education Students

You may wish to motivate students with a spelling-bee round robin. Set up teams of three or four students, and have a helper dictate a word to students in the group. The first student names the first letter, the second student names the second letter, and so on. As the team names letters, the helper should record the letters on the chalkboard or on a transparency. The helper may want to prompt students with phonics clues.

English-Language Learners

Hmong. The Hmong language's Romanized Popular Alphabet uses unpronounced final consonants as tonal markers. The only purpose of these consonants is to indicate a word's stress and pitch. Therefore, when reading, Hmong students may leave final consonants in English unpronounced. Because pronunciation is so crucial to spelling, Hmong spellers may also drop final consonants when writing words. Have students practice reading aloud, emphasizing final consonants as they read, until they begin to pronounce end consonants with regularity.

MECHANICS

STYLE  TIP

Different dictionaries show variations in spelling in different ways. To understand a dictionary's arrangement of such variations, check the guide (usually found in the front) that explains how to use the book.

When you look up the spelling of a word, make sure that its use isn't limited by a label such as *British* or *chiefly British* (*honour* for *honor*), *obsolete* (*vail* for *veil*), or *archaic* (*innocency* for *innocence*). In general, optional spellings that are not labeled, such as *jeweler* and *jeweller,* are equally correct.

- Second, study the word. Notice especially any parts that might be hard to remember.
- Third, write the word from memory. Check your spelling.
- If you misspelled the word, repeat the three steps of this process.

(2) Use a dictionary.

Whenever you find that you have misspelled a word, look it up in a dictionary. Don't guess about correct spelling.

(3) Spell by syllables.

A ***syllable*** is a word part that is pronounced as one uninterrupted sound.

EXAMPLES thor • ough [two syllables]

sep • a • rate [three syllables]

Instead of trying to learn how to pronounce a whole word, break it up into its syllables whenever possible. It's easier to learn a few letters at a time than to learn all of them at once.

Oral Practice **Pronouncing Spelling Words Correctly**

Study the correct pronunciations in parentheses after each of the following words. Then, pronounce each word correctly three times.

1. athlete (ath′ • lēt′)
2. children (chil′ • drən)
3. drowned (dround)
4. escape (e • skāp′)
5. library (lī′ • brer • ē)
6. lightning (līt′ • ning)
7. perhaps (pər • haps′)
8. probably (prŏb′ • ə • blē)

Exercise 1 **Spelling by Syllables**

Look up the following words in a dictionary, and divide each one into syllables. Pronounce each syllable correctly, and learn to spell the word by syllables.

EXAMPLE 1. possibility

1. *pos • si • bil • i • ty*

1. [*or* rep|re|sen|ta|tive]
9. [*or* ac|quain|tance]

1. rep|re|sent|a|tive
2. awk|ward
3. can|di|date
4. tem|per|a|ture
5. ap|par|ent
6. sim|i|lar
7. def|i|ni|tion
8. ben|e|fit
9. ac|quaint|ance
10. fas|ci|nate

(4) Proofread for careless spelling errors.

Re-read your writing carefully, and correct any mistakes and unclear letters. For example, make sure that your *i*'s are dotted, your *t*'s are crossed, and your *g*'s don't look like *q*'s.

(5) Keep a spelling notebook.

Divide each page into four columns:

COLUMN 1 Correctly spell the word you missed. (Never enter a misspelled word.)

COLUMN 2 Write the word again, dividing it into syllables and marking its accents.

COLUMN 3 Write the word once more, circling the letters that give you trouble.

COLUMN 4 Jot down any comments that might help you remember the correct spelling.

Here is an example of how you might make entries for two words that are often misspelled.

Correct Spelling	Syllables and Accents	Trouble Spot	Comments
probably	prob'•a•bly	prob(ab)ly	Pronounce both b's.
usually	u'•su•al•ly	usua(ll)y	usual+ly (Study rule 16f.)

Exercise 2 **Spelling Commonly Misspelled Words**

Copy each of the following words or expressions, paying special attention to the italicized letters. Then, without looking at this page or the copy you made of the correctly spelled words, write the words as a friend dictates them to you.

1. ans*w*er	**6.** *k*nowle*d*ge	**11.** r*h*ythm	**16.** toni*gh*t
2. aw*k*ward	**7.** *w*ritten	**12.** use*d* to	**17.** sure*l*y
3. *w*hole	**8.** of*t*en	**13.** inst*ea*d	**18.** tho*ugh*
4. to*w*ard	**9.** conde*mn*	**14.** me*a*nt	**19.** thr*ough*
5. *k*now	**10.** colum*n*	**15.** *a*isle	**20.** nin*e*ty

COMPUTER TIP

Spellcheckers can help you proofread your writing. Even the best spellcheckers aren't foolproof, however. Many accept British spellings, obsolete words, archaic spellings, and words that are spelled correctly but used incorrectly (such as *affect* for *effect*). Always double-check your writing to make sure that your spelling is error-free.

DIFFERENTIATING INSTRUCTION

Learners Having Difficulty

Encourage students to spell and pronounce new or problematic words aloud as they practice writing the words. You might suggest that students pronounce words and give exaggerated stress to troublesome letters. For example, students might pronounce any silent consonants, such as the *w* in *answer*.

English-Language Learners

Vietnamese. Many of the problems Vietnamese speakers have with pronunciation and spelling in English stem from the relatively small number of vowel sounds in their native language. They will have difficulty discerning the difference between any vowel sounds other than /e/ as in *pet*, /a/ as in *pot*, and /u/ as in *shut*. The difficulty in hearing and reproducing other sounds prevents them from sounding words out when reading and from spelling by sound. Introduce words with unfamiliar vowel sounds by exaggerating and lengthening the vowel sound to help students hear it. Some students benefit from instruction on how to produce the vowel sounds by placing their tongues, lips, and teeth in the correct positions. Vietnamese students may learn to spell by memorizing lists of words but may still have difficulty pronouncing the words.

TEACHING TIP

Exercise 2 Have students circle the italicized letters as they copy the words for the first part of this exercise. This reinforcement should help students with the dictation part of the exercise. You may want to have students continue to circle silent letters while they work on exercises throughout the chapter.

CONTENT-AREA CONNECTIONS

All Subjects

Difficult Words. Encourage students to use their spelling notebooks for all subjects, not just for language arts. Ask students to record in their notebooks any words they misspell and any difficult words they encounter in other subjects. Then students can check this chapter for the rules that apply to the words in their lists.

Spelling Rules

Rules 16b–p *(pp. 362–374)*

OBJECTIVES

- To proofread sentences to correct spelling errors
- To spell correctly words with prefixes and suffixes
- To form the plurals of regular and irregular nouns, compound nouns, Latin and Greek loan words, numerals, letters, symbols, and words used as words
- To determine whether numbers in sentences should be spelled out

DIRECT TEACHING

Modeling and Demonstration

Spelling Rules. Model how to spell correctly words that contain *ie* or *ei* by using the examples *brief, deceit, veil, foreign, protein,* and *friend.* First, ask what sound *ie* makes in *brief.* [*long* e] Point out that a word is spelled with *ie* when the sound is *long* e. Next, ask what sound *ei* makes in *deceit.* [*long* e] Explain that after *c* the *long* e sound is spelled *ei.* Point out that *ei* is also the correct spelling when the sound is not *long* e, or when the sound is *long* a. [*veil, foreign*] Show that *protein* and *friend* represent exceptions to these rules. Now, have a volunteer use another example from this chapter to demonstrate how to spell words with *ie* or *ei.*

Exercise 3 Proofreading Sentences to Correct Spelling Errors

ANSWERS

1. freind—friend
2. sheild—shield

MECHANICS

16 b–p

TIPS & TRICKS

Remember this rhyme:
I before e except after *c*
or when sounded like *a*
as in *neighbor* and
weigh.

Spelling Rules

ie and *ei*

16b. Write *ie* when the sound is long e, except after c.

EXAMPLES	achieve	chief	niece	shield	ceiling
	believe	field	piece	thief	deceit
	brief	grief	relief	yield	receive

EXCEPTIONS either, leisure, neither, seize, protein

16c. Write *ei* when the sound is not long e.

EXAMPLES	counterfeit	height	reign	forfeit
	foreign	heir	veil	weigh

EXCEPTIONS friend, mischief, kerchief

NOTE Rules 16b and 16c apply only when the *i* and the e are in the same syllable.

EXAMPLES de • i • ty sci • ence

–cede, –ceed, and *–sede*

16d. Only one English word ends in *–sede: supersede.* Only three words end in *–ceed: exceed, proceed,* and *succeed.* Almost all other words with this sound end in *–cede.*

EXAMPLES	accede	intercede	recede
	concede	precede	secede

Exercise 3 Proofreading Sentences to Correct Spelling Errors

The following sentences contain errors involving the use of *ie, ei, –ceed, –cede,* and *–sede.* For each sentence, identify the misspelled word or words and then write them correctly. If a sentence has no spelling errors, write *C.*

EXAMPLE 1. On my birthday I recieved a wonderful gift.
1. *recieved—received*

1. My neighbor, who is a good freind of mine, went on a trip out West.
2. He sent me a Dream Catcher like those used by the Sioux to sheild themselves from bad dreams.

RESOURCES

Spelling Rules

Practice

- *Language & Sentence Skills Practice,* pp. 341–356

Differentiating Instruction

- *Developmental Language & Sentence Skills,* pp. 145–150

3. Charms like this once hung in each tepee, and mine hangs from the cieling near my bed.
4. According to legend, bad dreams get caught in the web and only good ones succede in reaching the sleeper.
5. I do not really believe that my Dream Catcher can interceed on my behalf, but I have not had one bad dream since my birthday!
6. The Plains Indians moved their homes often, so their possessions could be niether bulky nor heavy.
7. Consequently, the Sioux who made the Dream Catcher used common, lightweight materials.
8. The twig bent into a ring is willow wood, and tiny glass beads represent nightmares siezed by the web.
9. Gracefully hanging from either side is a beautiful feather or a horsehair tassel.
10. Wonderful peices of workmanship like this help ensure that the culture of the Sioux will never resede into the past.

Adding Prefixes

16e. When a prefix is added to a word, the spelling of the original word itself remains the same.

EXAMPLES im + mobile = im**mobile** mis + spell = mis**spell**
un + certain = un**certain** over + rule = over**rule**

Adding Suffixes

16f. When the suffix *–ness* or *–ly* is added to a word, the spelling of the original word itself remains the same.

EXAMPLES time + ly = **time**ly even + ness = **even**ness
real + ly = **real**ly late + ness = **late**ness

EXCEPTIONS

1. Words ending in *y* usually change the *y* to *i* before *–ness* and *–ly:* empty—emp**ti**ness; easy—eas**i**ly
2. However, most one-syllable adjectives ending in *y* follow Rule 16f: shy—**shy**ly; dry—**dry**ness
3. *True, due,* and *whole* drop the final e before *–ly:* truly, duly, wholly.

Exercise 3 Proofreading Sentences to Correct Spelling Errors

ANSWERS continued

3. cieling—ceiling
4. succede—succeed
5. interceed—intercede
6. niether—neither
7. C
8. siezed—seized
9. C
10. peices—pieces; resede—recede

PRACTICE

Activity. To make students aware of how to spell words they hear, you might tape-record and play a segment from a familiar television show. Stop the tape when there is a word you want students to spell. After they have created a list, provide the correct spellings. Have students read **Rules 16b–p** and write the appropriate rule by any troublesome words.

DIFFERENTIATING INSTRUCTION

Learners Having Difficulty

To make the number of rules less intimidating to students, help them personalize applying rules. You might suggest that students add spelling rules one at a time to their notebooks, adding a sample word that they know how to spell. Encourage students to think of this word when applying the rule to other words. For example, when adding *ing* to a word with a silent *e,* they can use a sample word like *living* as a clue.

MECHANICS

Exercise 4 Spelling Words with Prefixes and Suffixes

Spell each of the following words, including the prefix or suffix that is given.

EXAMPLE **1.** un + common

1. uncommon

1. un + necessary — 1. unnecessary
2. il + legal — 2. illegal
3. occasional + ly — 3. occasionally
4. cleanly + ness — 4. cleanliness
5. mean + ness — 5. meanness
6. im + moral — 6. immoral
7. sly + ly — 7. slyly
8. speedy + ly — 8. speedily
9. same + ness — 9. sameness
10. un + usual — 10. unusual

16g. Drop the final silent e before adding a suffix that begins with a vowel.

EXAMPLES tame + ing = **tam**ing; noble + er = **nobl**er; tickle + ish = **tickl**ish; loose + est = **loos**est; admire + ation = **admir**ation; move + able = **mov**able

EXCEPTIONS

1. Keep the final silent e in most words ending in *ce* or *ge* before a suffix that begins with *a* or *o*:

   *knowledg**e**able, courag**e**ous.*

   Sometimes the e becomes *i,* as in *grac**i**ous* and *spac**i**ous.*

2. To avoid confusion with other words, keep the final silent *e* in some words:

   *dy**e**ing* and *dying, sing**e**ing* and *singing*

3. mile + age = mil**e**age

Exercise 5 Spelling Words with Suffixes

Spell each of the following words, including the suffix that is given.

EXAMPLE **1.** write + ing

1. writing

1. become + ing — 1. becoming
2. guide + ance — 2. guidance
3. continue + ous — 3. continuous
4. surprise + ed — 4. surprised
5. determine + ation — 5. determination
6. sense + ible — 6. sensible
7. save + ing — 7. saving
8. advantage + ous — 8. advantageous
9. dine + ing — 9. dining
10. hope + ed — 10. hoped

MINI-LESSON Grammar

Suffixes and Parts of Speech. You may want to point out to students that adding or changing a suffix will often change the part of speech of the original word. Write the following examples on the chalkboard or on a transparency.

1. *nice* (adj.) + *–ly* = *nicely* (adv.)
2. *kind* (adj.) + *–ness* = *kindness* (n.)
3. *sense* (n.) + *–ible* = *sensible* (adj.)

16h. Keep the final silent *e* when adding a suffix that begins with a consonant.

EXAMPLES safe + ty = saf**e**ty large + ly = larg**e**ly
hope + ful = hop**e**ful awe + some = aw**e**some
care + less = car**e**less pave + ment = pav**e**ment

EXCEPTIONS awe + ful = **aw**ful true + ly = **tru**ly
nine + th = **nin**th argue + ment = **argu**ment

Review A Spelling Words with Suffixes

Spell each of the following words, including the suffix that is given.

EXAMPLE 1. use + less
1. useless

1. announce + ment 1. announcement
2. use + age 2. usage
3. imagine + ary 3. imaginary
4. care + ful 4. careful
5. write + ing 5. writing
6. station + ary 6. stationary
7. hope + less 7. hopeless
8. type + ing 8. typing
9. advertise + ment 9. advertisement
10. use + ful 10. useful

16i. When a word ends in *y* preceded by a consonant, change the *y* to *i* before any suffix except one beginning with *i*.

EXAMPLES tidy + er = tid**i**er glory + ous = glor**i**ous
worry + ed = worr**i**ed terrify + ing = terrif**y**ing

EXCEPTIONS **1.** Some one-syllable words:
shy + ness = sh**y**ness sky + ward = sk**y**ward

2. *lady* and *baby* with most suffixes:
lad**y**like lad**y**ship bab**y**hood

16j. When a word ends in *y* preceded by a vowel, simply add the suffix.

EXAMPLES play + ful = **play**ful boy + hood = **boy**hood
array + ed = **array**ed gray + est = **gray**est
pray + ing = **pray**ing pay + ment = **pay**ment

EXCEPTIONS day + ly = **dai**ly pay + ed = **paid**
say + ed = **said** lay + ed = **laid**

Differentiating Instruction

Special Education Students

Spelling may present problems for students with visual-processing deficiencies. To help students, offer a multisensory approach. Have the students or a helper print in large letters on flashcards the correct spellings of words they are studying. Students can then study the words by simultaneously tracing the letters with their fingers and pronouncing the word on the card. For an added sensory dimension, letters can be written in puff paint so that students can actually feel the letters once the paint has dried.

MECHANICS

4. *use* (v. *or* n.) + *–ful* = *useful* (adj.)

5. *argue* (v.) + *–ment* = *argument* (n.)

Ask volunteers to use both words from each example in a sentence. Conclude by explaining that being familiar with how suffixes change a word's part of speech can help students expand their vocabularies.

Differentiating Instruction

Learners Having Difficulty

You may want to initiate a discussion about the necessity of rules. On the chalkboard, write *stop sign, referee,* and *lifeguard.* Ask students what these words have in common. [*They are associated with rules.*]

Stress that rules make life safer and easier. Just as understanding and obeying traffic rules may prevent accidents, understanding and following spelling rules may prevent unclear communication.

Have students suggest other words to add to the list on the chalkboard, and then discuss what might happen if the rules associated with the words did not exist.

MECHANICS

Exercise 7

DISTRIBUTED REVIEW

Ask students to identify all the possible parts of speech for the following words.

1. swim [*noun, verb*], swimmer [*noun*]

2. accept [*verb*], acceptance [*noun*]

5. riot [*noun, verb*], riotous [*adjective*]

Exercise 6 Spelling Words with Suffixes

Spell each of the following words, including the suffix that is given.

EXAMPLE **1.** ply + able
1. pliable

1. extraordinary + ly — 1. extraordinarily
2. try + ing — 2. trying
3. deny + al — 3. denial
4. satisfy + ed — 4. satisfied
5. rely + able — 5. reliable
6. baby + ish — 6. babyish
7. say + ing — 7. saying
8. joy + ful — 8. joyful
9. bray + ing — 9. braying
10. fly + ing — 10. flying

Doubling Final Consonants

HELP

The final consonant in some words may or may not be doubled. In such cases, both spellings are equally correct.

EXAMPLES
travel + er = trave**ler** *or* trave**ller**

shovel + ed = shove**led** *or* shove**lled**

16k. When a word ends in a consonant, double the final consonant before a suffix that begins with a vowel only if the word:

- has only one syllable or is accented on the last syllable

and

- ends in a *single* consonant preceded by a *single* vowel

EXAMPLES
dim + est = di**mm**est — red + ish = re**dd**ish
plan + ed = pla**nn**ed — propel + er = prope**ll**er
sit + ing = si**tt**ing — refer + ed = refe**rr**ed

Otherwise, simply add the suffix.

EXAMPLES
jump + ed = **jump**ed — tunnel + ing = **tunnel**ing
sprint + er = **sprint**er — appear + ance = **appear**ance

Exercise 7 Spelling Words with Suffixes

Spell each of the following words, including the suffix that is given.

EXAMPLE **1.** rebel + ed
1. rebelled

1. swim + er — 1. swimmer
2. accept + ance — 2. acceptance
3. number + ing — 3. numbering
4. excel + ed — 4. excelled
5. riot + ous — 5. riotous
6. prepare + ing — 6. preparing
7. control + ed — 7. controlled
8. slim + er — 8. slimmer
9. prefer + ing — 9. preferring
10. glamor + ous — 10. glamorous

Review B Spelling Words with Prefixes and Suffixes

The following paragraph contains spelling errors involving the use of prefixes and suffixes. For each sentence, write the misspelled word or words correctly. If a sentence is already correct, write *C*.

EXAMPLE **[1]** Few people know that a teenage boy helped create the awsome Mount Rushmore monument.

1. awesome

[**1**] Begining when he was fifteen, Lincoln Borglum helped his famous father, Gutzon Borglum, who planed and made this gigantic sculpture. [**2**] First, Gutzon Borglum built a plaster model one-twelfth as large as the completted sculpture would be. [**3**] On top of this model Borglum attached the equipment from which he controlled a plumb line. [**4**] The plumb line could be dangled in front of each president's likness to record carefuly each feature. [**5**] Lincoln Borglum helped in making these measurments. [**6**] Then, on top of the cliff, they fastenned an identical machine twelve times as large. [**7**] Lincoln Borglum was one of the workers who operatted this machine. [**8**] Using it, he copyed the movements of the smaller machine and marked exactly where to cut away the rock. [**9**] The closer the workers got to finishing the faces, the more carefully the Borglums studyed the heads. [**10**] There were numerous problems, but the monument was finally inaugurated in 1941.

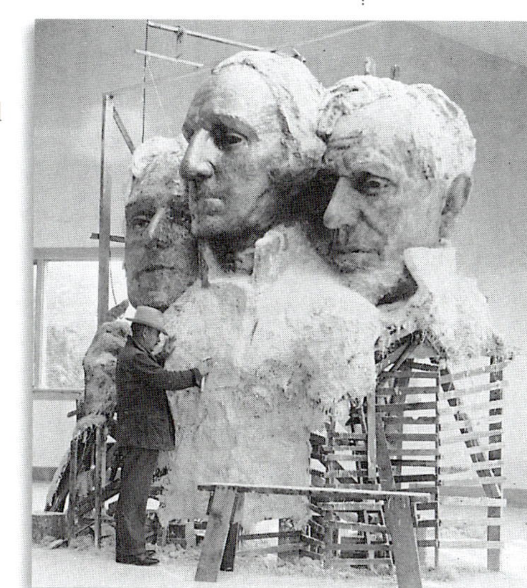

HELP
No proper nouns in Review B are misspelled.

Forming Plurals of Nouns

16l. To form the plurals of most English nouns, simply add *s*.

SINGULAR	boat	care	storm	radio	Jim
PLURAL	boat**s**	care**s**	storm**s**	radio**s**	Jim**s**

Review B Spelling Words with Prefixes and Suffixes

ANSWERS

1. Beginning; planned
2. completed
3. C
4. likeness; carefully
5. measurements
6. fastened
7. operated
8. copied
9. studied
10. C

DIRECT TEACHING

Modeling and Demonstration

Forming the Plurals of Nouns. Model how to spell the plural forms of nouns by using the examples *ship, branch, party, knife, joy, radio,* and *echo.* First, ask what the plural of *ship* is. [*ships*] Point out that most nouns just add an *s* to form the plural. Then, ask how to form the plurals of the other examples. [*branches, parties, joys, knives, radios, echoes*] Point out that some nouns form the plural in different ways, depending on the endings of their singular forms. Now, have a volunteer demonstrate how to spell the plural forms of nouns, using another example from this chapter.

EXTENSION

Critical Thinking

Metacognition. Write on the chalkboard a list of correctly and incorrectly spelled words that apply to **Rules 16l** and **16m.** Ask students if the words are spelled correctly. Next, have students think about how they came to their conclusions. You might have volunteers share their responses or suggest that all students record their processes in their spelling logs.

Synthesis and Evaluation. Tell each student to choose five rules from **16b** to**16m** and to write a brief narrative paragraph including five words that exemplify those rules but that are intentionally misspelled. Students will also want to include correctly spelled words using the same rules.

Have students trade papers with each other and underline any misspelled words in their classmates' paragraphs. Then, they should correct the spelling and give the number of the rule that applies to each misspelled word.

MECHANICS

16m. **To form the plurals of other nouns, follow these rules.**

(1) **If the noun ends in *s, x, z, ch,* or *sh,* add *es.***

SINGULAR	moss	fox	Sanchez	clutch	dish
PLURAL	moss**es**	fox**es**	Sanchez**es**	clutch**es**	dish**es**

NOTE Some one-syllable words ending in *z* double the final consonant when forming plurals.

EXAMPLES	quiz	fez
	qui**zz**es	fe**zz**es

Exercise 8 Spelling the Plurals of Nouns

Spell the plural of each of the following nouns.

EXAMPLE 1. Evans

1. Evanses

1. guess 1. guesses
2. ax 2. axes
3. tongue 3. tongues
4. cafeteria 4. cafeterias
5. wash 5. washes
6. boss 6. bosses
7. student 7. students
8. Owens 8. Owenses
9. box 9. boxes
10. ditch 10. ditches

(2) **If the noun ends in *y* preceded by a consonant, change the *y* to *i* and add *es.***

SINGULAR	fly	pony	cry	story
PLURAL	fl**ies**	pon**ies**	cr**ies**	stor**ies**

EXCEPTION plurals of proper nouns: the Hard**ys,** the Car**ys**

(3) **For some nouns ending in *f* or *fe,* add *s.* For other nouns ending in *f* or *fe,* change the *f* to *v* and add *s* or *es.***

EXAMPLES	giraffe	roof	self	life	elf	thief	wolf
	giraffe**s**	roof**s**	sel**ves**	li**ves**	el**ves**	thie**ves**	wol**ves**

NOTE Some nouns can correctly form their plurals either way.

EXAMPLES	hoof	scarf
	hoo**ves**	scar**ves**
	or	*or*
	hoof**s**	scarf**s**

TIPS & TRICKS

Noticing how the plural is pronounced will help you remember whether to change the *f* to *v.*

Exercise 9 Spelling the Plurals of Nouns

Spell the plural of each of the following nouns.

EXAMPLES
1. shelf
   1. *shelves*
2. poppy
   2. *poppies*

1. thief	1. thieves	6. wife	6. wives
2. chef	2. chefs	7. loaf	7. loaves
3. theory	3. theories	8. comedy	8. comedies
4. gulf	4. gulfs	9. trophy	9. trophies
5. ally	5. allies	10. self	10. selves

HELP To correctly complete Exercise 9, you may wish to refer to a recent dictionary.

(4) If the noun ends in *o* preceded by a vowel, add *s*.

SINGULAR	radio	cameo	kangaroo	Julio
PLURAL	radio**s**	cameo**s**	kangaroo**s**	Julio**s**

(5) If the noun ends in *o* preceded by a consonant, add *es*.

SINGULAR	echo	hero	tomato	veto
PLURAL	echo**es**	hero**es**	tomato**es**	veto**es**

EXCEPTIONS Some common nouns ending in *o* preceded by a consonant (especially musical terms) and proper nouns form the plural by adding only *s.*

SINGULAR	peso	sombrero	photo	alto
	piano	solo	Sotho	Sakamoto
PLURAL	peso**s**	sombrero**s**	photo**s**	alto**s**
	piano**s**	solo**s**	Sotho**s**	Sakamoto**s**

NOTE A number of nouns that end in *o* preceded by a consonant have two correct plural forms.

SINGULAR	cargo	grotto	mosquito
PLURAL	cargo**s**	grotto**s**	mosquito**s**
	or	*or*	*or*
	cargo**es**	grotto**es**	mosquito**es**

The best way to determine the plurals of words ending in *o* preceded by a consonant is to check their spellings in a dictionary.

MECHANICS

CONTENT-AREA CONNECTIONS

Science

Scientific Terms. Words from students' science textbooks can provide extra spelling practice. Ask students to find in their science textbooks examples of words that fit the rules covered in this chapter and to add the words to their spelling notebooks.

MECHANICS

HELP
To correctly complete Exercise 10, you may wish to refer to a recent dictionary.

Exercise 10 Spelling the Plurals of Nouns

Spell the plural of each of the following nouns.

EXAMPLE 1. stereo
1. stereos

1. igloo 1. igloos
2. soprano 2. sopranos
3. patio 3. patios
4. veto 4. vetoes
5. torpedo 5. torpedoes
6. banjo 6. banjos [*or* banjoes]
7. taco 7. tacos
8. cello 8. cellos
9. Romeo 9. Romeos
10. studio 10. studios

(6) The plurals of some nouns are formed in irregular ways.

SINGULAR	child	foot	goose	man	tooth
PLURAL	child**ren**	f**ee**t	g**ee**se	m**e**n	t**ee**th

(7) Some nouns have the same form in both the singular and the plural.

SINGULAR and PLURAL Japanese spacecraft sheep

Compound Nouns

(8) For most compound nouns, form the plural of only the last word in the compound.

SINGULAR	spoonbill	smashup	icebox	six-year-old
PLURAL	spoonbill**s**	smashup**s**	icebox**es**	six-year-old**s**

(9) For many compound nouns in which one of the words is modified by the other word or words, form the plural of the word modified.

SINGULAR	sister-in-law	notary public	attorney at law
PLURAL	sister**s**-in-law	notar**ies** public	attorney**s** at law

NOTE Whenever you are not sure about how to spell the plural form of a compound noun, check a recent dictionary.

Exercise 11 Spelling the Plurals of Nouns

Spell the plural form of each of the following nouns.

EXAMPLE 1. ox
1. oxen

1. Vietnamese 1. Vietnamese
2. earmuff 2. earmuffs
3. mouse 3. mice
4. cross-reference 4. cross-references
5. goose 5. geese
6. brother-in-law 6. brothers-in-law
7. aircraft 7. aircraft
8. woman 8. women
9. runner-up 9. runners-up
10. twenty-year-old 10. twenty-year-olds

Latin and Greek Loan Words

(10) Some nouns borrowed from Latin and Greek form the plural as in the original language.

SINGULAR	PLURAL
alumnus [male]	alumn**i**
alumna [female]	alumn**ae**
analysis	analys**es**
crisis	cris**es**
datum	dat**a**
phenomenon	phenomen**a**

NOTE A few Latin and Greek loan words have two correct plural forms.

SINGULAR	appendix	formula
PLURAL	append**ices** *or* append**ixes**	formul**as** *or* formul**ae**

Check a dictionary to find the preferred spelling of a plural loan word. The preferred spelling is generally the one listed first.

Numerals, Letters, Symbols, and Words Used as Words

(11) To form the plurals of numerals, most capital letters, symbols, and words used as words, add either an *s* or an apostrophe and an *s*.

EXAMPLES Put the ***4*'s** (*or* ***4*s**) and the ***T*'s** (*or* ***T*s**) in the second column.

Change the **&'s** (*or* **&s**) to ***and*'s** (*or* ***and*s**).

My parents were teenagers during the **'60's** (*or* **'60s**).

Many immigrants came to this country during the **1800's** (*or* **1800s**).

BORN LOSER reprinted by permission of Newspaper Enterprise Association, Inc.

RETEACHING

Spelling Rules

If students are having trouble with spelling rules, have them learn the rules by playing a game. First, have students work in randomly chosen groups of five to list spelling rules in order of increasing difficulty. Then, have the entire class discuss their rankings and give a point value for each rule based on its difficulty. Next, have students return to their original groups, and assign each group a set of rules for which they will create a list of words giving two spelling words per rule. Finally, have an assigned scribe in each group write each word, its rule number, and its point value on separate slips of paper. Gather all slips into separate containers based on the assigned point value.

Appoint one student to read the spelling words and a scorekeeper to tally points for each group. Have groups compete against each other. Begin the game by having a player chosen randomly from a group choose a point value. The host will draw a word from the appropriate container. The contestant will attempt to spell the word correctly. (The contestant's team receives the designated point value if he or she spells the word correctly.) Continue the game by alternating teams until the words are all used or the class period ends.

Exercise 12 **Spelling the Plurals of Nouns, Numerals, Letters, Symbols, and Words Used as Words**

ANSWERS

1. +'s *or* +s
2. parentheses
3. *so*'s
4. *9*'s or *9*s
5. fulcrums *or* fulcra
6. *C*'s or *C*s
7. 1840's *or* 1840s
8. indexes *or* indices
9. *!*'s or *!*s
10. *ho-ho-ho*'s

MECHANICS

PRACTICE

Guided and Independent

Review C You may wish to use the first five sentences as guided practice and the last five as independent practice. **HOMEWORK**

Review C **Spelling the Plurals of Nouns**

ANSWERS

1. oxen; geese; calves
2. butterflies; mice; burros; giraffes *or* giraffe
3. Armies; jalopies
4. wives; sons-in-law; children
5. ponies; sheep; C [*or* deers]
6. heroes
7. mosquitoes *or* mosquitos; kangaroos
8. *p*'s; *q*'s
9. leaves
10. C

STYLE TIP

When forming the plurals of numerals, letters, symbols, and words used as words, using both an apostrophe and an *s* is never wrong. Therefore, if you have any doubt about whether or not to use the apostrophe, it is best to use it.

HELP

Even though some of the items in Exercise 12 and Review C have two correct plural forms, you need to give only one form for each. You may wish to refer to an up-to-date dictionary.

HELP

When corrected, some lines of the poem in Review C will no longer rhyme.

To prevent confusion, always use an apostrophe and an *s* to form the plurals of lowercase letters, certain capital letters, and some words used as words.

EXAMPLES What do these ***a*'s** in the margins mean?

Ramon got **A's** last semester.

Her muffled ***tee-hee*'s** did not interrupt the speaker.

Exercise 12 Spelling the Plurals of Nouns, Numerals, Letters, Symbols, and Words Used as Words

Give the plural form of each of the following words, numerals, symbols, and words used as words.

EXAMPLE **1.** *o*

1. o's

1. +	**6.** *C*
2. parenthesis	**7.** 1840
3. *so*	**8.** index
4. *9*	**9.** *!*
5. fulcrum	**10.** *ho-ho-ho*

Review C Spelling the Plurals of Nouns

Most lines in the following silly poem contain misspelled words. Correct each misspelled word. If a line contains no misspellings, write *C*.

EXAMPLES **1.** A group of mans and womens started up a local zoo.

1. men; women

2. They bought a lot of animales and put them all on view.

2. animals

1. They caged the oxes with the gooses, the lion with the calfs,
2. The butterflys and mouses with the burroes and giraffs.
3. Armys of people soon arrived. In jalopys they were piled,
4. With wifes and husbands, son-in-laws, and lots of little childs.
5. The boys and girls rode poneys, and they fed the sheeps and deer,
6. And thought their folks were heros to bring them all right here.
7. The mosquitoses had a fine time feasting on the kangarooes;
8. Most of the other animals minded their *p*s and *q*s.
9. The moon shone brightly through the leafs as night began to fall.
10. Why do you think the lion had the nicest day of all?

Spelling Numbers

16n. **Spell out a number that begins a sentence.**

EXAMPLE **One thousand five hundred** band members attended this year's State Marching Band Festival.

16o. **Within a sentence, spell out numbers that can be written in one or two words; use numerals for other numbers.**

EXAMPLES I have only **one** week in which to write **four** reports.

We picked **twenty-one** quarts of peaches.

Agnes has sold **116** magazine subscriptions.

EXCEPTION 1 If you use some numbers that have one or two words and some that have more than two words, use numerals for all of them.

EXAMPLE Our school had **563** freshmen, **327** sophomores, **143** juniors, and **90** seniors.

EXCEPTION 2 Use numerals for dates when you include the name of the month. Always use numerals for years.

EXAMPLES School closes on June **6.** [This example could also be correctly written as *the sixth of June,* but not *June 6th.*]

Egypt fell to the Romans in **30** B.C.

16p. **Spell out numbers used to indicate order.**

EXAMPLE My brother graduated **second** [not *2nd*] in his class.

Reference Note

For more about **writing dates,** see page 287.

MECHANICS

Spelling Rules 373

Exercise 13 **Spelling Numbers**

POSSIBLE ANSWERS

1. Ninety people applied for the job.
2. Of the candidates, fifty-two seem qualified, but only one can be hired.
3. The contest jar held 231 red jelly beans, 83 green ones, and only 15 yellow ones.
4. Jim finished fourth in the Memorial Day Marathon.
5. My birthday is December 23.

Words Often Confused

(pp. 374–385)

OBJECTIVES

- To distinguish between words that are often confused
- To proofread sentences for correct use of words that are often confused

MECHANICS

Exercise 13 **Spelling Numbers**

Write five original sentences, following the directions given below.

EXAMPLE 1. Write a sentence giving the year in which your best friend was born.

1. *Rudy Garza was born in 1986.*

1. Write a sentence beginning with a number.
2. Write a sentence containing two numbers, both of which can be written in one or two words.
3. Write a sentence containing three numbers, two of them with one or two words and one of them with more than two words.
4. Write a sentence using a number to indicate the order in which a person placed in a race.
5. Write a sentence giving the month and date of your birthday.

Words Often Confused

You can prevent many spelling errors by learning the difference between the words grouped together in this section. Some of them are confusing because they are ***homonyms***—that is, they are pronounced alike. Others are confusing because they are spelled the same or nearly the same.

advice	[noun] *counsel* Why don't you ask your father for *advice*?
advise	[verb] *to give advice* The weather service *advises* boaters.
affect	[verb] *to influence* Do sunspots *affect* the weather?
effect	[verb] *to bring about, to accomplish*; [noun] *result, consequence* Our new boss *effected* some startling changes in our use of technology. Name three *effects* of the Industrial Revolution on family life.
all ready	[adjective] *everyone or everything prepared* We were *all ready* to go.
already	[adverb] *previously* Sharon has *already* gone.

RESOURCES

Words Often Confused

Practice

- *Language & Sentence Skills Practice*, pp. 357–361

Differentiating Instruction

- *Developmental Language & Sentence Skills*, pp. 151–156

all right	[This is the only acceptable spelling. Although the spelling *alright* is in some dictionaries, it has not become standard usage.]
all together	[adjective or adverb] *everyone or everything in the same place* *All together* at last, the travelers relaxed. The band simply must play *all together*.
altogether	[adverb] *entirely* You're *altogether* mistaken, I fear.
altar	[noun] *a table used for a religious ceremony* The *altar* was draped with a white cloth.
alter	[verb] *to change* This actor can *alter* his appearance.
brake	[noun] *a stopping device*; [verb] *to stop* The *brakes* on our car are good. I *brake* for deer.
break	[verb] *to shatter, sever* A high-pitched sound can *break* glass.
capital	[noun] *center of government*; *money or property used in business*; [adjective] *punishable by death*; *of major importance; excellent*; *uppercase* Raleigh is the *capital* of North Carolina. We need more *capital* to buy the factory. Is killing a police officer a *capital* crime? I made a *capital* error in judgment. This is a *capital* detective story. You need a *capital* letter here.
capitol	[noun] *building, statehouse* The *capitol* is on East Edenton Street.
choose	[verb, used for present and future tense] *select* You may *choose* your own partner.
chose	[verb, past tense, rhymes with *nose*] *selected* They *chose* to postpone the meeting.

(continued)

Reference Note

In the Glossary of Usage, Chapter 9, you can find many other words that are often confused or misused. You can also look them up in a dictionary.

TIPS & TRICKS

To remember the correct spelling of *capitol,* use this memory aid: There is a d**o**me on the capit**o**l.

DIRECT TEACHING

Modeling and Demonstration

Words Often Confused. Model the correct use of often confused words with the example *The builders did not alter the historic altar in that church.* First, point out that correct use can often be determined by asking what the confusing words mean in a sentence. Ask what *alter* means. [*change*] Ask what *alter* is or does in the sentence. [*is part of the verb* did alter] Next, ask what *altar* means. [*a table used in a religious ceremony*] Ask what *altar* does in the sentence. [*it is the direct object of the verb*] *Altar* is a noun and should be used only as a noun. Now, have a volunteer demonstrate the correct use of confusing words, using another example from this chapter.

DIFFERENTIATING INSTRUCTION

Learners Having Difficulty

Divide the **Words Often Confused** list among students, and have each student create a large chart for his or her assigned group of words. Students might want to vary the materials used for each chart. (For example, students with tactile orientation might write the words with puff paint or cut the words out of a fabric like velour to trace with their fingers while learning the words.) Then, as the class studies each group of words, hang the corresponding chart in the classroom.

Direct Teaching

Correcting Misconceptions

Homographs. Several pairs of the **Words Often Confused** in this chapter are **homonyms,** words that are pronounced alike but spelled differently (*brake/break; coarse/course*). Students are often less familiar with **homographs,** words that are spelled the same but are different parts of speech and are pronounced differently (*lead/lead*). You may want to introduce students to several other pairs of homographs to help them pronounce, spell, and use these words correctly.

For example, when *address* is used as a noun, the stress is on the first syllable. When it is used as a verb, the stress falls on the second syllable. Other examples include *con*flict—con*flict*, *per*mit—per*mit*, *pre*sent—pre*sent*, and *pro*duce—pro*duce*. Have students repeat these words as you model the correct pronunciations. Have students work with partners to create sentences using the word pairs—for example, "My father won't per*mit* me to get a driving *per*mit until next year."

MECHANICS

(continued)

coarse	[adjective] *rough, crude* This *coarse* fabric is very durable. He never uses *coarse* language.
course	[noun] *path of action or progress; unit of study; track or way; part of a meal;* [also used with *of* to mean *naturally* or *certainly*] The airplane strayed off its *course* in the storm. I'm taking an algebra *course*. She's at the golf *course*. The main *course* at the banquet was roasted turkey with dressing. Cats, of *course*, are predators.

Exercise 14 Distinguishing Between Words Often Confused

Choose the correct word or expression from the pair in parentheses.

EXAMPLE 1. I was proud to (*accept, except*) the award.
1. accept

1. Betty has (*all ready, already*) handed in her paper.
2. (*All right, Alright*), I'll wrap the package now.
3. The mechanic adjusted the (*brakes, breaks*).
4. Do you know which city is the (*capital, capitol*) of your state?
5. They were (*all together, altogether*) at dinner.
6. The rule goes into (*affect, effect*) today.
7. His (*coarse, course*) manners offended everyone.
8. A fragile piece of china (*brakes, breaks*) easily.
9. Our state (*capital, capitol*) is built of limestone and marble.
10. When will they (*choose, chose*) the winners?

Exercise 15 Proofreading for Words Often Confused

Correct the errors in word choice in the following sentences.

EXAMPLE 1. After taking that class, we were already to shoot our own videos.
1. all ready

HELP— Some sentences in Exercise 15 contain more than one error.

1. advice

1. The best moviemaking ~~advise~~ I ever received came from Ms. Herrera.

Mini-Lesson Mechanics

Confusing Words. Give students the following dictation to test their ability to distinguish between words often confused.

Counselors advise that correct spelling is important. You may fear that *it's already too* late, that your skills are *too weak* to be improved. However, if *you're* willing *to* learn a few basic *principles,* you can *break* the pattern of failure and *effect quite* a change in *your* life.

Next, have each student exchange papers with a classmate and use a colored pen to

2. She taught the video coarse that I choose as an elective last semester.
3. Once we would-be moviemakers were altogether, she said simply, "Rule number one: Take the lens cap off."
4. Everyone laughed, but she said, "It's no joke—in every class at least one person brakes this one basic rule."
5. "Of coarse," she added, "forgetting to put a videocassette in the camera has much the same affect."
6. If you chose to make your own home videos, I'd advice you to remember Ms. Herrera's words.
7. They will seriously effect you.
8. I remembered her advice when I went to the steps of the capital for my first shoot.
9. I checked the lighting and angle and chose a subject that was all together satisfactory.
10. When I started to shoot, I realized I had made a capitol error—I had forgotten to take the lens cap off!

complement	[noun] *something that completes or makes perfect;* [verb] *to complete or make perfect* The office now has a full *complement* of personnel. The rug *complemented* the cozy room.
compliment	[noun] *a remark that expresses approval, praise, or admiration;* [verb] *to pay a compliment* Ms. Garcia paid me a *compliment.* The review *complimented* Rosemary on her performance.
consul	[noun] *the representative of a foreign country* Did you meet the Greek *consul* at the reception?
council	[noun] *a group called together to accomplish a job* Our town *council* meets next Tuesday.
counsel	[noun] *advice;* [verb] *to give advice* Her *counsel* is invaluable to the president. The engineers *counsel* them to use additional support for the crossbeams.

(continued)

2. course/chose
3. all together
4. breaks
5. course/effect
6. choose/advise
7. affect
8. capitol
9. altogether
10. capital

TIPS & TRICKS

To remember the correct spelling of *complement*, use this memory aid: A compl**e**ment compl**e**tes.

Differentiating Instruction

Learners Having Difficulty

Students may find the following design helpful in learning the frequently confused words presented in this section.

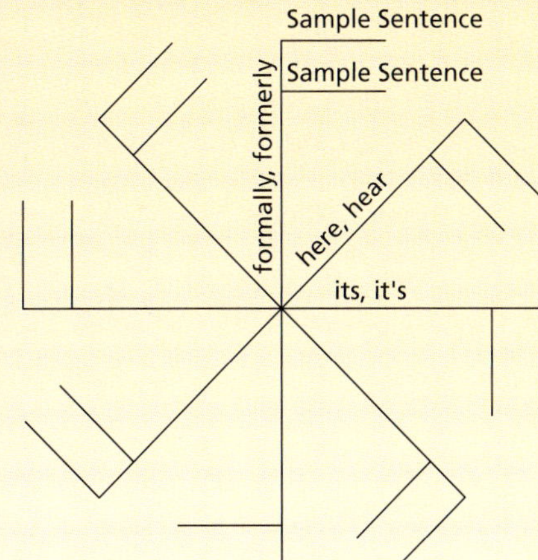

Each shorter line contains a sentence using both of the words being studied, while each longer line lists the pair of words. Suggest that students develop this diagram for the words that are frequently confused and put the diagram in their notebooks. Ask volunteers to share a few sample sentences they have written.

MECHANICS

circle any incorrect words. Explain to students that these are words that a spellchecker in a word-processing program would not correct and that they usually require extra practice or memorization to learn. Suggest that students make flashcards for the words in this section, or, if time permits, you could give students a different word pair from this section each day and have them write example sentences in their notebooks.

RETEACHING

Words Often Confused

Word Origins. Many of the word pairs in this section (for example, *moral* and *morale*) have similar origins. You might want to assign each student a pair of words, and have him or her research whether the two words have similar roots (for example, *brake* and *break*, *plane* and *plain*, *quiet* and *quite*, and *stationary* and *stationery*). Then, have students present their findings to the class.

MECHANICS

(continued)

councilor	[noun] *a member of a council* At the council meeting, my mother plans to introduce Dr. Watkins, the new *councilor.*
counselor	[noun] *one who gives advice* I don't think I'm qualified to act as your *counselor.*
desert	[noun, pronounced des′•ert] *a dry region* The Sahara is the world's largest *desert.*
desert	[verb, pronounced de•sert′] *to leave* She would never *desert* her comrades.
dessert	[noun, pronounced des•sert′] *a sweet, final course of a meal* What would you like for dessert tonight?

Exercise 16 Distinguishing Between Words Often Confused

Choose the correct word from the choices in parentheses.

EXAMPLE **1.** The town (*counselor, councilor*) voted on the bill.
1. councilor

1. The funds are for a (*desert, dessert*) irrigation project.
2. The Security (*Consul, Council, Counsel*) of the United Nations consists of fifteen members.
3. The new tie will (*complement, compliment*) my suit.
4. Miss Jee is my guidance (*councilor, counselor*).
5. The house looks (*deserted, desserted*).
6. Listen to your parents' (*consul, council, counsel*).
7. I passed on your charming (*complement, compliment*) to Isabel.
8. All the members of the city (*council, counsel*) agreed.
9. Frozen yogurt is my favorite (*desert, dessert*).
10. The American (*consul, counsel*) in Bahrain announced the recent trade agreement.

formally	[adverb] *properly, according to strict rules* Should he be *formally* introduced?
formerly	[adverb] *previously, in the past* The new consul was *formerly* a professor.

hear	[verb] *to receive sounds through the ears* Did you *hear* the president's speech?
here	[adverb] *at this place* The bus will be *here* soon.
its	[possessive of *it*] *belonging to it* The lion stopped in *its* tracks.
it's	[contraction of *it is* or *it has*] *It's* snowing! *It's* started snowing!
lead	[verb, present tense, rhymes with *deed*] to *go first* I'll *lead* the way.
led	[verb, past tense of *lead*] *went first* Last week she *led* us to victory.
lead	[noun, rhymes with *red*] *a heavy metal; graphite in a pencil* We made fishing sinkers out of *lead.* Use a sharp *lead* to draw fine lines.
loose	[adjective, rhymes with *noose*] *not tight, not securely fastened; not close together* The string on the package is too *loose.*
lose	[verb, rhymes with *choose*] *to suffer loss* Don't *lose* your ticket.
moral	[adjective] *having to do with good or right;* [noun] *a lesson in conduct* It's a *moral* question. These fables all have a *moral.*
morale	[noun] *mental condition, spirit* Letters from home raised our *morale.*
passed	[verb, past tense of *pass*] *went by* He *passed* us in the corridor.
past	[noun] *history, what has gone by;* [adjective] *former;* [preposition] *farther than; after* I didn't ask him about his *past.* Her *past* employer recommended her. I went *past* the house. It's ten minutes *past* noon.

(continued)

MECHANICS

Words Often Confused 379

To remember the correct spelling of *piece,* use the following memory aid: a **pie**ce of **pie.**

(continued)

peace	[noun] *absence of conflict* Only after war is *peace* truly appreciated.
piece	[noun] *a part of something;* [verb] *to assemble slowly* Have a *piece* of my homemade bread. We *pieced* together the puzzle.

Exercise 17 Distinguishing Between Words Often Confused

Choose the correct word of the pair in parentheses.

EXAMPLE 1. The two countries settled their dispute and now live in (*piece, peace*).
1. peace

1. The coach's praise after the game raised the team's (*morale, moral*).
2. It's already (*passed, past*) nine o'clock.
3. The searchers hoped that the search dog would (*lead, led*) them to the missing skier.
4. The two forwards (*led, lead*) the team to victory.
5. I'm more interested in math than I (*formally, formerly*) was.
6. Several children asked what the (*moral, morale*) of the story was.
7. I need a pencil with soft (*led, lead*).
8. Everyone at the dance was dressed (*formally, formerly*).
9. Molly (*past, passed*) the open doorway.
10. Is the bank offering good interest rates on (*it's, its*) savings accounts and loans?

Exercise 18 Proofreading for Words Often Confused

Correct the errors in word choice in the following sentences.

EXAMPLE 1. My dad's promotion lead to a move for our family.
1. led

1. Sometimes relocating can feel like abandoning everything and everyone you ~~formally~~ cared about. 1. formerly
2. However, before my family and I moved, one of my friends gave me very good ~~council~~. 2. counsel
3. "Moving away," she said, "doesn't mean that you are ~~desserting~~ your old friends." 3. deserting

CONTENT-AREA CONNECTIONS

Art/Home Economics

Spelling Quilt. Have each student involved in art or home economics design a quilt square illustrating a pair of words often confused. (For example, a student might illustrate *peace* and *piece* by drawing a large *peace* sign and a *piece* of pie.) Encourage students to use various methods (needlework, batik, collage, computer graphics, and so forth) they have learned in art or home economics classes to create their squares. Then, have students stitch or tape their squares together to make a spelling quilt to display in the classroom.

4. After my family moved across the country, I remembered that peace of advice. **4.** piece
5. For the first few months after we moved hear, I felt as though I'd been cut lose from everything I loved. **5.** here/loose
6. To boost my morale, my parents told me something that I needed to here. **6.** hear
7. If you dwell on the passed, you will loose out on the present. **7.** past/lose
8. They both moved often when they were young, so I guess they know what its like. **8.** it's
9. Now that a year has past, I understand that every place has it's good points. **9.** passed/its
10. I've made quite a few new friends, and I'm finally at piece with myself—and with my parents. **10.** peace

plain	[adjective] *clear, not fancy;* [noun] *a flat area of land* She made her point of view *plain.* Steven wears very *plain* clothes. The storm lashed the open *plain.*
plane	[noun] *a flat surface; a level; a tool; an airplane* Each *plane* of the granite block was smooth. The debate was conducted on a high *plane.* Chris smoothed the wood with a *plane.* The *plane* arrived on time.
principal	[noun] *head of a school;* [adjective] *main, most important* Our new *principal* addressed the assembly. Product design is my *principal* responsibility.
principle	[noun] *a rule of conduct; a law* His *principles* do not allow compromise. Please explain the *principle* of gravity.
quiet	[adjective] *silent, still* The library is usually fairly *quiet.*
quite	[adverb] *to a great extent or degree, completely* My little brother is *quite* clever for his age. I'm not *quite* finished.

(continued)

TIPS & TRICKS

To remember the correct spelling of *principal,* use the following memory aid: The princi**pal** is your **pal**.

DIFFERENTIATING INSTRUCTION

Learners Having Difficulty

Vocabulary and spelling problems are closely linked in the words covered in this segment. Ask students to choose five words from the **Words Often Confused** list that are not part of their usual vocabularies and to record the definitions in their spelling logs. Then, have students write several original sentences using each word on their lists correctly. Finally, have students revise the sentences to create a fill-in-the-blank or a multiple-choice exercise. Assign the exercises to class members needing extra practice.

TECHNOLOGY 

Remind students that computer spellcheckers do not identify words that have been confused with other words, because the program finds only misspellings, not incorrect usage. For example, a spellchecker will not point out that *affect* has been confused with *effect* since *affect* is a correctly spelled word in other contexts.

MECHANICS

Practice

Guided and Independent

Exercise You may wish to use **Exercise 19** as guided practice and **Review D** as independent practice.

HOMEWORK

MECHANICS

To remember the correct spelling of *stationery*, use the following memory aid: "You write a lett**er** on station**er**y."

Reference Note

For information on **possessive pronouns,** see page 184. For information on **adverbs,** see page 200. For information on **forming contractions,** see page 335.

(continued)

shone	[verb, past tense of *shine*] *emitted light* The sun *shone* brightly this morning.
shown	[verb, past participle of *show*] *revealed, displayed* Li Hua has just *shown* me her scrapbook.
stationary	[adjective] *in a fixed position* These chairs are *stationary.*
stationery	[noun] *writing paper* Use white *stationery* for business letters.
than	[conjunction, used for comparisons] Jimmy enjoys tennis more *than* golfing.
then	[adverb] *at that time; next* Did you know Bianca *then*? I revised my paper, and *then* I proofread it.
their	[possessive of *they*] *belonging to them* The girls gave *their* opinions.
there	[adverb] *at that place;* [also an expletive used to begin a sentence] I'll be *there* on time. *There* isn't any milk left.
they're	[contraction of *they are*] *They're* at the station now.

Exercise 19 Distinguishing Between Words Often Confused

Choose the correct word from the pair in parentheses.

EXAMPLE 1. Mrs. Tanaka is our school's (*principal, principle*).
1. *principal*

1. An elephant eats more vegetation (*then, than*) any other animal does.
2. One scene of the movie was not (*shone, shown*) on TV.
3. The deer was (*stationary, stationery*) for a full minute.
4. Gossiping is against his (*principals, principles*).
5. Last night many stars (*shone, shown*) brightly.
6. I wrote the letter on blue (*stationary, stationery*).
7. Rosa learned how to use a (*plain, plane*) in industrial arts class.

Learning for Life

Continued on pp. 383–384

Editing Services. Proofreading for spelling errors is a good way to confront personal spelling problems. Tell the class that they will be offering their proofreading services to another class. The class may be another language arts class at the same grade level.

Obtain from another teacher a set of papers that need proofreading, allowing the students who have written the papers to maintain anonymity by using identifying numbers rather than names on their papers.

8. My (*principal*, *principle*) problem is learning to spell.
9. I hope they remembered (*there*, *their*) homework.
10. Is he (*quite*, *quiet*) sure?

Review D Proofreading for Words Often Confused

Correct each error in word choice in the following sentences.

EXAMPLE 1. Our principle let us out of class early to welcome home our victorious volleyball team.

1. *principal*

1. King High School won quiet a victory last year—the girls' regional volleyball championship.
2. Everyone wanted to complement the team's abilities.
3. The victory had a positive affect on the whole student body.
4. Hundreds of students went to the airport to meet the team's plain.
5. The flight arrived on time, but than it took more then an hour for the aircraft to reach the gate.
6. Finally someone shouted, "Their they are!"
7. "There coming up the ramp!"
8. Coach Janos asked for quite and introduced each of the girls.
9. They're were loud cheers for each of them, even though quite a few hadn't played in the final game.
10. It was plane that they were quite excited about there success and were looking forward to the official victory rally the next day.

HELP — Some sentences in Review D contain more than one error.

1. quite
2. compliment
3. effect
4. plane
5. then/than
6. There
7. They're
8. quiet
9. There
10. plain/their

threw	[verb] *tossed; pitched* Freddy *threw* three strikes.
through	[preposition] *in one side and out the opposite side* The firetruck raced *through* the heavy traffic.
to	[preposition; also used before the infinitive form of a verb] They've gone *to* the store. She told us *to* wash the windows.
too	[adverb] *also; excessively* I like soccer, and Ted does, *too.* He was *too* tired to think clearly.
two	[adjective or noun] *the sum of one + one* I noticed *two* packages on the sofa.

(continued)

MECHANICS

Have each student become an "expert" on a particular spelling rule or on a set of words from the **Words Often Confused** list. Each student will read the papers for his or her specialty only (for example, forming plurals of words ending in *y*).

Have students brainstorm to develop a process that the whole class will use, such as learning a particular rule, reading the paper to find words related to that rule,

Exercise 20

DISTRIBUTED REVIEW

Have students identify the correct part of speech for each word or contraction below as it is used in the specified sentence.

3. next [*adverb*]

6. around [*preposition*]

9. –n't [*adverb*]

MEETING THE CHALLENGE

Your textbook lists many pairs of words that writers often confuse, pairs like *compliment* and *complement*. Come up with five pairs of words that could be confused that are not listed in your textbook. For each pair, write a sentence that uses both words correctly. For example, you could write, "My *compliments* to the chef—these flavors *complement* each other perfectly!" The sentences should function as reminders about each word's meaning and spelling. Share your five sentences and your five new pairs of words with your classmates.

ANSWERS

Sentences will vary.

(continued)

waist	[noun] *the middle part of the body* This skirt is too big in the *waist.*
waste	[noun] *unused material;* [verb] *to squander* *Waste* is a major problem in the United States. Don't *waste* your money on that.
weak	[adjective] *feeble, lacking force, not strong* The fawn is still too *weak* to walk.
week	[noun] *seven days* Carol has been gone a *week.*
weather	[noun] *conditions outdoors* The *weather* suddenly changed.
whether	[conjunction indicating alternative or doubt] She wondered *whether* to enter the contest.
who's	[contraction of *who is* or *who has*] I can't imagine *who's* at the door now. *Who's* been marking in my book?
whose	[possessive of *who*] *belonging to whom* *Whose* bicycle is this?
your	[possessive of *you*] *belonging to you* What is *your* idea?
you're	[contraction of *you are*] R.S.V.P. so that I'll know whether *you're* planning to be there.

Exercise 20 Distinguishing Between Words Often Confused

Choose the correct word from the ones given in parentheses.

EXAMPLE **1.** Lourdes speaks Portuguese, (*to, two, too*).

1. too

1. Next (*weak, week*) the Bearcats will play the Wolverines.
2. The ball crashed (*threw, through*) the window.
3. (*Your, You're*) up next, Leshe.
4. Giving a speech makes me (*weak, week*) in the knees.
5. (*Your, You're*) sleeve is torn.
6. Each band member wore a gold sash around the (*waist, waste*).
7. (*Whose, Who's*) bat is this?

Learning for Life

Continued from p. 383

checking a dictionary to be sure the word is not an exception to the rule, and writing an appropriate rule designation, such as **"16i,"** on the paper being read.

Provide a day that students may spend as proofreaders. Ask them each to write brief entries in their writing logs to summarize their experience and to tell what they learned from the activity.

8. (*Whose, Who's*) going to be first?
9. No, this isn't a (*waist, waste*) of time.
10. (*Whose, Who's*) seen my black sweater?

Exercise 21 Proofreading for Words Often Confused

Correct the errors in word choice in the following sentences.

EXAMPLE 1. Have you ever had the whether ruin you're plans?
1. weather, your

1. Last Labor Day weekend, my brother Jorge and I got up early Saturday morning and rode our bikes four miles too the beach. **1.** to
2. The two of us were to busy talking too notice that the sky was growing darker as we rode along. **2.** too/to
3. Just as we through our towels on the sand, it started to rain heavily. **3.** threw
4. We waisted the next hour huddled under one of the beach shelters, arguing about weather to stay or to go home. **4.** wasted/whether
5. We also got into an argument about who's fault it was. **5.** whose
6. "Your the one who had the bright idea," said Jorge. **6.** You're
7. "Whose the one who said it would be sunny?" I retorted. **7.** Who's
8. Finally, we pedaled back home threw the driving rain. **8.** through
9. It rained all day Sunday and Monday, to. **9.** too
10. We spent the weekend cooped up in the house while whether forecasters predicted sunny skies for the next weak. **10.** weather/week

Review E Identifying Correctly Spelled Words

Choose the correct word or expression from the pair in parentheses.

EXAMPLE 1. a (*stationary, stationery*) exercise bicycle
1. stationary

1. a (*brief, breif*) talk
2. (*neither, niether*) one
3. (*course, coarse*) cloth
4. some good (*advice, advise*)
5. fruit for (*desert, dessert*)
6. many (*heros, heroes*)
7. on the (*cieling, ceiling*)
8. two (*copies, copys*)
9. looking (*passed, past*) him
10. (*weather, whether*) to stay
11. the (*altar, alter*) boys
12. building (*patioes, patios*)
13. recycled (*34, thirty-four*) cans
14. we will go (*than, then*)
15. a (*mispelled, misspelled*) word
16. (*happyly, happily*) ever after
17. that's (*awsome, awesome*)
18. a (*week, weak*) voice
19. this sharp pencil (*led, lead*)
20. (*their, they're*) his

Words Often Confused 385

ASSESSING

Monitoring Progress

Chapter Review. To assess student progress, you may want to compare the types of items missed on the **Diagnostic Preview** to those missed on the **Chapter Review.** If students have not made significant progress, you may want to refer them to **Chapter 17: Correcting Common Errors, Exercises 35–39,** for additional practice.

MECHANICS

Numerals and terms in brackets refer to rules and concepts tested by the items in the Chapter Review.

1. niece/succeed [16b,d]
2. evenness [16f]
3. C [16a]
4. Occasionally [16f]
5. sensible [16g]
6. bookshelves [16m(3)]
7. O'Daniels [16l]
8. awesome / swimmer [16h, k]
9. Extraordinarily [16f, i]
10. fifteenth [16p]
11. chief/speeches [16b, m(1)]
12. All right/icy [*all right,* 16g]
13. boxes [16m(1)]
14. Council [*consul, council, counsel*]
15. C [16a]
16. brief [16b]
17. precedes [16d]
18. daily[16j]

Chapter Review

A. Proofreading Sentences to Correct Spelling Errors

Most of the following sentences contain spelling errors. Write the misspelled words correctly. If a sentence is already correct, write *C.*

1. Silas has no doubt that his favorite neice will succede in whatever career she chooses to follow.
2. The winter snow and ice damaged the eveness of the road surface.
3. Some critics' reviews were largely favorable; others said the movie was awful.
4. Occasionaly, we stay home on Saturdays to clean the yard.
5. Cousin Mark bought that car because he thinks it is a senseible compromise between style and economy.
6. I read all the recommended books from cover to cover for the finals, and now that exams are over, the books are safely back on the library bookshelfs where they belong.
7. I asked Patrick O'Daniel how long the O'Daniel's had lived in Texas.
8. In his twenties, Grandpa was an awsome swimer.
9. Extraordinaryly quickly, the snake disappeared into the undergrowth.
10. "As you know," said Ms. Garza, "February 15th—that is, tomorrow—is Colleen's birthday."
11. My cheif objection to attending the ceremony was having to listen to all those speech's.
12. "Alright, then," said Mom. "You can go outside, but be careful on those icey sidewalks."
13. How many boxs were stacked near the door?
14. The members of the United Nations Security Counsel are the United States, Russia, China, France, and the United Kingdom.
15. The engineer accidentally shut down the transmitter.
16. Vivian's account of her experiences in New Guinea was breif but vivid.
17. What do you call the passage that preceeds the main body of our Constitution?
18. The paper is delivered dayly, except on Mondays.

RESOURCES

Spelling

Review

- *Language & Sentence Skills Practice,* pp. 362–365

Assessment

- *Holt Handbook Chapter Tests with Answer Key,* pp. 31–32, 52

19. The elephant was ^ ~~considerring~~ coming into the clearing.
20. I'm grumpy because I just had an ^ ~~arguement~~ with a friend.

19. considering [16k]
20. argument [16h]

B. Distinguishing Between Words Often Confused

Choose the correct word from the pair in parentheses.

21. Last night I went (*too, to*) the theater.
22. How did the news (*effect, affect*) him?
23. We need to order some letterhead (*stationary, stationery*) and paper for the photocopier.
24. At the graduation ceremony, Mr. Garcia, the (*principle, principal*), gave a short speech.
25. The (*plain, plane*) finally took off after a two-hour delay.
26. First we sketched the outline, and (*than, then*) we filled in the features of the house.
27. Her duties in her old job were (*quiet, quite*) different from those in the new job.
28. "Son," said Dad, "I'd (*advice, advise*) you to keep at it. Quitters never get anywhere."
29. For (*desert, dessert*) they had frozen yogurt and shredded pineapple.
30. We were all very pleased when we heard that Shawna's dad had been named U.S. (*Counsel, Consul*) in Pretoria, South Africa.
31. Please permit me to introduce (*formerly, formally*) Dr. Villanueva, my sponsor.
32. When parking on an incline, always remember to set the (*break, brake*).
33. I think that tonight's debate is on the subject of (*capital, capitol*) punishment.
34. "(*All together, Altogether*) now," said the choir director.
35. Going to the Christmas concert with the whole family certainly raised my (*morale, moral*).
36. The (*capital, capitol*) of New York State is not New York City, but Albany.
37. I wonder (*who's, whose*) parka this is.
38. From Fran's point of view, volunteering to help clean up the city park was as much a question of (*principal, principle*) as goodwill.

21. [*to, too, two*]
22. [*affect, effect*]
23. [*stationary, stationery*]
24. [*principal, principle*]
25. [*plain, plane*]
26. [*than, then*]
27. [*quiet, quite*]
28. [*advice, advise*]
29. [*desert, dessert*]
30. [*consul, council, counsel*]
31. [*formally, formerly*]
32. [*brake, break*]
33. [*capital, capitol*]
34. [*all together, altogether*]
35. [*moral, morale*]
36. [*capital, capitol*]
37. [*who's, whose*]
38. [*principal, principle*]

MECHANICS

Chapter Review 387

39. [*your, you're*]
40. [*all ready, already*]
41. [*desert, dessert*]
42. [*lead, led, lead*]
43. [*loose, lose*]
44. [*passed, past*]
45. [*its, it's*]
46. [*moral, morale*]
47. [*shone, shown*]
48. [*coarse, course*]
49. [*quiet, quite*]
50. [*plain, plane*]

39. "Was that really (*you're, your*) best effort?" asked Ms. Yokoyama impatiently.
40. He opened his mouth to reply, but Babs had (*all ready, already*) gone.
41. Friends never (*dessert, desert*) each other.
42. Use a (*led, lead*) pencil to sketch the outlines.
43. "How could you (*loose, lose*) an entire bag of groceries?" asked Belinda incredulously.
44. The same truck (*past, passed*) us three times on the same stretch of highway.
45. Please remember that every journey has (*it's, its*) good and bad points.
46. "Improving communication, as many of you will find out, can boost (*moral, morale*)," said Ms. Lockheed.
47. The amber harvest moon (*shown, shone*) through the rustling branches and onto the badger's burrow.
48. "All the caddies will be paid in full, of (*course, coarse*)," said Mr. Glendinning.
49. When the office workers go home, a strange (*quiet, quite*) descends on the downtown business district.
50. The tornadoes raced across the barren (*plane, plain*).

DILBERT reprinted by permission of United Feature Syndicate, Inc.

Writing Application

Using Correct Spelling in a Letter

Spelling Words Correctly The junior varsity volleyball team is having its best season in several years, but no one else in school seems to know about it. Write a letter to the coach explaining the three best things the team can do to raise awareness and interest throughout the school. Use at least five words from the spelling lists and five words from the lists of words that are often confused.

Prewriting Begin by making a list of all the ideas you can think of to promote the team. Look at the other successful sports and activities at your school. What do they do to promote themselves? Narrow your list down to the three ideas that are most likely to work.

Writing Begin your letter by clearly explaining your purpose. Then, list each of your ideas and explain why you think they may help. Include estimates of how much money and time each of the ideas might involve. Conclude by offering to take charge of one part of the effort.

Revising First, read your letter to make sure all of your ideas are clearly and completely explained. Ask yourself if you have thought about all of your ideas thoroughly. Have you considered all the expenses that each plan may involve? Would anyone be offended or hurt by any of your plans? You may want to have an adult friend or family member look at your ideas to see if they are appropriate. Make sure you have used at least five words from the spelling lists and five words from the lists of words that are often confused.

Publishing Check your letter carefully for errors in grammar, usage, and punctuation. Then, think about a sport or other activity at school that does not get the recognition and support you think it deserves. Show your letter to the coach or sponsor of the activity, and offer to help carry out some of the ideas to get the activity more recognition.

APPLICATION

Writing Application

Prewriting Tip. You may wish to hold a brainstorming session to help students come up with ideas about how to promote the team.

Scoring Rubric. While you will want to pay particular attention to students' use of correct spelling, you will also want to evaluate overall writing performance. You may want to give a split score to indicate development and clarity of the composition as well as spelling skills.

Differentiating Instruction

Advanced Learners

Some students will not have problems spelling the words in the **75 Commonly Misspelled Words** list. Allow such students to work as a group to compile a list of words that they have encountered in their reading and have had difficulty spelling. Students can then study the words from the list they have compiled instead of spending time studying words they already know how to spell.

MECHANICS

75 Commonly Misspelled Words

The following list contains seventy-five words that are often misspelled. To find out which words give you difficulty, ask someone to read you the list in groups of ten. Write down each word, and then check your spelling. In your spelling notebook, make a list of any words you misspelled. Keep reviewing your list until you have mastered the correct spelling.

ache
across
again
all right
almost
always
answer

belief
built
business
busy
buy

can't
color
coming
cough
could
country

doctor
doesn't
don't

eager
easy
every

February
forty

friend

grammar
guess

half
having
heard
hour

instead

knew
know

laid
likely

making
meant
minute

often
once

ready
really

safety
said
says
shoes
since

speak
speech
straight
sugar
surely

tear
though
through
tired
together
tomorrow
tonight
tough
trouble
truly
Tuesday

until

wear
Wednesday
where
which
whole
women
won't
write

300 Spelling Words

Learn to spell the following words this year if you don't already know how.

absence
absolutely
acceptance
accidentally

accommodate
accompany
accomplish
accurate

accustomed
achievement
acquaintance
actually

administration
affectionate
agriculture
amateur
ambassador
analysis
analyze
announcement
anticipate
apology
apparent
appearance
approach
approval
arguing
argument
assurance
attendance
authority
available

basically
beginning
believe
benefit
benefited
boundary

calendar
campaign
capital
category
certificate
characteristic
chief
circuit
circumstance
civilization
column
commissioner
committee
comparison
competent
competition
conceivable

concept
confidential
conscience
conscious
consistency
constitution
continuous
control
cooperate
corporation
correspondence
criticism
criticize
cylinder

debtor
decision
definite
definition
deny
description
despise
diameter
disappearance
disappointment
discipline
disgusted
distinction
distinguished
dominant
duplicate

economic
efficiency
eighth
elaborate
eligible
embarrass
emergency
employee
encouraging
environment
equipped
essential
evidently

exaggerate
exceedingly
excellent
excessive
excitable
exercise
existence
expense
extraordinary

fascinating
fatal
favorably
fictitious
financier
flourish
fraternity
frequent
further

glimpse
glorious
grabbed
gracious
graduating
grammatically
gross
gymnasium

happiness
hasten
heavily
hindrance
humorous
hungrily
hypocrisy
hypocrite

icy
ignorance
incidentally
indicate
imagination
immediately
immense
indispensable

MECHANICS

Spelling Words 391

inevitable
innocence
inquiry
insurance
intelligence
interfere
interrupt
interpretation
investigation

jealous

knowledge

leisure
lengthen
lieutenant
likelihood
liveliness
loneliness

magazine
maneuver
marriage
marvelous
mechanical
medieval
merchandise
minimum
mortgage
multitude
muscle
mutual

narrative
naturally
necessary
negligible
niece
noticeable

obligation
obstacle
occasionally
occurrence
offense
official
omit
operation
opportunity
oppose
optimism
orchestra
organization
originally

paid
paradise
parallel
particularly
peasant
peculiar
percentage
performance
personal
personality
perspiration
persuade
petition
philosopher
picnic
planning
pleasant
policies
politician
possess
possibility
practically
precede
precisely
preferred
prejudice
preparation
pressure
primitive
privilege
probably
procedure
proceed
professor
proportion
psychology
publicity
pursuit

qualities
quantities

readily
reasonably
receipt
recognize
recommendation
referring
regretting
reign
relieve
remembrance
removal
renewal
repetition
representative
requirement
residence
resistance
responsibility
restaurant
rhythm
ridiculous

sacrifice
satire
satisfied
scarcely
scheme
scholarship

392 Spelling

scissors
senate
sensibility
separate
sergeant
several
shepherd
sheriff
similar
skis
sponsor
solemn
sophomore
source
specific
straighten

substantial
substitute
subtle
succeed
successful
sufficient
summary
superior
suppress
surprise
survey
suspense
suspicion

temperament
tendency

thorough
transferring
tremendous
truly

unanimous
unfortunately
unnecessary
urgent
useful
using

vacancies
vacuum
varies

MECHANICS

Spelling Words 393

CHAPTER 17

INTRODUCING THE CHAPTER

- This chapter focuses on some of the aspects of grammar, usage, and mechanics that students often have difficulty mastering. Students who do not master these concepts make serious grammatical errors in their writing; they miss or introduce new errors when proofreading; and they cannot effectively find grammatical errors on standardized tests that measure language skills.
- Since this chapter concentrates attention on the areas of greatest concern, you may find it useful in a variety of ways. You could use the exercises as diagnostic tools as you prepare to teach related chapters; you could use them as a resource for reteaching to provide extra practice for concepts you feel need more emphasis; or you could use them as a review of key concepts to help students prepare for standardized tests of language skills mastery.

CHAPTER 17

Correcting Common Errors

Key Language Skills Review

This chapter reviews key skills and concepts that pose special problems for writers.

- **Sentence Fragments and Run-on Sentences**
- **Subject-Verb and Pronoun-Antecedent Agreement**
- **Verb Forms**
- **Clear Pronoun Reference**
- **Comparison of Modifiers**
- **Dangling and Misplaced Modifiers**
- **Standard Usage**
- **Capitalization**
- **Punctuation—End Marks, Commas, Quotation Marks, Apostrophes, Semicolons, and Colons**
- **Spelling**

Most of the exercises in this chapter follow the same format as the exercises found throughout the grammar, usage, and mechanics sections of this textbook. You will notice, however, that two sets of review exercises are presented as standardized tests. These exercises are designed to provide you with practice not only in solving usage and mechanics problems but also in dealing with these kinds of problems on standardized tests.

CHAPTER RESOURCES

Internet

- Web resources: go.hrw.com

go.hrw.com

Practice & Review

- *Language & Sentence Skills Practice,* pp. 371–406
- *Language & Sentence Skills Practice Answer Key,* pp. 148–164

Application & Enrichment

- *Language & Sentence Skills Practice,* pp. 370, 407–410
- *Language & Sentence Skills Practice Answer Key,* pp. 164–166

Exercise 1 Revising Sentence Fragments

Each of the following word groups is a sentence fragment. Rewrite each fragment to make it a complete sentence. Add whatever words are necessary to make the meaning of the sentence complete.

EXAMPLE 1. having already read the book

1. Having already read the book, I was not surprised by the film's end.

1. television, radio, newspapers, billboards, magazines, and now the World Wide Web
2. beside the cold, clear spring tumbling down the rocky slopes
3. when we passed through the turnstile
4. to appreciate adequately the complexity of these drum rhythms
5. according to the most recent experiments
6. exercising regularly for thirty minutes at least three times a week
7. trained as a lab assistant at the local junior college
8. who had once actually stood on the Great Wall of China
9. one of the first women of that rank in the Navy
10. where the laundry had been hung on a line in full sunlight

Reference Note

For information on **correcting sentence fragments,** see page 434.

Exercise 2 Identifying Sentences and Revising Sentence Fragments

Identify each numbered word group in the following paragraph as either a sentence fragment (*F*) or a complete sentence (*S*). Then, make each fragment part of a complete sentence either by adding words to it or by combining it with another fragment or sentence in the paragraph. Change the punctuation and capitalization as necessary.

EXAMPLES **[1]** I discovered that the jacket was made of linen.
[2] When I got home.

1. S

2. F—When I got home, I discovered that the jacket was made of linen.

[1] Before you spend your money on that expensive shirt. **[2]** Read the label carefully! **[3]** Because some clothes must be sent to the dry cleaner. **[4]** They will cost you extra money. **[5]** A lot of money in the long run. **[6]** Other clothes must be washed by hand. **[7]** Requiring extra time and care for their upkeep. **[8]** If you are looking for quality clothes. **[9]** That are both attractive and inexpensive to own. **[10]** It pays to read the label.

1. F **2.** S
3. F **4.** S
5. F **6.** S
7. F **8.** F
9. F **10.** S

COMMON ERRORS

Differentiating Instruction

- *Developmental Language & Sentence Skills,* pp. 157–158
- *Developmental Language & Sentence Skills Guided Practice Teacher's Notes and Answer Key,* p. 39

Assessment

- *Holt Handbook Chapter Tests with Answer Key,* pp. 33–34, 53

Exercise 1

OBJECTIVE

- To write complete sentences from sentence fragments

Exercise 1 **Revising Sentence Fragments**

POSSIBLE ANSWERS

1. Advertisers can promote products through television, radio, newspapers, billboards, magazines, and now the World Wide Web.
2. Mother took Jon's picture beside the cold, clear spring tumbling down the rocky slopes.
3. We showed our admission passes when we passed through the turnstile.
4. Because I lack a strong sense of rhythm, I am not able to appreciate adequately the complexity of these drum rhythms.
5. According to the most recent experiments, that new drug is still not effective in stopping all seizures.
6. My doctor recommends exercising regularly for thirty minutes at least three times a week.
7. I hope to be trained as a lab assistant at the local junior college.
8. My aunt Hatty wrote a historical novel concerning a warrior who had once actually stood on the Great Wall of China.
9. I believe my history textbook has a picture of one of the first women of that rank in the Navy.
10. The children played in the backyard where the laundry had been hung on a line in full sunlight.

Exercise 2

OBJECTIVE

- To identify and revise sentence fragments

Exercise 2 **Identifying Sentences and Revising Sentence Fragments**

POSSIBLE ANSWERS

[1–2] Before you spend your money on that expensive shirt, read the label carefully! [3–4] Because

(continued)

COMMON ERRORS

Reference Note

For information on **correcting run-on sentences,** see page 441.

Exercise 3 Revising Run-on Sentences

Each of the following numbered items is a run-on sentence. Revise each run-on, using the method given in brackets after it. Be sure to change punctuation and capitalization as necessary.

EXAMPLE
1. Today's world offers many kinds of popular entertainment earlier Americans relied mainly on music and dancing. [*Use a comma and coordinating conjunction.*]
1. *Today's world offers many kinds of popular entertainment, but earlier Americans relied mainly on music and dancing.* Revisions may vary.

1. Just imagine your life without TV, audio and video recordings, and movies surely you would spend your time quite differently from the way you do now. [*Make two sentences.*]
2. In a world without recorded music, a musician could often attract a crowd even today, good musicians can make a living on the streets of a large city. [*Use a semicolon.*]
3. Music was important to the early settlers they often made their own instruments. [*Use a comma and a coordinating conjunction.*] 3. so
4. Many of the settlers owned fiddles, dulcimers, flutes, and guitars music could be a part of everyday life. [*Use a semicolon, a conjunctive adverb, and a comma*] 4. consequently
5. Long before the settlers arrived, there was already plenty of music in North America American Indians prized music and song. [*Use a semicolon.*]
6. The Seneca used rattles similar to the instruments known as maracas Northern Plains Indians used the hand drum. [*Use a comma and a coordinating conjunction.*] 6. and
7. The Maidu played flutes and whistles musicians today often incorporate such American Indian instruments into popular music. [*Make two sentences.*]
8. The banjo is widely regarded as a traditional American musical instrument the banjo originated in Africa. [*Use a semicolon, a conjunctive adverb, and a comma*] 8. however
9. West Africans made banjo-like instruments out of gourds for strings, they used dried animal gut. [*Use a semicolon.*]
10. Early banjos had no frets and only four strings frets are the ridges positioned at intervals on the necks of banjos and guitars. [*Make two sentences.*]

Exercise 4 Revising Sentence Fragments and Run-on Sentences

Most of the following word groups are either run-on sentences or sentence fragments. Identify and correct each sentence fragment and run-on sentence. If a word group is already a complete sentence, write *C*.

EXAMPLE
1. The area where I live used to be a prehistoric sea, sometimes my friends and I find fossilized sharks' teeth.
   1. *The area where I live used to be a prehistoric sea, and sometimes my friends and I find fossilized sharks' teeth.*

1. Walking slowly over the rocky terrain. 1. F
2. A strange rock caught our attention Jackie broke it open. 2. R
3. Inside were rows and rows of brilliant quartz crystals, we gasped at our discovery. 3. R
4. Gold lies hidden in the West, many people still seek their fortune there. 4. R
5. Is one of the best places in the world for prospectors. 5. F
6. When rainfall, a landslide, or some other act of nature alters the landscape. 6. F
7. Easier to find gold, silver, platinum, and other precious metals. 7. F
8. Although most commonly used for jewelry, gold has numerous industrial uses. 8. C
9. You can grow your own crystals, some grow quite quickly. 9. R
10. With a kit from a hobby shop only two blocks away from my house in Colorado Springs. 10. F

Oral Practice Choosing Verbs That Agree in Number with Their Subjects

Read each of the following sentences aloud, and choose the correct form of the verb in parentheses.

EXAMPLE
1. One of the customs most readily shared among cultures (*is, are*) games.
   1. *is*

1. Almost everybody (*has, have*) played games that originated in faraway places.
2. Few of these games (*is, are*) difficult to play.

Reference Note

For information on **subject-verb agreement,** see page 121.

Exercise 2 Identifying Sentences and Revising Sentence Fragments

POSSIBLE ANSWERS continued

some clothes must be sent to the dry cleaner, they will cost you extra money. [5] That can add up to a lot of money in the long run. [6–7] Other clothes must be washed by hand, requiring extra time and care for their upkeep. [8–10] If you are looking for quality clothes that are both attractive and inexpensive to own, it pays to read the label.

Exercise 3

OBJECTIVE

- To revise run-on sentences

Exercise 4

OBJECTIVE

- To identify and revise run-on sentences and sentence fragments

Exercise 4 Revising Sentence Fragments and Run-on Sentences

POSSIBLE ANSWERS

1. Walking slowly over the rocky terrain, we saw patches of algae.
2. A strange rock caught our attention; Jackie broke it open.
3. Inside were rows and rows of brilliant quartz crystals. We gasped at our discovery.
4. Gold lies hidden in the West, and many people still seek their fortune there.
5. This is one of the best places in the world for prospectors.
6. When rainfall, a landslide, or some other act of nature alters the landscape, gold can be exposed.
7. These changes make it easier to find gold, silver, platinum, and other precious metals.

(continued)

COMMON ERRORS

Exercise 4 Revising Sentence Fragments and Run-on Sentences

POSSIBLE ANSWERS continued

8. C
9. You can grow your own crystals, and some grow quite quickly.
10. You can start to grow crystals with a kit from a hobby shop only two blocks away from my house in Colorado Springs.

Oral Practice

OBJECTIVE

- To choose verbs that agree with subjects

Exercise 5

OBJECTIVE

- To identify and correct errors in subject-verb agreement

COMMON ERRORS

3. Pictures on ancient Greek pottery (*show, shows*) people playing with yo-yos.
4. (*Was, Were*) the first people who ever played the game lacrosse American Indian?
5. Arctic peoples, Africans, the Maori of New Zealand, and others as well (*plays, play*) cat's cradle.
6. Somewhere, somebody in one of the world's cultures probably (*is, are*) spinning a top right now.
7. Not all card games (*uses, use*) a standard deck of cards.
8. Most of these games (*requires, require*) at least two players, and some require four.
9. Several ancient African games still (*enjoys, enjoy*) popularity among children.
10. None of those colorful Chinese tangrams (*turns, turn*) out to be easy to solve.

Exercise 5 Proofreading a Paragraph for Subject-Verb Agreement

Identify the errors in subject-verb agreement in the following paragraph. Then, change each incorrect verb to agree with its subject.

EXAMPLE [1] Many a building design don't meet the needs of people with disabilities.

1. don't—doesn't

1. presents 2. has 3. make 4. pose 5. is 6. seeks 7. are 8. help 9. don't 10. gives

[1] Ordinary houses or a public building sometimes present problems for people with disabilities. [2] For example, a person using a wheelchair or crutches often have difficulty maneuvering in narrow halls. [3] Flights of stairs and a front stoop makes access difficult for anyone using a wheelchair or a walker. [4] Moreover, inadequate shower access or high counters needlessly poses problems for people with wheelchairs. [5] One homebuilder and solver of these problems are Craig Johnson. [6] Johnson, with a team of advisors and decorators, seek to make life easier for people with various disabilities. [7] Johnson recognizes that easy access and freedom from barriers is becoming both an issue for our aging population and a growing business opportunity. [8] Creating designs and making modifications for people with disabilities helps others, too. [9] For instance, doesn't most people find that levers are easier to operate than doorknobs are? [10] Also, neither a handrail nor a ramp give anyone any difficulty; in fact, both can come in handy for everyone.

Exercise 6 Identifying Antecedents and Writing Pronouns

Each of the following sentences contains a blank where a pronoun should be. Identify the antecedent for each missing pronoun. Then, complete the sentence with a pronoun that agrees with that antecedent.

Reference Note

For information on **pronoun-antecedent agreement,** see page 135.

EXAMPLE 1. At about the age of fifteen, Janet Collins followed ____ dream to the Ballet Russe de Monte Carlo.

1. Janet Collins—her

1. Until Janet Collins, nobody of African heritage had ever made ____ debut on the stage of the Metropolitan Opera House. — 1. his or her
2. While waiting to audition, she saw other ballerinas on a winding staircase backstage doing ____ warm-up exercises. — 2. their
3. All of the people who saw Janet at her audition clapped ____ hands. — 3. their
4. However, because of Collins's color, Mr. Massine, the choreographer, could not hire her for ____ production. — 4. his
5. Collins continued practicing, and in the end ____ was rewarded. — 5. she
6. The Metropolitan Opera opened ____ doors to the prima ballerina. — 6. its
7. Rudolph Bing admired her adagio dancing so much that ____ gave her many opportunities to leap and jump. — 7. he
8. Two of her roles were in *Carmen* and *Aida,* and ____ helped to make her famous. — 8. they
9. To be successful, a ballerina must discipline ____. — 9. herself
10. Either Ms. Lawton or Ms. Vicks will show the class ____ autographed picture of Collins. — 10. her

Exercise 7 Proofreading for Pronoun-Antecedent Agreement

Proofread the following sentences, and identify pronouns that do not agree with their antecedents. Give the correct form of each incorrect pronoun. If a sentence is already correct, write *C.*

EXAMPLE 1. From the earliest times, people all over the world have decorated himself or herself.

1. himself or herself—themselves

1. Whether for war, religious rituals, or beauty, cosmetics have always had its place in human society. — 1. their
2. In ancient Egypt, both men and women used various kinds of cosmetics to make himself or herself more attractive. — 2. themselves

Exercise 6

OBJECTIVE

- **To identify antecedents of missing pronouns and then to supply pronouns that agree with the identified antecedents**

EXTENSION

Relating to Vocabulary

Ask your students to find *antecedent* in the dictionary and to read its etymology. The word consists of two parts, both from Latin. *Ante–* means "before" and *cedent,* derived from *cedere,* means "going." Ask students how the etymology of the word can help them remember its meaning as applied in grammar. [*An antecedent usually goes before the pronoun that refers to it.*]

Exercise 7

OBJECTIVE

- **To identify and correct errors in pronoun-antecedent agreement**

3. C

3. In addition, nearly all Egyptians painted their eyelids with green paste to prevent sunburn.

4. his

4. One of the Egyptian kings was even buried with rouge and lip color in their tomb.

5. their

5. Ancient cosmetics were usually made from natural ingredients, some of which were poisonous to its users.

6. they

6. Arsenic and mercury were two of the most dangerous, and it ruined many lives.

7. himself or herself

7. The Roman man or woman who used cosmetics containing arsenic was slowly killing themselves.

8. her

8. Similarly, in Queen Elizabeth I's time, the English girl or woman who used a skin whitener containing mercury risked having their teeth fall out.

9. C

9. Since before the time of Cosmis—who sold makeup during the reign of Julius Caesar—to the present, enterprising people have made their fortunes by providing products that help others meet their cultures' standards of beauty.

10. he

10. Galen, a man of science in ancient Rome, would be pleased to find that today's cold cream is based on the formula they invented.

Exercise 8

OBJECTIVE

- To identify and correct errors in subject-verb and pronoun-antecedent agreement

Exercise 8 Revising Sentences for Agreement

Each of the following sentences contains either an error in subject-verb agreement or an error in pronoun-antecedent agreement. Revise the sentences to correct each error in agreement.

EXAMPLE 1. Either Mr. Baker or Mr. Perez have promised to drive his van on the field trip.

1. Either Mr. Baker or Mr. Perez has promised to drive his van on the field trip.

1. her
2. are
3. his or her
4. was
5. their
6. was
7. they
8. are

1. Many a girl has taken Shirley Chisholm as ~~their~~ model of success.
2. Here, class, ~~is~~ several classic examples of Aztec art.
3. Each member of the cast knows all of ~~their~~ lines for the play.
4. Beautifully illustrated and written, *Saint George and the Dragon* ~~were~~ awarded the Caldecott Medal.
5. Have Ms. Ivy and Mr. Lee played ~~her and his~~ music for the school?
6. Two dollars ~~were~~ once considered generous pay for an hour's work.
7. All of the travelers were surprised when ~~he or she~~ saw the old purple-and-yellow bus.
8. An international team of archaeological researchers ~~is~~ assembling, one by one, at the site of this exciting discovery.

9. Do Cindy and Brenda practice ~~her~~ dance routine here every day?
10. The two performers ~~has~~ become one of the most popular teams in the history of comedy.

9. their
10. have

Exercise 9 Writing Correct Verb Forms

Complete each sentence with the correct past or past participle form of the verb in italics.

EXAMPLE 1. *do* Have you ____ any research on the Cajun culture?
1. done

1. *blow* Yesterday, a hurricane ____ through Louisiana, where most Cajuns live.
1. blew
2. *begin* The Cajun culture ____ after French immigrants to Acadia, Canada, traveled south.
2. began
3. *come* While in Canada, these immigrants ____ to be known as Acadians.
3. came
4. *take* In Louisiana, the name Acadian ____ on a different pronunciation—"Cajun."
4. took
5. *choose* The Cajuns ____ to befriend the Choctaws, as well as settlers from Germany and Spain.
5. chose
6. *put* Cajun cooks ____ to their own use what they learned from the Choctaws about native plants and animals.
6. put
7. *eat* They ____ seafood seasoned with the Choctaws' filé, which is powdered sassafras leaves.
7. ate
8. *drink* They ____ coffee flavored with chicory.
8. drank
9. *raise* German settlers in the bayou country ____ the beef and pork that the Cajuns used in their tasty dishes.
9. raised
10. *bring* The Cajuns were also delighted with okra, called gumbo by the Bantu, who had ____ it with them from Africa.
10. brought

Reference Note
For information on **using verbs correctly,** see Chapter 6.

Exercise 10 Identifying Correct Forms of Irregular Verbs

Choose the correct form of the verb in parentheses in each of the following sentences.

EXAMPLE 1. For many years, teams of scientists have (*took, taken*) the opportunity to study the Antarctic Peninsula during the summer.
1. taken

1. The scientists (*went, gone*) there to study the delicate balance of the ecosystem.

Reference Note
For information on **using irregular verbs,** see page 147.

Exercise 9

OBJECTIVE

- **To give the correct past or past participle forms of verbs**

DIFFERENTIATING INSTRUCTION

Learners Having Difficulty

If your students need additional review before attempting **Exercise 9,** you may want to give them some guided practice. Form study groups of two or three students each, and assign the even-numbered items. Go over the answers orally to identify students who are struggling with the material, and reteach concepts as needed. Then, assign the odd-numbered items for students to complete as independent practice.

Exercise 10

OBJECTIVE

- **To select the correct forms of irregular verbs**

COMMON ERRORS

Differentiating Instruction

English-Language Learners

General Strategies. Some English-language learners who speak languages such as Indonesian, Japanese, Korean, Turkish, and Vietnamese might not understand the idea of irregular verbs because their native languages have few or no irregular verbs. Students might write the present tense forms of these verbs when they should use the past tense. Give students copies of a comprehensive list of the principal parts of irregular verbs with blank spaces left for the past form. Tell students to fill in the past forms of the verbs and to keep the lists in their notebooks.

Exercise 11

OBJECTIVE

- To identify and correct errors in verb forms

2. These scientists (*knew, knowed*) that worldwide weather patterns are influenced by events in Antarctica.
3. Before the twentieth century, few people (*choosed, chose*) to brave the frigid voyage to the Antarctic.
4. However, new means of transportation have (*brought, brung*) more people, especially scientists, to Antarctica.
5. Such countries as Chile, Britain, and Russia have (*began, begun*) exploring what's beneath Antarctica's ice and snow.
6. No one knows how long Antarctica's waters have (*ran, run*) red with krill, tiny creatures at the bottom of the food chain.
7. Many times, the Ross Ice Shelf has (*shook, shaken*) as a huge iceberg known as B9 has crashed into it.
8. An oil rig could have (*fallen, fell*) if struck by a roving iceberg.
9. If that had happened, a huge oil spill would likely have (*did, done*) major damage to Antarctica's ecosystem.
10. In Antarctica, the nations of the world have been (*gave, given*) an opportunity to work together in peace.

Exercise 11 Proofreading for Correct Verb Forms

Most of the following sentences contain incorrect verb forms. If a form of a verb is wrong, write the correct form. If a sentence already is correct, write *C.*

EXAMPLE **[1]** The brave galleon had rode the waves to an icy grave.

1. *ridden*

1. broken
2. driven
3. rang
4. dived
5. raised
6. C
7. sit
8. lies
9. shrunk
10. grown

[**1**] Over thousands of years of seafaring, many a ship has been ~~broke~~ on the rocks or lost in a storm. [**2**] Thirst for the treasure of these sunken ships has ~~drove~~ opportunists and scholars alike to the dark bottoms of the world's oceans. [**3**] The invention of scuba equipment in 1943 ~~rung~~ in a new era in underwater exploration. [**4**] Since then, treasure hunters and scientists have ~~dove~~ into waters all over the world and surfaced with gold and historical artifacts. [**5**] Expeditions have successfully ~~rose~~ entire ships, such as the *Vasa,* a seventeenth-century Swedish vessel. [**6**] Astonishingly, divers have swum down and inspected the remains of crafts more than forty centuries old! [**7**] Not only ships but also towns ~~set~~ on the ocean floor. [**8**] One such site is the community of Port Royal, which ~~lays~~ near Jamaica. [**9**] Ironically, although many treasures have been found, the search for treasure has not ~~shrinked~~. [**10**] On the contrary, as technology has improved, the number of underwater expeditions has ~~growed~~.

Exercise 12 Proofreading for Correct Verb Forms

Most of the following sentences contain an incorrect verb form. If the form of a verb is wrong, write the correct form. If a sentence is already correct, write *C.*

EXAMPLE 1. His horse weared a braided bridle.
1. wore

1. Luis Ortega has been describe as history's greatest rawhide braider. — 1. described
2. For years, collectors and cowhands alike have spoke of him with respectful awe. — 2. spoken
3. Ortega was lucky to have had a fine teacher; many braiders do not teach their craft because students have stole their secrets. — 3. stolen
4. However, even after a generous American Indian taught Ortega to braid, it taked young Luis many years of practice to perfect his skill. — 4. took
5. Ortega has never shrinked from hard work. — 5. shrunk
6. Once a vaquero himself, he throwed many a lasso in his younger days. — 6. threw
7. Since the 1930s, Ortega has wore the title of professional braider. — 7. worn
8. Ortega not only mastered the traditional craft, but also striked out on his own by adding color to braiding. — 8. struck
9. Unlike whips, which have stinged many a runaway steer, a riata is a type of lariat used for roping. — 9. stung
10. Pity the cowhand whose heart must have sunk as a steer ran off with his treasured Ortega riata! — 10. C

Exercise 13 Identifying Correct Forms of Pronouns

Choose the correct pronoun in parentheses in each of the following sentences. Then, tell whether the pronoun is used as a *subject,* a *predicate nominative,* a *direct object,* an *indirect object,* an *object of a preposition,* or an *appositive.*

EXAMPLE 1. Mr. Kwan and (*we, us*) members of the recycling club picked up all the litter along the highway last Saturday.
1. we—subject

1. Do you know (*who, whom*) safely disposes of old batteries? — 1. sub.
2. The two Earth Club members who collect items for recycling are James and (*she, her*). — 2. p.n.
3. (*Who, Whom*) threw these cans in the garbage? — 3. sub.
4. Save all recyclable material for (*we, us*) club members. — 4. o.p.

Reference Note

For information on **using pronouns correctly,** see Chapter 7.

Exercise 12

OBJECTIVE

- To correct errors in verb forms

Exercise 13

OBJECTIVE

- To identify correct forms of pronouns and tell how the pronouns are used

DIFFERENTIATING INSTRUCTION

Learners Having Difficulty

You may want to pair students for **Exercise 13.** One student will be responsible for the even-numbered sentences, and the other student will work with the odd-numbered sentences. Tell them to write the sentences in sequence but to answer alternately. Then, they should check each other's work.

COMMON ERRORS

5. app. 5. Give the co-chairpersons, Lisa and (*she, her*), all of the cans that you have collected.

6. d.o. 6. Ask (*whoever, whomever*) you know to save old newspapers for us to collect.

7. p.n. 7. (*Who, Whom*) could the next recycling team leader be?

8. o.p. 8. To (*whom, who*) do we give this cardboard?

9. d.o. 9. The city gave Mr. Kwan, (*who, whom*) everyone in the school respects, an award.

10. i.o. 10. Please give Carl and (*he, him*) the maps you three drew yesterday.

Exercise 14

OBJECTIVE

- To correct inexact pronoun references

Exercise 14 Correcting Inexact Pronoun References

Correct each inexact pronoun reference in the following sentences. If a sentence is already correct, write *C*. Answers will vary.

EXAMPLE 1. When you take medication for your allergies, be sure to read them carefully.

1. *When you take medication for your allergies, be sure to read the directions carefully.*

1. Annie said that she must have sneezed two dozen times today and that it was really bothering her. 1. the pollen
2. Annie asked Heather several good questions about her new allergy medication. 2. Heather's
3. Everyone knows that Heather has more problems with pollen allergies than I have. 3. C
4. Pollen, molds, and animal dander are widespread in our environment; they are three of the most common causes of allergies. 4. C
5. Different plants release pollen at different times of the year, which is why people have discomfort at various times. 5. ; consequently
6. Annie asked Sarah about summer allergies because she is especially uncomfortable during July. 6. Annie
7. To take a pollen count, they place a glass slide coated with oil outside for twenty-four hours. 7. scientists
8. The slide is then placed under a microscope, and the grains of pollen sticking to it are counted. 8. the slide
9. When it rains, the pollen count drops because the rain washes the pollen grains from the air. 9. C
10. In the news reports, they often give the pollen count.

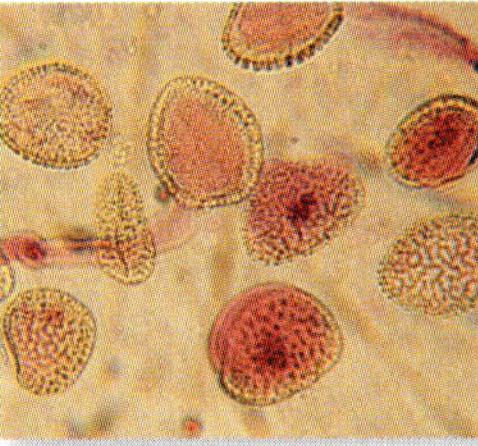

Pollen Grains

COMMON ERRORS

Exercise 15 Proofreading for Clear Pronoun Usage

Most of the following sentences contain inexact pronoun references. Revise each incorrect sentence. If a sentence is already correct, write *C*.

EXAMPLES
1. In India, they belong to laughing clubs.
   1. In India, some people belong to laughing clubs.
2. These clubs are popular with the people of India because of the conflicts they face every day.
   2. C

1. Scientists believe that long ago an island slammed into Asia; it created the Himalayas and joined the island to the continent.
2. That landmass is now India, and worlds still collide there, which is seen in the contradictions and conflicts of modern India.
3. India has been independent for more than fifty years, and it has caused many changes in this growing nation.
4. For instance, the famous city of Bombay has been renamed Mumbai, which honors the Hindu goddess Mumba.
5. However, British influences still exist, and that is apparent in English-language street signs.
6. Free-market policies have now been adopted, and many people have taken advantage of that; small, independent businesses are booming.
7. To the refugees who come to Calcutta from Bangladesh, it offers a little hope.
8. There are as many as thirty-seven laughing clubs in Mumbai (members believe it fights stress).
9. At the same time, beside the wall of an alleyway in Calcutta, a woman prepares food for her daughter while she sits in a nearby tree.
10. A country with ample natural resources and millions of highly educated people, India is taking its place on the world stage.

Reference Note

For information on **using pronouns correctly,** see Chapter 7.

Exercise 15

OBJECTIVE

- To identify and correctly revise sentences with unclear pronoun usage

Exercise 15 Proofreading for Clear Pronoun Usage

POSSIBLE ANSWERS

1. Scientists believe that long ago an island slammed into Asia; the force of the collision created the Himalayas and joined the island to the continent.
2. That landmass is now India, and worlds still collide there, a situation which is seen in the contradictions and conflicts of modern India.
3. India has been independent for more than fifty years, and independence has caused many changes in this growing nation.
4. For instance, the famous city of Bombay has been renamed Mumbai, a name which honors the Hindu goddess Mumba.
5. However, British influences still exist, and this influence is apparent in English-language street signs.
6. Free-market policies have now been adopted, and many people have taken advantage of this change; small, independent businesses are booming.
7. To the refugees who come to Calcutta from Bangladesh, the city offers a little hope.
8. There are as many as thirty-seven laughing clubs in Mumbai (members believe laughing fights stress).
9. At the same time, beside the wall of an alleyway in Calcutta, a woman prepares food for her daughter who sits in a nearby tree.
10. C

Exercise 16

OBJECTIVE

- To provide the appropriate comparative or superlative form of a given word

Exercise 17

OBJECTIVE

- To correct errors in the use of the comparative and superlative forms of modifiers

COMMON ERRORS

Reference Note

For information on **using modifers correctly,** see Chapter 8.

Exercise 16 Using Comparative and Superlative Forms

Complete each sentence with the correct comparative or superlative form of the word given in italics.

EXAMPLE 1. *well* Carl can perform CPR ____ than I can.
1. *better*

1. fewer
2. more
3. worst
4. more
5. better
6. worse
7. best
8. more
9. most
10. best

1. *few* Bicyclists who wear helmets have ____ serious injuries from accidents than bicyclists who do not wear helmets.
2. *many* Our family follows ____ safety procedures than we used to follow in the past.
3. *bad* Some of the ____ accidents are more likely to happen in the home than anywhere else.
4. *much* Is it ____ common to have an accident in the kitchen or in the bathroom?
5. *well* Emergency crews can spot luminous house numbers ____ than numbers that do not glow in the dark.
6. *bad* A grease fire will become ____ if you put water on it.
7. *good* Do you know the ____ way to extinguish an electrical fire?
8. *many* Smoke detectors are found in ____ homes than ever before.
9. *much* In many small fires, smoke causes ____ of the damage.
10. *good* Of course, the ____ safety procedure of all is preventing fires from starting in the first place.

Exercise 17 Proofreading Sentences for Correct Comparative and Superlative Forms

Correct each error in the use of comparative and superlative forms in the following sentences. If no modifiers need to be corrected, write *C.*

EXAMPLE 1. Most oftenest, I plan my day in the morning.
1. *Most often*

1. most important
2. C
3. most common
4. more comfortable
5. more likely

1. One of the ~~importantest~~ skills is the ability to set priorities.
2. You can establish your priorities more easily if you know your goals.
3. Owning a good car, having a rewarding job, and owning a house are three of the ~~most commonest~~ goals people share.
4. You, however, may want a pilot's license, a medical degree, an eighteen-wheeler, or just a ~~comfortabler~~ bed.
5. Whatever your goal, you will be much ~~more likelier~~ to achieve it if you plan your time carefully.

6. Look at even the ~~most small~~ unit of your time.
7. Can you think of ways that you could use your time ~~more better~~ than you do?
8. Try every day to work on your ~~most highest~~ priority.
9. Try ~~more hard~~ to stick to your schedule.
10. With a plan, you can meet your goals ~~quicklier~~ than you could without one.

6. smallest
7. better
8. highest
9. harder
10. more quickly

Exercise 18 Writing Comparative and Superlative Forms

Write the comparative and superlative forms of the following modifiers.

EXAMPLE 1. kind
1. kinder, kindest; less kind, least kind

1. alone	**6.** bad	**11.** natural	**16.** contentedly
2. loudly	**7.** delightful	**12.** wet	**17.** green
3. late	**8.** fiercely	**13.** mysterious	**18.** bravely
4. secretly	**9.** exact	**14.** gleefully	**19.** poor
5. lucky	**10.** childishly	**15.** timid	**20.** cautiously

Exercise 19 Correcting Double Negatives

Revise each of the following sentences to correct the double negative that it contains. Answers may vary.

EXAMPLE 1. The jurors couldn't say nothing about the trial.
1. The jurors could say nothing about the trial.
or
The jurors couldn't say anything about the trial.

1. Those machines don't take ~~no~~ dollar bills.
2. My grandfather ~~doesn't~~ hardly ~~let~~ anything bother him. 2. lets
3. Don't ~~never~~ accept a ride from a stranger! 3. ever
4. Why didn't ~~no one~~ take a message when Mom called? 4. anyone
5. Never use ~~none~~ of those microwave oven pans in a regular oven. 5. any
6. The movie ~~hadn't~~ scarcely started when the power went off.
7. I can't see ~~nothing~~ from here. 7. anything
8. There aren't ~~none~~ of those tamales left now. 8. any
9. Don't let ~~nobody~~ tell you that you can't win! 9. anybody
10. Neither cold nor heat nor ~~nothing~~ else discouraged them. 10. anything

HELP Although two possible answers are shown, you need to give only one answer for each item in Exercise 19.

Reference Note
For information on **double negatives,** see page 237.

Exercise 18

OBJECTIVE

- To write the comparative and superlative forms of modifiers

Exercise 18 Writing Comparative and Superlative Forms

ANSWERS

To indicate decreasing comparison, add *less* or *least* to the base form.

1. more, most alone
2. more, most loudly
3. later, latest
4. more, most secretly
5. luckier, luckiest *or* more, most lucky
6. worse, worst
7. more, most delightful
8. more, most fiercely
9. more, most exact
10. more, most childishly
11. more, most natural
12. wetter, wettest
13. more, most mysterious
14. more, most gleefully
15. more, most timid
16. more, most contentedly
17. greener, greenest
18. more, most bravely
19. poorer, poorest
20. more, most cautiously

Exercise 19

OBJECTIVE

- To revise sentences to correct double negatives

Exercise 20

OBJECTIVE

- To revise sentences to correct misplaced modifiers

Exercise 21

OBJECTIVE

- To revise sentences with dangling modifiers

Exercise 21 Correcting Dangling Modifiers

POSSIBLE ANSWERS

1. The coach and the fans in the stands cheered and applauded as the batter rounded third base.
2. Making a schedule will help you manage your time better.
3. C
4. While we were studying for exams, a storm knocked out the electricity.
5. You must select a specific topic or category before beginning your library research.
6. Right in the middle of making a copy of my report, I saw the out-of-paper message flash.
7. Tired from the long hike, we were glad to see our camp.
8. After we hung the new plants, the room appeared larger.
9. To save money, you need a realistic budget.
10. C

COMMON ERRORS

Exercise 20 Correcting Misplaced Modifiers

Revise the following sentences to correct errors in the use of modifiers. You may need to rearrange or add words to make the meaning clear. Answers may vary.

EXAMPLE 1. Cold and overcast, the tour group left the city.

1. *The tour group left the cold and overcast city.*

1. I watched the hawk swoop down and grab its prey with my new pair of binoculars.
2. He is such a hard-working student that he did every bit of his homework when he even got the flu.
3. Running through town, soft moonlight fell on the freight train.
4. You should accept rides from people only you know.
5. A kingfisher sat alertly on the fence post that had been hunting by the creek.
6. I figured out the answer studying the problem.
7. Bulky and dusty, we moved all of the boxes out of the attic.
8. Filled with wildflowers, Amy put that vase on her desk.
9. Suddenly, the bats swarmed out of the cave that we had awakened.
10. A package sat on the doorstep with Michael's name on it.

Exercise 21 Correcting Dangling Modifiers

Most of the following sentences contain a dangling modifier. If a sentence is incorrect, revise it to correct the dangling modifier. If a sentence is already correct, write *C.*

EXAMPLE 1. Following the path, a tiny cottage came into view.

1. *As we were following the path, a tiny cottage came into view.*

1. Rounding third base, the coach and the fans in the stands cheered and applauded.
2. To manage time better, making a schedule will help.
3. Modified to allow space for an additional bedroom, the floor plan's lack of closets became a problem.
4. While studying for exams, a storm knocked out the electricity.
5. Before beginning your library research, a specific topic or category must be selected.
6. Right in the middle of making a copy of my report, the out-of-paper message flashed.
7. Tired from the long hike, our camp was a welcome sight.

8. After hanging the new plants, the room appeared larger.
9. To save money, a realistic budget is necessary.
10. While we watched the children play, our problems seemed small.

Exercise 22 Correcting Misplaced and Dangling Modifiers

The following sentences contain misplaced and dangling modifiers. Revise each sentence to correct the misplaced or dangling modifier.

EXAMPLE
1. Seeing the rescue helicopter, shouts of joy burst out.
1. Seeing the rescue helicopter, the crew burst out with shouts of joy.

1. Customers lined up for copies of the new film about extraterrestrials in the video store.
2. To save a file, a name must be given to it.
3. The spaceship drifted toward the small moon that had lost its engines.
4. Dozens of white daisies decorated the tables, which had been grown in our own garden.
5. Marked by signs saying "Reserved," we couldn't find anywhere to park.
6. Did George Washington ever meet Robert E. Lee, whose face is on our dollar?
7. Following the trail, camp was quickly found.
8. Having advertised all week, all the tickets had been sold.
9. Patient hawks watched for fish soaring over the lake.
10. Mother packed a picnic lunch humming quietly.

Exercise 23 Correcting Errors in Standard Usage

Identify and correct each error in the use of formal, standard English in the following sentences. Answers may vary.

EXAMPLE
1. I ain't going to the movies on Saturday.
1. ain't—am not

1. Please ~~bring~~ this note to Ms. Nichols in the gym. 1. take
2. Who else was late to the party ~~beside~~ Ronnie and Ed? 2. besides
3. My science project took ~~alot~~ of time last weekend.
4. Oh, no! I can't find my raincoat ~~anywheres~~. 4. anywhere
5. Common elements include oxygen, hydrogen, iron, ~~and~~ etc.
6. The weather can ~~effect~~ people's moods. 6. affect
7. Starting next year, each student will wear ~~an~~ uniform. 7. a

Reference Note

For more on **common usage problems,** see Chapter 9. For information about **formal, standard English,** see page 223.

3. a lot [*or* a great deal]

5. [*or* . . . iron, and others.]

Exercise 22

OBJECTIVE

- **To revise sentences with misplaced and dangling modifiers**

Exercise 22 Correcting Misplaced and Dangling Modifiers

ANSWERS

Answers will vary. Accept reasonable responses.

1. Customers lined up in the video store for copies of the new film about extraterrestrials.
2. To save a file, one must name it.
3. The spaceship that had lost its engines drifted toward the small moon.
4. Dozens of white daisies, which had been grown in our own garden, decorated the tables.
5. Because of the signs saying "Reserved," we couldn't find anywhere to park.
6. Did George Washington, whose face is on our dollar, ever meet Robert E. Lee?
7. Following the trail, we quickly found the camp.
8. Having been advertised all week, all the tickets had been sold.
9. Patient hawks soaring over the lake watched for fish.
10. Humming quietly, Mother packed a picnic lunch.

COMMON ERRORS

Exercise 23

OBJECTIVE

- **To correct errors in the use of standard English**

8. Look out! You almost ~~busted~~ my CD player! 8. broke
9. Gradually, our dog ~~excepted~~ the new kitten. 9. accepted
10. The little steam engine pulled ~~all the faster~~ it could. 10. as fast as

Exercise 24

OBJECTIVE

- To revise sentences containing errors in standard English usage

TECHNOLOGY TIP

Remind students that they can check for proper grammar and usage within their writing by using the grammar-checking function that is common to many popular word-processing programs. Grammar-checking programs will catch a number of mistakes, including double subjects, double negatives, and nonstandard usage such as *anywheres* and *had ought*. Emphasize that such programs are not foolproof, however. Sometimes a grammar-checking feature will do little more than highlight a word or phrase and ask the user "Is this word used correctly?" The user of the program must understand the rules of grammar and usage.

COMMON ERRORS

Exercise 24 Correcting Errors in Standard Usage

Revise the following sentences to correct all errors in the use of formal, standard English. Answers may vary.

EXAMPLE 1. Like you would expect, the use of color is very important to artists.
1. *As you would expect, the use of color is very important to artists.*

1. Artists ~~which~~ study color know that color, value, and contrast form the foundation of a good painting. 1. who [*or* that]
2. Many artists would not even begin ~~no~~ painting ~~without~~ they first planned how they would use these elements. 2. a/unless
3. One of the basics that nearly all artists learn is ~~where~~ color is divided into warm colors and cool colors. 3. that
4. ~~Like~~ you might ~~of~~ guessed, red is a warmer color ~~then~~ blue, while green is cooler than orange. 4. As/have/than
5. The value, or darkness, of a color can indicate that objects differ ~~some~~ in distance from the viewer. 5. somewhat
6. For example, a dark color may be used to indicate that something is a long ~~ways~~ off. 6. way
7. ~~Contrast is~~ when two very different colors are placed ~~besides~~ each other. 7. beside/, they are said to contrast.
8. Contrasting values help to show detail, as does the contrast ~~among~~ this ~~here~~ white page and black type. 8. between
9. For ~~them~~ artists that work only in black and white, contrast and value are major concerns. 9. those [*or* artists who]
10. Many people feel that the ~~affect~~ of a painting can depend more on color ~~then~~ on other elements. 10. effect/than

Grammar and Usage Test: Section 1

DIRECTIONS Either part or all of each of the following sentences is underlined. Using the rules of formal, standard English, choose the answer that correctly expresses the meaning of the underlined word groups. If there is no error, choose A. Indicate your response by shading in the appropriate oval on your answer sheet.

EXAMPLE 1. In 1990, restoration began on the Sphinx, it is an ancient Egyptian statue.

(A) Sphinx, it is an ancient Egyptian statue

(B) Sphinx because it is an ancient Egyptian statue

(C) Sphinx, an ancient Egyptian statue

(D) Sphinx, being an ancient Egyptian statue

(E) Sphinx when it was an ancient Egyptian statue

ANSWER 1.     

1. The magnificent glass pyramids at the Louvre, which were designed by the American architect I. M. Pei.

(A) The magnificent glass pyramids at the Louvre, which were designed by the American architect I. M. Pei.

(B) Being designed by the American architect I. M. Pei, the magnificent glass pyramids at the Louvre.

(C) The American architect I. M. Pei, who designed the magnificent glass pyramids at the Louvre.

(D) The American architect I. M. Pei designed the magnificent glass pyramids at the Louvre.

(E) I. M. Pei, an American architect, designing the magnificent glass pyramids at the Louvre.

2. Have you read about the tornado that damaged so many homes in today's paper?

(A) about the tornado that damaged so many homes in today's paper

(B) in today's paper about the tornado that damaged so many homes

(C) about the tornado in today's paper that damaged so many homes

(D) about the destructive tornado in today's paper

(E) today about the destructive tornado in the paper

TEACHING 

Using the Grammar and Usage Tests. A **Correcting Common Errors Standardized Test Answer Sheet** that students may use for this **Grammar and Usage Test** is provided in the ***Holt Handbook Chapter Tests*** booklet.

Students may benefit from reading "Test Smarts" (pages 505–510 of their textbook) before they take the **Grammar and Usage Tests.**

Grammar and Usage 411

COMMON ERRORS

3. Most people believe that the Loch Ness monster is just a myth, sightings of the monster continue to be reported.
   (A) myth, sightings of the monster continue to be reported
   (B) myth, and people report still seeing the monster
   (C) myth. Sightings of the monster continue to be reported
   (D) myth; sightings of the monster continue to be reported
   (E) myth; however, sightings of the monster continue to be reported

4. Tamara told Jenny that she probably made an A.
   (A) that she probably made an A
   (B) that an A was probably what she made
   (C) that Jenny probably made an A
   (D) about her making an A probably
   (E) that her grade was probably an A

5. To fully appreciate many of Gary Soto's stories, some knowledge of Mexican American culture is necessary.
   (A) some knowledge of Mexican American culture is necessary
   (B) the reader needs some knowledge of Mexican American culture
   (C) you must learn all about Mexican American culture
   (D) knowing something about Mexican American culture
   (E) the necessity is to know about Mexican American culture

6. In this article, it says that the Chinese were using paper money by the thirteenth century.
   (A) In this article, it says that the Chinese were using paper money by the thirteenth century.
   (B) According to this article, it says that the Chinese were using paper money by the thirteenth century.
   (C) By the thirteenth century, the Chinese in this article were using paper money.
   (D) In this article, they say that the Chinese were using paper money by the thirteenth century.
   (E) According to this article, the Chinese were using paper money by the thirteenth century.

7. The capital of Liberia, Monrovia, which was named by freed slaves in honor of President James Monroe.
   (A) The capital of Liberia, Monrovia, which was named by freed slaves in honor of President James Monroe.
   (B) Monrovia, the capital of Liberia, named by freed slaves in honor of President James Monroe.

412 Correcting Common Errors

(C) Named by freed slaves, Monrovia, the capital of Liberia, in honor of President James Monroe.

(D) In honor of President James Monroe, freed slaves named the capital of Liberia Monrovia.

(E) In honor of President James Monroe, freed slaves who named Monrovia the capital of Liberia.

8. I bought a collar for my kitten that has a reflective tag and a breakaway buckle.

(A) for my kitten that has a reflective tag and a breakaway buckle

(B) for my kitten with a reflective tag and a breakaway buckle

(C) that has a reflective tag and a breakaway buckle for my kitten

(D) for my kitten having a reflective tag and a breakaway buckle

(E) for my kitten, and it has a reflective tag and a breakaway buckle

9. Henry Ford wanted to make his cars affordable to everyone; that is why he developed an efficient assembly-line method for manufacturing them.

(A) Henry Ford wanted to make his cars affordable to everyone; that is why he developed an efficient assembly-line method for manufacturing them.

(B) Henry Ford wanted to make his cars affordable to everyone so that he could develop an efficient assembly-line method for manufacturing them.

(C) Henry Ford wanted to make his cars affordable to everyone because he developed an efficient assembly-line method for manufacturing them.

(D) Henry Ford developed an efficient assembly-line method for manufacturing his cars because he wanted to make them affordable to everyone.

(E) To develop an efficient assembly-line method for manufacturing his cars, Henry Ford wanted to make them affordable to everyone.

10. Having seen that people in some countries were denied basic civil rights, my uncle's appreciation for the Bill of Rights grew.

(A) Having seen that people in some countries were denied basic civil rights, my uncle's appreciation for the Bill of Rights grew.

(B) My uncle, having seen the Bill of Rights, knew that people in some countries were denied basic civil rights.

(C) When basic civil rights are denied people in some countries, my uncle's appreciation for the Bill of Rights grows.

(D) My uncle's appreciation for people denied basic civil rights in some countries grew as he read the Bill of Rights.

(E) My uncle's appreciation for the Bill of Rights grew after he had seen that people in some countries were denied basic civil rights.

Grammar and Usage 413

Grammar and Usage Test: Section 2

DIRECTIONS Read the paragraph below. For each numbered blank, select the word or word group that best completes the sentence. Indicate your response by shading in the appropriate oval on your answer sheet.

EXAMPLE More powerful than optical microscopes, electron microscopes __(1)__ researchers to study extremely small objects.

1. (A) has enabled
   (B) is enabling
   (C) enabling
   (D) enable
   (E) enables

ANSWER 1.  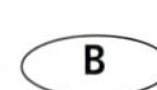   

An electron microscope, using a beam of electrons, __(1)__ a magnified image. Unlike an optical microscope, __(2)__ instrument does not depend on __(3)__ light rays. Instead, an electron lens __(4)__ a system of electromagnetic coils that focus the electron beam. The electrons __(5)__, of course, aren't visible to the naked eye. Rather, __(6)__ are directed at a specimen to form __(7)__ image on a photographic plate. The wavelength of an electron beam is __(8)__ than the wavelength of light. Therefore, __(9)__ magnification is possible with an electron microscope __(10)__ optical microscope.

1. (A) create
   (B) is creating
   (C) creates
   (D) will create
   (E) will have created

2. (A) this here
   (B) this
   (C) these
   (D) these kind of
   (E) that there

3. (A) any
   (B) not one
   (C) no
   (D) hardly any
   (E) barely some

4. (A) use
   (B) has used
   (C) will use
   (D) uses
   (E) had been using

COMMON ERRORS

5. (A) themself
(B) themselves
(C) theirself
(D) theirselves
(E) itself

6. (A) them
(B) it
(C) that
(D) this
(E) they

7. (A) its
(B) their
(C) they're
(D) its'
(E) it's

8. (A) short
(B) shorter
(C) more short
(D) more shorter
(E) shortest

9. (A) good
(B) gooder
(C) better
(D) more better
(E) more good

10. (A) then with an
(B) then with a
(C) than with an
(D) than with a
(E) then a

COMMON ERRORS

Grammar and Usage 415

Exercise 25

OBJECTIVE

- To proofread for correct capitalization

Exercise 26

OBJECTIVE

- To correct the capitalization of words and phrases

COMMON ERRORS

Reference Note

For information on **capital letters,** see Chapter 10.

Exercise 25 Correcting the Capitalization of Words and Phrases

Correct the following words and phrases by either changing lowercase letters to capital letters or changing capital letters to lowercase letters.

EXAMPLE 1. Hank's poem "Waiting for morning in july"

1. Hank's poem "Waiting for Morning in July"

1. geometry I, latin, and civics
2. *national geographic* magazine
3. the god of abraham, isaac, and jacob 3. [*or* God]
4. an Island in the gulf of mexico
5. liberty bell
6. during the great depression
7. readings from "the scarlet ibis"
8. internal revenue service forms
9. mother's day
10. an episode of *party of five*
11. Grandfather Ben and my Cousin
12. Hiroshige's painting *The Moon Beyond The Leaves*
13. an italian custom
14. bill of rights
15. a passage from the koran
16. is that an okidata® printer?
17. dr. and mrs. Dorset
18. a congressional medal of honor recipient
19. chief joseph
20. *King Of The Wind*

Exercise 26 Proofreading for Correct Capitalization

Each of the following sentences contains at least one capitalization error. Correct each error by changing capital letters to lowercase letters or lowercase letters to capital letters.

EXAMPLE 1. In the barn my Dad is building an ultralight plane that we have named the *hummingbird.*

1. dad, Hummingbird

1. The slave knelt at the feet of the statue and said, "Zeus, o, Zeus, Oh please, help me."
2. long ago, Africans shaped tools from stones; we find these stones wherever they lived.

3. My grandma told me that she used to go to Wrigley field with her father and mother.
4. This saturday, instead of going to eagle lake, let's go to the Riverdale High School Festival.
5. A Yale student laid out the plans for a submarine that was used in the American revolution.
6. Fred started sewing kites for himself and his friends and now has a small business known as Fred's fliers.
7. "Have you read *Changes in Latitudes*?" i asked.
8. Because the Panama Canal is too narrow for some supertankers, they sometimes must pass through the waters of the strait of Magellan at the Southern tip of south america.
9. The chess club meets every day after school in the large room East of the auditorium.
10. We think our team, the Kennedy middle school bobcats, is the best in Baker county.

Exercise 27 Proofreading for Correct Capitalization

Each of the following sentences contains errors in capitalization. Correct each error by changing capital letters to lowercase letters or lowercase letters to capital letters.

EXAMPLE 1. Often, i feel like a World traveler in my hometown.
1. I, world

1. When I ride the bus down central avenue, I can hear people speaking spanish, hindi, japanese, arabic, and some other languages I don't even recognize.
2. On independence day, my Mother and I drove our old ford thunderbird to Taylor park.
3. Near there we saw mr. Narazaki and Ms. white eagle talking.
4. They were in front of the Lincoln building, where the federal bureau of investigation has offices.
5. On that same Saturday, we also saw several muslim women wearing long robes and veils in front of hill medical center next to the Park.
6. After the band played John philip Sousa's "the Stars And Stripes Forever," people stood beside a statue of the Greek deity Athena and gave readings from the declaration of independence and the bible.
7. Later, mayor Mendoza read a telegram from the president of the united states, gave a speech, and awarded Medals to several people for their public service.

Exercise 27

OBJECTIVE

- To proofread for correct capitalization

COMMON ERRORS

Exercise 28

OBJECTIVE

- To correct sentences with errors in comma usage

DIFFERENTIATING INSTRUCTION

Learners Having Difficulty

As a review before assigning **Exercise 28,** write the following sentences on the chalkboard without commas and have students read them aloud, first without pausing for commas, then with the appropriate pauses. Ask students to discuss the differences in meaning they perceive.

1. My brother, Rico, thinks about cars all the time.
2. My brother Rico, who thinks about cars all the time, is out in the garage.
3. My, Rico thinks about cars all the time!

Exercise 29

OBJECTIVE

- To correct sentences with errors in comma usage

COMMON ERRORS

Reference Note
For information on **using commas correctly,** see page 271.

8. As soon as the big dipper was clearly visible, the fireworks started, and I thought, "this is definitely the greatest place on Earth!"
9. Next year, I plan to take United States history II at West creek high school.
10. I am going to look in my new history book for a list of all the peoples that make up our country, from the inuits of alaska to the hawaiians of hilo bay.

Exercise 28 Using Commas Correctly

Add and delete commas to punctuate the following sentences correctly.

EXAMPLE 1. A first-aid kit should contain adhesive tape scissors antiseptic and a variety of bandages.

1. A first-aid kit should contain adhesive tape, scissors, antiseptic, and a variety of bandages.

Optional commas are underscored.

1. Yes, I have a screwdriver and some screws and wood glue.
2. On the balcony of a second-floor apartment, a large macaw sat watching us.
3. We moved on October 15; our new address is 5311 East Baker Street, Deerfield, Illinois, 60015.
4. All you need to bring are a change of clothes, shoes, socks, a toothbrush, and toothpaste.
5. Phobos is, I believe, one of the moons around Mars, Mrs. Farris.
6. Fire damaged a number of houses, yet no one was injured, not even any pets.
7. Because acrylic, a type of water-based paint, dries rapidly, you must work quickly with it.
8. Birds sang, frogs jumped, and children played on that hot sunny day.
9. Malfunctioning dangerously, the robot moved jerkily toward the table, picked up a dish, dropped it on the floor, and rolled out the door.
10. Easing up on the throttle, she coasted in for a smooth landing.

Exercise 29 Using Commas Correctly

Add and delete commas to punctuate the following sentences correctly.

EXAMPLE 1. They made beads out of small white seashells Ed.

1. They made beads out of small, white seashells, Ed.

Optional commas are underscored.

1. Deer thrived, sea life flourished, and all manner of edible plants grew in the region, that is now California.

2. Up and down the coastline of California communities of American Indians have lived for centuries.
3. The Karok Pomo Yurok and Modoc are just four of the dozens of peoples living in this area.
4. Skilled in basketwork the Pomo became known for the decoration variety and intricate weaving of their baskets.
5. The Yurok developed an elaborate monetary system which they used in fixing a price on every privilege or offense.
6. While many peoples favored dentalium shells as currency they also exchanged other items in trade.
7. Yurok marriages were arranged with care for marriage was an important public and historic alliance.
8. Yes Helen, the Gabrielino hunted with a stick that is similar to the boomerang the famous Australian weapon.
9. Traditionally, the Coast Miwok peoples were each represented by a male chief, and a female chief and a female ceremonial leader called a *maien.*
10. Kintpuash who was also called Captain Jack was the Modoc leader, who escaped capture on November 29 1872.

Exercise 30 Proofreading for Correct Use of Semicolons and Colons

Add or delete semicolons and colons to correct the punctuation in the following sentences.

EXAMPLE 1. The party starts at 7 30, we will need to leave our house by 7 00.

1. *The party starts at 7:30; we will need to leave our house by 7:00.*

1. John is bringing the drinks, ice, and cups and Wanda is bringing the plates, knives, and forks.
2. Compare these three translations of King David's famous song, Psalm 23 1–6.
3. Don't forget to pick up; Carlos, Kam, Lisa, and Mary at 7 15 sharp.
4. Twin koalas are rare in captivity consequently, Australia's Yanchep National Park prized Euca and Lyptus, the two born there in 1996.
5. The dance committee still needs to get the following equipment a CD player, outdoor speakers, and a microphone.
6. During our party on the Fourth of July last year, a huge storm forced everyone inside then lightning knocked the power out.

HELP
In Exercise 30, you may need to use colons and semicolons to replace incorrectly used commas.

Reference Note

For information on **semicolons and colons,** see Chapter 12.

Exercise 30

OBJECTIVE

- To correct sentences with errors in the use of semicolons and colons

Exercise 31

OBJECTIVE

- To correctly revise sentences containing errors in punctuation

7. California's seagulls will eat just about anything: clams, chicks, berries, and even the occasional starfish.
8. We have invited exchange students from Dublin, Ireland; Paris, France; and Tokyo, Japan.
9. At 10:30 P.M., he neatly printed the title page, which read "Alfredo in Wonderland: A Tale of an Exchange Student in New York."
10. Bamboo is a versatile and flexible building material; in Indonesia, as in many countries, it has a wide variety of uses.

Exercise 31 Using Punctuation Correctly in Sentences

Add periods, question marks, commas, semicolons, and colons to correct the punctuation in the following sentences.

EXAMPLE 1. In almost every corner of the world dogs do useful work for people

1. *In almost every corner of the world, dogs do useful work for people.*

Optional commas are underscored.

1. Herding flocks, collies and briards and other varieties of sheepdog are on the job wherever there are sheep.
2. Did you know that German shepherds, which make good guard dogs, can also herd sheep?
3. Dogs guard our homes, assist people with disabilities, herd sheep, and hunt game.
4. Sled dogs include the following breeds: Samoyeds, huskies, Alaskan malamutes, and a few other strong breeds with thick fur.
5. Partners with police the world over, bloodhounds are feared by criminals and praised by the parents of lost children whom these dogs have found.
6. The basenji comes from Africa and is, in fact, called the Congo dog; many people share their homes with these animals, whose ancestors date back to 3000 B.C.
7. Although Mexican Chihuahuas are tiny, they fiercely take on any foe; they don't back down even when facing a larger dog.
8. Brave little Chihuahuas ignore the good advice given in Ecclesiastes 9:4.
9. Those famous lines make an obvious point: "A living dog is better than a dead lion."
10. My favorite neighbor, Edward Nichols, Jr., bought his Pekingese on Wednesday, January 6, 1999.

Exercise 32 Correcting Errors in the Use of Quotation Marks and Other Punctuation

For each of the following sentences, correct any error in the use of quotation marks, commas, and end marks.

EXAMPLE 1. The troop leader said that we should bring the 'barest essentials': a change of clothes, a toothbrush, and a comb.

1. The troop leader said that we should bring the "barest essentials": a change of clothes, a toothbrush, and a comb.

1. James seemed excited and said, "Did you see the news last night?"
2. "Sorry, Emma," Becky began, "but I'm late already."
3. When Coach Myers announced the tryouts this morning, she said, "that anyone could try out."
4. Ms. Waters asked us to read "The Tell-Tale Heart" and one other short story of our choice this weekend.
5. They are watching reruns of *The Magic School Bus;* this episode is "Lost in the Solar System."
6. For tomorrow's assignment, read "The Price of Freedom," the next chapter in your textbook.
7. My favorite part of *Reader's Digest* is "Humor in Uniform."
8. "Why don't you title your poem "Words and Music"?" Tom asked.
9. The recent article "Carbon Monoxide: The Silent Killer" details the effects of this deadly gas.
10. "Didn't you hear me yell Call 911! asked Erik. 10. 'Call 911!'?"

Exercise 33 Punctuating and Capitalizing Quotations

For each of the following sentences, correct any error in the use of quotation marks, commas, end marks, and capitalization.

EXAMPLE 1. Larry told me that "you were sitting in the library."

1. Larry told me that you were sitting in the library.

1. "I can't decide which selection to use for my project" sighed Fran.
2. Mary nodded and said "I haven't made up my mind either." "Are you going to choose a poem or a story"?
3. "I'm going to make a diorama of "Stopping by Woods on a Snowy Evening," interrupted Greg.
4. What if Ms. Hill says 'that you can't'? asked Mary.
5. Didn't she say "anything goes?" Greg answered.
6. "You're right." The instructions say 'write a song, present a play, or draw a picture, added Mary.

Reference Note

For information on **using quotation marks,** see page 314.

Exercise 32

OBJECTIVE

- To correct sentences with errors in the use of quotation marks and other punctuation

Exercise 33

OBJECTIVE

- To correct sentences with errors in the use of quotation marks, commas, end marks, and capitalization

Exercise 33 Punctuating and Capitalizing Quotations

ANSWERS

1. "I can't decide which selection to use for my project," sighed Fran.
2. Mary nodded and said, "I haven't made up my mind either. Are you going to choose a poem or a story?"
3. "I'm going to make a diorama of 'Stopping by Woods on a Snowy Evening,'" interrupted Greg.
4. "What if Ms. Hill says that you can't?" asked Mary.
5. "Didn't she say, 'Anything goes'?" Greg answered.
6. "You're right. The instructions say, 'Write a song, present a play, or draw a picture,'" added Mary.

Exercise 33 **Punctuating and Capitalizing Quotations**

ANSWERS continued

7. "You play the guitar," Fran pointed out. "Maybe you could write a song."
8. Mary smiled and said, "Great idea!"
9. "What I'd really like to do is write extra verses for Woody Guthrie's song 'This Land Is Your Land,'" Fran said.
10. "Perhaps even," Mary added, "make a video of it!"

Exercise 34

OBJECTIVE

- To correct sentences and groups of words with errors in the use of apostrophes

Exercise 35

OBJECTIVE

- To correct sentences with errors in spelling

COMMON ERRORS

7. You play the guitar, Fran pointed out. Maybe you could write a song."
8. Mary smiled and said, "great idea!
9. What I'd really like to do is write extra verses for Woody Guthrie's song This Land Is Your Land, Fran said.
10. Perhaps even," Mary added "make a video of it"!

Reference Note

For more information on **using apostrophes,** see Chapter 14.

Exercise 34 Using Apostrophes Correctly

Add or delete apostrophes to punctuate the following items correctly. If an item is already correct, write *C.*

EXAMPLE 1. Weve got Matts tickets'.
1. We've got Matt's tickets.

1. Dont use so many *so*s.
2. Its time for Janes report.
3. Ronnies and Eriks desks
4. Mom and Dads only car
5. PBSs most popular show
6. Who's your brother? 6. C
7. my sister's-in-laws cars
8. geeses caretaker
9. that baby birds' beak
10. Kerrys and your project
11. anyone's guess 11. C
12. Russs' *U*s look like *N*s.
13. Youre right!
14. those foxes dens
15. The blame is theirs'.
16. Lets eat at six oclock.
17. my March of Dimes donation 17. C
18. She says that shell bring ours'.
19. There's still time. 19. C
20. Bobs dog

Reference Note

For information on **spelling rules,** see Chapter 16.

1. daily/surely

Exercise 35 Proofreading for Spelling Errors

Correct each spelling error in the following sentences.

EXAMPLE 1. To succede, you must keep triing.
1. succeed; trying

1. I cannot easily make dayly visits, even though I would surly like to.

2. The judge ~~finaly~~ ~~conceeded~~ that the other driver had been ~~exceding~~ the speed limit.
3. The members of the procession ~~carryed~~ ~~one hundred twenty-five~~ baskets of beautiful flowers.
4. The desert heat and dryness ~~stoped~~ both ~~armys~~.
5. My neighbor's ~~childs~~ are always getting into ~~mischeif~~.
6. A word with two ~~es~~, such as *deer,* has a long vowel sound.
7. The children ~~truely~~ ~~enjoied~~ hearing ~~thier~~ echoes bounce off the canyon walls.
8. The candidate ~~siezed~~ the opportunity to give a ~~breif~~ statement of his ~~beleifs~~.
9. ~~Leafs~~ fluttered off the trees and down the ~~desertted~~ ~~beachs~~ during that ~~1st~~ day of winter.
10. ~~5~~ years ago, each of my ~~brother-in-laws~~ was working two jobs.

2. finally/conceded/exceeding
3. carried/125
4. stopped/armies
5. children/mischief
6. e's
7. truly/enjoyed/their
8. seized/brief/beliefs
9. Leaves/deserted/beaches/first
10. Five/brothers-in-law

Exercise 36 Proofreading for Spelling Errors

For each of the following sentences, write the misspelled word or words correctly.

EXAMPLE 1. Six concrete elfs guarded the doorway to my nieghbor's house.

1. elves, neighbor's

1. Leisure activities may be ~~wholely~~ ~~unecessary~~ for survival, but they make life enjoyable.
2. On the way to Japan, his ~~neice~~ met a Chinese man who spoke perfect English.
3. After the clouds ~~receeded~~, the sun glinted on the wet ~~rooves~~.
4. Three ranch hands were teaching ~~ropeing~~ to the tourists who had ~~payed~~ for lessons.
5. These attachments are interchangeable, I ~~beleive~~.
6. While my ~~freinds~~ and I were ~~siting~~ on the porch, we saw a white rabbit ~~hoping~~ across the street.
7. Place two heaping ~~spoonsful~~ of flour in a saucepan; then, slice three small ~~tomatos~~.
8. Yes, several ~~attorney-at-laws~~ at our offices are ~~alumnuses~~ of the state university.
9. There must have been over ~~one hundred and fifty~~ people standing in line longer than that.
10. Mr. Brady said that suddenly the ~~terrifing~~ possibility of going to school all year had not seemed so bad to the ~~Bradies~~.

Reference Note

For information on **spelling rules,** see Chapter 16.

1. wholly/unnecessary
2. niece
3. receded/roofs
4. roping/paid
5. believe
6. friends/sitting/hopping
7. spoonfuls/tomatoes
8. attorneys-at-law/alumni
9. 150
10. terrifying/Bradys

Exercise 36

OBJECTIVE

- To correct sentences with errors in spelling

COMMON ERRORS

COMMON ERRORS

Exercise 37

OBJECTIVE

- To correct sentences with errors in the use of words often confused

Exercise 38

OBJECTIVE

- To correct sentences with errors in the use of words often confused

Reference Note

For information on **words often confused,** see page 374.

1. plane's/quiet
2. It's/your
3. dessert/it's
4. their/passed
5. led/their
6. break/pieces
7. chose/through
8. loose/to
9. hear/weak
10. Whose/choose

Exercise 37 Proofreading for Words Often Confused

For each of the following sentences, correct any error in word usage.

EXAMPLE 1. A camel caravan in the dessert is a noble sight.
1. *A camel caravan in the desert is a noble sight.*

1. The roar of the plain's engine broke the quite of the night.
2. Its time to get you're suitcase packed.
3. I put my desert right here on the kitchen table, and now its gone.
4. As the mustangs picked they're way through the canyon, they unknowingly past a cougar hiding in the rocks.
5. Who was the warrior who lead the Zulus in there famous battle against the Boers?
6. Be careful, or you will brake that mirror into a million peaces.
7. Every knight choose his own way threw the forest.
8. First, the pigs got lose; then we spent all day trying too catch them.
9. He couldn't here us; he was too week from the fever.
10. Who's biography did you chose to read?

Exercise 38 Distinguishing Between Words Often Confused

Choose the correct word in parentheses in each of the following sentences.

EXAMPLE 1. Is Korean food for dinner (*all right, alright*) with you?
1. *all right*

1. I believe that Andrew Young began his political career during the 1960s; (*than, then*) he became a U.S. representative before being named ambassador to the United Nations.
2. Millie, would you care to explain the first (*principle, principal*) of thermodynamics to the class?
3. A (*stationery, stationary*) cold front has been responsible for this week's wonderful weather.
4. Recycling helps cut down on the (*waist, waste*) of resources.
5. Did you (*all ready, already*) qualify for the race?
6. How would you (*council, consul, counsel*) someone in this situation?
7. What (*effects, affects*) will the Internet have on your future career?
8. There's nothing (*plain, plane*) about these stylized medieval reliefs.
9. I think that when it came to scat singing, Sarah Vaughan really was (*all together, altogether*) the best.
10. Designing a golf (*coarse, course*) must be a challenging task.

Exercise 39 Proofreading a Business Letter

For each numbered item in the following business letter, correct any errors in mechanics. An item may contain more than one error. If an item is already correct, write *C*.

EXAMPLE **[1]** 813 E Maple St

1. 813 E. Maple St.

813 East Maple Street

[1] Belleville, IL, 62223

[2] February 12th, 2001

[3] Customer Service

Super Sport Shoes

14 Magenta Road

Woodinville, WA, 98072

[4] Dear Sir or Madam:

[5] Thank you for your prompt response to my order (number 51238) for two pairs of white jogging shoes. 5. C **[6]** These shoe's are the most comfortable ones I have ever worn.

[7] However, one of the pairs that I recieved is the wrong size. 7. received **[8]** This pair is to small; consequently, I am returning these shoes with this letter. 8. too **[9]** Please exchange them for one pair of white joggers two sizes larger. 9. C

[10] Your's truly,

Neville Walters

Neville Walters

Exercise 39

OBJECTIVE

- To proofread a business letter to correct errors in mechanics

COMMON ERRORS

TEACHING 

Using the Mechanics Tests. A **Correcting Common Errors Standardized Test Answer Sheet** that students may use for this **Mechanics Test** is provided in the ***Holt Handbook Chapter Tests*** booklet.

Students may benefit from reading "Test Smarts" (pages 505–510 of their textbook) before they take the **Mechanics Tests.**

COMMON ERRORS

Mechanics Test: Section 1

DIRECTIONS Each of the following sentences contains an underlined word or word group. Choose the answer that shows the correct capitalization, punctuation, and spelling of the underlined part. If there is no error, choose answer E (Correct as is). Indicate your response by shading in the appropriate oval on your answer sheet.

EXAMPLE 1. Marla asked, "did you see the meteor shower last night?"

(A) asked, "Did
(B) asked "Did
(C) asked "did
(D) asked did you
(E) Correct as is

ANSWER 1.  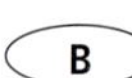 C  

1. We keep a variety of emergency equipment in the trunk of our car, a first-aid kit, jumper cables, a blanket, a flashlight, and road flares.

(A) car a first-aid
(B) car: a first-aid
(C) car; a first-aid
(D) car: a 1st-aid
(E) Correct as is

2. Alvin Ailey, who's choreography thrilled audiences for years, formed the dance company that still bears his name.

(A) Ailey who's choreography
(B) Ailey whose choreography
(C) Ailey who's choreography,
(D) Ailey, whose choreography
(E) Correct as is

3. Jerome said, "I cant believe that Ben Franklin wanted the turkey to be the symbol for the United States!"

(A) said, "I can't believe
(B) said "I can't believe
(C) said, "I can't beleive
(D) said, 'I can't believe
(E) Correct as is

4. "Do you," asked Kay 'Know the story of Icarus?"

(A) you, asked Kay, "know
(B) you?" asked Kay. "Know
(C) you," asked Kay, "know
(D) you," asked Kay, 'know
(E) Correct as is

5. I often struggle to open my gym locker; its lock is probably rusty.

(A) locker, its
(B) locker; Its
(C) locker. It's
(D) locker: It's
(E) Correct as is

6. Please bring too tomatos, a head of lettuce, and some feta cheese from the market.

(A) bring: two tomatoes,
(B) bring 2 tomatoes
(C) bring two tomatoes,
(D) bring to tomatoes,
(E) Correct as is

7. "Did Principal Reeves really say, 'We need *less* discipline?" asked Cassandra.

(A) discipline,'"
(B) discipline'?"
(C) discipline?'
(D) discipline'"?
(E) Correct as is

8. Grandfather enjoyed the childrens storys about their visit to the wildlife sanctuary.

(A) childrens story's
(B) childrens' stories
(C) childrens stories
(D) children's stories
(E) Correct as is

9. The Leonards visited: Rome, Italy, Athens, Greece; and Istanbul, Turkey, on their vacation.

(A) visited Rome, Italy;
(B) visited: Rome, Italy;
(C) visited, Rome, Italy;
(D) visited Rome; Italy;
(E) Correct as is

10. Did aunt Susan, bring the coleslaw?

(A) aunt Susan
(B) aunt, Susan,
(C) Aunt Susan
(D) Aunt, Susan,
(E) Correct as is

COMMON ERRORS

Mechanics 427

Mechanics Test: Section 2

DIRECTIONS Each numbered item below contains an underlined group of words. Choose the answer that shows the correct capitalization, punctuation, and spelling of the underlined part. If there is no error, choose answer E (Correct as is). Indicate your response by shading in the appropriate oval on your answer sheet.

EXAMPLE **[1]** 200 north Vine Street

(A) 200 North Vine street
(B) 200 North Vine Street
(C) Two-Hundred North Vine Street
(D) 200, North Vine Street
(E) Correct as is

ANSWER **1.**     

200 North Vine Street
Austin, TX 78741

[1] May, 5 2001

Athena Wilson
Worldwide Travel, Inc.
4135-A Anderson Avenue
[2] San Antonio, Tex. 78249

[3] Dear Ms. Wilson:

[4] Thank you for you're prompt response to my request for information about traveling to Australia. The color brochures describing the **[5]** different, Australian tours were especially helpful. My family and I are interested in the "Natural Wonders" **[6]** package, that includes day trips to **[7]** the great Barrier reef. **[8]** Well also want to schedule a three-day stay in Sydney. How much will the entire package **[9]** cost, for three adults and one child?

[10] Yours truly

Naomi Baskin

Naomi Baskin

1. (A) May 5 2001
(B) May Fifth 2001
(C) May 5th 2001
(D) May 5, 2001
(E) Correct as is

2. (A) San Antonio, Tex 78249
(B) San Antonio Texas 78249
(C) San Antonio, TX 78249
(D) San Antonio TX 78249
(E) Correct as is

3. (A) Dear Ms. Wilson,
(B) Dear ms. Wilson:
(C) Dear Ms Wilson,
(D) Dear Ms. Wilson;
(E) Correct as is

4. (A) Thank you for youre
(B) Thank you for youre'
(C) Thank you for your
(D) Thank you for your'
(E) Correct as is

5. (A) different australian
(B) different Australian
(C) different, Australian,
(D) different, australian,
(E) Correct as is

6. (A) package that includes
(B) package that, includes
(C) package: that includes
(D) package that includes:
(E) Correct as is

7. (A) the Great Barrier Reef
(B) the great Barrier Reef
(C) the Great Barrier reef
(D) The great Barrier reef
(E) Correct as is

8. (A) Well, also
(B) We'll, also,
(C) We'll also
(D) We'll, also
(E) Correct as is

9. (A) cost for 3
(B) cost? For three
(C) cost: for three
(D) cost for three
(E) Correct as is

10. (A) Yours' truly,
(B) Yours truly:
(C) Your's truly,
(D) Yours truly,
(E) Correct as is

COMMON ERRORS

RESOURCES

Correcting Common Errors

Review

- *Language & Sentence Skills Practice*, pp. 404–406

Assessment

- *Holt Handbook Chapter Tests with Answer Key*, pp. 33–34, 53

PART 2 Sentences

go.hrw.com
GO TO: go.hrw.com

CHAPTER

18

INTRODUCING THE CHAPTER

- Complete sentences are the foundation of good writing. In this chapter, students will learn to evaluate sentences for completeness. They will identify and revise sentence fragments, phrase fragments, subordinate clause fragments, and run-on sentences. Use this chapter to teach the concept of complete sentences and also as a reference that students may consult throughout the year as they complete their writing assignments.

CHAPTER

Writing Complete Sentences

Diagnostic Preview

A. Identifying Sentences and Sentence Fragments

Identify each of the following word groups as a *sentence* or a *sentence fragment.*

EXAMPLE 1. Falling into a deep, dreamless sleep.
1. *sentence fragment*

Terms in brackets refer to concepts tested by the items in the Diagnostic Preview.

1. frag. [frag.]
2. frag. [frag.]
3. sent. [sent.]
4. frag. [frag.]
5. sent. [sent.]
6. frag. [frag.]
7. sent. [sent.]
8. frag. [frag.]
9. sent. [sent.]
10. frag. [frag.]

1. To begin on page 10 and read the rest of the chapter.
2. Because we did not have any other homework over the weekend.
3. Learning to speak a second language is one of my goals.
4. If you will be allowed to leave class early next Tuesday afternoon.
5. Irritable from lack of sleep, the child began to whine.
6. Lettuce, a cucumber, a bell pepper, and some shredded carrots.
7. The full moon, rising above the trees, illuminated the snowy fields.
8. These muffins, which are made with whole-wheat flour and buttermilk.
9. As we entered the cave, our guide pointed to some interesting formations.
10. Max, who is one of my cousins from Michigan.

B. Revising Sentence Fragments

Rewrite each of the following sentence fragments to create a complete sentence.

CHAPTER RESOURCES

Internet

- Web resources: go.hrw.com

Practice & Review

- *Language & Sentence Skills Practice,* pp. 411–424
- *Language & Sentence Skills Practice Answer Key,* pp. 167–171

EXAMPLE **1.** Underneath one of the cushions on the couch.

1. I found ten pennies underneath one of the cushions on the couch.

Answers will vary; here are sample revisions.

11. Encouraging her to become a doctor.

12. Excited about the approaching vacation.

13. The fishing boats that were tied up at the dock.

14. After he finished folding the clothes.

15. One of the most thoughtful essays I have ever read.

11.–15. [sentence fragments]

11. The teacher was

12. , the children could hardly sit still on the last day of school

13. rocked gently as the tide came in

14. He started his homework

15. Marian's essay was

C. Identifying and Revising Run-on Sentences

Identify each of the following word groups as a *sentence* or a *run-on sentence.* Then, revise each run-on sentence to make it one or more complete sentences. Here are possible revisions.

EXAMPLE **1.** Don't leave your lunch on that table, did I tell you what happened to me at the park last week?

1. run-on sentence Don't leave your lunch on that table. Did I tell you what happened to me at the park last week?

16. The morning was warm and sunny, I agreed to take my younger sister and her friends to the park.

17. While I packed lunch, Sarah, Ellen, and Annie put on their bike helmets and checked the air pressure in their tires.

18. The park is only a mile from our house, the ride was easy and pleasant.

19. When we reached the park, we locked our bikes and walked over to the playground, we put our helmets and lunch on a nearby picnic table.

20. The girls climbed on the playscape while I sat under a tree and read.

21. After an hour, Sarah announced that she was hungry, and we all agreed to stop and eat lunch.

22. As we approached the picnic table, we heard squealing and chattering, a family of squirrels had started lunch without us.

23. A big squirrel was perched on one of the bike helmets, in its paws was a piece of one of our sandwiches.

24. One squirrel was eating an apple, and another was tearing at a paper bag, searching for more good things to eat.

25. The squirrels ran away when we appeared, of course, we had to go back home to eat lunch.

16. run-on/and [run-on]

17. sent. [sent.]

18. run-on [run-on]

19. run-on [run-on]

20. sent. [sent.]

21. sent. [sent.]

22. run-on [run-on]

23. run-on [run-on]

24. sent. [sent.]

25. run-on/and [run-on]

SENTENCES

ASSESSING

Entry-Level Assessment

Diagnostic Preview. You may want to use the **Diagnostic Preview** to identify areas in which students need instruction and practice in writing complete sentences. You could use the results of the preview to decide which lessons to teach to the entire class and which ones to assign to small groups.

Differentiating Instruction

- *Developmental Language & Sentence Skills,* pp. 159–162
- *Developmental Language & Sentence Skills Guided Practice Teacher's Notes and Answer Key,* p. 40

Assessment

- *Holt Handbook Chapter Tests with Answer Key,* pp. 35–38, 52

SENTENCES

PRETEACHING

Lesson Starter

Motivating. Write the following quote on a chalkboard.

"When people will not weed their own minds, they are set to be overrun with nettles."

(Horace Walpole, 1717–1797, Fourth Earl of Orford, British writer and author of an early Gothic novel)

Motivating. After you write the quotation on the chalkboard, explain to students that nettles are weeds with prickly leaves that irritate the skin. Ask students to respond to Walpole's idea. In what ways is writing like tending a garden? [*Plants need water, sunlight, and nutrients in the soil to grow; sentences that lack essential parts cannot communicate. Sentences, like gardens, must also be pruned and weeded so that the ideas are clear.*] Present the idea that sentence fragments, like stunted plants, are incompletely "nourished," and run-on sentences contain unwanted material that must be trimmed. Tell students that in this chapter they will learn to identify and revise sentence fragments and run-on sentences.

Sentence Fragments

OBJECTIVES

(pp. 434–441)

- **To identify and revise sentence, phrase, and subordinate clause fragments**
- **To use subordinate clauses in complete sentences**

Sentence Fragments

A ***sentence*** is a word group that has a subject and a verb and that expresses a complete thought. A ***sentence fragment*** is a word group that is missing a subject or a verb or that does not express a complete thought.

Sentence fragments usually occur when you write in a hurry or become a little careless. You may leave out a word, or you may chop off part of a sentence by putting in a period too soon.

To find out whether you have a complete sentence or a sentence fragment, you can use a simple three-part test:

1. Does the group of words have a subject?
2. Does it have a verb?
3. Does it express a complete thought?

If you answer *no* to any of these questions, your word group is a fragment. It is missing at least one basic part.

FRAGMENT Was the best sharpshooter in the United States. [The subject is missing. Who was the best sharpshooter in the United States?]

SENTENCE Annie Oakley was the best sharpshooter in the United States.

FRAGMENT Annie Oakley with Buffalo Bill Cody's Wild West show. [The verb is missing. What did she do with the Wild West show?]

SENTENCE Annie Oakley performed with Buffalo Bill Cody's Wild West show.

FRAGMENT As it fell through the air ninety feet away. [This group of words has a subject (*it*) and a verb (*fell*), but it does not express a complete thought. What happened as something fell through the air?]

SENTENCE Annie could shoot a playing card as it fell through the air ninety feet away.

Annie Oakley

RESOURCES

Sentence Fragments

Practice

- *Language & Sentence Skills Practice,* pp. 411–418

Differentiating Instruction

- *Developmental Language & Sentence Skills,* pp. 159–160

NOTE By itself, a fragment does not express a complete thought. However, fragments can make sense if they are clearly related to the sentences that come before or after them. These sentences give the fragments meaning by helping the reader fill in the missing parts.

The following passage is from an essay that describes the death and the cutting down of a great white oak on the writer's family homestead. The author's grandfather has carefully cut at the dead tree and is about to aim the final blows. See how the author uses fragments to describe the fall of the great tree.

> Then came the great moment. A few last, quick strokes. A slow, deliberate swaying. The crack of parting fibers. Then a long "swoo-sh!" that rose in pitch as the towering trunk arced downward at increasing speed.
>
> Edwin Way Teale, "The Death of a Tree"

Experienced writers like Teale sometimes use sentence fragments to achieve a certain effect. As a developing writer, however, you need to practice and master writing complete sentences before you begin to experiment with writing fragments.

Oral Practice Identifying Sentence Fragments

Some of the following items are sentence fragments. Read each item aloud. Then, tell whether the item is a complete sentence, is missing a subject, is missing a verb, or does not express a complete thought.

EXAMPLE 1. After he wrote "A Christmas Memory."

1. Not a complete thought

1. Truman Capote was an American author. 1. C
2. Was born in New Orleans in 1924. 2. S
3. Grew up in Alabama. 3. S
4. Because he hated attending boarding schools. 4. N
5. A movie version of *Breakfast at Tiffany's,* probably his most famous novel. 5. V
6. When he moved to New York City. 6. N
7. Capote's short story "A Christmas Memory" was made into a television movie. 7. C
8. His characters lively and eccentric. 8. V

Direct Teaching

Modeling and Demonstration

Sentence Fragments. Model how to determine whether a group of words is a sentence or a sentence fragment by using the example *Sat on a bench in the park.* First, ask students whether the group of words has a subject. [*no*] Then, ask whether the group of words has a verb. [*yes;* Sat] Point out that the sentence doesn't tell us who sat on a bench, and ask what subject could make the group of words a sentence. [*Answers will vary.*] Finally, ask whether the word group expresses a complete thought, now that a subject has been added. [*yes*] Now, have a volunteer use another example from this chapter to demonstrate how to identify and correct a sentence fragment.

Differentiating Instruction

English-Language Learners

General Strategies. To help students understand the parts of a complete sentence, provide them with a chart like the one below. Let students work in pairs to match subjects, verbs, complements, and modifiers to express complete ideas.

Possible Subjects	People The boys I
Possible Verbs or Verb Phrases	worked play will go
Possible Complements and Modifiers	in the sun baseball to school

Application

Sentence Fragments

Activity. Bring to class or have students find and bring in examples of recent print advertisements. Ask each student to work with a randomly assigned partner to circle sentence fragments or phrase fragments used in the advertisements to capture readers' attention. Direct students to identify the types of fragments or phrases and to rewrite them as complete sentences. Assign one student to act as recorder and the other to present and explain the pair's work to the class. Discuss how the use of complete sentences changes the advertisement.

9. Is one of his most moving stories. 9. S
10. Spent six years researching the nonfiction book titled *In Cold Blood.* 10. S

TIPS & TRICKS

To find phrase fragments in your writing, read the sentences in your paragraphs from the last to the first. Reading this way helps you to listen for complete thoughts that make sense.

Phrase Fragments

A ***phrase*** is a group of words that does not have a subject and a verb and that is used as a single part of speech. Three kinds of phrases that can easily be mistaken for complete sentences are *verbal phrases, appositive phrases,* and *prepositional phrases.*

Verbal Phrases

Verbals, forms of verbs that are used as other parts of speech, sometimes fool us into thinking that a group of words has a verb when it really does not. Some verbals end in *–ing, –d,* or *–ed* and are used the same way adjectives are. Other verbals have the word *to* in front of the base form (*to go, to play*).

A ***verbal phrase*** is a phrase containing a verbal and its modifiers and complements. By itself, a verbal phrase is a fragment because it does not express a complete thought.

Reference Note

For more on **verbals** (participles, gerunds, and infinitives), see page 77.

FRAGMENT Learning about the Civil War.
SENTENCE I enjoy learning about the Civil War.

FRAGMENT Gaining glory for itself and for all black soldiers.
SENTENCE Gaining glory for itself and for all black soldiers, the 54th Massachusetts Regiment led the attack on Fort Wagner.

FRAGMENT Inspired by the 54th Massachusetts Regiment.
SENTENCE Inspired by the 54th Massachusetts Regiment, other black soldiers fought bravely.

FRAGMENT To become good soldiers.
SENTENCE Black volunteers trained hard to become good soldiers.

Appositive Phrases

An ***appositive*** is a word that identifies or explains the noun or pronoun it follows. An ***appositive phrase,*** a phrase made up of an appositive and its modifiers, is a fragment. It does not contain the basic parts of a sentence.

Learning for Life

Using Fragments. While this chapter will make clear that sentence fragments should not be used in formal writing assignments, students should be aware of fragments in everyday use of language. Ask your class to brainstorm possible situations in which sentence fragments are regularly used to communicate messages. Students may suggest the following situations:

- conversation
- making lists

FRAGMENT	A twenty-five-year-old soldier.
SENTENCE	The 54th Massachusetts Regiment was commanded by Colonel Shaw, a twenty-five-year-old soldier.

Prepositional Phrases

A ***prepositional phrase*** is a group of words containing a preposition and a noun or pronoun object. A prepositional phrase cannot stand alone as a sentence because it does not express a complete thought.

FRAGMENT	With great courage on the battlefield.
SENTENCE	The 54th Massachusetts Regiment acted with great courage on the battlefield.

The 54th Massachusetts Regiment

Exercise 1 Revising Phrase Fragments

Use your imagination to create sentences from the following phrases. You can either (1) attach the fragment to a complete sentence, or (2) develop the phrase into a complete sentence by adding a subject, a verb, or both.

EXAMPLE
1. landing on the planet
1. *Landing on the planet, the astronauts immediately began to explore.*

or

The astronauts were landing on the planet.

1. in a huge spaceship
2. setting foot on the planet
3. to explore the craters
4. walking around in a spacesuit
5. finding no sign of life
6. the astronauts' spaceship
7. checking the spaceship for damage
8. the planet's moon
9. to return to Earth
10. on a successful mission

MEETING THE CHALLENGE

You may have already noticed that many advertisements use fragments rather than complete sentences. Search through a popular magazine, and clip out an ad that uses fragments. Then, revise the ad so that it contains only complete sentences. How does the ad change when you revise the fragments? Do you think the new ad would appeal to the same audience that the original ad did? Write a brief paragraph in which you explain your conclusions.

ANSWERS
Revisions and paragraphs will vary.

SENTENCES

DIRECT TEACHING

Correcting Misconceptions

Prepositional Phrases. Students may think that every phrase beginning with the word *to* is a prepositional phrase. Explain to students that the word *to* may begin an infinitive or infinitive phrase. Provide the following examples:

Prepositional phrase: I walked *to the store.* (*to* + noun)

Infinitive/Verbal phrase: The plane prepared *to land.* (*to* + verb)

Exercise 1 Revising Phrase Fragments

ANSWERS
Here are some possible revisions.

1. The astronauts landed in a huge spaceship.
2. They were setting foot on the planet for the first time.
3. To explore the craters, the astronauts had to wear spacesuits.
4. Walking around in a spacesuit is not easy.
5. Finding no sign of life, the astronauts returned to their spaceship.
6. The astronauts' spaceship was struck by a meteor.
7. After checking the spaceship for damage, the astronauts prepared to leave.
8. Giganta, the planet's moon, was a beautiful reddish color.
9. The astronauts were anxious to return to Earth.
10. On a successful mission, they gathered valuable information about the planet's surface.

- writing headlines for a news story or dialogue for a short story
- composing an advertisement

Ask students to work in groups to create and act out brief scenes from real life in which they use fragments to communicate. If you have time, ask volunteers to act out the scenes again, this time using complete sentences. Discuss the differences between the scenes.

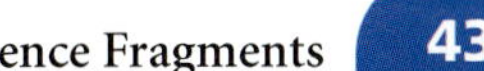

SENTENCES

Differentiating Instruction

Learners Having Difficulty

As you discuss the terminology used in this section of the chapter, some students may benefit from drawing illustrations to explain and provide context for terms such as *independent* and *subordinate*. For example, a student could illustrate how a locomotive, which can operate on its own power, is connected to a boxcar, which lacks its own power. They may do the same with the terms *fused, splice,* and *compound* that appear in later sections of the chapter. Students can display their drawings in the classroom for reference.

English-Language Learners

Cantonese. Sentences in Cantonese tend to be short, with only one clause. Cantonese speakers may need help with the concepts of compound and complex sentences. They will tend to write subordinate clauses as complete sentences. They will benefit from sentence combining exercises. Ask them to review any compositions they write to see where short sentences might be combined with appropriate connecting words.

Subordinate Clause Fragments

A ***clause*** is a group of words that has a subject and a verb. One kind of clause, an ***independent clause,*** expresses a complete thought and can stand on its own as a sentence. For example, the group of words *I ate my lunch* is an independent clause. However, another kind of clause, a ***subordinate clause,*** does not express a complete thought and cannot stand by itself as a sentence.

FRAGMENT When Paris carried off the beautiful Helen of Troy. [What happened when Paris carried off Helen?]

SENTENCE When Paris carried off the beautiful Helen of Troy, he started the Trojan War.

FRAGMENT Who was a great hero of the Greeks. [The reader needs to know more—whom does this subordinate clause describe, and what did that person do?]

SENTENCE Odysseus, who was a great hero of the Greeks, took part in the Trojan War.

FRAGMENT Because the wooden horse concealed Greek soldiers. [What was the result of the concealment?]

SENTENCE Because the wooden horse concealed Greek soldiers, the Greeks finally won the Trojan War.

FRAGMENT Which was Achilles' only vulnerable spot. [What was Achilles' only vulnerable spot?]

SENTENCE An injury to his heel, which was Achilles' only vulnerable spot, led to that hero's death.

NOTE A subordinate clause telling *why, where, when,* or *how* is called an ***adverb clause.*** Usually you can place an adverb clause either before or after the independent clause in a sentence.

EXAMPLE **After he started home from the Trojan War,** Odysseus had many more adventures.

or

Odysseus had many more adventures **after he started home from the Trojan War.**

If you put the subordinate clause first, use a comma to separate it from the independent clause. The comma makes the sentence easier for the reader to understand.

Reference Note

For more on **punctuating introductory adverb clauses,** see page 281.

Mini-Lesson Mechanics

Using Commas with Adverb Clauses. Remind students that an adverb clause can be placed at various locations in the sentence. Point out, however, that if an adverb clause is placed at the beginning of a sentence, a comma will need to follow that clause. Ask students to read the following sentences to determine whether a comma is needed. If a comma is needed, have students identify the word it should follow and add the comma. If a sentence is correct, have students write C.

Exercise 2 Revising Subordinate Clause Fragments

The following paragraph contains some subordinate clause fragments. First, find these clause fragments. Next, revise the paragraph, joining the subordinate clauses with independent clauses. (There may be more than one way to join them.) Change the punctuation and capitalization as necessary. Here is a possible revision.

EXAMPLE When you look at eyeliner. You may not think of ancient Egypt.

When you look at eyeliner, you may not think of ancient Egypt.

People have been using cosmetics for thousands of years. In Africa, the ancient Egyptians used perfumes, hair dyes, and makeup. That they made from plants and minerals. While they often used cosmetics to improve their appearance. They also used them to protect their skin from the hot sun. Today, cosmetics are made from over five thousand different ingredients, including waxes, oils, and dyes. The cosmetics business is a huge industry. Advertisers are extremely successful in selling cosmetics. Because they appeal to our desire to be attractive. Advertisers often hint. That their products will make us beautiful, happy, and successful.

Exercise 3 Using Subordinate Clauses in Sentences

Use each of the following subordinate clause fragments as part of a complete sentence. Add whatever words are necessary to make the meaning of the sentence complete. Add capitalization and punctuation as necessary. Possible sentences appear below.

EXAMPLE 1. when our windows started glowing

1. We were eating dinner when our windows started glowing.

1. as we watched the spaceship land 1. , we were terrified.
2. who approached the house in long leaps 2. An alien, /, was ten feet tall.
3. which startled the dog 3. The alien made a strange sound,
4. so that we could get a better look 4. , we went outside.
5. when they handed me a glowing sphere 5. , we knew the aliens were friendly.

Differentiating Instruction

Advanced Learners

Remind students that in poetry, sentence fragments, phrase fragments, subordinate clause fragments, and series of items are often used for effect. Invite students to look through poetry anthologies for examples, or show students Naomi Shihab Nye's poem "Daily."

Read Nye's poem aloud and ask students what they notice about it. Guide the discussion with the observation that the first six lines of the poem sound like a series of sentence fragments. The sentences are not constructed in the traditional subject-verb-object order, and they do not have end marks. This construction creates the effect of an ongoing series of daily activities.

SENTENCES

Extension

Critical Thinking

Analysis. Ask students to work with partners to list reasons why sentence fragments are more often used successfully in conversation than in writing. [*Speakers use tone of voice, inflection, pauses, and gestures along with words to convey meaning. The listener can see the speaker and can respond to nonverbal speech as well as verbal messages. In spoken conversation, two-way communication allows a speaker to judge whether meaning is clear to a listener. Writing is, at least in this respect, one-way communication. The reader has to rely solely on the writer's words for understanding.*]

1. Before you leave look at this picture. [*leave,*]
2. I should leave at the sound of the bell. [*C*]
3. Because Mother worked all day she is tired tonight. [*day,*]
4. While he was singing at the top of his lungs Lou attracted quite a bit of attention. [*lungs,*]
5. A larger boat is being built next to the kayak. [*C*]

SENTENCES

Reteaching

Sentence Fragments

Having students remove phrases and subordinate clauses from complete sentences might help them see how these sentence parts function in a complete sentence and why the parts are fragments when left on their own. Write the following sentences on the chalkboard and ask students to work in pairs to identify the indicated sentence parts. You may want to review the types of phrases and clauses first.

Verbal Phrases

1. Emilio wanted to go to law school.

2. He enjoyed researching past cases.

[1. *to go to law school;* 2. *researching past cases*]

Appositive Phrases

3. Marlene moved to New York from Greenville, a small town in Texas.

4. Her aunt, a freelance writer, took her to London.

[3. *a small town in Texas;* 4. *a free-lance writer*]

Prepositional Phrases

5. Hasina graduated with honors.

6. She received job offers from many large companies.

[5. *with honors;* 6. *from many large companies*]

Subordinate Clauses

7. Toshio completed his homework as the baseball game began.

8. Because he was a fan, he didn't want to miss the game.

[7. *as the baseball game began;* 8. *Because he was a fan*]

6. The aliens invited us inside the spaceship

6. because they liked us.
7. which looked very complex. **7.** We stared at the controls,
8. before we could object, **8.** , the spaceship lifted off.
9. so we didn't complain. **9.** Zooming above our neighborhood was amazing,
10. even though no one would believe our story, **10.** , we knew we'd had an amazing adventure.

NOTE A **series of items** is another kind of fragment that is easily mistaken for a sentence. Notice that, in the following example, the series of items in dark type is not a complete sentence.

FRAGMENT I ate several things for lunch. **A sandwich, an apple, four pieces of celery, and some popcorn.**

To correct the fragment, you can

- make it into a complete sentence

or

- link it to the previous sentence with a colon

SENTENCE I ate several things for lunch. I ate a sandwich, an apple, four pieces of celery, and some popcorn.

or

I ate several things for lunch: a sandwich, an apple, four pieces of celery, and some popcorn.

Review A Identifying and Revising Fragments

Some of the following groups of words are sentence fragments. Identify each fragment, and make it part of a complete sentence, adding commas where necessary. When you find a complete sentence, write *C.*

EXAMPLE **1.** Originally raised to hunt badgers. Dachshunds are now popular as pets.

1. Originally raised to hunt badgers, dachshunds are now popular as pets. Possible revisions follow.

1. Humans have kept dogs as pets and helpers. For perhaps ten thousand years.
2. Herding sheep and cattle and guarding property. Many dogs more than earn their keep.
3. Descended from wolves. Some dogs are still somewhat wolflike.
4. There are over one hundred breeds of dogs now. **4.** C
5. If you have a Saint Bernard. You have one of the largest dogs.

Reference Note

For more on **punctuating introductory phrases,** see page 281.

6. Because Yorkshire terriers are very tiny and cute, many people keep them as pets.
7. Since they are all born blind and unable to take care of themselves, puppies need their mothers.
8. Most dogs are fully grown by the time they are one year old. 8. C
9. Dogs live an average of twelve years, although many live to be nearly twenty.
10. If you like dogs, consider having one for a pet.

Run-on Sentences

A ***run-on sentence*** is two or more complete sentences run together as one. Because they do not show where one idea ends and another one begins, run-on sentences can confuse your reader. There are two kinds of run-ons. In the first kind, called a ***fused sentence,*** the sentences have no punctuation at all between them.

RUN-ON Schools in the Middle Ages were different from ours students usually did not have books.

CORRECT Schools in the Middle Ages were different from ours**.** **S**tudents usually did not have books.

In the other kind of run-on, the writer links together sentences with only a comma to separate them from one another. This kind of run-on is called a ***comma splice.***

RUN-ON Schools today have books for every student, many schools also have televisions and computers.

CORRECT Schools today have books for every student**.** **M**any schools also have televisions and computers.

Revising Run-on Sentences

There are several ways you can revise run-on sentences. As shown in the examples above, you can always make two separate sentences. However, if the two thoughts are equal to one another in importance, you may want to make a ***compound sentence.***

RUN-ON Canada has ten provinces each province has its own government. [fused]

Canada has ten provinces, each province has its own government. [comma splice]

COMPUTER TIP 

You can use a grammar-checking program to flag sentences in your writing that are longer than a certain number of words—sentences that have a higher chance of being run-ons. You can then use the information in this chapter to determine whether or not the flagged sentences are run-ons.

TIPS & TRICKS

To spot run-on sentences, read your writing aloud. Each point where you hear yourself making a pause as you read is a point where you should ask, *Do I need to create separate sentences here? Do I need to add a semicolon or period? Do I need a comma and a conjunction instead? Do I need additional punctuation here?*

SENTENCES

Run-on Sentences

OBJECTIVE
(pp. 441–444)

- **To revise run-on sentences by forming two sentences or one compound sentence**

DIRECT TEACHING

Modeling and Demonstration

Run-on Sentences. Model how to determine whether a group of words is a run-on sentence by using the example *My family enjoys movies, we want to visit Hollywood someday.* First, ask students how many complete thoughts are expressed in the example. [*two*] Ask whether each group of words that expresses a complete thought has a subject and a verb. [*yes;* family, enjoys; We, want] Point out that the word group contains two complete sentences that contain closely related ideas. Ask whether two sentences can be joined with a comma to make a compound sentence [*no*]. Ask how the two word groups can be joined to make a compound sentence. [*by inserting the coordinating conjunction* so *after the comma; answers may vary*] Ask students to suggest other ways to correct the run-on sentence. [*Answers will vary.*] Now, have a volunteer use another example from this chapter to demonstrate how to identify and correct a run-on sentence.

RESOURCES 

Run-on Sentences

Practice

- *Language & Sentence Skills Practice,* pp. 421–422

Differentiating Instruction

- *Developmental Language & Sentence Skills,* pp. 161–162

SENTENCES

TECHNOLOGY TIP

If you have a computer that can be used with a projector screen, open a word-processing program and type some of the sample run-on sentences that appear on pp. 441–443. Then, as students read the instruction and the examples in their textbooks, you or a student may demonstrate on the computer how to revise each sentence. Students may benefit from seeing the actual changes being made for them.

DIRECT TEACHING

Evaluating Ideas in Run-on Sentences

Students may have trouble evaluating the importance of ideas in a run-on sentence. Remind students that some run-ons will be better divided into separate sentences (when the ideas are not closely related). Others will be better joined in one sentence by a comma and a coordinating conjunction or by a semicolon (when the ideas are closely related and of equal importance.) Still others will be better joined by a semicolon and a conjunctive adverb (when the ideas are closely related in a particular way). Make the process of evaluation visual by writing a run-on sentence on the chalkboard and drawing a box around each of the important ideas. Then, have students evaluate the ideas by asking the following questions:

- Does one idea seem more important than another?
- Does one idea have to happen before the other can? If so, the first idea is more important.
- Does inserting the words *and, or,* or *but* make a difference in the meaning of the sentence? If *and* or *but* makes the sentence seem wrong, then you have a clue about the equality of the ideas.

Model the evaluation process before asking students to try it on their own.

1. You can make a compound sentence by using a comma and a coordinating conjunction (such as *and, but,* or *or*).

CORRECTED Canada has ten provinces**, and** each province has its own government.

2. You can make a compound sentence by using a semicolon.

CORRECTED Canada has ten provinces**;** each province has its own government.

3. You can make a compound sentence by using a semicolon and a word such as *therefore, instead, meanwhile, still, also, nevertheless,* or *however.* These words are called ***conjunctive adverbs.*** Follow a conjunctive adverb with a comma.

CORRECTED Canada has ten provinces**; also,** each province has its own government.

Reference Note

For more on **compound sentences,** see page 109.

NOTE Before you join two sentences in a compound sentence, make sure that the ideas in the sentences are closely related to one another. If you link unrelated ideas, you may confuse your reader.

UNRELATED Canada is almost four million square miles in size, and I hope to visit my relatives there someday.

RELATED Canada is almost four million square miles in size, but most of its people live on a small strip of land along the southern border.

Exercise 4 Revising Run-on Sentences

The following items are confusing because they are run-on sentences. Clear up the confusion by revising the run-ons to form clear, complete sentences. To revise, use the method given in parentheses after each sentence.

EXAMPLES

1. Hollywood is still a center of American moviemaking fine films are made in other places, too. (Use a comma and a coordinating conjunction.)

1. Hollywood is still a center of American moviemaking, but fine films are made in other places, too.

2. How much do you know about the history of movies how much would you like to know? (Make two sentences.)

2. How much do you know about the history of movies? How much would you like to know?

CONTENT-AREA CONNECTIONS

Mathematics

Punctuating Equations. Explain to students that run-on sentences may be a sign that students are becoming sophisticated writers, as they are trying to connect several ideas in their writing. Stress that run-ons are usually the result of incorrect punctuation. Equations, like sentences, grow longer and more complicated as the problems become more sophisticated. In addition, equations

1. Movies entertain millions of people every day. The cinema is popular all over the world. (Make two sentences.)
2. Many films take years to make they require the skills of hundreds of workers. (Use a comma and a coordinating conjunction.) **2.** , and
3. The director of a movie has an important job; the cast and crew all follow the director's instructions. (Use a semicolon.)
4. The director makes many decisions the producers take care of the business end of moviemaking. (Use a semicolon and a conjunctive adverb.) **4.** ; however,
5. The first movie theaters opened in the early 1900s. They were called nickelodeons. (Make two sentences.)
6. Thomas Edison was a pioneer in early moviemaking; he and one of his assistants invented the first commercial motion-picture machine. (Use a semicolon.)
7. The machine was called a Kinetoscope it was a cabinet that showed moving images through a peephole. (Make two sentences.) **7.** .
8. Edison worked with George Eastman, another inventor, to make roll film. Eastman is now remembered for his contributions to film-making. (Make two sentences.)
9. The first sound films were shown in the late 1920s; they marked a milestone in moviemaking history. (Use a semicolon.)
10. Movies are great entertainment they are also an art form. (Use a semicolon and a conjunctive adverb.) **10.** ; however,

George Eastman and Thomas Edison

Review B Revising Fragments and Run-on Sentences

The following paragraph contains several sentence fragments and run-on sentences. Revise all fragments and run-ons, adding words and changing the punctuation and capitalization as necessary to make each sentence clear and complete.

EXAMPLES
1. I just started researching my paper on American women in the military would you like to know what I've learned so far?
   1. *I just started researching my paper on American women in the military. Would you like to know what I've learned so far?*
2. Women served in the Civil War. Not just men.
   2. *Women, not just men, served in the Civil War.*

Review B Revising Fragments and Run-on Sentences

DISTRIBUTED REVIEW
After students complete **Review B,** consider having them use it as a review of the types of phrases discussed in the chapter. A list of phrases appears below.

- During the Civil War [*prepositional phrase*]
- of sick and wounded soldiers [*prepositional phrase*]
- carrying supplies [*verbal phrase*]
- To military hospitals [*prepositional phrase*]
- in the South [*prepositional phrase*]
- of two women captains [*prepositional phrase*]
- in the Confederate Army [*prepositional phrase*]
- Caring for sick and wounded soldiers [*verbal phrase*]
- in the North [*prepositional phrase*]
- In 1864 [*prepositional phrase*]
- of nurses [*prepositional phrase*]
- for the Union Army [*prepositional phrase*]
- of the Red Cross [*prepositional phrase*]
- Until 1904 [*prepositional phrase*]

are punctuated with specific symbols to show what parts of the equation belong together and how the different parts of the equation are related. Ask a math teacher at your school to provide students with a few examples of equations and to explain how the mathematical symbols punctuate the equation.

SENTENCES

Here is a possible revision.

and

was

, and

became

and/its

During the Civil War, Women who were nurses showed remarkable heroism. They took care of sick and wounded soldiers, they risked their lives carrying supplies. To military hospitals. Sally L. Tompkins one such woman. She ran a military hospital in the South she was one of two female captains in the Confederate Army. Clara Barton was another heroic Civil War nurse, she worked tirelessly. Caring for sick and wounded soldiers in the North. In 1864, Barton superintendent of nurses for the Union Army. She later founded the American Red Cross Society. Served as president ~~of the Red Cross~~. Until 1904.

Clara Barton

444 Writing Complete Sentences

Chapter Review

Terms in brackets refer to concepts tested by the items in the Chapter Review.

1. frag.—Malcolm takes pictures [frag.]
2. run-on [run-on]
3. run-on—and [run-on]
4. frag.—I want you to see [frag.]
5. sent. [sent.]
6. frag.—, was leading the elephant [frag.]
7. sent. [sent.]
8. run-on—?/. [run-on]
9. frag.—, the princess was working on her embroidery [frag.]
10. sent. [sent.]

11.–15. [revising run-ons]

12. ; still,

14. ; however,

A. Identifying Sentences, Sentence Fragments, and Run-ons

Identify each of the following word groups as a *sentence*, a *sentence fragment*, or a *run-on sentence*. If a word group is a sentence fragment, rewrite it to make a complete sentence. If a word group is a run-on sentence, rewrite it to make it one or more complete sentences.

Here are possible revisions.

1. Whenever the class goes on a field trip.
2. Let's go skating instead, everyone has already seen that movie.
3. The rain had been falling for days, the creeks were full to their banks.
4. The house on our street that was recently painted bright blue.
5. Crouching in the tall grass, the cat watched the birds closely.
6. A young boy, not more than ten years old.
7. When we went to Virginia last summer, we visited several Civil War battlefields.
8. May I borrow your ruler, I think I left mine at home?
9. Meanwhile, in another room of the castle.
10. That restaurant, owned by the same family for thirty years, is very popular.

B. Revising Run-on Sentences

Rewrite each run-on sentence to form clear, complete sentences. For some of the items, the revision method you should use is given in parentheses. Here are possible revisions.

11. On Sunday mornings, my family always makes a big breakfast, everyone especially likes omelets.
12. Making an omelet is not very difficult, you must have all the ingredients ready and take your time. (Use a semicolon, a conjunctive adverb, and a comma.)
13. I like chopped tomatoes, onions, and green peppers in my omelets, my sister likes to add mushrooms, too.
14. Sometimes I grate a little cheddar cheese for the top of the omelet, you don't have to use cheese if you don't like it. (Use a semicolon, a conjunctive adverb, and a comma.)

ASSESSING

Monitoring Progress

Chapter Review. To assess student progress, you may want to compare the types of items missed on the **Diagnostic Preview** to those missed on the **Chapter Review.** If students have not made significant progress, you may want to provide them with additional practice.

RESOURCES

Writing Complete Sentences

Assessment

- *Holt Handbook Chapter Tests with Answer Key,* pp. 35–38, 52

15. but [revising run-ons 1]
16. [revising run-ons 2]
17. [revising run-ons]
18. or [revising run-ons 1]
19. ; instead, [revising run-ons 3]
20. yet [revising run-ons 1]

15. An omelet pan looks much like a frying pan, the bottom of an omelet pan is slightly rounded.

16. These eggs are very fresh, we bought them at the farmers' market yesterday. (Use a semicolon.)

17. Carefully break three eggs into a deep bowl, wash your hands after you break the eggs. (Make two sentences.)

18. Use a whisk to beat the eggs, you can use a fork if you don't have a whisk.

19. Don't stir the eggs while they are cooking, lift the edge of the eggs and let the uncooked part run under the cooked part.

20. Sometimes my omelets look like scrambled eggs, they still taste great. (Use a comma and a coordinating conjunction.)

C. Revising Sentence Fragments and Run-on Sentences

The following paragraphs contain sentence fragments and run-on sentences. Revise the paragraphs, making each sentence clear and complete. You will have to add words and change the punctuation and capitalization in some sentences. Here are possible revisions.

Of all the great apes, the gorilla may be the most mysterious and misunderstood, many people think gorillas are aggressive and ferocious, but researchers have found that gorillas are actually quite shy. Unless they are threatened or disturbed. The leader of a gorilla group will beat his chest, roar, and rush at an intruder, rarely does his display lead to a fight. ; however,

Gorillas, the largest of the great apes, have long, powerful arms and short, thick legs, adult males, who are sometimes twice the size of the females, can grow to almost five and a half feet. Up to six hundred pounds. Although the hair of the gorilla is usually black, grown males have an area of gray or silver hair on their lower backs, sometimes mature males are called "silverbacks." and

446 Writing Complete Sentences

Gorillas in the forests of equatorial Africa. You may be surprised to learn that gorillas are vegetarians they eat leaves and shoots and spend a lot of time looking for food. Gorilla family groups are made up of six to twenty animals one or two silver-backs lead and defend each group. Each group has a territory, between ten and six-teen square miles, several groups may share the same area. Every night, each gorilla in a group builds a new nest of leaves and branches. Sometimes in a tree and sometimes on the ground.

Like its close relative, the chimpanzee, the gorilla is highly intelligent gorillas have demonstrated the capacity to remember, to anticipate, and to solve problems. Gorillas have shown that they can learn sign language from humans. Maybe even more readily than chimpanzees.

Gorillas have become more and more endangered in Africa the destruction of the gorilla's habitat continues humans clear the forests for farming, grazing, and lumbering. In addition, female gorillas typically give birth only once every four years, most births are single. Baby gorillas weigh less than five pounds and are completely helpless. For several months. The destruction of habitat and the gorilla's slow reproduction rate have made the gorilla vulnerable to extinction, illegal hunting also threatens the animal's survival. One kind of gorilla, the mountain gorilla, is especially rare only five hundred to one thousand mountain gorillas survive today.

live

but

and

and

SENTENCES

Chapter Review 447

CHAPTER

19

INTRODUCING THE CHAPTER

- In the first half of this chapter, students will learn strategies for writing effective sentences, including the techniques of combining sentences by inserting words and phrases, using compound subjects and verbs, and creating compound and complex sentences. Students will then learn about improving their sentence style by using parallel structure, identifying and revising stringy and wordy sentences, and varying their sentence beginnings. You may use this chapter to teach students the concepts of combining sentences and improving sentence style or as a reference tool for students as they complete writing assignments throughout the year.

CHAPTER

19 Writing Effective Sentences

Diagnostic Preview

A. Combining Sentences by Inserting Words or Phrases

Combine the sentences in the following items by inserting words or phrases from one sentence into the other sentence.

Here are possible revisions.

EXAMPLES

1. The miners trudged up the mine shaft. They were covered with coal dust.
1. *The miners, covered with coal dust, trudged up the mine shaft.*
2. The baby is sleepy. The baby is ready for his afternoon nap.
2. *The sleepy baby is ready for his afternoon nap.*

Terms in brackets refer to concepts tested by the items in the Diagnostic Preview.

1.–5. [Inserting words and phrases]
1. barking
2. , a talented artist,
4. Laughing and shouting with excitement,
5. gold

1. I'm tired today because a dog disturbed my sleep last night. ~~The dog was barking.~~
2. My sister designed the invitation to the wedding. ~~She is a talented artist.~~
3. Rita won the math contest. ~~She won~~ by answering all the questions correctly.
4. The children ran toward the playground. ~~The children were laughing and shouting with excitement.~~
5. The team looked great in the new uniforms. ~~The uniforms are gold.~~

CHAPTER RESOURCES

Internet

- Web resources: go.hrw.com

Practice & Review

- *Language & Sentence Skills Practice,* pp. 425–450
- *Language & Sentence Skills Practice Answer Key,* pp. 172–181

B. Combining Sentences by Using Compound Subjects and Compound Verbs

Combine the sentences in the following items by using compound subjects or compound verbs. Here are possible revisions.

EXAMPLE 1. The American history test lasted one hour. The test had fifty questions.

1. *The American history test lasted one hour and had fifty questions.*

6. I carefully washed the ripe grapes. I put them in a bowl in the refrigerator.
7. Neil is a good writer. Kate is also a good writer. They have written many articles for the school newspaper.
8. Selma and James ride the bus most of the time. Selma and James decided to walk to school today.
9. We will visit the museum on Saturday morning. We will have lunch at that restaurant afterward.
10. Charles plays the violin in the student orchestra. Charles's sister Anita also plays the violin in the student orchestra.

6.–10. [Compound subjects and verbs]
6. and
7. Neil and Kate are good writers and
8. but
9. and
10. and his sister Anita

C. Combining Sentences by Forming Compound and Complex Sentences

Combine the sentences in the following items by forming compound or complex sentences. Here are possible revisions.

EXAMPLE 1. Our part of the state rarely gets snow. Last week was certainly an exception!

1. *Our part of the state rarely gets snow, but last week was certainly an exception!*

11. The snow started in the morning. By early evening a foot of new snow had fallen.
12. No one could drive or even ride bicycles. The roads were barely visible.
13. We tried to clear a path from the door to the road. Drifting snow covered our work.
14. The cold was bone chilling. Everyone in our neighborhood wanted to go sledding.
15. We are not used to the cold and snow. We couldn't stay out more than an hour.

11.–15. [Compound sentences and complex sentences]
11. , and
12. because
13. , but
14. Although
15. , so

SENTENCES

ASSESSING

Entry-Level Assessment

Diagnostic Preview. You may want to use the **Diagnostic Preview** to identify areas in which students need instruction and practice in writing effective sentences. You could use the results of the preview to decide which lessons to teach to the entire class and which ones to assign to small groups.

Differentiating Instruction

- *Developmental Language & Sentence Skills,* pp. 163–176
- *Developmental Language & Sentence Skills Guided Practice Teacher's Notes and Answer Key,* pp. 41–43

Assessment

- *Holt Handbook Chapter Tests with Answer Key,* pp. 39–43, 52

SENTENCES

PRETEACHING

Lesson Starter

Motivating. Write the following quotation on a chalkboard.

"That writer does the most, who gives his reader the most knowledge, and takes from him the least time."

(Charles Caleb Colton, 1780–1832, English writer and clergyman)

Ask students to rephrase the quotation in their own words. [Here is a possible response: *The best writers give a lot of information without taking up a lot of my time.*] Guide students in discussing some of the obstacles they meet in reading for information and in writing informative essays.

Next, write the following quotation on a chalkboard.

"Trifles make perfection, and perfection is no trifle."

(Michelangelo Buonarroti, 1475–1564, Italian Renaissance sculptor, painter, and poet as quoted by C. C. Colton in *Lacon*)

After explaining that trifles are things of little importance, ask students to think about Michelangelo's contradiction and put it into their own words. Students may write their paraphrase or read it aloud. Ask students how the idea applies to their own writing. Guide them toward understanding that in revising, proofreading, and polishing their own writing, they are attending to the small things, the trifles, that, once corrected, make for perfection. Finally, ask students how the ideas in the two quotations on this page might be related. [*The writer who is concise, precise, and careful with details can communicate more clearly and quickly with the reader.*]

D. [Varying sentence beginnings, using parallel structure, revising stringy sentences, revising wordy sentences]

D. Revising a Paragraph to Improve Sentence Style

Revise the following paragraph to improve the writing style by varying sentence beginnings, correcting nonparallel structures, and revising stringy or wordy sentences. Possible revisions follow.

EXAMPLE 1. The purpose of this essay is to convey my interest in applying for the summer science program and to let you know that I have been fascinated by botany for many years, at least from the time I was five or six years old.

1. *I am applying for the summer science program because I have been fascinated by botany since I was five or six years old.*

While/most/plants

studying/much/free time

my magnifying glass,

and

In a large garden next to the greenhouse, I grow vegetables and some flowers.

dates/and/I also note

I am including my illustrated notebooks

When other children were collecting insects and shells, I was looking at leaves and flowers, and whenever my brother and I went fishing, I spent more than a majority of the time studying the vegetation on the riverbanks. Now collecting, drawing, and study of plants take up many of my recreational hours. I never go anywhere without my magnifying glass, and I never leave the house without my notebook, and also, I always remember to bring my watercolors and my colored pencils. I have built a small greenhouse in our backyard. The greenhouse is where I experiment with seeds; I also grow tropical plants in the greenhouse. Outside the greenhouse, plants are grown by me in a large garden. The plants are mostly of the type that can be consumed by humans, but in addition, some are being raised simply because they are considered by many to have beautiful flowers. I keep careful records of the products of my cultivation, including, but not limited to, date of planting, and germination for each particular variety of seed, date of appearance of first true leaves, date of harvesting, and how I control pests and diseases. The written records of my efforts in the garden, in the form of my notebooks, including the illustrations, are being included by me as a part of this application.

Combining Sentences

Short sentences are often effective; however, a long, unbroken series of them can sound choppy. For example, notice how dull the following paragraph sounds.

> I have seen a lot of earthling-meets-alien movies. I have seen <u>The Last Starfighter</u>. I have seen all the <u>Star Trek</u> movies. I have noticed something about these movies. I have noticed that there are good humans in these movies. There are bad humans. There are good aliens. There are bad aliens. The humans and aliens are actually not so different from each other.

Notice how much more interesting the paragraph sounds when the short, choppy sentences are combined into longer, smoother sentences.

> I have seen a lot of earthling-meets-alien movies, including <u>The Last Starfighter</u> and all the <u>Star Trek</u> movies. I have noticed that there are good and bad humans in these movies, as well as good and bad aliens. The humans and aliens are actually not so different from each other.

Inserting Words

You can combine short sentences by inserting a key word from one sentence into another. You usually need to eliminate some words in sentences that are combined. You may also need to change the form of the key word.

Using the Same Form	
Original	Edgar Allan Poe led a short life. His life was tragic.
Combined	Edgar Allan Poe led a short, **tragic** life.
Changing the Form	
Original	Edgar Allan Poe wrote strange stories. He wrote horror stories.
Combined	Edgar Allan Poe wrote strange, **horrifying** stories.

RESOURCES

Combining Sentences

Practice

- *Language & Sentence Skills Practice,* pp. 425–436

Differentiating Instruction

- *Developmental Language & Sentence Skills,* pp. 163–168

Combining Sentences
(pp. 451–461)

OBJECTIVES

- To combine sentences by inserting words and phrases
- To combine sentences by creating compound subjects and verbs
- To combine sentences by creating compound sentences
- To combine sentences by creating complex sentences

SENTENCES

DIRECT TEACHING

Modeling and Demonstration

Combining Sentences. Model how to combine sentences by using the example *Edgar Allan Poe was a writer who wrote stories and poems. Edgar Allan Poe was an American writer.* First, ask whether the two sentences are about the same subject. [*yes; Edgar Allan Poe*] Next, ask whether the two sentences repeat any information. [*yes; he was a writer*] Point out that when information is repeated in two sentences, it is often possible to take information from one sentence and insert it into the other sentence. Next, ask what information could be moved from the second sentence to the first sentence. [*Poe's nationality*] Ask which word can be used. [*American*] Point out that students will have to change the article *a* to *an* when they insert *American* before *writer.* Now, have a volunteer use another example from this chapter to demonstrate how to combine two sentences by inserting a word.

SENTENCES

TEACHING TIP

Participles. Students may need a review of participles and their function before they begin **Exercise 1.** Remind students that there are two types of participles, *present participles,* which end in *–ing,* and *past participles,* most of which end in *–d* or *–ed.* Also, participles can be used as adjectives describing a person, place, thing, or idea. Here are a few examples: *paved driveway, estimated cost, moving truck.*

DIFFERENTIATING INSTRUCTION

English-Language Learners

Spanish. Inserting key words that are adjectives may be confusing to some Spanish speakers. In Spanish, descriptive adjectives usually follow the nouns they modify. In addition, when an adjective appears before the noun, it often has a different meaning. Working through **Exercises 1** and **2** orally can help focus attention on the placement of adjectives in relation to the nouns they modify.

NOTE Some verbs can be made into adjectives by adding *–ed* and *–ing,* and some adjectives can be made into adverbs by adding *–ly.*

EXAMPLES to bore—boring, bored quick—quickly
to tilt—tilting, tilted modest—modestly

Exercise 1 Combining Sentences by Inserting Words

In the following sets of sentences, some words have been italicized. Combine each set of sentences by inserting the italicized word (or words) into the first sentence. The directions in parentheses will tell you how to change the word form if it is necessary to do so.

EXAMPLE 1. Edgar Allan Poe was a writer who wrote stories and poems. Edgar Allan Poe was an *American* writer.

1. Edgar Allan Poe was an American writer who wrote stories and poems.

Here are some possible combinations.

1. The mother of Edgar Allan Poe died three years after he was born. She was *young.*
2. Poe was taken in by Mrs. John Allan and her husband. Their taking him in was *fortunate.* (Add *–ly* to *fortunate.*) 2. Fortunately,
3. Poe created stories. He created *detective* stories.
4. Poe inspired the author of the Sherlock Holmes stories. The author had *talent.* (Add *–ed* to *talent.*) 4. talented
5. Poe had theories about the writing of fiction. His theories were *original.*
6. Poe also wrote poems. The poems were *numerous.*
7. Poe wrote the poem "The Raven." It is a *well-known* poem.
8. Poe worked for literary magazines. He worked for *several* of them.
9. Poe wrote literary criticisms about authors. The authors were *comtemporary.*
10. I enjoy Edgar Allan Poe's short stories. His short stories are *terrifying.*

Exercise 2 Combining Sentences by Inserting Words

In Exercise 1, the words you needed to insert were italicized. Now, try using your own judgment to combine sentences. There may be more than one way to combine each set; do what seems best to you. Add commas and change the forms of words when needed.

MINI-LESSON Mechanics

Sentence Style. Your students probably already have an intuitive sense of sentence style—when they are looking at someone else's writing. Show them the following sentences and ask the questions that follow.

Lacrosse is a game. Lacrosse is played with sticks with nets on the ends. Lacrosse was first played by the Iroquois. Lacrosse gets its name from the French. Lacrosse comes from the French words for "the hooked stick."

EXAMPLE 1. Luis Valdez is a talented and famous playwright. He is a Mexican American.

1. *Luis Valdez is a talented and famous Mexican American playwright.*

Possible combinations are shown below.

1. Valdez was born in Delano, ~~Delano is in~~ California.
2. He grew up in a family of farm workers. ~~They were migrant workers.~~ 2. migrant
3. As a child, Valdez began to work in the fields. ~~He was six years old.~~ 3. six-year-old
4. He champions the cause of underpaid migrant farm workers. ~~He also champions the cause of migrant farm workers who suffer from overwork.~~ 4. , overworked
5. He organized the Farm Workers' Theater, a troupe of actors and musicians. ~~The troupe travels.~~ 5. traveling
6. The Farm Workers' Theater has performed in the United States, ~~It has also performed in~~ Europe, and Mexico.
7. Valdez received ~~an award~~ in 1990. ~~It was the Governor's Award.~~ 7. the Governor's Award
8. Valdez wrote the play *Zoot Suit.* ~~It was a success.~~ 8. successful
9. The play was produced on Broadway. ~~The play was popular.~~ 9. popular
10. Valdez is a member of the California Arts Council. ~~He is a founding member of the council.~~ 10. founding

Inserting Phrases

You also can combine closely related sentences by taking a phrase from one sentence and inserting it into another sentence.

Prepositional Phrases

A ***prepositional phrase,*** a preposition with its object and any modifiers of that object, can usually be inserted into another sentence with no changes. Just omit some of the words in one of the sentences.

ORIGINAL Twelve million immigrants came to the shores of the United States. They came through Ellis Island.

REVISED Twelve million immigrants came to the shores of the United States **through Ellis Island.**

Participial Phrases

A ***participial phrase*** contains a verb form that usually ends in *–ing* or *–ed.* The entire phrase acts as an adjective, modifying a noun or a pronoun. Sometimes, you can change the verb from one sentence into a participle by adding *–ing* or *–ed* or by dropping the helping verb if the

COMPUTER TIP

You can use a word-processing program's cut and paste commands to find the best placement for a participial phrase within a sentence.

DIFFERENTIATING INSTRUCTION

Learners Having Difficulty

Some students may not understand or retain terms such as *appositive phrase, conjunctive adverb,* and *coordinating conjunction,* and yet they may be able to use sentence-combining techniques correctly. Using simple language, such as "moving a group of words from one sentence to another," instead of "inserting a prepositional phrase," may be more effective.

English-Language Learners

General Strategies. All languages have shortcut versions of certain structures. Explain to students that an appositive phrase is a shortened form of an adjective phrase. An appositive phrase can be created from an adjective phrase by eliminating the pronoun *who, which,* or *that* and the form of the *be* verb. For example, in the sentence "My grandfather, who was a carpenter, built tables," the adjective phrase "who was a carpenter" can be shortened to the appositive phrase "a carpenter." Now the sentence reads "My grandfather, a carpenter, built tables." Ask students to find or create examples of sentences with adjective phrases and to use the phrases to create appositive phrases.

SENTENCES

- Could you write the same thing in a different way? [*Sample answer: Lacrosse is a game played with sticks with nets on the ends. It was invented by the Iroquois and gets its name from the French words for "the hooked stick."*]
- How is your version different from the first? Is it shorter or longer? How many sentences did you use?

SENTENCES

DIRECT TEACHING

Combining Sentences by Inserting Phrases

Activity. Give students an example of how to combine sentences using infinitive phrases and gerund phrases:
Original: The principal established a committee. It has the responsibility for choosing the mascot for the new high school.
Combined with an infinitive phrase: The principal established a committee to choose the mascot for the new high school.
Original: Joel slammed my locker door. I was irritated by that.
Combined with a gerund phrase: I was irritated by Joel's slamming my locker door.

Finally, give students the following pairs of sentences, and have them use infinitive phrases and gerund phrases to combine the pairs.

1. Dr. Smith solved my problem. He did this by extending the deadline on my paper. [Dr. Smith solved my problem by extending the deadline on my paper.]
2. Saul has a goal. He wants to be a policeman. [Saul has a goal to be a policeman.]

main verb already ends in *–ing* or *–ed.* Then, you can combine the two sentences. To avoid confusing your reader, place the participial phrase close to the noun or pronoun it will modify.

ORIGINAL Many immigrants faced long months of waiting at Ellis Island. They were weakened by their journeys.

REVISED Many immigrants, **weakened by their journeys,** faced long months of waiting at Ellis Island.

Appositive Phrases

An ***appositive phrase*** usually follows a noun or pronoun and helps to identify it. Sometimes you can combine sentences that have nouns or pronouns referring to the same thing by changing one of the sentences to an appositive phrase.

ORIGINAL My grandfather was an immigrant. My grandfather brought with him photographs that are now souvenirs.

REVISED My grandfather, **an immigrant,** brought with him photographs that are now souvenirs.

Reference Note

For more information on **phrases,** see page 68.

Exercise 3 Combining Sentences by Inserting Phrases

Revise each of the following sets of sentences to create one sentence. There may be more than one way to combine the sentences. In numbers 1 through 5, the words you need to insert are italicized. In numbers 6 through 10, change the forms of words or omit words as indicated in parentheses, and add commas wherever they are needed.

EXAMPLE 1. Auguste Piccard was a Swiss physicist who studied the upper atmosphere. He studied it *by going up in balloons.*

1. Auguste Piccard was a Swiss physicist who studied the upper atmosphere by going up in balloons.

Possible combinations appear below.

1. Auguste Piccard was an inventor, scientist, and explorer. He was *from Switzerland.*
2. Piccard once spent sixteen hours in a balloon. He was *floating across Germany and France.*

Learning for Life

Writing Effective E-mail. Tell students that one advantage of the Internet is that they can communicate their ideas instantly to many people. These people might be friends or relatives, but they might also be politicians or business owners. Remind students that effective e-mail is short and informative.

Work with students to create a set of rules for e-mail. Some rules might be:

3. Piccard attended the Swiss Institute of Technology. The institute is *in Zurich, Switzerland.*

4. Piccard was a young man when he became a professor. He became a professor *at the Swiss Institute.*

5. Piccard created an important invention. ~~He invented an airtight gondola.~~ **5.** , an airtight gondola

6. The gondola took Piccard ten miles into the air. ~~The gondola was attached to a balloon.~~ (Omit *The gondola was.*) **6.** Attached to a balloon,

7. Piccard then made numerous balloon trips. ~~He studied electricity.~~ (Change *studied* to *studying.*) **7.** Studying electricity,

8. Piccard turned his interest to the ocean depths. ~~He designed a deep-sea diving ship.~~ (Change *designed* to *designing.*) **8.** Designing a deep-sea diving ship,

9. Piccard and his son Jacques went two miles below the surface of the Adriatic Sea. ~~They went in 1953.~~ (Omit *They went.*) **9.** In 1953,

10. Another deep-sea diving ship went almost ten miles below the surface of the ocean. ~~It set the world's depth record in 1960.~~ (Change *set* to *setting.*) **10.** Setting the world's depth record in 1960,

Using Compound Subjects and Verbs

Another way to combine sentences is to make compound subjects and verbs. First, look for sentences that have the same subject or the same verb. Then, make the subject or verb compound by adding a coordinating conjunction such as *and, but, for, or, nor, so,* or *yet.*

ORIGINAL The Angles were fierce people. The Saxons were fierce people. [different subjects with same verb]

REVISED The **Angles and the Saxons** were fierce people. [compound subject with same verb]

ORIGINAL The Angles and Saxons invaded Britain. The Angles and Saxons conquered Britain. [different verbs with same subject]

REVISED The Angles and Saxons **invaded and conquered** Britain. [compound verb with same subject]

ORIGINAL The Angles conquered Britain. The Saxons also conquered Britain. They both pushed back the native Celts. [different subjects and different verbs]

REVISED The **Angles and the Saxons conquered** Britain and **pushed back** the native Celts. [compound subject and compound verb]

SENTENCES

TEACHING TIP

Joining Subjects and Verbs. Remind students that when a singular subject and plural subject are joined by *or* or *nor,* the verb should agree with the subject nearer the verb.

EXAMPLES

Neither the roller coaster nor the game *booths were* open.

Neither the game booths nor the *roller coaster was* open.

- be brief and to the point
- do not use unnecessary words
- correct any errors before sending
- include the writer's name and e-mail address for a reply

SENTENCES

Direct Teaching

Correcting Misconceptions

Compound Subjects, Compound Verbs, and Compound Sentences. Some students may still be confusing compound sentences with sentences that have compound subjects, compound verbs, or both. Model how to distinguish compound subjects and verbs from compound sentences by using the following lines from a familiar nursery rhyme:

Jack and Jill went up the hill
to fetch a pail of water.
Jack fell down and broke his
crown, and
Jill came tumbling after.

Ask how many subjects are in the first sentence. [*two*] Ask how many verbs are in the sentence. [*one*] Point out that the sentence has a compound subject—two subjects performing the same action. Now, ask how many subjects and verbs are in the second sentence. [*two; three*] Now, ask if the two subjects, Jack and Jill, are performing all the actions. [*no; Jack is performing two of the actions, and Jill is performing a different action*] Ask if the second sentence can be divided into two complete sentences. [*yes*] Point out that the second sentence is a compound sentence—two subjects performing different actions—and that the first clause has a compound verb—one of the subjects is performing two actions.

Reference Note

For more information on **agreement of subjects and verbs,** see page 121.

NOTE When you combine sentences by making compound subjects and compound verbs, make sure that your new subjects and verbs agree in number.

ORIGINAL The Angle dialect is an ancestor of Modern English. The Saxon dialect is also an ancestor of Modern English.

REVISED The Angle and Saxon dialects **are** ancestors of Modern English. [The plural subject *dialects* takes the plural verb *are.*]

Oral Practice Creating Compound Subjects and Compound Verbs

Possible combinations appear below.

Here are five sets of short sentences. Read each set aloud. Then, combine each set into one sentence that has a compound subject, a compound verb, or a compound subject and a compound verb.

EXAMPLE
1. Yesterday Tina and I bought a coconut. We cracked it open.
1. *Yesterday Tina and I bought a coconut and cracked it open.*

1. Bananas are a popular tropical fruit. Coconuts are another popular tropical fruit. 1. Bananas and coconuts are popular tropical fruits.
2. Brazil produces bananas. India produces bananas. Both countries export bananas. 2. Brazil and India produce and export bananas.
3. Some bananas are cooked ~~as vegetables are. They are~~ eaten as vegetables are. 3. and
4. By A.D. 600, the Egyptians ~~were eating coconuts.~~ Indians and Koreans were ~~also~~ eating coconuts.
5. Coconuts are not a major crop in the United States. Bananas are not a major crop in the United States, either. 5. Neither coconuts nor bananas are a major crop in the United States.
6. The United States imports much of the world's banana crop. ~~Likewise, Great Britain imports much of that crop.~~ 6. and Great Britain
7. Christopher makes dried banana chips. ~~Christopher eats dried banana chips, too.~~ 7. and eats
8. Coconut ~~is delicious in fruit smoothies. Banana is~~ delicious in fruit smoothies. 8. and banana are
9. My mother ~~has~~ many recipes that use bananas. ~~My uncle also has many recipes that use bananas.~~ 9. and my uncle have
10. Did you know that vitamin C ~~is~~ found in bananas? ~~Potassium is also~~ found in bananas. 10. and potassium are

Creating a Compound Sentence

You can combine two sentences by creating a compound sentence. A ***compound sentence*** is two or more simple sentences linked by

- a comma and a coordinating conjunction

  or

- a semicolon

  or

- a semicolon, a conjunctive adverb, and a comma

Before linking two thoughts in a compound sentence, make sure that the thoughts are clearly related and equal in importance. Be sure that you do not link two thoughts in a compound sentence when one thought is clearly more important than the other.

ORIGINAL The cat knocked over a lamp. The dog chewed up my shoe.

REVISED The cat knocked over a lamp**, and** the dog chewed up my shoe. [comma and coordinating conjunction]

The cat knocked over a lamp**;** the dog chewed up my shoe. [semicolon]

The cat knocked over a lamp**; meanwhile,** the dog chewed up my shoe. [semicolon and conjunctive adverb]

NOTE You can use the coordinating conjunctions *and, but, nor, for, yet, or,* and *so* to form compound sentences. However, you should avoid overusing them. Too many coordinating conjunctions can be a sign that you are writing stringy sentences. When you join two sentences with a coordinating conjunction, remember to use a comma before the conjunction.

Exercise 4 Combining Simple Sentences to Create Compound Sentences

Possible combinations appear below.

The sentences in the following pairs are closely related in meaning. Using the methods you have learned, combine each pair into a compound sentence. Remember to add commas and semicolons where they are needed in your combined sentences.

EXAMPLE **1.** My class is studying American Indians. We will use our research to create an encyclopedia.

1. My class is studying American Indians, and we will use our research to create an encyclopedia.

Reference Note

For more information on **compound sentences,** see page 109.

TIPS & TRICKS

Using conjunctive adverbs to join sentences allows you to emphasize the relationship between ideas. Some of the frequently used conjunctive adverbs are *also, besides, consequently, however, meanwhile, moreover, otherwise, then,* and *therefore.*

Reference Note

For more about **stringy sentences,** see page 463.

TEACHING TIP

Creating a Compound Sentence. You may want to introduce this section by drawing a seesaw on the chalkboard. Explain to students that in creating a compound sentence, both ideas included in the sentence should be equal in importance. Ask students to imagine placing each idea on the seesaw, one on each end. Have them visualize the balance between the two ideas. If one idea were more important, then the seesaw would tip down on that side. In such a case, the ideas probably do not belong in the same sentence.

EXTENSION

Relating to Literature

To demonstrate how writers use compound sentences, have students read the chase scenes in Richard Connell's short story "The Most Dangerous Game." Then, ask students to consider why Connell uses so many semicolons to combine sentences. Explain that Connell uses semicolons to separate sentences that describe events or thoughts occurring almost simultaneously. Using periods would cause readers to stop fully at the end of each sentence; semicolons allow the reader to continue reading at a quick pace.

TEACHING TIP

Creating a Complex Sentence. Some students, despite their proficiency with the meanings of most subordinating conjunctions, struggle with the conjunction *although.* Often, telling students that the word means "even though" does not help. Explain that *although* signals a situation that is the opposite of what the reader expects. Provide straightforward examples based on everyday experiences like the following ones:

1. Although I ate a big breakfast, I am still hungry.
2. Although I ran five miles every day, I still did not lose weight.

1. The Hopi live on a reservation. They have many separate villages. 1. , but
2. Many Hopi grow crops. Some make jewelry, baskets, pottery, and other crafts.
3. Hopi crops include corn, beans, and pumpkins. The Hopi have farmed these crops successfully for generations. 3. , and
4. The Hopi live in houses made of stone and plaster. The houses are built by women of the tribe.
5. The Hopi are peaceful people. Their religion is very important to them. 5. , and
6. The Hopi religion includes a profound respect for nature. One of the most famous Hopi rituals is a rain dance called the Snake Dance. 6. , and
7. The Hopi are one of several Pueblo peoples. My class is planning to study at least three different Pueblo groups. 7. , and
8. The various groups of Pueblo peoples traditionally spoke different languages. The cultures of the different villages are closely related. 8. ; howe
9. Some Pueblo peoples live in Arizona. Others live in New Mexico.
10. Spanish settlers noted the distinctive villages made of apartment-like stone and adobe structures built by Southwestern Indian tribes. The name *Pueblo* comes from the Spanish word for "village." 10. ; in fact,

Creating a Complex Sentence

A ***complex sentence*** includes one independent clause—a clause that can stand alone as a sentence. It also has one or more ***subordinate clauses***—clauses that cannot stand alone as sentences.

Adjective Clauses

You can make a sentence into an ***adjective clause*** by inserting *who, which,* or *that* in place of the subject. Then you can use the adjective clause to provide information about a preceding noun or pronoun.

ORIGINAL Many people are afraid of bats. They are usually harmless creatures.

REVISED Many people are afraid of bats, **which are usually harmless creatures.**

NOTE When you use adjective clauses to combine sentences, remember that *which* is not used to refer to a person, only to places and things. Use *who, whom, whose,* and *that* to refer to people.

Adverb Clauses

You can turn one sentence into an ***adverb clause*** and combine it with another sentence. The adverb clause may modify a verb, an adjective, or another adverb in the sentence (the independent clause) to which it is attached.

Adverb clauses begin with subordinating conjunctions like *after, although, because, if, when,* and *where.* You have to choose these conjunctions carefully. They show the relationship between the ideas in the adverb clause and those in the independent clause. For example, *when* shows how the ideas are related in time, *where* shows how the ideas are related in space, and *although* shows under what conditions the ideas occurred. When you use an adverb clause at the beginning of a sentence, you need to be sure to separate it from the independent clause with a comma.

ORIGINAL Many people are afraid of bats. Bats have a bad reputation.

REVISED Many people are afraid of bats because bats have a bad reputation.

ORIGINAL Some people think bats are dangerous. Bats rarely attack humans.

REVISED **Although some people think bats are dangerous,** bats rarely attack humans. [Note that a comma follows the adverb clause that begins the sentence.]

Noun Clauses

You can make a sentence into a ***noun clause*** and insert it into another sentence just as you would an ordinary noun. You create a noun clause by inserting a word like *that, how, what, which,* or *who* at the beginning of the sentence. When you place the noun clause in the other sentence, you may have to change or remove some words.

ORIGINAL Dracula is such a frightening character. This does not help the bat's reputation.

REVISED **That Dracula is such a frightening character** does not help the bat's reputation. [The word *that* introduces the noun clause, which becomes the subject of the verb *does help.*]

REVISED **What does not help the bat's reputation** is that Dracula is such a frightening character. [The word *what* introduces the noun clause, which becomes the subject of the verb *is.*]

Reference Note

This in the original sentence is an unclear (general) pronoun reference. General references can be corrected by creating a noun clause, as in the revised sentence. For more on **clear pronoun references,** see page 193.

DIFFERENTIATING INSTRUCTION

English-Language Learners

Cantonese. Cantonese sentences are sometimes patterned in ways that allow an adverb clause to act as a coordinating rather than a subordinating element: ***Although she*** *looked for her book,* ***but she*** *could not find it.*

Show students that complex sentences that begin with a subordinating conjunction, or connecting word, do not also have *and* or *but* between the clauses.

Vietnamese. In Vietnamese, an introductory clause may be followed by a "balancing" word in the main clause: ***Because*** *she studies hard,* ***therefore*** *she makes good grades.*

Some Vietnamese speakers may omit the subordinating word and use just the balancing word. Others may use *also* as a balancing word with a range of uses: *Even if I knew her well, I would* ***also*** *not call her house after 10:00 P.M.*

Show students that they usually need only one subordinating conjunction, or connecting word, to form a complex sentence. Have them identify connecting words in sample sentences, and check their writing for correct usage.

TEACHING TIP

Punctuation with Clauses. To help students write and punctuate sentences that contain adjective, adverb, and noun clauses, such as those in **Exercise 5,** review the related grammar and mechanics rules in small groups. Then, ask each group to write several original sentences using each clause type. You might want to be available for help as students write.

RETEACHING

Combining Sentences

Activity. Provide students with excerpts of at least five sentences from children's nonfiction books or magazines. (These excerpts should contain sentences that are repetitive and choppy.) Then, ask students to work in pairs or groups to rewrite the sentences using the combining techniques they have learned in this chapter. Suggest that students use each of the combining techniques at least once. If all your students revise the same excerpt, ask volunteers to read aloud their revised versions, and draw attention to the fact that many different versions are possible.

Exercise 5 Combining Simple Sentences to Create Complex Sentences

Possible combinations are shown below.

Following are five sets of short, choppy sentences that need revision. Use subordinate clauses to combine each set of sentences into a single complex sentence. You may see different ways to combine some of the sets; choose the way that seems best to you. You may need to change or delete some words to make smooth combinations.

EXAMPLE
1. My sister is fascinated by sharks. My sister is studying biology.
   1. *My sister, who is studying biology, is fascinated by sharks.*

1. My sister first saw a shark on a family vacation. We took ~~the vacation~~ five years ago. **1.** that
2. The sharks scared me. They intrigued her. **2.** Even though
3. My sister took me to a large outdoor aquarium. ~~It~~ had sharks on display. **3.** that
4. She told me a lot about the sharks. ~~The sharks~~ were swimming in circles in the aquarium. **4.** , which
5. The shark is a member of ~~a~~ fish family. ~~The family~~ includes the largest and fiercest fish. **5.** the / that
6. Most sharks have long bodies, wedge-shaped heads, and pointed back fins. ~~The back fins~~ sometimes stick out of the water. **6.** that
7. Sharks live mostly in warm seas. Some sharks have been found in bodies of cold water. **3.** Although
8. The whale shark is harmless to people. ~~It feeds on plankton.~~ **4.** , which feeds on plankton,
9. The whale sharks eat plankton. They strain ~~the plankton~~ out of the water. **9.** , which
10. However, many sharks are ruthless killers. ~~They~~ feed on flesh. **5.** that

Review A Revising a Paragraph by Combining Sentences

Using all of the sentence-combining techniques you have learned, revise and rewrite the following short paragraph. Use your judgment about what sentences to combine and how to combine them. Work for clear, varied sentences that read smoothly; however, do not change the meaning of the original paragraph. Here is a possible revision.

EXAMPLE Audrey visited England last April. She sent us a postcard.

When Audrey visited England last April, she sent us a postcard.

Stonehenge is in southwestern England. ~~It is a series of stones. They are huge stones. They~~ weigh as much as fifty tons each. ~~Stonehenge~~ was built about five thousand years ago. The stones were moved to their present site. ~~They were moved~~ by as many as one thousand people. There are many theories about the purpose of the stones. One popular theory is that the stones served as an observatory. ~~The observatory was astrological.~~ At one point in the summer, the sun rises over one of the stones. ~~It rises directly over that stone.~~

a series of huge stones

that

It

, and

astrological

directly

Improving Sentence Style

In the first part of this chapter, you learned some techniques for making smooth sentence combinations. Now you will learn how to style your sentences by making them clear, balanced, and varied.

Using Parallel Structure

When you combine several related ideas in one sentence, it is important to make sure that your combinations are balanced. You create balance in a sentence by using the same form or part of speech to express each idea. For example, you balance a noun with a noun, a phrase with a phrase, and a clause with a clause. This balance is called parallelism, or ***parallel structure.***

NOT PARALLEL I am not much of an athlete, but I like softball, soccer, and playing hockey. [two nouns and a phrase]

PARALLEL I am not much of an athlete, but I like **softball, soccer,** and **hockey.** [three nouns]

RESOURCES

Improving Sentence Style

Practice

- *Language & Sentence Skills Practice,* pp. 439–448

Differentiating Instruction

- *Developmental Language & Sentence Skills,* pp. 169–176

Improving Sentence Style
(pp. 461–470)

OBJECTIVES

- To revise sentences to create parallel structure
- To revise stringy and wordy sentences
- To vary sentence beginnings

SENTENCES

DIRECT TEACHING

Modeling and Demonstration

Using Parallel Structure. Model how to identify and correct problems with parallel structure by using the following sentences:

I like softball.
I like soccer.
I like to play hockey.
I like softball, soccer, and to play hockey.

Ask students how the last sentence was formed. [*The writer combined the sentences to eliminate repetition of the subject.*] Ask students what the word *softball* is. [*noun*] Ask students what the word *soccer* is. [*noun*] Ask students what the words *to play hockey* are. [*phrase*] Point out to students that nonparallel structures often occur when writers combine sentences. Ask students how the sentences could be combined so that all the direct objects of the verb *like* are nouns. [*I like softball, soccer, and hockey.*] Ask students if they can think of another way to combine these sentences using a parallel structure. [*I like to play softball, soccer, and hockey.*]

DIFFERENTIATING INSTRUCTION

Learners Having Difficulty

Some students may find it easier to identify a sentence that needs revision if they can hear the sentence as they read it. Ask volunteers to read aloud the examples of nonparallel structure on pp. 461–462. Have students discuss the differences between the two versions of the sentences. You may also want to use this strategy later as students revise stringy sentences.

NOT PARALLEL Dominic does not have enough time to play soccer, join the debating team, and band. [two phrases and a noun]

PARALLEL Dominic does not have enough time **to play soccer, to join the debating team,** and **to participate in band.** [three phrases]

NOT PARALLEL He said that he would meet you at the soccer field and not to be late. [clause and phrase]

PARALLEL He said **that he would meet you at the soccer field** and **that you should not be late.** [two clauses]

Exercise 6 Revising Sentences to Create Parallel Structure

Bring balance to the following sentences by putting the ideas in parallel form. You may need to add or delete some words. If a sentence is already correct, write *C*. Here are possible answers.

EXAMPLE 1. My favorite subjects are art, taking Spanish, and geography.

1. *My favorite subjects are art, Spanish, and geography.*

1. I find geography most interesting; I like to study faraway locations and ~~learning~~ about famous cities. 1. to learn
2. Do you believe that reading about a beautiful place is almost as good as ~~to visit~~ it? 2. visiting
3. My favorite sources of information are *National Geographic* magazine, encyclopedias, and ~~on~~ the Internet.
4. I'm working on a presentation on European capitals for my social studies class and a report about Parisian culture for my French class. 4. C
5. For my report, I included photos of famous Paris monuments such as the Eiffel Tower, the Arc de Triomphe, and ~~showing~~ the Louvre.
6. Paris, the capital of France, is famous for its history, culture, and ~~eating in~~ excellent restaurants.
7. The Seine River runs through the city and supplies water to all Parisians. 7. C
8. Visiting the Notre Dame Cathedral, walking through the Louvre Museum, and the Eiffel Tower are all favorite pastimes of tourists. 8. seeing
9. It is interesting that Paris has always attracted artists and refugees ~~have always been welcome.~~ 9. welcomed
10. Many famous Americans, including Ernest Hemingway, lived and ~~were writing~~ in Paris during the 1920s. 10. wrote

Revising Stringy Sentences

Linking together related ideas is a good way to bring variety to your writing. If you overdo it, however, you may end up with a *stringy sentence.*

A ***stringy sentence*** just goes on and on. It usually has too many independent clauses strung together with coordinating conjunctions like *and* or *but.* Since all the ideas are treated equally, your reader may have trouble seeing how they are related.

There are three ways you can fix a stringy sentence. You can

- break the sentence into two or more sentences
- turn some of the independent clauses into subordinate clauses or phrases
- use a combination of the above strategies

STRINGY The fire alarm bell rang, and everyone started to file out of school, but then our principal came down the hall, and he said the bell had been rung by mistake, and we went back to class.

BETTER The fire alarm bell rang, and everyone started to file out of school. Then our principal came down the hall to say the bell had been rung by mistake. We went back to class.

BETTER When the fire alarm bell rang, everyone started to file out of school. Then our principal came down the hall. He said the bell had been rung by mistake, and we went back to class.

Exercise 7 Revising Stringy Sentences

Decide which of the following sentences are stringy and need revision. Then, revise the stringy sentences by (1) breaking each sentence into two or more sentences, (2) turning some independent clauses into subordinate clauses, or (3) turning some independent clauses into phrases. If you find a sentence that is effective and does not need to be improved, write *C.* Possible revisions are shown below.

EXAMPLE 1. Alexandre Gustave Eiffel was a French engineer, and he designed the Eiffel Tower, and he designed the frame for the Statue of Liberty, but his greatest accomplishment may have been proving that metal was an important building material.

1. *Alexandre Gustave Eiffel was a French engineer who designed the Eiffel Tower and the frame for the Statue of Liberty. His greatest accomplishment may have been proving that metal was an important building material.*

MEETING THE CHALLENGE

Journalists, especially if they write for newspapers, develop a style that uses mostly short sentences. Cut a short article out of a newspaper, read it, and then rewrite the article, using stringy sentences. Next, revise the sentences once again, using a blend of sentence structures. Compare the three articles now. Which is easiest to read? Which has the most impact? Which version do you prefer?

ANSWER
Revisions will vary.

DIFFERENTIATING INSTRUCTION

Learners Having Difficulty

Many students can eliminate stringy sentences in a focused exercise, yet stringy sentences reappear in their own writing. Some students may benefit from the following strategy for identifying stringy sentences in their own work: Starting at the beginning of a piece of writing, students should highlight the text until they come to the end of an independent clause, whether there is punctuation at that point or not. Then, they should highlight the next clause in a different color. After all the clauses have been highlighted, students can examine the text to see how the clauses are connected, looking especially for three or more clauses connected by *and.*

1. Alexandre Gustave Eiffel was a famous Frenchman, and he was born in 1832, and he died in 1923. 1. who
2. Eiffel graduated from the College of Art and Manufacturing, and then he worked with a Belgian company, and then he founded his own company.
3. Eiffel was an engineer, and he designed the Eiffel Tower, and it was built for the World's Fair of 1889.
4. In 1889, the French government planned the World's Fair, and the World's Fair celebrated the hundred-year anniversary of the French Revolution. 4. which
5. The Centennial Committee held a contest for the design of an appropriate monument, and over one hundred plans were submitted, but the committee chose Eiffel's plan.
6. After the Eiffel Tower was built, it served as the entryway to the fair. 6. C
7. Eiffel specialized in bridges, and he designed an arching bridge, and it was the highest bridge in the world for many years. 7. that
8. Eiffel's chief interest was bridges, and the Eiffel Tower displays his bridge-designing skills, and so does another historical monument, and it is a monument that you know.
9. In 1885, Eiffel used his engineering knowledge to design part of a great American symbol, the Statue of Liberty in New York Harbor. 9. C

464 Writing Effective Sentences

10. Toward the end of his life, Eiffel studied the effects of air on airplanes; ~~and then~~ In 1912, he built a wind tunnel and an aerodynamics laboratory; ~~and~~ Later he conducted experiments from the Eiffel Tower, which is now a favorite tourist attraction.

Revising Wordy Sentences

If someone says, "It would please me greatly if you would diminish the volume of your verbalizing during the time I am perusing this reading material," you might wonder what language is being spoken. How much easier and clearer it is to say "Please be quieter while I am reading."

Here are three tips for creating sentences that are not too wordy.

- *Do not use more words than you need.*
- *Do not use fancy words where simple ones will do.*
- *Do not repeat yourself unless it is absolutely necessary.*

WORDY It is with deepest sorrow and regret that I come to you to beg your forgiveness for my thoughtlessness.
IMPROVED I am really sorry, and I want to apologize for my thoughtlessness.

WORDY In the event that we are unable to go to the movie, we can play basketball at Alicia's house.
IMPROVED If we cannot go to the movie, we can play basketball at Alicia's house.

WORDY My friend Ken is a talented drummer who plays the drums with great skill.
IMPROVED My friend Ken is a talented drummer.

Exercise 8 Revising wordy Sentences

The writer of the following letter wants to make a complaint, but the wordiness of the letter gets in the way. Revise the letter, making it clearer and more effective. Replace fancy words with simple ones, and eliminate unneccessary repetition. You may add details if you wish.

EXAMPLE 1. I was so upset at the horrendous occurrences that occurred on the day in question that was yesterday that I felt it was my only option to write a letter to the child's parents.

1. *I was so upset at the horrendous occurrences yesterday that I had to write a letter to Charles's parents.*

Direct Teaching

Revising Wordy Sentences

Activity. Explain to students that gerunds and infinitives can be used to reduce the wordiness in sentences, thereby creating clarity and conciseness in writing. Put the following pairs of sentences on the chalkboard and work with students to reduce clauses to gerunds or to infinitives and to combine sentences.

1. John bought a boat because he wanted to surprise his wife. [John bought a boat to surprise his wife.]
2. That she called her mother was important. [Calling her mother was important.]

Application

Revising Sentences

Activity. Have students form groups of three. Then, provide them with a picture, a piece of art, or a scene on videotape. Ask one member of the group to be the primary viewer of the picture, art, or scene, and to watch it carefully once or twice. Without looking any further, the viewer should tell the others in the group exactly what he or she saw. One group member should act as a scribe and write down exactly what the viewer says. The viewer may use many short, repetitive sentences or longer stringy or wordy ones in the description. Ask the trio to work together to revise the sentences in the description by using the strategies in this chapter. The third student is responsible for checking that all the strategies are used and for reading the revised description aloud.

Exercise 8 Revising Wordy Sentences

ANSWER
Here is a possible revision.

Dear Mr. and Mrs. Wilson,

I am sorry to tell you that I won't be able to baby-sit Charles anymore. You hired me to baby-sit him on July 13, and I did the best job I could; however, Charles behaved very badly. He threw things at me and locked me in a closet. Because he posed a danger to me, I won't baby-sit him again.

Sincerely,

Miguel Garza

EXTENSION

Critical Thinking

Synthesis. To help students be more alert to wordiness in their writing, have them create wordy sentences from short sayings or proverbs. Provide students with a book of famous quotations and a thesaurus and ask them to choose a saying or proverb and transform it into a wordy sentence. You may make this activity into a contest by posting the wordy versions and having students guess at the original proverbs. Here is an example:

Currency is many things but it is first and foremost and above all things the radical of all terrible grievances. [*Money is the root of all evil.*]

Dear Mr. and Mrs. Wilson,

At this point in time, it is my unhappy duty to inform you of the fact that I will no longer be available to baby-sit Charles. On the evening of July 13, I was hired by you to perform the duties of baby sitter for your three-year-old son. These duties were performed by me to the best of my ability. However, I do not feel that any baby sitter should be in a position of having to deal with the threat of harm to the baby sitter's person. I feel that Charles's hurling of objects at my person and his action of locking me in the closet were threats to my safety. The situation being what it is, I feel I cannot safely perform my duties, and I will no longer place myself in danger by sitting with your son.

Sincerely,

Miguel Garza

Beyond Sentence Style

Previously in this chapter, you learned how to combine sentences smoothly and how to make sentences clear, balanced, and varied. Now you will learn how sentences work together in the larger structure of the paragraph.

Varying Sentence Beginnings

Basic English sentences begin with a subject followed by a verb. However, beginning every sentence with a subject makes your writing dull. Notice how boring the following paragraph sounds.

The theater was packed. Jan and I managed to find our seats. The play began thirty minutes late. We were bored. We read the program four times. Jan wanted to find out the reason for the delay. She asked an usher. The usher was amused. The usher said that the star's costume had been damaged by her dog. We laughed because the play was *Cats*.

CONTENT-AREA CONNECTIONS

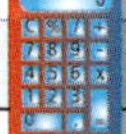

Physical Education

Varying Strategies in Sports. Students may benefit from a comparison of the strategy of varying sentence beginnings to strategies players use in different sports in laying up shots, scoring goals, or throwing pitches. Ask them to consider why a football player changes runs for the goal, why a basketball player uses different approaches to the net, or why a pitcher varies pitches. Students will probably comment on how the different strategies keep the opponents

Now, notice how much more interesting the same paragraph sounds with varied sentence beginnings. To create the varied beginnings, the writer has combined sentences. Some sentences became words, some became phrases, and others became subordinate clauses.

> Although the theater was packed, Jan and I managed to find our seats. The play began thirty minutes late. Bored, we read the program four times. To find out the reason for the delay, Jan asked an usher. Amused, the usher said that the star's costume had been damaged by her dog. We laughed because the play was Cats.

Varying Sentence Beginnings

Single-Word Modifiers
Excitedly, Marcia opened her presents. [adverb]
Hungry, the family stopped at the restaurant. [adjective]
Swaying, the couple danced to the music. [adjective]
Phrases
With tears of joy, Carla received her prize. [prepositional phrase]
Smiling happily, Tanya told us the good news. [participial phrase]
To make good grades, you must study. [infinitive phrase]
A fine teacher, Mr. Ramos is also a master gardener. [appositive phrase]
Subordinate Clauses
Because the coach was angry, the team had to run ten laps. [adverb clause]
When Tom found the kitten on his doorstep, he decided to keep it. [adverb clause]

NOTE If you use a prepositional phrase telling *when, where,* or *how* to vary your sentence beginnings, you can sometimes put the verb of the sentence before the subject. In the following example sentence, the subject is underlined once, the verb twice.

EXAMPLE Down the street rumbled an old cart.

TIPS & TRICKS

To check your writing for varied sentence beginnings, put parentheses around the first five words of each of your sentences. If most of your subjects and verbs fall within the parentheses, you need to begin more of your sentences with single-word modifiers, phrases, or subordinate clauses.

SENTENCES

DIFFERENTIATING INSTRUCTION

Advanced Learners

Encourage students who are avid readers to write a five- or six-sentence paragraph about any topic in the style of their favorite author. Then, have them display their text next to an excerpt from a work by the author. Ask students to write a brief statement about the author's style (students should consider how the author used any of the strategies mentioned in this chapter, such as parallel structure and varied sentence beginnings) and any problems they encountered in mimicking the author's style.

guessing or how they are a response to the situation as the player sees it. Guide students to see how the same comments apply to writing sentences with varied beginnings.

If possible, use videotaped examples of different sports strategies, which your school coaches should be able to provide.

Beyond Sentence Style 467

Exercise 9 **Varying Sentence Beginnings**

ANSWERS

Here are some possible answers.

1. In many different parts of the world, animals are in danger of extinction.
2. A small animal, the aye-aye is related to the monkey, and it is one of the less well-known of the endangered animals.
3. Because the rain forest on its home island is being destroyed, the aye-aye is endangered.
4. To see the desman, a water-dwelling mammal, you must travel to the Pyrenees, Portugal, or the former Soviet Union.
5. By damming mountain streams, people are threatening the desmans' survival.
6. Although the giant otter of South America is protected, poachers continue to threaten its survival.
7. Cautious, mountain lions generally stay away from humans, who hunt them relentlessly.
8. Because its home is being damaged by acid rain, the great peacock moth of Europe is in trouble.
9. Expert hunters, wolves prey on large animals.
10. Sadly, gray wolves are an endangered species.

Exercise 9

DISTRIBUTED REVIEW

Ask students to use the facts in the ten sentences of **Exercise 9** to write a paragraph about endangered animals. They do not need to use all the sentences, but they should organize the ones they do use into an interesting paragraph, varying sentence beginnings.

Exercise 9 Varying Sentence Beginnings

The following sentences are all good, but they would make a boring paragraph. Here is your chance to practice varying sentence beginnings. The notes in parentheses tell you whether to start your revised sentence with a single-word modifier, a phrase, or a clause. In some cases, you may also want to add or delete a word to make the sentence sound better.

EXAMPLE 1. We are learning many interesting facts in our biology class. (phrase)

1. *In our biology class, we are learning many interesting facts.*

1. Animals are in danger of extinction in many different parts of the world. (phrase)
2. The aye-aye is a small animal related to the monkey, and it is one of the less well-known of the endangered animals. (phrase)
3. The aye-aye is endangered because the rain forest on its home island is being destroyed. (subordinate clause)
4. You must travel to the Pyrenees, Portugal, or the former Soviet Union to see the desman, a water-dwelling mammal. (phrase)
5. People are threatening the desman's survival by damming mountain streams. (phrase)
6. The giant otter of South America is protected, but poachers continue to threaten its survival. (subordinate clause)
7. Mountain lions are cautious and generally stay away from humans, who hunt them relentlessly. (single-word modifier)
8. The great peacock moth of Europe is in trouble because its home is being damaged by acid rain. (subordinate clause)
9. Wolves are expert hunters, and they prey on large animals. (phrase)
10. Gray wolves, sadly, are an endangered species. (single-word modifier)

Exercise 10 Revising Sentences to Create Variety

Use what you have learned about varying sentence beginnings to revise the following paragraph. Reword some sentences so that they begin with single-word modifiers, phrases, or clauses. Some sentences may be reworded in several ways; choose the way that seems best to you. (Consult the chart on page 467 for help.)

EXAMPLE 1. Some find it disturbing that land animals aren't the only creatures at risk of extinction.

1. *Disturbingly, land animals aren't the only creatures at risk of extinction.*

Ocean animals unfortunately are often on endangered-species lists. Penguins are at risk in oceans of the Southern Hemisphere. Many penguin species have problems today because of oil pollution and commercial fishing. Turtles are endangered because they are slaughtered for food and for their beautiful, highly prized shells. Lobsters become threatened when people overfish. Mediterranean monk seals also are threatened by increased land development and tourism.

Review B Revising a Paragraph

The following paragraphs have many of the problems you have reviewed in this section. Show your writing style by rewriting and revising the paragraphs (1) to correct nonparallel structures, (2) to correct stringy and wordy sentences, and (3) to vary sentence beginnings. You may add or delete details as necessary.

EXAMPLE 1. My family loves animals, the outdoors, and to go on picnics.

1. *My family loves animals, the outdoors, and picnics.*

One time in the recent past, we went on a picnic in Big Bend National Park in Texas. It had rained heavily all night north of the park. A friend of ours, Mrs. Brown, went with us. She had lived in that part of Texas for a large number of years. She knew all about what to expect if it rained. She told us that there could be a flash flood in the park and about how the park could be

Exercise 10 Revising Sentences to Create Variety

ANSWER
Here is a possible revision.

Unfortunately, ocean animals are often on endangered-species lists. Because of oil pollution and commercial fishing, many penguin species in oceans of the Southern Hemisphere are at risk. Turtles are endangered because they are slaughtered for food and for their beautiful, highly prized shells. When people overfish, lobsters become threatened. Also, Mediterranean monk seals are threatened by increased land development and tourism.

Review B Revising a Paragraph

ANSWER
Here is a possible revision.

Recently, we went on a picnic in Big Bend National Park in Texas with our friend, Mrs. Brown. North of the park, it had rained heavily all night. Having lived in that part of Texas for years, Mrs. Brown knew what to expect. She said that even if it didn't rain in the park, there could be a flash flood because the water could run across the dry desert sand.

She made us turn our cars around so we could leave the low area quickly if a flood came. The sun was shining brightly, and everyone thought Mrs. Brown was crazy, but as we started to eat, suddenly a wall of water four feet high came toward us. We jumped into the cars and got away just in time. We were glad to be alive, and we thanked Mrs. Brown.

dangerous even if it did not rain there because the water could run across the dry desert sand.

Mrs. Brown made us turn our cars around to face in the other direction because she wanted us to be able to leave the low area quickly if a flood came. The sun was shining with great brightness, and everyone thought Mrs. Brown was crazy, and we started to eat our picnic.

A very high wall of water four feet high came toward us suddenly. We jumped into the cars and getting away just in time. We were glad to be alive, and we thanked Mrs. Brown.

Terms in brackets refer to concepts tested by the items in the Chapter Review.

1. [inserting phrases]
2. and [compound verbs]
3. After [complex sentences]
4. or six [inserting words]
5. [inserting phrases]
6. , but [compound sentences]
7. and her brother/ and [compound subjects and verbs]
8. French and Canadian [inserting words]
9. because [complex sentences]
10. Clapping and stomping, [inserting words]

11. heavy rain [wordy]
12. and [stringy]

Chapter Review

A. Combining Sentences

Combine the following sentences by inserting words or phrases, forming compound subjects or compound verbs, or forming compound or complex sentences. Possible revisions follow.

1. The tall woman over there is Mrs. Randolph, ~~She is~~ the editor of the newspaper.
2. Frank picked up the shovel and the rake. He put them away in the garden shed.
3. We saw the school play last night. We went over to Trisha's house.
4. I think she said the game was at five o'clock. ~~Maybe she said the game was at six.~~
5. Announcements are made at the end of the day. ~~Announcements are made~~ during the last class period.
6. In one of the offices, a telephone was ringing constantly. No one answered it.
7. Kathy heard the knock at the door. ~~Her brother heard the knock at the door. Kathy and her brother~~ ran downstairs to greet Aunt Marci.
8. The flags flapped wildly in the gusty wind. ~~The flags were French and Canadian.~~
9. I couldn't watch that program last night. I had to finish my math homework.
10. The crowd rose to its feet when the team scored. ~~The crowd was clapping and stomping.~~

B. Revising Stringy or Wordy Sentences

Revise the following stringy or wordy sentences. Some of the sentences may be both stringy and wordy. Possible revisions follow.

11. ~~The game, which was~~ the final game of the series, was postponed because of the ~~excessive downpour~~.
12. We took the subway, ~~and then we got off at our stop, and then we got on~~ a bus, ~~and we went~~ to the museum.

ASSESSING

Monitoring Progress

Chapter Review. To assess student progress, you may want to compare the types of items missed on the **Diagnostic Preview** to those missed on the **Chapter Review.** If students have not made significant progress, you may want to provide them with additional practice.

SENTENCES

RESOURCES

Writing Effective Sentences

Assessment

- *Holt Handbook Chapter Tests with Answer Key,* pp. 39–43, 52

13. Because/now [wordy]
14. probably/admire [wordy]
15. [wordy]
16. car/driving west [wordy]
17. [stringy]
18. had [stringy, wordy]
19. I think you would enjoy reading the book I just finished. [wordy]
20. author's/accurately [wordy]

13. Owing to the fact that no one in the class has finished the assignment to completion, we will have a pop quiz at this point in time.

14. The woman who is my great-grandmother is in all probability the person of whom I am the most admiring.

15. The reason they were late to school was because John had set his alarm clock to a time that was an hour later than he was supposed to have set it.

16. The passenger vehicle was proceeding in a westwardly direction.

17. First, Nora borrowed my book, and then Nathan wanted to look at my notes, and then Naomi needed to use my pen, and by the time I got to class, my backpack was almost empty.

18. I knew I would have to study for the test when I got home, so I didn't answer the phone because I didn't want to be disturbed, but my father called because he wanted to let me know that he was going to be late, but I missed the call.

19. The book, which I just finished reading, has many characteristics that could cause me to recommend it to you as a book you should schedule some time to read in the future.

20. The style of the writing of the author of the book is difficult to describe with any degree of accuracy.

C. Revising a Paragraph to Improve Sentence Style

Revise the following paragraph, combining choppy sentences, correcting unparallel structures, improving wordy or stringy sentences, and using a variety of sentence beginnings to improve the style of the writing. Possible revisions follow.

Neither of/likes/but Spike/them
ing

Getting
putting
is no easy task
ing
and splashing water

No one in my family enjoys giving our two dogs baths. Our dogs do not like baths. One of the dogs really hates baths. His name is Spike. Spike somehow seems to know when we want to give him a bath. Spike runs away and hides under the bed when we fill up the tub. It's no easy task to get that dog out from under the bed, put him in the tub, and keeping him there. Ike, our other dog, handles baths differently. He knocks over the tub. Water splashes everywhere. Water pools on the floor, and drips from the walls. Water thoroughly soaks whoever is giving the dogs a bath. Then, Ike leaps away from the tub and tears through the house. He speeds from room to room, and then he jumps onto the couch and shakes off all the water. We always have to clean the utility room after we bathe the dogs. We usually have to clean up the rest of the house, too. We spend hours mopping up the floors, wiping down the walls, and to wash all the towels. The last time we bathed the dogs, we reminded ourselves that using a professional dog-grooming service would be better than to exhaust the whole family.

and

leaping
tearing/Ike

After bathing the dogs,
and

washing
take us hours

exhausting

SENTENCES

CHAPTER

20

INTRODUCING THE CHAPTER

- Diagramming gives students the opportunity to use their spatial skills to help them analyze language. You may find diagrams especially useful in helping students understand sentence structure and relationships between parts of sentences.
- The system of diagramming used in this chapter is generally referred to as the Reed and Kellogg system; it was first presented by Alonzo Reed and Brainerd Kellogg in their book *Higher Lessons in English.*

CHAPTER

20 Sentence Diagramming

The Sentence Diagram

A ***sentence diagram*** is a picture of how the parts of a sentence fit together and how the words in a sentence are related.

Reference Note

For more about **subjects** and **verbs,** see page 42.

Subjects and Verbs

The sentence diagram begins with a horizontal line intersected by a short vertical line that divides the complete subject from the complete predicate.

EXAMPLE Fish swim.

Fish | swim

HELP

Notice that a sentence diagram shows the capitalization but not the punctuation of a sentence.

Reference Note

For information about **understood subjects,** see page 51.

Understood Subjects

EXAMPLE Wait!

(you) | Wait

Nouns of Direct Address

EXAMPLE Sit, **Fido.**

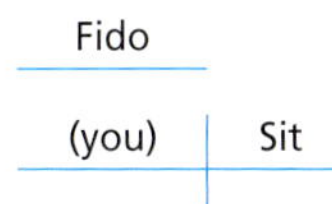

Sentences Beginning with *There*

EXAMPLE **There** is hope.

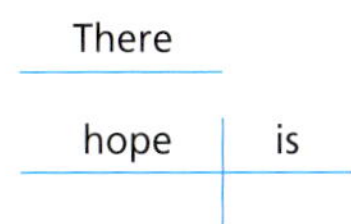

Compound Subjects

EXAMPLE **Carmen** and **Basil** were fishing.

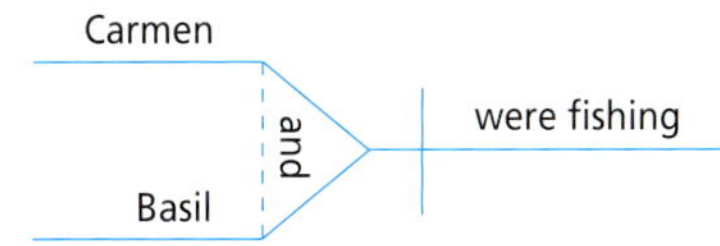

Compound Verbs

EXAMPLE They **stopped** and **ate.**

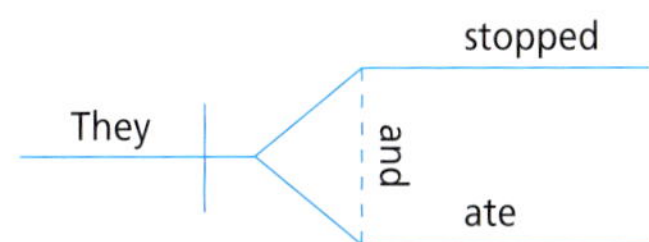

The following diagram shows how a compound verb is diagrammed when the helping verb is not repeated.

EXAMPLE They are **sitting** and **reading.**

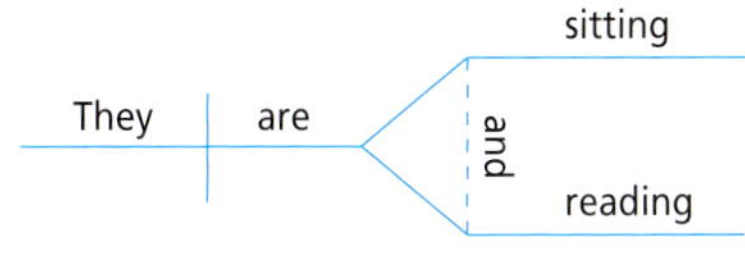

Reference Note

For information about **nouns of direct address,** see page 284.

Reference Note

For information about **sentences beginning with *there*,** see page 50.

Reference Note

For more about **compound subjects,** see page 52. For more about **compound verbs,** see page 53.

SENTENCES

The Sentence Diagram 475

Compound Subjects and Compound Verbs

EXAMPLE **Coaches** and **players jumped** and **cheered.**

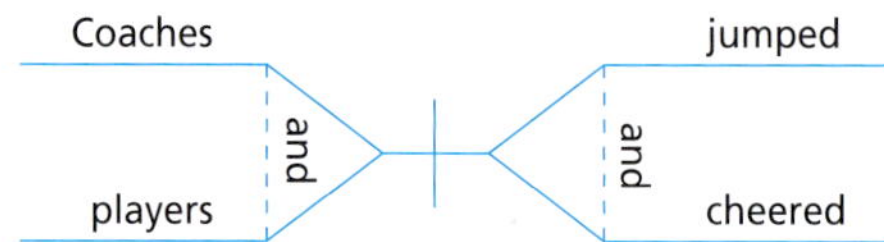

Sometimes the parts of a compound subject or a compound verb are joined by correlative conjunctions. Correlatives are diagrammed like this:

EXAMPLE **Both** Bob **and** Teri can **not only** draw **but also** paint.

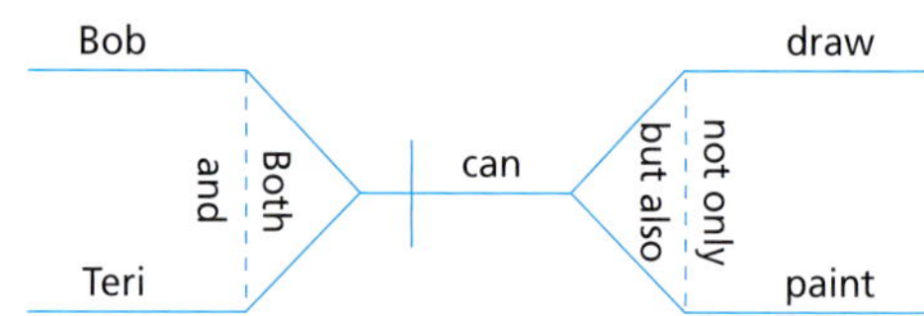

Adjectives and Adverbs

Reference Note

For more about **adjectives,** see page 10. For more about **adverbs,** see page 21.

Both adjectives and adverbs are written on slanted lines connected to the words they modify.

EXAMPLE **That old** clock has **never** worked.

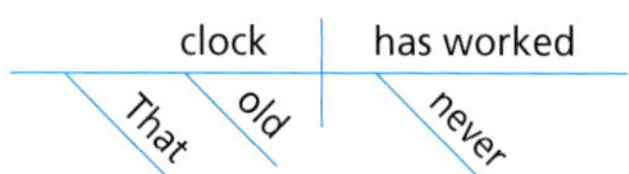

When an adverb modifies an adjective or an adverb, it is placed on a line connected to the word it modifies.

EXAMPLE This **very** beautiful glass **almost** never breaks.

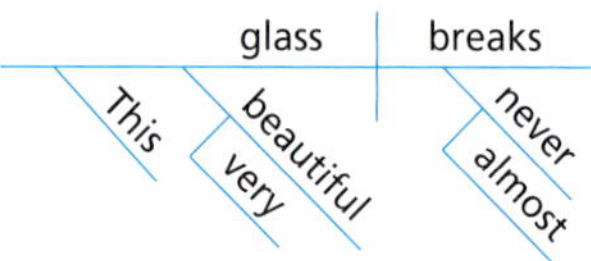

476 Sentence Diagramming

Notice the position of the modifiers in the following example:

EXAMPLE **Soon** Anne and **her** sister will graduate and will move.

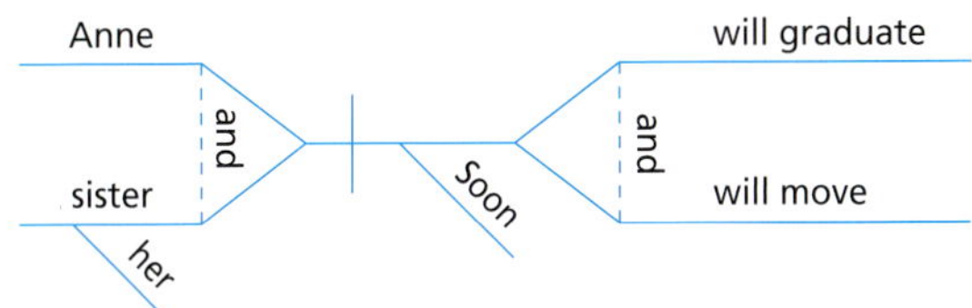

Above, *her* modifies only one part of the compound subject: *sister.* *Soon* modifies both parts of the compound verb: *will graduate* and *will move.*

When a conjunction joins two modifiers, it is diagrammed like this:

EXAMPLE The **English** and **Australian** athletes worked **long** and **very hard.**

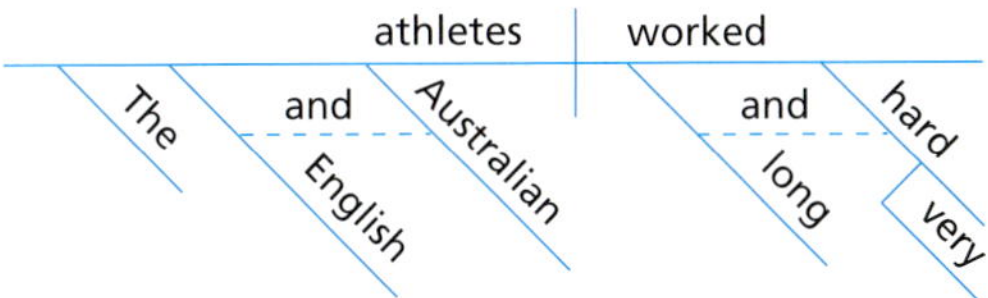

Subject Complements

The subject complement is placed on the horizontal line with the subject and verb. It comes after the verb. A slanted line separates the subject complement from the linking verb.

Predicate Nominatives

EXAMPLE Cathedrals are large **churches.**

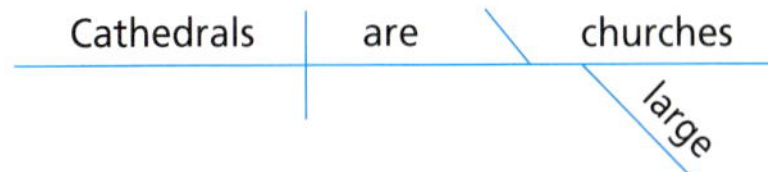

Reference Note

For more about **predicate nominatives,** see page 58.

SENTENCES

The Sentence Diagram 477

SENTENCES

Reference Note

For more about **predicate adjectives,** see page 58.

Predicate Adjectives

EXAMPLE Cathedrals are **large.**

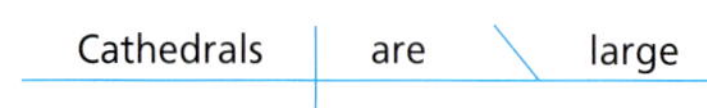

Compound Subject Complements

EXAMPLE My friend is **small** and **quiet.**

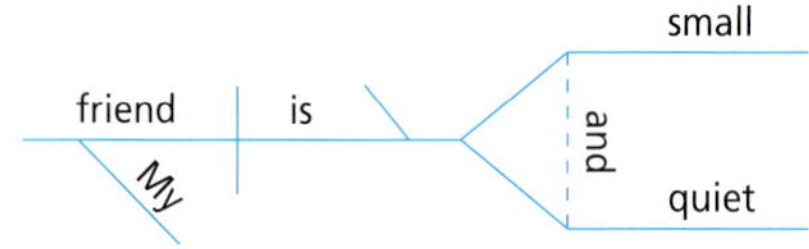

Objects

Reference Note

For more about **direct objects,** see page 59.

Direct Objects

A vertical line separates a direct object from the verb.

EXAMPLE We like **music.**

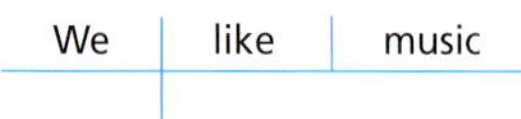

Compound Direct Objects

EXAMPLE We like **plays** and **movies.**

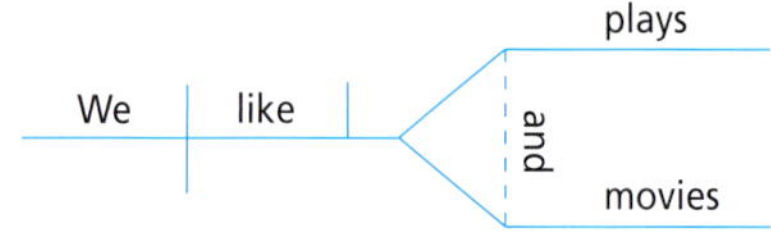

Reference Note

For more about **indirect objects,** see page 60.

Indirect Objects

The indirect object is diagrammed on a horizontal line beneath the verb.

478 Sentence Diagramming

EXAMPLE Pete bought **Mario** a sandwich.

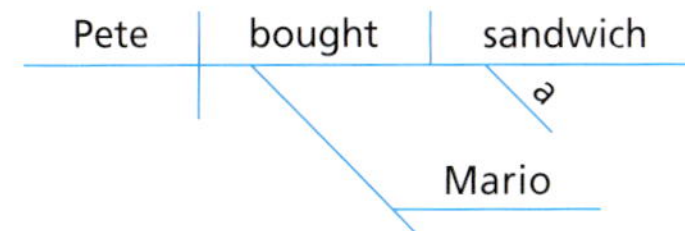

Compound Indirect Objects

EXAMPLE Latoya gave her **family** and **friends** free tickets.

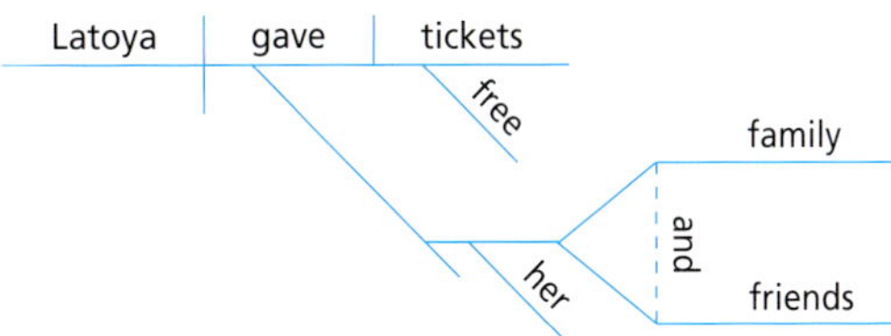

Phrases

Prepositional Phrases

The preposition is placed on a line slanting down from the word the phrase modifies. The object of the preposition is placed on a horizontal line connected to the slanting line.

Reference Note

For more information about **prepositional phrases,** see page 70.

EXAMPLES **By chance,** a peasant uncovered a wall **of ancient Pompeii.** [*By chance* is an adverb phrase modifying the verb; *of ancient Pompeii* is an adjective phrase modifying the direct object.]

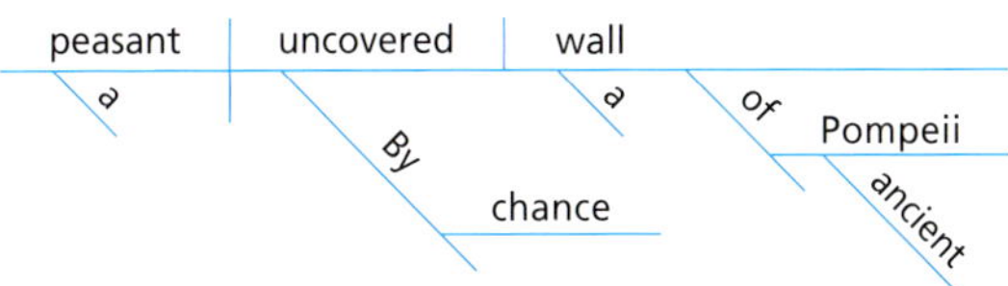

Our team practices late **in the afternoon.** [adverb phrase modifying an adverb]

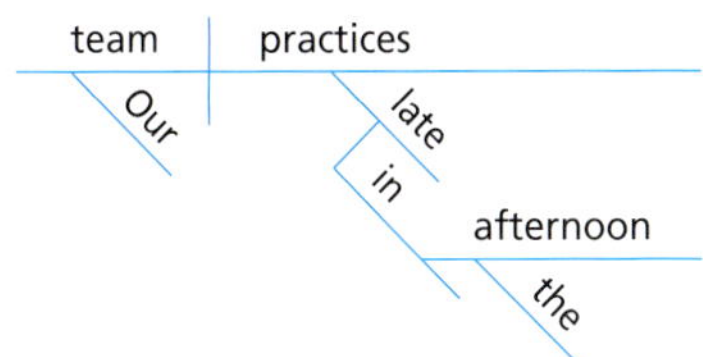

SENTENCES

The Sentence Diagram 479

They drove **through the Maine woods** and **into southern Canada.** [two phrases modifying the same word]

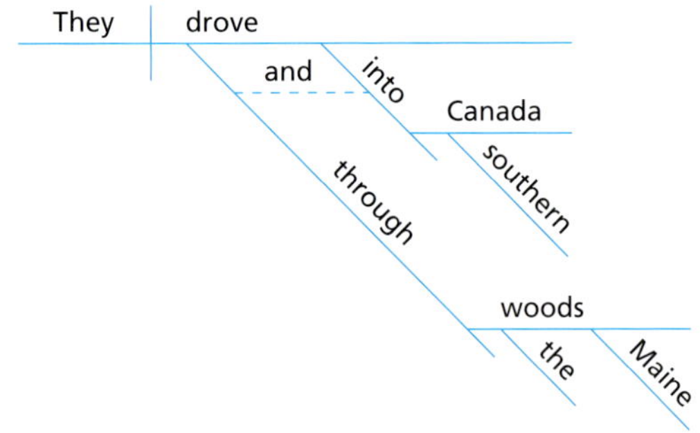

Mom taught the game **to my father, my uncles, and me.** [compound object of preposition]

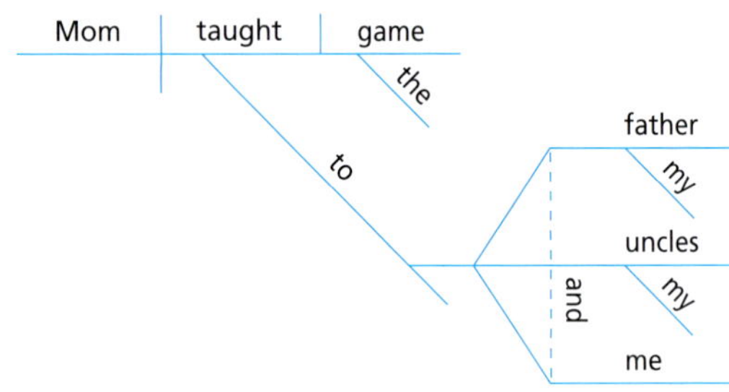

Follow the signs **to Highway 3 in Laconia.** [*In Laconia* is a prepositional phrase modifying the object of another preposition.]

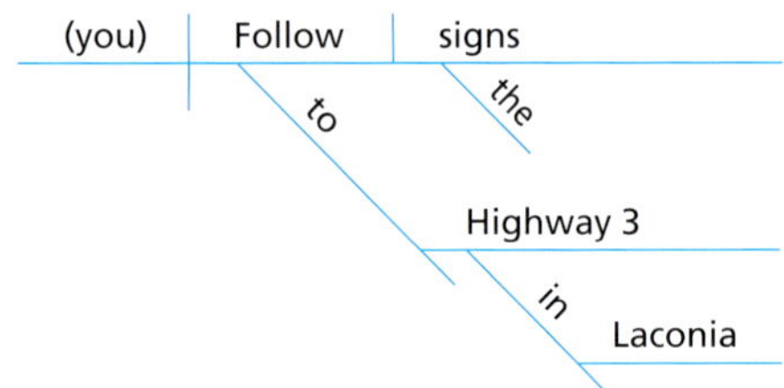

480 Sentence Diagramming

Participles and Participial Phrases

EXAMPLES I found him **crying.**

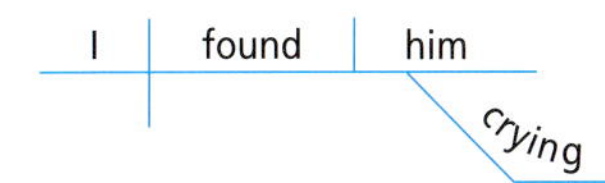

Wagging its tail, the large dog leaped at me.

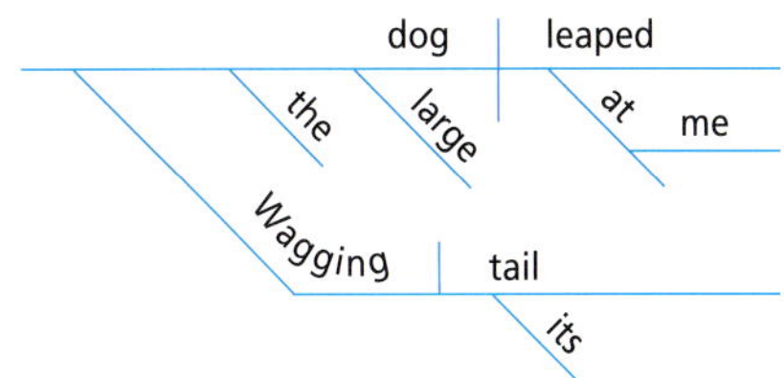

Notice that *tail*, the direct object of the participle *Wagging*, is diagrammed like any other complement.

> **Reference Note**
> For more information about **participles** and **participial phrases,** see page 77.

Gerunds and Gerund Phrases

EXAMPLES **Walking** is healthful exercise. [gerund used as subject]

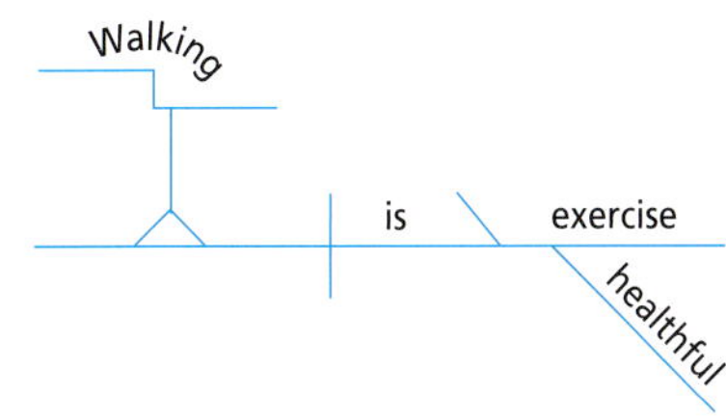

The constant cold is a good reason for **taking a vacation in the winter.** [gerund phrase used as the object of a preposition]

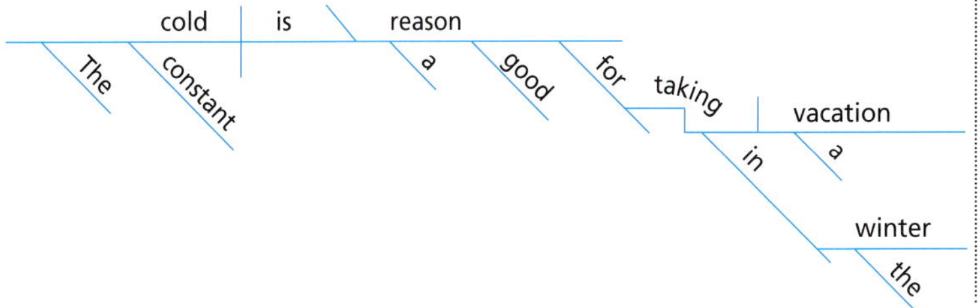

> **Reference Note**
> For more about **gerunds** and **gerund phrases,** see page 81.

The Sentence Diagram 481

SENTENCES

Reference Note

For more information about **infinitives** and **infinitive phrases,** see page 85.

Infinitives and Infinitive Phrases

EXAMPLES **To leave** would be rude. [infinitive used as subject]

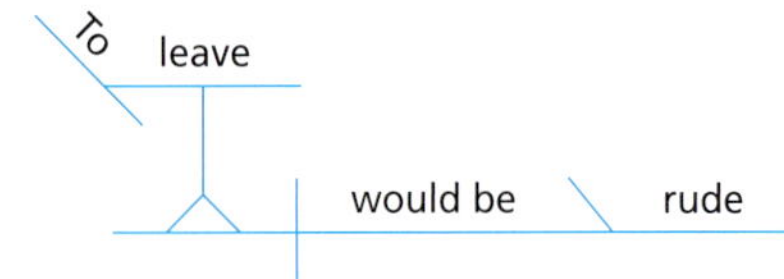

To join the Air Force is her longtime ambition. [infinitive phrase used as subject]

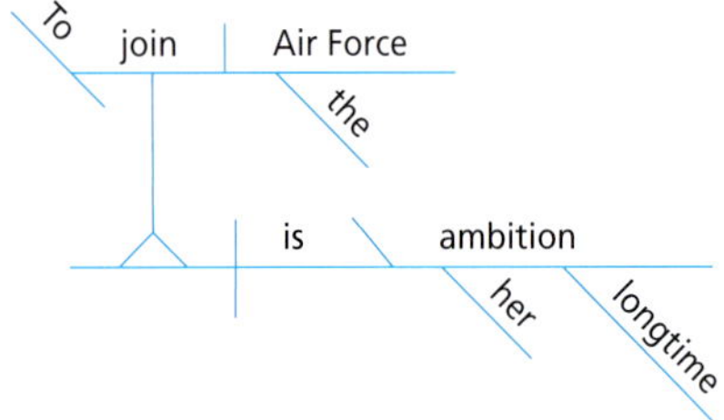

Infinitives and infinitive phrases used as modifiers are diagrammed much as prepositional phrases are.

EXAMPLES I am happy **to help.** [infinitive phrase used as adverb]

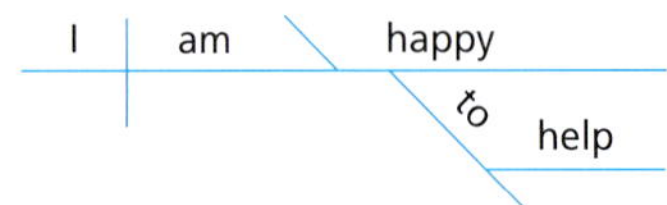

I am leaving early **to get the tickets.** [infinitive phrase used as adverb]

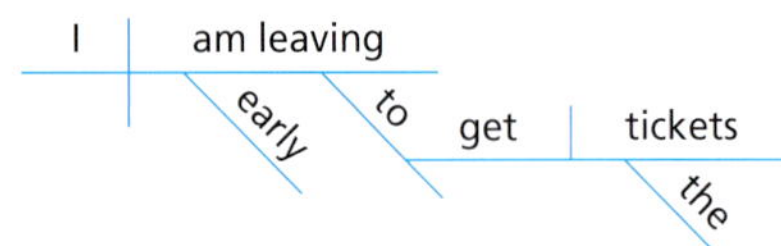

482 Sentence Diagramming

Appositives and Appositive Phrases

Place the appositive in parentheses after the word it identifies or explains.

EXAMPLES My brother **Josh** is a drummer in the band.

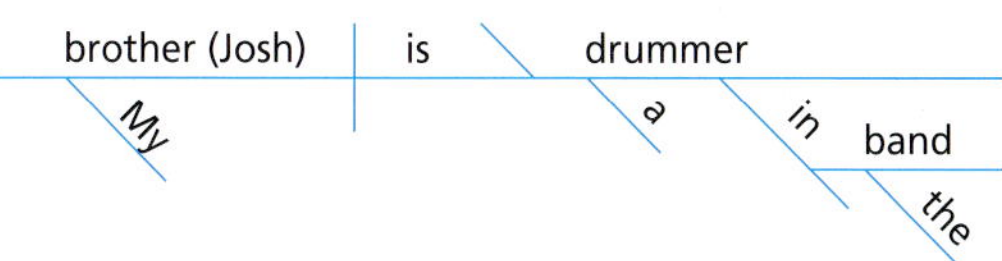

The next show, **a musical comedy,** was written by Mike Williams, **a talented young playwright.**

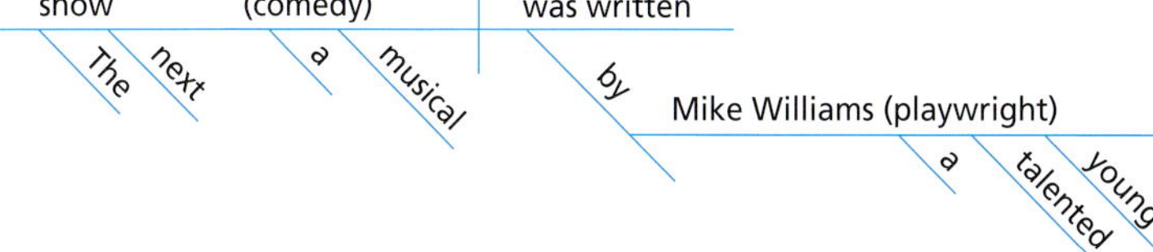

Reference Note

For more information about **appositives** and **appositive phrases,** see page 89.

Subordinate Clauses

Adjective Clauses

An adjective clause is joined to the word it modifies by a broken line leading from the relative pronoun to the modified word.

EXAMPLES The restaurant **that we like best** serves excellent seafood.

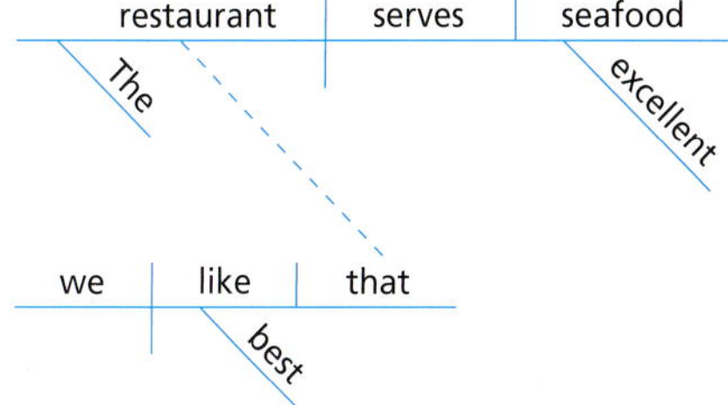

Reference Note

For more about **adjective clauses,** see page 101.

SENTENCES

The Sentence Diagram 483

SENTENCES

He is the teacher **from whom I take lessons.**

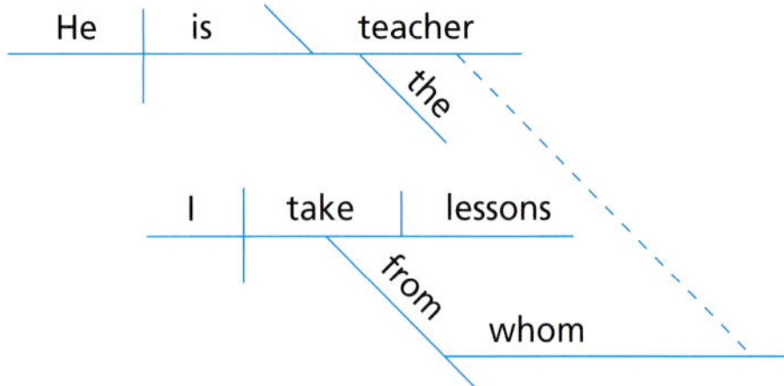

Reference Note

For more about **adverb clauses,** see page 104.

Adverb Clauses

Place the subordinating conjunction that introduces the adverb clause on a broken line leading from the verb in the adverb clause to the word the clause modifies.

EXAMPLE **If you visit Texas,** you should see the Alamo.

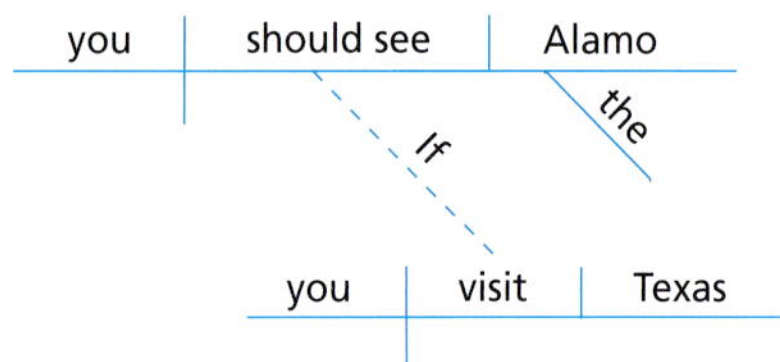

Reference Note

For more about **noun clauses,** see page 106.

Noun Clauses

Noun clauses often begin with introductory words such as *that, what, who,* or *which.* These introductory words may have a function within the subordinate clause, or they may simply connect the clause to the rest of the sentence. How a noun clause is diagrammed depends upon its use in the sentence. It also depends on whether or not the introductory word has a grammatical function in the noun clause.

EXAMPLES **What you eat** affects your health. [The noun clause is used as the subject of the independent clause. The introductory word *What* functions as a direct object in the noun clause.]

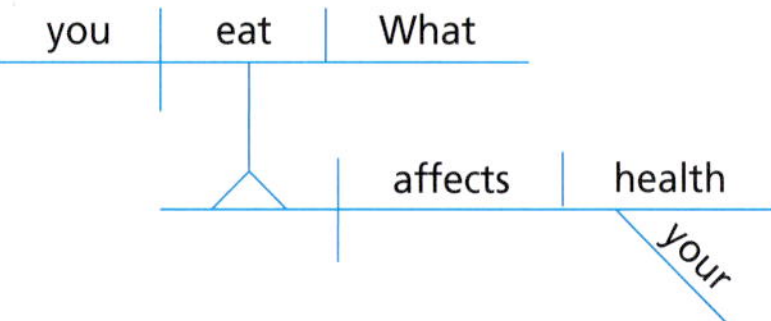

We strongly suspected **that the cat was the thief.** [The noun clause is the direct object of the independent clause. The introductory word *that* does not have a grammatical function within the noun clause.]

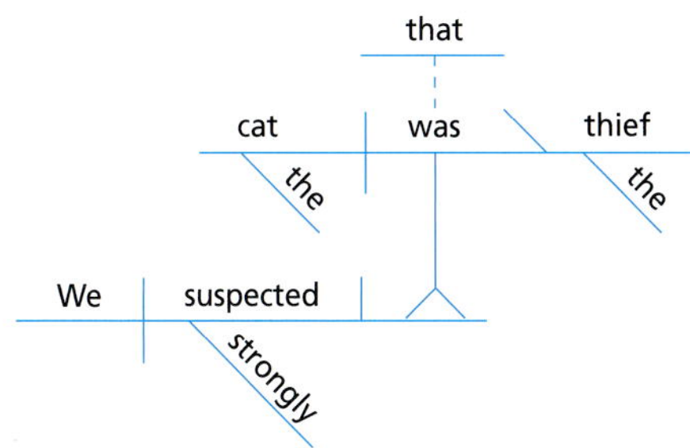

Sometimes the introductory word in a subordinate clause may be omitted. In the example above, the word *that* can be left out: *We strongly suspected the cat was the thief.* To diagram this new sentence, simply omit the word *that* and the solid and broken lines under it from the diagram above. The rest of the diagram stays the same.

Sentences Classified According to Structure

Simple Sentences

EXAMPLES George Vancouver was exploring the Northwest.

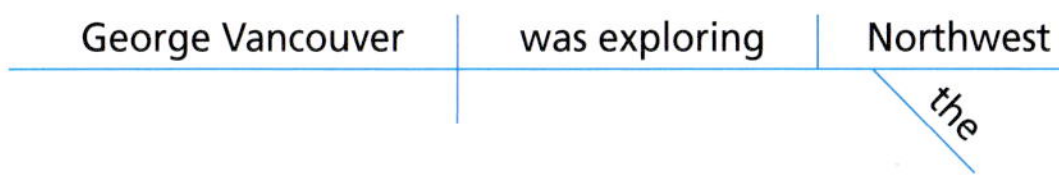

Cities in Washington and British Columbia are named for him.

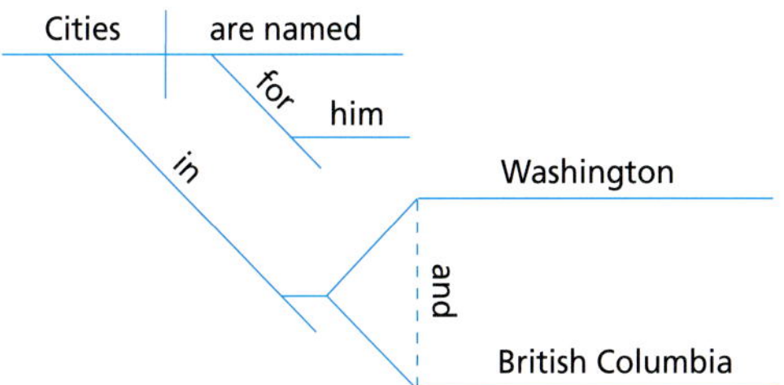

Reference Note

For more about **simple sentences,** see page 109.

SENTENCES

The Sentence Diagram 485

Reference Note

For more information about **compound sentences,** see page 109.

Compound Sentences

EXAMPLE James Baldwin wrote many essays, but he is probably more famous for his novels.

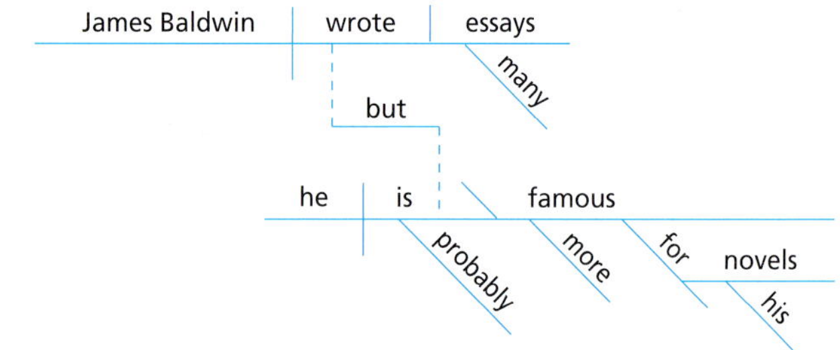

If the compound sentence has a semicolon and no conjunction, place a straight broken line between the two verbs.

EXAMPLE Baldwin was a distinguished essayist; his nonfiction works include *Notes of a Native Son.*

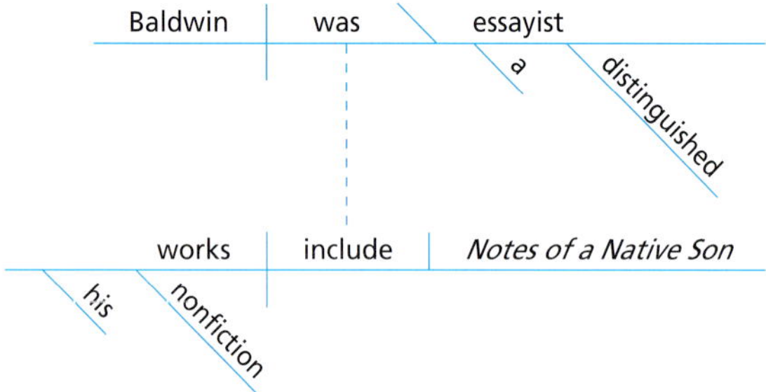

If the clauses of a compound sentence are joined by a semicolon and a conjunctive adverb, place the conjunctive adverb on a slanting line below the verb it modifies.

EXAMPLE Baldwin was born in New York; however, he lived in France for a while.

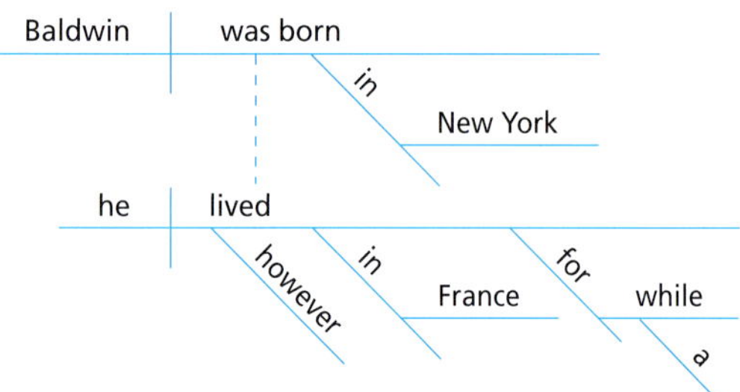

486 Sentence Diagramming

Complex Sentences

EXAMPLE Jaime Escalante always believed that his students could do well in math.

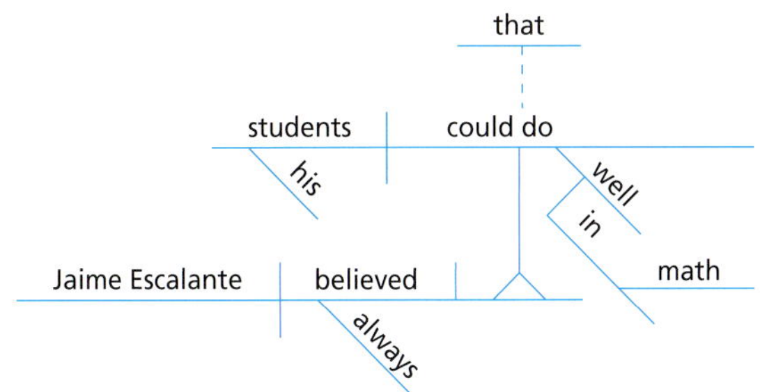

> **Reference Note**
> For more about **complex sentences,** see page 110.

Compound-Complex Sentences

EXAMPLE Before her plane mysteriously disappeared in 1937, Amelia Earhart had already forged the way for women in aviation, and she was later recognized for her achievements.

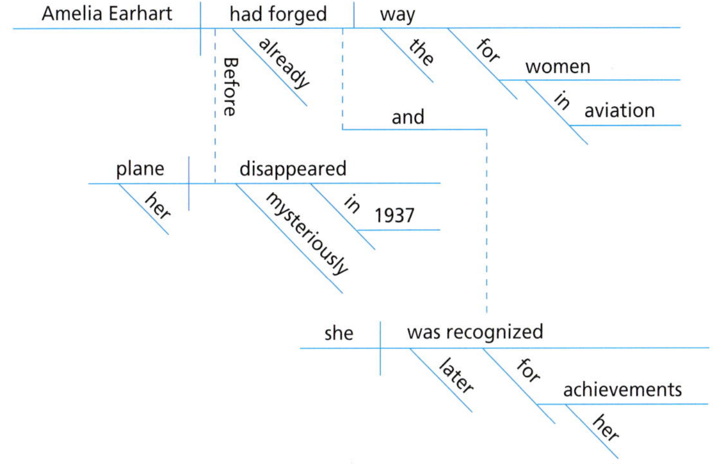

> **Reference Note**
> For more about **compound-complex sentences,** see page 110.

SENTENCES

The Sentence Diagram 487

PART 3 Resources

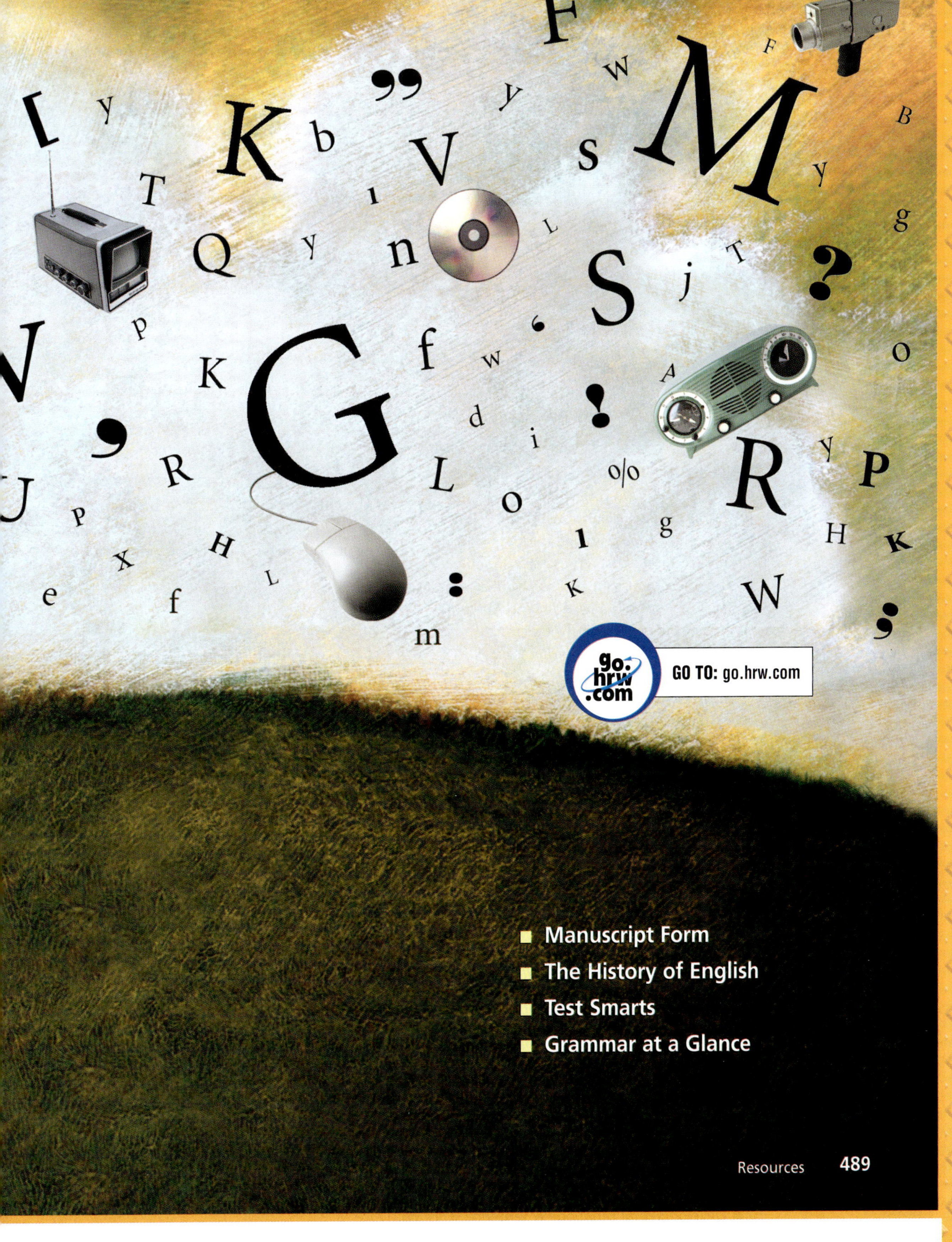
GO TO: go.hrw.com
Manuscript Form
The History of English
Test Smarts
Grammar at a Glance
Resources 489

Manuscript Form

Why Is Manuscript Form Important?

What is manuscript form, and why should you care about it? ***Manuscript form*** refers to the overall appearance of a document. A legible, professional-looking manuscript gives the impression that the writer cares not only about what he or she has to say but also about what the reader thinks. A manuscript that is an illegible jumble, on the other hand, gives the impression that the writer is careless, is not thinking clearly, or does not respect the reader.

Such impressions affect our lives every day. For example, a busy employer faced with the task of evaluating multiple job résumés may simply discard the sloppy ones without ever reading them. If we value what we write and want others to understand and value it too, then we should present our ideas in the best form possible. To help you present your ideas as effectively as possible, this section of the book covers basic guidelines for preparing and presenting manuscripts and provides a sample research paper as a model.

General Guidelines for Preparing Manuscripts

The following guidelines are general style rules to use in formal, nonfiction writing. Such writing includes papers and reports for school, letters of application for jobs or colleges, letters to the editor, and press releases for clubs and other organizations.

Content and Organization

1. Begin the paper with an introductory paragraph that contains a thesis sentence.
2. Develop and support your thesis in body paragraphs.
3. Follow the principles of unity and coherence. That is, develop one and only one big idea (your thesis), and make sure that your paragraphs and sentences flow smoothly without any gaps in the sequence of ideas.
4. Place charts, graphs, tables, and illustrations close to the text they illustrate. Label and number each one.

RESOURCES

Manuscript Form

Practice

- *Language & Sentence Skills Practice,* pp. 451–452

Differentiating Instruction

- *Developmental Language & Sentence Skills,* pp. 177–178

5. Follow the conventions of standard grammar, usage, capitalization, punctuation, and spelling.
6. Include a conclusion.

Appearance

1. Submit manuscript that is legible. Type or print out your paper using black ink; or when your teacher permits handwriting, write neatly using blue or black ink. (Other colors are harder to read.) If the printer or typewriter you are using is printing words that are faint and hard to read, change the ink cartridge or the ribbon.
2. Keep all pages neat and clean. If you discover errors and if you are working on a word processor, you can easily correct the errors and print out a fresh copy. If you write your paper by hand or on a typewriter, you generally may make a few corrections with correction tape and insert the revisions neatly. To replace a letter, word, or phrase, neatly cross out what you want to replace. Then, insert a caret mark (^) below the line, and write the inserted item above the line.

EXAMPLE

weekly
The ~~daily~~ ^ broadcasts continued all that summer.

Paper and Font

1. Use quality $8\frac{1}{2} \times 11$ inch paper.
2. Use only one side of the paper.
3. When using a word processor, use an easy-to-read font size. Size twelve is standard.
4. Use a standard font, such as Times New Roman, that does not call attention to itself. Flowery, highly stylized fonts are hard to read. They look unprofessional, and they distract the reader from the ideas you are trying to convey.

Plagiarism

Do not plagiarize. Plagiarism is the unacknowledged borrowing of someone else's words or ideas and the submission of those words or ideas as one's own. Honest writers document all borrowings, whether those borrowings are quoted or merely paraphrased.

Back-up files

When you are ready to submit your work, be sure to save a copy—a printout, a photocopy, or an electronic file—for yourself.

Academic Manuscript Style

In school you will write some very formal papers—research reports or term papers, for example. For such assignments, you will need to follow not only general manuscript guidelines but also some very specific guidelines especially for academic manuscripts.

The academic manuscript style summarized on the following pages follows the style recommended by the Modern Language Association in the *MLA Handbook for Writers of Research Papers.* Two other popular manuscript styles are the format recommended by the American Psychological Association, known as APA style, and the one published in *The Chicago Manual of Style.* Style manuals are updated from time to time, so be sure you are using the most current version. When formatting papers for school, be sure to follow your teachers' instructions on which manuscript style to use.

Manuscript Form 491

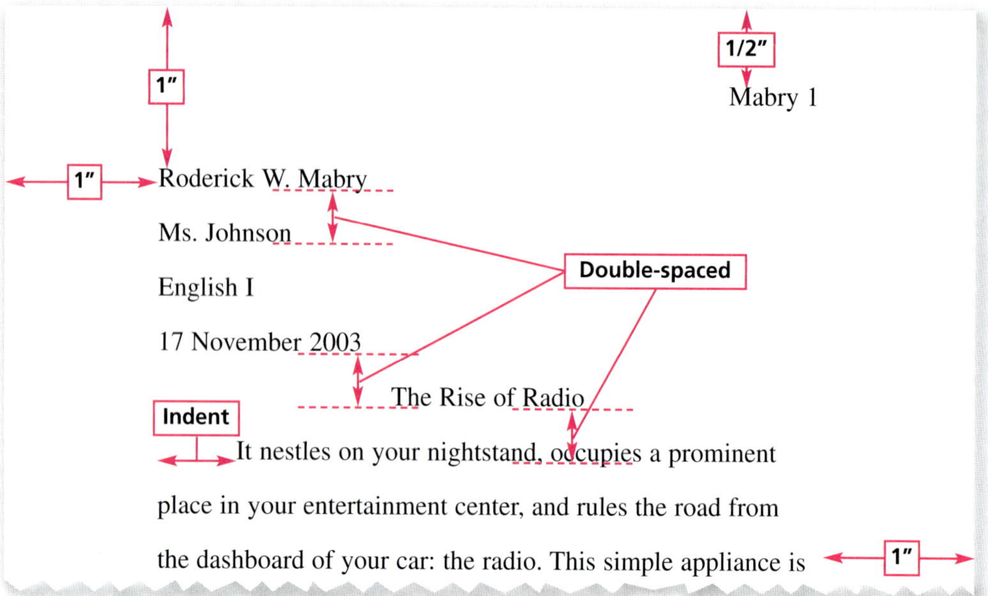

Title Page, Margins, and Spacing

1. Leave one-inch margins on the top, sides, and bottom of each page.
2. Starting with the first page, number all your pages in the upper right-hand corner. Precede each page number with your last name. Computer software can help you create this "header."
3. Place your heading—your name, your teacher's name, your class, and the date—in the upper left-hand corner of the first page. (If your teacher requires a separate cover sheet, follow his or her instructions.)
4. Double-space between the header and the heading. Double-space the lines in the heading. Double-space between the heading and your title. (This rule does not apply if your teacher requires a cover sheet.)
5. Center the title, and capitalize the appropriate letters in it.
6. Double-space between the title and the body of the paper.
7. Do not underline or use quotation marks to enclose your own title at the head of your own paper. If you use someone else's title within your title, use quotation marks or underlining, as appropriate, with the other person's title only.

EXAMPLE

An Analysis of Symbolism in Yeats' **"**The Second Coming**"**

8. When typing or word-processing, always double-space the lines. (In a handwritten paper, skip every other ruled line unless your teacher instructs you otherwise.)
9. Do not use more than a double-space, even between paragraphs.
10. Indent the beginning of each paragraph one-half inch (five spaces).

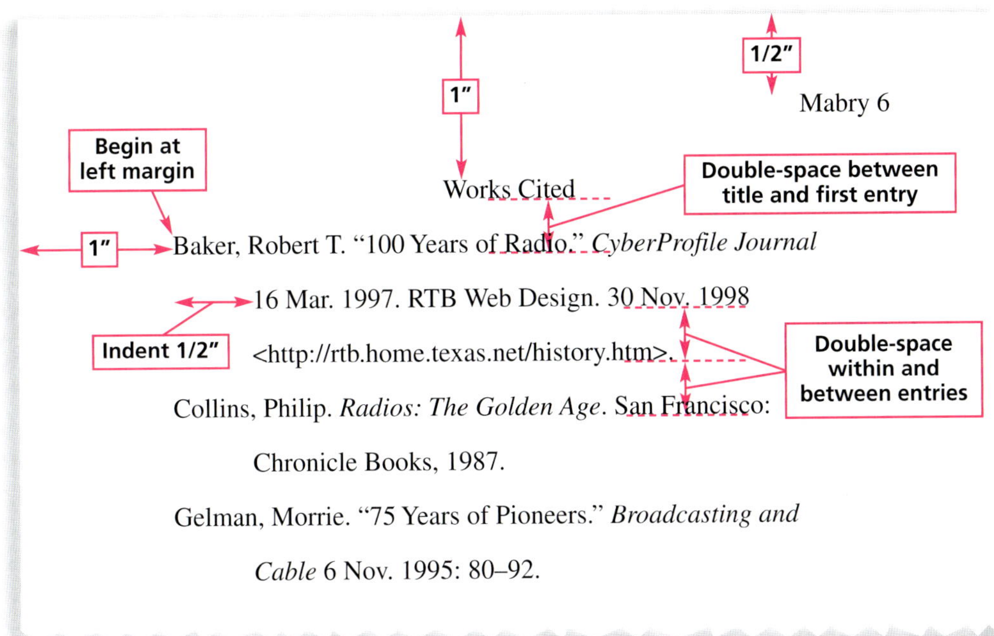

Mabry 6

Works Cited

Baker, Robert T. "100 Years of Radio." *CyberProfile Journal* 16 Mar. 1997. RTB Web Design. 30 Nov. 1998 <http://rtb.home.texas.net/history.htm>.

Collins, Philip. *Radios: The Golden Age*. San Francisco: Chronicle Books, 1987.

Gelman, Morrie. "75 Years of Pioneers." *Broadcasting and Cable* 6 Nov. 1995: 80–92.

Documenting Sources

Works Cited Page

1. In a research paper or any other paper that incorporates information from other sources, add a works cited page at the end.
2. Continue numbering the pages of your paper through the works cited page.
3. The entries on the works cited page should be in alphabetical order, according to the last name of the author. For works with no author, the entry should be alphabetized according to the first main word in the title.
4. Do not number the sources on your works cited page.

Documentation in the Body of the Essay

1. Use parenthetical citations within the body of your paper to acknowledge any paraphrased idea or quotation that you have borrowed from someone else. The parenthetical citation refers to specific source documentation on the works cited page. Place the parenthetical citations at the **end** of the material that you borrowed from some other source.

EXAMPLE

Newspapers worried that radio would drive them out of business (Henderson 90).

2. If the citation appears at the end of a sentence, the citation comes before the closing period, as shown above. If the citation appears at the end of a dependent clause or after the first half of a compound sentence, the citation comes before the sentence comma.

EXAMPLE

Newspapers worried that radio would drive them out of business (Henderson 90), but it did not.

Manuscript Form 493

3. For quotations of five or more lines, indent all of the lines one inch (about ten spaces) from the left margin. Do not use quotation marks to enclose indented quotations. Also, place end punctuation at the end of the quoted material, not after the closing parenthesis.

In the following passage, we see how effectively the author sets the mood. With a little imagination, we can almost feel the moist air and hear the murmured conversations.

1"

> The streetlights along Toole Street, which meandered downhill from the Language Academy to the town, were already lit and twinkled mistily through the trees. Standing at the gates were small groups of students, clustered together according to nationality. As Myles passed by, he could not help overhearing intense conversations in Spanish, German, and Japanese; all of his students had momentarily abandoned English in the urgency of deciding where to go for the weekend and how to get there. (Boylan 58)

494 Manuscript Form

Model Research Paper

The following final draft of a research paper closely follows the guidelines for MLA style given on the preceding pages. (Note: The pages of the model paper are smaller than 8½ × 11, and the margins of the paper are less than one inch wide to allow room for annotations.)

Mabry 1

Roderick W. Mabry

Ms. Johnson

English I

17 November 2003

HEADING
your name
your teacher's name
your class
date

The Rise of Radio

It nestles on your nightstand, occupies a prominent place in your entertainment center, and rules the road from the dashboard of your car: the radio. This simple appliance is so common that most people take it for granted, yet radio is a relatively new invention. In fact, the first commercial radio station, KDKA in Pittsburgh, did not go on the air until 1920 (Stark 120). Before long, however, the new medium dramatically affected the nation's entertainment, information delivery, and economy.

THESIS SENTENCE: tells focus of the paper

The invention of radio was made possible by a number of earlier developments. German physicist Heinrich Hertz, drawing on established mathematical principles, discovered the existence of radio waves in 1887. Eight years later, in Italy,

TOPIC SENTENCE: tells focus of the paragraph and is a subtopic of the thesis

(continued)

RESOURCES

RESOURCES

(continued)

FIRST REFERENCE: Full name of inventor is used.

SECOND REFERENCE: last name only

This parenthetical citation indicates that paraphrased information in the paragraph comes from Yenne, page 77. *Yenne* refers to *Yenne, Bill* on the works cited page.

In the Baker citation, no page number is listed because this information comes from an unpaginated online source.

Mabry 2

Guglielmo Marconi successfully completed the first wireless transmission of Morse code signals. An American invention helped move radio closer to reality: Lee De Forest's 1907 Audion, which made it possible to transmit sounds, not just signals. A full decade before KDKA debuted, De Forest broadcast a live performance by famed Italian tenor Enrico Caruso from New York City's Metropolitan Opera House (Yenne 77).

Few people were equipped to hear that landmark broadcast, however, because radio was still very much a do-it-yourself project; most people built their own receivers. In 1921, one such "tinkerer," twenty-eight-year-old Franklin Malcolm Doolittle of New Haven, Connecticut, even used his homemade transmitter to broadcast the Yale-Princeton football game from his home (Gelman 80). The first commercially produced receivers became available in 1920, when a Pittsburgh department store began offering sets for ten dollars. The response was so enthusiastic that Westinghouse began mass producing the appliances (Baker).

When radio found its way into the majority of American households, it brought the nation together in an unprecedented

496 Manuscript Form

Mabry 3

way. Radio reached into "once dreary homes, reducing the isolation of the hinterlands and leveling class distinctions" (Henderson 44). At first radio programming simply duplicated existing forms of entertainment: singers, musicians, comedians, lecturers. Coping with technical difficulties left little time for creating new types of shows. Later, as the technical problems were resolved, programmers began adapting existing formats and experimenting with new types of shows, including variety shows, serials, game shows, and amateur hours ("Radio as a Medium of Communication"). As programming expanded, radio truly became, in researcher Amy Henderson's words, "a theater of the mind" (144).

The introduction of radio also radically altered the way people learned about events in the outside world. For the first time in history, everyone could receive the same information simultaneously. As sociologists Robert and Helen Lynd, writing in the 1920s, noted, "With but little equipment one can call the life of the rest of the world from the air . . ." (qtd. in Monk 173). Live coverage gave news events an immediacy far greater than newspapers or newsreels could provide. In fact, most people

When parenthetical documentation follows closing quotation marks at the end of a sentence, the period should be placed after the parentheses.

These parentheses contain only the page number because the author is named in the text.

This citation tells us that the quotation from Robert and Helen Lynd was found in a book edited by Linda R. Monk.

(continued)

RESOURCES

(continued)

Mabry 4

first learned of such historic events as the 1941 Japanese attack on Pearl Harbor from the radio (Stark 120).

Note again how strong topic sentences control the content of the paragraph and develop a subtopic of the thesis sentence.

Equally important was radio's impact on the economy. The first, and most noticeable, effect was to add a new consumer product to people's wish lists. Most early sets were strictly functional—"a box, some wire, and headphones" (Baker). Once the initial demand was satisfied, however, manufacturers began stimulating repeat sales by offering new models each year, with the goal of placing a "radio in every room" (Collins 10).

The demand for sets was a boon to manufacturers, but it struck fear into some other segments of the economy. Newspapers worried that radio would drive them out of business (Henderson 90). Similarly, members of the traditional entertainment industry feared that the new technology would cut into the sales of tickets and recordings (Stark 120).

The parenthetical citation for Henderson is placed directly at the end of the paraphrase.

Surprisingly, advertisers were slow to realize the opportunities radio offered. At first, most business people assumed that profits would come solely from the sale of sets and replacement parts. In addition, paid advertising was considered

RESOURCES

improper for what was initially viewed as a "new, pure instrument of democracy" (Weiner). Instead, early programs were underwritten by "sponsors," with companies receiving only a brief, discreet acknowledgment in return for their support. Eventually, however, this approach gave way to the direct advertising that is familiar today (Weiner).

Reviewing the rise of radio makes clear how instrumental the medium was in shaping the nation's entertainment, information delivery, and economy. Today, with the advent of television and the Internet, radio is no longer the primary source of news and entertainment for most people, nor is its impact on the economy as far-reaching. Still, each day millions of listeners wake, work, and play to the rhythms of radio, and many would be lost without it. The radio may have been muted, but it has not been unplugged.

Mabry ends his paper with a concluding paragraph that is entirely his own statement. First, he restates the thesis in the form of a conclusion. Then, he places the history of the radio in its modern context.

(continued)

Manuscript Form 499

RESOURCES

(continued)

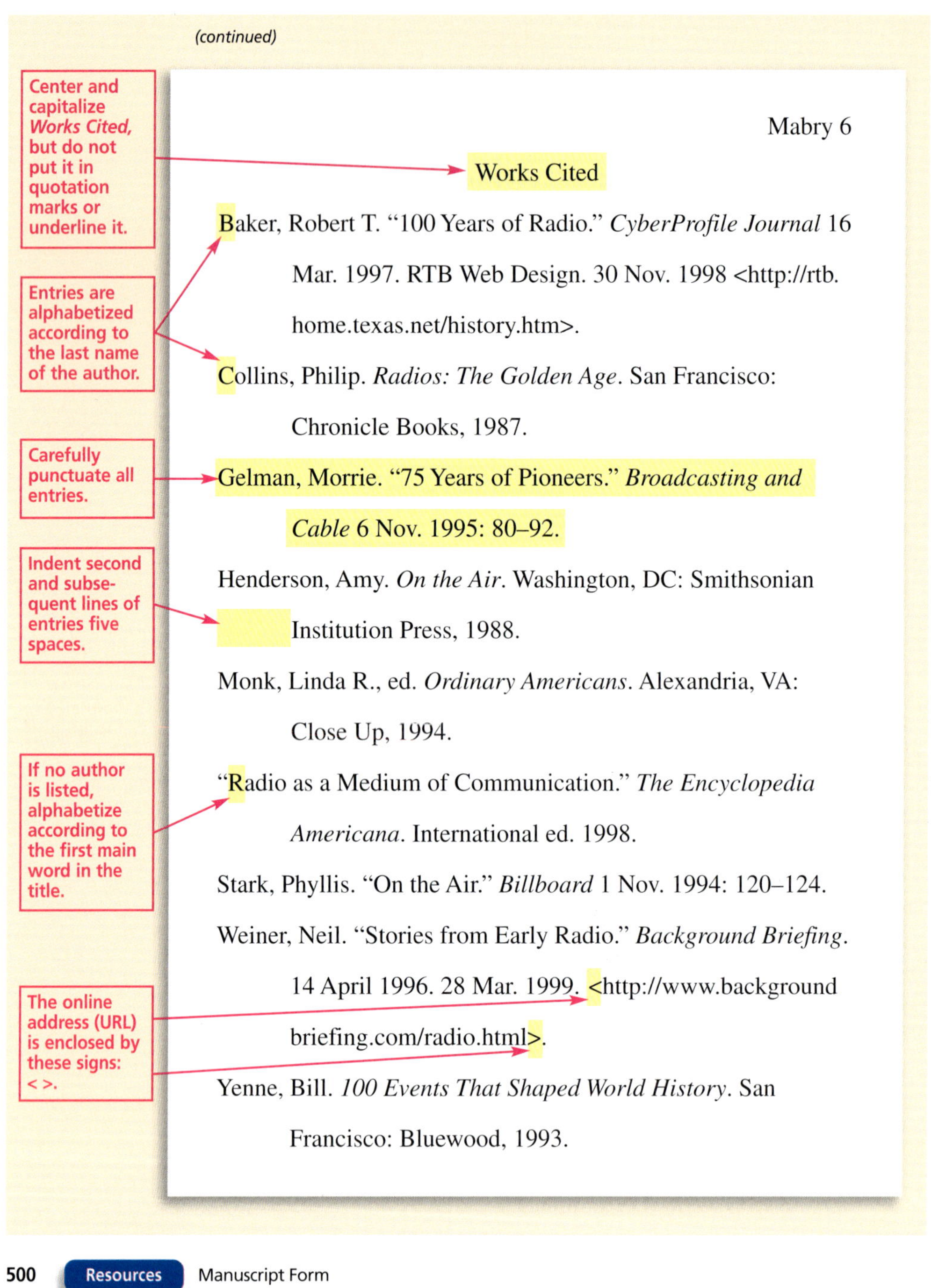

Mabry 6

Works Cited

Baker, Robert T. "100 Years of Radio." *CyberProfile Journal* 16 Mar. 1997. RTB Web Design. 30 Nov. 1998 <http://rtb.home.texas.net/history.htm>.

Collins, Philip. *Radios: The Golden Age*. San Francisco: Chronicle Books, 1987.

Gelman, Morrie. "75 Years of Pioneers." *Broadcasting and Cable* 6 Nov. 1995: 80–92.

Henderson, Amy. *On the Air*. Washington, DC: Smithsonian Institution Press, 1988.

Monk, Linda R., ed. *Ordinary Americans*. Alexandria, VA: Close Up, 1994.

"Radio as a Medium of Communication." *The Encyclopedia Americana*. International ed. 1998.

Stark, Phyllis. "On the Air." *Billboard* 1 Nov. 1994: 120–124.

Weiner, Neil. "Stories from Early Radio." *Background Briefing*. 14 April 1996. 28 Mar. 1999. <http://www.backgroundbriefing.com/radio.html>.

Yenne, Bill. *100 Events That Shaped World History*. San Francisco: Bluewood, 1993.

500 Resources Manuscript Form

The History of English

Origins and Uses

The English language was first written about 1,300 years ago, but was spoken long before that. Over the centuries, English has grown and changed to become the rich, expressive language we use today. The history of this development is a story of people, places, and times.

Beginnings of English Many of the world's languages come from an early language called ***Proto-Indo-European.*** We have no records of this parent language, but it was probably spoken by Eastern Europeans six or seven thousand years ago. Tribes of these people slowly migrated across Europe and to India. As they wandered in different directions, each tribe developed its own ***dialect,*** or distinct version of the language. The dialects eventually developed into separate languages. The map on this page shows how the Indo-European root word *mater* (mother) developed in some of these languages. The arrows indicate directions of migration.

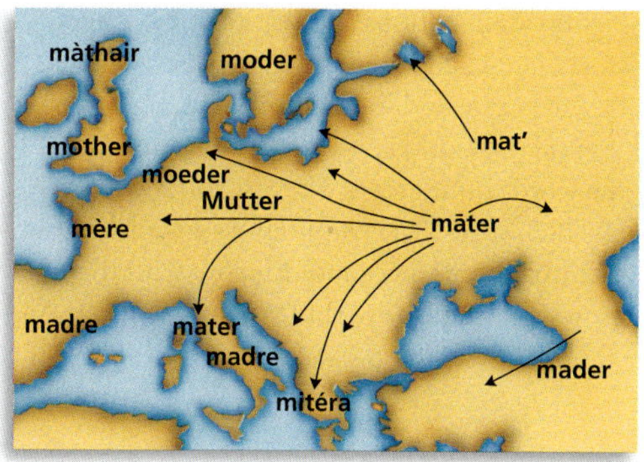

Old English Around A.D. 450, tribes known as the Angles and the Saxons invaded Britain. They took over land that had been settled earlier by the Celts. The separate dialects these tribes spoke eventually blended into one language—***Old English,*** sometimes called Anglo-Saxon. Modern English still bears traces of its Anglo-Saxon roots. For example, the words *eat, drink,* and *sleep* come from the Old English words *etan, drincan,* and *slæp.* The Anglo-Saxons used an *–s* to form the plurals of many nouns, just as we do. We also have Old English to thank for irregular verb forms such as *swim, swam,* and *swum.*

Middle English In 1066, the Normans from France seized control of England. For the next 150 years, French was the official language of government, business, and law. Therefore, many

RESOURCES

Origins and Uses 501

RESOURCES

English words that are connected with wealth and power, such as *governor, attorney,* and *fashion,* come from the French. The common people of England, however, still spoke English—a changing form of the language we call ***Middle English.*** The grammar of English was becoming simpler as many of the complicated word endings disappeared.

The following lines are matching excerpts from the Lord's Prayer (Matthew 6:9–13) in Old English and Middle English. As you can see, Middle English looks much more like the English you know.

Old English: Fæder ure þu þe eart on heofonum, si þin nama gehalgod.

Middle English: Fader oure þat art in hevene, i-halwed bee þi name.

Modern English

Before 1476, speakers and writers in different parts of England used different versions of the language, and therefore they often had trouble understanding each other. When William Caxton set up the first printing press in England around 1476, all of this changed. Early printers standardized spelling, and since London was the center of English trade and culture, they printed all books in London English. London English soon became the standard throughout England. Once standards were set, people wanted to learn the proper way to speak and write their language. Soon, grammar and usage handbooks sprang up, along with the first English dictionaries.

Two other factors influenced Modern English. One factor was its expansion into an international language through the discovery of new lands. From the sixteenth century through the nineteenth century, English merchants, explorers, and settlers spread English to other parts of the globe. They also learned new words from other languages, enriching English with international imports.

EXAMPLES

Japanese: soy	**Dutch:** cruise
Turkish: yogurt	**Spanish:** siesta

The language was also affected by the scientific revolution of this time. Words had to be created to name the new discoveries being made.

EXAMPLES

atmosphere **pneumonia** **skeleton**

American English

Immigration to the American colonies brought about a new version of the language—***American English.*** Like the United States itself, American English represents a variety of cultures and peoples. Native Americans, Africans, and immigrants from most countries around the world have enriched the language with words from their native tongues. For example, Native Americans gave us *coyote* and *squash; jazz* and *gumbo* came from Africa; and Italian immigrants added *spaghetti* and *ravioli* to the menu.

English in the Twenty-first Century

English has become the most widely used language in the history of the world, with over 750 million users. It is an official language in eighty-seven nations and territories. It is the world language of diplomacy, science, technology, aviation, and international trade. As people around the world contribute to the language, the word count grows. The last count was over 600,000 words. The count grows so quickly that dictionary makers cannot keep up with the growth of English vocabulary.

502 The History of English

Varieties of English

English is a rich and flexible language that offers many choices. To speak and write effectively—at home, at school, and on the job—you need to know what the varieties of English are and how to choose among them.

Dialects of American English Like all languages, American English has many distinct versions, called ***dialects.*** Everyone uses a dialect, and no dialect is better or worse than another. Each has unique features of grammar, vocabulary, and pronunciation.

- **Regional dialects** The United States has four major regional dialects: the *Northern,* the *Midland,* the *Southern,* and the *Western.* Pronunciations of words often vary from one dialect region to another. For example, some Southerners pronounce the words *ten* and *tin* the same way—as "tin." Similarly, regions differ in grammar and vocabulary. For example, you may say "sick *to* my stomach" if you come from New York but "sick *at* my stomach" if you come from Georgia. You may drink *soda, tonic,* or *pop* depending on what part of the country you come from.

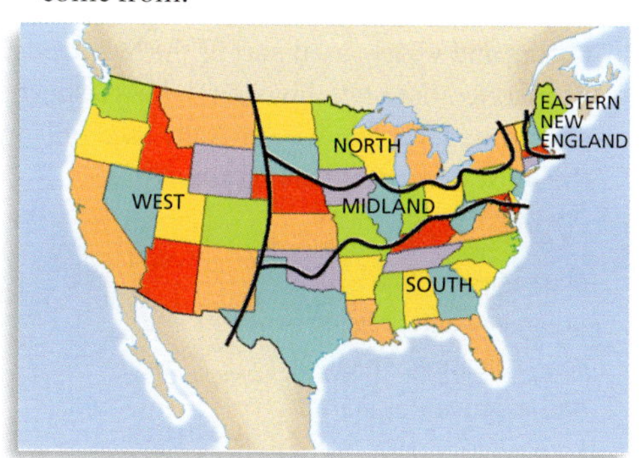

- **Ethnic dialects** An ethnic dialect is used by people who share the same cultural heritage. Because Americans come from many different cultures, American English includes many different ethnic dialects. The most widely used ethnic dialects are African American Vernacular English and Hispanic Vernacular English. Many everyday words began as ethnic dialect words but then became part of the general English vocabulary. For example, African Americans introduced the words *banana* and *tote* into English, and Hispanic Americans added words such as *avocado* and *patio.*

Standard American English Every variety of English has its own set of rules and guidelines. No variety is the best or the most correct. However, ***Standard American English*** (SAE) is the one variety of English that is more widely used and accepted than others in the United States. Because it is commonly understood, SAE allows people from many different regions and cultures to communicate with one another clearly. It is the variety of English you read and hear most often in books and magazines, on radio and television. It is the kind of English that people are expected to use in most school and business situations. This textbook presents many of the rules and guidelines for using Standard American English. To identify the differences between Standard American English and other varieties of English, this book uses the labels *standard* and *nonstandard.* Nonstandard does not mean wrong language. It means language that is inappropriate in situations where standard English is expected.

DIFFERENTIATING INSTRUCTION

Advanced Learners

Show students that the source language of a word can determine its spelling. Point out words from Spanish that contain the pattern *le* found in *tamale,* such as *chile* and *frijole.* Then, divide the class into five groups and assign each group to one of the following language groups: Latin, Spanish, German/Dutch, Greek, and French. Each group member should use a dictionary to search for three to five words from the source language. Then, group members should compile a list of all of the words found and try to identify two spelling patterns common to words from the source language. Finally, each group should present its findings in a poster that highlights the spelling patterns identified and lists all of the words found.

RESOURCES

Standard English—Formal to Informal

Depending on your audience, purpose, and occasion, the language you use can be formal, informal, or somewhere in between. The following chart shows some of the appropriate uses of very formal and very informal English.

Uses of Formal and Informal English

Formal

Speaking: formal, dignified occasions, such as banquets and dedication ceremonies

Writing: serious papers and reports, tests, business letters

Informal

Speaking: everyday conversation at home, school, work, and recreation

Writing: personal letters, journal entries, and many newspaper and magazine articles

You can say the same thing in many different ways. For example, *chow down* and *dine* both mean "eat," but one is much more formal than the other. The main differences between formal and informal English are in sentence structure, word choice, and tone.

Features of Formal and Informal English

Formal

Sentence Structure: longer and more complex

Word Choice: precise, often technical or scientific

Tone: serious and dignified

Informal

Sentence Structure: shorter and simpler

Word Choice: simple and ordinary; often includes contractions, colloquialisms, and slang

Tone: conversational

Uses of Informal English In informal speaking and writing, people constantly make up new words and give new uses to old ones. This makes informal English flexible. Dictionaries help you to see this flexibility by giving labels to different informal uses of words. The two most commonly listed usage labels are **colloquialisms** and **slang.**

- **Colloquialisms** *Colloquialisms* are the informal words and phrases of conversational language. They bring flavor and color to everyday speech and a friendly, conversational tone to writing. Many are figures of speech that aren't meant to be taken literally.

  EXAMPLES

  I may have made a mistake, but you don't have to **fly off the handle** about it.

  Today, many young couples **foot the bill** for their weddings rather than having their parents pay for them.

  My mother told us to quit **making such a racket.**

- **Slang** ***Slang*** is made up of newly coined words or of old words used in unconventional ways. It is usually clever and colorful. It is often a special language for specific groups of people, such as students and military personnel. Some people use slang to be up-to-date. Sometimes a slang word becomes a lasting and widely used part of the language. More often than not, however, it lives a short and limited life. Slang is generally used only in the most informal speaking situations.

  EXAMPLES

  beat—tired

  bummer—a depressing experience

  cool—pleasing, excellent

  hassle—to annoy, harass

  kooky—strange

504 The History of English

Test Smarts

Taking Standardized Tests in Grammar, Usage, and Mechanics

TEACHING TIP

You can reinforce the material in this part of the book with practice tests found on pages 411–415 and 426–429 of the pupil's textbook and with chapter tests found in the ancillary booklet *Holt Handbook Chapter Tests.*

Becoming "Test-Smart"

Standardized achievement tests, like other tests, measure your skills in specific areas. Standardized achievement tests also compare your performance to the performance of other students at your age or grade level. Some language arts standardized tests measure your skill in using correct capitalization, punctuation, sentence structure, and spelling. Such tests sometimes also measure your ability to evaluate sentence style.

The most important part of preparing for any test, including standardized tests, is learning the content on which you will be tested. To do this, you must

- listen in class
- complete homework assignments
- study to master the concepts and skills presented by your teacher

In addition, you also need to use effective strategies for taking a standardized test. The following pages will teach you how to become test-smart.

General Strategies for Taking Tests

1. **Understand how the test is scored.** If no points will be taken off for wrong answers, plan to answer every question. If wrong answers count against you, plan to answer only questions you know the answer to or questions you can answer with an educated guess.

2. **Stay focused.** Expect to be a little nervous, but focus your attention on doing the best job possible. Try not to be distracted with thoughts that aren't about the test questions.

3. **Get an overview.** Quickly skim the entire test to get an idea of how long the test is and what is on it.

4. **Pace yourself.** Based on your overview, figure out how much time to allow for each section of the test. If time limits are stated for each section, decide how much time to allow for each item. Pace yourself, and check every five to ten minutes to see if you need to work faster. Try to leave a few minutes at the end of the testing period to check your work.

5. **Read all instructions.** Read the instructions for each part of the test carefully. Also, answer the sample questions to be sure you understand how to answer the test questions.

6. **Read all answer choices.** Carefully read *all* of the possible answers before you choose an answer. Note how each possible answer differs from the others. You may want to make an *x* next to each answer choice that you rule out.

7. **Make educated guesses.** If you do not know the answer to a question, see if you can rule out one or more answers and make an educated guess. Don't spend too much time on any one item, though. If you want to think longer about a difficult item, make a light pencil mark next to the item number. You can go back to that question later.

8. **Mark your answers.** Mark the answer sheet carefully and completely. If you plan to go back to an item later, be sure to skip that number on the answer sheet.

9. **Check your work.** If you have time at the end of the test, go back to check your answers. This is also the time to try to answer any questions you skipped. Make sure your marks are complete, and erase any stray marks on the answer sheet.

Strategies for Answering Grammar, Usage, and Mechanics Questions

The questions in standardized tests can take different forms, but the most common form is the multiple-choice question. Here are some strategies for answering that kind of test question.

Correcting parts of sentences

One kind of question contains a sentence with an underlined part. The answer choices show several revised versions of that part. Your job is to decide which revised version makes the sentence correct or whether the underlined part is already correct. First, look at each answer carefully. Immediately rule out any answer in which you notice a grammatical error. If you are still unsure of the correct answer, try approaching the question in one of these two ways.

- **Think how you would rewrite the underlined part.** Look at the answer choices for one that matches your revision. Carefully read each possible answer before you make your final choice. Often, only tiny differences exist between the answers, and you want to choose the *best* answer.

- **Look carefully at the underlined part and at each answer choice, looking for one particular type of error, such as an error in capitalization or spelling.** The best way to look for a particular error is to compare the answer choices to see how they differ both from each other and from the underlined part of the question. For example, if there are differences in capitalization, look at each choice for capitalization errors.

After ruling out incorrect answers, choose the answer with no errors. If there are errors in each of the choices but no errors in the underlined part, your answer will be the "no error" or "correct as is" choice.

EXAMPLE

Directions: Choose the answer that is the **best** revision of the underlined words.

1. My neighbor is painting his house and my brother helped him.
   A. house; and my brother is helping him.
   B. house, and my brother had helped him.
   C. house, and my brother is helping him.
   D. Correct as is

Explanation: In the example above, the possible answers contain differences in punctuation and in verb tense. Therefore, you should check each possible answer for errors in punctuation and verb tense.

A. You can rule out this choice because it has incorrect punctuation.
B. This choice creates inconsistent verb tenses, so you can rule out this answer.
C. This choice has correct punctuation and creates consistent verb tenses.
D. You can rule out this choice because the original sentence lacks correct punctuation between the clauses.

Answer: Choice C is the only one that contains no errors, so the oval for that answer choice is darkened.

Correcting whole sentences This type of question is similar to the kind of question previously described. However, here you are looking for mistakes in the entire sentence instead of just an underlined part. The strategies for approaching this type of question are the same as for the other kind of sentence-correction questions. If you don't see the correct answer right away, compare the answer choices to see how they differ. When you find differences, check each choice for errors relating to that difference. Rule out choices with errors. Repeat the process until you find the correct answer.

EXAMPLE

Directions: Choose the answer that is the **best** revision of the following sentences.

1. After Brad mowed the lawn, he swept the sidewalk and driveway, then he took a shower. And washed his hair.
   A. After Brad mowed the lawn, he swept the sidewalk and driveway. Then he took a shower and washed his hair.
   B. After Brad mowed the lawn, he swept the sidewalk and driveway. Then he took a shower, and washed his hair.
   C. After Brad mowed the lawn. He swept the sidewalk and driveway; then he took a shower and washed his hair.
   D. Correct as is

Explanation: The original word groups and answer choices have differences in sentence structure and punctuation, so you should check each answer choice for errors in sentence structure and punctuation.

A. This choice contains two complete sentences and correct punctuation.
B. This choice contains two complete sentences and incorrect punctuation.
C. This choice begins with a sentence fragment, so you can rule it out.
D. You can rule out this choice because the original version contains a sentence fragment.

Answer: Choice A is the only one that contains no errors, so the oval for that answer choice is darkened.

Identifying kinds of errors This type of question has at least one under-lined part. Your job is to determine which part, if any,

Test Smarts 507

contains an error. Sometimes, you also may have to decide what type of error (capitalization, punctuation, or spelling) exists. The strategy is the same whether the question has one or several underlined parts. Try to identify an error, and check the answer choices for that type of error. If the original version is correct as written, choose "no error" or "correct as is."

EXAMPLE

Directions: Read the following sentences and decide which type of error, if any, is in the underlined part.

1. Marcia, Jim, and Leroy are participating in Saturday's charity marathon. they are hoping to raise one hundred dollars for the new children's museum.
   A. Spelling error
   B. Capitalization error
   C. Punctuation error
   D. Correct as is

Explanation: If you cannot tell right away what kind of error (if any) is in the original version, go through each answer choice in turn.

A. All the words are spelled correctly.
B. The sentences contain a capitalization error. The second sentence incorrectly begins with a lowercase letter.
C. The sentences are punctuated correctly.
D. The sentences contain a capitalization error, so you can rule out this choice.

Answer: Because the passage contains a capitalization error, the oval for answer choice B is darkened.

Revising sentence structure Errors covered by this kind of question include sentence fragments, run-on sentences, repetitive wording, misplaced modifiers, and awkward construction. If you don't immediately spot the error, examine the question and each answer choice for specific types of errors, one type at a time. If you cannot find an error in the original version and if all of the other answer choices have errors, then choose "no error" or "correct as is."

EXAMPLE

Directions: Read the following word groups. If there is an error in sentence structure, choose the answer that best revises the word groups.

1. Mary Lou arranged the mozzarella cheese and fresh tomatoes. On a platter covered with lettuce leaves.
   A. Mary Lou arranged the mozzarella cheese and fresh tomatoes on a platter covered with lettuce leaves.
   B. Mary Lou arranged the mozzarella cheese and fresh tomatoes, on a platter covered with lettuce leaves.
   C. Mary Lou arranged the mozzarella cheese and fresh tomatoes; on a platter covered with lettuce leaves.
   D. Correct as is

Explanation: The original word groups and answer choices have differences in sentence structure and punctuation.

A. This choice is correctly punctuated and contains a correct, complete sentence.
B. This choice contains an incorrect comma, so you can rule it out.
C. This choice contains an incorrect semicolon, so you can rule it out.
D. The original word groups contain a sentence fragment, so D cannot be correct.

Answer: Choice A is the only one that contains no errors, so the oval for that answer choice is darkened.

Questions about sentence style

These questions are often not about grammar, usage, or mechanics but about content and organization. They may ask about tone, purpose, topic sentences, supporting sentences, audience, sentence combining, appropriateness of content, or transitions. The questions may ask you which is the *best* way to revise the passage, or they may ask you to identify the *main* purpose of the passage. When you see words such as *best, main,* and *most likely* or *least likely,* you are not being asked to correct errors; you are being asked to make a judgment about style or meaning.

If the question asks for a particular kind of revision (for example, "What *transition* is needed between sentence 4 and sentence 5?"), analyze each answer choice to see how well it makes that particular revision. Many questions ask for a general revision (for example, "Which is the *best* way to revise the last sentence?"). In such situations, check each answer choice and rule out any choices that have mistakes in grammar, usage, or mechanics. Then, read each choice and use what you have learned in class to judge whether the revision improves the original sentence. If you are combining sentences, be sure to choose the answer that includes all important information, that demonstrates good style, *and* that is grammatically correct.

EXAMPLE

Directions: Choose the answer that shows the **best** way to combine the following sentences.

1. Jacques Cousteau was a filmmaker and author. Jacques Cousteau explored the ocean as a diver and marine scientist.
   - **A.** Jacques Cousteau was a filmmaker and author; Jacques Cousteau explored the ocean as a marine scientist.
   - **B.** Jacques Cousteau was a filmmaker and author, he explored the ocean as a diver and marine scientist.
   - **C.** Jacques Cousteau was a filmmaker and author who explored the ocean as a diver and marine scientist.
   - **D.** Jacques Cousteau was a filmmaker, author, diver, and scientist.

Explanation:

- **A.** Answer choice A is grammatically correct but unnecessarily repeats the subject *Jacques Cousteau* and leaves out some information.
- **B.** Choice B is a run-on sentence, so it cannot be the correct answer.
- **C.** Choice C is grammatically correct, and it demonstrates effective sentence combining.
- **D.** Choice D is grammatically correct but leaves out some information.

Answer: Because answer choice C shows the best way to combine the sentences, the oval for choice C is darkened.

Fill-in-the-blanks This type of question tests your ability to fill in blanks in sentences, giving answers that are logical and grammatically correct. A question of this kind might ask you to choose a verb in the appropriate tense. A different question might require a combination of adverbs (*first, next*) to show how parts of the sentence relate. Another question might require a vocabulary word to complete the sentence.

To approach a sentence-completion question, first look for clue words in the sentence. *But, however,* and *though* indicate a contrast; *therefore* and *as a result* indicate cause and effect. Using sentence clues, rule out obviously incorrect answer choices. Then, try filling in the blanks with the remaining choices to determine which answer choice makes the most sense. Finally, check to be sure your choice is grammatically correct.

Test Smarts 509

EXAMPLE

Directions: Choose the words that **best** complete the sentence.

1. When Jack _____ the dog, the dog _____ water everywhere.
   - **A.** washes, splashed
   - **B.** washed, will be splashing
   - **C.** will have washed, has splashed
   - **D.** washed, splashed

   D

Explanation:

- **A.** The verb tenses (present and past) are inconsistent.
- **B.** The verb tenses (past and future) are inconsistent.
- **C.** The verb tenses (future perfect and present perfect) are inconsistent.
- **D.** The verb tenses (past and past) are consistent.

Answer: The oval for choice D is darkened.

Using Your Test Smarts

Remember: Success on standardized tests comes partly from knowing strategies for taking such tests—from being test-smart. Knowing these strategies can help you approach standardized achievement tests more confidently. Do your best to learn your classroom subjects, take practice tests if they are available, and use the strategies outlined in this section. Good luck!

Grammar at a Glance

A

abbreviation An abbreviation is a shortened form of a word or a phrase.

- **capitalization of**

TITLES USED WITH NAMES	**M**r.	**D**r.	**J**r.	Ph.**D.**
KINDS OF ORGANIZATIONS	**A**ssn.	**I**nc.	**D**ept.	**C**orp.
PARTS OF ADDRESSES	**A**ve.	**S**t.	**B**lvd.	**P.O. B**ox
NAMES OF STATES	[without ZIP Codes]		**K**y.	**T**ex.
			Tenn.	**N. D**ak.
	[with ZIP Codes]		**KY**	**TX**
			TN	**ND**
TIMES	**A.M.**	**P.M.**	**B.C.**	**A.D.**

- **punctuation of** (See page 267.)

WITH PERIODS	(See preceding examples.)
WITHOUT PERIODS	VCR ESPN NAACP FCC
	DC [D.C. without ZIP Code]
	kg lb tsp km ft
	[Exception: inch = in**.**]

action verb An action verb expresses physical or mental activity. (See page 15.)

EXAMPLES Kurt **ran** toward the ledge.

Owen correctly **guessed** the number of jelly beans in the jar.

active voice Active voice is the voice a verb is in when it expresses an action done by its subject. (See page 163. See also **voice.**)

EXAMPLE Napoleon's armies **conquered** most of western Europe.

HELP

Grammar at a Glance is an alphabetical list of special terms and expressions with examples and references to further information. When you encounter a grammar or usage problem in the revising or proofreading stage of your writing, look for help in this section first. You may find all you need to know right here. If you need more information, **Grammar at a Glance** will show you where in the book to turn for a more complete explanation. If you do not find what you are looking for in **Grammar at a Glance,** turn to the index on page 537.

RESOURCES

Grammar at a Glance 511

adjective An adjective modifies a noun or a pronoun. (See page 10.)

EXAMPLE **The** peninsula has **high** mountains and **winding** roads.

adjective clause An adjective clause is a subordinate clause that modifies a noun or a pronoun. (See page 101.)

EXAMPLE The man **who disappeared** was soon found again.

adjective phrase A prepositional phrase that modifies a noun or a pronoun is called an adjective phrase. (See page 71.)

EXAMPLE We approached the highest peak **in the Alps.**

adverb An adverb modifies a verb, an adjective, or another adverb. (See page 21.)

EXAMPLE Helen **rarely** loses her temper.

adverb clause An adverb clause is a subordinate clause that modifies a verb, an adjective, or an adverb. (See page 104.)

EXAMPLE We will try to get indoors **before the storm arrives.**

adverb phrase A prepositional phrase that modifies a verb, an adjective, or an adverb is called an adverb phrase. (See page 73.)

EXAMPLE Terry cleaned his room **in a few minutes.**

agreement Agreement is the correspondence, or match, between grammatical forms. Grammatical forms agree when they have the same number and gender.

- **of pronouns and antecedents** (See page 135.)

SINGULAR **Ethan** politely asked for an increase in **his** allowance.
PLURAL Ethan's **brothers** politely asked for an increase in **their** allowances.

SINGULAR **Everyone** in the play made **his or her** own costumes.
PLURAL **All** of the performers made **their** own costumes.

SINGULAR Is **Matthew or Terence** looking forward to reciting **his** poem in front of **his** classmates?
PLURAL **Matthew and Terence** are looking forward to reciting **their** poems in front of **their** classmates.

512 Grammar at a Glance

- **of subjects and verbs** (See page 121.)

SINGULAR The art **teacher has painted** a mural on a wall of the cafeteria.

The art **teacher,** with the help of her students, **has painted** a mural on a wall of the cafeteria.

PLURAL The art **students have painted** a mural on a wall of the cafeteria.

PLURAL The art **students,** with the help of their teacher, **have painted** a mural on the wall of the cafeteria.

SINGULAR **Everyone** in this class **is learning** sign language.

PLURAL **All** of the students **are learning** sign language.

SINGULAR **Neither Diego nor I was** ready to compete in the battle of the bands.

PLURAL **Salsa, reggae, and zydeco were** among the kinds of music played at the band competition.

SINGULAR Here **is** your book **bag.**

PLURAL Here **are** your **books.**

SINGULAR **Ten dollars is** the cost of the ticket.

PLURAL In this stack of bills, ten **dollars are** torn.

SINGULAR **Two thirds** of the freshman class **has voted.**

PLURAL **Two thirds** of the freshmen **have voted.**

SINGULAR ***Symphonies of Wind Instruments*** **was composed** by Igor Stravinsky.

PLURAL Stravinsky's other **symphonies were** also well **received.**

SINGULAR **Is mathematics** your favorite school subject?

PLURAL **Are** my **binoculars** in your locker?

ambiguous reference Ambiguous reference occurs when a pronoun incorrectly refers to either of two antecedents. (See page 193.)

AMBIGUOUS Martina is supposed to meet Jada at the library after she practices her cello lesson.

CLEAR After **Martina** practices **her** cello lesson, **she** is supposed to meet Jada at the library.

CLEAR After **Jada** practices **her** cello lesson, **she** is supposed to meet Martina at the library.

RESOURCES

Grammar at a Glance 513

antecedent An antecedent is the word or words that a pronoun stands for. (See page 6.)

EXAMPLE **Alfred** sent **Julie** and **Dave** the money **he** owed **them.** [*Alfred* is the antecedent of *he. Julie* and *Dave* are the antecedents of *them.*]

apostrophe

- **to form contractions** (See page 335.)

  EXAMPLES couldn't let's o'clock '99

- **to form plurals of letters, numerals, symbols, and words used as words** (See page 337.)

  EXAMPLES *p*'s and *q*'s *A*'s and *I*'s

  10's and *20*'s *$*'s and *¢*'s

- **to show possession** (See page 337.)

  EXAMPLES gymnast's routine

  gymnasts' routines

  children's toys

  everyone's opinion

  Whitney Houston's and Denzel Washington's performances

  a year's [*or* twelve months'] leave of absence

appositive An appositive is a noun or a pronoun placed beside another noun or pronoun to identify or describe it. (See page 89.)

EXAMPLE My great-aunt **Rina** was born in Poland.

appositive phrase An appositive phrase consists of an appositive and its modifiers. (See page 89.)

EXAMPLE Kublai Khan, **the first emperor of the Yuan dynasty,** united China under his rule.

article The articles, *a, an,* and *the,* are the most frequently used adjectives. (See page 12.)

EXAMPLE On **an** overpass south of **the** city, **an** incident occurred that convinced John that he needed **a** new car.

RESOURCES

bad, badly (See page 203.)

NONSTANDARD Do you think these leftovers smell badly?

STANDARD Do you think these leftovers smell **bad**?

base form The base form, or infinitive, is one of the four principal parts of a verb. (See page 145.)

EXAMPLE This computer program has helped me [to] **learn** Spanish.

brackets (See page 354.)

EXAMPLE The history book points out that "the name Hundred Years' War is a misnomer **[**a wrong name**]**, for the name refers to a series of wars that lasted 116 years **[**1337–1453**]**."

capitalization

- **of abbreviations and acronyms** (See **abbreviations.**)
- **of first words** (See page 246.)

EXAMPLES **M**y sister writes in her journal every night.

Omar asked, "**W**ould you like to play on my soccer team?"

Dear Ms. Reuben:

Sincerely yours,

- **of proper nouns and proper adjectives** (See page 248.)

Proper Noun	Common Noun
James **L**ovell, **J**r.	astronaut
Alexander the **G**reat	leader
South **A**merica	continent
Appalachian **M**ountains	mountain chain
Minnesota **V**ikings	team
Democratic **P**arty (*or* **p**arty)	political party
French and **I**ndian **W**ar	historical event
Jurassic **P**eriod	historical period
Mother's **D**ay	holiday
General **M**otors **C**orporation	business

RESOURCES

Grammar at a Glance 515

- **of titles** (See page 257.)

EXAMPLES **G**overnor Pataki [preceding a name]

Pataki, the **g**overnor of New York [following a name]

Thank you, **G**overnor. [direct address]

Aunt Ramona [*but* our **a**unt Ramona]

***D**ust **T**racks **on a R**oad* [novel]

***T**he **L**ion **K**ing* [movie or play]

***N**ova* [TV program]

***M**ona **L**isa* [work of art]

"**T**he **S**tar-**S**pangled **B**anner" [song]

"**A**migo **B**rothers" [short story]

"**N**othing **G**old **C**an **S**tay" [poem]

case of pronouns Case is the form a pronoun takes to show how it is used in a sentence. (See page 177.)

NOMINATIVE **He** and **I** are making vegetable quesadillas.
Two of the class officers are Eric and **she.**
Either player, Cheryl or **she,** can play shortstop.
We volunteers have worked very hard on the recycling campaign.
Is Ernesto Galarza the author **who** wrote *Barrio Boy*?
Do you know **who** they are?
I helped Ms. Wong as much as **he.** [meaning "as much as he helped Ms. Wong"]

OBJECTIVE This jacket will not fit Yolanda or **her.**
Aunt Calista brought **him** and **me** souvenirs of her trip to the Philippines.
Were you three cheering for **us** or **them**?
The mayor thanked **us** volunteers for our contributions.
Maya Angelou, **whom** many readers admire, is certainly my favorite author.
One of the candidates for **whom** I will vote is Tamisha.
I helped Ms. Wong as much as **him.** [meaning "as much as I helped him"]

POSSESSIVE **Your** interpretation of **her** poem was different from **mine.**

516 Grammar at a Glance

clause A clause is a group of words that contains a verb and its subject and is used as part of a sentence. (See page 98.)

INDEPENDENT CLAUSE Theo installed the blinds

SUBORDINATE CLAUSE while Dorothy worked on the wiring

colon (See page 303.)

- **before lists**

EXAMPLES The recipe calls for the following herbs**:** thyme, basil, cilantro, and oregano.

The documentary profiled three women artists of the twentieth century**:** Audrey Flack, a painter; Louise Nevelson, a sculptor; and Margaret Bourke-White, a photographer.

- **in conventional situations**

EXAMPLES 6**:**30 A.M.

Ecclesiastes 11**:**7–10

*Computers and You***:** *A Video Guide*

Dear Sir or Madam**:**

comma (See page 271.)

- **in a series**

EXAMPLES Tony**,** Julian**,** and Katie helped me make the fruit salad by cutting up the oranges**,** bananas**,** grapes**,** and papayas.

We rode our bicycles to the park**,** bought snacks at the juice bar**,** found a picnic table**,** and then played chess for an hour.

The silly cat had run through the living room**,** over the sofa**,** between my feet**,** through the door**,** across the hall**,** and up the stairs.

- **in compound sentences**

EXAMPLES I like all kinds of music**,** but jazz is my favorite.

The students listened to each candidate's speech**,** and then they left the auditorium to cast their votes.

- **with nonessential phrases and clauses**

EXAMPLES Didn't Mount Etna**,** Europe's largest volcano**,** erupt a few years ago?

Grammar at a Glance 517

In the mid-1900s, the Inuit, whose ancestors had led nomadic lives of hunting and fishing, began settling in urban areas of the Arctic region.

David will be bringing fresh salsa, which his father makes from tomatoes and herbs that they grow in their garden.

- **with introductory elements**

EXAMPLES In the first match of the tennis tournament, Pablo competed against the player who was ranked first in the state.

When the exciting game was over, many of the fans raced onto the field to praise and congratulate the winning player.

- **with interrupters**

EXAMPLES The most memorable part of our vacation, however, was our visit to the Smithsonian Institution.

You might consider making a mobile, for example, or some other simple present.

The most demanding role, I believe, is that of King Lear in Shakespeare's tragedy of the same name.

- **in conventional situations**

EXAMPLES On Monday, June 5, 2000, the Walkers flew from Detroit, Michigan, to San Juan, Puerto Rico, to attend their family reunion.

I mailed the package to 1620 Palmetto Drive, Tampa, FL 33637, on 15 September 2000.

comma splice A comma splice is a run-on sentence in which two sentences have been joined with only a comma between them. (See page 441. See also **fused sentence** and **run-on sentence.**)

COMMA SPLICE My sister Eileen has a paper route, I help her sometimes, especially when the weather is bad.

REVISED My sister Eileen has a paper route, **and** I help her sometimes, especially when the weather is bad.

REVISED My sister Eileen has a paper route; I help her sometimes, especially when the weather is bad.

REVISED My sister Eileen has a paper route. I help her sometimes, especially when the weather is bad.

comparison of modifiers (See page 205.)

- **comparison of adjectives and adverbs**

Positive	Comparative	Superlative
strong	strong**er**	strong**est**
happy	happ**ier**	happ**iest**
ambitious	**more** ambitious	**most** ambitious
quietly	**less** quietly	**least** quietly
well/good	**better**	**best**

- **comparing two**

EXAMPLES Which is **longer,** the Nile River or the Amazon River?

Of the cheetah and the gazelle, which animal can run **more swiftly**?

Mount Everest is **higher** than **any other** mountain peak in the world.

- **comparing more than two**

EXAMPLES Of all of the lakes of the world, the Caspian Sea is the **largest.**

In the school's walkathon, one of the freshmen walked the **farthest.**

complement A complement is a word or word group that completes the meaning of a verb. (See page 55.)

EXAMPLES I gave **Sally** that **picture.**

This is an old **sofa,** but it's very **comfortable.**

complex sentence A complex sentence has one independent clause and at least one subordinate clause. (See page 110.)

EXAMPLE Beethoven, who had a hearing impairment most of his adult life, wrote his ninth symphony after he had become deaf.

compound-complex sentence A compound-complex sentence has two or more independent clauses and at least one subordinate clause. (See page 110.)

RESOURCES

Grammar at a Glance 519

EXAMPLES While Arianna was at the shopping mall, she checked both bookstores for Barbara Kingsolver's latest novel, but neither store had a copy in stock.

At the cookout on Saturday, we served yakitori; it is a Japanese dish of bite-sized pieces of meat and vegetables that are placed on skewers and grilled.

compound sentence A compound sentence has two or more independent clauses and no subordinate clauses. (See page 109.)

EXAMPLES My family and I recently moved into a new house, and now I have a room of my own.

By area, New York City is the largest city in the world; however, by population, Tokyo-Yokohama is the world's largest urban area.

conjunction A conjunction joins words or groups of words. (See page 31.)

EXAMPLES **Both** Robin **and** Michelle arrived early, **but** all the good seats were taken.

While you were sleeping, I worked out.

contraction A contraction is a shortened form of a word, a numeral, or a group of words. Apostrophes in contractions show where letters or numerals have been omitted. (See page 335. See also **apostrophe.**)

EXAMPLES

you're [you are]	there's [there is *or* there has]
who's [who is *or* who has]	they're [they are]
weren't [were not]	it's [it is *or* it has]
'91–'94 model [1991–1994 model]	o'clock [of the clock]

D

dangling modifier A dangling modifier is a modifying word, phrase, or clause that does not clearly and sensibly modify a word or a word group in a sentence. (See page 213.)

DANGLING Riding the Ferris wheel, most of the park's other attractions could be seen.

REVISED **Riding the Ferris wheel, we** could see most of the park's other attractions.

520 Grammar at a Glance

dash (See page 349.)

EXAMPLE One of the substitute teachers**—**Ms. Narazaki, I believe**—** will accompany us on the field trip.

declarative sentence A declarative sentence makes a statement and is followed by a period. (See page 63.)

EXAMPLE People still enjoy going to movies, despite the popularity of videos**.**

direct object A direct object is a word or word group that receives the action of the verb or shows the result of the action. A direct object answers the question *Whom?* or *What?* after a transitive verb. (See page 59.)

EXAMPLE They gave the **oats** to the horse.

double comparison A double comparison is the nonstandard use of two comparative forms (usually *more* and *–er*) or two superlative forms (usually *most* and *–est*) to express comparison. In standard usage, the single comparative form is correct. (See page 210.)

NONSTANDARD These small boxes are much more heavier than they appear.

STANDARD These small boxes are much **heavier** than they appear.

double negative A double negative is the nonstandard use of two or more negative words to express a single negative idea. (See page 237.)

NONSTANDARD The annual sports banquet doesn't cost the athletes nothing.

STANDARD The annual sports banquet **doesn't** cost the athletes **anything.**

STANDARD The annual sports banquet costs the athletes **nothing.**

NONSTANDARD Yesterday, my throat was so sore that I couldn't hardly eat no solid food.

STANDARD Yesterday, my throat was so sore that I could **hardly** eat **any** solid food.

double subject A double subject occurs when an unnecessary pronoun is used after the subject of a sentence. (See page 231.)

RESOURCES

Grammar at a Glance 521

NONSTANDARD Laura and her sister they have a large aquarium of tropical fish.

STANDARD **Laura and her sister have** a large aquarium of tropical fish.

end marks (See page 265.)

- **with sentences**

EXAMPLES Tiger Woods has won the golf tournament**.** [declarative sentence]

How long has Tiger Woods been playing professional golf**?** [interrogative sentence]

Oh**!** [interjection]

What a remarkable golfer Tiger Woods is**!** [exclamatory sentence]

Imagine how you would feel if you were playing in a tournament with Tiger Woods**.** [imperative sentence]

Don't talk while someone is hitting the ball**!** [strong imperative sentence]

- **with abbreviations** (See **abbreviations.**)

EXAMPLES We are planning to go to Washington, D.C**.**

When are you going to Washington, D.C.**?**

essential clause/essential phrase An essential, or restrictive, clause or phrase is necessary to the meaning of a sentence and is not set off by commas. (See page 277.)

EXAMPLES The man **whose sudden appearance caused the uproar** rose to identify himself. [essential clause]

Students **going on the field trip** should meet in the gym. [essential phrase]

exclamation point (See **end marks.**)

exclamatory sentence An exclamatory sentence expresses strong feeling and is followed by an exclamation point. (See page 64.)

EXAMPLE That's absolutely incredible**!**

F

fragment (See **sentence fragment.**)

522 Grammar at a Glance

fused sentence A fused sentence is a run-on sentence in which sentences have been joined together with no punctuation between them. (See page 441. See also **comma splice** and **run-on sentence.**)

FUSED According to my research, the Dome of the Rock was built in Jerusalem during the seventh century it is the oldest existing Muslim shrine.

REVISED According to my research, the Dome of the Rock was built in Jerusalem during the seventh century**. It** is the oldest existing Muslim shrine.

REVISED According to my research, the Dome of the Rock was built in Jerusalem during the seventh century**; it** is the oldest existing Muslim shrine.

G

general reference A general reference is the incorrect use of a pronoun to refer to a general idea rather than to a specific noun. (See page 193.)

GENERAL The illusionist escaped from a locked trunk, made various fruits and vegetables dance in the air, and levitated. This thrilled her audience.

REVISED The illusionist thrilled her audience by escaping from a locked trunk, making various fruits and vegetables dance in the air, and levitating.

REVISED The illusionist escaped from a locked trunk, made various fruits and vegetables dance in the air, and levitated. These illusions thrilled her audience.

gerund A gerund is a verb form ending in *–ing* that is used as a noun. (See page 81.)

EXAMPLE **Fishing** for blue crabs is especially popular in the Gulf Coast states.

gerund phrase A gerund phrase consists of a gerund and its modifiers and complements. (See page 83.)

EXAMPLE **Photographing old stone bridges** is one of Tracy's hobbies.

good, well (See page 203.)

EXAMPLES Benita is a **good** saxophone player.

Benita played extremely **well** [not *good*] at the tryouts for the school orchestra.

RESOURCES

Grammar at a Glance 523

H

hyphen (See page 344.)

- **to divide words**

  EXAMPLE In their flower garden, they planted zinnias, mari-golds, and dahlias.

- **in compound numbers**

  EXAMPLE They planted twenty-three varieties of those kinds of flowers.

- **with prefixes and suffixes**

  EXAMPLES All of the flowers were in full bloom by mid-July.

  Our garden is pesticide-free.

I

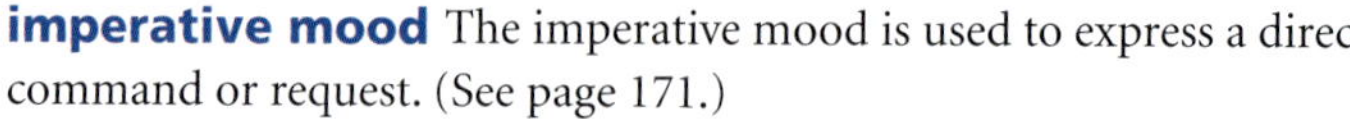

imperative mood The imperative mood is used to express a direct command or request. (See page 171.)

EXAMPLES **Sit** down! [command]

Please **read** the minutes of our last meeting. [request]

imperative sentence An imperative sentence gives a command or makes a request and is followed by either a period or an exclamation point. (See page 63.)

EXAMPLES Please return this to the display case. [request]

Clean this room now! [command]

incomplete construction An incomplete construction is a clause or phrase from which words have been omitted. (See page 192.)

EXAMPLE I like cheddar cheese more **than he [likes cheddar cheese].**

indefinite reference An indefinite reference is the incorrect use of the pronoun *you, it,* or *they* to refer to no particular person or thing. (See page 193.)

INDEFINITE In the first issue of the school newspaper, it shows a calendar of the school's major events.

REVISED The first issue of the school newspaper shows a calendar of the school's major events.

REVISED In the first issue of the school newspaper is a calendar of the school's major events.

524 Grammar at a Glance

independent clause An independent clause (also called a *main clause*) expresses a complete thought and can stand by itself as a sentence. (See page 98.)

EXAMPLE **Shawna planted the sunflower seeds and tried to imagine** what the flowers would look like.

indicative mood The indicative mood is used to express a fact, an opinion, or a question. (See page 171.)

EXAMPLES Georgia O'Keeffe **is** famous for her abstract paintings. [fact]

Georgia O'Keeffe, in my opinion, **was** the most talented American artist of the twentieth century. [opinion]

Didn't O'Keeffe **paint** *Cow's Skull: Red, White, and Blue*? [question]

indirect object An indirect object is a noun, pronoun, or word group that often appears in sentences containing direct objects. An indirect object tells *to whom* or *to what* (or *for whom* or *for what*) the action of a transitive verb is done. Indirect objects generally precede direct objects. (See page 60.)

EXAMPLE Sandy gave **Grandma** the watch.

infinitive An infinitive is a verb form, usually preceded by *to*, used as a noun, an adjective, or an adverb. (See page 85.)

EXAMPLE Patty tried **to play** the trumpet but decided she preferred **to learn** the clarinet.

infinitive phrase An infinitive phrase consists of an infinitive and its modifiers and complements. (See page 86.)

EXAMPLE Ms. Snyder tried **to explain the meaning of the phrase,** but we still found it hard to understand.

interjection An interjection expresses emotion and has no grammatical relation to the rest of the sentence. (See page 33.)

EXAMPLE **Oh no!** I completely forgot!

interrogative sentence An interrogative sentence asks a question and is followed by a question mark. (See page 64.)

EXAMPLE Did you visit Las Cruces when you were in New Mexico**?**

RESOURCES

Grammar at a Glance 525

intransitive verb An intransitive verb is a verb that does not take an object. (See page 14.)

EXAMPLE The queen **waved** good-naturedly.

irregular verb An irregular verb is a verb that forms its past and past participle in some way other than by adding *–d* or *–ed* to the base form. (See page 147. See also **regular verb.**)

Base Form	Present Participle	Past	Past Participle
be	[is] being	was, were	[have] been
drive	[is] driving	drove	[have] driven
fall	[is] falling	fell	[have] fallen
go	[is] going	went	[have] gone
run	[is] running	ran	[have] run
sing	[is] singing	sang	[have] sung
speak	[is] speaking	spoke	[have] spoken
think	[is] thinking	thought	[have] thought
write	[is] writing	wrote	[have] written

italics (See page 311.)

- **for titles**

EXAMPLES *Their Eyes Were Watching God* [book]

U.S. News & World Report [periodical]

The Ascent of Ethiopia [work of art]

Mozart Portraits [long musical recording]

- **for words, letters, and symbols used as such and for foreign words**

EXAMPLES Notice that the word *Tennessee* has four *e*'s, two *n*'s, and two *s*'s.

A *jeu de mots* is a pun or a play on words.

its, it's (See page 379.)

EXAMPLES **Its** [The coyote's] howling frightened the young campers.

It's [It is] six o'clock.

It's [It has] been raining all day.

L

lie, lay (See page 167.)

EXAMPLES I think I will **lie** down and take a short nap before dinner.
I think I will **lay** this quilt over me.

linking verb A linking verb connects the subject with a word that identifies or describes the subject. (See page 16.)

EXAMPLE Renata's grandma **looked** great at the party.

M

misplaced modifier A misplaced modifier is a word, phrase, or clause that seems to modify the wrong word or words in a sentence. (See page 215.)

MISPLACED Standing in line behind us, we thought we saw the great baseball player José Canseco.

REVISED We thought we saw the great baseball player **José Canseco standing in line behind us.**

modifier A modifier is a word, phrase, or clause that makes the meaning of another word more specific. (See page 200.)

EXAMPLE We **closely** watched him apply the finish **during his demonstration.**

mood Mood is the form a verb takes to indicate the attitude of the person using the verb. (See page 171. See also **imperative mood, indicative mood,** and **subjunctive mood.**)

N

nonessential clause/nonessential phrase A nonessential, or nonrestrictive, clause or phrase adds information not necessary to the main idea in the sentence and is set off by commas. (See page 276.)

EXAMPLE Granddad's Hudson convertible**, which he bought new in 1951,** was the next item up for auction.

noun A noun names a person, place, thing, or idea. (See page 3.)

EXAMPLE Before the **war,** most **people** I know never gave the **Balkans** a **thought.**

noun clause A noun clause is a subordinate clause used as a noun. (See page 106.)

RESOURCES

EXAMPLE **What's really going to amaze you** is how much I paid for it!

number Number is the form a word takes to indicate whether the word is singular or plural. (See page 120.)

SINGULAR	bird	I	foot	woman
PLURAL	birds	we	feet	women

O

object of a preposition An object of a preposition is the noun or pronoun that completes a prepositional phrase. (See page 28.)

EXAMPLE Faced with a huge **pile** of **papers** when she arrived, she took a deep breath and plunged in. [*With a huge pile* and *of papers* are prepositional phrases.]

P

parallel structure Parallel structure is the use of the same grammatical forms or structures to balance related ideas in a sentence. (See page 461.)

NONPARALLEL My parents promised to buy a video camera and that they would let me take it on my school trip.

PARALLEL My parents promised **to buy a video camera** and **to let me take it on my school trip.** [two infinitive phrases]

parentheses (See page 348.)

EXAMPLES Ganymede **(**see the chart on page 322**)** is our solar system's largest satellite.

Ganymede is our solar system's largest satellite. **(**See the chart on page 322.**)**

participial phrase A participial phrase consists of a participle and its complements and modifiers. (See page 79.)

EXAMPLE At the wildlife park, we were startled by the gibbons **swinging through the trees.**

participle A participle is a verb form that can be used as an adjective. (See page 77.)

EXAMPLE The **exhausted** hikers headed for home.

528 Grammar at a Glance

RESOURCES

passive voice The passive voice is the voice a verb is in when it expresses an action done to its subject. (See page 163. See also **voice.**)

EXAMPLE The posters on the bulletin board outside the principal's office **were changed** once a week.

period (See **end marks.**)

phrase A phrase is a group of related words that does not contain both a verb and its subject and is used as a single part of speech. (See page 70.)

EXAMPLES **A man of elegance and style,** Uncle Jesse lives **in Georgia.** [*A man of elegance and style* is an appositive phrase. *Of elegance and style* and *in Georgia* are prepositional phrases.]

Press this lever **to open the cage door.** [*To open the cage door* is an infinitive phrase.]

Smiling at her fans, the actress signed autographs. [*Smiling at her fans* is a participial phrase. *At her fans* is a prepositional phrase.]

Being on time for appointments is courteous. [*Being on time for appointments* is a gerund phrase. *On time* and *for appointments* are prepositional phrases.]

predicate The predicate is the part of a sentence that says something about the subject. (See page 42.)

EXAMPLE They **had been living in California for twenty years.**

predicate adjective A predicate adjective is an adjective that is in the predicate and that modifies the subject of a sentence or a clause. (See page 57.)

EXAMPLE Does the garage smell **strange**?

predicate nominative A predicate nominative is a word or word group that is in the predicate and that identifies the subject or refers to it. (See page 57.)

EXAMPLE Federico Fellini was a famous **filmmaker.**

RESOURCES

Grammar at a Glance 529

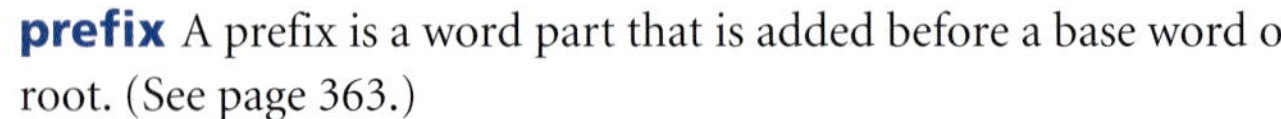

prefix A prefix is a word part that is added before a base word or root. (See page 363.)

EXAMPLES un + known = **un**known il + legible = **il**legible

re + write = **re**write pre + school = **pre**school

self + confidence = **self**-confidence trans + Siberian = **trans**-Siberian

mid + August = **mid**-August ex + president = **ex**-president

preposition A preposition shows the relationship of a noun or a pronoun to some other word in a sentence. (See page 28.)

EXAMPLE He came **from** Mexico and settled **near** Houston to find jobs **for** his family.

prepositional phrase A prepositional phrase is a group of words that includes a preposition, the object of the preposition (a noun or a pronoun), and any modifiers of that object. (See page 70.)

EXAMPLE Having breakfast **on the Bar X Ranch** was a real treat **for all of us.**

pronoun A pronoun is used in place of one or more nouns or pronouns. (See page 6.)

EXAMPLES Colin thinks **he** might be moving upstate.

Did **you** paint **your** room by **yourself**?

Some of the puppies look like **their** mother.

question mark (See **end marks.**)

quotation marks (See page 314.)

- **for direct quotations**

  EXAMPLE **"**Before the secretary of state returns to Washington, D.C.,**"** said the reporter, **"**she will visit Dar es Salaam, Tanzania, and Nairobi, Kenya.**"**

- **with other marks of punctuation** (See also preceding example.)

  EXAMPLES **"**In which South American country is the Atacama Desert**?"** asked Geraldo.

Which poem by Edgar Allan Poe begins with the line "Once upon a midnight dreary, while I pondered weak and weary"?

Carlotta asked, "Did Langston Hughes write a poem titled 'A Dream Deferred'?"

- **for titles**

EXAMPLES "The Rockpile" [short story]

"Muddy Kid Comes Home" [short poem]

"River Deep, Mountain High" [song]

regular verb A regular verb is a verb that forms its past and past participle by adding *–d* or *–ed* to the base form. (See page 146. See also **irregular verb.**)

Base Form	Present Participle	Past	Past Participle
ask	[is] asking	asked	[have] asked
drown	[is] drowning	drowned	[have] drowned
suppose	[is] supposing	supposed	[have] supposed
use	[is] using	used	[have] used

rise, raise (See page 169.)

EXAMPLES The hot-air balloon is **rising.**

She is **raising** the windows to let in some fresh air.

run-on sentence A run-on sentence is two or more complete sentences run together as one. (See page 441. See also **comma splice** and **fused sentence.**)

RUN-ON In 1903, Marie Curie and her husband, Pierre, won the Nobel Prize in physics in 1911 she alone won the Nobel Prize in chemistry.

REVISED In 1903, Marie Curie and her husband, Pierre, won the Nobel Prize in physics**. I**n 1911, she alone won the Nobel Prize in chemistry.

REVISED In 1903, Marie Curie and her husband, Pierre, won the Nobel Prize in physics**; i**n 1911, she alone won the Nobel Prize in chemistry.

Grammar at a Glance 531

semicolon (See page 296.)

- **in compound sentences with no conjunction**

EXAMPLE Salma decided to read Amy Tan's *The Joy Luck Club*; her English teacher recommended it.

- **in compound sentences with conjunctive adverbs**

EXAMPLE Elizabeth went to the library to check out Carson McCullers's *The Member of the Wedding*; **however,** another reader had already checked out the library's only copy.

- **between items in a series when the items contain commas**

EXAMPLE This summer I read three great books: *The House on Mango Street,* a collection of short stories by Sandra Cisneros; *Pacific Crossing,* a novel by Gary Soto; and *The Piano Lesson,* a play by August Wilson.

sentence A sentence is a group of words that contains a subject and a verb and expresses a complete thought. (See page 41.)

EXAMPLE The leaves [S] scattered [V] on the autumn wind.

sentence fragment A sentence fragment is a group of words that is punctuated as if it were a complete sentence but that does not contain both a subject and a verb or that does not express a complete thought. (See page 434.)

FRAGMENT The spider monkey, found chiefly in Costa Rica and Nicaragua.

SENTENCE The spider monkey, found chiefly in Costa Rica and Nicaragua, is an endangered species.

simple sentence A simple sentence has one independent clause and no subordinate clauses. (See page 109.)

EXAMPLES Dr. Mae C. Jemison is an astronaut.

Who first walked in space?

sit, set (See page 168.)

EXAMPLES The music students **sat** quietly, enjoying a sonata by Frédéric Chopin. [past tense of *sit*]

The music director **set** the sheet music on each student's desk. [past tense of *set*]

slow, slowly (See page 204.)

EXAMPLE Proceeding **slowly** [not *slow*] through the food court, the mariachi band played festive music to entertain the diners.

stringy sentence A stringy sentence is a sentence that has too many independent clauses. Usually, the clauses are strung together with coordinating conjunctions like *and* or *but.* (See page 463.)

STRINGY Yesterday afternoon, my friends and I were playing kickball in my backyard, and when Rahm kicked the ball to the fence, we spotted a wren, and it was hobbling on one leg, so I gently picked up the bird and carried it inside to my mother, and she tried hard to make a splint for the injured leg, but she was unsuccessful, so finally she and I decided to take the wren to our veterinarian.

REVISED Yesterday afternoon, my friends and I were playing kickball in my backyard. When Rahm kicked the ball to the fence, we spotted a wren hobbling on one leg. I gently picked up the bird and carried it inside to my mother. Although she tried hard to make a splint for the injured leg, she was unsuccessful. Finally, she and I decided to take the wren to our veterinarian.

subject The subject tells whom or what a sentence is about. (See page 42.)

EXAMPLE Isn't the **mayor** going to be there?

subject complement A subject complement is a word or word group that completes the meaning of a linking verb and identifies or modifies the subject. (See page 57.)

EXAMPLE My grandfather, who is usually **cheerful,** is an **optimist.**

subjunctive mood The subjunctive mood is used to express a suggestion, a necessity, a condition contrary to fact, or a wish. (See page 171.)

EXAMPLES It is essential that Luisa **attend** the meeting on Monday. [necessity]

If I **were** you, I would apply for the scholarship. [condition contrary to fact]

Ashley wishes she **were** able to go with you to the Juneteenth picnic. [wish]

RESOURCES

Grammar at a Glance 533

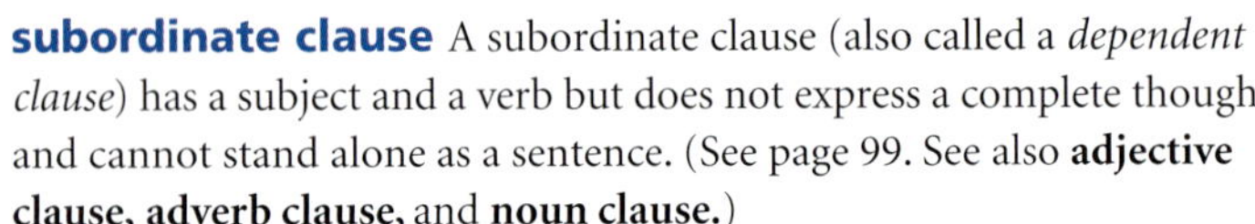

subordinate clause A subordinate clause (also called a *dependent clause*) has a subject and a verb but does not express a complete thought and cannot stand alone as a sentence. (See page 99. See also **adjective clause, adverb clause,** and **noun clause.**)

EXAMPLE **After they had dinner,** they sat on the porch and remembered old times.

suffix A suffix is a word part that is added after a base word or root. (See page 363.)

EXAMPLES

brave + ly = brave**ly**	kind + ness = kind**ness**
happy + ness = happi**ness**	obey + ing = obey**ing**
drop + ed = dropp**ed**	dream + er = dream**er**

tense of verbs The tense of verbs indicates the time of the action or the state of being expressed by a verb. (See page 156.)

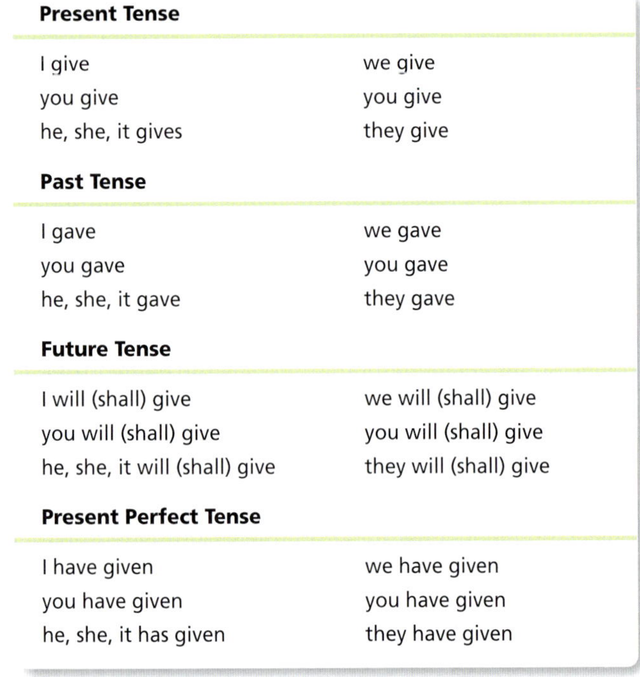

Present Tense	
I give	we give
you give	you give
he, she, it gives	they give
Past Tense	
I gave	we gave
you gave	you gave
he, she, it gave	they gave
Future Tense	
I will (shall) give	we will (shall) give
you will (shall) give	you will (shall) give
he, she, it will (shall) give	they will (shall) give
Present Perfect Tense	
I have given	we have given
you have given	you have given
he, she, it has given	they have given

(continued)

534 Grammar at a Glance

(continued)

Past Perfect Tense

I had given	we had given
you had given	you had given
he, she, it had given	they had given

Future Perfect Tense

I will (shall) have given	we will (shall) have given
you will (shall) have given	you will (shall) have given
he, she, it will (shall) have given	they will (shall) have given

transitive verb A transitive verb is an action verb that takes an object. (See page 14.)

EXAMPLE Ms. Southall **excused** me when I **explained** the situation.

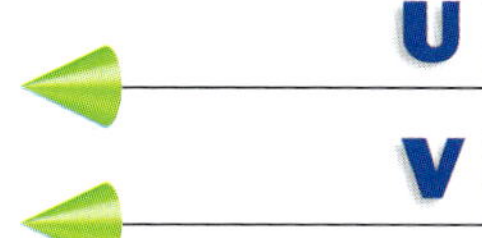

underlining (See **italics**.)

verb A verb expresses an action or a state of being. (See page 14.)

EXAMPLES The waters of the Brahmaputra River **flow** from the Himalayan snows.

He **is** happy.

verbal A verbal is a verb form used as an adjective, a noun, or an adverb. (See page 77.)

EXAMPLES **Chattering** and **screaming,** the monkeys disappeared into the treetops.

I especially enjoyed the **dancing.**

Is that hard **to see**?

verbal phrase A verbal phrase consists of a verbal and its modifiers and complements. (See page 77. See also **participial phrase, gerund phrase,** and **infinitive phrase.**)

EXAMPLES **Pleased to see his master,** Alf the dachshund wagged his tail vigorously.

Studying together helps me.

He'd like **to give Ella a gift.**

RESOURCES

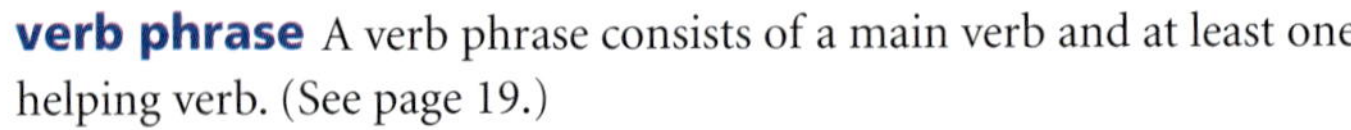

verb phrase A verb phrase consists of a main verb and at least one helping verb. (See page 19.)

EXAMPLE Strange as it **may seem,** I **have** never **eaten** an avocado.

voice Voice is the form a transitive verb takes to indicate whether the subject of the verb performs or receives the action. (See pages 163.)

ACTIVE VOICE Steven Spielberg **directed** the movie.
PASSIVE VOICE The movie **was directed** by Steven Spielberg.

weak reference A weak reference is the incorrect use of a pronoun to refer to an antecedent that has not been expressed. (See page 193.)

WEAK I was surprised to learn that my aunt Frances, who is a programmer for a computer company, does not have one in her home.

REVISED I was surprised to learn that my aunt Frances, who is a programmer for a computer company, does not have a computer in her home.

well (See *good, well.*)

who, whom (See page 187.)

EXAMPLES Enrique, **who** had applied for a part-time job at the animal clinic, asked me to write a letter of recommendation.

Enrique, **whom** I had recommended for a part-time job at the animal clinic, learned today that he will start working this weekend.

wordiness Wordiness is the use of more words than necessary or the use of fancy words where simple ones will do. (See page 465.)

WORDY In spite of the fact that my friend Akira, who is my best friend, is moving to another state, we think that, in our opinion, we will continue to remain good friends due to the fact that we have so much in common.

REVISED Although Akira, my best friend, is moving to another state, we think we will remain good friends because we have so much in common.

536 Grammar at a Glance

INDEX

Index 537

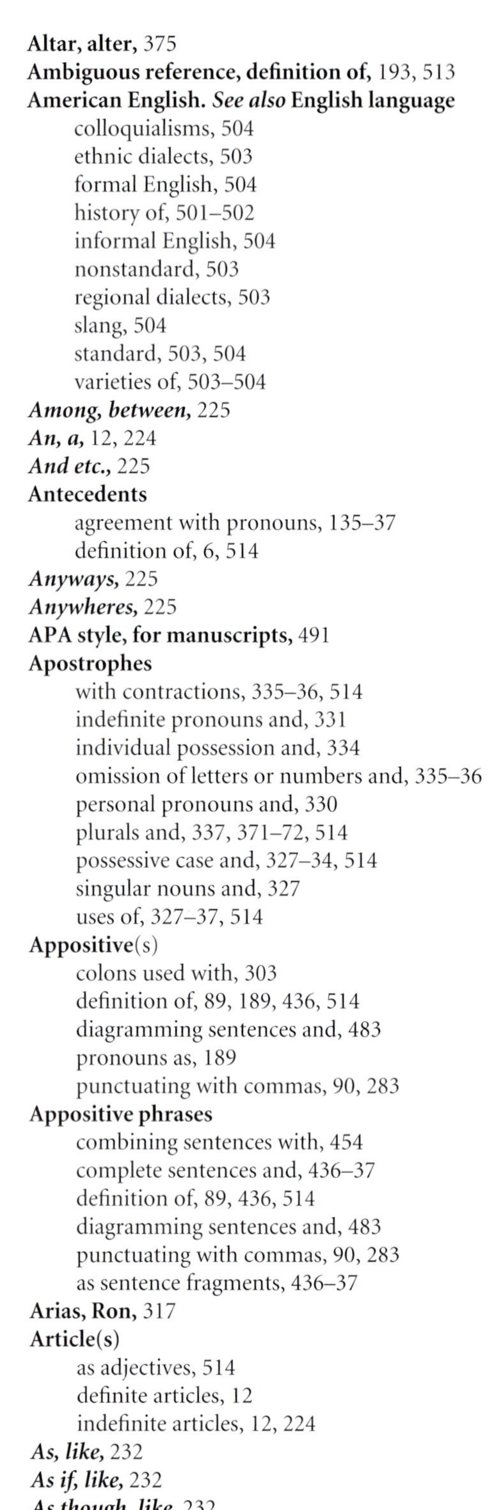

538 Index

Index 539

D

Index 541

H

542 Index

Index 543

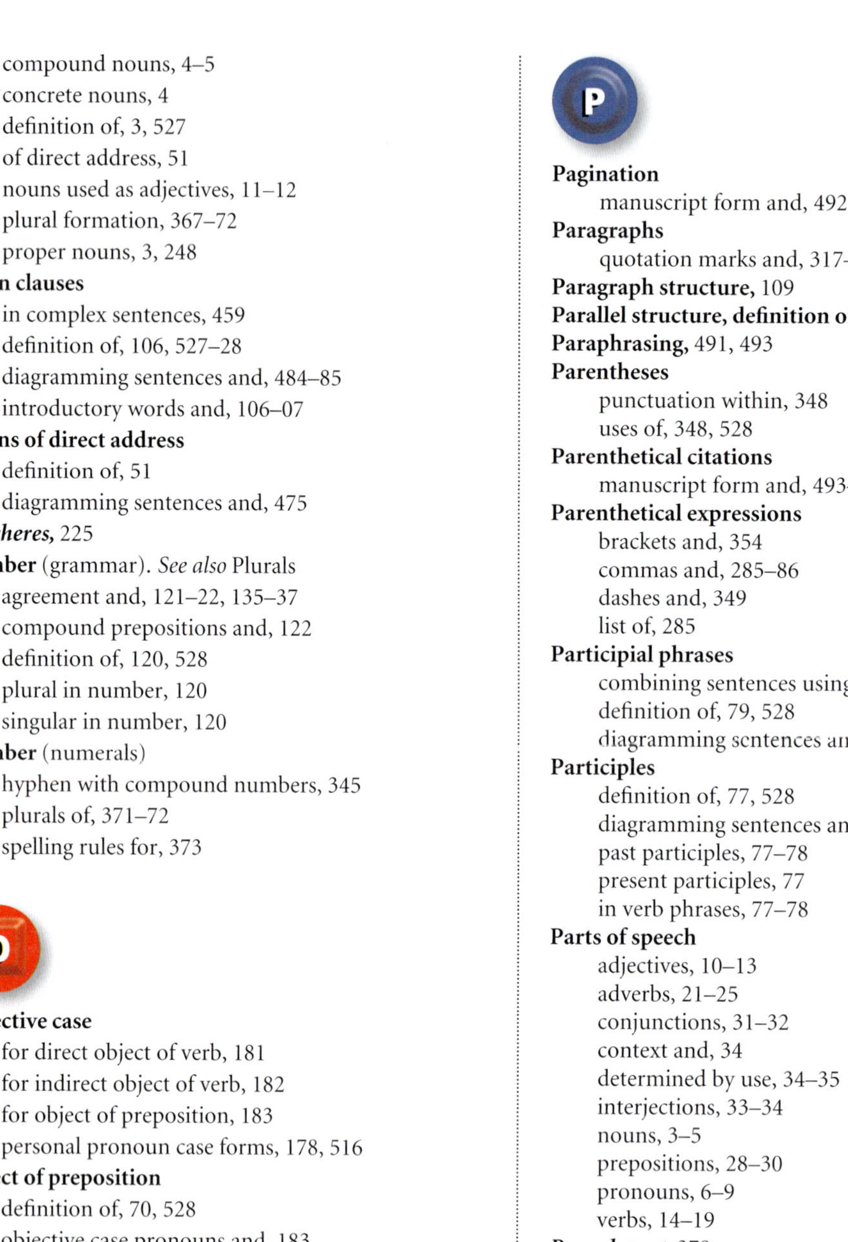

O

P

Index 545

546 Index

Index 547

548 Index

Index 549

ACKNOWLEDGMENTS

For permission to reprint copyrighted material, grateful acknowledgement is made to the following sources:

Ronald Arias: From "El Mago" by Ronald Arias from *El Grito: A Journal of Contemporary Mexican-American Thought,* Spring 1970. Copyright © 1970 by Ronald Arias.

PHOTO/ILLUSTRATION CREDITS

Abbreviation used: (tl) top left, (tc) top center, (tr) top right, (l) left, (lc) left center, (c) center, (rc) right center, (r) right, (bl) bottom left, (bc) bottom center, (br) bottom right.

COVER: Kim Taylor/Bruce Coleman, Inc.

TABLE OF CONTENTS: Page iv, Scala/Art Resource, NY; v, Pat Street; vi, Jerez/Viesti Collection, Inc.; vii, Image Copyright © 2003 Photodisc, Inc.; viii, Image Copyright © 2003 PhotoDisc, Inc./HRW, ix, Shaker Village of Pleasant Hill; x, Pete Saloutos/ Corbis Stock Market; xi, The Granger Collection, New York; xii, Louis Psihoyos/Matrix International; xiii, Jerome Wexker/ Photo Researchers, Inc.; xiv, Image Copyright © 2003 PhotoDisc, Inc./HRW; xv, Peter Steiner/Corbis Stock Market; xviii, Sam Dudgeon/HRW; xix, Sam Dudgeon/HRW; xx, Sam Dudgeon/HRW.

CHAPTER 1: Page 6, Walter Choroszewski; 9, Culver Pictures Inc./SuperStock; 23, John Lemker/Earth Scenes; 25, © 1984 by Sidney Harris-Punch; 27, SuperStock.

CHAPTER 2: Page 43, Fairfield Processing Corp.; 56, Image Copyright © 2001 Photodisc, Inc.; 60, Image Copyright © 2001 Photodisc, Inc.; 64, Image Copyright © 2003 Photodisc, Inc.

CHAPTER 3: Page 73, (tr) (rc), John Harrison; 76, (rc) (br), Archive Photos; 84, Cartooning Fundamentals, Al Ross, Stravon; 88, HRW Photo Research Library; 89, HRW Photo; 91, Culver Pictures, Inc.

CHAPTER 4: Page 100, Robert E. Daemmrich/Tony Stone Images; 106, Archive Photos; 108, Eadweard Muybridge/Culver Pictures, Inc.; 111, International Museum of Children's Art, Oslo, Norway; 112, Jerome Wexler/Photo Researchers, Inc.; 114, (bl) (br),Courtesy of Ursula Gibson.

CHAPTER 5: Page 120, Torquay Natural History Society; 122, (lc) (l) (bl) (bc), Kodansha International Ltd.; 126, Copyright 1905 Fred Harvey; 132, Eric Beggs/HRW Photo; 138, Image Copyright © 2003 Photodisc, Inc.

CHAPTER 6: Page 152, Richard Tomkins/Liaison International; 155, Marian Anderson/Culver Pictures, Inc.; 162, Image Copyright © 2001 Photodisc, Inc.; 166, Image Copyright © 2001 Photodisc, Inc.; 170, The Granger Collection, New York; 172, From Prairie Fires and Paper Moons: The American Photographic Postcard:1900-1920, Hal Morgan and Andreas Brown, David R. Godine (Publisher), Boston, 1981.

CHAPTER 7: Page 179, Brown Brothers; 185, David R. Frazier Photolibrary; 191, (cr), Scala/Art Resource, NY; 191, (br), National Portrait Gallery, London/SuperStock; 194, Image Copyright © 2001 Photodisc, Inc.; 184, David R. Frazier Photolibrary.

CHAPTER 8: Page 203, Image Copyright © 2003 Photodisc, Inc.; 212, (lc), Gary Griffen/Animals Animals/Earth Scenes; 212, (bc), Pete Saloutos/The Stock Market; 217, Cosmo Condina/Tony Stone Images; 208, Jerez/Viesti Collection.

CHAPTER 9: Page 227, Louis Psihoyos/Matrix International; 230, Andrew Eccles/Alvin Ailey American Dance Theater; 233, Corbis images; 236, Eric Brissaud/Gamma Liaison.

CHAPTER 10: Page 255, Random House, Inc.

CHAPTER 11: Page 279, Gutzon Borglum/FPG International; 282, The Newark Museum/Art Resource, NY; 286, Image Copyright © 2001 Photodisc, Inc.

CHAPTER 12: Page 297, (rc), CORBIS/Philip Gould; 297, (br), Library of Congress/HRW; 299, Image Copyright © 2003 Photodisc, Inc.; 301, Doug Perrine/Innerspace Visions Photography; 303, Photo courtesy of TEXAS HIGHWAYS magazine.

CHAPTER 13: Page 317, Greenwich Suit of Armour, c. 1550. Christie's Images, London, UK/Bridgeman Art Library; 322, Image Copyright © 2003 Photodisc, Inc.

CHAPTER 14: Page 330, The Stock Market; 332, Shaker Village of Pleasant Hill, KY; 333, Shaker Village of Pleasant Hill; 337, Joe Viesti/Viesti Associates, Inc.

CHAPTER 15: Page 351, One Mile Up, Inc.; 352, HRW Photo Library/courtesy Gibbs Memorial Library, Mexia, Texas

CHAPTER 16: Page 363, Pat Street; 367, Gutzon Borglum/FPG International; 377, Image Copyright © 2003 Photodisc, Inc.

CHAPTER 17: Page 397, Image Copyright © 2003 Photodisc, Inc.; 401 Image Copyright © 2003 Photodisc, Inc.; 404, Image Copyright © 2003 Photodisc, Inc.; 405, HRW Photo/Mary Miller; 417, Image Copyright © 2003 Photodisc, Inc.; 420, Image Copyright © 2003 Photodisc, Inc.

CHAPTER 18: Page 434, Culver Pictures, Inc.; 437, Archive Photos; 443, HRW Photo Research Library; 444, Bettmann/ CORBIS.

CHAPTER 19: Page 453, Fotos International/Archive Photos; 454, (lc), Ted Horowitz/The Stock Market; 454, (tl) Seidman/ HRW Photo Library; 455, Michael Krasowitz/FGP International; 461, SuperStock; 464, Doug Armand/Tony Stone Images; 468, K.G. Vock/Okapia, 1989/Photo Researchers, Inc.; 470, Zandria Muench/Tony Stone Images; 460, James D. Watt/Mo Yung Productions/ © 2000 Norbert Wu.

ILLUSTRATION CREDITS: Page 36 (c), Leslie Kell; 63 (tr), Joann Daley; 80 (cl), Uhl Studios, Inc.; 103 (tr), Keith Bowden; 290 (b), Ortelius Design; 338 (bl), Uhl Studios, Inc.; 361 (c), Leslie Kell; 373 (t), Steve Shock.

Photo/Illustration Credits 551